THE BEST OF
YANKEE MAGAZINE

50 Years of New England

Edited by Judson D. Hale, Sr.

YANKEE BOOKS

A division of Yankee Publishing Incorporated
Dublin, New Hampshire

Editorial Acknowledgments:

Interior design, caring, creativity, and hard work:
Margo Letourneau

Photo research, author-photographer-artist representation, and diplomacy:
Andrea Norman Meagher

Proofreading, production, money matters, and stick-to-it-iveness:
Ben Watson and Sharon Smith

Caption writing and jumping into the editorial breach when needed:
Susan Mahnke and Tim Clark

Paste-up, stripping, and willingness to work well for long hours:
Brenda Ellis, Ray Self, Lucille Rines, Maryann Mattson, and others of the merry Graphics crew

Typing and good humor:
Karen Dionne and Ann Grow

Problem solving, talent spotting, behind-the-scenes force, and editor extraordinaire:
John Pierce

Collecting the employee names and worrying about omissions:
Ann Card

. . . plus every person Ann listed and/or inadvertently omitted (pages 318–320)

About the Jacket Painting:

"A Yankee Rack Picture," [a detail] oil on masonite (35½″ by 42″) by David Brega of Marshfield, Massachusetts. This is a particular style of trompe l'oeil (a painting that creates a strong illusion of reality) characterized by the ribbon and made popular during the 19th century by American painters John F. Peto and William Michael Harnett. Among the objects depicted (and none is real, nor are the background boards) are at least one *Yankee* cover from each of the past five decades, an 1857 *Old Farmer's Almanac* (Yankee purchased *The Old Farmer's Almanac* from Little, Brown and Company in 1939), and a snapshot of Yankee founder Robb Sagendorph (1900–1970). Note: the 50th anniversary seal at lower right is *not* part of the painting.

Yankee Publishing Incorporated
Dublin, New Hampshire
FIRST EDITION
Second printing, 1985
Copyright 1985 by Yankee Publishing Incorporated

Library of Congress Catalog Card Number: 85-50089
ISBN: 0-89909-079-6

WE DEDICATE THIS BOOK TO:

Mrs. Olive Thompson of Fall River, Massachusetts; Mrs. C.W. Lane of Foxboro, Massachusetts; Mrs. David Hannum of Putney, Vermont; Helen Morland of Essex, Massachusetts; Clifford Deer of Fayville, Massachusetts; Mrs. Anna Campi of Torrington, Connecticut; and Henry B. Hough of Martha's Vineyard — all seven of whom have been *Yankee* subscribers for 45 or more years; to the 1,000,278 subscribers as of September 1985; to the 612 first subscribers, wherever they may be today; and to all the millions of subscribers in between.

AND ALSO TO:

The Hanover Inn, Hanover, New Hampshire, and the State Street Bank and Trust Company, Boston, both of whom have been Yankee Publishing Incorporated advertisers since 1935, and to the 220,368 companies, resorts, and individuals who have advertised with us since then.

CONTENTS

The Best of *Yankee* Magazine • 50 Years of New England

Foreword

On September 27, 1984, I mailed or handed a letter to 72 people who, through friendship, family, or professional affiliation, I knew had been reading Yankee Magazine for a long time. (The youngest on the list was 22, the oldest 84 — so the term "long time" is obviously relative.)

After a short description of how I generally envisioned the format of our proposed 50th Anniversary book, I made to each one a specific request:

"Please write down which Yankee Magazine articles stand out in your memory as being something you particularly enjoyed. If you can't remember the title or the author, fine. Just give me an idea of what it was about and, if you can, approximately when you remember reading it. I'll find it.

"I'll ask that you not look through back issues to remind yourself of things. Please rely only on your memory. This is important to me. If you can think of only one or two, that's terrific and will be a big help. If you can remember more as being specifically your favorites, all the better. Incidentally, include, if you like, cartoons, readers' letters, specific photographs, an 'I Remember,' a recipe — ANYTHING! But . . . from your memory only.

"As a reward, you'll be listed in the Foreword, you'll have a free lifetime pass to Jud's Museum [cruelly described by a recent visitor as "probably the rattiest, dustiest, most useless little collection of stupid junk ever labeled a 'museum' "], and you'll be part of what I hope will be a fun book for Yankee's birthday."

Over the next month, I heard from no fewer than 71 of the 72 people to whom I had written. (I was sorry to learn that the 72nd, my friend Arpiar Saunders, once of Greylock Photoengraving, North Adams, Massachusetts, had passed away.)

Some wrote two or three typewritten pages, listing over a dozen special articles or stories they remembered, going into some detail explaining why each was memorable — and then adding a list of what they particularly didn't like! A few were brief and vague, saying simply, "Anything by Edie Clark" (no, it wasn't Edie who said that!) or "Just be sure to include some of those Swanberg murder stories." One friend returned my letter with a scribbled note on the top that said, "The story about the Radcliffe girl who filed her teeth to points." I knew instantly which story she meant. (See "The Bracelet," Chapter 10.)

Many of the 71 complained about my stipulation that they not look through back issues to refresh their memories. My feeling was that I wanted the book to contain those past things in Yankee that have remained in people's minds. It wouldn't necessarily be a literary evaluation, but rather a sort of endurance test. Determining the most memorable items, I felt, was probably as good a way as any to arrive at "the best."

Because the response resulted in so many more stories than could possibly fit into one book, I've included "Samplers" at the end of each chapter. These include short excerpts from the overflow of favorites submitted, as well as letters, cartoons, and other remembered tidbits. But even so, I had to leave out so much it was truly painful. On the other hand, it's comforting to know that 50 long, turbulent, wonderful years of hard and creative work by hundreds of people have resulted in so many things at least 71 Yankee readers can remember!

Judson D. Hale, Sr.
Editor, Yankee Magazine and
The Old Farmer's Almanac

THE SEVENTY-ONE . . .

Phyllis Worcester	Lew Dabney	Vrest Orton	Larry Willard
Dottie Guy	Ed Phippard	Jamie Trowbridge	Doug Christensen
Clarissa Silitch	John Pierce	Bob Johnson	Susan Mahnke
George Kendall	Sandy Taylor	Linda Clukay	Karl Lipsky
Jim Dodson	Steve Muskie	Rick Wasowicz	Patricia Whitcomb
Ken Fredericks	Sally Hale	Steve Avery	Frank Gardner
Andrea Meagher	Rob Trowbridge	Polly Bannister	Mary Lewis
Peter Sykas	Charlie Jordan	J.H. Drake	Marian Simonetta
Steve Klett	John Scott	Earl Proulx	Lorna Trowbridge
Tim Clark	Deb Navas	Jean Burden	Mary Walker
Dick Heckman	Jane Black	Edie Clark	Margo Letourneau
Carolee Barrett	Kenny Hooker	Jane Kauppi	Esther Fitts
Joan Hayes	Don Cuddihee	Sharon Smith	Bob Ginna
Anna Larson	Mel Allen	Reta Huberlie	Mary Sheldon
J Porter	Ben Watson	Ann Marie Aldrich	Ann Grow
Mark Bastian	Anne Thompson	Geoffrey Elan	Cornelia Trowbridge
Joyce Swanson	Jody Saville	Betty Doyle	Kenison Smith
Austin Stevens	Clint Sperry	Dougald MacDonald	

Many thanks, everyone.
J.D.H.

What Rob Trowbridge does not include in this brief, personal, and revealing
history of Yankee Magazine is that it was his vision, energy, enthusiasm, and business expertise that
fueled the phenomenal growth of Yankee Publishing Incorporated
over the past 20 years — an achievement that would have made Yankee's
founder, Robb Sagendorph, were he alive today, so very, very proud of his son-in-law.
But then, how could he have said that? (J.D.H.)

The First 50 Years

BY ROB TROWBRIDGE

Publisher, *Yankee* Magazine, *The Old Farmer's Almanac,*
and *New England Business*

How *Yankee* Was Born, or
The Ultimate Definition of Low Overhead

Town Meeting Day on March 12, 1935, was snowy and cold. The 246 residents of Dublin, New Hampshire, gathered at the Town Hall, built in 1882, to debate such typical questions as "To see if the Town will vote to sell the land formerly used as the Town Dump or take any other action related thereto." They also met to vote on a budget of $58,266 (by 1985 it had risen to over half a million), and to choose a selectman for a three-year term.

One candidate for the job was a relative newcomer, Robb Sagendorph, age 35, who had summered in nearby Peterborough since 1914. When he had tired of selling steel in New York City for his father's firm, the Penn Metal Company, this graduate of both Harvard College and Harvard Business School (1922 and 1924, respectively) looked around the Monadnock Region for a place to settle. He found a large, rambling, Italian-villa-style summer home that was located on a dirt road and had a commanding view of Mount Monadnock.

Since 1931, Sagendorph had actively pursued his chosen profession of writing; however, publishers had not matched his enthusiasm to the extent that Sagendorph could claim writing as his livelihood. Without a steady stream of dollars generated by the Northern Trust Company out of the estate of his wife Beatrix's father, the late George Arthur Thorne of Chicago, the Sagendorphs would have been living on meagre fare. Having more spare time than he liked, Sagendorph filed for the position of town selectman.

The townsfolk of Dublin were not so easily convinced that they needed the services of this tall (6'5") Harvardian, and the selectman's job went to someone else. However, the town fathers liked Robb Sagendorph and did not want to discourage him. "Just can't let him get a swelled head by winning the first time he runs for something," Henry Gowing was heard to say. Gowing, a local farmer who would become one of Robb's close friends, advised the selectmen that perhaps they should appoint Robb to a vacancy existing on the Library Committee. As usual, the selectmen took Henry Gowing's advice.

By coincidence — or was it fate? — the Library Committee, including new member Robb Sagendorph, decided to contract for the printing of various forms and the reprinting of an article from a 1901 issue of *New England Magazine* called "Historic Dublin, New Hampshire." Word spread quickly about the printing job, and Arthur Bennett, an itinerant printer, appeared at Robb Sagendorph's house that same week to ask if he could do the job. He had debts to pay, he said, and he needed the work "bad."

Robb Sagendorph asked Bennett if he could print a magazine on his equipment. "Sure could. What would you call it?" asked Bennett. "We'll call it 'The Yankee,' " Robb Sagendorph replied. And on that March day an enterprise was begun that would take up the rest of Sagendorph's life, a good deal of his wife's money, and much of the time and talent of his close friend and editorial colleague Benjamin Rice of Peterborough.

Between March and September 1935, a seven-month gestation, *Yankee* Magazine was conceived and born. Articles would be written by professional but country-oriented authors. Traditions like square dancing that had begun to disappear from the scene would be rediscovered through the pages of *Yankee*, and even older customs, such as bundling (in which a courting couple shares the same bed — without undressing), would be fondly remembered.

Beth Tolman, wife of Newton Tolman, whose family dominated the neighboring town of Nelson, New Hampshire, as well as local square dancing, became Associate Editor of *Yankee*, traveling each day by car, horse, or bicycle, depending on the weather and/or status of the various vehicles. Phyllis Worcester, a local woman with secretarial skills, signed on as treasurer and office manager. All three were housed in a little six-sided shack that Robb had built behind his garden, just out of sight of the house and with a gorgeous view of Mount Monadnock. Since it is impossible to name in this short account all the people who have helped *Yankee* grow and prosper, we have printed, in the back of this book (see page 318), all the names of employees who have worked for the company during its first 50 years.

The First Subscribers

What the new magazine needed next was subscribers, so Robb Sagendorph hired a consultant (who remains nameless for reasons that will become obvious). The man claimed that he could provide *Yankee* with a mailing list that would produce paid orders for subscriptions. All that *Yankee* had to do was pay him 75¢ per name and he would turn over the signed orders. *Yankee* would then bill each customer for $2.50, the subscription price. Faithfully the man arrived with fistfuls of signed orders, and after paying him his fee, Robb and Phyllis did the billing. Slowly but surely it dawned on them that this slippery soul had flown the coop with $600 worth of commissions on subscriptions he had concocted himself — the names were totally fictitious.

After that experience Robb Sagendorph decided to drum up his own business. Most of the early promotion was limited to New Hampshire, but by 1938, when *Yankee* was three years old, Robb envisioned a future for the magazine throughout

7

YANKEE
DECEMBER · 1973
50 CENTS

The December 1973 cover, one of the last of hundreds painted by Yankee co-founder Beatrix Sagendorph, depicts an early view of the Yankee buildings (foreground) in the village of Dublin, New Hampshire.

New England. On a September morn in 1938, he sent out a mailing of more than 300,000 pieces. Postage had been paid at the Dublin post office and the mail truck was on its way to Keene by way of a bridge spanning the Minnewawa Brook. But this was no ordinary day. The rising wind suddenly strengthened and blew the mail truck right off the bridge and into the stream. Robb's big promotion became one of the many victims of the 1938 Hurricane!

How the "Swopper's Column" Began

Yankee's printer, Arthur Bennett, had a personal habit that was directly responsible for the creation of a popular feature in the magazine. During the printing process, Bennett would remove his "uppers" and place them on the windowsill. (He would also take a little gin at this time. How he could hold register on that swaying press on a swaying floor only the gin might explain.) Robb Sagendorph, none too pleased with the teeth, placed a small announcement in an early issue: "Will swop one set of false teeth for a broom." A lady from Marlborough responded with alacrity. Robb took the broom and handed over Bennett's denture — thus creating one of *Yankee*'s perennial favorites, the "Original Swopper's Column."

Bennett could only mumble angrily, but he eventually struck back in his own subtle way. Robb Sagendorph had been soliciting advertising from the tourist industry for some time, and he finally convinced two lovely maiden ladies in Bethlehem, New Hampshire, to advertise their inn in *Yankee* Magazine. The headline was to read "A lovely place to come and play." Bennett, who did all the typesetting, managed to leave off the first letter of the last word and the ad went to press. Imagine Robb's surprise when the little ladies innocently called to say that the response to their ad had been phenomenal! Word spread throughout the North Country, and *Yankee* was well on its way toward becoming a leader in travel and resort advertising in New England.

The Old Farmer Buys an Almanac

In the early 1930s, the Swan family of Boston inherited the venerable publication known as *The Old Farmer's Almanac*, which had been founded in 1792 and which was (as it is today) the oldest continuously published periodical in the country. The Swans licensed the *Almanac* to Little, Brown and Company in the mid thirties, but the venture was not a success and circulation fell off rapidly. The Swans knew *Yankee* and felt that Robb Sagendorph was the kind of person who could make the *Almanac* regain its lost stature. After a short lunch with the Swans at the Union Club in Boston, Robb Sagendorph emerged as the 11th editor of *The Old Farmer's Almanac*.

If ever there was a perfect "fit" between an editor and a publication, it was between Robb Sagendorph and *The Old Farmer's Almanac*. While preserving its original format and style (you could hardly tell the difference between issues 100 years apart), Robb was able to surprise the reader with a mixture of fact, fantasy, and pure down-home humor. This made the *Almanac* a real favorite, especially with the press.

The first issue Robb Sagendorph edited was the 1941 edition, and some old friends helped him out. Robert Frost wrote original poetry; Ben Rice wrote the Farmer's Calendar. Robb either wrote the rest himself or reprinted sage advice from the past, and he did the weather forecasts as well, using an old

formula that had been devised by the *Almanac*'s founder, Robert B. Thomas. With a lot of work and promotion, the *Almanac* thrived again.

The War Years: Cutting *Yankee* Down to Size

The arrival of World War II caused *Yankee* to change its format to its current 6″ by 9″ size. Not only was paper scarce, but as Robb Sagendorph said in the January 1942 issue, "We should have adopted the digest size in the beginning to show the reader that there was nothing fancy or city-like in this Yankee product." During 1942, *Yankee* was published in digest size, but then it literally vanished from sight. The *Yankee* reader became used to hearing from Robb Sagendorph in various printed forms, mostly letters, which he published to keep the copyright and trademark alive while he was in New York working his heart out for the Bureau of Censorship, a job that wore him out mentally, partially because he could not discuss his work with anyone, including his family.

The War Years: How the *Almanac* Almost Became Too Successful

At his New York apartment on East End Avenue, Robb did find time to publish *The Old Farmer's Almanac* for the years 1943 through 1946, but it was the '43 edition that became the most famous since 1816 (when a forecast for snow in July, printed by error, actually came true). In April 1943, the Coast Guard arrested several Nazi saboteurs who had landed on Long Island. The public commotion was enormous! The Nazis were found to be carrying the 1943 *Old Farmer's Almanac*. Robb was fond of explaining that perhaps the submariners were using the *Almanac*'s tide tables and weather forecasts. "After all," he would say, with facetious modesty, "Germany *did* go on to lose the war!" The Navy took things more seriously and insisted the *Almanac* state that the weather forecasts were only "indicators."

Making Headway...

In July 1945 Robb Sagendorph brought forth a slim, 10-page issue of *Yankee*. Somehow his faithful subscribers had remained faithful throughout the war, although they were not receiving much of a magazine.

The offices had moved from the shed at the Sagendorphs' house to a building right next to the IGA store on the south side of Main Street in Dublin. The local telephone operator, Mrs. Bell (yes, Ma Bell), was housed on the second floor, where she could see everything in town. If Robb did not answer the office phone, she would tell the caller that he had "just left and should be home in 10 minutes." Now a selectman, he would spend Mondays over at the Town Hall, a stone's throw away.

In those early years, *Yankee* Magazine would not have survived had it not been for the success of *The Old Farmer's Almanac*. But in time *Yankee* began to grow to a level where it could cover its overhead and then make some headway. Several things contributed to this advance. First, Judson D. Hale, Robb's nephew, joined *Yankee* in 1958 and by the early sixties was able to lay out and design the magazine in such a way as to make it more readable and inviting. Second, the centennial of the Civil War created an increased interest in historical subjects. *American Heritage* swept onto the stage, and Americans began to look back at their past with fondness and nostalgia. All of a sudden people were attracted to *Yankee*, which had been publishing such material for years.

There were only a handful of employees at this time: Phyllis Worcester, Treasurer, on board since 1935; Annabelle Dupree, Advertising Manager; Jud Hale, Managing Editor and Chief Bottlewasher (in 1958 Robb Sagendorph paid his nephew $50 a week for his first job); Esther Fitts, Associate Editor; Anthony Anable, Sales Director. Beatrix Sagendorph, Robb's wife, was Art Editor and, until 1969, produced the majority of *Yankee* covers. I came on in 1964 as the assistant publisher.

Also in place by this time was a loyal group of mail-order advertisers. The Small Business and Crafts column each month brought such tremendous response to the person featured that he or she often would advertise in subsequent issues or at least give such glowing testimonials that the story of *Yankee*'s unique "pull" became legend. All advertising was solicited by mail; Annabelle Dupree took orders by phone.

Robb had always done his own newsstand distribution for *Yankee*, but in 1964, upon my recommendation, he had a national distributor handle both the magazine and the *Almanac*. As the magazine began to sell, more and more people accepted our offer of gift subscriptions and we went from 200,000 subscribers in 1966 to 325,000 in less than two years. Consequently, the Christmas rush became a nightmare and we fell hopelessly behind. The computer systems of the day did not know how to keep track of who gave what to whom. We definitely needed help.

Compounding the Chaos — Circulation Woes

Yankee had been so successful in inspiring gift subscriptions that perhaps 30 percent of our list represented a gift from someone else. That's nice and friendly, but when you realize that Uncle Harry forgets whom he gave to, and Aunt Alice sent the order in without Harry knowing, but she gave the wrong address for their niece Susie because she thought she knew it but did not, you can imagine the potential for chaos that exists. Add to that mix of signals the fact that 75 percent of this activity happens in a three-month period before Christmas, and the chaos becomes compounded.

The service bureau we had hired to process subscriptions was failing us. Over 40,000 complaints were on my desk; the attorneys general of most of the New England states were on my neck; and cancellations were coming in faster than orders.

Out of Chaos . . . Order!

In 1974 we acted swiftly to purchase the old A&P grocery store in Peterborough and install our own computer system. By 1980 the Yankee fulfillment crew had become so efficient that we in turn became a service bureau for other publishers. What was one of our weakest points is now one of our strongest.

Why readers exclaim, "We love the little ads in the *Yankee*."

When the sales force began to form after 1964, we knew that subscribers were already "hooked" on the small advertiser in *Yankee*. They liked the ads as much as they liked the rest of the magazine. The rates were so low that no self-respecting mail-order advertiser could afford *not* to be in *Yankee*. The public began to enjoy shopping by mail, especially if the featured product was not available from retail stores. *Yankee* began to

build a reputation for trustworthy advertisers, and the whole process blossomed nicely.

The greatest challenge was to get the small advertiser to accept the fact that, as the magazine grew, higher circulation meant higher rates. Annabelle Dupree sometimes gave up on fancy explanations and could be heard on the phone saying, "I don't know why they raised the rates. They just *did*."

The "Idea" of *Yankee*: "That Great Culture"

Yankee's theme was stated in the very first issue. "Yankee's destiny," Robb Sagendorph wrote, "is the expression and perhaps indirectly the preservation of that great culture in which every Yank was born and by which every real Yank must live."

For years I wondered why I would hear from a lady in Kansas who would state clearly that she did not come from New England, she did not intend to travel to New England or retire here, she had no relatives in New England — but she loved *Yankee* Magazine. What, I asked, is she getting? What is it about *Yankee* that is so attractive to her?

"There is no power to see in the eye itself any more than in any other jelly," wrote Henry David Thoreau. "We cannot see anything until we are possessed with the idea of it — and *then* we can hardly see anything else." So it was that people across America were becoming possessed with "the idea" of New England — and *Yankee* Magazine helped them see it.

From 1935 until about 1969, *Yankee* was the creation of Robb Sagendorph. Then Judson Hale took over the reins. At this point *Yankee* turned the corner from being an edited compilation of articles, chosen from a vast group of submissions, to a truly planned collection of articles, features, and departments, all designed to please the reader.

Instrumental in the transition were John Pierce, the Managing Editor; Austin Stevens, a Contributing Editor, who came to *Yankee* from *Boston* Magazine along with Dick Heckman, now Director of our Book Division; Margo Letourneau, Art Director; and later J Porter, the design genius who recast *New England Business*, the *Travel Guide*, and *Yankee* itself. Tim Clark, Mel Allen, Susan Mahnke, Edie Clark, Steve Muskie, and many others among those listed on pages 318-320 brought young, professional talent.

It is clear, however, that the editorial side of the business has been the expression of the tastes of two individuals — Robb Sagendorph and Judson Drake Hale. It is rare for any magazine to have only two editors in 50 years — and probably rarer still that they be related!

Yankee Today

Yankee Magazine continues to be the mainstay of the organization. One million circulation seems as though it will be a realistic resting place for the magazine.

The Old Farmer's Almanac continues to grow steadily over the four million mark for total distribution, and in 1992 we will celebrate the 200th anniversary of its founding.

The Book Division, which will sell more than $2.5 million worth of books and calendars this year, has broadened its scope with the arrival of Foremost Books, giving Yankee Books an entrée into the field of expensive coffee-table volumes.

New England Business, published since 1979 as the regional voice of the business community, has grown to 50,000 circulation, a circulation we call "elective" because the reader is "elected" by us to receive the magazine in the first place. Then, each year, the reader may elect to continue receiving it.

Yankee Magazine's Travel Guide to New England, published since 1971, has established itself as the premier travel annual in the region.

The Yankee Intern Program grew out of a combined desire to support historic preservation projects, to give college students meaningful summer jobs, and to attract more younger readers and especially college students, who represent the readers of tomorrow. Administered by the National Trust for Historic Preservation and funded by *Yankee* (partly through reader contributions), the program sends dozens of students out into communities to perform the nuts-and-bolts work of preserving our heritage.

Here's to the NEXT 50 Years. . . .

Sometimes people ask us whether we are presenting the "real" New England. Are those pristine village greens, white church spires, covered bridges, fishing shacks, and church sup-pers really there? We have only to look around us throughout the six-state region to give a firm and enthusiastic "yes!" If anything, New Englanders — natives, visitors, and newcomers — have become increasingly aware of what the New England image *ought* to be, and thus reality has been rapidly catching up to that image through the actions of community-minded citizens and the historic preservation movement. So many of New England's cities today — Lowell, Newburyport, Portsmouth, Portland, Providence, Burlington, Concord (New Hampshire *and* Massachusetts), Hartford, Boston, and innumerable others in varying stages of restoration, beautification, and revitalization — prove the point. New England, the essence of America's heritage, is far more "New England" today than it was when Robb Sagendorph began a little publication he called "The Yankee" 50 long years ago. And, the good Lord willing, *Yankee* Magazine, now a million subscribers strong, will continue into the next half century showing "that great culture" to the world.

During a morning meeting in October of 1968, a shirt-sleeved Robb Sagendorph gives some advice and counsel to his son-in-law, Rob Trowbridge (left), now the Publisher of Yankee, *and his nephew, Jud Hale, now its Editor. Since that October morning 17 years ago, Yankee's monthly paid circulation has increased from 297,000 to well over one million.*

CHAPTER 1

January

*J*anuary has always been the month to get lost. Invariably in a "raging blizzard." Sometimes at sea, often on mountains, or even, as in "A Message in the Wind," in an old roadster with a wife in labor! But other kinds of trouble have occurred in January, too. For instance, it was in the January 1961 issue that we announced "an 874-foot bridge connecting Campobello with Lubec, Maine, was opened last month." What a furor that simple statement caused! In writing the article, it seems we misread a newspaper statement saying construction "bids opened last month." There was no bridge, as hundreds of readers wrote and called to inform us. One even said that he'd "rowed that stretch of water all afternoon looking for your confounded bridge."

Sometimes January trouble has come to us in the form of true statements, statements many wished had gone unmade — like mentioning that in Stonington, Connecticut, lived "some of the wealthiest people in New England" (1983), or that when one leaves Thomaston, Maine, one is "hit by the eyesore of the Dragon Cement Company" (1959). Worse still, we were scolded in 1983 by over a hundred readers who said the farmer in the cover painting was milking his cow "on the wrong side."

Yes, January has always been the month to "get lost," at least for us! So we'll begin our best of Januarys with an article about the sun. Nothing controversial about the sun . . . is there?

Mt. Washington looms over Berlin, New Hampshire, and the James River Corporation pulp mill.

– photograph by Candace Cochrane

13

Like the location of the "birthplace" of the American Navy,
the creator of the deep-fried clam, or the origin of the doughnut hole,
here was a subject Yankee readers loved to good-naturedly (most of the time) argue
about. Maybe it would have been more fun if we hadn't settled the matter....

Where
(in these United States)
Does the Sun Shine First?

BY BLANTON C. WIGGIN

Engineer, Chairman, Advanced Instruments, Inc.,
Route 128, Massachusetts, and Puzzle Editor for
the *Old Farmer's Almanac.*

"Does the sun rise first on Mt. Katahdin?" or . . . "Is West Quoddy Head the easternmost point in the United States?" Sacrilege! "Of course these headlines must be fooling. Is someone putting me on?" you ask. Untold generations of Maine-iacs know about Katahdin, and Quoddy Head. I was brought up on them. So were my ancestors. Everyone knows the sun rises first on Mt. Katahdin.

Everyone except people in Washington County, Maine, where a welcome sign proclaims it "The Sunrise County of the U.S.A."

Now Mt. Katahdin is about 40 miles *west* of any part of Washington County, and 110 miles nor'west of Quoddy Head.

So, who is right? Who gets the sun first? We'll see shortly.

And what about West Quoddy Head? Any map shows that this is clearly the easternmost point in Maine. Our ancestors were correct that Quoddy Head was easternmost in the U.S., but as we shall see later in the article, times have changed. After we solve the sunrise problem, we will show you how to win a bet anytime on the "easternmost" question.

Taken in Hamlin, Maine, shortly after sunrise, January 27, 1971.

– John P. Adams

Let's look at the sunrise. The problem is that, while the sun rises generally in the east, if you've ever been up early on a summer's morn, you've probably noticed that it rises well *north* of east. And in the winter, it swings way to the south of east. About 35 degrees, in Maine.

It's only on March 21 and September 21 that the sun rises due east.

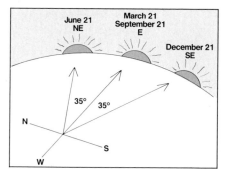

Now, suppose you're up early and you're watching the sunrise. If you move toward the sun you will see it rise sooner, or earlier. If you back away it will come up later, and if you move right or left it will move with you and will rise at the same time. Nothing difficult about that.

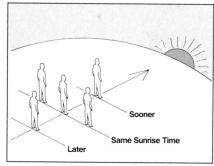

That is the meaning of a "Same Sunrise-Time" line. All points on a particular line see the sun at the same time.

Let's draw the June 21 sunrise direction arrows for Maine. And then let's draw at right angles some "Same Sunrise-Time" lines. (*See Figure 1, next page.*)

On this basis it looks like Hamlin, Maine, would see the first sun in the summer. And this is true on a first approximation. But Hamlin is a St. John River town, basically in a valley. Perhaps Mt. Katahdin, or some hill located behind Hamlin, would look right over and see the sun earlier.

The map shows several possibilities.

– illustrations by Jill Shaffer

15

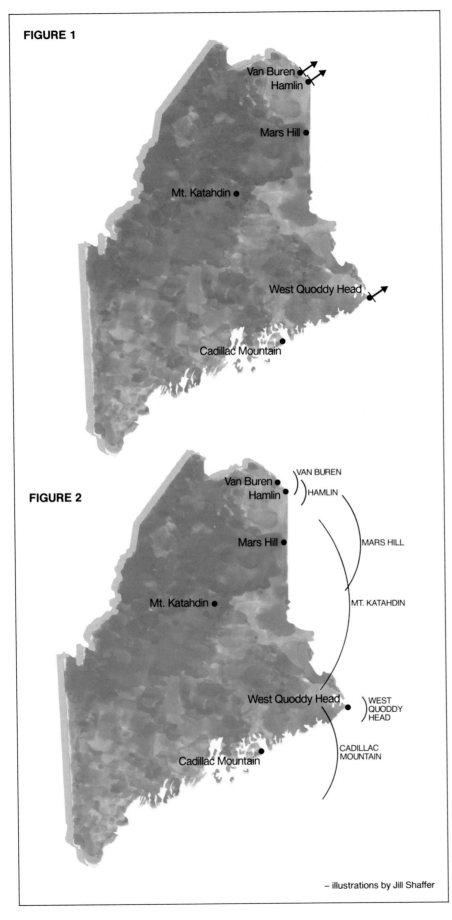

FIGURE 1

Van Buren
Hamlin

Mars Hill

Mt. Katahdin

West Quoddy Head

Cadillac Mountain

FIGURE 2

Van Buren   VAN BUREN
Hamlin   HAMLIN

Mars Hill   MARS HILL

Mt. Katahdin   MT. KATAHDIN

West Quoddy Head   WEST QUODDY HEAD

CADILLAC MOUNTAIN

Cadillac Mountain

– illustrations by Jill Shaffer

Katahdin is nearly a mile (5268 feet) high, and surveyors tell us it can see a sunrise 95.8* miles away. There is Cadillac Mountain, on the coast at Bar Harbor, with a 51.7-mile* lookout. West Quoddy Head Lighthouse claims a 15-mile range, although possibly a little less by calculation. And then there is a sleeper, Mars Hill, 1660 feet high, right on the New Brunswick line, north of Washington County, with a 52.8-mile* view.

Next step is to draw circles around these points, showing the horizon where the sun would rise. (*See Figure 2.*)

If we combine the sunrise direction lines with the horizon circles and "Same Sunrise-Time" lines, it becomes obvious. (*See Figures 3, 4 and 5.*)

So the sun actually rises first at different places, depending upon the time of year. It turns out on close analysis that despite Mt. Katahdin's height, and despite Washington County's eastness, other points usually get an earlier sunrise.

Here is the rough schedule:

Dec. 21–Mar. 6	**Cadillac Mountain**[1]
Mar. 7–Mar. 24	**West Quoddy Head**
Mar. 25–Sept. 18	**Mars Hill**[2]
Sept. 19–Oct. 6	**West Quoddy Head**
Oct. 7–Dec. 20	**Cadillac Mountain**[1]

1. Between about January 11 and March 6, and between October 7 and November 29, the hills of Grand Manan Island, N.B., near and higher than West Quoddy Head, usually block the sunrise (for up to four to five minutes), giving most mornings to Cadillac Mountain.

2. In spring and summer, the hills of Carleton County, N.B., may block the

FIGURE 3

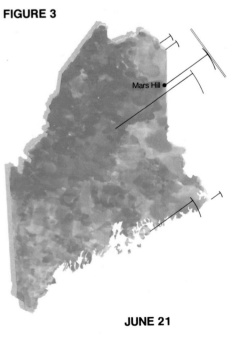

Mars Hill

JUNE 21

sunrise at Mars Hill a minute or so, giving some mornings to Mt. Katahdin.

Only actual timings at each spot throughout the year would tell exact dates. All four places are within a minute or two, but unfortunately Mt. Katahdin is another minute or two behind the other spots, other things being equal, all year round, and Washington County's Quoddy Head may be first only about 10 percent of the year.

There are some good questions that people ask when they get to this point:

1. What about Daylight Saving Time?
2. How about the sun's rays in the earth's atmosphere?
3. Does the speed of light make any difference at all?

Actually none of these factors has any effect on the earliest sunrise. Daylight Saving Time, or any other time, is simply a number that society places on a natural phenomenon. A particular spot will have the earliest sunrise regardless of the kind of time numbers that people might use. All of Maine uses the same time anyway.

It can be argued that there is a bit more refraction of sunlight coming over the horizon to a high hill than arriving at sea level. If the light passed through the bulk of the earth's atmosphere twice, there would be nearly twice as much bending. However, the second bend was figured in our horizon-distance calculations.

The speed of light is infinitely faster than the slow turning of the earth toward the rising sun, so there is no effect here.

An interesting thing develops if you extend a "Same Sunrise-Time" line to the southwest on December 21. It very nearly crosses Sankaty Head on Nantucket Island, and also North Key Largo in the chain south of Miami, Florida. There is 116 feet of elevation at Sankaty Head, and one calculation places the sunrise only 30 seconds behind Cadillac Mountain on the winter date.

Now the interesting part: how to win that bet about the easternmost point in the United States.

Start off by asking your friend about the other three "-most" compass directions. Which state is

Southernmost?	Hawaii
Northernmost?	Alaska
Westernmost?	Alaska

Does this give you a clue? The easternmost point in the United States is not in Maine, but it is, also . . . Alaska! Whether your opponent is an expert or a layman, the reasoning is sound: The measure of "eastness" is longitude.

Longitude climbs to a maximum of 180 degrees east, which you will find passing through the state of Alaska, near Anvil Peak on Semisopochnoi Island. The western Aleutians are the easternmost part of America!

Doesn't that make Alaska the earliest sunrise state? The answer is no, because all of Alaska, including the western Aleutians, observes the same day. The International Dateline swings west of the Aleutians to follow political boundaries in this region. It's a practical and sensible convenience. The Aleutian Near Islands and nearby Siberian Commander Is-

lands see the sun rise within a few minutes of each other, but for the Siberians it is Tuesday morning, whereas for the Aleuts, it is only Monday morning. The Aleuts are seeing the last sunrise instead of the first.

To adapt Kipling's "The Ballad of East and West":

"Oh East is East, and West is West,
and only the twain shall meet,
"Where Earth and Sky meld with
the sea by 'laska's Anvil Peak."

But the first sunrise still occurs in *Maine*, anyway.

*JUST TO BE TECHNICAL . . .

Our calculations, based on the most current value for the radius of the earth, differ slightly from Mr. Wiggin's figures for the distance at which a sunrise can be seen from Mt. Katahdin, Cadillac Mountain, and Mars Hill, though these differences in no way refute Mr. Wiggin's overall conclusions. Our figure for Katahdin is 88.8 miles, for Cadillac, 47.9 miles, and for Mars Hill, 49.8 miles. These figures do not correct for refraction of light.

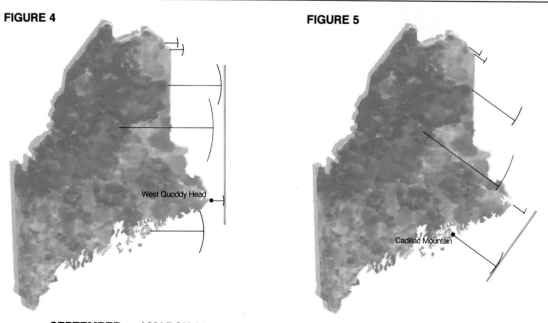

FIGURE 4

West Quoddy Head

SEPTEMBER and MARCH 21

FIGURE 5

Cadillac Mountain

DECEMBER 21

At the time this article was published (January 1978),
Floyd Davis of Foster, Rhode Island, had devoted every spare minute for thirty
years to ridding his two-acre field of rocks. What was really making him boil the week
Carol McCabe visited him, however, was that the tax assessor saw no difference
in value between what he had done and what he had not done. Yet
something about the perseverance and toughness of this man engraved
him into the minds of many, many readers....

Floyd Davis Versus the Rocks

BY CAROL MCCABE

Some people will stumble over a rock all their lives and never stoop and pick it up." Floyd Davis said that. Floyd Davis was at the time standing in a two-acre field alongside Route 6 in western Rhode Island, his foot resting on a chunk of stone the size of a woodstove, explaining how he'd spent certain parts of the last 30 years cleaning up that particular piece of land. He's about three-quarters of the way through the field now, moving into his own mid-seventies close behind the century, and hoping to last long enough to finish the job he's set for himself.

"When I'm gone, somebody who comes along after me will have something halfway decent to look at," he said, turning to view with modest satisfaction the finished portion of his field where lush green meadow grass lies smooth and level as a tablecloth. He started working on that eastern end of the field shortly after World War II, about the time that Princess Elizabeth and Lt. Mountbatten were married. At the other end of his field, rocks are set in the earth as thick as tapioca in a pudding, in sizes ranging from teacup to Tradesman van, representing the years of work still ahead of him. "It's one of those before-and-after deals," he explained. "You really had to see it before to see the difference."

Davis is a heroic figure to some of his neighbors, who have watched the land emerge from beneath the rocks year by year. Foster, the town near the Connecticut border where he lives, still fits, as few New England places do, the description that appeared in the classic state guidebook published in the 1930s by the WPA. It was, that book's writers observed, "a very rugged, hilly township whose soil is a gravelly loam better suited to grazing than farming," a soil "derived from immediately underlying rock," rocks which are "largely granite of several different ages, but all several hundred million years old," rocks "which have withstood erosion." They have not, however, withstood the inexorable drive of Floyd Davis.

"It was all wooded when I bought it," he said of his two acres, which lie between the Providence-to-Hartford highway and his pretty white house on a hillside above. "I bought the house after World War II, then I bought this piece to protect myself, to keep somebody else from building right in front of me," an undertaking that would not have occurred to any lesser man than another Floyd Davis. "You like to have a little space to walk around and not trespass."

The first two years were spent felling the trees that once grew among the rocks. "What good was it if it looked like that?" he asked, jabbing an indignant finger at a wooded patch on the far side of the highway. The wood from the field went to fuel the stoves in the house, which had been a country store when Davis, who

---

"Sometimes the old-timers around here will
give me the devil for moving rocks," he said. "They
say, 'Leave 'em be. They look kinda pretty.' Tell you the
truth, I think that's just an excuse for laziness."

18

was then a construction worker, and his bride bought the place. "Our house was in about the same shape as the land. You'd never know it for the same place. They'd used it for a village store and a barroom. The kitchen still had the meathooks on the walls. Why, my wife's sister came up to visit her and went home crying. 'Poor Del,' she said, 'having to live in a place like that.' "

In those days, Davis was working on construction jobs, sometimes as far as 300 miles from Foster, working six days a week and coming home to do his chores on the seventh. "I'd drive all Saturday night to get home and all Sunday night to get back to work."

By 1953, the year when Edmund Hillary and Tenzing Norkay became heroes by climbing Mt. Everest, he was well into

that two-acre field. "A lot of the rocks here are on the surface, comparatively. They go down only four or five feet." He examined a bathtub-size rock lying in freshly disturbed earth. "One trouble with them, though, is the biggest part is sometimes below the surface. Some of them you have to break up a little to get them out." Those are the ones he blasts down to a size that his John Deere 450 loader can handle. "Sometimes you just knock off the tops of them and cover them over with dirt to make it level."

He figures he has spent about $3000 bringing earth in to level the smooth end of the field. "Trouble with rocks is when

---

Floyd and his dog, deaf from dynamite blasting, survey the west side of the field, yet to be cleared.

you get them out, there's nothing but a big hole there."

If some of Davis' neighbors admire him, others are puzzled by his obsession. "Sometimes the old-timers around here will give me the devil for moving rocks," he said. "They say, 'Leave 'em be. They look kinda pretty.' Tell you the truth, I think that's just an excuse for laziness. To my thinking, it's no more work to get rid of them than it is to walk around them half your life."

Davis moved implacably westward across his field during the fifties and sixties. When the Army fired the first U.S. earth satellite into orbit, Floyd Davis blew the tops off rocks. While other men were digging the St. Lawrence Seaway, Floyd Davis was shoveling up rocks.

His patience was as steady as the tem-

perament of the Labrador ice sheet that, thousands of years ago, visited its largesse upon the field he now owns. The great glacier, 12,000 feet thick in some sections, edged its way down from the Arctic, covering most of eastern Canada and moving across New England south to New York. All around a central core of stagnant ice, a moving frozen river stripped the surface of all its details, transporting the materials outward and dumping them as moraines.

Floyd Davis thinks his place must have been on the edge. "Cat rocks is what they call them," he said, walking past a vast natural rock dump behind the house, pointing out rocks as big as a summer cottage. "There may have been places where the glacier stopped moving. Oh, there's numerous places in town look pretty much the same. Other people in Foster have them," he said modestly. "I'm not the only one at all, but I have my share."

So, while Yuri Gagarin and Alan Shepard, Jr. and Virgil Grissom and Gherman Stepanovich Titov looked up and out into space during the early 1960s, Floyd Davis just kept on looking down at the surface of the earth in a two-acre field beside Route 6. He kept doing other chores around the place at the same time, of course. He had fixed up the house, put on a new roof, and raised the second story to make the bedrooms cooler. He decided that a cellar was needed under the west side of the house, so he blasted one out of the earth beneath the living room. "And don't you know," his wife Del recalled recently, "when he went down there to blast, he left the cellar door open and we had rock dust all over this place for weeks." And she continued with considerable pride, "There was a rock down there half the size of a house and he never even cracked a window when he blasted it."

"I like to fix up a place to where it looks halfway decent," her husband said.

The Davis house is filled with Mrs. Davis' collections of antiques that range from Royal Bayreuth china to wooden roller skates. Beside it, as summer finally began this year, perfect rows of green shoots pierced the rich-looking soil of a vegetable garden. "Took 25 truckloads of stone out of there to make that garden," Floyd Davis observed.

As the years went on during the 1960s, Mrs. Fischer of South Dakota was busy producing quintuplets and Dr. Barnard of South Africa was transplanting hearts and Floyd Davis of Rhode Island was

gouging rocks and building walls. He had bought a five-acre piece next to the house, "to have a little more space to walk around and not trespass," he said. He cleaned that up and became interested in the low area down the slope from the house and barns that he had rebuilt. Black cattle browsed dreamily this summer around a pond where that low spot once held only "a swamp hole, a brush hole with brush 10 feet high, a swale and good for nothing to anybody." He had the pond dug almost as soon as the brush was cut. "A pond is useful for cattle, and in the country if you have a fire, a pond can save your buildings."

A sweetly sloping field descends from the barns to the pond, bisected by a tightly made gray stone wall of the sort that surrounds every field in this part of New England. "That hill was so steep you

---

"There was a rock down there [in the cellar] half the size of a house, and he never even cracked a window when he blasted it."

---

couldn't do anything with it," Davis said. "So I thought, 'I'll put in a stone wall across that steep part. It'll look better and be of some use. It'll give me a place to put some of these stones.' "

Davis' son Floyd Jr. happened to walk through the barnyard as his father was speaking to a neighbor, passing several tidy woodpiles, in each of which was stovewood or kindling of a different diameter. "You wouldn't want any rocks up at your place, would you?" the younger man asked hopefully.

Davis Senior was, meanwhile, bending to pick up the one visible scrap of detritus in his rich, green field, an anonymous red plastic object. "I don't like to see a mess," he observed. "Some people will just stumble over something every day and never pick it up. I can't understand that."

And each spring he takes a wheelbarrow and walks the roadsides near his property, picking up bushels of candy wrappers and beer cans.

Del Davis says her husband never sits for long.

"Well," he says, "tell you the way I was brought up was I had chores to do. If I ran off and played, they were right there for me to do when I got back. Nobody did them for me. And after a while I got

the idea I might as well do them and get them out of the way. And that got to be a habit, you might say. Well, you live longer working than you ever will sitting around."

The gross national product reached a trillion dollars and Evel Knievel failed to rocket 1600 feet across Snake River Canyon, but he tried. Catfish Hunter signed a $3.75 million contract with the New York Yankees, a Japanese woman climbed Mt. Everest, and an eight-year-old girl climbed Mt. Blanc. Floyd Davis advanced relentlessly across a field in western Rhode Island, pulling a coverlet of green meadow over the land the way the glacier once tucked the earth under a sheet of cold.

He is proud of having brought some of this land into use for the first time and believes that others should make the same effort to reclaim rocky soil. "Someday the people are going to have to come back to the land and live on these farms or starve to death," he said. "It'll be just like in China, where every bit of land will be used. I think they ought to take some of these people that are out of work in this country and bring them out to some of these farms and put them to work cleaning up these fields."

The first American space station was launched and a Colorado woman produced sextuplets. Frank Robinson became the first black manager in the major leagues and Floyd Davis continued to go to bed at eight each night so as to get an early start on the rocks next day.

"There's this one thing that makes me boil," he finally said. "The tax man comes around and he looks at that end of the field and then he looks at this end and he can't see any difference. He says it's all worth the same. Now you look. Which would you rather have, that end or this? It makes me boil to hear him say it's all the same," he said, bouncing furiously on his feet at the implication that all of the years of digging and blasting and filling and smoothing don't count for a cent. "Well, tell me, which would you rather have if 'twas you?"

A slow, shaggy dog, deaf from the sound of blasting, creased the tall, wet grass as she tagged her master's feet across the two-acre field beside Route 6. Floyd Davis gave her an affectionate whap, then looked back at his field as he closed the wide, swinging gate. "Tell you," he said, "I wish I was 25 or 30 years younger. It's just beginning to get where it looks halfway decent."

This is the shortest fiction piece we've published in 50 years and, for some, the most haunting. . . .

Gabriel, Gabriel

FICTION BY B.J. CHUTE

There was nothing strange about it. Nothing to indicate that it would be different from a hundred days.

The clothes on the line were as stiff and bright as they had been on other Mondays; Anna's starched blue housedress was blurred amorously against Tom's faded overalls, jerking in the wind.

Anna glanced out of the kitchen window and smiled at the overalls affectionately. Tom would need a new pair soon, and there was no extra money. There never was. She didn't care.

She moved lazily and aimlessly about the kitchen, touching things, straightening them. She was thinking of Tom, and their loving each other. Thinking that he would be home soon from the village; thinking of the long winter nights and the short winter days, and of all the days and nights that stretched ruggedly ahead of them.

She stopped by the sink and brushed the tops of her fingers across its shining metal surface. Coffee grounds. Half past one of a January day, and the coffee grounds not emptied yet. She took a newspaper from a shelf and spread it slowly on the table, holding the grounds high to drip before she tilted them onto the pages.

Then, with the damp mass pulping the newsprint, she bent over, her elbows on the table, and read mindlessly through an article on diet. Dull. She skimmed another headline. This one was familiar. It had been talked over and laughed at.

"World Will End at Two O'Clock Monday, Eminent Scientist Predicts."

There were no explanations, no jargon about sunspots and light years. Just a simple statement from Dr. Gerhard Lutz of a place called the Konhagen Institute. A wise, patient man, they said, with a brilliant record. Curious.

So many people had predicted the end of the world, so many times. Anna, with her elbows on the table, gazed at the wall and remembered. When she was a little girl, the grown-ups had given soothing assurance that the end would come on a Sunday, so that the good people would be caught in church — alert dispensation on the part of a devout Providence.

Two o'clock, Monday. That would be two o'clock today. The paper was nearly a week old.

They had joked about Dr. Lutz' theory, down in the village. "Buyin' a week's supply, Mrs. Lane?" the grocer had asked her solemnly. "Ain't that goin' to be a terrible waste, with the world so near finishin' itself? That's four days' good food nobody'll get to use."

Anna remembered the way Tom had laughed, and she paused in the dutiful act of wrapping up the coffee grounds. If they had a son, she hoped he would inherit his father's laugh. It had a trick of making everything seem suddenly right.

Her heart pounded above a rising tide of joy as she thought of bearing Tom's child, and she let the folded edges of the newspaper slip back. Dull brown stains crept over Dr. Lutz' prediction.

Five minutes of two.

In five minutes, the world would end. And in fifteen minutes — in fifteen minutes, she would make the cake frosting, unless Tom came home early. He might, if the car hadn't broken down again.

She went to the door and stood looking out, leaning against the jamb. The thought of Tom made her feel gentle and reverent. The thought of their children, and their children's children.

The valley was full of snow, and the trees stood bare against it. It was still and soft and gentle, like the sensation in her heart. Slow to break the peace of the moment, she glanced reluctantly at her watch. It was two o'clock.

Very faint, but very clear and golden, came the first notes of the trumpet.

Anna thought it was Tom's horn, and started to run down the hill.

Have you ever been hopelessly stuck on a back road in the middle of a New England blizzard in a wind-leaking roadster without a heater accompanied by a two-year-old child and your wife who is in labor? Here is a true story that gave our readers two different kinds of goose-pimples. . . .

A Message in the Wind

BY PETER LaROCHE

Blizzards and below-zero temperatures are not out of the ordinary in a New Hampshire winter. I've seen it as low as 42 below, and I've seen 20 inches of snow over a period of 24 hours come driving in before a gale, straight from the top of Mount Washington.

Such a storm, with the thermometer standing at 18 below zero, caught me on a day in January of 1934. A day I shall never forget!

Since 1932 I had been caretaker on Governor's Island on Lake Winnipesaukee in New Hampshire. After the summer homes were closed for the season, my sole duty was to patrol once a day to see that all was well. As the heavy snows came we dug in and it didn't matter if we did not get to Laconia for a week or 10 days. Both my wife Edna and I are natives of New Hampshire and, not given to caring much for bright lights, didn't mind the isolation. Our only child, Beverly, was then only 20 months old, so there was no school problem.

The large farmhouse where we lived on the island stood about two-thirds of a mile from the highway. (The island is joined to the mainland by a long causeway broken by a high bridge to allow for boat traffic underneath.) As the island was private property, we had no plow service, but this did not matter much as most of my travel about the island was on snowshoes or skis. And when we had to go to Laconia, I had plenty of time to break out a passage for my little roadster.

But January of 1934 was not just another winter month. That was the month our second child was supposed to be born. Beverly had given my wife quite a rough time before and during birth, and now the doctor was not sure as to when the child would be born. As soon as it became evident that the time was drawing near, we were to come immediately to the hospital. "Take no chances this time," Dr. Armand Normandin warned us. "It will be best to come a week or so ahead of time, just to make sure."

We knew the good doctor had our best interests at heart, but those were the Depression years, and $5 had to go a whole week for food. An extra week at the hospital could really hurt. So we watched the weather and kept everything prepared to make a run for it. Snow was light, days were fine, and we hung on.

Then it struck!

In the middle of the night the wind came lashing at the house sitting on top of the hill. I jumped out of bed and looked out the window. It was only the wind, no snow, except for what was being blown about. With a sigh of relief I climbed back into bed and fell asleep.

About seven o'clock in the morning my wife woke me up to tell me the pains had started. The wind was still battering at the house as I hurriedly dressed, stoked up the fire, and put on the coffee.

Then I looked outside, and I'm sure my heart skipped a beat. Sometime during the night it had started snowing and had turned into a blizzard. It was impossible to see more than a few yards, and the snow was already piled well over a foot deep, where it hadn't drifted to twice that depth.

I grabbed the phone and started to call the doctor. I jiggled the hook, banged the phone, and pounded on the box, but it was no use . . . the phone was dead.

Thirty minutes later, dressed as warmly as possible and having had a quick breakfast, we climbed into the roadster, roared out of the barn, and started for the highway. Two hundred feet from the barn I realized I was going to have a battle on my hands. When the car bogged down, the snow was even with the top of the radiator. I opened the trunk, took out my big snow shovel and cleared away in front of the car, then hopped in, reversed as far as I could go, and, with the car in

**The car would never take us back,
for the road was drifted in solid behind us. . . .**

low gear and the motor roaring, I slammed ahead into the ever-mounting snow. I gained about 25 feet.

For the next hour I worked like a man possessed. Icicles formed on my face as I jumped out of the car and shoveled with all my might, then jumped back in, reversed, and slammed the little car ahead.

My wife sat huddled in the seat with Beverly wrapped close to her in a blanket. The car had no heater and the snow came in through the flimsy side curtains. I was mighty scared and tried to hide it in the loud voice I usually used when denouncing the weather and the state of New Hampshire in winter. But while I shoveled, I prayed to God for help.

At the end of an hour I was less than halfway across, and I knew then that I'd never make it. My lungs ached with a burning pain, and I could hardly lift my arms. There was only one thing to do — go back to the house.

Then I found that the car would never take us back, for the road was drifted in

solid behind us. And in my exhausted state, I could never carry the two of them up that hill through those drifts. And to leave one behind. . . .

I opened the door, climbed into the car, and looked over at my wife. "How . . . how is the pain?"

"Not too bad. I think I can wait. You'd better rest a little while."

I didn't know what to say. I just nodded, then looked away. I don't know why I looked away. There was no longer anything to hide. Little Beverly began to cry.

I thought of trying to get across the lake to Harold Mitchell's farm and have him come over with his team of horses to pull us out, but I knew I could never get back in time to find my wife and child alive. At 18 below zero nothing lives for very long.

Then my wife said, "Why don't you try shouting? Someone might hear you."

Suddenly I felt like laughing. Shouting in a blizzard! Even inside the car we had to speak loudly to hear ourselves. She

insisted that I try, so I stepped out and started shouting as loud as I could. Every time I did, it brought on a coughing spell, and after a few tries I had to stop.

Feeling a bit rested, I decided we might as well die trying, so I resumed shoveling, but was making no headway as a languorous feeling started to come over me. I rested against the car.

Then I saw him, and I jumped in astonishment. Out of the blizzard he came. A big man dressed in a heavy mackinaw and a fur cap. He came on strongly through the drifted snow and stopped before me. I peered at him to see if it was someone I knew who might have guessed my predicament, but this was a stranger.

"Why th' devil are you out here in a car!" he shouted.

In my joy at seeing him, my words tumbled one over the other as I told him that I was trying to get my wife to the hospital.

He grabbed the shovel and began clearing snow like a plow. I continued to

January 19, 1934 — the day after the blizzard. The author is standing on the snowbank in front of the door of his home on Governor's Island, Lake Winnipesaukee, New Hampshire.

ram ahead to gain every foot. When we hit the causeway where the road was elevated and the wind kept most of the snow blown away, my helper rode the back bumper to give me traction, and we managed to get all the way across the causeway without shoveling.

From the end of the causeway to the highway this man must have shoveled tons of snow. When I tried to relieve him, he'd wave me back into the car, shouting that this was just exercise for him.

Two or three times I looked at my wife and knew by the whiteness of her face and the tightly pressed lips that the cold was getting to her, and the pain was increasing. I was badly frightened and my nerves were jangled to the extent that my foot bounced up and down on the accelerator and I couldn't stop it.

I prayed to God that the big figure ahead of the car who shoveled snow like a madman would hold out. And hold out he did. Two and a half hours after leaving the house, the little car broke through onto the partly cleared highway, and we were on our way.

When I made as if to stop, our benefactor waved us on, and in the rearview mirror, I saw him standing in a drift at the roadside — a big figure encased in a mantle of snow. He waved once more before the blizzard shut off the view between us.

At two o'clock the next morning, in the warm safety of the hospital, our daughter Norma was born.

Then I began the search to find the big man who had come to us in our greatest hour of need. For days I snowshoed from one bobhouse (these are little huts and cabins put on the lake for ice fishing) to another asking about the man.

At first I was confident I would find him close in along the channel by the causeway, but after I had eliminated the few that were there, I began to range farther out.

It was ridiculous to think that anyone

The author Peter LaRoche and daughter Norma LaRoche Fish, who, born in the aftermath of the blizzard of January 1934, now resides in Sherman Oaks, California.

that far away could have heard me shouting. But then, it was ridiculous to think that anyone 500 feet away could have heard me calling. Maybe he had been caught out on the lake and was trying to make his way to our house on the hill? This seemed the only logical answer.

Four days later I found him in a bobhouse by Eagle Island, about a mile and a half from where he had come looming out of the blizzard. It was an unusually large house and I figured whoever owned it must have it equipped for long fishing sessions. I was right. I banged on the door and in a moment it opened, and there he stood. He looked at me quizzically for a moment, then smiled.

"What was it, a boy or a girl?" he boomed.

I told him it was a girl, over eight pounds, and that the wife and daughter were doing well. He invited me in and I shook off my snowshoes and stepped inside. The hut was fitted out like the cabin on a cruiser, with a little galley, bunks, and a drop table that made into a dinette.

My first question, after my profound thanks, which he waved away, was how he had come to be near us.

"Well, it's a funny thing," he said. "I've been fishing here in the channel by Eagle Island for about eight years. Now, here about 10 days ago, I got the idea I could do better if I set my house in the channel north of the causeway bridge. So, I drugged it over there, and would you know it, I never caught a fish! So, day or two after the blizzard let up, I drugged it back. I'm doin' all right here. Averagin' two, three a day."

He stuck out his hand. "Oh, by the way, the name's Schrader. Nick Schrader. Pavin' contractor in the summer, fisherman in the winter."

I introduced myself and shook hands. Then I asked what had been in my mind for the past week. "Mr. Schrader, what brought you out of your bobhouse at the height of the blizzard?"

A surprised expression came across his face. "Why, I heard you shout."

"You heard me shout over a quarter of a mile away in a roaring blizzard, and you inside your bobhouse?"

"As plain as I'm hearin' you now."

In a moment of silence it became evident to Mr. Schrader that what he had said was physically impossible. He cleared his throat and looked away. Then said, "It . . . it must have carried on the wind, eh?"

"It must have," I agreed.

— courtesy of Peter LaRoche

ANOTHER WINTRY RECOLLECTION

It was a few minutes after midnight, and the official Canadian Pacific thermometer at the railroad station in Newport, Vermont, read well below zero. The passenger train from Montreal to Boston had just pulled in and was chuffing impatiently while mail bags and baggage were being hustled on and off.

A young man opened the rear door of the last car and stepped onto the observation platform for a breath of that cold air. He was expensively dressed and wore a pair of soft, furlined gloves, which he pulled off to light a cigarette. He laid the gloves on the railing.

As the train rattled and banged, pulling itself together for departure, one of the gloves fell to the roadbed. One of the mail handlers saw it fall, grabbed it up, and ran after the accelerating train. He threw it toward the young man but his throw fell short.

The young man waved, smiled, and tossed the other glove to the ground.

One glove is of little use. Two gloves can warm both the hands and the heart.

John Cleary

*Most of us at Yankee can recall the half-dozen or so
articles that, through the years, have elicited the most requests for reprints.
This is definitely one of them. . . .*

Abby Rockefeller's
Greywater Greenhouse

BY EDIE CLARK

American social theorist Thorstein Veblen considered waste to be an indication of wealth. "Conspicuous consumption" was what he called it, and he further suggested that the United States was affluent by virtue of both its ravenous consumption of goods and its resultantly overflowing garbage pails.

When the world was vaster and more slimly populated, solutions for waste disposal were perhaps simpler. There were even times when entire cities picked up and moved a good distance away rather than have to deal with their surroundings, so thoroughly polluted were they with their own wastes.

And as the world gets smaller, waste disposal schemes become less and less effective. With all good intentions, we try to bury it, burn it, drown it, or entomb it, yet waste seems to be waste and somehow comes back to us, often in the nastiest ways: landfill dumps are running out of space; our lakes, oceans, rivers, and groundwaters are becoming polluted by seeping industrial and household wastes; septic systems are undergoing closer scrutiny and are being subjected to tougher regulations; and wastes from nuclear power plants are radioactive problems no one seems able to deal with.

Abby Rockefeller believes waste is a resource. In a confident and articulate manner, she presents her theory, simultaneously unveiling concrete evidence of its validity: over the past six years, she has gradually transformed her Cambridge, Massachusetts, home into a state-of-the-art, self-reliant dwelling that would be the envy of any rural homesteader, yet she has still retained a sophisticated environment. Schizophrenic this may be, yet it demonstrates clearly that ecologically sound living does not have to be either rustic or primitive.

First impressions of Abby's comfortable, tastefully decorated home in a sleepy Cambridge neighborhood prove deceptive: two chubby, Heinz-57 dogs snooze on the living room couch; books and records line the walls adjacent to an impressive fieldstone fireplace. The kitchen, open and airy by virtue of a line of skylights over the counter, is modern and obviously the kitchen of an interested cook: exotic spices, imported coffee, and organic dry goods line the open shelves. Sliding glass doors open outside off the kitchen onto an attractive wooden deck from the center of which rises a gnarled fruit tree. So far, it seems a home fairly typical of a Boston humanities professor, which is just one of Abby's professions. Just beyond the deck is a greenhouse, a standard three-sided, lean-to style that could easily be taken for the weekend workshop of an amateur orchid grower — which is exactly what it's not. So much for first impressions.

Within this gracious, homey atmosphere resides the oldest functioning Clivus Multrum in the country, along with a filter system that prepares "greywater"

(household washwater) for recycling in a solar greenhouse, which in turn provides a significant harvest of both summer and winter vegetables. In essence, Abby recycles much of the waste generated in her home without in any way detracting from a gracious style of living. In fact, she claims, all these additions make her life more comfortable and more convenient than before.

Abby's interest in the Clivus (pronounced Clee-vus) Multrum (a Swedish composting toilet that's been in use in that country since the forties) began in 1971 when she purchased two of the units, one for her farm in New Hampshire and one for her home in Cambridge. Subsequently, she was so impressed that she obtained the exclusive U.S. rights to sell the Clivus Multrum and has been president of this small, Cambridge-based operation ever since. The first in a now somewhat crowded composting toilet market, the Clivus has been called the "Cadillac" of composting toilets: over a period of time, using no energy or chemicals, it organically converts toilet and garbage wastes into a rich garden compost. It's large but can be installed in houses both new and old, even those without full basements. It was invented by Rikard Lindstrom more than 30 years ago when conditions on the Baltic Sea became serious enough to merit alternatives.

Mr. Lindstrom's son, Carl, a former division head in Sweden's equivalent to the Environmental Protection Agency, is now head of Research and Development at Clivus Multrum USA and has been responsible for many of the progressive features now being offered in addition to the Clivus Multrum. Abby credits much of the unique design of the greywater greenhouse to Carl's ingenuity and his engineering background, though they worked on the project together.

Carl and Abby began by refining the strengths of the Clivus. In addition to its composting function, the Clivus also effectively separates toilet wastes from the sink and tub wastewater exiting the house to the septic or sewer system. Realizing this potential, Carl designed a device called a roughing or trickling filter that filters hair, lint, food particles, and grease from household wastewater, making it possible for it to be reused at the same time that it is being purified. The

Abby Rockefeller in her Cambridge (Massachusetts) home, where she proved that ecologically sensible living can be maintained in urban as well as rural areas — and without sacrificing either comfort or beauty.

trickle filter is about the same size as *Star Wars'* celebrity robot Artoo-Detoo, and can nestle comfortably into even the smallest basement.

Initially, they piped this filtered greywater to a perforated pipe running through Abby's pile of leaf mulch behind her house. The results there triggered the idea of the greywater greenhouse, which is now attached to the south side of Abby's house. Together, Abby and Carl incorporated solar greenhouse concepts, deep soil beds, and greywater irrigation to produce a truly remarkable year-round source of vegetables in the midst of an urban environment in New England — that is, tomatoes in midwinter.

Solar greenhouses are popping up all over the country, not all of them as im-

pressive or streamlined as Abby's. Hers needs little maintenance (she can be away for over a week without having to call in a neighbor to water or tend the garden in any way). It uses passive solar design and simple heat exchangers from her furnace for heat, thus eliminating the need for solar collectors or bulky hot-water storage units and, because of the deep soil beds, which are in themselves a unique greenhouse concept, it can produce root crops and possibly even trees, items not within the reach of a conventional greenhouse, solar or no solar.

Thus, even though water conservation is a strong advantage to the Clivus system (a family of four flushes about 40,000 gallons of pure drinking water down the toilet every year using conven-

tional plumbing), it is by no means the only advantage. Abby's setup dramatizes that the recovery of nutrients otherwise lost is as important as conserving water, possibly more so, and fosters a holistic approach to living. The system has the potential for making each family responsible for treating its own wastes, possibly eliminating complex and centralized sewage- and waste-disposal systems.

Some people may view all this as an eccentric departure for the daughter of the chairman of the board of one of the world's most powerful banks. And well it may be. Chase Manhattan and Clivus Multrum share initials only. There have been times when the financial health of Clivus Multrum USA has been questionable. But Abby's persistent and energetic

Using passive solar design, Abby's greywater greenhouse required very little maintenance and provided a thriving environment for her plants year round. Her system has since been copied extensively.

By combining her Clivus Multrum composting toilet with a special filtering system, Abby was able to recycle household washwater ("greywater") for her greenhouse.

efforts to keep it afloat have been successful. At this writing, there are Clivus Multrums in most of the U.S. states, more than 700 altogether, with the highest number here in New England. And she's even sold a few to other Rockefellers, although the Chase Manhattan Bank has not yet installed one.

But that's still not enough, and one of the biggest obstacles has been what Abby regards as the indifference, sometimes hostility, of state and local officials. And it's true that from the start Clivus has met with a healthy amount of controversy, on which Abby comments: "One of the most persistent problems has been that the states approve the system, subject to local approval. That way, no matter how positive the state's attitude is, it can be quickly negated by local officials who often haven't taken the time to consider the Clivus Multrum's advantages. It is still the very committed who purchase and advocate the Clivus," Abby continues. "Even those who are terribly enthusiastic can lose steam when confronted with stubborn town officials."

The uninitiated think of it as some sort of indoor outhouse, thus considering it more a backward step than anything as progressive as Abby and other Clivus owners insist. "The Clivus is not just a toilet; it is a treatment plant and a garbage disposal as well. Unlike an outhouse, the Clivus doesn't smell, doesn't pollute the groundwater, doesn't lose all that fertilizer, and isn't outdoors!" Listening to Abby, one can't help but conclude that selling this system must take a touch of the evangelist. She's a believer.

"For most people there are some psychological adjustments that must be made in living with a Clivus," Abby admits, and adds that they are working on a new design that visually will more closely resemble the conventional flush toilet.

And it may be the addition of the greywater greenhouse that will conclude the Clivus controversy: it is the logical extension of the Clivus concept, completing the cycle of waste to resource. Abby considers the Clivus/greenhouse system satisfying aesthetically, psychologically, and environmentally. It con-

verts wastes, recovers nutrients normally lost in conventional methods of treatment, purifies water, and produces vegetables. It can be built almost anywhere, in an urban or rural environment, does not require a lot of space, and is not prohibitively expensive. And it's convenient. "A Clivus makes a house *more* convenient. The point is not to eliminate convenience but to increase it without increasing environmental damage. *All* waste is a resource. We should eliminate the word 'waste' from our vocabulary. What is waste treated one way is a resource treated another," Abby says. Such transformations do not require complex or centralized technologies.

"Huge sacrifices need not be made in creating an ecologically sound environment. It is very possible to retain a good standard of living without the destruction of resources and great expenditures of energy."

Her home is a testimony to this. *But* — if Thorstein Veblen were alive today to inspect Abby Rockefeller's garbage, he might write her off as a pauper. ॐ

The Champion Sleepwalker

BY W.A. SWANBERG

In 1845, the wealthy Tirrell family of Weymouth, Massachusetts, was holding frequent grave conferences with one question on the agenda: What to do about Albert?

Tall, 25-year-old Albert Tirrell seemed determined to dive headfirst into ruin and drag the proud family name with him. The possessor of a pretty wife, Prudence, and two small children, he had made a commendable start only to fall into horrendous error. When his father died in 1843 Albert was left a large inheritance and the nominal control of the Tirrell shoe factory, the biggest in Weymouth. Such a young man could scarcely be given full authority over an enterprise employing scores of men and machines, but he labored diligently and was showing considerable promise late in 1844 when he made that regrettable business trip to New Bedford. It was in New Bedford, then a rip-snorting whaling port, that he met a young lady named Maria Bickford whose aims in life were as dubious as her appearance was alluring.

That was when the Tirrell troubles began. Albert promptly dropped the shoe business, forsook his family, and concentrated his time on Maria Bickford. Maria, described in an old account as "a beautiful and designing wench who played the concertina with skill," fell in wholeheartedly with this arrangement, charmed not only by Albert but by the largesse he tossed her way. The next thing the Tirrells knew, he had installed her in a Boston apartment and seldom put in an appearance except to draw money.

Time and again, Nathaniel Bayley, Albert's 32-year-old brother-in-law, sat down with him to deliver a stern lecture on the duties of a husband and a businessman. Albert would raise his hand and vow, "So help me, I will put that woman out of my life." Yet he seemed mesmerized by Maria, and although they often quarreled violently he always returned to her. His forlorn wife was in

tears. The Tirrell inheritance was dwindling at a merry clip, for Maria had expensive tastes in jewelry and clothing. Gossip was rife in both Boston and nearby Weymouth. In September 1845, Albert and Maria were ejected from the staid Hanover House in Boston after an uninhibited party climaxed by a fight. That was the last straw. To teach him a lesson, the family had Albert arrested and charged with adultery.

No sooner had they done this than they realized what a disgrace it would be to have one of their clan besmirched with a criminal record. They now begged the court for leniency. On October 21, Albert was freed after paying a bond and agreeing to keep the peace for six months — above all, to shun Maria.

He kept his word for less than 24 hours. Maria had meanwhile taken lodging in a house on Cedar Lane in Beacon Hill. Sure enough, Albert, hopelessly bewitched, showed up there on October 22. He was with Maria so much during the next five days and home so little that the Tirrell family must have wondered what, if anything, would bring the black sheep back to the fold.

At about four on the morning of October 27, smoke issued from the house on Cedar Lane and someone raised the alarm. Firemen, coming on the run, discovered a smouldering mattress on the upstairs landing. Another mattress was blazing in Maria Bickford's room. More important, Maria herself lay on the floor in her chemise, dead, her throat cut deeply. A bloody razor lay some eight feet away. Matches had been stuffed into the mattresses, making it clear that someone had murdered Maria and then tried to burn down the house to destroy the evidence.

Next to arrive were the police, who learned that Albert Tirrell had been with Maria that night and, in fact, had left without taking his fancy figured vest.

Meanwhile a disheveled Albert was

racing across nearby Bowdoin Square and pounding at the door of Timothy Fullam, who kept a livery stable. Fullam knew him, having previously furnished him with rigs at odd hours. He got up and harnessed a horse while Albert muttered vaguely, "Someone tried to murder me — I'm in a scrape." He seemed in a stupor, speaking in a disconnected way, but Fullam was not surprised, for he had seen the young aristocrat in his cups on other occasions.

They drove to Weymouth, where Albert had a quick conference with Nathaniel Bayley. The brother-in-law, well aware that Albert had violated his probation, advised him to keep out of sight. It was not until later that the police came looking for Albert and the shocked Bayley found that he was wanted not for a petty misstep but for murder. Bayley told the officers he had no idea of Albert's whereabouts. After they left, he sought out the scapegrace, accused him of the crime, gave him some money, and told him to clear out of the country.

According to Bayley's later story, Albert seemed "strangely confused" and denied any knowledge of the murder. Nevertheless, he apparently agreed that his position would be embarrassing if he stayed. He took the money, went to Boston, shipped as a seaman aboard the freighter *Sultana,* and vanished for four months. Not until February, when the *Sultana* docked in New York, was he arrested and brought back for trial.

It was the sensation of the decade. The whole Boston area was agog when County Attorney Samuel Parker opened the trial on March 24, 1846, with the demand that Albert Tirrell be hanged for murder. There was evidence aplenty that he had been with Maria on the fatal night and that they had often quarreled violently. There was proof that he had fled to the livery stable after the crime and been driven home. Nor did his flight to sea seem the act of a man with an unsullied conscience. All in all, seasoned observers said that Prosecutor Parker's job was easier than rolling off a log, since nothing could save Albert from the gallows.

By this time one might think the long-suffering Tirrells would have decided that hanging was, all things considered, the most certain and permanent method of keeping Albert out of trouble. On the contrary. No Tirrell had ever been hanged, and they did not propose to start now if they could help it. They retained Rufus Choate to avert such a disgrace.

Choate, who had recently completed Daniel Webster's unexpired term in the United States Senate, was one of the most eloquent pleaders of the day, a man whose services came high. Some observers sniffed that the Tirrells were carrying their snootiness pretty far when they insisted on paying a fat fee for an attorney who could no more save Albert's neck than the courthouse chimney sweep.

But Choate, a resourceful fellow, had made a close study of the evidence. He had been struck by the statements of both Timothy Fullam and Nathaniel Bayley that Albert seemed in a stupor after the crime, as if he did not know where he was. After talks with the family, he hit on a line of defense that would make American legal history. When he rose in the courtroom, he staggered Prosecutor Parker, the judge, and the jury by what he said.

"If Albert Tirrell murdered Maria Bickford," he told them, "he was not responsible for what he did because he was asleep at the time and unaware of what he was doing."

As people stared at him pop-eyed, he proceeded to paint Albert as the champi-

on sleepwalker of the whole New England area. From earliest childhood, Choate said, the boy had been even more active while asleep than when awake. When he was three, his parents had found him missing from his crib. They were horrified to discover that he had climbed out on the roof of an adjacent porch and was toddling along the edge of it, sound asleep, only a step from disaster. His father rescued him and put him back to bed. The lad remembered nothing of it in the morning. On another occasion he had paid a night visit to the kitchen, taken a quart jar of maple syrup, and distributed its contents over the parlor rug so thoroughly that the rug had to be discarded.

His nocturnal athletics were so alarming that for his own safety his parents had been forced to bar his windows and lock his door after putting him to bed. However, as he grew older he complained about this restraint so that the practice of locking his door was discontinued for a time. One night when he was 16, he had left the house clad only in his nightshirt and his father's best beaver hat, harnessed the horse, and driven to his uncle's home a mile distant. The uncle, aroused by the arrival of the horse, was amazed to find Albert unhitching the beast at the stable. He was clearly asleep, performing this operation in a daze, heedless of the early winter chill. When the uncle shook him, he awoke with a start, unaware of how he had got there.

Young Prudence Tirrell related that Albert, a lover of whist, had once left his bed in the small hours. When she became aware of his absence she found him in the library, playing whist with me-

chanical motions in his sleep although he had no companions. Again, she had awakened to find him pressing his fingers around her neck, apparently bent on strangling her. Her sharp cry brought him to his senses, whereupon he apologized profusely.

A seaman from the *Sultana* testified that Albert had slept alone on deck by choice, saying he was a restless sleeper and did not wish to disturb the others. Early one freezing morning the second mate had seen him climbing at a perilous height on ice-covered rigging. Everyone was in a sweat until he got down safely, when it was seen that he was in a daze. The mate seized him by the arm. Albert started, stared around in surprise, and said, "Mate, where have I been?"

"That was precisely my client's condition on the morning of October 27 when he reached the livery stable," Choate said. "He was just awakening from somnambulistic sleep. He did not know where he had been or what he had been doing."

Drs. Walter Channing and Samuel Woodward gave expert testimony for the defense about the remarkable things sleepwalkers could do. "In this somnambulistic state," said Dr. Woodward, "a person can dress himself, set a house on fire, or commit a homicide. The somnambulist, however, is not insane. He is dreaming asleep, while the insane person is dreaming awake."

During the beginning of all this talk about sleepwalking, Prosecutor Parker had assumed the expression of a man enjoying a hilarious joke. As it progressed, however, his amusement gave way to indignation. When his turn came, he allowed that he had never heard such nonsense in all his life. Albert's condition of semi-stupor after the crime, he declared, was due simply and solely to an excess of rum, a beverage of which he was known to be inordinately fond. If the jury found him anything but guilty, Parker hinted, they must indeed be sleepwalking.

But Attorney Choate had cast his spell. As the jurors retired to deliberate, according to one waggish report, "many of them appeared to be in a somnambulistic state." They returned two hours later and pronounced Albert Tirrell not guilty. A free man, Albert walked happily out with his family.

Very probably he pinched himself to make sure that he was awake.

– illustration by Hamilton Green

A·JANUARY
SAMPLER

☞ Memorable thoughts, quotes, and assorted tidbits from the last 50 January issues. ☜

NOW IS THE GOOD OLD DAYS

☞ "We didn't know it was hard to read by oil lamps because nobody had anything better. The kerosene lamp seemed so much better than the candles that we could remember. I thought it was wonderful to be able to get a light just by pressing a button and not to have to bother with matches and a chimney. But I can remember a woman who told me that she preferred the kerosene lamps to electricity. She was a queer specimen." **Miss Ruby Hemenway, weekly columnist for the Greenfield (Massachusetts)** *Recorder,* **at the time of her 100th birthday.** *(From "The Oldest Newspaper Columnist on Earth" by Edie Clark.)*

— Carole Allen

Miss Ruby Hemenway.

ONE MUFFIN AND A LITTLE CHEESE

☞ "True, some of our customers were a bit demanding and, as I look back on the scene, I realize now that some were just plain spoiled. Take, as an example, the 'Cheese Grande Dame,' as we occasionally spoke of her (in private). Along with her small slice of cheese (coon, cut from a fresh wheel, never a piece that had been lying around) she would select one raisin bran muffin. These two items were to be sent to her home in Louisburg Square. Up the hill from the Tremont Street store she would hike accompanied by an S.S. Pierce stock boy. He kept a respectable three paces to the rear and carried the cheese and muffin around to the rear door, where he would wait while the lady let herself in by the front door, opened the rear door, received her eleven o'clock repast, and handed the boy a nickel for his trouble." **James W. Spring, Jr., long-time employee of the S.S. Pierce Co. in Boston.** *(From "Here at S.S. Pierce, Madam, We Do Not Permit Profanity.")*

I HATE TO BOTHER ANYONE

☞ Mr. Pariseau keeps his household accounts on the back of an envelope, each item printed in a fastidious hand: $46 a month mortgage, $22.50 a week for food stamps, $19 a month for electricity, $5 for phone, $18 a month for bottled gas, and $40 a month for medication for his wife and himself.

Their living expenses exceed Mr. Pariseau's Social Security payment. He owes the Welfare Department $400 borrowed before his first check came in. His own operation was covered by Medicare, but his wife recently had her gall bladder removed and that added another $1700 to their indebtedness. Mrs. Pariseau is so crippled with arthritis that she has to slide in and out of a chair. Her son drives her to a faith healer in Quebec twice a month. The faith healer believes Mrs. Pariseau can be helped — if she can afford it.

The "Outreach" worker wants to get Mrs. Pariseau on Social Security and somehow restore Mr. Pariseau's lost $72. But the Northeast Kingdom [in northern Vermont] doesn't have a permanent Social Security office. The traveling representative comes to Newport on the first and third Wednesday of each month, and one case like the Pariseaus' among so many doesn't bubble to the top that quickly.

The Pariseaus don't understand what happened to them. He repeats over and over in English and French, "I hate to bother anyone." He is both afraid and ashamed. He believes he lost benefits because he did something "wrong" but he can't imagine what that could be. *(From "The End-of-the-Road People" by Stan Bicknell.)*

— Don Bousquet

"How's the Indian pudding today, Eleanor?"

THAT'S NOT THE WAY IT WAS

☞ "I don't know why they wanted those San Juan Hills. It was summer, I remember that, and we were in a valley looking up at that blockhouse, and a ranch house. Now that ranch house was directly up there ahead of us. There wasn't much of an army up there on that hill. It was the snipers. They were firing down on us.

"Now everybody thinks Teddy Roosevelt called out 'Charge!' and we all went galloping up that hill on our horses waving swords and shooting away at everything. That's not the way it was. Teddy was the only one up on a mule. He claimed it was a horse, but it was a mule. He wasn't up there to be a hero, either. Up there, the snipers had a better chance of spotting him. He was up there so the men could see him — so they'd know which way he was headed.

The charge up San Juan Hill by an artist who didn't know the facts!

"He said 'Forward!' That's what he said. And as we were moving along, he'd call out, 'Up the hill' and 'Let's Go!' Things like that.

"I don't remember exactly how many of us there were charging up that hill behind him. If it was 50, it was a lot. Some got hit on the way up. I didn't. Those Spaniards weren't very good shots." **William Bickford of South Boston, aged 103.** *(From "The Man Who Walked Up San Juan Hill While Teddy Roosevelt Rode a Mule" by Keith Douglas.)*

Jean Burden

ABOUT *YANKEE'S* POETRY . . .

☞ An unsuccessful poet takes himself too seriously, his poem not seriously enough. The pompous attitude results in an inflated tone to the poem — it promises more than it delivers, or it gives off an air of earnestness that is more offensive than enlightening. A really good poem is often about a very ordinary, commonplace thing or event; but because the poet sees it with more than ordinary insight he chooses the poem's ingredients to communicate all that he sees — plus an indefinable magic that opens up the poem, sometimes in almost an explosion of sensibility and connotation. It liberates the subject and, in so doing, ourselves. **Jean Burden, *Yankee*'s prize-winning Poetry Editor since 1954.** *(From "Poetry is a Celebration of the Concrete.")*

BE ON THE SAFE SIDE — THE LEFT

☞ In your January 1974 issue, Mary C. Lowe, of Assonet, Massachusetts, stated that her father taught her that you sat on the left side of a carriage or wagon and mounted from the left.

I asked my husband if he knew why, as he is a former teamster, and he said that usually the quiet horse was placed on the street side, or left. Since many wagons had their mounting steps on the front, it was far safer to mount from the side where the quiet horse was. Many times you had to use the harness itself to help you get in the wagon. Some people even used the whippletree. You can imagine what a nervous horse would do when suddenly whacked in the rear with a tipping whippletree.

Dorothy N. Hadder
Oxford, Connecticut

 "I don't admire *Moby Dick* and I don't admire Melville. I think he's a jughead and a pansy and a few other things like that. He said they steered the *Pequod* with a tiller made from a whale's jawbone. They never would have trusted it. Too brittle. It might have snapped like a pipe stem in a seaway. . . .

"There's always somebody who is trying to take me for a ride. I had quite a skirmish with a fellow on the answer I gave about the name Opodeldoc. I knew perfectly well that Opodeldoc wasn't anything but a liniment from the early 1800s. He thought that I was talking about a

"THE ORACLE" ALWAYS SPOKE HIS MIND.

The late Joseph Chase Allen.

comic strip that was published maybe 60 years ago with a character called Opie Dildock, and he wrote me a scathing letter telling me about this comic strip. I told him that he came

late to the party. I gave him the recipe for making Opodeldoc, because I've got it right here in the dictionary. I told him if he suffered from liver trouble I sympathized with him — I had a relative who did, and no one could get along with him, either. *Yankee* published that.

"Another homely old-fashioned expression I have run across here and in various other places where I have lived is 'catouse' — have you heard of it? It has to do with a mild sort of a squabble or argument, maybe more than mild. They will say some fellow was gonna get married but the folks didn't care for his choice and they raised a hell of a catouse about it. It would be proper to spell it c-a-t-h-o-u-s-e, because originally the word was 'cat house' and it meant something absolutely disorderly, improper, and everything that goes with it. That's what it was and that's what I told them." **Joseph Chase Allen of Martha's Vineyard who, for over 30 years, answered readers' questions in *Yankee*'s "Sayings of the Oracle" column.** *(From "Who is 'The Oracle,' Anyway?" by Susan Mahnke.)*

THE FIRST SNOWMOBILES

 Back in 1913, Virgil D. White, a West Ossipee, New Hampshire, Ford dealer, invented and patented the "Snowmobile." What's more, he coined the name and copyrighted it — though both copyright and patent have long since expired. The rig was a combination of runners and caterpillar traction fitted to Ford cars of that era. Seventy such machines were built by hand in 1923, and then some 3500 a year were turned out on an assembly-line basis until 1929, when demand ceased and the company was liquidated. White's Snowmobile devices were shipped to 21 states, Canada, Sweden — even to Egypt, where extra wheels replaced the runners to form the "Sandmobile."

Over 20,000 snowmobiles like the above were manufactured during the 1920s in Ossipee, New Hampshire. At right is the late Virgil D. White, inventor of the snowmobile.

– courtesy of Jean L. Schillare

THE GENTLE ART OF LISTENING TO SPEECHES

by Garnette Wassen

☞ As a result of all the listening to dinner speeches I've done in my life, I've worked out a basic posture. It consists of placing my left elbow on the table and resting my cheek in the palm of my left hand. Not only does this convey the impression that I am following every word, but in case my eyes grow heavy I can use the tip of my forefinger to prop an eyebrow up while I draw the lower lid down with my thumb.

But the first thing a listener should learn is to anchor himself securely. Some listeners court disaster during an after-dinner speech by lacing the fingers together and resting the chin on them like a hammock. The danger here is that, in the course of a very long speech, the fingers are apt to come unlaced without warning, plunging the chin into your hot cup of coffee.

The safest plan is to grip the table and scowl intently, pursing your lips and nodding your head rhythmically whenever the speaker's glance comes to rest on you. But don't nod *too* rhythmically, because the steady movement tends to have a decidedly soporific effect.

Naturally, the listener should vary his expression according to the circumstances. For children's recitations I always assume an indulgent smile, with my head tilted quizzically. The trouble is that after the first 12 stanzas my smile starts getting rigid, my jaw muscles tighten into knots, and my lips draw back in a sinister smile. This sometimes frightens a reciting child — but hardly enough to call off the recitation.

Sooner or later every listener must face the problem of how to stifle a yawn. Swallowing is not recommended, because the gulp is apt to be audible and the effort to strangle it without being detected produces an expression of acute anguish, causing the eyes to pop and tears to course inexplicably down the cheeks.

This is bad enough if the narrator is telling a funny story, but it is worse if the story is emotional, since he will then be flattered into thinking that he has touched some deep sympathetic chord in his audience and will make his story even longer.

If a yawn cannot be suppressed, I usually resort to some ruse like upsetting my drink or dropping a lighted cigarette

– Austin Stevens

EAST FALMOUTH, MASS. (AP) — After 46 years of staring at the ocean, Joseph and Charlotte Hindley, the last civilian lighthouse keepers in New England, confessed that it was all pretty boring. About the biggest problem they faced was learning to live with the fog horn. . . .

NEWS ITEM: ROBERT W. LINLEY, JR. MONROE, CONN.

...AND WHO KNOWS, WE MAY EVEN DISCOVER THAT WE MISS IT A LITTLE...

HOME SWEET HOME

Eno Nash

down behind the upholstery of the sofa. While I'm on my hands and knees during the ensuing excitement, I can get rid of my yawn safely, and if I'm really alert I can continue creeping on all fours out of the room.

WHEN SLEEP IS NOT IN MY BED

☞ I once heard a sound that I like to remember when sleep is not in my bed waiting for me. It was at a hunting camp in Maine. There was a skim of ice out from the shore a ways and the wind was having fun breaking it up with the waves and trying to pile it on the shore. It sounded like 600 wind chimes accompanying a flock of blackbirds that have congregated to go south and are arguing about the best route. It was a very pretty tinkly sound, and as I went to sleep I made up my mind then to remember it. I can still hear it. . . . *(From "Sounds to Remember" by Russell G. Willcox.)*

P.S. on the above: *While* Yankee *has never been accused of being a Lonely Hearts magazine, Russell G. Willcox did become part of a*

Russell Willcox and his "Swopper" bride, Rachel, 1971.

nice little Yankee love story. An avid user of our "Swopper's Column" during the 1960s, Mr. Willcox often swopped things with and then began to write a lady named Rachel in Alaska. In the spring of 1971 they met, married, honeymooned in Alaska, and then moved to his home in South Egremont, Massachusetts. We published this photo of the happy couple in our June 1971 issue.

CHAPTER 2

February

*I*n "the old days," we always began our February issue planning with three articles, one about George Washington, one on Abraham Lincoln, and the third having some connection with St. Valentine's Day. February just wasn't February without those three subjects covered. So it was a bit of a shock that not one of the reader/selectors for this book mentioned any of them! The favorite Lincoln piece was in an April issue (see Chapter 4) and nobody had a favorite Washington or valentine story.

Besides the articles about a death on Katahdin, volleyball, boiled mittens, snowbanks, an unusual priest, and those Russian fireplaces, the most remembered February subject was the series of readers' letters attempting to determine "the shortest distance between Rhode Island and New York as the crow flies." It was a trick question because the answer was "no distance." "Picture a seagull floating out in Long Island Sound," the final letter read. "His head could be in Rhode Island while his wings are in Connecticut and his tail in New York!"

February is also the month in which the worst Yankee poem was published. Although the year was 1959, some readers still remember it, with nausea. The last four lines: "A home is more than four square walls/ With a ceiling up above./ It's a place for someone to love us/ And where there's someone to love."

Happy Washington's, Lincoln's, and Valentine's Day.

Storm-driven winter waves toppled Old Orchard's first pier, built in 1898. The new pier houses summer concessions and game rooms.

– photograph by Stephen O. Muskie

– illustration by Bruce Hammond

*Although the rescue and death occurred in February 1974,
the tragedy is still discussed among New England mountaineers. Mel Allen interviewed
some of the survivors six years later for our February 1980 issue and still there were
traces of guilt. Yet, as everyone allows, that storm truly eliminated all choices
but the final one, between life and death.*

Making the Final Choice on Katahdin

BY MEL ALLEN

On Thursday evening, January 31, 1974, a fierce winter storm cut a swath of destruction across northern New England. It tore roofs off of mobile homes and tossed them into nearby trees, and sent tree limbs crashing into power lines, leaving thousands of homes without electricity. And it trapped six men on a tiny ledge below Pamola Peak on Mt. Katahdin, 4600 feet above sea level, yet still 300 feet below a ridge that offered escape.

They awoke that day to a breathtaking vista from their camp at Chimney Pond in Baxter State Park in northern Maine. Mt. Katahdin, 5207 feet at its summit, was bathed in a red glow, a beautiful yet ominous warning that within the next 12 to 18 hours the unseasonably balmy weather of the past week would change, though to what extent was unknown.

They were six men who had come to Katahdin to climb its ice and snow gullies, which for size and grandeur were unparalleled in the Northeast. They had met at the Pinkham Notch headquarters of the Appalachian Mountain Club, where three of them now worked.

Bob Proudman, the leader of the expedition, had come to Katahdin twice the previous winter. He was 25, a highly skilled technical climber (requiring ropes and specialized equipment). He had climbed since he was a teenager and like most good climbers was competitive, taking special satisfaction in being

Tom Keddy looking up at Katahdin the day before the group was to climb Pamola Peak. His last words two nights later were, "Tell my parents I was doing what I loved."

the first to scale a mountain in winter. He had earned the reputation of being somebody who would try anything, once trying to climb Cannon Mountain in a hurricane. But now, after taking a bad fall, he had toned down, and the closer he came to making a climb, the more cautious he became.

Paul Dibello, 23, had come to Pinkham Notch in 1971 to ski, and found that climbing "put me more on the *edge* than anything I'd ever done." The delicate movements necessary on fragile ice reminded him of ballet, and in summer he ignored the bare granite cliffs and strapped crampons (climbing spikes) to his boots, and went looking for dead pine trees to climb.

Michael Cohen, 30, had climbed ice for two years, often with Bob Proudman. "We never hesitated to tell each other we were frightened," he says. To Michael winter climbing was the perfect blending of mind and body; he had never seen anything so beautiful as a wall of ice close up. He was steady and cool. "Nothing gets Michael down," his friends would say.

Doug George, 23, a student at the University of New Hampshire, had skied since age three. He was serious and deliberate, a careful planner. With Bob, Paul, and Michael he had climbed on Katahdin the year before, and had written Bob saying, "If you're planning another Katahdin trip I'd like to be included."

Page Dinsmore, 19, was the youngest. He had grown up only 17 miles from Pinkham Notch in Shelburne, where scrambling on rocks was as natural as breathing. He had never climbed big routes like those on Katahdin, but had gotten out of a lot of tough spots in winter. While taking a semester off from

---

There was no place to turn on the ledge. They could only crouch together, yelling their names over and over, making certain nobody dozed. With faces pressed close, they yelled, "Endure!" a hundred times.

Doug refused to let Tom sleep, hugging and punching him, until he felt himself dangerously weak.

Doug George especially enjoyed packing gear into the base camp — a 15-mile trip on skis each way.

Michael Cohen now leads outing club expeditions, showing young people how to persevere, no matter what.

Dartmouth he had worked at Tuckerman Ravine, where he met Paul. Invited in December to join the expedition he had declined, saying he would be back in college. However, early in January he reconsidered his decision.

Tom Keddy, 26, was the least experienced climber. An avid skier, he had endured Navy duty in the Gulf of Tonkin by telling himself, "This winter I'll be skiing Wildcat!" When discharged he moved into Pinkham Notch, a half mile from Wildcat, and began climbing with Paul. "I have a natural ability on ice," he wrote his parents. When a more experienced climber dropped out at the last moment, Paul, who had been impressed by Tom's calmness on a recent hard

climb, invited him along. Tom reassured his parents, "One thing we're not planning to do is to have accidents."

They would climb two steep, long gullies on Pamola cliff, 2200 feet to its summit. It would be their first real climbing after a week of supply packing and wet weather. At 8:30 it was sunny and mild. They had no radio, unreliable in Baxter's rugged terrain; unknown to them, the Portland Weather Bureau updated its forecast to read:

HIGH WIND WARNING IN EFFECT LATE TODAY. MOSTLY SUNNY THIS MORNING. INCREASING CLOUDINESS THIS AFTERNOON. CHANCE OF SNOW BY EVENING FOLLOWED BY CLEARING. HIGHS AROUND 50. MUCH COLDER WITH LOWS 5 TO 10 TONIGHT.

They arrived at the base of their gullies by 9:30. Because of the warm day they traveled light, expecting to complete their climb in eight hours or less. In addition to the standard climbing outfit (double boots, wool pants, wind pants, gaiters, hats, wool shirts, and windbreakers), they threw sweaters and down vests in their packs, except for Page and Bob, who also carried down parkas.

They would climb in teams of three, linked by a rope. Paul led Page and Tom up a steep gully packed with dense ice from refrozen water, the most challenging ice to climb. To Paul it would prove exhilarating, "the best ice of my life," but also unexpectedly difficult and slow. Meanwhile, Bob led Mike and Doug up a more moderate gully filled with more snow than ice, which made for faster climbing.

Soon Bob lost sight of Paul's party as the gullies deepened and by 5 P.M. he had chopped from the snow a small ledge, three feet wide and five feet long, while Doug and Mike waited at the end of the rope 150 feet below. He was in the clouds, and it was growing dark rapidly. He wondered how far he was from the ridge where Dudley Trail, a popular hiking path, led to their base camp. Peering into the mist with his headlamp, he tried to see the route above but saw only the glare from the mist. He grew anxious waiting to hear from Paul's team, sensing the storm's approach. "It was so still, like before a thunderstorm," he says.

There was a shout from the other gully. It was Paul saying he would hook up soon, but not until three hours later was Mike able to lower a headlamp to Page

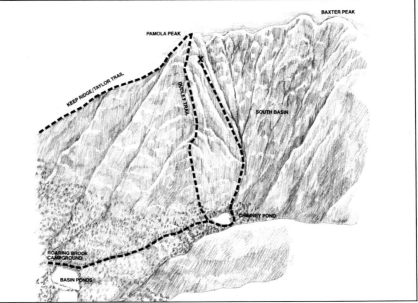

The route of the group's ascent is the dotted line parallel to and to the right of Dudley Trail. The "X" marks the location of the small ledge where the storm trapped the six climbers. Blinded by frostbite and blowing snow, Bob and Page wandered down the Keep Ridge/Taylor Trail, missing the Dudley Trail — the shortest route.

coming into view. With no warning the storm hit, pinning everyone in their tracks. "It was like someone just hit me in the face in a dark room," Page says. Tom and Paul flattened themselves against the slope, pressing their faces to the ice. Bob crouched on his ledge, his face to his knees, unable to look up because his face would fill with snow.

As it snowed, the sky rocked with thunder and lightning flashed. Through the snow and furious gusts they inched their way toward the ledge where Bob waited, his rope held taut. Two hours after the storm hit, the snow abated; stars shone painfully bright through the swirling snow and the winds intensified. In nearby Millinocket temperatures plummeted from 40 to zero in a few hours. First Doug, then Page, followed by Mike, Paul, and Tom, climbed to the ledge where they tied into anchoring pins placed by Bob. Bob was frightened, especially upon seeing Tom stumble onto the ledge after falling several times, while Paul quickly lapsed into dazed exhaustion. Options swirled in his mind: he knew their strength would never be greater than it was at this point. Soon they would face a wind chill of 80 degrees below zero, and if they did not keep warm and awake they would die.

But to leave now would mean climbing in the dark, in the raging wind with tangled ropes, onto unknown terrain, where if the leader fell he could pull his ropemates with him. They opted to stay, and they huddled together, embracing each other for warmth.

At Chimney Pond, Baxter Park ranger Arthur York had come on duty. He was troubled, but not deeply worried to find the men had not returned. The rangers had all been impressed by the group's knowledge of mountains, and had granted them blanket permission to camp out on the mountain so that they could climb some distant gullies. He called on his radio for other rangers to see if Proudman had mentioned overnight plans to them, but failed to reach anyone. He decided he would give them until Friday morning.

There was no place to turn on the ledge. Packs and ropes crowded their legs. They struggled for 45 minutes to put Tom's windbreaker on him; it became impossible in the wind to search for sweaters in the packs. Except to gulp food they could only crouch together, yelling their names over and over, making certain nobody dozed. They tried singing but the wind drove their voices

away. With faces pressed close, they yelled "Endure!" a hundred times. But the wind and cold tore confidence from them, and as the night wore on, their shouts lessened, and enduring became each man's private war with cold.

Mike pressed himself into a narrow crack in the ledge until he felt he was part of the rock. Concentrating on every part of his body, he willed himself to stay warm. He told himself he had been uncomfortable before, that the storm would pass, and he'd be needed to make decisions in the morning.

Paul was silent, appearing to the others as though he was drunk. In the middle of the night he became aware that he no longer had feeling in his legs, but he didn't care that much, only that they no longer felt cold. When the others tried to make him stand in the middle of the night he discovered he couldn't unbend his legs. He knew then he could never climb off the ledge, that his only chance was rescue. Tom had slipped from being an active leader of yells into a groggy state and Bob grew very frightened looking at them.

"I knew we couldn't leave them," he says. "We'd have to get them out. But I didn't know how. We could slap them, tie ropes around them, carry them out. Whatever we tried I knew it would be dangerous for everyone."

Daylight startled them. For the first time they could see the ridge, only 300 feet away. They would have to climb a steep snowfield, but if somehow they could untangle the frozen knot of ropes, the attempt would be reasonable. Page,

his face ghostly white, said quietly, "I've got to leave. I'm freezing to death." Bob looked at Page, who obviously was suffering, and warned, "If you fall there's nothing to stop you." Page, his hands immobilized and unable to help untangle the ropes, climbed off the ledge.

Shocked by their condition that only now they could see, Bob and Mike worked desperately to free the ropes. With enough rope tied together, Bob could carry it to the ridge, loop it around a rock, and descend to the ledge. With the rope as a handline he was certain they could escape.

They were all now going blind from frostbitten eyes. With blurred vision Bob found a large, perpendicular boulder near the ridge, perfect for securing the rope. He rappelled swiftly down the cliff, exulting that they would all soon be out, when suddenly he was clutching the end of the rope, dangling over space; the knots had untied in the wind. He hung onto the rope for what seemed an eternity. He couldn't see. He yelled for Mike but he knew it was futile. He wondered if he could even find the ledge; he knew it might be suicidal to climb down with blurred vision, with no rope anchoring him to the mountain. He decided to leave, hoping there was time for a rescue. "I wish I could have told them that it was probably, here on in, every man for himself," he says.

Mike and Doug realized something had gone wrong. For the next three hours Mike concentrated on helping Paul while Doug refused to let Tom sleep, hugging and punching him, until he felt

Page Dinsmore — his helmet was so encrusted with ice that it had to be cut and melted off his head.

Bob Proudman stands at the head of Diamond Gully. He led the first ascent of this route before the tragic 1974 climb.

himself dangerously weak. He knew he wouldn't survive another night. Mike was reaching the same conclusion. He tried to think through his options, but there were no data except that he was freezing and had no more warmth to give Paul. He told Paul he was going for help. He told himself that if he didn't get off soon, there would be three men helpless on the ledge.

Mike and Doug climbed unroped and separated. On his way to the ridge, Doug's glove blew away as he momentarily placed it under his arm. He screamed, watching his hand shrivel in 60 seconds. Miraculously the glove blew past Mike, then when the wind slackened, slid back down. Using his teeth, Mike tugged the glove over Doug's now useless hand. When he reached the ridge Doug walked around in circles until he came to his senses and started down Dudley Trail.

As he slid down the trail he couldn't understand why he didn't pass a rescue team. He crawled the last 100 yards through the snow to the ranger's cabin and pounded on the door. When Arthur York opened the door it was 1:15 P.M., the first time anybody knew there was trouble on the mountain.

Ten minutes later Mike arrived. Shortly past 2 P.M. Page broke into the ranger's cabin at Roaring Brook, 3.3 miles from Chimney Pond, and radioed for help; he was exhausted from bushwhacking through the woods after blindly wandering with Bob down the wrong trail. Soon a helicopter arrived to transport them to a hospital; already crack mountain rescue units from New Hampshire and Maine had started for Katahdin.

The body is resourceful; cutting off blood to Paul's feet and legs caused more blood to flow to his brain and he started to think clearly. When he felt his hands also begin to freeze he became scared, and realized his hopes for a rescue were remote. He looked at Tom with dismay. Six months earlier Paul's best friend had been killed falling off Cannon Mountain and Tom had become his new best friend. Tom could make a stone laugh, and was a tireless worker, volunteering to pack blankets with Paul into the AMC huts whenever he could. "It's time to go!" he yelled to Tom. "We're not going to stay here and die." Every time Tom would slip off the ledge where a rope held him in place, Paul would drag him up, cursing at his gray face, demanding he talk, get up, MOVE. But Tom had nothing left to give, except to murmur, "Tell my parents I was doing what I loved."

Paul beat his hands against his legs incessantly for two hours; when he tried to stand it felt as if he had two wooden legs. He could not see except for a blur of white. He found 30 feet of rope, tied it to Tom's waist, and unhooked him from the anchoring pins. He heaved on the rope to pull Tom up, but failed. Carefully he anchored Tom again to the mountain, and with the edge of his ice axe cut the rope that linked them. Groping his way upwards he forced Tom from his mind. Twice he fell, but the wind gusted so hard up the gully it held him in place until he could dig his crampons into the snow.

Without his sight Paul knew he had to keep facing into the biting wind, his only bearing to the southwest toward Dudley Trail and the way down. The one burning thought in his mind was that the minute he took his face from the wind he'd be off the other side of the mountain and helplessly lost.

As he crawled off the ridge he heard a helicopter and thought it was watching for his descent. He groped for handholds, bumping into boulders, falling repeatedly into snow. The effort warmed him enough that his eyes began to thaw, and Paul was certain he saw a shortcut; taking three steps he plunged 60 feet into a thick stand of spruce and deep snow. He lay dazed and badly scratched, but otherwise unhurt. He thought, "That's it. I've had it. I can't go any farther. I'll just lie here until they pick me up. I'm done." But the sound of the helicopter faded, and then disappeared completely. It was silent where he lay. "It was as if I was the only one on earth. I knew I had to keep moving."

He crawled for several hours, periodically collapsing in the snow to catch his breath. It grew dark and he saw a candle a long way away. He headed for the candle, and crashed into the ranger's cabin, whose window light he had been following, falling against the door at 7 P.M., four hours after leaving the ledge.

They carried him inside and started cutting away his clothes. When they reached his favorite climbing britches, he roared, "Leave them alone," and with his remaining strength he yanked his pants off, sparing them the knife; then he collapsed into unconsciousness.

Rescue teams arrived late that night. The temperatures were still below zero and the winds made climbing treacherous. An elite group of mountaineers attempted a rescue, for they knew that Tom's slim hopes rested on them, but they were forced to abandon the climb. They left at dawn, on Saturday, February

2. By 11:30 they had reached the ledge and found Tom, frozen, eight feet below the ledge, where the rope still protected him from falling farther.

Until the winds ceased, it would be too dangerous to carry his body up the mountain; and they did not cease until Wednesday, February 6, when Tom Keddy finally reached Pamola.

Bob Proudman, the least injured, was hospitalized five days for serious frostbite. It would be several weeks before Mike, Doug, and Page could leave. Paul would be hospitalized for eight months, finally losing a thumb and both his feet.

Tom's father put two pictures of Tom in his den, both showing Tom posed on an outcropping of rock in the White Mountains, with a burst of foliage behind him. At first Mrs. Keddy could not look at the pictures, but in time they became a part of her life, so that today she says, "When I walk past him now I tip my hat. He always said he felt so alive when he was climbing, and he had fun, he had so much fun!"

Paul operates a successful garage and from his doorstep views snowcapped mountains. He plans to ice climb again soon. He says the storm taught him humility, but figures people won't understand when he says in some ways it was the best thing that ever happened to him.

Doug lives near Paul, working at a half dozen things at once, including building solar homes. Page went back to college, and in two years will be a veterinarian. Bob stopped climbing soon after the storm, his heart no longer in it; but he stayed active in the outdoors, continuing to work for the Appalachian Mountain Club. Michael lives in western Maine, where he is an educator. He also leads outing club expeditions, where one of his goals, among others, is to show young people they can persevere, no matter what the circumstances.

They say there will always be traces of guilt in having left, yet they acknowledge there was nothing else they could have done. Bob Proudman looks his questioner in the face and asks, "What would *you* have done?"

They are the survivors of a night without heroes, though surviving that storm may be heroic enough; for the storm cut short all choices but the final one, between life and death — choices for which no rules exist, not for them, not for any of us on mountains of our own, in storms we cannot foresee, storms that catch us with no warning.

One result of our publishing "On the Trail of the Volleyball Hall of Fame" in February 1978 was an upgrading of the facility and a renewed interest in it. On the other hand, we felt it was perfect just as described here!

On the Trail of the Volleyball Hall of Fame

BY STEPHEN ORAVECZ

Almost everyone in western Massachusetts knows that basketball in this country originated in Springfield, now the home of the Basketball Hall of Fame. But only a few people are aware that the only other Olympic sport invented in this country, volleyball, comes from Holyoke, a city just north of Springfield. Signs there proclaim: Welcome to Holyoke, Birthplace of Volleyball, Home of the Volleyball Hall of Fame. When I saw one of those signs, I was intrigued.

Having grown up near the Football Hall of Fame in Canton, Ohio, I knew that its dome looked like a giant football sticking out of the ground. I wondered if this hall of fame would look like a giant volleyball. I also wondered what would be inside. I could not think of a single famous volleyball player.

I noticed there were no directions on those signs about the Volleyball Hall of Fame. I asked a friend who suggested I start on High Street. He said he remembered seeing the Hall of Fame there, but I could not find it. And I could not find any address in the phone book or from the operator. I began asking directions at a gas station, but it must have been obvious I was not buying anything — the attendants ignored me. When I did get their attention, they could not give me any help. I asked at other stations, but the response was always the same: "You know, I've seen those signs. Let me think

a minute. I should know where it is." They didn't.

Like me, they assumed the Hall of Fame was a well-established institution. Some, like my friend, had even thought they had seen it.

Finally, an employee of a Getty station suggested that I try the fire station just around the corner.

Three firemen sat in front of the red brick building that housed the engines. I was confident. And, when I asked about the Hall of Fame, they looked at each other expecting someone to know. "You've seen those signs," one said to the next. They seemed a little embarrassed that they did not know, so I explained that everyone in Holyoke seemed to have seen the signs, but no one had seen the real thing.

"The cops will know," they said. "We'll call the cops."

One of them called the police and explained he had a guy standing there who had been to 10 or 12 gas stations looking for the Volleyball Hall of Fame.

The fireman hung up smiling. I figured the police must have known; you can count on them. But they did not know, although they had seen the signs.

Then the fireman remembered that he knew the commissioner of volleyball — a John O'Donnell, or something like that. I imagined Bowie Kuhn, Commissioner of Baseball, or Larry O'Brien, Commissioner of Basketball, living in Holyoke. But it seemed worth a try. We pulled out a phone book and found six John O'Donnells. On the second try we got the right one; or rather, the right house. He was not at home, and whoever answered the phone did not know where the Hall of Fame was located. But someone else at O'Donnell's knew, and he announced that the Volleyball Hall of Fame was on the second floor of the Wistariahurst Museum on Cabot Street.

I found the museum. I knew the Hall of Fame was on the second floor, and was glad not to bother the receptionist by asking more directions. Even though she was surrounded by a collection of 18th- and 19th-century furniture, I still expected to be greeted by banners and volleyball nets at the top of the stairs.

In 15 minutes I had been through every room on the second floor without seeing one volleyball. A guide who noticed my by now aimless wandering asked if I was looking for anything special. When I said the Volleyball Hall of Fame, she said, "Oh," and pointed down to the end of the hall.

There, in two glass showcases, were several tournament programs, a short history of the game, four volleyballs, and a net. The guide suggested I might enjoy the Basketball Hall of Fame. She understood it was bigger.

*We were proud to publish the only instructions in print anywhere
for this special kind of wool mitten. Kindly reader reaction, however, almost made us
feel as though we'd helped save the very cornerstone of our New England culture!
Well, they* are *wonderful mittens and something more....*

New England Boiled Mittens

BY ROBIN HANSEN

Time was that when a man went out in his boat in winter, he took his mittens off a nail on board, dipped them in the warm water from the engine, wrung them out, and put them on wet. Then he clapped and beat his hands and swung his arms until his fingers were so red they stung. After that he could work all day, hauling traps from the frigid salt water, working with sloppy, half-frozen bait, or even clamming, and his hands would stay warm.

When he peeled his mittens off at the end of the day, his hands were red and so warm they steamed in the cold air. He hung the mittens up again by little loops on their cuffs and went ashore.

The wool mittens had an amazing insulating quality when wet. They may have been knit by his wife, or he may have bought them — handknit — from the same store that sold him his trap stock, boots, netting shuttles, and other gear. Wherever he got them, they were big, maybe a third bigger than his hand, and made of oily, cream-colored yarn.

Some men took them home and soaked them in hot water; others put them in the bilge of their boats and walked on them all day while doing other work. And they shrank. The wool became thicker, the stitches tighter than can be knit, and as the fisherman wore them, wetting them each time in salt water, they shrank and matted even more until they were shaped to his hands and quite stiff when dry.

Fishermen wore mittens like these in New England and the Canadian Maritime Provinces for hundreds of years. Some still do, when they can get them.

The downfall of the fishermen's wet mitten came with the rise of the insulated glove, which on the surface sounds a lot more reasonable. Bulky and rubbery, the insulated glove is warm enough, but doesn't permit much fine finger movement or any feeling through its layers. Some fishermen use them only for the prickly work of handling bait, complaining that they "can't work in them."

Elizabeth Bergh was one of the Chebeague Island ladies to revive the special mitten-knitting skill.

In many fishing communities, the art of knitting fishermen's mittens has been lost, and even those women who wanted to knit them for their husbands couldn't. There were no mittens left to measure, and no women left who knew how to make them.

This was the case on Chebeague Island, off Portland, until a few years ago. Minnie Doughty, the one woman who had maintained the skill, died, taking her knowledge with her. Like many other coastal women, Mrs. Doughty had had a difficult life and had lost several of her six sons to the sea. In her lifetime she had knitted a great many pairs of fishermen's mittens — so many that when she died, the single remaining new pair was treasured as a keepsake by her daughters.

One of the expert knitters of the Chebeague Island Methodist Church Ladies Aid, Elizabeth Bergh, took these old mittens, counted stitches, measured, found a loose end to determine the thickness of the yarn, and put together instructions for fishermen's mittens. The Ladies Aid knitters tried out the instructions, then continued knitting until they had a small pile of mittens. They "sold like hotcakes" at their fair, Miss Bergh recalled.

If you have a fisherman in the family, or if you spend much of the winter by the sea, try knitting a pair of these remarkably warm, thick, almost water-repellent mittens for someone in your family.

Here are Elizabeth Bergh's instructions, based on Minnie Doughty's mittens. They are probably the only instructions in print anywhere for this kind of mitten. But beware! They make a huge mitten that must be shrunk in salt water, and really can be used only in the traditional way.

The yarn traditionally used for these mittens on Chebeague Island is cream-colored, 3-ply natural Fisherman Yarn from Bartlettyarns in Harmony, Maine.

The brown mittens have been repeatedly soaked in salt water, as they should be.

– photographs by Kip Brundage

This is half again as heavy as worsted-weight yarn and makes an astoundingly dense mitten. Some women use Bartlett-yarns 2-ply Fisherman Yarn, a worsted-weight, oiled, wool yarn, which is easier to knit and makes a lighter, more flexible mitten. The pattern is the same for the two weights of yarn. Any oiled fisherman yarn in these weights can be substituted for the Bartlettyarns Fisherman Yarn.

Instructions are for a man's medium-size mitten. To knit a child's size, find a mitten pattern for worsted-weight yarn and knit a full size larger — for example, a size 8 for a six-year-old — then shrink the mittens. Wool mittens shrink anyway, but only a few patterns take this into account.

FISHERMEN'S WET MITTEN DIRECTIONS

Yarn: Two skeins Bartlettyarns 2- or 3-ply Fisherman Yarn, or other worsted-weight wool with lanolin, used singly.
Equipment: Four number 4 double-pointed needles, or size needed to knit correct gauge.
Gauge: 5 stitches equal 1 inch.

On size 4 double-pointed needles, cast on 12, 15, and 15 stitches, a total of 42 stitches on 3 needles. Knit 2, purl 1 until wristband measures 4 inches.

Then, first round: place last purl stitch on first needle. Purl 1, knit 2, purl 1. Knit rest of round, increasing 2 stitches on each needle for a total of 48 stitches.

Second round: start thumb gore. Purl 1, increasing 1 stitch in each of the next 2 stitches, purl 1. Knit around, and knit rounds 3, 4, and 5, maintaining the 2 purl stitches as a marker.

Sixth round: purl 1, increase in the next stitch, knit 2, increase in the next stitch, purl 1 (8 stitches, including 2 purls). Knit around. Knit 3 more rounds.

Continue to increase this way every fourth row until you have 14 stitches for the thumb gore, including the 2 purl stitches. Knit 3 more rounds and place the 14 stitches on a string.

Cast on 10 stitches to bridge the gap and divide the stitches 18 to a needle (total 54 stitches). Knit up 4 to 4½ inches from thumb for the hand.

Begin decreasing in next round:
Knit 2 together, knit 7. Repeat around. Knit 2 rounds. Knit 2 together, knit 6, and repeat around. Knit 2 rounds. Knit 2 together, knit 5, and repeat around. Knit 2 rounds. Knit 2 together, knit 4, and

repeat around. Knit 1 round. Knit 2 together, knit 3, and repeat around. Knit 1 round. Knit 2 together around. Break the yarn and draw up the remaining stitches on the tail, using a yarn needle. Darn the tail back and forth across the tip of the mitten. Thumb: Pick up from thumb gore 7 stitches on each of 2 needles and 1 stitch from each side of the thumbhole, a total of 16 stitches on 2 needles. Pick up the 10 stitches from the palm side of the thumbhole on a third needle. Knit 2 rounds. Next round, decrease 1 stitch on each end of the third needle. There are now 8 stitches on each needle. Knit 2 to 2½ inches.

Next round, decrease: knit 2 together, knit 2, and repeat around. Knit 1 round. Next round, knit 2 together, knit 1, and repeat around. Break yarn and draw up

remaining stitches on the tail, using a yarn needle. Darn the end into the tip of the thumb. Work all other loose ends into the fabric of the mitten.

Crochet a loop at the edge of the cuff for hanging the mitten to dry. Use the tail left from casting on, if possible.

To shrink: soak the mittens in boiling hot water, squeeze them out, and dry them on a radiator. I shrink mine in the drier on the hot setting, but this takes out some of the oil. Some men say to dry them in the freezer. This takes a long, long time. Some claim they soak their mittens in fish gore, then wash them in hot water. However you choose to shrink your mittens, the first shrinking will not complete the trick, but the mittens will continue to shrink with use.

૭∽

ADDITIONAL SHRINKING INSTRUCTIONS
(That we should have included with the original article)

☞Before you start the shrinking process, trace around one mitten on a sheet of newspaper. Then you'll not only know *if* it shrinks but also *how* it shrinks. You may want to knit your next shrinking mittens longer — or more narrow.

Stir soap into a bowl containing water as hot as your hands can stand and fill another bowl with ice-cold rinse water, as cold as your hands can stand. Salt it if you want to, about a tablespoon per gallon.

Submerge the mittens in the hot soapy water and squeeze water through them. Let them sit to get used to the heat (What a shock they're going to get!), then scrub them on the bumpy surface, repeatedly wetting them in the hot soapy water, until they begin to look fuzzy or until you feel like doing something different.

Then, squeeze them out and *plunge* them into the cold water and rinse all the soap out. You'll actually feel the wool tense up as you do this. Change the water every so often to keep it really cold and clear.

Squeeze (but don't wring) the cold water out. Then back to the hot water with them and more soap and scrubbing. Replenish the hot water as needed, and add soap each time. Rub some soap right into the mittens.

Repeat this back-and-forth process four or five times. I sometimes let the mittens rest after a cold salt rinse, squeezed out on the drainboard,

thinking they're finished with their torment, while I have breakfast or a cup of coffee. Then I put them back into more hot soapy water for more scrubbing.

After a few such violent temperature changes, you will feel a change in the texture of the fabric. It will feel thicker, stiffer, and tighter, and it will be visibly smaller in the cold water. If you've knitted with natural white wool, it will also be much whiter than when you started.

Put a tablespoon or two of vinegar in the last cold salt rinse to soften the wool, squeeze the rinse thoroughly through the mittens, then wring them out for real. Roll them up in a towel and lean on them to remove all the excess water.

Now for the finishing touch, which fishermen don't do but you can: take a stiff brush — a scrub brush, a vegetable brush (I squeeze the broom-straws of a whiskbroom together at the bottom) — and brush each mitten from the cuff toward the fingertips. Brush and brush, and all the fuzzed fibers that aren't matted will go one way and look beautiful. When dried, your mittens will look like authentic Maine fishermen's mittens knitted by a little old lady in Sweden for her favorite grandson.

The whole shrinking and brushing procedure for one pair of mittens may take up to 90 minutes.

Robin Hansen, 1985

Life in a Snowbank

BY K.L. BOYNTON
© K.L. Boynton, 1974

New England in winter is a busy place. And, of all things, certain insects are the first to prove it.

Now it is a fact that, not being equipped to function actively in cold weather, the insect tribe by and large shuts up shop in the fall. Some kinds survive as adults only because they are hidden away in the ground or tucked under logs, debris, or in tree cavities in a kind of cold storage. Others long ago gave up on this and simply carry their species on by wintering in the egg or pupal stage. So it is most unusual for insects to be out at all and astonishing that some would pick the coldest season of the year to do their wooing.

First and foremost amongst these are the snow fleas, since their idea of a perfect place for frolicking is a good snowbank — and who cares about temperature? A sunny day in February with a bit of thaw brings these minute dark-colored insects out of the soil and ground debris by the thousands, their social gatherings looking as if somebody had scattered fine cinders over the snow.

Small and wingless, they have soft bodies covered with hairs, big heads, and rather a truculent look, what with their antennae, dark eye patches on their faces, and puffed-out cheeks. Inside of these hollow face cones are their mouth parts, which have to be stuck outside to work.

While snow fleas have the standard insect number of six legs attached properly to their chest region for walking, a fancy spring mechanism has also been added. This is what produces the mighty leaps so characteristic of these insects, and it consists of a tailpiece made of a pair of appendages joined at their base and attached to the fourth segment of the belly area. This tailpiece is normally carried tucked up underneath the body, pointing forward, and is held in place by a trigger catch. It is worked by muscles, and when the snow flea slaps this tailpiece down hard, it straightens with a snap, propelling him upward and forward perhaps several feet.

Hence the name "springtails" given to his clan — and there are many kinds, some living even in water. The snow flea belongs to the land-based springtails, who live in decaying vegetation and most of whom breed later in the spring. Specific kinds inhabit various soil layers and, along with beetle mites, are among the most important producers of humus.

Land springtails, including the frolicking snow fleas, lay their eggs in the soil and in vegetative debris. The youngsters hatch as miniature carbon copies of the adults, shedding their skins at various growth intervals. The winter springtails abroad on New England snow dine on windborne pollen and fungus spores, in this aping their Arctic cousins, the glacier fleas, who actually live on the ice, leaving it only to deposit their eggs on stones. For ice and snow are not just white stuff devoid of life. Microscopic life forms are there: bacteria of various kinds, algae, pollen, fungus spores, primitive protozoa. A bit of a thaw, and a snowbank can spring to life.

Soil animals by and large are tolerant of cold, and hence the springtails as a clan are adapted to chill circumstances. The snow fleas have gone further in their

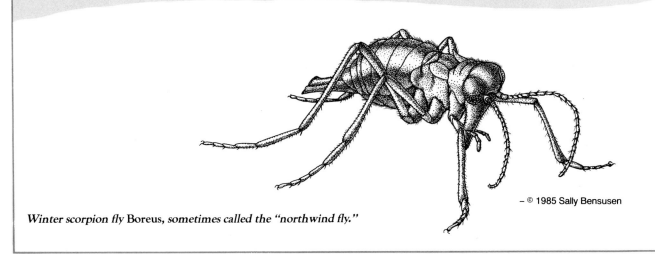

Winter scorpion fly Boreus, sometimes called the "northwind fly."

– © 1985 Sally Bensusen

adaptation with a reproductive setup apparently touched off by first thaws and increasing sunlight at the turn of the year.

The crane flies — those long-legged fellows that look like outsize mosquitoes fluttering and swarming over water during spring and summer evenings — also have offbeat relatives who are snow lovers. Unlike the summer crane flies, these snow-goers are wingless, and what with their long, hairy legs, look more like spiders than insects as they trudge around in the snow. These too are snow breeders, clambering up from their warm hiding places in leaf litter or around tree roots, attracted by the bright sunlight. Air temperature again seems to make no difference, it being zero one fine day when the winter crane flies were socializing. The females, after mating, return through the snow to their leaf-litter homes to deposit their eggs.

Nor are the scorpion flies to be outdone. These fellows are the strange-looking little flies seen in summertime around streams and brooks, particularly in rank vegetation. The name comes from the fact that the posterior end of the adult male does resemble the tail of a scorpion, although it is in reality only the genital organs enlarged and modified into a clasping organ. Standard scorpion flies have four wings; most kinds are carnivorous, with a long, stout beak and biting mouth parts, and they use their long legs to capture and hold living prey.

The winter scorpion flies include the "snowborne *Boreus*" — the "northwind flies" as they are also called — so indifferent to weather they may appear in vast numbers on the snow any time from November on. Again, they do not look much like their summer relatives. Small and black, these snow enthusiasts are without functional wings, but their long legs make them look like tiny grasshoppers skipping about in a winter hoedown. The adults live only in winter and are probably predaceous, though they also feed on mosses. Mrs. Scorpion Fly, equipped with an ovipositor perhaps nearly as long as her body, pokes her eggs deep into leafy ground litter and soil, and the larvae hatching out in about 10 days resemble small grubs with brown heads. They live in moss and vegetable debris, dining on what's at hand since they are mostly vegetarian. Their pupal stage is spent under rotten wood or under stones where, by the way, they are to be found until the season rolls around for their turn to be snow adults.

Also out courting in winter are certain species of stone flies — good-size dark insects whose long wings are carried folded over their backs. Old in time, stone flies are the most primitive of all winged insects, and today's models gracing the New England scene look almost exactly like their ancient ancestors of some 150 million years ago. Stone flies seem to have developed a good thing through the long time of evolution and stick to it, carrying on the clan with a kind of staggered production schedule covering much of the year. With a setup like this, plenty of stone flies are bound to make it regularly, and hence their long evolutionary success.

Stone flies, being aquatic insects, spend their early days in the water, the nymphs living in masses of leaves and ground debris, eating algae, diatoms, and dead organic matter. When the last metamorphosis is finished, each naiad leaves the water and takes a firm hold on stones or a bit of shrubbery preparatory to the final molt. A slit occurs down its back, and the adult form emerges in about a minute. As soon as its wings are expanded and hard, it is ready to fly, albeit rather clumsily, leaving the empty skin behind. It may live as long as a month as an adult.

The stone flies that emerge in winter are the hardiest of the lot. The naiads leave the water through the first available cracks in the ice and go through the last molt. As brand-new adults they crawl over ice and snow, feeding voraciously on blue-green algae growing on tree trunks, stones, old logs, etc. Concrete bridges over icy streams are scenes of much socializing, and in due time each lady returns to the frigid waters to deposit her 5000 to 6000 eggs.

Naturally enough, the nymphs produced by the summer end of the clan are also in the same stream and these will become adults with the arrival of spring. The question immediately arises as to how it is that this winter-laid lot does not go ahead and mature in the next few months too, long before their scheduled winter appearance. Biologists Harper and Hynes, investigating the affairs of these winter stone flies, found that indeed the eggs do hatch directly and that the nymphs proceed to grow to a certain stage in the cold water of late winter and early spring. But as the water warms, something happens. Their bodies become filled with fat globules and they burrow down into the stream bottom to enter a kind of holding period during which they live on accumulated fat.

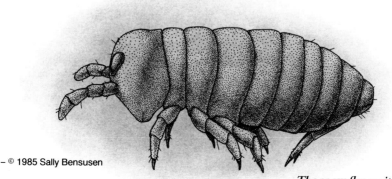

– © 1985 Sally Bensusen

The snow flea — it loves sunny February days.

Not that these snowbank Romeos have a corner on winter lovemaking, for it seems that certain other local residents among New England's wildlife are also very sociably inclined at this time.

Here, then, is an adaptation that these winter-operating stone flies have developed to survive the high temperatures of summer and to wait for the proper time for their winter emergence. It is particularly neat since it allows the egg to hatch promptly; the nymph can then use the late winter and early spring for partial growth, be inactive during the unfavorable time, and resume its development immediately upon return of cool weather in early fall. Prompt egg-hatching is a great advantage: otherwise the egg must simply sit out the unfavorable period where it happened to land, and stone fly eggs are on many a water-dweller's menu. A nymph, on the other hand, is active, and can find a far better place to hide during its time out of circulation — a matter of no small importance in species survival.

Species survival is the big thing in the insect world and, having been in business for millions of years, insects have come up with a surprisingly large number of ways to achieve it. Not the least of these is "cold hardiness," which is chiefly a matter of prevention of freezing and naturally enough is particularly evident in these winter-active numbers.

In the fall, treetop insects and many others migrate to the forest floors which, heavy with fallen leaves and decaying vegetation, stay warm enough under a blanket of snow. Other insects that winter as adults or as larvae may not find such favorable hibernation places and may well be subjected to freezing. Physiological changes must occur if they are to survive. One such change is that as the temperature falls the production of metabolic water lessens and more of the free body water combines with body proteins; this apparently lowers the in-

sect's freezing point. The next step is to undergo a kind of gradual "supercooling" — a period of deep chill reached just before the insect's freezing point is reached. This involves a lowering of body temperature along with that of the air to almost the critical point, a rebound upward through the liberation of latent heat, and then a temperature drift downward to a stable equilibrium with the environment. The critical point where freezing begins varies with different insects, being about minus 22 degrees Fahrenheit in many hibernating insects.

Supercooling seems to play a decisive role in the insect's ability to stand being frozen stiff, as indeed some can. Arctic zoologist L. Keith Miller found further that some ground beetles collected in winter survived lab temperatures as low as minus 126 degrees Fahrenheit without apparent injury, but that the same kind of beetles collected in summer could not stand any freezing at all.

Highly important also is the fact that many hibernating insects (these Arctic ground beetles certainly) have a high concentration of glycerol or other polyhydric alcohols in their haemolymph that act as a life-preserving antifreeze. And it is probable that the snow fleas, winter stone flies, and the like are similarly equipped, since chilling conditions favor the synthesis of these protective substances — hence they can be out courting on a winter's day.

Not that these snowbank Romeos have a corner on winter lovemaking, for it seems that certain other local residents among New England's wildlife are also very, very sociably inclined at this time.

Take *Daphnia*, the water flea, for instance. Being a crustacean and thus a member of the crab-crayfish-lobster

tribe, she is only a distant relative of the insect snow flea. But even before the ice melts on the surface of cold ponds, she's busy with family affairs. A strange, fat little creature she is, with a body covering so transparent that all her interior machinery is on display. So too is the neat brood-pouch knapsack on her back. Inside this her eggs, and later the young when hatched out but still aboard, can be clearly seen. Her antennae, besides adding undeniable charm to her appearance, are highly useful in swimming, which she does by jerking them downward. This propels her upward, and as she slowly sinks, the antennae, fluffing out, act as parachutes. Neat as a pin, she uses the tip end of her trunk, which is turned downward and forward and has spines and claws, to keep her body covering clean.

Fairy shrimps are also active in the ice-cold water, dining on microscopic protozoa and algae, and extremely busy with their domestic affairs since their season is a short one. These are slightly larger members, perhaps an inch long, of the crustacean tribe, who swim on their backs and have some 20 segments to their bodies. They are decorated with leaflike appendages, which are used not only for swimming but also in breathing and food gathering. After mating, the adults die, this year's eggs being next year's potential population held over during the summer waiting period to hatch finally in cold waters. The larvae that have made it this far grow rapidly then, becoming adults just in time for the big winter hoedown.

Other cold-water dwellers are in the family-raising turn of mind, but a word must be said about what is going on topside — in the forests where the air is frigid, the snow deep, and the north wind

The stone flies are the hardiest of all.

on the howl. For even here things are definitely afoot. Under many a feathered and furry bosom beats a romantic heart, undaunted by the winter cold.

Even the fierce great horned owl, old bad news himself to the rodent community, has midwinter tender feelings. Expressed in soft tremulous hooting as early as the first January thaw, his basso-profundo love song floats out over the wintery woods. And it brings a lady winging to his side to sit and watch his bowing, wing spreading, and bill snapping — but alas, she is apparently unmoved by it all. Still, all is not lost, for the suitor flies off to return in nothing flat with a fresh rabbit. If she accepts it, they're engaged.

Things can move apace now. But since great horned owls are dead set against nest building, a last year's abode of some red-tailed hawk is selected and furbished up slightly, and household chores begin. Now nobody needs to point out to owls that New England is a very cold place at this time of year and that their eggs have got to be kept warm. Mrs. Owl starts her incubation the minute the first round egg is laid, and from then on somebody is on nest duty all the time. There is a lag of a few days before the second egg is laid and again before number three, which is about par for a clutch. Incubation is around 28 days, so the chicks arrive in frigid weather and must be further brooded. This becomes no small job since they are of different sizes because of the original delay in the egg-laying sequence and consequent staggered hatching. The parent owls are extra busy at night, then, working the grocery detail, for what with a nestful of voracious youngsters clacking their bills for food, trip after trip has to be made carrying

cargo before they are at last stuffed for the night. Additional supplies are still brought and stowed on the nest's edge for in-between snacks, and this helps keep up chick metabolism until the next evening's dinner hour rolls around.

While raising owlets in winter may seem like making a hard enough job even tougher, the thing is that the youngsters of these big raptors take a long time to develop fully and to become efficient hunters and therefore are dependent on their parents for months. An early start is a must. It also nets the owls the best nesting sites, for they are already ensconced in the hawks' nests by the time the rightful owners get around to their family raising. This means that the hawks have to delay their own affairs while building another abode, a matter of importance since they too dine on the same local rodent and rabbit supply. There first, the owls have already set up hunting territories. All intruders get the bum's rush so that the owl family is assured of a good supply of food.

Downstairs in the forest the minks, skunks, and raccoons are off on their family-raising stints as early as February. Also, upon observing squirrels chasing each other up and down trees, lugging around dead leaves, and peering into this dead tree hole and that, Sherlocks among biologists have concluded that apartment hunting is in order with these buck-toothed forest inhabitants too.

Biologically speaking, all the winter breeders from the snow fleas to the great horned owl, by jumping the gun, have their youngsters off to a good start before competition gets bad in the spring, an obvious advantage for species maintenance. But there is even more to it.

The snow fleas, for example, being

springtails, are most valuable members of the great fraternity of soilmakers. They eat organic matter already being worked over by soil bacteria and protozoa and, in their role as secondary decomposers, help break down this dead matter into a usable form necessary to plant growth. Out working during the snow thaw times, they keep the soil-making cycle going even in winter.

The winter stone flies and their like supply the streams with additional eggs and larvae, which form an important part of fish food — particularly that of trout. The minute water fleas and fairy shrimp, being so small, form a part of the freshwater plankton eaten by small water dwellers who are in turn eaten by bigger ones, and so the water food chain is kept going even in spite of an ice cover.

The great horned owl and mink assure a supply of predators needed to keep rodent numbers in check; the skunks supply more scavengers and insect eaters; the squirrels additional tree planters.

So Old Man Winter can fling down as much snow as he likes. True enough, in New England a good many wildlife characters who do the work of keeping that part of the world in balance during warmer seasons are absent in winter, either vacationing in the South or tucked away in a hibernating or survival nook. Still, a surprisingly large number of local residents are on the job. It is due to their efforts that the making of the earth, the stocking of the shelves for the great food chain goes right on all year around, and the delicate balance of life is maintained.

New England in winter is indeed a busy, busy place.

During the late 1970s, Father Ralph DiOrio of St. John's in Worcester, Massachusetts, was attracting worshipers to his services from all over New England, New York, New Jersey — and even Europe. So we asked writer Donald Gropman to attend one and we sent three of our editors, too. Yes, in some ways we found it shocking. Yet intriguing.

Thursday Morning at St. John's

BY DONALD GROPMAN

photography by Jeff Jacobson

No one ever knows, including Father DiOrio, what will happen or where events will lead once the service begins. He is careful to point out that Divine Healings take place in random ways.

Outside the air has cooled down into the breathable seventies, but inside St. John's even the church-high ceiling cannot provide enough space to dissipate the communal heat of several hundred steaming worshipers and one Roman Catholic priest on fire with what he and many others believe to be the healing grace of God. Father Ralph DiOrio, the healer in spite of himself, "the channel of God," addresses the congregation, all of whom are here hoping to experience healings, or at least to witness them. DiOrio, robed in a handmade cassock of unbleached yarn, moves up the center aisle, away from the altar and out among his flock. He is saying, particularly to the newcomers, "Don't try to touch me. It's not necessary. You're not going to touch anything. You have to touch . . ." and here DiOrio pauses. He spreads his arms, palms up, and smiles to indicate the insignificance of his mere human body. "You have to touch God," he says, and pauses again to look around the church.

When he speaks again his tone has changed, and there is a note of wonder in his voice. "Some of you will feel electricity. Heat. A jolt of lightning, so to speak." He shrugs. It is a meaningful shrug, an expressive shrug, for it signifies a view of the world that accepts all God's wonders, mysteries, and surprises without demanding always to know why. He confesses in a loud whisper, "I don't know how God does it," and the smile that often plays over his face breaks into soft laughter.

Father DiOrio looks out over the church. Downstairs the pews are packed and it's standing room only. Upstairs the shallow balcony is almost as full. DiOrio looks out over the congregation and says, "Some of you will be falling down. I don't want you newcomers to think we are passing out Blue Nun or Chianti on the side." He laughs and a responsive scattering of laughter comes back to him. "And there is no ether in the holy water, either." Another exchange of laughter. "What is happening when someone falls is a phenomenon of God's presence called the 'Slaying in the Spirit' or the overpowering of the spirit. The resting in the Lord. The Lord usually likes to pass through people; it's a spirit of prayer. The saints used to experience this type of prayer — it's called Ecstatic Union. They were just lost in God. Their bodies, with their external senses, became suspended and they would just float in the Lord."

The Slaying in the Spirit is frequently associated with a divine healing, but the two phenomena are not necessarily linked. Some swoon, but are not healed; some are healed, but never swoon. Others have both, the swoon and the cure of an illness or the healing of a wound.

The crowded people, many of whom arrived hours early to be sure of getting good seats, hang on every one of Father DiOrio's words, respond to each expression on his face and each gesture of his body. One can sense but not quite see the high-level energy exchange that is taking place between Father DiOrio and his flock. The air is charged with hope and expectation. Suddenly a gray-haired woman rises from her seat, moves slowly into the center aisle, and keels over — stiff as a board, flat on her back. While the echo of her fall is still palpable in the density of the church, another woman crumples from her seat and slides softly into a swoon stretched out beneath a pew. It is a rule of the house that swooners must be left alone. So nobody bothers the fallen women and Father DiOrio, the smile on his face warmer and bigger than ever, resumes his introductory remarks. So begins another Thursday morning service of the Charismatic Renewal in an old red-brick church on the edge of downtown Worcester, Massachusetts.

At the center of the Charismatic Renewal Movement is the ancient Greek word *charisma*, which we have come to know best in recent years (certainly since the earliest public days of John F. Kennedy, to whom it was attributed in mythic amounts) as the peculiar magnetic quality that draws great crowds to certain public figures. But the root meaning of the word has to do with *gifts,* the gift itself and not the specific thing that has been given. In Roman Catholic doctrine the charism is a gift of God and from God, and healing is its most common content. The charism is both *of* and *from* God because it never ceases to be God, never ceases to be God's power that is traveling through the mortal charismatic. Catholic charismatics like Father DiOrio view themselves as the instruments chosen to deliver God's divine healing, as the channels through which God's power flows, and nothing more, nothing special in and of themselves. In fact, Catholic doctrine specifies that a charismatic is not even necessarily a holy person and that the gift is not for the glorification of the individual, but for the good of others. The theological meaning of the word humbles the charismatic while the popular usage flatters, so the two meanings of the word are opposite. Nevertheless, both meanings apply equally well to Father DiOrio.

The Charismatic Renewal is Father DiOrio's second religious career. He spent the first 20 years of his priesthood in more traditional social involvements: he worked with street gangs in Chicago; with Indians in Canada; with ecumenists in upstate New York. His first contact with the Charismatic Renewal Movement came after repeated requests by his Spanish-speaking congregation in Fitchburg, Massachusetts, that they be allowed to "go charismatic." He resisted at first, but after several visits to charismatic services he became more open to the idea. After a series of signs and intimations that something powerful was going to happen to him, his own gift revealed itself during a charismatic service in a Boston church about two years ago. After delivering a guest sermon he was confronted by a frantic woman who ran

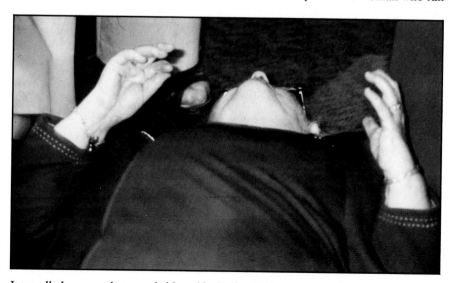

It usually happens that people blessed by Father DiOrio — even if he hasn't actually touched them — swoon dead away in a faint.

51

up to him in the room behind the altar: "Father, hurry up!" she cried. "My husband is bleeding inside his stomach!"

"Bleeding!" DiOrio answered. "Let's call an ambulance right away, get him to a hospital!"

"No, no!" she insisted, *"pray* over him!"

"Pray over him? Come on," DiOrio said, "call the doctor."

But the woman would not back down. She only grew more insistent. "Father," she demanded, *"pray!"*

As Father DiOrio recalls this scene he shrugs his shoulders and says with wonder in his voice, "Eh, all right. I pray. POOM! The man goes down! He says, 'I feel great. My ulcers don't seem to be bleeding anymore.' I think, 'Is this man pulling my leg? He's bleeding, I pray over him, and all of a sudden he's okay?' I think he's pulling my leg or he's crazy. But he gets up and goes back to his seat singing 'Hallelujah!' Then a nun rushes up and says 'Father, there's a woman here, she wants to kill her son and daughter! She's going crazy. Will you do a deliverance over her?' 'Deliverance?' I think, but the nun quickly brings the lady into the hallway where I am. I lay hands on her for about 10 minutes. This woman," DiOrio says, his voice compressed into an amazed whisper, "this woman gets totally *freed!* I say, 'Holy mackerel! Is this real? Is this happening to me?' This lady goes back happy too. And now a schoolteacher comes out, a young girl about 25 or 26 from Cambridge, and she says, 'Father, I have some problems, serious problems. Will you pray with me?' 'All right,' I say, 'let's sit down.' So I'm sitting with a girl in the stairwell holding her hand. If some old priest walked by he'd probably complain to Rome. I'm holding her hand praying with her and she's overpowered. She says, 'I felt the heat go through my body, a healing through my brain!' And then she goes back happy and peaceful. Now I'm in the back of the church and I'm saying to myself, 'There's something wrong here, something crazy. I gotta get out of here, gotta get out!' "

As soon as the service was over Father DiOrio rushed up the side aisle of the church trying to flee, but he was called back by the priest in the pulpit and asked to pray over a crippled boy. "I couldn't say no in front of all those people, so I went up to the little kid and placed hands on him and the kid started *moving* and

people saw this. I pulled away, and a lady says to me, 'Father, pray over me, touch me!' and when I do POOM! she goes right down! 'Father, touch me!' they shout. POOM! One after the other they go down! By the time I got up to the other end of the church the whole place was laid out! Then I knew I had broken out!"

Two years have passed since Father DiOrio's charism became manifest, two years in which his healing ministry has drawn people from all religions. They come in private cars, in campers, by chartered busloads from places in New England and New York, from as far away as Norway and Italy. He receives hundreds of letters each week: invitations to hold services all over the world and testimonials from men and women who believe they have been healed. Through it all Father DiOrio maintains that he is only God's instrument, only a pipeline and not the power itself, the power that acts in ways beyond his mortal control.

The Divine Healings and the Slayings in the Spirit both take place in random ways. There are no set patterns. No one

WHAT WAS IT LIKE?

(AN EYEWITNESS REACTION)

It was a curious mixture of emotion and technology, spontaneity and choreography, God and show business. We three *Yankee* editors (Anna Larson, Susan Mahnke, and Deb Stone) who attended half of the November 30 morning service came away feeling ambivalent, but intrigued, about what we were seeing. Part of the ambivalence may have been because we came to observe, not to be healed. Father DiOrio seemed real — genuinely moved to heal, a gentle, peaceful, strong man of the Church. Some of the trappings — the small pieces of polyester knit that his attendants handed out as "prayer cloths," the prolonged testing of the sound system, the anticipated fainting of the members of his ministry as he blessed them — were jarring notes. But the air of hope, the emotional release that seemed to be found by the people DiOrio touched, made the experience moving and worthwhile.

Susan Mahnke

ever knows, including Father DiOrio, what will happen or where events will lead once the service begins. Events often are propelled by DiOrio's direct involvement, but he is not needed all the time. People swoon throughout the service, in all parts of the church. And the events called Healings frequently occur in the same way.

In the middle of a prayer Father DiOrio is facing the altar, his back to the congregation. Suddenly he interrupts his prayer, "I see a woman in a white beaded blouse . . . I think there's a gold chain . . . there's a respiratory problem . . . I see her chest area . . . there's perhaps a spot of cancer. . . ." At this point a woman wails in recognition of her grief. "There's been a healing," DiOrio says. "Thank You, Jesus!"

His hands are moving all the time, never stopping, all the while modeling their messages in the air. They seem to throb, yet they are steady and calm. Whatever it is that flows through and out of DiOrio's body, it exists in such abundance and in such a volatile state that it easily leaps through space and arcs across the gap between his fingers and their flesh, because most of the time he does not even touch them at all, merely brings his hand to within six inches of their foreheads and down they go.

His hand approaches and every muscle in her face goes lax. It all happens quickly. She sways a moment, then keels over. Her knees are stiff, but a friendly hand eases her to the floor. She falls with her head turned to the side. Her eyes are closed. She lies flat. Her hand rests on her stomach and her stomach moves steadily up and down. A smile sits lightly on her face.

When she is safely down in her swoon DiOrio moves on. The pace is quick and getting quicker. They are falling as soon as he gets to them. Most go down like boards, stiff as planks, but some few crumple, like marionettes whose strings are cut. Then the blessings are over and the floor space at the front of St. John's is filled with the supine bodies of those who have floated into the Lord.

Father DiOrio returns to the altar to conclude the service. Though many healings have been claimed, there is still much energy in St. John's Church, energy not yet used, and some of it seems to crackle around DiOrio.

We could understand the fact that our readers might be interested in a stove that will burn up to four-foot logs, hold the heat for 12 hours or more, and burn with 90 percent efficiency. But considering the fact that it's constructed of 100 tons of brick and mortar, we were very surprised at the hundreds of reprint requests that continue to this day!

What's So Hot About a Russian Fireplace?

BY MEL ALLEN
photography by Carole Allen

Basilio Lepuschenko built his first two Russian-style wood-burning brick stoves 20 years ago in his new home in Richmond, Maine, 5000 miles from his native Byelorussia, where such brick stoves have heated houses for three centuries and are known as "grub-kas." There are some 300 Russian families living in the environs of Richmond in the lower Kennebec Valley, the largest concentration of Russians in rural America, but only a few Russian brick stoves — each one built or supervised by Basilio Lepuschenko. Until recently, oil was cheap and plentiful. Masons skilled in the craft of building Russian stoves, with their labyrinthine system of convoluted flues to retain maximum heat, were not.

Basilio Lepuschenko is not a mason by trade. Now 52, he has been a carpenter and cabinetmaker on three continents since the age of 19. "Not a helper," he says to be sure there is no misunderstanding, "a carpenter." When he was seven he helped his uncle lay the bricks for a grubka in a typical Byelorussian house of logs with tiny windows. Because of their importance to family comfort during harsh Russian winters, the building of a grubka, especially in a small village, was no small matter. Discussions centered on the relative merits of the chosen masons, who mysteriously were able to construct stoves that would not draw until the traditional gift of vodka was proffered.

"We filled the stove twice at most each 24 hours," says Lepuschenko. "The heat from the stove was highest four or five hours after the fire was just coals. The house was 80 degrees during the day. When we woke up it was 60 degrees."

Basilio Lepuschenko stands in front of the brick heater he built for his father-in-law in Richmond, Maine.

When he first came to Richmond he built two stoves and placed them at opposite ends of the house. He spent $16 that winter for two cords of hickory scraps to heat the house, and that was all. "The stoves are so efficient because they burn everything inside," he said.

"I have known this from a boy," he said. "There is very little creosote with grubkas because everything burns. But we burn poplar wood three times a year to clean the chimney."

There is no brick stove at present in the house he has just completed. His former house no longer has brick stoves, either. "Oil was 16¢ a gallon," he sighed. "We thought why bother getting wood. So I knocked them down." To show a visitor a Russian stove he drives to his father-in-law's house.

It is a small stove, utilizing perhaps only 500 bricks, he said. The stove is six feet high, two feet wide, and three and a half feet long. The house was designed around the stove. Portions of masonry protrude in three rooms. "It heats all three," he said.

Lepuschenko is surrounded by neighbors who return his Byelorussian greeting of "Dobra" with one of their own. His son plays in the balalaika orchestra and he himself is on the board of directors of the Slavophile Society. He receives two newspapers each week from Russia, and miraculously has reestablished contact with relatives and friends from the small village of his youth, which was destroyed in the war and no longer exists. He thinks his new house is lovely, but he misses one thing: he misses heating with his Russian stoves.

Scientists and engineers are hungrily quantifying the seemingly inexhaustible aspects of wood heat. There are so many reports that soon they will be stacked by the cord. What are the most efficient, economical, convenient, and safe ways to burn wood? Suddenly the answers to these questions seem terribly important. Researchers sometimes come upon methods of other times, other places, that seem so logical, so practical, we are taken aback; how could we, in our sophistication, have missed them?

So it was, for instance, with herbal cures. And so, too, it may yet be with the great brick-enclosed stoves now becoming known to the rest of us simply as Russian fireplaces.

In an essay on catching colds, Ben Franklin chided popular notions that chilly houses contributed to hardy bodies. The Russians, observed Franklin, were said to be remarkable physical specimens and they "live in rooms, compared to ours, as hot as ovens." Furthermore, Franklin wrote, the stoves by which the Russians kept so warm seemed "remarkably more efficient" than America's open fireplaces. While perhaps 10 percent of the heat generated by such fireplaces warms the house (the rest disappearing up the chimney), it is said that perhaps 90 percent of the heat generated in the firebox of a Russian fireplace ultimately warms the house.

Rob Pfeiffer built a massive Russian fireplace 18 months ago in the center of his rambling farmhouse on the coast of Maine. He was aided by Will Moran, a 67-year-old third-generation New York-Irish mason who had built six Russian fireplaces in the past 15 years. They used 100 tons of bricks and mortar to build what is essentially a brick radiating wall. The wall, in reality, is a double wall, two bricks thick. It is 10 feet tall, five feet long (four-foot lengths fit easily in the firebox), nearly three feet wide, with 12 feet of chimney — all within the living space of the two-story house. With nearly 20 times the bricks of the Russian fireplaces constructed by Lepuschenko, it is as if a shrine to wood heat stands between the kitchen and the dining room.

Before exiting, smoke must curl up and around five horizontal passageways spaced 18 inches apart. Flue passages are eight by 10 inches. Each passageway is supported by a set of 1946 Studebaker leaf springs and ¾-inch steel reinforcing rods. Few Russian fireplaces contain such support. Not only are they an extra precaution against weaknesses in the structure due to the heavy weight, but they were a time-saver in the construction as well.

Last winter Rob Pfeiffer ascended the roof of his house while the fire blazed 22 feet below. He was checking to see if combustion was as complete as he had been told. He thrust his arm down the throat of the chimney. "It was amazing," he said. "I couldn't feel heat. Or smoke. I

"Any good mason with patience can build one. Some masons are fussy and some are sloppy. Be sure you get a fussy one."

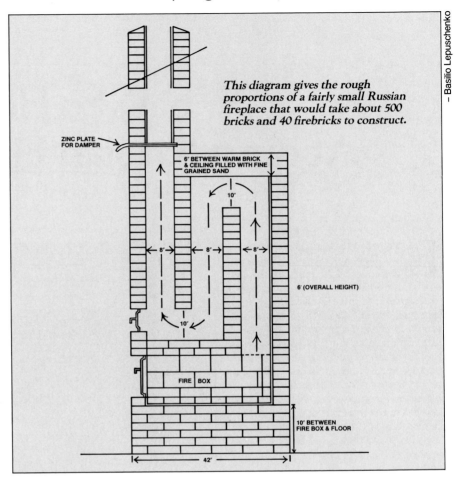

— Basilio Lepuschenko

ZINC PLATE FOR DAMPER

This diagram gives the rough proportions of a fairly small Russian fireplace that would take about 500 bricks and 40 firebricks to construct.

6" BETWEEN WARM BRICK & CEILING FILLED WITH FINE GRAINED SAND

10"

8" 8" 8"

6' (OVERALL HEIGHT)

10"

FIRE BOX

10" BETWEEN FIRE BOX & FLOOR

42"

could hardly feel anything that said there was a fire down there."

At the same time, the intense heat of the firebox needed for complete combustion, 1200 degrees Fahrenheit, was being stored within the massive masonry chambers. Hours later, long after the Pfeiffers had retired, the wall of brick, to the touch about 150 degrees, was keeping the 800 square feet on the first floor at 70 degrees. The second floor was too hot for comfort.

The heat-retaining properties of their Russian fireplace are prodigious. "We have left on a Friday night," said Kitty Pfeiffer, "and when we returned on Sunday the bricks were still warm."

People have traveled many miles to see the few Russian fireplaces functioning in New England. Accustomed to the usual fireplace openings, they are struck by the appearance of the Russian fireplace. The massive brick around the long and narrow opening closed by a cast iron door sets off questions:

"How does it work? How do we build one? How much does it cost? How long do they last? Are they safe?" And they want to know one other thing. "How come if we're so smart, it took us 300 years to catch up to the Russians?"

How does it work?

The heat-storing properties of bricks have been utilized to keep people warm for centuries, and a Russian fireplace takes maximum advantage of this capacity. By slowing the passage of hot gases through the stove without having to slow the intensity of the fire, you have optimum combustion without the extreme fluctuations of temperature resulting from hot fires in metal stoves. In a Russian fireplace, a big fire gives off the same heat as a small fire, but for a longer period of time.

The warm masonry heats the living space. It also radiates heat back toward the fire, where it is needed for highly efficient combustion. With adequate heat

(1200 degrees) and air, the gases burn. Without them, they do not. Instead they pass into the sides of chimney walls, eventually clogging them as they form creosote deposits.

Merely hooking a brick oven, for instance, to a conventional chimney will provide a heat-storing mass. But without the refractory passages within the stove, to slow the combustible gases, most of the heat would be lost.

Russian fireplaces have a minimum of three switchbacks, and the convolutions of the flues seem limited only by the builder's ingenuity. In 1940, a Maine dairy farmer named Sam Jakola, a native of Finland, constructed what essentially we call a Russian fireplace. He called his a Finnish fireplace. Using fieldstones rather than bricks, he built a 45-foot flue within the fireplace.

The flue extended from the top center of the firebox to within a foot of the ceiling. It curved to the right, then dropped down below the floor. It turned left under the firebox before curving ultimately to the roof and chimney. Sam Jakola, who built six more, forced the heat to spend itself within his fireplace. A newspaper report in 1950 said, "If the weather is below zero, Sam builds a fire every evening. But when winter temperatures are normal he doesn't have to touch the firebox for two days."

A curious feature of Russian fireplaces is that many fires are started from scratch. The warm house diverts attention from the firebox until it is too late to catch coals. The Pfeiffers light their fire-

This is the Russian fireplace in the Rob Pfeiffer house, built in 1976 for $600. He also incorporated a flue for the cookstove.

place every 12 hours. However, from early December until spring, when they rely on a wood cookstove in the kitchen, the masonry never cools.

How do we build one?

"Any good mason with patience can build one," said Will Moran. But he warns: "Some masons are fussy and some are sloppy. Be sure you get a fussy one." Albie Barden for three years has operated the Maine Wood Heat Company in Norridgewock, Maine. Soon he hopes to study with skilled masonry stove-builders in Europe, while he researches a book he is writing about Russian fireplaces. He will conduct workshops this spring for masons. Aided by a Maine mason who has constructed several in the past year, the participants will construct Russian fireplaces during the workshop.

"I am being conservative in my approach," Barden said. When an article mentioned him as a source of information on Russian fireplaces, he was swamped with calls, visits, and letters. One letter came from Africa, another from Italy. A teacher just returned from Afghanistan visited Barden, saying he had heated his house in Afghanistan with a brick stove. He had called it a Russian fireplace there as well. "There are still problems to be worked out," Barden said. "But they would seem to dovetail perfectly with passive solar heating. We could see a great increase in the number of Russian fireplaces in the future."

How much do they cost?

Rob Pfeiffer built his Russian fireplace for $600. He provided much of the labor, and many bricks were available from a previous fire. Russian fireplaces constructed today in Maine are ranging from $1500 to $4000. With care they should last at least 30 years. Basilio Lepuschenko said he knows some in Byelorussia that date back to his great-grandfather's day.

Are they safe?

"It can be a beautiful thing if you have confidence in it," said Kitty Pfeiffer. "But if it worries you it can be a nightmare." There are dangers inherent in any heating system, but a properly built Russian fireplace minimizes many of them.

According to the Chimney Sweep Guild, last year there were 41,000 chimney fires, causing $19 million in damages. A wood-burning system that prevents creosote formation provides a safety bonus. If used with a little com-

mon sense, Russian fireplaces would seem to be among the safest wood-heating systems available.

The fireplace must be constructed on a firm foundation. There must be adequate space between the warm brick and the ceiling and floor. Lepuschenko allows 10 inches of space from the firebox to the floor. He fills in the six inches below the ceiling with fine-grained sand as a fire barrier.

There are no stovepipes to become disconnected, sending flames shooting against a wall. There is no thin-walled metal that could burn through if a fire burns out of control, and no sparks shooting out.

There must be disadvantages?

Obviously, a Russian fireplace is a more costly, more complex alternative than many are willing to invest in. You do not go down to the local hardware store and order a Russian fireplace. In Eastern Europe there are national guilds for builders of masonry stoves. Our masons here in America are still learning this particular craft.

Ironically, a major disadvantage for some is the steady outpouring of heat from the masonry. Our houses are generally lighter, less massive than those in Eastern Europe. Our houses respond quickly to fluctuations in outside temperatures. If a day warms suddenly, there is no thermostat to shut off heat in a Russian fireplace. This could be especially troublesome in south-facing homes with lots of glass to allow sunshine in.

And in this increasingly mobile society, we cannot pack up our treasured grubka and move it across town. Nevertheless, an impressive number of people seem able and willing to renew a tradition that, once begun, does not seem likely to die again.

Plans and Designs:

Masonry stove designs are available from the Maine Wood Heat Company. Write to Albie Barden, RFD 1, Box 640, Norridgewock, Maine 04957, to receive a catalog with upcoming workshops, or to obtain information about a book on Russian fireplaces.

Basilio Lepuschenko is preparing detailed plans that he will sell to aid masons who are interested in constructing Russian fireplaces. Write to Mr. Lepuschenko at Alexander Road, Richmond, Maine 04357.

A · FEBRUARY
SAMPLER

☞ Memorable thoughts, quotes, and assorted tidbits from the last 50 February issues. ☜

THE FATHER OF AN AMERICAN HERO RECALLS "THE GOAL"

☞ "Every time you expect something from Michael he comes through. The good Lord must have been on his side from the start. It was uncanny. The score was 3–3 in the Russian game and I'm sitting next to my wife and I said, 'You know, Helen, Michael's not done nothing yet.' I says, 'C'mon, he's due.' I no sooner got through talking than I see the puck slide across to him. And as soon as he got the stick on it I yelled, 'Shoot, Mike, shoot! Don't waste time!' And he did. He just let it go. I saw that net stretch and I said, 'Oh my God, that's it?' It was beautiful.

"And I started to think — this goal here could be a big thing. If it could stay up with no other team scoring. I knew the impact it was going to have. I held tight to my St. Anthony's medal. 'This is for my Michael,' I said. 'Make this thing end 4–3. No more. No less.' 'Cause I knew what would happen. He's the captain. He's got the winning goal. And the people will *never* forget that.

"Now after we got home I'm still thinking he'll turn pro and play NHL. The clubs were interested. To tell you

The Eruzione family outside their three-family house in Winthrop, Massachusetts.

— Ulrike Welsch

the truth, I wanted him to play. The guys in the bar always said he was too small for the NHL. I'd say, 'C'mon. He's got heart and can dig in the corners; he passes and he's smart.' But then I'm hearing Michael talking, why he doesn't want the NHL. He said, 'Dad, you can't beat this — what we just achieved. I'll never score another goal to equal the one against the Russians. This is something I'll never forget.' So he got me thinking.

So he signs for forty grand. He'd get kicked around. Maybe bust up his knees, then have to sweat it out the following year. All that at 25. And I started seeing things coming into the house for him, like a free car, and I said to myself, 'This kid's got it made.' " **Mike Eruzione's father, Jeep, of East Boston.** *(From "The Celebrity" by Mel Allen, published one year after the February 1980 Olympics in Lake Placid, New York.)*

"Didn't realize I had to be ready the very first minute!"

— Alan Ferguson

THE SHORTEST FEBRUARY TRUE-LIFE STORY

☞ Will swop handmade size 5 champagne-colored wedding dress with appliquéd lace and chiffon skirt, and size 5½ keepsake .17-karat diamond ring for a wood- and coal-burning stove. F 115 MA *(From the February 1984 "Original Swopper's Column," established in November 1935.)*

THE PRESIDENT IS NO MORE

☞ "In a back room over a back building, on a common bedstead covered with an Army blanket and a colored woolen coverlid, lay stretched the murdered President, his life's blood slowly ebbing away. The officers of the government were there and no lady except Miss Harris whose dress was spattered with blood, as was Mrs. Lincoln's, who was frantic with grief beside him, calling on him to take her with him, to speak one word to her . . . but her agonizing appeals were of no avail!

"I held and supported her as well as I could and twice we persuaded her to go into another room. All night long, we watched in this way, from half past 11 to seven the next morning.

"At that hour, just as the day was struggling with the dim candles in the room, we went in again. Mrs. Lincoln must have noticed a change, for the moment she looked at him she fainted and fell upon the floor. I caught her in my arms and held her to the window which was open, the rain falling heavily. She again seated herself by the President, kissing him and calling him every endearing name, the surgeons counting every pulsation and noting every breath gradually growing less and less. Then they asked her

Mary Todd Lincoln.

to go into the adjoining room, and in 20 minutes came in and said, 'It is all over! The President is no more!'

"At nine o'clock we took her home to that house so changed for her and the doctor said she must go immediately to bed. She refused to go into any of the rooms she had previously occupied. 'Not there! Oh, not there!' she said, and so we took her to a room she had arranged for the President for a summer room to write in." **Elizabeth L. Dixon, wife of Senator James Dixon of Connecticut, quoted from an 1865 letter to her sister, Louisa, and provided to *Yankee* by David C. Andrews, great-grandson of Mrs. Dixon.** *(From "A Night to Remember.")*

shirt and holding his line — a knot and small coil in his right hand, the rest in his left hand extended in front of him.

There was an air of doomed resignation among the crewmen lining the rail, when our ship took a heavy roll to starboard and rolled back to even keel before starting down to port. At that precise moment, Spike McShay whipped his line high into the air toward the wreck, and what a roar from his shipmates when the rope dropped across the man's shoulders. As the man desperately wrapped the rope around his body, his boat disappeared beneath the waves. Time has erased that lucky soul's name from my memory, but neither he nor I will ever forget Spike McShay.

Walter M. Price

A·FAVORITE LETTER

ON KEEPING THINGS SHIPSHAPE

☞ As a retired Navy man, I can't figure out why the fellow who queried the Oracle in the December issue had never heard the Navy version of why a ship is called "she." I refer to "A Man and His Ship," which says, "There are many reasons: there's always a great deal of bustle about her. There's usually a group of men around. She has a waist and stays. She takes a lot of paint to keep her looking good. It's not the initial expense that breaks you, it's the upkeep. She's all decked out. It takes a good man to handle her right. She shows her topsides, but always hides her bottom. And, when coming into port, she always heads for the nearest buoy."

Gerry Morton, Arnold, Maryland

. . . . I learned in Marblehead that it was because the rigging costs more than the hull.

Andrew E. Kanders, Oakton, Virginia

∽∾ I REMEMBER ∿∾

A STORMY NIGHT IN FEBRUARY 1926

☞ Frank "Spike" McShay was old, stooped, and near blind when I last saw him, but that didn't dim my memory of him on a dark, stormy night the first week of February 1926. I was a deckhand aboard the Eastern Steamship liner *Camden,* and Spike was the boatswain, reputed to be the finest line thrower that ever sailed the Penobscot River. On this particular passage we were 25 hours late departing Boston for Rockland, Maine, due to a severe blizzard, and we hit such heavy seas when we passed Deer Island that it was almost impossible to keep our feet on deck. About an hour later most of the crew not on duty were in their bunks in the forecastle when the whistle sounded all hands on deck. We were about abreast of Thatcher's Island.

Clinging to lifeboats and stanchions, I made my way to the starboard side where the crew was helplessly watching a man held in our ship's powerful spotlight. He stood waving a little light on the deck of a small craft, near awash and obviously sinking. We were headed into the wind just maintaining steerage, but with each swell we drifted a little from the foundering craft.

At the first mate's order, six strong men threw lines, but the longest throw was 30 feet short of the target. Spike had not thrown his line, but the situation seemed hopeless. We were drifting astern of the sinking boat and her top rail was already level with the water. There was no time to come around for a second try. Spike stood at the rail, stripped to his

– Alan Ferguson

"Y'know, Earl, Florida climate wouldn't agree with me . . . if I ain't miserable half the time, I don't get the full use outa feelin' good the other half."

A MAINE FISHERMAN TELLS IT LIKE IT IS

☞ "People may think we're rowdy because we go up to Rockland and have a few drinks on a Saturday night, or maybe once in a while during the week if the weather report is bad and we know we won't have to get up at three o'clock in the morning to go out on a trawler. More likely we'll stay home in our dry little village and play cribbage. But what's this about our being superstitious? Like it's bad luck to have a blue boat? Ridiculous! I wouldn't paint a boat blue myself — I don't like the color — but I don't call it a *superstition.* Same with using the word 'pig.' I hear tourists say we won't allow the word to be used and some fishermen won't even eat pork. Well, I for one won't eat pork but that ain't *superstition.* I don't *like* pork. And, well, I'll admit a few of my friends won't use the word 'pig,' but it doesn't bother me much. So long as I'm clear of the boat." *(From "Living the Good Life in Port Clyde, Maine" by Lawrence F. Willard.)*

EARL KNOWS EVERYTHING

☞ Can you identify the sketched object? It is sterling silver with a beaded edge and is about 4½ inches end to end. There is a *sharp* hook on the bottom. It belonged to my great-aunt, whose initials appear on it, and it is about 100 years old.

K.C., Middlesex, N.J.

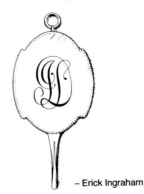

– Erick Ingraham

Back in the 1800s ladies wore gloves that buttoned up to the elbows. Some were made of kidskin and some of linen. The buttons were apt to be linen also. These gloves stained easily, so the hook was used to reach through the buttonhole and pull in the button, keeping the gloves cleaner than they would have been if fingers had been used. (From Earl Proulx's monthly "Plain Talk" column.)

I REMEMBER

WHAT MAINE IS LIKE

☞ I was in Hollywood, far from my Maine home, because a Hollywood producer was interested in buying the film rights to a book I had written. In his office there was a middle-aged woman who was elaborately uphol-stered and had ornate fingernails and roguishly painted eyes. She sat in a murmurous sea of secretaries. For four days she watched me come and go and then on my last day there she came and stood next to me at a large window facing the buildings of Century City.

"This is no place to live," she said in a confessional tone.

"How long have you been here?" I wanted to know.

"All my life. But since I was a little girl," she said melodiously, "I've thought about what it must be like to live in Maine."

"Really?" I asked. I wondered what her image of Maine was like and I supposed it included the heavily advertised rhapsodies — lobster dinners, the tourist gift shops?

"No, nothing like that," she said. "I've always wanted to be able to walk across the road every morning in my nightgown to get the mail."

Don J. Snyder

– Don Bousquet

"It must be a bleak sort of life — holed-up in there with only occasional refillings of our feeder to relieve the tedium. . . ."

THE ONLY MOBILE SLAUGHTERHOUSE IN NEW ENGLAND

☞ In only a few flashes of the knife, the innards are removed. The kidneys, heart, and liver are deposited in a baggie; they are some of the best eating parts. The remainder is discarded into a five-gallon plastic pail. With the pig gutted, Sherburne reaches for a power saw on the shelf. The electric saw is much like a giant carving knife and rattles to life when Pete depresses the trigger. He saws the pig in half, starting at the hind end and finishing at the head. Once the halves are sprayed off with a hose, the animal is ready for butchering.

Children dart in and out of the swinging doors at the front of the bus. Seldom does one peek in without saying, "Hi, Pete." Sherburne looks up each time and grins, not remembering all the names yet personalizing every reply with a "Hi there, Red," or a "How ya doin' today, Blondie?"

"I put this bus on the road to help the little guy. I did it for that and for another reason," Pete says. "I just

Pete Sherburne, "The Pigman."

can't live on Social Security, not the way expenses are today. You just can't do it." *(From "Pete the Pigman" by Matt Beebe.)*

— © 1981 R. Terry Walker

THE RECIPE SOME THOUGHT WE SHOULD NOT HAVE PUBLISHED

FIELDMOUSE PIE
5 fat fieldmice
1 cup macaroni
½ medium onion, thinly sliced
1 medium-size can tomatoes
1 cup cracker crumbs

Boil the macaroni 10 minutes. While it is cooking, fry fieldmice long enough to try out excess fat. Grease casserole with some of the fat and put a layer of macaroni in it. Add onion and tomato, then salt and pepper it well. Add fieldmice and cover with the remaining macaroni. Sprinkle the top with cracker crumbs seasoned with salt, pepper, and butter. Bake at 325° for 20 minutes or until mice are well done. (Note: if insufficient mice are available, substitute sausages.) **Published originally in a 19th-century cookbook put out by a group of ladies in Grafton, Vermont.** *(From "If You Want a Foolproof Recipe for Fieldmouse Pie" by Annie Proulx.)*

RHODE ISLAND'S FIRST RECKLESS ROAD RASCAL

He was the scourge of the highway, reaching speeds of 15 to 18 miles per hour....

by Murray T. Pringle

☞ Michael Woods isn't listed in the *Guinness Book of World Records,* but he probably should be. After all, he was the first motorist in history to be bagged for speeding. And back in 1904 that took a bit of doing.

One day Mike was tooling along in a snappy foreign landaulet limousine that he was chauffeuring for one of the residents of Newport, Rhode Island. With him as he zipped along was his employer.

As they proceeded over the cobblestones of swank Bellevue Avenue they caught the eye of Patrolman Sullivan. The officer was shocked to observe that the open black limousine was causing a virtual breeze. With the conscientiousness and dedication that is to be found in every traffic cop who has ever patrolled the highways and byways since, Officer

Sullivan sprang astride his bicycle (that's right, bicycle) and pedaled off furiously in hot pursuit.

Aided by a downgrade and a stiff tail wind, Officer Sullivan drew abreast of the limousine and waved Mike to the curb. Stern-faced, he demanded: "Do you realize you were driving faster than a horse can trot?"

And like every motorist since, Mike expressed innocent surprise. "Was I really? I had no idea, officer."

Next thing Mike knew, he was in court. Officer Sullivan informed the judge that he was charging the errant motorist with operating his machine at 18 miles an hour! In 1904 that was considered just a shade short of being supersonic. Judge Darius Baker (later to become a justice of the Rhode Island Supreme Court) tsk-tsked and levied a fine of $15, plus $2.60 in court costs. Mike paid up and that was that. Only it wasn't.

A week later, his employer sent Mike Woods out to the garage to crank up the limousine for another trip to town. The purpose of this trip is not recorded in police or court records. They may have been hurrying to meet the steamboat from Providence or perhaps they were

just out joyriding. Be that as it may, Mike really had her down to the floorboard when he turned the corner at the edge of the Newport polo field.

Oh, oh! Coming from the opposite direction was another car. Now that's no big thing these days, but in 1904 all highways (if they could be called such) were one-lane. The driver of the other car, W.P. Thompson, later told police that he really had to stand on his brakes to avoid a collision. He had to stop so quickly, in fact, that he never could get his machine started again and it had to be towed away. Mike himself played a return engagement in the courthouse.

Judge Baker glowered at the miscreant standing before him as though he were confronting a male Lizzie Borden. No doubt about it; he was coping with an incorrigible speed demon. Two charges of driving "faster than a common traveling pace" in just one week! Obviously the horseless carriage was getting out of hand. Something would have to be done to teach reckless drivers a lesson.

"Five days!" roared the red-faced judge, and the hapless Mike Woods found himself in the slammer. Thus was highway history made.

CHAPTER 3

March

March — maple syrup, mud season, and town meetings. But, above all, town meetings. "Town meeting will be about the same as usual," longtime Yankee editor Ben Rice once wrote, "But say what you will, it does perk a man up to hear old John rant and spiel out all the figures he's been working on since last March to show that education costs more'n it used to and don't give half as much as it used to. General feeling will be the town is gone to hell and there's nothing to be done about it. This is the best tonic a man can have in March, and Ma and I will drive home as sweet as any doves."

Over the years, March Yankees have addressed every "town meeting issue" from road salt, zoning, and conservation matters to energy, waste disposal, and the various levels of argument about historic districting ("Historic districting is an excellent way to protect homogeneous neighborhoods from encroaching urban blight" versus "If putting a plaque on my house means I can't afford the taxes, then they can have their plaque back"). But one year's hot issue is often forgotten a year later, and so the more memorable, lasting stories sometimes reflect the haunting, windy, shutter-banging-in-the-night mood of March, exemplified by one of our all-time favorites, "Horror on Smuttynose."

As Josh Billings wrote, March is a month "to make men swear and women balky."

In East Granville, Vermont, school director Margaret Handley walks with her neighbors, John and Kelly Flood.

– photograph by Carole Allen

61

This New England

Granville, Vermont

BY EDIE CLARK

photography by Carole Allen

At around 8:30 on the morning of March 3, Town Meeting Day throughout Vermont, Margaret Handly will lace up her winter boots, put a lined nylon windbreaker on over her heavy sweater, and pull down the flaps on her wool plaid hunter's cap. She will go out to the barn to warm up her four-wheel-drive Ram Charger and wait there for her neighbor across the street, Stanford Jarvis, to join her. They will ride the 45 miles down through Bethel, west over Route 107, and then north into Rochester and on up to the Granville town hall. If the weather's not too bad, they'll get there by 10, just when the meeting's being called to order. Stanford is one of the town's selectmen and Margaret is the school director and town constable. For something like 30 years, Margaret and Stanford have made this trip together from East Granville to their town meeting. At best, they won't return home until six or seven that night. "It makes for kind of a long day," Margaret says. On the map, Granville and East Granville are only about eight miles apart. Between them runs Braintree Gap. In the summer, there's a road that runs up over the mountain and connects the two towns, but in this part of Vermont summer doesn't last and the road closes when the snows come in. Ever since anyone can remember and for no very good reason that anyone can think of, East Granville has been part of Granville.

Granville is an unprepossessing little town with its backside in the Green Mountains. There really isn't a main street, unless Route 100, the skier's freeway, could be called a main street. The houses sit right tight on the road and seem to huddle together for protection. In town, there's a general store, a wooden bowl mill, a clapboard mill, and a gas station. There's also a one-room schoolhouse where Granville's 13 grade-school-age children attend grades 1 through 6. (The children over in East Granville go to school in Randolph.)

Eula Bannister, known to most people in town as Mrs. Bannister, has taught these six grades for 19 years. Fully 80 percent of the town's budget is spent on the school. Mrs. Bannister lives down in Hancock so she makes a point of not attending town meeting, when delicate issues of budget allocations are discussed, sometimes heatedly, by the town's taxpayers. "I want to give them a chance to fight out their differences without feeling they have to hold back because I'm there."

Town meeting is a time for settling differences, and it has been so for generations. In fact, the very subject of town meeting involves disagreement. Some say the meetings are a waste of time, a time when everything *but* town business gets talked about and a time when some people who attend just plain talk too much. Others, like Stanford Jarvis, say the meetings are vital, the only way town decisions can be made.

Gene Bagley is the chairman of Granville's board of selectmen. He lives only about an eighth of a mile from the Granville town hall, in a big white farmhouse that looks out over his cow barns. He says he doesn't get over to East Granville more than a couple of times a year, but nevertheless he feels it's very much a part of the town.

Overall, he characterizes Granville as "a quiet hill town. If you want excitement, you have to go out of town for that."

Maybe over to East Granville. Margaret Handly thinks it has its own excitement. "We've got a cardinal staying here for the first time this winter, a coon we'd all like to get hold of, and, of course, there's Old Henry, who lives up on the hill." She laughs. "If we want a good time, we've got to make it ourselves."

Margaret Handly is a small, good-humored woman of 66 with lively eyes and lots of energy. She smokes tiny cigars and calls the people of East Granville "rocky people," referring, it would seem, to their grit. There are 18 houses in town, and if you stand in the right place, you can see just about all of them in one glimpse. Margaret owns 12 of those 18 houses, which makes her the town's biggest landlord. She's the town's road agent and keeps the roads plowed in the winter, with either her jeep or her John Deere bulldozer. She takes a lot of pride in East Granville, and the fact that the town is somewhat of a stepchild seems to make it even more interesting to her.

Margaret can sit at her dining room table and count off the population of her town: "There's the Scotts, that's two, the Cooks are three more, and then the Curriers make nine . . ." and come up with an accurate head count: 70 (that includes the two babies expected within the next two months), almost a quarter of Granville's total population of 284.

Back in the twenties, Margaret's grandfather used to go over the mountain on snowshoes in order to get to the town meeting, then stay overnight and return the next day. "A lot more people went to town meeting in those days. And it was sure a lot harder to get there."

Four generations of Margaret's family have lived in East Granville but none to her knowledge has ever lived over in Granville. "Granville's not exactly around the corner. It's around a lot of corners."

Gene Bagley puts it another way: "East Granville isn't so far away. It's just a lot of travel to get there."

(photography continued on next two pages)

62

Above: *The Granville town center. Eight miles away, across Braintree Gap, is East Granville.*

Left: *Margaret Handly votes "Yes" at town meeting in the Granville Town Hall.*

Granville, Vermont

Houses line Route 100 in Lower Granville.

Granville's one-room schoolhouse is the oldest of its kind in the country.

Above: *Town meeting can last a bit too long for some of the younger townspeople.*

Left: *Town moderator Rodney Brown (standing) owns the gas station in town.*

As Porcupines Go...

BY NICHOLAS HOWE

The porcupine population waxes and wanes. Some say that this is inversely proportional to the fisher cat population. Fishers, so this theory goes, are the only natural enemy of the porcupines, the only animal in the woods that can kill them, or that cares to try. The fisher is supposed to tip the porcupine over and rip him up the belly, where there are no quills, and then eviscerate him. When this operation has been performed often enough, the porcupine population falls below a level critical to the fisher's eating habits, and the fisher moves on to quillier pastures, leaving the porcupine to rebuild his numbers. Then the fisher returns, begins tipping over porcupines again, and so on.

I have never been convinced by this line of reasoning: if this habit is so characteristic of the fisher cat, why is it called a fisher? Porcupines don't have much to do with water; their quills are hollow and they float rather high, like ping-pong balls. I would think that this would make it difficult for them to get a good purchase on the water with their short legs. Fishers, on the other hand, are habitués of the watercourses.

Whatever the truth of these cyclical theories, there were very few porcupines around northern New England during the last 10 or 15 years, but now the woods are crawling with them. They have never been much interested in my house, but now they are very interested indeed in my outbuildings. They're out there every night and most days, chewing the outbuildings to pieces. I really can't afford to lose my outhouse and toolshed, but I go way back with porcupines, and I can't bring myself to shoot them.

The first pet I ever had was a porcupine. The summer I was five I had awakened one night to hear a baby crying outside our summer house in Jackson, New Hampshire. It turned out to be a tiny porcupine in an apple tree near the front porch. It had apparently been left behind by its mother during a tree-climbing lesson, and now it was sitting on a low limb, desolate, and sobbing as if its heart would break. A porcupine baby crying sounds exactly like a human baby crying, and I was touched. Without quite realizing it, I moved him into my imagination, and took him back to Massachusetts in the fall. His name was "Porkie," and he went with me everywhere.

At night, Porkie retired with me to my

bedroom. I didn't like to sleep in my daytime clothes, and I assumed he wouldn't either, so I always unbuttoned his quilly coat for him and hung it on a chair. That chair was an old wooden one, with most of the black paint chipped off the legs, showing a layer of older tan paint underneath. With the sometimes vagrant world view of the five year old, I took it for granted that the black paint was really bark on the wood from which the chair had been made, and where Porkie had gnawed it off the lighter sapwood showed through. I believed that Porkie stayed in my room all night, and although I had never actually seen him chewing on the chair, it was the obvious explanation.

My mother made no objection to this arrangement, since Porkie cost nothing to feed and was perfectly housebroken. In fact, most people weren't even aware

of his existence. He was, at any rate, far less troublesome than a pet that had been similarly adopted by one of my mother's younger sisters when she was about my age. Its name was "Buttocks." No one was quite certain just what this pet was, but it always accompanied Aunt Patty to the living room, and the six other people in the family had to remember to leave a vacant chair for it to sit in. This worked well enough when only the family was present, but if a guest went to sit in the empty chair, Patty would fly to the rescue, shrieking, "Oh, no — you *can't* sit there. *Buttocks* is sitting there!"

I don't remember what happened to Porkie. He stayed with me for most of the year, but eventually we got a cocker spaniel puppy whose birthday was the same day as mine, and Porkie and I drifted apart. By the time we went to Jackson for the next summer, he was gone.

The next close meeting I had with a porcupine was a year later on a family hike. Toward the end of what had seemed to me an excessively long afternoon, I was getting cranky, and to distract me, Mother said she'd give a nickel to the first person who saw a porcupine. This was a safe enough offer for her, since they rarely come out in the daytime, but it incited me to a frenzy of watchfulness. In those days my allowance was a penny a week, paid on Saturday. This was a sum so large, and of such vast purchasing power, that it usually took until Wednesday to decide what combination of things would be the best value for the money. A nickel was more money than I had ever hoped to have at one time in my life. Almost immediately I spotted a lumpish-looking thing in a tree, and asked how a pocketbook had gotten left up there. It wasn't a pocketbook, and I got the nickel.

During the war the Jackson house was closed. With so little gasoline, no one could get up there from our family's winter bases in southern New England, and I was sent to camp for two summers. One of the big deals at camp was to go on overnight trips to "Sunset Point." This was a projection into the lake that was probably no more than a few hundred yards from our regular cabins, but at our age it might as well have been a thousand miles into the wilderness.

One evening at Sunset Point someone found a porcupine in a tree, and the counselor in charge shot it with a bow and arrow. The arrow went in through its stomach and stuck out of its back. The poor animal fell backwards and landed in a crotch of the tree lower down. Wedged there, sitting upright like a little old man, he tried to pull the arrow out of his stomach with his handlike paws, sobbing piteously as his life oozed away. It was exactly the same sound I had heard in the apple tree in Jackson. The other boys shook him out of the tree, shouting and stamping in triumph as he fell to the ground. The counselor skinned him and gutted him, and put him in a pot of salty water to soak overnight. The next morning he was fried, and the boys ate him for breakfast. I ate some too. At that age it's hard to refuse a dare like that. But after I went to bed that night I summoned Porkie from the mists of five years gone, and apologized.

Eventually the war ended, and our far-flung family and the usual throng of loose connections once again congregated at the summer place in Jackson. Two things happened that year. The first one was supposed to mark me for life, and didn't. The second wasn't supposed to, and did.

The first was the atomic bomb. It has been an article of faith in the popular sociology of the last 30 years that the central fact of our lives is the threat of The Bomb. At one time or another every malaise that has afflicted the psyche of modern man has been laid at the door of this dread clap of doom that is supposed to be hanging over our heads at every moment of the day and night. I've never known quite what they meant by that. Atomic warfare is a little too abstract for me, and I'm not sure that I believe them when they say that worry about The Bomb has irreversibly scarred our psyches. I know that there are a great many bombs scattered around the world, and I agree that this is absolutely a bad thing. But I don't worry about it in a personal way, a way that would scar my psyche. I've never known anyone who was killed

by an atomic bomb. There are infinitely more automobiles than atomic bombs in the world, and I know many people who have been killed by automobiles. Among my friends, automobiles are unquestionably the leading cause of death. Statistics assure me that I have a fair chance of being killed by an automobile myself. But automobiles have not scarred my psyche. I have not spent a single minute of my life actively worrying about automobiles as an imminent source of calamity in a practical, personal sense.

The other thing happened when my generation of cousins and friends moved into the barn. This was a place of wonder and dread. It hadn't been used for animals for many years, and one end had been cleaned out and provided with wall paneling. In the summer one set of cousins slept there with their parents. Over this rough apartment was "the shelf": the older boys who helped out around the place slept there, with blankets hung from the beams and a birch sapling railing to keep them from falling over the edge into the center section of the barn.

I have never killed another animal since that night, and that is why I am so ambivalent about the porcupines that are eating up my outhouse and toolshed.

This center section was two and a half stories high, filled with odds and ends, and with a long rope hung from the high beam that crossed the center span. This swinging rope was the vehicle for incredible feats of derring-do for those who dared. Farther along there was a dark upper level packed with old bedsprings and trunks full of relics — old World War I uniforms, with a sticky, primitive gas mask that we were afraid to put on. Still farther along, at ground level, there had been a large woodshed. A space was always left behind the last tier of wood, and secret things were done there by people older than I. Later this end was enlarged and rebuilt to form a huge room, finished in old barn boards, and with a large center fireplace. There were parties there that went on long after we went to bed. There were also porcupines that lived under the barn and chewed their

way up through the massive planks of the old floor.

Now my cousins and I and several friends who were up for the summer had moved up onto the shelf. This was an important step, establishing our spiritual kinship with the heroic tenants we remembered from before the war. After a few nights on the shelf, we realized that the porcupines were coming in to gnaw on the lower elements of the barn. We resolved to kill them.

There was a bounty on porcupines then, and the fire warden would pay 50¢ for each severed nose that was brought to him. It was the high road to riches. There followed lengthy debates on the most effective strategies for the attack and the best methods of killing. We assembled armories of croquet mallets and wooden balls and iron pipes and baseball bats, and for several nights thereafter we jumped out of bed and rushed the porcupines with a grand show of yelling and throwing things. Then we realized that sooner or later we would have to call each other's bluff and get serious about the business of death. Sleeping on the shelf had its responsibilities. The next time we heard a porcupine down below, Ben and I went down and hit it, but it just chattered its teeth at us. We hit it again, and it backed into a corner. We hit it again, and it tried to climb the wall. We had a clear shot at its nose now, and we hammered away at its face with what we understood were lethal strokes. It was cornered, and we smashed away at its nose with full strokes of our baseball bats and croquet mallets. It blinked at us and tried to wipe away the blood with its paw. Porcupines are very tough, and this one didn't stop crying and holding its face until we had smashed its face to pulp.

The next morning neither of us ate any breakfast, and we spent most of the day slumped on the sofa. About the middle of the afternoon Mother came and asked us if we had buried the dead porcupine. We dug a hole in the north meadow and went back to the carnage in the barn. When we rolled our trophy into a pail to take it out to the meadow, we realized that it was a female, and she was pregnant. Back at the house my mother, still playing it straight, asked us if we had cut off the nose for the fire warden's bounty.

I have never killed another animal since that night, and that is why I am so ambivalent about the porcupines that are eating up my outhouse and toolshed. When I first built my own house, there were no porcupines around at all. The

My brother had a huge malamute who lived to be 15 and never lost his enthusiasm for biting porcupines. He'd travel miles to find one.

celebrated fisher-cat effect, I told myself. Then, one spring, they were back. My first thought was for Arcturus, my Newfoundland dog. He weighed 215 pounds, and his friendliness bordered on pathology. With his size, and his disposition, he could pick up a porcupine in a single mouthful if the thought occurred to him — dogs are susceptible to that impulse. My brother had a huge malamute who lived to be 15 and never lost his enthusiasm for biting porcupines. He'd travel miles to find one. It was impossible to pull the quills from his mouth without anesthesia, and eventually he made so many trips to the hospital that he became virtually immune to the anesthetic — perhaps even addicted to it. The veterinarian would pump vast quantities into the dog's veins with no more effect than a sort of bemused look in his eyes. When we worked on the quills he would bite at our hands in a good-natured way, hardly penetrating farther than the bone.

I cautioned Turi about the new hazard in his backyard, but I needn't have worried. One evening I heard gnawing sounds coming from the toolshed, and heard Turi rouse himself from his customary state of watchful sleep and climb down from the porch to investigate. I thought I'd follow him and allow the first inevitable bite. Given Turi's nature, it seemed more likely that this would be more of a friendly nudge — just enough to lodge a few quills lightly in his nose. Then I'd step in and scare the porcupine away. I pictured myself pulling out the quills and explaining the facts of life to my grateful friend, who would then never go near a porcupine again, but only bark loudly to scare them away. Very modern and wise, I thought, in the best tradition of both child-rearing and enlightened self-interest.

When I reached the shed, Turi was sitting quietly, watching the porcupine as he ate up the handle of my best shovel. Not a flicker of hostility, or even interest, animated my friend's noble brow. After a minute or two, he lay down and went to sleep, his nose less than two feet from the dreaded foe. I felt relieved, but also a little let down. I shook Turi awake, and showed him how to bark at porcupines. As I pranced around on all fours, barking at the puzzled porcupine, Turi went back

to sleep. Obviously I was going to have to deal with them without his help.

A few weeks later I got my first chance. I was coming home after dark, and as I passed the shed I realized that there was a porcupine working away on the west wall. There were two of them, in fact: one large adult and one baby. The adult was chewing through the wood in the usual professional manner of his kind, apparently demonstrating the proper technique for the tiny beginner. I could have held the baby in one hand, and might have at that, for the quills at that age are hardly more than stiff hairs. The adult cast an apprehensive glance at me, and then at the trainee. The idea seemed to be to stand fast, in the interest of a longer practice session. Indeed, the baby needed it; a vigorous surge of chewing produced no chips at all — only a damp shiny place on the wood.

After a few minutes the adult became alarmed. Its quills went up, accompanied by the usual angry chattering of the teeth, and it began the familiar slue-footed retreat, switching its tail menacingly. Attentive to every nuance, the baby erected its feathery quills and, switching its finger-size tail smartly, turned to run after the adult. This must have been its first time out, for it was obviously unfamiliar with the drill practiced so deftly

by its mentor. It turned 360 degrees instead of 180 and retreated straight into my booted foot. With a small squeak, the baby reversed itself, but at the same time apparently decided that valor was the better part of discretion and began to thrash the toe of my boot with its wispy tail. It gave me several hearty swats, which I was barely able to feel through the leather, and then looked around to see if I had fled in disarray. I hadn't. Five more swats, and another look. I was standing firm. Realizing the high stakes in the encounter, the infant David hunched its shoulders and delivered a volley of tiny pats with its rapidly fatiguing tail and then, panting and gasping for breath, it stole another look, dreading the discovery that the foe was unmoved.

I realized that Goliath also had his responsibilities in this epic confrontation and, taking my cue, I howled in pain and escaped the precincts, hopping on one leg and dragging my crippled foot behind me. Looking back, I could see the victor reeling with exhaustion as he tried to find that trail back to the den. Then, squaring his slender shoulders, he marched away to tell his littermates and the admiring elders of the stirring victory against such towering odds. They probably thought the child had imagined me.

The author's house at 2424 feet atop Mount Cleveland in the White Mountains of New Hampshire. Hawks, small porcupines, and humans on foot are frequent visitors.

*Since 1968, we've annually awarded cash prizes for the three best poems published in
Yankee the previous year. The judges, each serving terms of up to four years, have been Hayden Carruth,
May Sarton, Peter Viereck, Maxine Kumin, Josephine Jacobsen, and Donald Hall (the judge for 1985 poetry).
For some reason, more winners were published in March issues than in any other months. Here they are . . .*

March Brings Out the Best Poetry

Sugaring
by Mary Oliver

Between winter and spring
the maples become rivers
of giving, the horses labor

in the white woods, the fire
blazes and the sap flows
into the metal pails and the pails

fill. What more
can you hope to be than a creature
apart and yet so welcomed

by things that have no name?
Such old roots and such sweetness
just has to rise.

I enter the building,
and roll up my sleeves
and stir the steaming pans

offering their dark glaze
to this kingdom of one and many.
Later, walking the tired horses home,

I think I speak their language, I look
    down
at my fingers expecting to see
leaves.

A Present from Ireland
by Eric Barker

That is what it says
under the harp
on the wallet
that you bought for me in Shannon.

American bills are foreign to it; they
    don't fit,
and it doesn't need them anyway,
being brimmed with notes enough, God
    knows,
when the harp recalls the wind
in those blackthorn hedges
between Limerick and Killarney;

remembers it now
where I walk in another wind
and something is frail inside me,
knowing no song
from those white bridesmaid hedges
can ever reach you now.

The lightest note subdues me.
I am shaken by a wisp of wind.

Flowers Are a Gentle Weapon
by Virginia Brasier

The flowers are real and look endearing
Over the ear, or in soft-blowing young
    hair.
Flowers are a gentle weapon and worth
    fearing.
Flowers are fair.

Over the ear, or in soft-blowing young
    hair,
Flowers are a sign (less love, perhaps,
    than compassion:
A new green comprehension here and
    there.)
Flowers are the fashion.

Flowers are a gentle weapon, worth
    fearing,
Over the ear or in young hair,
    soft-blown.
A flower has changed the heart, just by
    the wearing,
And cracked a stone.

The Flower
by Lois R. Baskett

Hepatica: medieval Latin for liver,
    wort or leaf
                        the ground is star
crowned with them spattered like
snow melting in the glistening low
leaves. Let them weave in groups
to the path at your feet
                        so frail
no, tough: bent to the wind's sharp
cuffs and bowed by the insistent
bees in train they toss and quail
then rise in a crowd again.
    A wavering line of them crosses
the cliff-face where
                        seeds were
caught by a fold up there and lace
    foams as stone-trim.
                        Flimsy things.
In their crack they are slowly
forcing both sides of the
    splintered rock back
                        and back.

A Geologist Speaks Strangely of Baughman's Spring
by J.E. Harrison

Peering at rocks, searching for garnets:
traces of red, shining like silica,
I was astonished in that mountain silence
to hear voices babbling behind me
sounding through the stillness
with a musical accompaniment.
Who would believe a flutter of angels
hovering thirty feet above the ground
and glittering — near Route 3?

My city ears were deaf to miracles,
my glass draws out the truth of stone,
and though I had been forty days
in those deserted places, tapping
the earth's veins with a small hammer,
I had not expected that spring
of sound to gush into my ears,
or such a glory of light to strike
from aspen leaves by the small stream.

Tomorrow and Tomorrow
by Lee Sutton

Listening to the politicians of a spring
    evening
my mind veers and I am occupied
with the eggs of crickets warming
under last year's leaves;
I think on the cold sparked
intelligence of spiders
and how dragonflies make love,
two sets of wings in flight
a synchronized brightness of air.

Factual voices chat of treacheries deceit
    and death
but I hold to the notion of crickets
    unfolding
cell by cell into spring light,
the dragonflies floating in pairs
flashing like daggers in the warm air.
One must consider a spider's sense,
the precise bright thread of a spider's
    calculations.

Death is a falling away of light
and these are light.

The Antique That's Never Advertised

BY SAMUEL PENNINGTON

photography by Stephen O. Muskie

A few years ago I asked an Aroostook County, Maine, antiques dealer why he never advertised his spruce gum boxes. His answer was, "I don't need to — I've got a spruce gum box collector."

In the 10 years I've been publishing *Maine Antique Digest,* I've seen only one spruce gum box advertised, and that one sold quickly to a collector. But if you know what you're looking for you can still find them in shops or at flea markets. Collectors don't get them all. I recently saw two of the boxes in a Hallowell, Maine, antiques shop for $90 apiece. They are still a surprisingly affordable thing to collect.

If you find one, you'll be holding part of the history of the great North Woods as well as an authentic piece of lumberman's folk art.

Spruce gum is the resinous pitch that oozes from the spruce tree wherever it is cut or injured. When dried slightly, it can be chewed — a cheap, if bitter, substitute for chewing gum or chewing tobacco. Carrying raw spruce gum in your pockets would make a mess, however, since it's sticky as well as chewy. Hence, the spruce gum box.

No two boxes are ever quite alike, but most of them were made in the form of books, hollowed out of a single piece of wood, usually spruce or fir, the two most available softwoods, but occasionally maple or birch, or some other hardwood. A sliding cover, either at the top of the "book" or along its "pages," serves to close it. The size is generally such as would fit into a large jacket pocket, about the size of a fat paperback novel, but I've seen them as large as a big dictio-

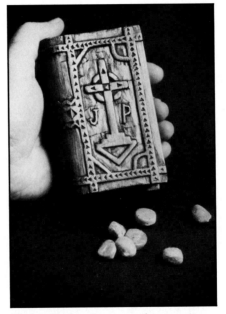

Harlan Taylor, shown on the opposite page with some of his favorite spruce gum boxes, bought the carved box with initials J.P. (pictured above) at an auction in Brunswick, Maine, for about $125.

nary and as small as a pocket Bible.

A variation of the spruce gum box is the spruce gum barrel, a small hollowed-out tube about the size of a beer can, made much like the old wooden canteens carried by soldiers and farmers in the field. Usually the barrel has a cap at either end, although sometimes there is one solid end.

Although the earliest dated box I've seen is 1887, I suspect they were made before that. They seem to date generally from the period of the logging camps — 1870 or so until the early 1940s, when

mechanization and better transportation effectively ended the camps. The latest dated one I've seen was inscribed "To Anne — France 1945," probably made by a soldier in Europe after the war.

The boxes range in quality from crude ones with minimal scratch-carved decoration to elaborately inlaid examples. Bible forms were popular — I once owned one that said "Bible," and some of the boxes may have been made to hold pocket Bibles or prayer books. As in most folk art, the woodsmen added all sorts of embellishments to the boxes. Hearts were a frequent motif, as were pinwheels, chip carving, deep relief carving, imaginative paint, inlay, secret drawers, small mirrors, sentimental sayings — anything a talented woodcarver could work into the form. I've even seen one with a tintype photograph worked into it.

One that I treasure is painted deep red and relief-carved on its cover is the title, "History of Maine." It cost me a then staggering $160 at a 1977 Maine auction. The only other one I own has a three-masted sailing ship inlaid with some black painted wood and cigar box mahogany. It brought $100 at the same auction. I've regretted not buying another one at that auction that had a woodsman's axe and a cant dog inlaid in the cover. I'd own more boxes, but we have a house rule that anything over two is a collection, and collections have a way of taking over their owners.

Not afraid to collect them is Harlan Taylor, a retired aeronautical engineer who lives in Kennebunk Beach, Maine. He hasn't counted his collection lately, but thinks it numbers around 40 spruce gum boxes. He started collecting them

The box in the center, inscribed 1887, is the earliest dated box the author has seen. The box at left, with inlaid mirror, is close to 100 years old; the box at right, with inlaid tintype, about the same.

about seven years ago, when his daughter sent him a magazine clipping about the boxes and suggested that he keep an eye out for them.

For a long time most of us who collected or wrote about them just assumed that spruce gum boxes were made by the woodsmen. It seemed logical. The boxes were generally found only in New England and the Canadian Maritime Provinces. Most looked as if they had been made for wives, daughters, or sweethearts, with inscriptions like "Remember Me," "Friendship and Love," "This is True," and "Maine Woods, Vol. I, by Iva Scott."

It remained for collector Harlan Taylor to confirm the theory. Two years ago Taylor found Ernest Lord, an 88-year-old retired woodsman, and interviewed him at length in the nursing home in Kennebunk shortly before he died. Woodsman Lord said a lot of boxes were made in the camps. He said the loggers would go into the woods camps in September and not come out until April, living in crowded bunkhouses.

"That was a rough bunch there. We worked hard every day but Sunday, and even then there wasn't much to do," recounted the old woodsman. "A lot of those guys would just as soon have fistfights — it was always tough competition for who got the best places to cut wood all week. We were always competing with each other. There wasn't much room in the bunkhouse, and some of those guys didn't wash their clothes even on Sunday; it was easy to let them get on your nerves. We'd carve those boxes just to have something to do to keep the tension down.

"We didn't have much money, and the wood was free and so was the spruce gum. We usually made what we could in one day; we'd cut them while the wood was still green. That was the only thing you could cut in the cold, but some fellows would work on their boxes a lot longer," said the old woodsman, explaining about the more elaborate boxes.

Lord said sometimes they'd make two or three boxes in a winter and fill them with pieces of spruce gum to mail back

to a wife or sweetheart or daughter.

Collecter Taylor said he'd found that only about half the antiques and flea market dealers he talked to really knew what a spruce gum box was, and maybe another 25 percent were vague. "I asked one fellow at a flea market how much his spruce gum box was. He said he didn't have one. Then I picked up a box and asked how much this thing was. That's the one I got for $5."

Taylor said that when he started he bought just about any box that came along, but now he's more selective. "They're just like coins or anything else collectible — the ones that are expensive, there's a reason for it. They have to be pretty elegant to be worth $250." Taylor said the most expensive ones he'd seen were two that were offered at a Portland antiques show last Christmas. They were $500 each, but he didn't buy them.

For a long time, my "History of Maine" was the most expensive box sold at auction. It was topped by one engraved "The Lumberman's Secret," which brought $380 (American funds) at an auction in Mahone Bay, Nova Scotia, in August 1981. The buyer was dealer, auctioneer, and collector Chris Huntington, who once ran a famous antiques shop in Mount Vernon, Maine. He said that he had another box in his collection by the same maker entitled "The Lumberman's Book."

SPRUCE GUM

☞ If you can't find a spruce gum box or can't get to the North Woods, you can still buy commercially prepared spruce gum at many Maine drugstores. If you're a real addict, you can buy it 24 hours a day, 365 days a year at L.L. Bean's famous store in Freeport, Maine. The old-timers dipped theirs in sugar and carried it in the boxes. The commercial brand is rolled in cornstarch and takes a bit of rolling around in your mouth before it's fit to chew.

Some swear by it, but I'd rather look at the boxes. They are true lumberman's folk art.

Huntington owns a box with the saddest tale of all. It says "Remember Me" on one side and "1917" on the reverse. But the gallant young man who made it never came back from that awful war. When Huntington bought it, the soldier's military insignia was still in the box, a treasured remembrance of a fallen soldier and sweetheart.

Huntington has another box entitled "Gum Book 1899," so we know for sure that at least one woodsman kept gum in a box. That's the sort of documentary evidence the historian likes to find — we deal with so many embellished legends in the antiques business.

For the historically minded, there are some spruce gum boxes in museums. Farthest north is Newfoundland's Provincial Museum in St. John's, which has one dated 1888 and found in Harbour Deep. The Billings Farm Museum in Vermont has 12 boxes, probably the largest museum collection. The Maine State Museum in Augusta has a couple of boxes, as does the Lumberman's Museum in Patten, Maine.

If you're looking to buy a spruce gum box, the best places to find one would probably be the small antiques shops of Maine, New Hampshire, Vermont, and the Maritime Provinces of Canada. Don't be afraid to ask the dealer if he has one. If he doesn't have one in stock, maybe he can find you a gum box, unless he already has a collector lined up. The boxes also turn up occasionally at country auctions.

Most of what we call folk art has gone up so in price in recent years that it's hard to recommend it to a beginning collector. Spruce gum boxes are an exception. Even though boxes are not plentiful, the prices have remained remarkably stable and affordable. If you'd like to start collecting something to do with the North Woods, keep your eyes open for the boxes. Do as the woodsmen did, and let your heart be your guide. But watch out you don't buy more than two. Things like spruce gum boxes have a way of taking over more than just the shelves they sit on.

Clearing Land

If rocks hold New England down, roots hold it together.

Four instructive years have left us with the deeper meaning of the pioneer phrase, "clearing land." Our place, you see, is virtually the only clearing in a 10,000-acre forest in western Massachusetts. By the time wilderness gets to this spot it has picked up lots of momentum.

Next to the garden, for example, is a pile of sofa-size boulders, apparently bulldozed down by the glacier from the cliff just to the north of the clearing. It's a neat pile, as these things go, high and rounded and distinct, composed of maybe 40 similar-size pieces. Marking both ends of the pile is a pair of room-size boulders. Among the trees in all directions from there, rocks peek up charmingly through the leaf mold.

The first year of the garden, before we had developed a system, I poked at the surface stones like a kid playing with his lima beans. Then I went after the ones I could see — couldn't avoid seeing because they stuck out of the ground. Today, knowing what's underneath, I laugh, but at that point I needed to believe that these were probably the only stones in the garden.

Stone clearing is spectacular in the spring when the water table has subsided below the surface a ways but the ground isn't dry. Rooting like a well-equipped boar, a pig with sonar, you pry and grapple hidden objects out of the mud, whether bone or stone or stump you can't always tell. Stones move more easily when they're practically floating.

Motorized equipment would be a handicap here, as in most natural New England soils except bottomland. So we work by hand with shovels, picks, axes, bars, and a few long, strong poles. In rare instances we employ the old Willys Jeep for a yank, though it doesn't do the transmission any good.

We start at the upper end of the piece to be cleared and loosen things up with the pick. When we come to a stump, we sit on it, to get a feel of it, of course, then dig and chop around it, finding hidden roots with the pick and chopping them free with a garden axe. If rocks hold New England down, roots hold it together. When I strip out roots, I understand that I have set the soil free, and it may run away to sea.

A root will spring mud into your face; ignore it. You will despair; ignore that, too. Perhaps two hours later the stump can be rolled away like a medicine ball with spikes, a piano without casters.

Now and then the pick strikes a stone. Each one is tried to see if it will wiggle. If so, it is worked loose and brought out and ceremoniously added to the waist-high shipping pile. Any stone too big to wiggle must either be named and left alone for the "character" it lends the garden, or excavated all around, a purchase found under it, and levers of escalating lengths brought to bear, always on a good fulcrum placed close to the stone. Once it budges, someone pries it up while someone else — carefully — wedges wood or stone underneath it. Archimedes is with you: the stone is lowered for a moment onto the supporting wedges, a higher fulcrum is arranged, and the object of your desire is pried up again. The whole process must be repeated until the thing is fully resting on two of the longest poles. These now, with the fulcrums removed, can become either skids or giant twin levers operated simultaneously with a giant twin partner. Thus the stone is either lifted, rolled, or slid out of its hole.

A profound sense of geologic history has influenced my handling of the stone situation. It is my understanding that the rocks were there first, before the garden, before the Extension Service, and even before much of the soil. Any soil around them blew or washed in from the receding glacier, or is the product of mastication by the molars of frost and roots. Thus I acknowledge their seniority before giving them the old heave-ho.

BY JONATHAN VON RANSON

Horror on Smuttynose

BY MARK BASTONI

Louis Wagner was working alone, barely scratching out a living fishing the Maine and New Hampshire waters off the Isles of Shoals, when he had the good fortune to meet John Hontvet and his wife Maren. For two years John and Maren took a personal interest in seeing that Wagner was never in need of food or clothing, and even went so far as to include him in John's prosperous fishing business.

The Hontvets' trust in and kindness toward Wagner proved to be a mistake. On the morning of March 6, 1873, they discovered, much to their woe, how they were to be repaid.

When John Hontvet and Maren arrived from Norway in 1868, they were the only people living on Smuttynose Island in the Isles of Shoals. At dawn each day John would navigate his schooner, the *Clara Bella,* to the fishing grounds and draw his trawl lines, then sail to market in nearby Portsmouth, New Hampshire. After selling the fish he would buy bait, then sail for home in late afternoon. His industriousness earned the tall, light-haired man much respect from his friends and neighbors on other islands, whose numbers rarely reached above 50. Business was good, and in a short time the Hontvets prospered and lived comfortably in their island domain.

Maren Hontvet was a small woman, but not frail, with a gentle manner, especially in the company of others. She provided a fine household for her hard-working husband, applying her decorative touch by using bright paint and paper in their cottage. And she always kept the sunny window shelves filled with an assortment of plants.

Although quite content with their new lives, the Hontvets missed their families in Norway. Maren cherished their small red house, standing in contrast to the run-down fish sheds scattered on the whitened ledges of the island. But often her only companion while John fished was her small dog, Ringe, who ran over the treeless landscape through the low thickets of wild rose and bayberry.

The Hontvets lived on Smuttynose about two years before Louis Wagner came into their lives. Wagner was a dark, muscular, 28-year-old Prussian with a thick accent. He seemed friendly enough to the Hontvets but others viewed him less congenially. He never spoke of his shrouded past, and some had the impression he was always lurking and listening from the corner of the room, pretending not to hear the conversation.

Wagner fished alone from Star, Malaga, and Cedar islands, which are connected to Smuttynose by seawalls and breakwaters. The Hontvets would have been hard pressed to avoid so close a neighbor for, although second-largest in the Isles of Shoals, Smuttynose is only one-half mile long and not quite as wide. The three became close friends over the two years of their acquaintance — as close, it is said, as brothers and sister.

In May 1871 Maren's happiness swelled with the arrival of her sister, Karen Christensen, from Norway. The circumstances of Karen's arrival were somewhat grievous — she had lost a lover in Norway for whom she continually pined — but Maren was certain she could help her sister overcome her melancholy and build a new life. Several weeks after she came, Karen got a position as a live-in maid with a family on Appledore Island, the largest of the Isles of Shoals.

One year passed and John's business continued to grow, so he hired Louis Wagner in June 1872. Wagner was also given a room in the Hontvets' house and seemed more like part of the family than ever. But in October of that year John was to find himself with more help than he needed. His brother Matthew came from Norway to live on Smuttynose. With Matthew was Maren's brother, Ivan Christensen, and his wife Anethe. Ivan was tall and well proportioned, and his wife was beautiful, with blue eyes, bright teeth, and thick blonde hair that swept across her delicate face and fell to her knees when not braided. They had been married since Christmas.

The new arrivals were welcomed by John and Maren and the five lived together in the cottage. Ivan and Matthew went to work for John and Anethe helped Maren keep house. Louis Wagner stayed on with the Hontvets for five weeks after Matthew, Ivan, and Anethe arrived, then booked passage as a hand on another fishing schooner, the *Addison Gilbert,* and left Smuttynose in November. The Hontvets surely felt secure in the knowledge that they had helped Louis get on his feet. But Wagner's luck took a turn for the worse. The *Addison Gilbert* was wrecked and Louis was reduced to working along the Portsmouth wharves. He earned so little he barely managed to pay board to the Jonsens, with whom he lived. By March 1873 he was destitute. His shoes were worn, his clothes tattered, and he owed three weeks' rent.

After a long, severe winter, spring was finally in the air and the sun rose steadily in the clear sky as John, Matthew, and Ivan set sail on the morning of March 5, 1873. When the trawl lines were in they planned to sell the catch in Portsmouth and buy bait arriving on the early train from Boston. At sea they met a neighbor and asked him to stop at Smuttynose and tell the women the winds had changed in favor of sailing directly to the mainland, so they wouldn't be stopping to leave one of the men on the island, as was their usual custom. They'd be home later on that evening.

It was late afternoon when the women got the message. They had already prepared supper and decided to keep it hot until the men came home. Karen was now living on Smuttynose also. She had left her position to take a job as a seamstress in Boston, but was visiting with the family before moving.

When the *Clara Bella* docked in Portsmouth early that evening Louis Wagner was present to help tie the vessel to the wharf. He asked John and the others if they would be returning to Smuttynose that evening, a question they thought curious but hardly reason for suspicion. John explained they would return home if the bait arrived on schedule but, if it was late, they would stay in port, bait their trawl lines, and return home in the morning. He then asked Wagner to help bait the lines, a chore which could consume an entire night. Wagner agreed and left the wharf.

It was 7:30 that evening when Louis was last seen in Portsmouth. He apparently learned the bait hadn't arrived on the early train, and, knowing John's profitable business as he did, concocted

a bizarre scheme to burglarize the Hontvets' home. The quarter moon shed little light on this, the first calm night of the new year. On the shore of the Piscataqua River Wagner stole a dory (not one hour after the owner had replaced the worn tholepins), and rowed past the murky brick buildings with smoke streaming silently from their chimneys, into the harbor and out to sea. The 12-mile row to the Isles of Shoals was a feat, yet far from impossible for a skilled oarsman. In fact, John Hontvet had made the three-hour trip alone in a whaling boat dozens of times. Doubtless Wagner's desperation fueled his determination.

About 10:00 P.M. the three women in the Hontvet house decided not to wait up any longer. They changed into their nightgowns and Maren fixed a bed for Karen in the kitchen, where it was warmer than in the upstairs bedrooms. She and Anethe then retired to an adjoining bedroom.

The crusty snow glistened on shadowy Smuttynose as Louis approached in the dory. Rather than land in the cove where the *Clara Bella* was usually moored, he rowed to the far side of the island and disembarked on the rocky shore. He

watched the lone cottage for several hours after the light coming through the windows had disappeared. Confident the women were asleep, he trudged up the slope in his heavy rubber boots to the door of the house. He tried the door and found it was not bolted and swung open easily. In the darkness of the kitchen, he closed the door behind him, and jammed a piece of wood into the latch of the bedroom door behind which Maren and Anethe slept unsuspecting. He intended to accomplish his raid undetected but at that moment Ringe barked loudly, waking Karen. Seeing the dark figure silhouetted against a window she asked, "John? Is that you?"

Maren sat up in bed and called to her sister, "Karen? Is something wrong?"

"John scared me!" Karen replied, still half asleep. With that Wagner reached for a chair and struck a crippling blow out of the darkness. The young woman screamed frantically as Wagner continued his assault.

"Karen! Karen! What's wrong?" Maren shouted as she jumped out of bed and tugged at the door. Karen struggled to her feet as Wagner dealt another crushing blow. Battered and bleeding,

– Margo Letourneau and Maryann Mattson

75

she was thrown against the bedroom door, freeing the latch, and fell at Maren's feet. Wagner rushed again, swinging and hitting both women this time, but Maren somehow managed to drag her sister out of his reach. She closed and barricaded the door as Louis tried to force his way in.

Petrified, Anethe watched the gruesome scene from a corner of the room. "Anethe! Run! Hide!" Maren implored as she bolted the door from the inside. Nearly incoherent, Anethe clambered out a window and stood barefoot in the snow. She was frozen with fright. "Run!" Maren screeched, but it was too late. Wagner had given up trying to enter the room and had left the house. As he approached Anethe, his true identity was revealed in the moonlight. "Louis! Louis!" Anethe shrieked.

Maren was astonished to see through the window the man they had so willingly accepted now so fiendishly occupied. As Anethe stretched out her hands before him he reached to the woodpile and seized the long handle of the axe. In one swift motion he raised the instrument high into the starry night and drove the steel blade into Anethe's head. Her lifeless body shuddered violently and slumped as Wagner continued striking her, all in full view of Maren, who stood so close on the other side of the window she "could have reached out and touched his arm."

Seeing Anethe could no longer be helped, Maren turned her attention to saving herself and her sister. She rushed to the bed where Karen was kneeling with her head on the mattress and tried to revive the dazed woman. "Karen! Karen! We must run!" she begged, but her poor young sister was on the verge of fainting and could only manage to say, "No . . . too tired." Meanwhile, Wagner completed his butchery and was returning to the bedroom door with the axe.

Maren's keen sense of self-preservation told her they were both doomed if they stayed together. She hastily wrapped herself in a heavy skirt, and hearing Wagner entering the house, she climbed through the window into the bloodied snow with Ringe, now silent, close behind. As she ran, the spiny ice covering the undergrowth tore her bare feet. She expected to find Wagner's boat in the cove and was near panic upon discovering it wasn't there. Her first impulse was to hide in the cellar of a vacant building close by, but she thought better of it, realizing Wagner would be thinking likewise. Instead she ran along the shore to the far side of the island. As she passed the cottage, circumventing it as widely as possible, her ears captured the agony of Karen. Shivering and clutching Ringe close to her breast she crawled between two rocks near the water's edge where the pounding of the waves obliterated all other sound.

At the house Karen was trying to escape through a window when Wagner burst into the room. He swung the axe wildly at the feeble figure, first on the mark, then missing, splitting the sill, and breaking the handle. Karen's listless form melted into the room, where Wagner twisted a handkerchief around her

---

There, lying on the floor, her long gold hair matted in a pool of dried blood, was his adored lover.

---

throat and pulled mightily until he was sure his deed was final.

What anxiety Wagner must have felt seeing Maren had escaped the room! He left a bloody trail of footprints in the snow surrounding every building on the island in a vain attempt to forever silence the last person who could identify him. He searched as long as he could but knew he had to abandon hope of finding Maren if he were to escape under cover of darkness. He went back to the house and dragged Anethe's body by the feet into the kitchen. Exhausted, he then brewed a pot of tea, leaving bloodstains on the handle, and ate some food he had brought with him using a plate, knife, and fork from the Hontvets' kitchen. After ransacking the house and finding only $15 he departed, leaving Anethe's body on the floor beside a clock that had been knocked off the mantel in the struggle and had stopped at exactly seven minutes past one.

It was almost eight the next morning before Maren dared leave hiding. Unable to gain the attention of workmen on a neighboring island she staggered on frozen feet across the breakwater connecting Smuttynose and Malaga and waved her arms to the children of Jorge Ingerbredsen who were playing outside their home on Appledore. Once alerted, Jorge rowed the quarter mile to Maren's rescue. He returned her to the care of his wife, then gathered men with guns to search Smuttynose. When the party landed on the island they discovered Wagner's deed horribly documented.

Finding no one on Smuttynose the men returned to Appledore and searched there also. A few hours later, the *Clara Bella* was spotted on the horizon, her sails spread majestically, gliding through the warming sunshine on the icy sea. Seeing a signal on shore, Matthew and Ivan rowed a tender to Appledore and John sailed the schooner to its mooring on Smuttynose. When the tender landed the men were told of "some trouble on Smuttynose." They rushed to the Ingerbredsen house, where they found Maren in a deplorable state.

"Anethe! Where is Anethe?" Ivan pleaded. Tearfully Maren answered, "Anethe is . . . at home."

Ivan and Matthew flew to the tender and rowed furiously to Smuttynose. They landed at the same time as John and the three raced to the house. Ivan pushed open the door and entered the kitchen. There, lying on the floor, her long gold hair matted in a pool of dried blood, was his adored lover. Covering his face he pushed his way out the door and collapsed senseless in the snow. John and Matthew viewed the full contents of the destroyed home, then sailed the *Clara Bella* to Appledore. Later that afternoon John and others carried Maren's tale of terror to the authorities in Portsmouth.

Word of the calamity spread fast. A description of Louis Wagner was telegraphed to police throughout the coastal states and the evening editions were filled with all the gory details.

Two men, both of whom knew Wagner and were sure of their description, informed police they had seen Wagner in New Castle about six o'clock that morning. The stolen dory was also found in New Castle near a place called "Devil's Den." The new tholepins were worn almost a quarter of an inch.

After returning to the Jonsens', where he changed some of his clothes, Wagner had caught a 9:00 A.M. train for Boston. There he purchased some new boots and a new suit of clothes, then dallied with some women he knew at a boardinghouse. Certainly John Hontvet told the authorities of Wagner's usual haunts and that evening Boston police found him. When arrested Wagner was wearing his new suit over his old clothes. He offered no resistance.

The next day Wagner was transferred from jail to the Boston depot for the trip to Portsmouth, followed by a jeering crowd of 500. At each depot along the route the train was met by outraged citizens demanding his immediate demise. It is reported that a crowd of 10,000 filled the streets of Portsmouth and narrowly missed tearing Wagner to pieces when he arrived.

Smuttynose was in the jurisdiction of the state of Maine and Wagner would have to be tried there. Three days later, when he was moved from the Portsmouth jail to the train, a lynch mob of over 200 fishermen from the islands and the coast was waiting. The police escort drew their revolvers and a company of bayonet-wielding Marines was called from the Navy base, but the mob was not easily subdued. The escort was showered with stones and bricks.

The trial of Louis Wagner commenced on June 9, 1873. After nine days of testimony and 55 minutes of deliberation, he was found guilty as charged. He broke out of jail within a week, but was recaptured in New Hampshire. On June 25, 1875, 27 months after the crime, Wagner was led into the yard of the state prison in Thomaston, Maine, and hanged.

Maren and John Hontvet were never to live on the Isles of Shoals again. They moved to Portsmouth, where John continued working as a fisherman.

Ivan, his spirit broken, could not bear to leave the neighborhood where he and Anethe had spent so many happy times. He worked as a carpenter on Appledore for the rest of the summer of 1873, never out of sight of the cottage where he was robbed of his happiness. He never spoke unless spoken to, and never lifted his eyes from his work when speaking. At the end of the summer he returned alone to Norway and was never heard of again.

THE *REAL* HORROR ON SMUTTYNOSE

☞ Although certain oft-told stories are manifestly not true, the people to whom the stories belong keep telling them anyway, for they satisfy some deep need within. One of New England's favorite stories was retold in the March 1980 issue of *Yankee* — the story of the double murder committed on Smuttynose Island off Portsmouth, New Hampshire, in 1873. Whatever the real truth of these events was, the accepted story, as repeated by the author, is not true. It is not my purpose to criticize the author, who followed his sources scrupulously. The trouble is in the sources, the principal one being by Celia Thaxter, who, like quite a number of subsequent writers, failed to examine the trial record.

Louis Wagner, who was hanged for the crime, was most certainly innocent. Mrs. Maren Hontvet, who named Wagner as the killer and who was the woman alive after the night of bloodshed, was almost surely guilty. She testified that a big, powerful man entered the small house on Smuttynose Island on the night of March 5, 1873. According to Maren, the intruder first broke a chair over a sleeping Karen, then went outside, where he caught Anethe trying to flee and cut her down with three blows of an axe. Maren (with her little dog Ringe) then fled and hid throughout the cold night in the rocks under the sea. Maren had hauled Karen from under the blows of the killer, been hit herself, but had not been cut, nor had Karen been cut when Maren effected the rescue. After she fled, the killer axed Karen. Maren's testimony does not place her in proximity to the victims either when or after the axe fell.

Jorge Ingerbredsen, who first found Maren, testified that she was "in an over bad condition. She was in her nightdress crying and halooing, and blood all over her clothes, Mrs. Hontvet's clothes." John W. Parson, the physician who did the autopsy on Anethe, testified that she had 15 to 20 wounds on her head. Most of them were flesh wounds. Testifying to the defense, he observed that most of the flesh wounds would have "spurted." Although it went to some pains, prosecution failed to show that the dried blood found on Wagner's clothes could be positively identified as human blood. Wagner testified the blood was from fish. There was absolutely no testimony during the trial or evidence by report from outside the trial that Maren had suffered anything other than contusions and cold feet. She herself had not bled.

Thus, there was no place for the blood on Maren to have come from except from Anethe and from Karen, who had been as badly cut up as Anethe. Maren either did the killings herself, or closely collaborated in them. From the condition of the bodies, the former is more likely, for they were erratically hacked, and they were strangled unnecessarily. Even a casual account of the externals suggests that the murders were the work of a relatively weak arm and not the work of a powerful, deliberate, midnight thief, one capable of rowing a dory 20 miles in open ocean.

What is intriguing is this: Ingerbredsen's testimony comes on page 3 of the transcript. Maren's begins on page 10. The trial record, without summations, runs to 149 pages. That means that the evidence most damaging to prosecution was public, obvious, and massive right from the start of the trial. Why, then, we must ask, did all collaborate in what we should now call, and Wagner then called, a public lynching?

There are many ways of answering that question, but the simplest is to say that the alternative was, in that time and that place, unthinkable. Handsome, faithful, dutiful family women did not, could not, be allowed to do evil. Evil came into the human situation from without. It was not there, within, waiting to spring. At any rate that was the myth the major poets of the time, poets like Whittier and Longfellow and Emerson, were singing. Those presiding spirits taught there was no evil in New England. Melville and Hawthorne had found otherwise, but they were currently out of public favor.

One small item. The author, copying Thaxter — and who knows how many others in between — describes Wagner as dark, lowering, skulking. The *Eastern Argus* for March 7, 1873, describes him as "of light sandy complexion." Edward Mitchell, a reporter from the *Lewiston Journal,* who spent the afternoon and evening before the execution with Wagner, and who witnessed the execution, wrote that he was a "rosy-faced Prussian. His face was round and good-natured, his eyes mild; no wickedness discernible in his countenance." To make him evil, legend had to make him black; but he was, in fact, blond.

L. Morrill Burke
Associate Professor
University of Southern Maine

A·MARCH SAMPLER

☞ Memorable thoughts, quotes, and assorted tidbits from the last 50 March issues. ☜

LIFE IN A COMPANY TOWN

☞ Michael, he told me, finally had gone into the mill [Great Northern Paper Co., Millinocket, Maine] sometime after he turned 20, starting as a fifth hand in the paper room, as his father had, because that's where the money was, and the advancement. The next year, in 1974, he got married. The next year he was dead.

He had been on Number 10 paper machine. The levelator had risen from the floor to take off a roll of paper. Michael was in between working on the paper, and the hydraulic arm of the levelator came down and crushed him.

Wiggie was up by Number 5. There was a commotion, and someone ran past with a stretcher. Wiggie ran then.

"They tried to hold me back. When they did, I knew it was my son."

After they buried Michael, people came to him and said, "You ought to sue them, Wiggie. Something had to have

The paper mills of Millinocket, Maine, with Mount Katahdin in the distance.

— Stephen O. Muskie

gone wrong for the levelator arm to come down on him like that."

"Why didn't you?" I asked.

"What good would it do?" Wiggie asked. "I might get some money, but what is that? I still had to work in the mill. I still had to live in the town. I couldn't change my life." *(From "Millinocket Is a Company Town" by Willis Johnson.)*

REPORT FROM A FLY ON THE WALL

☞ During the war, the women set aside frivolous pieces and concentrated on work for the Red Cross. Such a project was in train when I went up to fetch Ma late one autumn afternoon.

For such a restrained, genteel group, they seemed to be in something of an uproar. Peeking in cautiously, I could see a phalanx of broad backs tensely bent over the table. Pink and white flannel was everywhere. The floor was covered with scraps, and pins had fallen like pine needles in a high wind. A sample on the back of a chair turned out to be pajamas — men's pajamas for the

Veterans' Hospital. The ladies had hit a snag.

Cora, at the head of the table, was reading directions from the pattern sheet. She looked agitated, the bun of her snow-white hair had slipped to one side, her face was flushed. Here was the sergeant whose troops were out of step and in disorder. The snafu was how to put the flies in the pajama bottoms. (In the instructions the flies were referred to as "closures.") So it was trouble, trouble, trouble.

"That can't be right — can't you see that's upside down?" Cora waved a frantic hand. "How could it work upside down, I ask you?" She turned back to the directions. "It says here, lay the upper flap on the right-hand side — Mabel, can't you tell which is the right-hand side? Just hold it up in front of you and use your right hand — yes, like that. Well, no, not like

that — he'd have to be left-handed. Oh, Sadie — you're making the opening over a foot long, whoever heard of a — well, never mind." She studied the sheet again. "Now, turn the flap to the front of the left side opening and stitch neatly along the edge. Which is the edge, where is the edge?" She stood up to get a view of the whole length of the table.

"Sarah, you're doing it on the backside — the man would have to be an acrobat." She coughed, sat down hurriedly. Putting her handkerchief to her mouth, she coughed in terrible spasms. *(From "A Pajama Party at the Ladies' Aid" by F.B. Tolman.)*

"Floppy" Tolman, here describing a meeting in Nelson, New Hampshire, during World War II, is one of many of the Nelson Tolmans who have contributed much to Yankee *over the years.*

I AM A LIVING NIGHTMARE

HOW TO WASH A QUILT

☞ A very old quilt must be given kind treatment if it is to be washed. First, colorfastness must be determined. To do so, fill a medicine dropper with a diluted washing agent, wet a small area, and blot dry. If any color comes out on the blotter, the colors are not fast, and you will probably choose not to wash the quilt. If all seems safe, proceed. When a quilt is heavy with water, the filler swells, and old, rotted threads will give way. Therefore, it is necessary to minimize the strain. One way of doing this is to make two sheets the size of the quilt by seaming together inexpensive nylon net. Place the quilt between the net pieces and baste together. The net will provide extra strength during the washing process. In order to cut down on handling, do the washing in a bathtub. *(From "On Taking Care of Your Own Favorite Quilt" by Bets Ramsey.)*

☞ I pay $400 to insure my 1972 pickup truck, without collision, and I have never made an insurance claim. Yet I have driven thousands of miles within the city limits of Boston and never hit a car, a pedestrian, or a bicyclist, though I have broken every traffic law in the book. When a light changes from green to yellow I step on the gas. I make illegal U-turns, and travel up or down a one-way street. I brake hard because I am often forced to. I park where I shouldn't and turn right on red, whether or not it is allowed. I turn left on red. I rarely pass in the breakdown lane, though if I'm rushed, this maneuver is an option for me. I always make progress in a traffic jam, regardless of its size or nature. I am a cog in a machine that has the ability to work when other parts break down. I am a purebred Boston driver, a living nightmare. *(From "Confessions of a Boston Driver" by Scott Cramer.)*

– illustration by Chris Demarest

A·FAVORITE LETTER

THE REAL LOBSTER EATING RECORD

☞ As an avid *Yankee* reader (and New Hampshire native) I must make haste to correct an inaccuracy in Jane and Michael Stern's "Traveler's Journal" in the March 1982 *Yankee*!

Is it because fame is fleeting? Is it because I moved to California? Or is it because I lost 250 pounds and with it my chances of repeating my record-breaking eating marathons? Whatever the case, the so-called record that pro wrestler André the Giant supposedly set of eating 40 lobsters at Custy's Restaurant in North Kingstown, Rhode Island, is a mere two-thirds of my record: a record that hung proudly in Custy's until their unfortunate fire last year. André's so-called record was an average day for me, *and my record was 61 lobsters!*

If I go back to Custy's it will be a moderate visit "for old time's sake." Gone will be the dozens of lobster shells left behind, but I do ask in the interest of journalistic accuracy and in memory of the Tom Shovan who used to break eating records coast-to-coast and sent buffet proprietors throughout New England into shudders and cold sweats for 40 years that *Yankee* print a correction to this gross misstatement that would lead the naive reader to believe that a mere 40 lobsters are enough to satisfy a truly voracious appetite!

Tom Shovan
Woodland Hills, California

– Austin Stevens

NEWPORT (R.I.) MERCURY — The 72-foot schooner *Mariah* left Goat Island yesterday with a crew of seven men and one woman for a round-the-world cruise they expect will take about 2½ years. . . .

NEWS ITEM: BEN SLATE BOSTON, MASS.

...AND JUST **WHAT**, PRAY TELL, DOES "SEVEN DAYS OF THE WEEK" HAVE TO DO WITH THE **EIGHT** OF US..?

March "Houses for Sale" Have Always Been a Little Odd!

A WHOLE TOWN

☞ In March of 1971 we featured an entire town for sale. Not an out-of-the-way, run-down set of buildings technically still a town. This was thriving Harrisville, New Hampshire, one of the most photographed towns in all New England and one just declared a Historic District. In all, there were 17 houses, mostly brick, many located on a river or a pond; the entire Cheshire Mill complex, built originally in 1799 and closed down in 1970; and almost 40 acres of land in the central village. We didn't have high hopes that anyone would want an entire town — but we were wrong! A manufacturer of water filters, Filtrene Corp., in New Jersey, decided Harrisville was just where they'd rather be. They bought the town, reopened the mill, rehired everyone, and provided a still-continuing happy ending to our story.

Harrisville, New Hampshire — virtually the whole town was for sale in 1971.

– Ann Card

– Paul Darling

Nayatt lighthouse, Barrington, Rhode Island — did it sell for $550,000?

AN OLD LIGHTHOUSE

☞ In March of 1982 we featured the Nayatt lighthouse, built in 1829 on Nayatt Point in Barrington, Rhode Island. We love lighthouses, and *Yankee* readers seem to also, although most prefer *imagining* living in one rather than *actually* living in one! This lighthouse was beautifully renovated as a luxurious seaside home, a fact certainly reflected in the $550,000 price tag! But we'll never forget the panoramic view of Narragansett Bay from the tower. Fantastic.

– Dick Smith

There's something about a caboose that Yankee readers just love.

A CABOOSE

☞ We featured an entire railroad for sale in April 1980 — station, three locomotives, several cars, and the tracks going from Kingston to Wakefield, Rhode Island. In November the year before we offered "697 well-insulated dwellings for $2000 each!" They were refrigerated railroad cars on a siding up in Bangor, Maine! But it's always cabooses that somehow strike *Yankee* readers' imaginations. This was a restored one up in North Conway, New Hampshire, available for $7500 in our March 1975 issue. We called the story "How to Get Back on the Track." (The only things as popular as cabooses are tugboats! Feature either a tugboat or a caboose in *Yankee* and the result is *instant* sale. No matter *what* the price.)

CHARLIE'S MOUNTAIN

☞ It was the oldest ski area continuously operated by the same family in the United States — consisting not only of 120 acres of Temple Mountain in southern New Hampshire, but also 23 woodstoves; snowmobiles, snowcats, etc. galore; and "a house from which you can ski to work!" We featured it in March 1984 for a half million dollars, and it sold within the first week. We felt that "skiing to work" every morning was what proved irresistible!

An entire New Hampshire mountain, ski trails and all, sold the first week.

– Stephen O. Muskie

A lovely old Cape and barn in Maine, at a pre-inflation price.

THE BEST MARCH BARGAIN

☞ It was a 150-year-old eight-room house, fully modernized, with a connecting shed and barn plus 50 acres that had a beautiful brook running through it. Location: up in the Brunswick area of Maine. Price: $8500. But of course that was back in March of 1962. Oh, for the good ol' days!

UNCLE SAM'S PLACE

☞ It seems that back in 1780 one Edward Wilson and his 11 children moved from Massachusetts to Mason, New Hampshire, where he built a seven-room house. One of his sons, named Sam, eventually moved to Troy, New York, where he established a successful meat-packing business. When the War of 1812 came along, Uncle Sam ("Uncle" being a general term of endearment in those days) was appointed government inspector of meat, which called for branding every meat barrel with the initials of the United States. But somehow "U.S." came to be thought of as "Uncle Sam" around those parts and the rest is history. At any rate, "Uncle Sam" Wilson often returned to the family house in Mason. The last Wilson to own it died in 1906 and the place was sold for $2000. The price on the house when we featured it in March of 1979 was $96,000.

– Ann Card

Uncle Sam's house, featured twice in Yankee over the years.

A • MARCH
SAMPLER

(continued)

– Gordon Brooks

IT NEVER COMES EASY — EVEN FOR THE GREAT ONES

☞ " . . . he brings together the jottings he finds he has written down concerning it, fusing them into a connected whole with additional material suggested at the time. His essays are then very slowly elaborated, wrought out through days and months, and even years of patient thought. . . . His essays are all carefully revised, again and again, corrected, wrought over, portions dropped, new matter added, or the paragraphs arranged in a new order. He is unsparing in his corrections, strikes out sentence after sentence; and paragraphs disappear from time to time. His manuscript is everywhere filled with erasures and emendations; scarcely a page appears that is not covered with these evidences of his diligent revision." **George Willis Cook, describing the writing habits of his friend Ralph Waldo Emerson.** *(From "Between the Lines with Ralph Waldo Emerson" by James Willert.)*

"All those in favor say 'ay-uh'."

NANA IS GOING TO DIE

☞ " . . . we were at my father-in-law's and that same weekend at his sister's. My son — he's psychic, too — was three at the time. He took his grandfather's picture and turned it face down at both houses. My father-in-law died the next day. He'd gotten out of his car to change a flat tire. He had a coronary and died.

"Four months later my mother went into the hospital for tests. The surgery was not supposed to be life-threatening, but I knew she was going to die, and my son knew too. He was saying his prayers one night and blessing everything in sight — to stall for time.

" 'And God bless Nana,' I said.

" 'No,' he said, 'No God bless Nana. Nana is going to die.'

"He wouldn't say it so I finally covered him and went downstairs. The call came at seven o'clock the next morning. My mother was dead.

"It was a year of devastation that I was psychically attuned to. I learned what it was like to live with the foreknowledge of misfortune, and I learned that you can't change fate. If it's meant to be, it's going to be. The only problem with psychic awareness is that you have to learn acceptance." *(From "Portrait of a Psychic" by Beth Lundyn.)*

TOWN MEETING DIPLOMACY

☞ There was a controversial article in our town warrant some years ago. A leading citizen who had enemies on both sides of the question was urged to declare his opinion. Negative or affirmative would make him equally unpopular.

Whispering that he was hoarse from a cold, he handed the moderator a slip of paper, quoting from John Selden, a leading British jurist. The moderator was motioned to read it aloud to the voters. The note read:

"Wise men say nothing in dangerous times. The lion, you know, called the sheep to ask if his breath smelt. She said, 'Aye.' He bit off her head for a fool. He called the wolf, and asked him. He said, 'No.' He tore him to pieces for a flatterer. At last he called the fox, and asked him. Replied the fox, 'I have got a cold and cannot smell.' "

J. Almus Russell
Bloomsburg, Pennsylvania

MISSING: THE HUMAN ELEMENT

☞ "As we looked at that agency (the Nuclear Regulatory Commission) overall, our most important judgment was that it is an agency that is hypnotized by equipment. It had a firm belief that equipment can be made fail-safe, and as a result it totally ignored the human element in nuclear power." **John Kemeny, then president of Dartmouth College and chairman of a presidential commission charged with studying the nuclear accident at Three Mile Island.** *(From "All the Things We Do He Does Better" by Tim Clark.)*

John Kemeny

– courtesy of Dartmouth College

82

THE DAY I MET HELEN KELLER

☞ Helen Keller was very young the day I met her, maybe 12 or 13, and I was only four or five. This meeting happened at the home of Mrs. Laura Richards. Mrs. Richards, daughter of Julia Ward Howe, lived in Gardiner, Maine, the small city where I was born. Her mother and father were directors of the Perkins Institute for the Blind, in Watertown, Massachusetts, where Helen Keller was a pupil.

My mother told me that morning I was going to meet a wonderful young girl. She didn't tell me any more, as I was too young to understand what it meant to live in the soundless darkness of being blind, deaf, and dumb. When we got to the "Yellow House," the Richardses' home, one of the Richards girls took my hand and led me across the lawn to where Helen was standing with her lifelong teacher, Mrs. Anne Sullivan Macy, and others.

Betty Richards said, "Helen, this is Alice." Mrs. Macy guided Helen's hand to my head. She kept it there a moment or two, and then she spoke. Her voice was a loud, rather hoarse sound that frightened me. She said "Baby." I thought, "What is the matter with this girl? I'm not a baby!"

There was an awed silence. "Did you hear that?" a woman whispered. "She said 'baby.'" Then they all crowded around Helen. I was pushed to one side, which suited me. That word "baby" was not her first word, but one of her first, I was later told.

I saw her once again when she was appearing at Keith's in Boston. The young girl I remembered had turned into a beautiful woman. But it is that day in my childhood that I shall always remember.

Alice P. Mullaney
Jamaica Plain, Massachusetts

HOW A NEW ENGLAND LEGEND CAME TO BE

☞ Ice sheathed the inside of the dory and had to be broken up and pitched overboard. A hard routine developed: pound ice, bail, watch the stealthy seas, row, row, row.

Welch did his part right up to his last gasp, and brave men have long paid tribute of sorrow to this humble hero. All the hardships of those sub-Arctic waters could not subdue his manhood. He fought to the very last, but the combination of evil things was just too much to bear. He slowly froze to death at his post of duty. He died on the third night and lay, an ice-shrouded passenger, on the dory's bottom. Thereafter, Blackburn fought alone.

By this time, he was conscious that his feet were frozen and that his utmost efforts to keep life in his stiffening hands were unavailing. Then, with a new and desperate urgency, death seemed to tap him on the shoulder. If a man could not close his hands around his oar-handles, how could he row?

His solution of this problem was as characteristic as it was direct. Here is what he said later about this phase of his martyrdom.

"My fingers are getting whiter and stiffer. I think too late now to stop 'em freezing. I knew that if my fingers froze straight and stiff I couldn't keep on rowing after they froze. So I made up my mind there was nothing else to do. If my fingers were bound to freeze, I'd make 'em freeze in such shape as to be of some use afterwards.

"So I curled 'em around the handles of the oars while yet they wa'nt too stiff and I sat there without moving while they froze around the handles of the oars."

And so he rowed — hands frozen, feet frozen, no sleep, no food, no water, and with a dead man as his silent passenger.

He finally raised the Newfoundland coast and landed in a tiny inlet. *(From "The Heart That Beat the Sea" by William P. Deering.)*

Howard Blackburn's saga occurred in the winter of 1883 but Blackburn, without hands, lived many years into this century — running a restaurant in Gloucester, Massachusetts, crossing the Atlantic several times single-handed (voluntarily), and generally enjoying his status as a New England legend. Although our story, excerpted above, appeared back in March 1955, we still receive an occasional request to repeat it.

– Alan Ferguson

"Earl ain't got anythin' really important t'say, but he likes t'know he's still got a finger on the wheel."

CHAPTER 4

April

*T*he first Spring issue — with material saved for it all during the late fall and winter. The ice goes out, the Red Sox are finally in full swing, Daylight Savings begins, the summer birds have arrived, and now is the time for something about Lexington and Concord, perhaps Easter, the Boston Marathon, and, above all, anything to remind us the long winter is over. Fine for an April issue to look like May — but never like March.

And yet so many articles concerning horrible deaths have been mentioned by readers to be among April's best: "The Only Man Who Didn't Go Down with the Thresher," "A Death in the Country," and, most gruesome of all, "The Man Who Last Saw Abraham Lincoln." Even April's favorite fiction, "The Odor of Fish," has an ending surprisingly different from the usual mood.

Of course it was April 1976 that saw the beginning of the great controversy, lasting for months in our letters column, concerning who possessed "the oldest biscuit in the world." Everyone eventually conceded the prize to a New England lady in Aiken, South Carolina. Her biscuit, carefully wrapped in muslin, was baked on April 20, 1828, by her great-great-grandmother on the day she died.

So much for the month beginning with All Fools' Day. . . .

Quahoggers at Old Orchard Beach, Maine, take advantage of the best clamming tide of the season, the "spring" tide that occurs when earth, moon, and sun are aligned.

– photograph by Stephen O. Muskie

85

Author John A. Gould opens his garage door to greet Aunt Emma, April 1979.

When we accepted this little piece in cold, dark December of 1979, we felt we'd jumped forward to every April forevermore! It's truly a special spring ritual of the nostalgic kind. . . .

Into the Sunshine — and Another Spring

BY JOHN A. GOULD

When I am certain spring is securely in place — and only then — I open my garage door. I have to have seen plenty of skunk cabbage, the maples starting to leaf out, and at least one heron. Grass must be going green, the wind coming warm out of the southwest. Most important, April showers must have already washed the roads clean of both the sullied March snow and the salt.

My garage is an old, wood-frame structure with a cement floor, standing a couple of blocks from where I live. (Actually, it isn't even mine; I rent it.) The distance creates no problem, really, since the door remains closed during the five months of the year when walking to it is least pleasant. Then, usually on a Saturday late in April, I finally decide that the season has arrived to rouse Aunt Emma from hibernation.

Aunt Emma is a 1951 Chevrolet Deluxe, a four-door sedan, black with modest chrome strips on the sides and with fender skirts. The word "cream puff" must have been coined with her in mind: 56,000 miles (original miles, by George), perfectly maintained interior, working clock and cigarette lighter, original engine and paint, and — with the exception of a couple of ochre spots on the bumpers — absolutely without rust. She has a split windshield (1951 was the last Chevrolet with flat panes; a year afterwards came the curved one-piece jobs that wrinkle the roadside as it slides by). The wipers run on the engine's vacuum, stopping dead when the accelerator is floored. Her enamel is glossy, seemingly an eighth of an inch thick.

Her condition does not, I'm afraid, reflect on me except in the most literal sense. I bought her in Brunswick, Maine, four years ago from Jon Lee, a used-car dealer with an avid interest in old automobiles. Jon himself drives a Packard straight out of the thirties, and his heart is pure. Like a certain few pet shop owners, he will not deal away a treasure unless he feels it will be well treated. I told him I was looking for a car that I could *use,* in good weather, at least; especially one that, if cared for, would not rust and fold into oblivion after 2.7 years. My motives must have sounded jake to him, because we shook hands the same day.

Aunt Emma is the genuine article. I had her history from Jon, whom I trust. Honor bright, a little old lady owned her first, keeping her out of all inclement weather for 13 years. When the lady died, her son inherited Emma and maintained her in a similar fashion: less than 2000 miles per year, frequent oil changes, no driving on rainy days (to say nothing of snowy or sleety ones). When, after much negotiation, the son finally sold her to Jon, he asked permission to keep her for a few days so he could take photographs of her for the family album.

I do not find this surprising. Aunt Emma is remarkably photogenic. Friends are forever snapping their Canons at her. People wave. Once, while we were traveling along the Maine Turnpike at our sensible 45 miles an hour, a fancy motorcycle pulled abreast of us. "What year is that?" the driver shouted across the slipstream.

"Fifty-one," I called back, flashing fingers, first five, then one.

He gave the thumbs-up sign and said something into a CB transmitter. "Some guy wanted to know," he yelled. With a roar, he pulled ahead of us and was gone.

Each spring the act of opening the garage door to bring Aunt Emma outside renews me. First, there is the scent of the wood garage — a musty, dusty, fusty sweetness, perfumed by oil and gasoline and dry rot and a few decaying leaves and Aunt Emma herself. To me this odor is as suggestive as the madeleine's taste was to Proust. It spins me back into the past to my grandfather's garage in the early fifties when I was small and his Chevrolet — almost a twin to this present one — sat gleaming in its own cool sweet dim cave.

Beneath a coat of dust, Emma's finish shines dully. Once inside the building, I have a few simple operations to perform. I have to jack up the bumpers and remove the blocks which have kept the wheels off the floor all winter. I have to put the battery back under the hood and reconnect the terminals. I have to check the oil. In order to avoid sludge deposits in the motor, I am careful to change the oil just before putting the car up each November; come spring it is always a pleasure to pull the dipstick and see a clean amber bead at the full mark.

Finally we are ready to try the starter. I pull the choke, put in the clutch, and press the button; Emma turns over, coughs once, and, with a few billows of exhaust that will rapidly clear as she warms, starts: *pahdadadadadada,* as smooth as a sewing machine. I close the door (which sounds like no automobile door built today — THWUNK! like an axe into an oak), time stops for an instant, and slowly, gloriously, Aunt Emma and I roll gingerly outside into the sunshine, into still another spring.

The assassination at Ford's Theater occurred on April 15, 1865, and April issues of many publications over the years have often published articles on some aspect of the tragedy. But we've never read anything like Charles Fitz-Gerald's contribution to our April 1980 issue. While it is gruesome (and we debated at some length before deciding to go ahead with it), it also represents a historically important story and the final chapter of the Lincoln assassination.

The Man Who Last Saw Abraham Lincoln*

BY CHARLES E. FITZ-GERALD

Fleetwood Lindley was 13 years old in 1901 when his father sent for him to come as quickly as possible to Abraham Lincoln's tomb in Springfield, Illinois.

The last time Fleetwood Lindley went to Oak Ridge Cemetery, he stayed. The funeral procession filed out of Springfield, in through the cemetery gates, and halted at the family plot. Lindley's coffin was lowered into its simple grave close to his father's. Not far away the towering monument of Abraham Lincoln's tomb dominated the Illinois plain. There, beneath the winter-tempered soil, Fleetwood and the "Great Emancipator" were rejoined for the first time since facing each other over a half century earlier. For with the death of Fleetwood Lindley on February 1, 1963, the world lost the last person to look upon Abraham Lincoln's face.

Almost a century had passed since Lincoln's own funeral made its way to Oak Ridge Cemetery. On that May 4 in 1865 the long journey back from Washington ended for the martyred president. His body's travels, however, were not over. Had officiating Bishop Matthew Simpson foreseen the chronic shuffling that would befall Lincoln's corpse, he might never have uttered, "Rest in peace." Over the next 36 years the coffin of Abraham Lincoln would be moved no fewer than 10 times.

The simple act of getting the president's body interred was marred by heated conflict. Immediately on hearing of the assassination, the city council of

---

* While this title was not exactly a "trick," it was a little like our 1975 article about a living Massachusetts man who had "sailed with John Paul Jones." He had been aboard the ship carrying the remains of John Paul Jones back from France to this country in 1905.

Springfield purchased a block in the heart of the city and workmen were hastily assigned to construct a vault to receive the body. On the morning of May 4, shortly before services were to begin, Mary Lincoln telegraphed Springfield stating unequivocally that her husband's remains were to be buried in Oak Ridge Cemetery or she would have his body returned to Washington and interred in an unused crypt in the Capitol originally prepared for George Washington. According to her wishes, the body was taken to Oak Ridge Cemetery. There, in the public receiving vault, Mr. Lincoln was laid to rest — for the first time.

Later that year the cemetery needed the public vault, and so the president's coffin was moved to a temporary chamber close by on December 21, 1865.

Soon after Lincoln's assassination, an association was formed to raise funds for an appropriate tomb within the cemetery to guard his remains. Ground was broken in 1869. In September of 1871, construction had progressed to a point where the coffin was able to be moved to a crypt in the tomb. After the entire structure was completed and dedicated in 1874, the president's coffin was taken from the crypt and placed in a white marble sarcophagus on October 15. At last, after three moves, the slain Lincoln lay in a fitting and supposedly final resting place.

At this same time a master engraver, Ben Boyd, was serving a 10-year sentence in Joliet Prison — his reward for faithful service to a large ring of counterfeiters. His associates had not forgotten him, however, mainly because of their inability to find another of his artistic accomplishment. They had a plan to get Ben out from behind bars. They would steal the corpse of Lincoln, precious to Illinois, and hold it for ransom; the ransom was to be Ben Boyd's freedom. They selected the night of election day, November 7, 1876, as perfect for their purpose, theorizing that the people of Springfield would be too distracted with a new president to worry over a dead one. At eight o'clock three men broke into the tomb. Quickly they pried open the sarcophagus and began to pull out the coffin. With success seemingly at hand, one of the men was sent to get their hidden wagon. When he failed to return quickly, the two remaining plotters went out to investigate and saved themselves immediate capture. Their fellow body snatcher was actually Louis Swegles, a detective who had gone to fetch waiting Secret Service men rather than the wagon. Although they escaped that night, the two grave robbers were arrested 10

By the time Fleetwood arrived at Oak Ridge Cemetery, workmen (above) had taken Lincoln's casket into Memorial Hall for final identification and interment in the new tomb.

They would steal the corpse of Lincoln,
precious to Illinois, and hold it for ransom. . . .

days later in Chicago. But they had raised doubts about the safety of Lincoln's remains in the minds of the group of men who cared for the tomb.

These men, the National Lincoln Monument Association, took action: they hid the body. On the night of November 15, 1876, three members of the association hauled the coffin deep into the tomb's interior. Quickly they dug a shallow grave, and just as quickly it filled with water. Not knowing what to do next, they rested the coffin on planks dis-

carded by workmen and covered it with debris. For over two years this "temporary" mausoleum housed the body. While Abraham Lincoln lay in the midst of refuse, thousands passed close by paying homage to a lovely but empty marble sarcophagus. Then on the night of November 18, 1878, six association members successfully scooped out a shallow grave to hide the coffin.

These six, joined by three associates, met on Lincoln's birthday, February 12, 1886, to form the Lincoln Guard of

Honor; their purpose was to protect the body of the late president. One of these men was Joseph P. Lindley.

The establishment of the Guard did not end worry for the body's safety or the uneasiness prompted by such an undignified burial. Still, nothing was done until April 15, 1887, the anniversary of the assassination. Then the coffin was lifted from its hidden grave for transfer to a brick vault beneath the tomb's floor, built to ensure the safety of the body. Rumors that Lincoln's corpse had actu-

ally been stolen had circulated ever since the aborted theft. The Guard of Honor decided to settle any questions and to make sure their precautions were not for the wrong corpse. The casket was cut open to expose the face of Lincoln. The Guard members were satisfied and signed affidavits attesting that the coffin indeed contained the remains of Abraham Lincoln. With that, the coffin was resealed and inhumed. This time Lincoln would rest undisturbed for 13 years.

When the Lincoln Tomb was built, the base had not been dug deep enough and each year it became more unsafe. By 1899 the structure was so dangerous it had to be completely dismantled in order to be rebuilt. A vault was excavated

Above: *Charles L. Wiley, left, and his uncle, Leon P. Hopkins, were called to Oak Ridge Cemetery on September 26, 1901, to cut open the lead lining of Lincoln's casket. They had performed the same grim task in 1887.*

near the tomb to house Lincoln's remains during construction, and on March 10, 1900, he was moved there.

About 200 people gathered at the reconstructed tomb on April 24, 1901, to witness the unearthing of Lincoln's coffin for removal back to the tomb. The nine tons or more of brick and stone that had been heaped on the temporary grave to disguise it had to be lifted by steam derrick, and it was late in the day when Lincoln's coffin was finally reached. The setting sun slanted an orange light as the workmen opened the protective outer crate and when it colored the cedar coffin, heads were spontaneously bared in reverence. Six workers then carried the coffin into the tomb to be placed in the same marble sarcophagus that had received it in 1874. But even this interment was not to be the last.

About a month after the tomb was reopened, Lincoln's oldest son, Robert, came to inspect it. Robert Lincoln had become an important man in his own right — one whose wishes were not lightly regarded. He had been anxious for the security of his father's body and what he found did not assuage his concern. The coffin lay in the same sarcophagus that thieves had easily violated previously. He returned to Chicago and studiously devised a new burial arrangement that he outlined in a letter of June 21, 1901, to Illinois Governor Yates saying, "I feel compelled to say that only by adoption of such a plan as this could I be satisfied that all danger of desecration be avoided." Governor Yates quickly contacted Colonel J.S. Culver, who had just rebuilt the tomb, with instructions to break through the floor of the catacomb and to

Left: *On April 24, 1901, a crowd gathered to watch workmen transfer Lincoln's coffin from a temporary vault to the securely rebuilt tomb.*

Voices used for speechmaking were muffled to church tones . . . then quietly the men converged to ring the coffin and look in.

The group who viewed Lincoln's remains before the final sealing of the casket included Joseph P. Lindley (circled), Fleetwood's father.

dig an opening 10 feet below the surface. The plan further stipulated that the body would lie in an east and west direction. A cage of flat steel bars resting in cement would enclose the coffin and over the whole of this would be poured enough cement to seal the contents forever.

On the morning of Thursday, September 26, 1901, the decision was made to go ahead with the interment. Plans to wait for Governor Yates to return from a trip before proceeding were scrapped for fear the delay would only draw curiosity seekers.

For 13-year-old Fleetwood Lindley, the day that would be a great part of his life began as usual. He and the sun were up together. He dressed for school and went into the kitchen for breakfast. There his father's demeanor charged the house with excitement and mystery. Joseph P. Lindley was a prominent citizen of Springfield, employed by the railroad and a member of the select Lincoln

Guard of Honor. Fleetwood knew from hearing him talk that the country was then passing through a frightening period. President McKinley had been recently murdered and that very day his convicted assassin was to be sentenced. For whatever reason, his father now spoke to him in a tone more grave than he could recall ever hearing before. "I want you to take your bicycle to school today. I may send for you this morning, and if I do, don't stop for anything but pedal as fast as you can to Oak Ridge Cemetery. The Guard will be in the Lincoln Tomb and you come right there."

Twenty people, including Acting Governor John J. Brenholt, other state officials, and the Lincoln Guard of Honor, assembled at the monument by 11:30.

An argument quickly broke out over the advisability of opening the casket to view the body. Those against such action cited Robert Lincoln's express wish that the coffin remain sealed, and since it had not been tampered with since it was opened in 1887, they questioned what purpose would be served. On the other side, it was argued that rumors still circulated that Lincoln was not in the coffin and that a continuous record of identification was needed. Only after peppery debate was it decided to view the body.

Two plumbers, Leon P. Hopkins and his nephew, Charles L. Wiley, had cut open the lead lining and cedar coffin of Lincoln's casket in 1887. They were sent for to do their grim work again. Joseph Lindley seized this opportunity to send word back to Springfield for Fleetwood to come quickly. "Fleet" lived up to his nickname, tearing the two miles under his wheels from school to cemetery.

Six laborers, preparing the bed of cement for the coffin, were hastily summoned to carry the wooden box containing the casket to the south room of the tomb known as Memorial Hall. One of the six, John P. Thompson, had assisted in transferring the coffin five times. At 11:45 they rested their load on two sawhorses and then were abruptly discharged from the hall. Soon Hopkins and Wiley arrived, followed shortly by young Fleetwood. Chest heaving, he rolled his bicycle into Memorial Hall and leaned it against the wall. His father motioned him to slip behind the room's only door. Newspapers had been fixed over its glass, so that when the door was closed it would block the view of the reporters and others banished outside.

The plumbers unpacked their tools and set to work. Fleetwood now knew what he was going to see and his heartbeat again quickened. The door was locked and the only light available beamed from two skylights, glimmering on the plumber's chisel as it divided the soft lead. Fleetwood made his way to the side of his father, who was in brisk conversation with fellow Guard members. When the coffin was opened 14 years earlier, Joseph Lindley had been present, and Fleetwood remembered his father's description of Lincoln's face as being the color of an old saddle. What would it look like now?

All at once the room grew quiet. Voices used for speechmaking were muffled to church tones. Chief plumber Hopkins lay his chisel aside and carefully gripped the incised rectangle of lead over Lincoln's head and tenderly drew it away. The fetid odor that escaped momentarily checked the viewers' curiosity, fixing them in place. Then quietly they converged to ring the coffin and look in.

The face of Lincoln was now alabaster white. "The features looked exceedingly white to me," said Judge B.D. Monroe. "Not a natural white but immaculate as a shirt bosom. Anyone who had seen a good picture of Lincoln could identify them." The headrest had disintegrated, allowing the head to fall back, and thrusting the chin forward, drawing first attention to the familiar whiskers. Though the eyebrows had vanished, there could be no mistaking the mole on the cheek and the thick black hair.

Except for small tendrils of mold covering the black suit originally worn at the second inauguration, his clothes had preserved well. Adjutant General J.N. Reece had viewed the remains in 1887, and "particularly remembered the beau-

tiful black stock that surrounded the President's neck. That was in a perfect state of preservation."

But what of the chalk-white coloring of the face that 14 years earlier had been close to black? It was recalled that on the funeral train's trek westward in 1865, the features had suddenly darkened, and a Philadelphia undertaker had covered Lincoln's face with powder so that the body could continue to be exhibited. That could not explain it, however, since the coating of powder could not disappear 14 years earlier and reappear in 1901. J.S. McCullough said, "Yes, the sight was somewhat gruesome. The white on the face was due to a mold that covered it." Later, the *Illinois State Journal* would say, "Fourteen years ago when the remains were opened the face was very dark, almost black, and the change to an immaculate white is not understood unless the suggestion that a mold has overspread the features is correct."

The viewers looked up to corroborate silently what there could be no doubt of — the face framed by the rectangle of jagged metal was Lincoln's. The assembly pulled back from the coffin to allow it to be resealed by the plumbers. Joseph Lindley drew his son in front of him and Fleetwood concentrated on the face of Lincoln as it disappeared under the covering for all time.

The workmen were recalled to carry out Robert Lincoln's plan of burial. These final pallbearers bore the casket back to the catacomb followed by the 23 witnesses. Fleetwood edged close to the deep, square chasm. Quickly leather straps were thrown across the opening and the coffin was inched out over the waiting cage of stout steel. Men grasped the straps and Fleetwood instinctively bent to seize the end of the one at his feet. Sliding hand over hand, straining his young arms, he watched with the others as the casket descended into the cage at the chamber's floor. There was a muted thump and the strap went limp in Fleetwood's grip. Reluctantly he dropped the leather, feeling the loss of a last physical connection to something very important in his life. Then wave after wave of fluid cement cascaded over the bars, inundating the compartment and discharging Robert Lincoln's instruction. Abraham Lincoln has rested undisturbed beneath the rock-hard mixture to this day.

Millions visit the Lincoln Tomb each year while nearby only family and a few remaining friends stop to remember Fleetwood Lindley, but together they shared a moment when Abraham Lincoln at last found peaceful rest, helped a little by a young boy with a fast bicycle.

Lincoln's cedar casket was finally placed in a steel-lined chamber beneath the floor of the sarcophagus room. Fluid cement was then poured into the compartment to insure its security against vandalism and theft.

Can an imaginary story be "too real"? Some readers thought so.
But it received the most votes for April fiction. . . .

The Odor of Fish

FICTION BY WILLIAM EVANS

– illustration by George Lawrence

The wharf is gone now, charred to the water line. All that remains are the stumps of a few pilings, smooth-worn and black as the heads of seals, and the shells of some dories grown up in brush so thick you have to know where to look to find them. There's a fish cooperative where the packing plant stood — a low, whitewashed building with several long ramps — that already looks ancient, though it can't be more than a dozen years old; and the plant-owned houses, once as stooped and gray as rheumatic old women, are now privately owned and restored.

I don't get up that way much any more, to Port Clyde Harbor where I grew up. My parents are gone now, too. My father, just before he died, worked up the coast in Warren for a company that built dragging nets, while my mother, her hands knotted from years of work in the fish-packing houses, spent her time at home knitting bait bags and lobster trap heads she sold to the local lobstermen. I live in Boston now, where I write for a newspaper, and Sharrie, my sister, is a housewife in Illinois — both of us far from the village in Maine. It's been 30-odd years since I was a boy and since she worked her first summer in the fish-packing plant.

In those days my father, a tough, bitter man who didn't own his boat, ran a trawler for the port. He'd be miles "outside" — the word then used for the sea beyond our harbor — long before the whistle, a shrieking blast, called the villagers to work at 6:30. At the whistle, my mother — a hale woman with blue eyes and hair the color of beach sand — would bind her fingers with sticky, gray protective tape, while my sister tried to vomit so she wouldn't have to go in that day. In the dim light of the bathroom in

the house we rented, I can see her still: her narrow shoulders hunched over the toilet bowl, her face pale as straw. My mother had cut Sharrie's red hair as short as mine so it wouldn't be in her way when she packed, and it curled around her ears and against the nape of her neck.

She was 16 that summer, when packers were either women or teenagers, and when workdays could be 12 to 16 hours long, depending on the load of the carrier. Some held 2000 bushels of fish, and packers worked until they were gone, often dragging from the packing rooms at nine or ten o'clock — no overtime, no bonus, and another carrier to unload the next morning. (Since the fish were perishable, labor laws didn't apply.)

Every morning but Sunday, packers waited in the half-dark packing rooms between long rows of rusting tables until the fish were pumped to conveyors. Then, on a shout from the overseer, they took their places. The conveyor belts keened in distress; 200 pairs of scissors clacked. The pumps chattered and whined over the sound of the grinding wheels where scissor-blades were sharpened, over the full-voiced yells of the workers as they tried to talk above the din. They stood all day at the waist-high tables. The woman nearest the conveyor, the scooper, slid her arm inside a rubber-lipped shunt and pulled down herring or sardines — occasionally an eel or a jellyfish — stiff with rigor mortis, preserved with salt. The vapor burned her eyes. Her partner, the woman opposite, picked cans from a conveyor belt above eye level, unable to see the ragged edges as she reached for them. Her hands were marked with tiny cuts that stung, then itched, when the salt seeped into them.

Besides scooping or picking cans, each packer scissored heads and tails and packed the fish belly up, five per can, not too full or slack. For a case of a hundred cans, she received 55 cents. She earned minimum wage, $1.05 at the time, or she lost her job. A good packer like my mother could earn $2.20 an hour. She got her whole body into a rhythm, didn't talk except to scream for more cans from supply, never looked up or away. But Sharrie could not make minimum wage, even with my mother and friends helping out now and then. She studied each fish, watched the clock. At her turn to be the scooper, she cried, clenching the sleeve of her Banlon sweater so the fish wouldn't touch her skin. When she walked home through the streets lit by window lamps — shuffled, really, as though she were still on the slippery floor of the packing

room — the coral-pink sweater sleeve hung to her knees.

To me she seemed silly. I was 10 that summer, yet to know the frustrations of breakdowns or late carriers — dead time for which there was no pay — yet to learn of layoffs when fishing was poor. I spent my days crabbing with Jacky Wallace or listening to the talk of the old men on the wharf. Two generations separated many of them from my father, who called them idlers. He had no time for Sharrie's queasy stomach or for the old men's stories I found so wonderful — about the Coffin family who invented doughnuts that turned themselves in the cooking fat and jumped out when they were done, about the man who fashioned a curved rifle barrel so efficient that when he shot from his door he had to pull his head in quick to escape the bullet whizzing around the house.

The wharf, which stood down the harbor from the fish-packing plant, was a place full of wood smell and tar smell. It seemed to me time had stopped there, or at very least had paused. The afternoon sun warmed your back and your neck and the planks at your feet, and a breeze often blew from the harbor. Though the old men still worked — and worked hard, to be sure, building lobster pots from red oak, painting marker-buoys and repairing hogshead bait barrels — they found time to swap yarns about the days before engines when lobstermen hauled their traps by hand and fished from Friendship sloops. They spoke their own language — a clear day, the ocean smooth as glass, they called a "grandmother's day"; rain with wind and chop, "some buggerish out there." Sometimes they argued the best way to cook sea moss pudding.

Lester Eckstrom was the oldest, the senior member of the wharf, and when he spoke the others gave serious ear, but often grinned and wisecracked, too. "Was out in a dory," Eckstrom might say. "First thing I hauled up a pot and this great big lobster was hanging on it, come up and bit that boat in two." Somebody, maybe Stilly Orcutt, would finish the tale: "Lester jumped in the stern, you know, and sculled that half to shore!" And someone else might holler over from his workbench, "By gol he's here to tell about it!"

He was white haired, a slightly built man, and he could walk at a pace that made me gasp. He gave every corner and field its own peculiar name and history — here an Indian massacre; there a witch was tried and hanged; no one lives in the

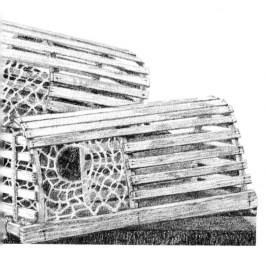

Baum house because footsteps are heard there at night. He could point to pocks in the shore dug by hunters of pirate treasure, and to ledges where ships had sunk.

"Did you ever *see* a pirate?" I once asked, as I tagged along after him.

He stopped and turned to look at me, narrowing his eyes. "Pirates," he said, "and plenty of them."

I thought it over as we walked. "What about a ghost?"

"Yes, sir, and ghosts," he said, and I took him at his word. With its mists and fog and black water at night, the Maine coast seemed to me a likely place for such things.

In his top vest pocket Eckstrom carried shark's teeth turned to stone by the sea. Some were triangular, the size of his fingernail, others heart shaped and as large as the first joint of his thumb. All were polished by the tides, were cool and surprisingly heavy. I watched him search for the teeth in tide pools, bending every few steps to finger the sand, hunkering down on rocks, and sometimes he'd weigh a stone in his hands, turn it this way and that like a jeweler with a gem. He sold the teeth to a man in Martinsville who set them into bracelets, necklaces, and ashtrays, marketed for sale in Old Orchard Beach.

He knew the species of his fossils, Blue Shark or Porbeagle, and he liked to explain how the seas dissolved the original tooth, leaving minerals in its size and shape. Certain times were best for finding fossils: after a northeaster when the slate-gray ocean churned up spars, wooden kegs and crates, strips of linoleum, every kind of fish; and with the extreme tides of the new and old moons. I learned to listen for trawler warnings on the radio, secretly glad when my father cursed the weather and the loss of a fishing day, and I learned the cycles of the moon. My collection of teeth numbered 20 or so, though some were broken, and I kept them in an empty peanut butter tub. When I showed them to Lester Eckstrom, he grinned. One of his own teeth was capped with gold.

Most nights after supper I'd take my shark's teeth from the peanut butter tub and spread them over the kitchen table, organizing them by size or by color — some glossy black, others grayish white. My mother, when she'd washed and dried the dishes, would sit on one of the kitchen chairs beside the front door jamb, where, screwed into the molding, there was a brass hook for knitting bait bags and lobster trap heads. These she made from sisal twine, stitching with a wooden needle she'd carved herself, knotting and burning the twine ends so quickly it was hard to see how she did it. Near her in the lamplight, Sharrie would read romance novels she'd borrowed from the school library, always so absorbed by the books you'd have to shout before she'd hear you — it made my father furious. He'd sit in his armchair by the radio, listening to the Coast Guard, the night conversations of other fishermen, or just the static of the citizen's band, and he'd sip from a mug of hot tea.

He wasn't especially tall, maybe five-foot-six, though in my memory, no doubt incorrect, he filled two-thirds of the bed he shared with my mother. His shoulders and arms were thick; I once bragged that he'd lifted a barrel full of fish cuttings from his boat to the wharf (most of the fishermen winched them up), though I'm sure I never saw him

---

They spoke their own language on the wharf — a clear day, the ocean smooth as glass, they called a "grandmother's day"; rain with wind and chop, "some buggerish out there."

---

perform the feat. He had run his boat aground — the boat that had belonged to his father — when he'd missed the entrance to the harbor in a storm. He was, as I've said, a bitter man.

The last week in July had been one of those still, hot weeks when tensions between people get as heavy as the air. Fishing had fallen off. My father complained nightly: 20 draggers in a mile square, draggers up from the Carolinas and down from New Brunswick. Carriers, when they came in, sat high in the water, half-loaded, watermarks dry; days were lost in dead time at the packing plant.

I sat at the kitchen table, counting and arranging my shark's teeth, feeling the coolness of them on my fingertips. My mother knitted by the door, trying to catch what breeze there was, while Sharrie lay on the rug propped on her elbows over a book. My father sat in his armchair. He cursed suddenly, angered by something he'd heard on the radio, and I turned to see him hit the switch with the

heel of his hand. My mother turned, too, with a look of quiet apprehension, her needle poised above her lap. She watched as he sat forward and ran his fingers through his dark brown hair. Then, as he eased back, she resumed her knitting. A little later he got up and lumbered out to the porch, where I could hear him chafing the sole of his boot on the pine planks. When he came back in, letting the screen door slap behind him, he stood beside my mother, thumbs in his pants waist.

"About time for bed then, ain't it?" he said.

My mother looked surprised — it was early yet, even for a family who'd be up before light. But she lifted her knitting from the hook on the jamb, stood, and placed the twine and needle on her seat. I gathered up my shark's teeth, snapped the lid on the peanut butter tub, and behind me felt silence. I slid from the chair. My father stood over my sister, scowling, shaking his head, his hands fisted. My mother quickly knelt and touched her shoulder. Sharrie glanced up like someone startled from a dream and, seeing my father, flinched.

The next morning I was wakened by the smell of dead fish. In the dim light I could taste it; waves of it would be rising from the carrier holds like steam. In the kitchen I sat at the table while my mother fried eggs, her fingers already bound. My father had gone. When the whistle blew she called Sharrie from the bottom of the stairs, the spatula in her hand. My sister didn't answer, but soon I heard her step on the stairs, and she dragged into the room.

"Mama, the smell," she said. She lowered herself into the chair beside me.

My mother didn't look from the pan on the stove. She turned, slid two eggs onto Sharrie's plate, and dunked the pan in the sink, where it hissed. Sharrie cut the eggs into triangles and pushed them with her fork in the runny yolk.

"Tape's on the stool when you're through," my mother said. At the counter she spooned jelly onto a slice of white bread and placed another on top. She wrapped the sandwich in waxed paper and dropped it into a bag.

Sharrie's fork clinked to the table. She held her head in her hands and whined, her red bangs hanging over her plate.

"Don't forget the dishes," my mother said to me, and swung around with the lunch sack. "I'll wait on the porch." She pushed open the door.

Sharrie sat still, staring at the tabletop.

Then she skidded back her chair and picked up the tape.

"Sissy," I whispered.

She spun to face me, her blue eyes gleaming. As she went out she let the screen door slam.

I washed and stacked the breakfast dishes and took out my tub of shark's teeth. I was about to lay my fossils on the table when Jacky hollered in. A freckled boy, his skin covered with dust, he stood on the porch with a broken fish-pole, his long-handled net, and a bucket of fish heads he'd freshened in the sun.

Passed only by a bus hauling commuters to the plant, we hiked half a mile to a backwater bridge. There, with the bait tied to a string at the end of the pole, Jacky lured the crabs to the surface, where I slipped the net under their swimming legs and hoisted them, pinching, into the air. By noon, as the water beneath the bridge became only a stream trickling through black mud, we left our sport.

At home I fixed a sandwich and stuffed it down, jelly oozing between my fingers, then trotted through town toward the harbor. The roofs of the neighborhood sloped; the houses sat on rotting sills. Near the packing plant the sound of engines pumping fish from carriers — a low rumble punctuated by metal screeching against metal — shook the ground. I headed for an island where I had often followed Lester Eckstrom, walked the path to a cliff that jutted into the sea, and the noise and smell were gone. From the motionless crescent of his boat, a lobsterman checked his traps.

I climbed down rock to the stringy mounds of seaweed. The current swept into crags, water ferns washing back and forth. In my sneakers I stepped in, careful not to stir the sand. Stooping and pushing rocks with my toe, I searched the bottom, occasionally plunging my arms to pull up a stone.

In an hour I'd found nothing; in two, a pebble speckled red that I folded into a handkerchief. The tide was rising and the sun shone hot through the haze. My T-shirt stuck to my back. On hands and knees I crawled over the seaweed, stood to scale the rocks. And there at my feet, as if it had meant to bite the shore, I saw the tooth — a wedge of gray stone half the size of my fist.

I weighed it, first in one hand, then in the other. I held it between my thumb and forefinger and pressed it into my dungarees, wincing as I imagined it biting through my leg. I opened the handkerchief, placed the tooth gently on top of the pebble, and folded the handkerchief again. I pushed it deep into my pocket and ran for the wharf.

Stilly Orcutt was there alone. He sat on a bucket in a flannel shirt, bent over a smoldering cigarette. Beyond him, on the water, a dory rocked at its mooring.

"Eckstrom!" I yelled, so excited and out of breath I couldn't think of what else to say.

Stilly, a bald, round-shouldered man, lifted his head and regarded me. "Ain't seen him," he said.

I turned and headed for town.

The boardinghouse was a three-story building with a mansard roof. On a bench set against its peeling clapboards sat the men my father called idlers — Griffin Alberts, Harley Maling, and others who lived there. They were quiet. One picked his tooth with a nail; another spat brown saliva to a dark spot in the dirt. Away from the wharf they'd lost their air of consequence.

Standing to one side, I asked for Eckstrom. A younger man, large and red faced, motioned to the doorless threshold. "Second floor," he said. "Two B."

I edged past them.

The stairwell led to a narrow hallway where a shaded window cast yellow light onto two doors along the far wall. I saw that neither bore numbers or letters, and a vague feeling of dread passed over me; I chose the left. Stacks of newspapers lay beside it, a shopping bag crammed with empty soup cans. I knocked softly. A swarm of gnats flitted from the bag. I knocked again, and waited. Nothing.

I made my way downstairs, into the sunlight, where I was startled by the high voice of the red-faced man: "Find him?"

I touched the handkerchief in my pocket. I meant to go home, but turned and shook my head.

Hands on his knees, he heaved himself up and yanked out a key chain. He motioned me to follow. We moved slowly up the stairs as he paused for breath on each step. At the door he banged and then tried the knob — open. Inside, a rubber boot stood upright on the broad floor planks near a clothes tree layered with khakis and flannels. Beyond, there was a small table littered with a bowl and plate, a can opener and spoons. In one corner a cot lay thick with blankets.

The man lumbered forward, dust spinning in slow motes behind him in the yellow light. He leaned over the cot. "Hey," he said, and prodded the blankets. "Eckstrom!" he said, prodding again. And then he straightened as if he'd been slapped.

I stood for a moment, confused. The man turned, gesturing with his hands as if to apologize, and through the heat it came in on me, an odor like fish. I stepped back and ran from the room.

That night the heat had not let up. Fishing had improved — "turned itself around," as my father put it — though he seemed not much happier than the night before. We ate silently, the four of us, until my mother felt my forehead to see whether I was well: I could not finish my supper.

"Don't you get like your sister," my father said. He stared at Sharrie as he chewed. She sat still, head down, hands hidden beneath the table; she had eaten only a biscuit and some applesauce. I said nothing, watching the muscles of my father's jaw work a bite of Spam.

Later I sat in my room, the peanut butter tub — the large tooth inside — unopened in the glow of the lamp. My mother had sent me early to bed. Downstairs she must've been knitting at the door, her chair faced into the night, while Sharrie lay beside her, lost in a book. My father would have been seated in his chair, arms squared, or maybe cupping a mug of tea in his hands. I remember a murmur of voices, then quiet. All at once, over the static of the radio: "I'd be happy I *had* the job . . . " followed by Sharrie's quick step on the stairs, ". . . and a roof over my head!" he shouted after her. His voice ran, menacing, all the way up the stairwell.

Sharrie's sobs came through the wall — her room, next to mine. The radio clicked off, my father said something to my mother, and the back door slammed. Slowly, quiet returned to the house, settling in like fog. Without knowing why, I left my room and crept through the hall. I found my sister sprawled on the bed.

"Sharrie?" I stood beside her. She lay still. "Sharrie?"

She rolled to her side. "What do you want?"

I stood by the bed, unable to answer. "I don't know," I said, and the tears started suddenly down my face.

She sat up, staring, and then she put her arms around me. She rocked me and smoothed my hair. I remember her breath on the top of my head. And in the dark, against my neck, I felt the damp sleeve of her sweater rolled tightly above her elbow.

Lots has been written about jonnycakes, mostly arguing over the "correct way" to make them, grind the corn, or even spell the word. Then, in April of 1981, we visited an active group of Rhode Islanders who had settled all the arguments! However, a few of our traditionalist subscribers later wrote us to say the recipes (herewith) were "simply outrageous — but good!"

The Jonnycake Revival

TEXT AND PHOTOGRAPHY BY
PAUL A. DARLING

Rhode Islanders have come to blows over jonnycakes for any number of reasons — over how they originated (Indians vs. settlers), over how to spell them (journey-cake vs. Johnny cake vs. Jonny Cake vs. jonnycake), over which kind of corn to grind for jonnycake meal (white flint vs. dent), and even over how to grind that corn (hot and round vs. flat and cool). Of course the most heated arguments occur over the "correct" way to make them; debates about the merits of South County-style (scalded meal) jonnycakes vs. Newport County-style (milk) jonnycakes have even reached the Rhode Island legislature.

The fine points of jonnycake lore have been chewed over by swamp Yankees for generations, but now there is an arbiter of such issues. Helene Tessler, president of the Society for the Propagation of the Jonnycake Tradition in Rhode Island (SPJTRI), allows that both the South County and Newport County versions are "correct."

It all began, she says, with the Narragansett Indians, who ground native corn between flat stones, mixed it with water into a stiff batter, and baked it in the hot ashes of their campfires. Settlers west of Narragansett Bay, now South County, borrowed the Indian tradition, but they scalded the cornmeal, added a little salt, milk, and molasses, and cooked their jonnycakes thick (one-half inch by three inches in diameter) on a board in front of an open fire. But over on the east side of Narragansett Bay, now Newport County, the settlers used just milk and a little salt, making their jonnycakes five inches in diameter, thin, and crisp. (See recipes, pages 100-101.) Either way, jonnycakes may be eaten with butter, butter and ma-ple syrup, butter and molasses (the most authentic way); with ham, bacon, or sausage; with applesauce or fried apple rings; or with creamed codfish, creamed chipped beef, or pot roast gravy.

Back in the early 1800s Shepherd Tom Hazard, whose colorful letters to the *Providence Journal* about olden days in Narragansett were bound into a book called *Jonnycake Papers of Shepherd Tom,* lamented that the art of baking the Rhode Island jonnycake was dying out. Shepherd Tom would have been delighted with the women of SPJTRI, who make available jonnycake recipes, history, fact sheets, and newsletters, and work with historical, educational, and agricultural institutions, as well as gristmills and restaurants, all for the purpose of promoting the jonnycake. The society's leading concern, says Helene Tessler, is assuring a steady supply of the proper corn for jonnycake cornmeal. The essential ingredient is stone-ground Rhode Island whitecap flint corn. This is a strain derived from the maize that the Narragansett and Wampanoag Indians grew.

Purists will tell you that flint corn doesn't grow anywhere but in Rhode Island; because of soil and climate variations, whitecap flint planted in other regions develops an entirely different taste and texture. Even under the best of Rhode Island conditions, flint corn has a lower yield per acre and does not possess the resistance to disease of modern hybrids. It requires lots of hot sun for all of the growing season, yet a severe drought destroyed a portion of the harvest in the summer of 1980. Whitecap flint must also be cultivated about one-quarter mile distant from sweet corn of other varieties or windborne pollen will ruin the results. The University of Rhode Island maintains a seed supply and furnishes limited amounts to such growers as Old Sturbridge Village, Mystic Seaport, and Prescott Farm in Portsmouth, Rhode Island. The other general types of corn grown today are flour corn, dent, popcorn, and sweet corn, but none of them makes satisfactory jonnycake meal, according to the SPJTRI.

Milling the grains is a bit of an art, too. The old-timers kept their fine-grained granite stones well balanced and adjusted, using either wind or water to power the mill. Even the best grain, wrote Shepherd Tom, would not avail if, "rushed through the stones in a stream from the hopper and rolled over and over in its passage, the coarse, uneven, half-ground stuff falls into the meal box below, hot as ashes and tasteless as sawdust." Quality meal is flat (not round), and is kept reasonably cool in the milling. The cornmeal supplied to grocers' shelves, incidentally, is *bolted,* if shipped from the big

Right: *Society member Martha Greig removes jonnycakes from a soapstone griddle. The table at the Prescott Farm in Middletown, Rhode Island, is laden with various Indian cornmeal goodies baked by members of the Society for the Propagation of the Jonnycake Tradition in Rhode Island — (clockwise from the top) chicken with jonnycake meal stuffing, cocktail jonnycakes, Anadama bread loaf, dish of whitecap flint corn, dish of Indian pudding with cream, bowl of Indian pudding (center), corn sticks in a cast-iron mold, Toads, muffins with assorted berries, traditional brown bread, bowl of jonnycake meal poultry stuffing, jonnycakes. Members Peggy Richmond and Anita Rich tend the jonnycakes baking on the hearth.*

Thomas Byrnes, Jr., and Aileen O'Neil spoon jonnycakes onto the griddle.

commercial mills. With the germ removed (and oil with it), the product will keep better, but is blander in flavor. Rhode Island cornmeal, containing all of the germ, should be refrigerated in order to remain fresh for extended periods.

The beauty of this hard flint corn is its versatility. The colonists couldn't improve the Indians' maize, but they soon invented numerous new ways of cooking it. They made dishes with names both familiar and half-forgotten: pone, suppawn, samp, bannock, Indian dumplings, and stir-abouts. Roger Williams wrote that "sukqutthhash" was corn, "seethed like beans." Until the 1920s, when Rhode Island flint corn planting went into decline, many families (especially rural) often had cornmeal in some form for three meals a day.

Reviving some of the old cornmeal delights, like those mentioned in the *Jonnycake Papers* or other historic accounts, is another function of the Society for the Propagation of the Jonnycake Tradition. Last October they held a Jonnycake Bake-off at the Culinary Division of Johnson & Wales College in Providence, which they hope to make a regular event. In addition to the prizes awarded to the winners, who baked both traditional forms of jonnycake, a special award was given to the individual who presented the most innovative adaptation. There were some variations using chopped pecans or shredded orange rind, thin cakes with Grand Marnier topping or with praline, and there were cocktail jonnycakes.

A relatively recent development is the jonnycake *cookie.* Alas, no one has volunteered to make the recipe public. So secret is the formula, in fact, that perhaps the interested amateurs of New England had better get in a supply of Rhode Island cornmeal and invent their own version of this *jonnycookie* delight!

Thick Scalded Jonnycakes

(South County/West-of-Bay Recipe)
1 cup white cornmeal
½ teaspoon salt
1 cup boiling water
3 or 4 tablespoons milk or cream
1 teaspoon sugar or molasses (optional)

Mix all ingredients to consistency of mashed potatoes, adding more liquid if necessary. Drop by spoonfuls onto hot, greased griddle to make cake ½-inch thick and 2 to 3 inches in diameter. Fry 6 to 8 minutes on each side, or until brown, crunchy crust is formed.

Thin Cold-Milk Jonnycakes

(Newport County/East-of-Bay Recipe)
1 cup white cornmeal
½ teaspoon salt
1⅞ cups cold milk

Mix all ingredients to thin, soupy consistency. Ease large spoonfuls onto hot, greased griddle to make cake about ⅛-inch thick and 5 inches in diameter. Fry 2 to 3 minutes on each side, or until brown.

Toads

1 cup cornmeal
1 cup flour
2 teaspoons baking powder
2 tablespoons of sugar *or* ¼ cup molasses
1 egg
1 cup milk

Mix all ingredients thoroughly and drop from teaspoon into very hot deep fat (370°).

Molasses gives a richer, more robust flavor than sugar. A little cinnamon and nutmeg may be added if desired.

These are delicate and tender when first cooked. A brief heating in the oven helps them the second day.

New England Corn Bread

1 cup white stone-ground cornmeal
1 cup sifted flour
1 teaspoon salt
3 teaspoons baking powder
1 egg, well beaten
1 cup milk
2 tablespoons melted shortening
1 tablespoon sugar *or* 2 tablespoons maple or corn syrup

Mix and sift dry ingredients. Beat egg until light and stir into milk. Add shortening and sweetening. (Syrup makes better corn bread than sugar.) Beat well. Add dry ingredients and beat again. Put batter in preheated, greased 8x10-inch pan and bake in hot oven (400°) for 25 to 30 minutes.

Indian Corn Muffins with Variations

1 cup stone-ground white cornmeal
1 cup sifted all-purpose flour
½ teaspoon salt
2½ teaspoons baking powder
4 to 6 tablespoons sugar
½ cup milk
½ cup light cream
2 eggs, beaten
2 tablespoons unsalted butter or margarine, melted

Preheat oven to 400°. Sift dry ingredients into mixing bowl. Combine milk and light cream with eggs and add to dry ingredients. Add shortening and stir until blended.

Grease 2-inch iron muffin pans and set in oven for short time before filling with batter (to keep baked muffins from sticking). Pour batter into pans and bake for 20 minutes. Makes 12 muffins.

Cranberry variation. Soak ¾ cup whole cranberries in 1 cup cranberry juice for 30 minutes. Drain and fold berries into batter. Use the larger amount of sugar with this variation.

Blueberry variation. Lightly flour ¾ cup blueberries before folding into the batter.

Indian Pudding

1 quart milk
7 tablespoons cornmeal
1 egg, beaten
½ teaspoon ginger
½ teaspoon cinnamon
¼ teaspoon salt
⅔ cup molasses
½ cup cold milk

Scald 1 quart milk in top of double boiler. Add cornmeal and place over boiling water. Cook, stirring, for about 15 minutes. Add remaining ingredients, except ½ cup cold milk. Cook 5 minutes more. Pour into buttered baking dish. Bake 3 hours at 300°. About halfway through cooking, add the ½ cup cold milk, pouring it on top of the pudding.

May be served warm with vanilla ice cream, or with butter or cream.

Apples, peeled, cored, cut into eighths, and put on the bottom of the baking dish make "Blackstone Pudding."

Brown Bread

1 cup rye meal (or flour)
1 cup cornmeal
1 cup whole wheat flour
¾ tablespoon baking soda
1 teaspoon salt
¾ cup molasses
2 cups sour milk

Combine dry ingredients, add molasses and milk, and mix well. Pour into well-greased mold, filling two-thirds full. Cover. Set on trivet in deep kettle and fill kettle with boiling water to one-half the depth of the mold. Steam 3½ hours. Keep water boiling and add water as necessary to maintain level.

Makes 2 loaves, using 1-pound coffee tins as molds.

South County-style jonnycakes are traditionally baked thick.

Helen Tessler (right), president of the Society for the Propagation of the Jonnycake Tradition, presents awards to bake-off winners.

Favorite April "I Remembers"

ADVICE FROM ROBERT FROST

☞ The high point of my college career was when Robert Frost, my idol of many years' standing, came to the campus for a couple of days. To make it even more exciting, however, the college president invited me to ride with Mr. Frost to the airport. Although it was a hectic time, since my wife had just given birth to our second child, I accepted immediately.

We climbed into the college limousine — a 1958 DeSoto. The chauffeur was the college plumber, Louie La Rose. I sat on the front seat in the middle, with Mr. Frost beside me.

The heat was stifling. With a sigh of relief, Frost undid his tie and stuck it into a side pocket. Louie did the same, even imitating the sigh. So I did, too, but omitted the sound effects. Then, succumbing to the discomfort of his recent meal sitting heavily on him, Frost undid his belt buckle and unzipped his fly. Then — would you believe it? — Louie undid his trousers, too! I just sat there looking back and forth at them in panic and thinking, "No way!"

We drove past the hospital where my wife and new baby were probably just turning in. Frost bent toward me. "President Lowry tells me that you and your wife have just had a son. What are you going to name him?"

"Well, to tell you the truth, sir, we've been thinking about calling him Robert Frost in honor of your visit."

"No," said Frost, "that's not a good idea at all. Never name a child after anybody famous. He spends his whole life either trying to live up to it, or living it down. Haven't you got any other ideas?"

"Well, yes, the alternative is the family name."

"What's that?"

I was really feeling stupid, but I said it very tentatively: "Willem Maurits Lange, the Fourth."

Frost gazed in silence at the soft June sunset and the rolling hills unfolding before the big DeSoto. At last he said, "You'd better call him Robert Frost." *Willem Lange*

ABOUT A VERY RUDE WOMAN

☞ It's pleasant to have a memory that, whenever recalled, makes one smile. I remember a crowded elevator at R.H. Stearns, probably the oldest and most respected department store in Boston. Among the passengers were an attractive young mother with a little girl about five years old, bound for the children's department on the fifth floor, and also an extremely stout woman and a mild-looking little man in a derby hat.

Suddenly the stout woman let swing a resounding slap on the cheek of the inoffensive-looking little man in the derby, then pushed her way out of the elevator.

The young mother was evidently apprehensive how such a show of bad manners would affect the little girl. "She was a very rude woman, wasn't she, Ellen?" she said.

"Yes," agreed Ellen, "she was. She stepped on my foot and I pinched her behind."
Laurie Hillyer

PLAYING HIDE-AND-SEEK WITH ADMIRAL BYRD

☞ It was the summer of 1939, when I was 11. We — my parents, six brothers and sisters, and I — had just arrived at our cabin on Tunk Lake, Maine. At daybreak I had dashed down to the lake and, churning with curiosity, rowed across to investigate the new family named Byrd who had moved into the long-abandoned log clubhouse. To my delight, I discovered a girl about my age named Helen, her older sisters, Bolling and Kay, and brother Dick.

That very night, the whole family came to visit. During the hubbub I cast side-glances at Admiral Byrd, a trim man of medium height with wiry gray hair. I tried to imagine him in a daring role — flying over the North Pole in a flimsy little plane; working alone, half frozen in his Antarctic hut.

"Could we all play hide-in-the-dark?" my sister Ruth was begging. We all found ourselves huddling in the kitchen while Ruth disappeared to hide. At the count of 100, everyone poured out into the caverns of our darkened cabin to find Ruth.

Since the admiral found her first it was now his turn to hide. The rest of us reassembled for the countdown and once again began groping through the darkness. Shadowy sleuths brushed by each other. Time dragged on, and my mother was beginning to exhibit signs of concern. Finally she could stand it no longer, so she called the roll. Five Byrds and eight Bryans answered "Here!"

"We're giving up," my mother shouted. "Give us a clue! Come out wherever you are!"

A little laugh escaped from the fireplace. We all gasped. Admiral Byrd was rising from the glowing logs. He climbed out and stretched his limbs.

For one hour he had been crouching behind the logs and now emerged unscathed. My father, sputtering with amazement, was inspecting the large fireplace as though he half expected to find a secret panel that he'd somehow overlooked for the past 10 years. Could the admiral have crouched between the andirons and the rear wall of the commodious fireplace?

"How could you stand the heat? How could you pick such a hazardous hiding place?" we Bryans asked.

Mrs. Byrd stood by, unable to conceal her merriment. Helen's smug expression said, "Obviously, you don't know my father."

A smile was flickering across the admiral's face. It seemed as if he was looking straight at me when he said, "It's just the challenge of the thing."
Joy Bryan Bacon

Name any good old American song and there's a fair chance it was written by a New Englander. We've covered about all of them in the last 50 years — even unto one, in 1965, about the first man to sing "Sweet Adeline"! (It was the late Harold W. Castner of Damariscotta, Maine.) But there was something special about "The Long, Long Trail"....

The Song That Made a Million
(For Somebody Else)

BY MARC DROGIN

Songwriter Alonzo "Zo" Elliott, 1964.

It was springtime in 1913 and this meant that the windows were open at 85 Connecticut Hall. The noise of the Yale students traveling to and from classes floated up to the second-floor lounge that morning. Ward Twitchell, one of the three students sharing the suite, sat comfortably on the window seat studying a textbook. The second student was out.

And Alonzo Elliott, the third roommate, was daydreaming.

It was a daydream about the Napoleonic Wars, and through "Zo" Elliott's thoughts roamed a fragment of melody — a melody in the well-known conventional harmony of thirds and sixths. When the melody bothered Elliott to the point of action, he ignored the fact that his playing would annoy the dean in his office below, and seated himself at the old upright piano.

Improvising in his mind and translating a few notes into two-hand accompaniment on the piano, Elliott pieced the melody together for a few moments.

"You should write it down," said the student from the window seat, "and make a fortune."

"Oh, I will," replied Elliott, working on the melody despite conversation and the outside noises. "I really will one of these days."

"You always say that but you never do," his friend remarked, and went back to the textbook. Elliott refined the melody — the next to the last note seemed to peter out since it was not sharped. A few moments later he had created something new in using the major seventh chord often as harmony.

It was a few moments later when their roommate, Stoddard King, came home with a "hello" to the two and made himself comfortable while Elliott played him the melody.

King thought a moment.

"That two-part harmony — I think the lower part is the melody, not the upper part, as you think. And it has just the kind of sticky harmony that we need for the song we promised the Zeta Psi Fraternity banquet."

Elliott played the melody again. He'd forgotten that he had been elected to write a song for his fraternity affair in Boston. He was almost finished when King made him stop.

"I have a splendid idea for this. This is the chorus, mind you, and it starts with,
There's a long, long trail a-winding. . . ."

Elliott found the point in the melody, smiled, and sang out,
"Into the land of my dreams. . . ."

King replied with a smile, and Elliott added:
"Where the nightingales are singing. . . ."

And King, knowing there was no sense to it at all, picked up the line with,
"And a white moon beams. . . ."

Elliott stopped for a fraction of a second, played the chord, and added:
"There's a long, long night of waiting,
Until my dreams all come true. . . ."

And then King, with his fine sense of logic, wrapped it up:
"Till the day when I'll be going down
That long, long trail with you."

They liked it. It sounded good.

The melody had taken a half hour to write, the rest of the lyrics not much longer, the chorus fewer moments than it might take to sing it twice through today. Elliott and King rehearsed it for a few evenings and were ready.

The banquet crowd loved it. American publishers abhorred it. And it was obvious that, nice as it was, it was not the key to fortune that their roommate had advised.

Later that year, though, Elliott was pursuing his studies at Trinity College, Cambridge, England, and a young London publisher admired both the new chord and the two-part harmony. He gambled recklessly, he thought, and published "The Long, Long Trail" in December 1913, never crediting "Zo" Elliott.

Before World War I had come to a close years later, the Yale students' impromptu song was an international legend, loved by many. In his victory speech, Great Britain's Prime Minister Lloyd George called it "the song that helped us win the war."

And so it has come down through the half century, composed and written by person or persons unremembered, a song believed to be English in birth and resident of everywhere.

Alonzo "Zo" Elliott died on June 24, 1964, at a convalescent home in rural Connecticut. I had met him only a week before, talked to him at length, and written this story, and we'd gone over it together a few days later. I remember how pleased he was that after 50 years of infrequent interviews, he had finally been asked about exactly how the song had been born. He liked the angle and it rang true. Some of the words took him a moment to recall in order.

"I've been asked so many times when I wrote the song and where I was, but I don't believe anyone has ever wondered exactly how it came about. And I recall that night of the banquet, when the fraternity brothers were so riotous that King and I saved that song for last and, even then, we didn't dare sing more than the chorus."

☞ Memorable thoughts, quotes, and assorted tidbits from the last 50 April issues.

THE CASE OF THE MISSING THORN

☞ The New Englander of today is made aware of his Colonial heritage by numerous, ever-present reminders of the past. The most noticeable of these reminders are the signs over the stores of modern Yankee traders that begin with "Ye." Ye Olde Nautical Shoppe. Ye Olde Pewter Shoppe. Ye Olde Book Shoppe. Ye Olde Antique Shoppe.

It is quite likely that neither the visitor nor the owner of the shop realizes that the correct pronunciation of "Ye," in this instance, is actually "The," and that the first letter of the word "Ye" isn't "Y" at all, but a "thorn," which was the Old English manuscript symbol for the "th" sound. Properly drawn it looks something like this:

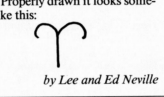

by Lee and Ed Neville

— Stephen Whitney

Governor Sherman Adams, 1978.

YOU CAN'T TAX REAL ESTATE TWICE!

Before 1975 it was fairly common for personal property — cows, for instance — to actually be moved off the property and even out of state on the April day the listers [as property tax assessors are known in Vermont] were due to arrive. A typical story involves a lister questioning a farmer who apparently had no cows anywhere on his property.

"I see you have a big pile of manure out in back of your barn there," said the lister with just a hint of sarcasm. "Since you haven't spread that on your field yet, guess I'll have to list that as personal property."

"Oh, no, you don't," said the farmer. "That ain't personal property."

"Why not?" asked the lister. "There it sits and it's yours."

"It's settin' on the ground."

"Makes no difference," said the lister.

"Yes, it does," was the reply. "If it were settin' on my barn floor or on my cement loadin' platform, then it's 'personal property.' But it's settin' on the ground and that makes it 'real estate.' And you already counted in my real estate once. You can't tax it twice." (*From "It's Hard to Raise Your Neighbor's Taxes" by Patricia Whitcomb.*)

THE LAST STRAW

☞ Duty was a very important thing — the duty to support the family and to see to it that the children had at least the three Rs. Opportunities were somewhat limited, but if a boy wanted to go to college. . . . There is the old story of the boy in one of our villages who decided to go to college. His people were willing to help him, but were unsure about some of the ideas he would pick up. And sure enough, the boy came back from college a Democrat. The family was very upset about that, and considered he'd been under the auspices of evil. To make it worse, the boy founded a Democratic movement, and on the Fourth of July organized a parade. His father pulled down all the shades in the house; wouldn't let anybody look out to see what was going on. But he got curious and picked up just a corner of the shade and took a peek. In horror he turned to his wife and said, "My God, Samantha, they've even stolen our flag!" **Sherman Adams in the first of our "New England Perspectives" series, April 1978, entitled "Sherman Adams: The Quintessential Doer" by Richard Meryman.**

PORTRAIT OF A MURDERER

☞ "If he could have, he would have been six-foot-six and an overachiever, a shining credit to his society. Even though he eventually killed someone, he was a man who had the highest regard for morals and standards. He wanted to be admired for what he stood for — a love of the outdoors, the loyalty and values that had been bred into him. In other circumstances he might have been the Lone Ranger.

On the outside everything looked so good for him. But privately he was at war inside himself. He still felt as if he'd not made the grade. He had turned to the things he dearly loved — the woods and independence — but they weren't enough in the end. He became, instead, like a man on a high pole." **Defense attorney Michael Carlin, speaking about his client, William Harvey, following the 1983 shooting of Tania Zelensky, daughter of Russian immigrants, in Pittsfield, Vermont.** (*From "A Death in the Country" by James Dodson.*)

Ted Williams and fishing crony Bud Leavitt on the Miramichi, waiting for the salmon.

ON THE MIRAMICHI WITH TED WILLIAMS

☞ He looked downriver where the fishermen were spaced at 100-foot intervals. "I can tell a guy by the style of his cast," he said. "The trick is the consistency of the cast, keeping the angle the same. And you have to know your limits — don't cast more than you can handle."

He stayed fairly close to the bank, feeling for the black rocks beneath him disguised in the flowing water. The bank to his left was a mound of high grass with a few dead tamaracks in a grove of young birch. Across the river was a knoll with houses painted white, a blue tent on a lawn where a campfire smoldered, a scattering of trailers, and two canoes beached on the shore. Four mergansers flew past and above them streaked an Air Force jet; for a moment the fly line, the ducks, and the jet shared the sky above the water. He looked up. "Four hundred fifty knots," he gauged.

"See that fly swinging now. That's a *hot* spot. There's plenty of action in the water, lots of oxygen for the fish. Now the next hundred feet will really be hot. I'm in a good place here, mercy, mercy." As he cast his mouth hung open just a bit and his body leaned toward the water on his follow-through. "Yi, yi, yi, I'm in a

good place! I remember all the spots, and that's a lot of memories. I remember where I cast, where I got a boil. Every time I approach that rock I remember that little roll I got, so slow and pretty. Fourteen pounds. This fish gets under your skin so bad, so bad."

Across the way a young native fisherman called out from his canoe. "Happy birthday, Ted. I heard it on the radio. Pretty soon, Ted, the salmon are going to put the shift on you."

Williams laughed. "Pretty good. Forty years ago," he shouted back, "I was whistling along at .413 right about now." (*From "Fishing Buddies" by Mel Allen.*)

BOSTON GLOBE — (Vineyard Haven, Mass.): An 84-year-old man drove down a one-way street in the wrong direction causing a series of collisions involving 15 cars.

WHAT TOWN IS THIS?

☞ A small town was passing under us when, suddenly, a schoolhouse erupted and children were shrilling, "Look at the balloon! Look at the balloon!" Dogs barked, chickens squawked, and men shouted. We now were at 2800 feet but could hear the sounds clearly. We also could be heard, but evidently not so clearly. Our pilot shouted, "What town is this?" and back came the answer, "Half past one." Later he was able to check our position from other landmarks and decided that we should be looking for a place to land. . . .

Our lift having been reduced, we started down. As we neared the ground, we emptied a couple of sandbags to slow our descent and then our drag rope was snaking across fields, through trees and over farmhouses. The wire wrapping at its end was supposed to prevent snagging. Evidently the rope was unaware of this, because it wrapped itself around a chimney, jerked it loose, and crashed it into a defenseless chicken coop. As if by magic the house door popped open and a very unhappy farmer rushed out and started shooting at us. Later the balloon had to be patched. (*From "I Flew in a Rubber Monster" by Alan A. Morse.*)

The time of the above reminiscence was World War I.

These balloons were trainers for World War I balloonists. The one at left carried just one person.

– Air Force Museum, Wright-Patterson A.F.B., Ohio

– Tom Payne

EVERY MAN SHOULD HAVE A TRACTOR

☞ Sure enough, when he started the grubby, six-ton monster and pulled the lever back, the blade heaved itself reluctantly aloft. A push on the lever sent it plunging back to earth, squashing in the process a small but beloved briefcase I had placed on top of the machine while it still stood silent and vibrationless during the earlier negotiations.

A considerable quantity of smoke arose while the bulldozer was running, but I was assured that "in a good wind you wouldn't hardly notice it."

The trip from the driveway to the garden plot could, I suppose, have been worse. At least no one was injured. But that may have been only because the smoke from the machine grew so thick that my family, who were present to applaud, elected to grope a retreat back to the house.

Upon turning into the garden, the great machine abruptly listed to starboard, settled about a foot, and then crawled level again.

"Underground stream," I announced with the knowledgeable air of the professional heavy-equipment operator.

In a manner of speaking it *was* an underground stream. Though more specifi-

cally it must be identified as our septic tank, or remains thereof.

As the bulldozer moved away from the disaster area and clanked slowly past the storage shed, which sits atop cement block pilings beside the upper part of the garden, vibrations set up by its great weight had an adverse effect upon the nearest of the supporting piers, and the building immediately fell down on that corner with a nasty crash.

Since the damage was done, there seemed nothing for it at the moment but to descend with terrible vengeance upon the corn stubble that had attacked my rotary tiller. Easing the control forward to lower the blade to what I figured to be about ground level, where it could scrape away the offending stalks, we chugged on through the corn patch.

On the journey, the machine's laboring became more pronounced. The volume of smoke increased, though it seemed impossible. Forward speed decreased. A funny noise was to be heard over the pounding of the engine. Ahead of the blade, and unbeknownst to me as I couldn't see that far in the smoke, an enormous pile of good topsoil was inching its way across the garden. I had set the blade a bit low. Yes, the corn stubble had been removed. But so had everything else. (*From "No Garden This Year" by Dwight Tracy.*)

FATE USED A BOTTLE OF LINIMENT

☞ "Most people have forgotten we actually left on Friday, April 5, to make the test dive," recalled Commander Raymond A. McCoole. "When we got out to sea, we discovered the main seawater suction valve wasn't functioning properly. We turned around and returned to Portsmouth, where the *Thresher* was put into dry dock.

"That was the purpose of those test runs — to check out the ship for problems, and to correct them."

At 2 A.M. on Sunday, McCoole was instructed to build up steam for a 4 A.M. departure by his skipper, John Wesley Harvey, a 1950 Annapolis graduate. He was in the process of doing this when he was notified of his wife's accident [a bottle of liniment she was holding had exploded and temporarily blinded her].

"Jim Henry, the assistant reactor officer, took charge," said McCoole, "and I rushed to the hospital to see Barbara.

Commander Raymond McCoole, reactor control officer on the Thresher, *was excused from the fateful voyage at the last hour because of an emergency.*

"I was back to the *Thresher* by three o'clock. I knew Barbara would be all right and there was somebody watching over the children. I was the reactor officer on the *Thresher,* and I was prepared to go to sea with her.

"The executive officer came up to me.

— courtesy of Richard Pritchett

He said, 'The old man wants to see you.' I went forward.

"'I think you should be with your family,' the skipper said. 'I think you should be with Barbara. Besides, your assistant Jim Henry needs some experience. Let him handle the reactor.'"

It was at this point that the skipper handed McCoole papers authorizing him to have two days' leave.

A few minutes later, the *Thresher* went to sea, and Ray McCoole, standing on the pier, watched her sail away forever.

He still gets "an eerie feeling" when he recalls it was "an exploding bottle of liniment" that saved his life.

"I wish I could have made that voyage," he said. "I know that sounds heroic. But that isn't the way I want it to sound. Look at it this way. Next to the skipper, as far as reactors were concerned, I was the most experienced officer on the *Thresher.* I had worked with that reactor, and I knew it well. I might have been able to spot the problem before anything happened." (*From "The Only Man Who Didn't Go Down With the* Thresher*" by Richard Pritchett.*)

– Austin Stevens

➤➤➤ FOOTNOTE TO HISTORY ⬅⬅⬅

THE FIRST BOSTON MARATHON

☞ April 19 is Patriots' Day in Massachusetts, and it marks two important events. One is the valiant stand of the minutemen from Lexington and Concord against British regulars in 1775 — the opening battles of the American Revolution. The other is the annual running of the Boston Marathon.

The official records say that John J. McDermott was the first man to run the 26-mile race from Hopkinton, Massachusetts, to Boston in 1897. But students of history contend that the honor should actually go to two "Praying Indians" who made approximately the same run 221 years earlier — on snowshoes!

It happened in the winter of 1676, when Massachusetts Bay colonists were at war with hostile Indians. The Indians were gathered in winter camp at Quabog, near the town now called Brookfield. Bay Colony magistrates chose two young Indian men, James Quonnapohit and Job Kattenanit, to join the hostile Indian camp as spies. The two young men were Christians, converts of the Reverend John Eliot, and the sons of sagamores, chiefs of their respective tribes.

The spies successfully infiltrated the Indian camp and learned that the hostiles were planning an attack on a group of colonists settled around Lancaster. With the help of Job Kattenanit, James Quonnapohit escaped from the war camp on January 24 and ran on snowshoes for 55 miles — more than two marathons — to warn the Bay Colony leaders. His path took him through Hopkinton all the way to Boston, where he arrived, famished and exhausted, with the news. His companion, Kattenanit, escaped two weeks later, and made the same grueling run through winter snows to arrive in Boston on February 8, warning that the attack was imminent.

Tragically, the elders of the Bay Colony did not heed the warnings of their faithful scouts, and two days later the settlement at Lancaster was destroyed, its inhabitants massacred or captured. The first two "Boston Marathons" had been run for nothing — unless, perhaps, for modern-day trivia enthusiasts.

Courtesy of Jerry Nason

CHAPTER 5

May

Memorial Day brings a New England community together like no other holiday. Although the gathering on the town green and the march to the cemetery are annual rites to honor the casualties of long-ago wars, the occasion is somehow a celebration of survival. The leaves are finally on the trees again, the grass is green, and the annual appearance of rather anachronistic old uniforms of another time on familiar friends and neighbors reminds us we've made it through another winter. Maybe the general is now too weak to walk in the parade, but he looks magnificent, with his battle ribbons, sitting in the front passenger seat of the open car carrying the gold star mothers. There are the Johnsons back from their winter in Florida — and could that handsome young man in a Marine uniform be their little grandson, Tommie? It's comforting to greet the usual women at the baked goods counter on the church lawn, the band sounds better than ever, the eulogy repeats those stirring words about "preserving our freedom," and it's always odd to suddenly confront the town postman dressed as a sailor!

Of all the articles and photos picked by readers for this book, more were originally published in May issues than in any other month. Beginning with the memorable photo, herewith, from May 1974, there follow the top favorites, including a lady with a conscience, a war hero, a man unusually devoted to his departed friends, a philosophy of simplicity, and an act of extraordinary personal courage. Together they fittingly represent the unifying emotions of Memorial Day, that time of grateful survival.

Preparing for the band concert on the common, Memorial Day, Grafton, Vermont.

– photograph by S.R. Gilcreast, Jr.

Wife of Malcolm Peabody, the retired Episcopal Bishop of central New York, and mother of both Endicott Peabody, the governor of Massachusetts, and Marietta Tree, an ambassador to the United Nations under Adlai Stevenson, Mary Parkman Peabody made world headlines in 1964 when, at age 72, she joined a civil rights demonstration in Florida and went to jail. This interview was conducted at her home 14 years later (and published in the May 1978 issue as part of the "New England Perspectives" series).

Mary Peabody:
The Committed Conscience

BY RICHARD MERYMAN

I've had an awfully happy life. I'm very lucky. I've had a good husband and good children I enjoyed. But to be happy I think it's very important to have a place in the world through work. I married a minister and there are always things that a minister's wife can be part of. Work is very stabilizing. It makes you feel that you have an identity — that you're contributing to the world and you're needed.

Let's see, what are the things that Calvin said? Work, play, love, and worship. It's very important to have a good time. That lifts your spirit, doesn't it? Sometimes I have to make myself look around and see if I can't have a better time.

And I think it is your duty in life to love your neighbor as yourself. I keep telling myself that — though I don't always succeed, I may say. But I do try not to talk about people in a critical way. A man once asked me what I thought was the most important thing for a wife to be. I said, "Compassionate." One must have compassion, unselfishness. That's really charity, isn't it?

Of course, I think that worship and being a member of a church is important. I don't know whether you can ever say that to a young person nowadays. The church seems to have lost its way. But it still stands for what is good in the community — truth, for example. I think everything is founded on truth. It's one of the foundation stones of people-to-people relations. Look at our politicians. They're terrible because they haven't told the truth. But I think my son Endicott was really very truthful in poli-

Mary Peabody, at home in Cambridge, Massachusetts, 1978.

tics. Young people are cheating on exams without compunction. That's terrible.

Naturally I believe in good morals, which are not practiced today. Those customs that have come down through many ages in the Christian/Jewish tradition, I feel are important. I think the Ten Commandments are important. But a lot of people I know and care for don't follow them. And this living around together doesn't seem to have spoiled their self-respect at all.

It's certainly been tried over the ages, but it's never been accepted as a good way to live. I hope, personally, that peo-

ple today will find it doesn't work in the long run. There's the problem of legitimacy of children. I think moving on from one person to another must leave terrible scars behind, somewhere. And you do have to move on, when you're trying out possible mates. They say they're doing it so they won't get divorced. But I think divorce is much more preferable because at least they go into a marriage thinking that they're going to make a go of it. It's a good thing to commit yourself.

It is important that you do what you say you will do. That means staunchness. Do your duty. Do your part in life. That's what "New Englander" means to me — doing your duty. Caring for things that are good and true. Being a terrible prig, I suppose. New Englanders are pretty straitlaced, and they don't have much give to them.

I think it was the climate they had to struggle with, don't you? They had to be very practical and face life as it is and take the cold with the heat. But those attitudes carry people through life pretty well. It means they don't expect too much. They don't always expect to have a good time.

I don't know how all that got into my bones. Osmosis, probably. My father was very nice to us and well liked, but he didn't talk very much. My mother did the talking for the family. She came from New Jersey and was more artistic and emotional — hers was not a New England temperament.

New Englanders may be happily amused or disgusted by things — but they don't tear a passion to tatters. They certainly don't go off the deep end with enthusiasm. I think that's a negative quality. I don't think they express themselves enough. Growing up in Boston, I felt that reserve all around me — and it was bred into me. I don't approve of it, but I can't help myself.

Perhaps because I've enjoyed my life, I have no great nostalgia for my childhood. But I had wonderful, happy times — every summer in Northeast Harbor, Maine. It's so beautiful just to look at. In Boston we lived on Commonwealth Avenue, just a half block from the Public Garden. When the fountains were dry, we used to play tag in the basins. Of course there were no automobiles, and in the winter in the snow we used to do what we called "punging." We'd run beside the livery sleighs and jump on the runners and ride on them. The cabs were called "booby hutches." My little brother was considered too young for punging and my mother forbade him to do it. I remember he jumped on the runners of a booby hutch and looked in the window and found his mother inside!

We used to take the trolley out to Heath Street and then walk a mile or more to the country club to skate on a pond. My father came out sometimes but he rode in a carriage. He worked his way through law school, became treasurer for the Provident Institution for Savings, and was eventually very affluent. But we were brought up on the idea of economy. And money was not spent on carriages for children.

Boston has always been famous for wealthy families who did not show it. I think they felt guilty spending too much money on themselves and they used it to do interesting things for other people. They had causes. They supported the symphony orchestra. There was never any talk at all about money at home. But without it being said, it was instilled in me that I was privileged and had a duty to give back in some way to the community... to life.

Of course, when I was growing up life was much simpler. We didn't have a war. Life was just a question of going from school into society and then into something you were interested in. The women weren't expected to do anything except get married. I'm certainly glad my girlhood wasn't like today's. It's too confusing now.

But I wish I'd had a little more freedom with boys. I didn't know how to get on with them very well. I didn't see boys except at dances; few girls did. There were dancing schools — Wednesday afternoon, Thursday afternoon, Friday afternoon — depending on your age. Then finally the Friday evening dances, which were the most exciting. After I came out at eighteen, there was the custom that on Sunday afternoons boys would come and call on you. I can see them now, coming down Commonwealth Avenue, two by two, all dressed up.

When you were a debutante, the great honor was to be invited to the Assembly. I was invited, and it was a pretty stupid affair. They were not exciting parties because they were for older people. But the debutantes invited were the members of the Sewing Circle. You came out and then joined the Sewing Circle. You never sewed. It was like the Junior League; you tried to be of some use to the world.

If you weren't thinking about getting married, you thought about volunteer work. I was maybe a little bit more churchy than most of the girls, and I had a great feeling for foreign missions — not just to convert people, but to educate them; give them a chance to live better. If I didn't become a missionary, I wanted to marry a minister, because he did a lot for people and his life could be much more shared than most men's lives. And suddenly along came Malcolm Peabody.

Throughout my lifetime I had cared a great deal about the blacks in the South. In 1964 there was a black minister in Boston who was recruiting people for a demonstration down in St. Augustine. But it was Easter week and my husband had to take charge of the church. I said, "Well, do they take women? Would I be of any use?" So they snapped onto me.

Just because I was mother of the governor, it got an awful lot of publicity. So now I'm picked out as being this wonderful old lady who went down South to demonstrate, but three other women went with me.

I was never afraid of anything happening to us. I just thought we might have some eggs thrown at us. The second day we heard that people in Boston were saying, "Oh, blacks are going to jail, but the whites aren't." So we felt we all had to go to jail — and we telephoned home to get permission. I called my son Endicott, who was governor, and he said, "All right, mother. What's right down there is right here."

Another white woman from Boston, Mrs. Campbell, and I and five black women — including the wife of Bishop Burgess — went to the restaurant at a large motel. The manager asked us to leave and we refused, and he sent for the sheriff and he asked us to leave. And I said we didn't have to without knowing the ordinance. I'd been coached on that. So he had to go get his ordinance and read it over our heads — that we were trespassing and conspirators and unwelcome guests. We still refused to leave. Oddly enough I saw a great friend of mine in the lobby. She was down South, visiting some people and had come there for lunch. She said, "Mary Peabody, what are you doing here?"

I said, "I'm getting arrested!"

We went to jail for two days and two nights. They separated the colors. Our cell supposedly held eight people, but we had fifteen in it. There were two girls in there for forgery and they were awfully good to us. They insisted Mrs. Campbell and I sleep in their beds. And the black woman we had spent the first night with sent over a blanket and a pillowcase.

People still say to me, "Oh, whites felt encouraged to do something themselves, and blacks felt encouraged when you went down there." So perhaps it was important, after all.

When I came back, it seemed the most I could do was raise money. I tutored some black children through one winter. I've been raising money, it seems, ever since; for a black school in Roxbury, for one thing. My life is too disjointed to take any volunteer work. I'm 86. I haven't got the strength I used to have. I tried working for the Quakers in their clothing department, but I couldn't keep it up. I only hope my old age doesn't last too long. I spend a lot of time at my desk, keeping up with people, keeping up with causes. I was interested in stopping the B-1 bomber, and I see no reason for having the Concorde and wasting all that fuel. So I write letters to the President, to the Congress. I think Mr. O'Neill is kind of tired of hearing from me. But I really haven't got any work to do anymore. That's why I'm losing my identity!

In my mother-in-law's Bible, after she died, I found a little note she had written to herself. It said, "Remember to be cheerful." I think that's very important — not to complain, not to say you're lonely all the time. All I say is I'm cold all the time! I don't allow myself a fire if I don't have anybody here. And I make myself keep the house at 65. I'm very frugal. Also the thing to do is to save energy. So I put on layers, just like the Chinese — my layers of clothes.

As a representative of the Chance Vought Aircraft plant in Stratford, Connecticut,
just after the war in the Pacific ended, Frank J. Delear was assigned to cover Major
"Pappy" Boyington's triumphant reunion with his Black Sheep Squadron after he had
already been awarded the Congressional Medal of Honor "posthumously."
Here is how it was. . . .

The Return of the Luckiest Unlucky Man Alive

BY FRANK J. DELEAR

– illustration by Austin Stevens

It was in early January 1944 when we got the bad news. Major Gregory L. Boyington, legendary leader of the U.S. Marine Corps Black Sheep fighter squadron of World War II, was missing in action in the South Pacific.

To some 13,000 employees of Chance Vought Aircraft in Stratford, Connecticut, it seemed almost like losing a personal friend. For nearly three months, in stories and pictures, we'd followed Boyington's exploits behind the .50-caliber machine guns of a Vought F4U-1 Corsair: how he'd shot down five planes on his first mission as skipper of the Black Sheep to become an overnight ace; how he'd downed 20 more in a few short weeks to win fame as the top active American ace; how he'd led his squadron through the skies of the Solomon Islands, taunting enemy pilots to come up and fight; how his men idolized him, calling him "Pappy" or "Gramps" in deference to his experience and advanced years (he was 31 to their average of about 21).

Now Pappy had flown his last mission, hurled his last taunt at the enemy. A few meager details filtered through: he'd taken off at dawn on January 3 from the island of Bougainville to lead a fighter sweep over Rabaul on New Britain Island, site of a strong enemy air base. Near Rabaul he'd been seen to shoot down one plane. Then silence. Months passed, becoming a year, then a year and a half, with no word from the enemy. Only the optimistic believed that Boyington was still alive. Someone recalled his boast to the Black Sheep that he'd meet them in a San Diego bar six months after the war even if he went down with 40 Zeros on his tail. So a faint hope still lingered on.

The Boyington legend grew: the bull-necked bruiser, an ex-collegiate wrestling champion, who'd built a bunch of misfits into one of the hottest fighter squadrons of the war; the hard-drinking bad boy of Marine aviation who'd shot down 26 planes to tie the records of Eddie Rickenbacker in World War I and Marine Major Joe Foss in the early days of World War II (later it was learned that Boyington had downed not one but three planes on his last flight, to raise his total to 28); the hell-for-leather Marine who was promoted to Lieutenant Colonel and awarded the Congressional Medal of Honor and the Navy Cross, all "posthumously."

Then the miracle: V-J Day and Boyington discovered alive in a prison camp in Japan 20 months after his disappearance. He returned to the United States a hero, wined and dined and shuttled around the country to promote the sale of war bonds and the greater glory of the Marine Corps. After that an up-and-down career saw him slide into alcoholism, fight his way back to health, and, in 1958, write a candid and colorful autobiography, *Baa, Baa Black Sheep.* Later an on-again-off-again TV series thrust him once more into the spotlight and brought republication of his book for a whole new audience. It also provided a nostalgic trip into the past for those few who retained personal memories of the exploits of the Black Sheep Squadron.

I first met Greg Boyington in August 1945 at the Oakland, California, airport upon his return from captivity. As Chance Vought publicity representative, I was to cover the event, assist with the ensuing festivities, and arrange a Boyington visit to the Corsair plant in Stratford.

Those of us from Vought felt we already knew him. His wrestler's physique, courage, deadly marksmanship, and years of flight experience had combined to make him the top Marine fighter pilot. His leadership qualities had also been proven beyond question. In addition, he was a tactician who, at a time when fighters were used chiefly for bomber escort and base defense, argued that they should be used as offensive weapons as well. His ideas helped to set the pace that eventually smashed Japanese air superiority in the Southwest Pacific.

We knew, too, that Boyington had always been a hero to his Black Sheep. As one of them remarked when they went into combat for the first time, "We still need plenty of smoothing out. There is one thing that's holding us together and that we know will pull us through — it's faith in Pappy."

That faith led to aerial exploits which would — and did — fill a book. The first time the Black Sheep went into action they shot down 12 Zeros, including the five by their leader. In four other sallies they destroyed 28 Zeros over enemy territory without losing a pilot. By the end of the first month they had sho

---

"I put myself on my back, and the fire — it was just like looking into a furnace. I grabbed my safety belt with one hand and the stick with the other; if I'd had a third hand I'd have opened the canopy. I gave the stick an awful kick and just crashed right through the canopy. It was cracked by gunfire."

Someone recalled his boast to the Black Sheep that he'd meet them in a San Diego bar six months after the war even if he went down with 40 Zeros on his tail.

down 55 Zeros and three dive-bombers. The Zeros were all bagged within sight of their own airfields.

Just before completing their first tour of duty the Black Sheep flew up to the most powerful enemy air base in the Solomons — Kahili, on Bougainville Island. They circled mockingly over the base until 20 Zeros finally came up to fight. The Black Sheep shot down 12 and went home.

The Black Sheep combat record for two tours of duty, September 12 to October 24, 1943 (operating from Munda and Russell islands), and November 27, 1943 to January 8, 1944 (from Vella LaVella and Bougainville), needs no embellishment: 96 enemy planes destroyed in air combat, all but three over enemy territory; 32 probably destroyed and 50 more damaged in the air; 21 destroyed on the ground; 23 barges destroyed and hundreds of air raids carried out on enemy bases throughout the Solomons and beyond. They flew almost 1100 combat missions, logging just under 4200 combat flight hours, all with the loss of 12 pilots missing in action and six wounded. Only one pilot sustained injuries and none was killed in operational (noncombat) accidents.

That was the background against which we watched Gregory Boyington's dramatic return.

Twenty of Pappy's squadron mates, rounded up by Vought's West Coast reps, greeted him uproariously as he emerged from the Navy DC-4 transport that had brought him from Honolulu, where he'd been recuperating for a week. Standing about 5'8", with a trim, compact build, heavy through the shoulders, he looked surprisingly fit for one who had spent 20 months in captivity. He wore his campaign hat at a jaunty angle and sported a pencil-thin mustache, raised, he said later, as part of an effort to soften his sometimes caustic personality in preparation for the publicity spotlight he'd soon have to face. His face, in repose, reflected a quiet self-confidence, the lips curled in just the hint of a chip-on-the-shoulder sneer. Yet he had a ready smile and at Oakland his grin wouldn't quit as he embraced one familiar figure after another.

For sheer spontaneity, tears along with shouts of joy, it was a meeting impossible to forget. Hoisting Pappy to their shoul-

ders, the young pilots carried him to the waiting microphones. Radio interviews, newsreel appearances, and a press conference followed. We learned for the first time how close to death Boyington had come on his last mission. He related how he had bailed out of his inverted and flaming Corsair barely 100 feet in the air by crashing headfirst through the bullet-shattered cockpit canopy, hit the water of St. George's Channel a split second after his chute popped, survived repeated strafings by enemy fighters, and, hours later, drifting wounded and semiconscious in his life raft, was picked up and brought to Rabaul by a cruising Japanese submarine.

Recently, by telephone from his home in Fresno, California, Boyington disclosed more about that final flight. At that time he had only two days left on his

combat tour and would never have had to fly another mission because of his age and rank.

"I'd just come back from a mission and my plane was riddled with bullet holes," he said. "My total number of kills then was 25, one short of the record. Major Marion Carl, an 18-plane ace and also a squadron commander, volunteered to let me lead his squadron the next day since, he said, he had no chance at the record. I didn't care about the record, but I said 'O.K., but do you mind if I change planes?' A little sarcasm there! So I went on that extra mission, and the only one of my own squadron with me was my wingman, George Ashmun. The rest were new men, and inexperienced. So what happened? When George and I dove down through the cloud layers those new guys should have followed us

Majajiro (Mike) Kawato was an 18-year-old Petty Officer Third Class in the Imperial Japanese Navy at the time he and other members of his squadron shot down Pappy Boyington on January 3, 1944.

 — courtesy of Frank Delear

Above: *In 1943, the Black Sheep squadron offered to shoot down a Japanese plane for every baseball cap sent to them by a World Series contender. The St. Louis Cardinals donated 20 caps, and the Black Sheep met the challenge many times over. Here, Pappy Boyington hands over 20 "meatballs," each representing a downed enemy plane, to First Lieutenant Christopher Magee. Below:* The Black Sheep, reunited in 1945 as Pappy had predicted, singing their version of the Yale Whiffenpoof Song.

down, but they didn't. So they never saw us again and never saw the rest of the flap we got into. I never said much about that before, but at this late date it can't hurt anyone. They didn't mean anything wrong; they were just inexperienced."

Boyington got three planes that day and Ashmun one. Their dive through the clouds was an overhead attack on 60 to 80 enemy planes they'd spotted far below. But there must have been other Zeros above them because Ashmun's Corsair began smoking, then flamed and crashed into the water.

"While George was going down they all piled on him," Boyington said. "I followed them down, squirting at all of them. I guess I was getting hit, too. I pulled out of my dive full gun just over where George crashed. I went about a mile when my main tank went 'woosh.' I put myself on my back, and the fire — it was just like looking into a furnace. I grabbed my safety belt with one hand and the stick with the other; if I'd had a third hand I'd have opened the canopy. I gave the stick an awful kick and just crashed right through the canopy. It was cracked by gunfire. I jerked the chute

115

"I wrote Mike that the irony of 12 pilots shooting at an empty plane was exceeded only by two ex-wives each trying to collect my insurance."

immediately and felt a tug on my shoulder just as I hit the water on my side."

After surviving the strafing by enemy planes, Boyington spent the rest of the day patching himself up. "I'd been badly hit," he said. "My scalp was hanging down in my eyes, my left ear was almost torn off and my throat was cut; I had a hole in my upper left leg and both arms had been hit by shrapnel; my left ankle had been broken by shrapnel."

In 1977 Boyington met one of the Japanese Navy pilots who had helped shoot him down: Majajiro Kawato, an 18-year-old Petty Officer 3rd Class at the time of the fight over Rabaul.

"He had flown to the United States from Japan in a single-engine Piper Comanche," Boyington said. "It was a 36-hour solo flight to honor all the U.S. and Japanese pilots and air crews lost in World War II, a total of about 7000. He barely made it to this country, being about out of gas and so exhausted that he was actually punchy. They'd had a big ceremonial farewell for the guy before he took off so he didn't get quite as much sleep as he wanted. We call him Mike and he's a great guy. He's staying in California and I've gotten to know him; in fact I'm doing a foreword for a book on the war he's writing. Anyway, Mike gave me his account of that last mission.

"As you know, I was busy trying to cover my wingman when these Zeros came at me from behind. Mike was one of those firing at me. He told me: 'You were a lot lower than you said in your book, maybe under 100 feet, when you got hit. You flipped out of the plane, but the plane righted itself and kept on flying. About 12 Zeros went chasing after it, firing at it. I yelled over the radio to stop firing as they were chasing an empty plane. I'll bet all 12 claimed kills on the pilotless plane!' Recently I was reviewing an article that Mike had submitted for my approval and I read that account. I wrote him back that the irony of 12 pilots shooting at an empty plane was exceeded only by two ex-wives each trying to collect my insurance. I never knew, before hearing it from Mike, that my Corsair had righted itself and continued to fly."

As a captive, Boyington was flown from Rabaul to the islands of Truk, Saipan, and Iwo Jima, and finally to Japan, where he spent the last 17 months of his captivity. Aboard a Japanese Betty light bomber en route to Truk, he wanted to take over the craft from the crew and fly it to an American-held island, but the five other captives aboard refused to take the risk — even though it appeared that only one of the enemy crew was armed.

"If I'd had five of you guys there we'd have taken that ship over," he told his Black Sheep upon his return. "Wouldn't that have been something, coming back in a Betty?"

At first, beatings with rifle butts and baseball bats punctuated his life as a prisoner, but Boyington soon learned it was best to say nothing and not to lose his temper no matter what indignities were heaped upon him. His weight dropped from 170 to 110, but soared to 190 after he was given a job in the kitchen at the prison camp in Ofuni, Japan.

At Oakland, with the arrival formalities over, the Black Sheep got down to the serious business of the reunion — two days and two nights at the swank St. Francis Hotel across the bay in San Francisco. A cocktail party featuring round after round of rousing songs by the squadron members, individually and collectively, kicked off the festivities. (*Life* magazine, departing for the first time from its policy of never covering a drinking party, used the Boyington soirée as its lead story with over six pages of candid photographs.) Dinner followed, with Pappy receiving a hastily inscribed gold watch.

In the cold gray of the next morning, Pappy and his men showed up for a CBS radio network show, live from a corner of the hotel ballroom. Without rehearsal, the Black Sheep boomed out their special version of the Yale Whiffenpoof Song for the edification of the housewives of the nation:

From that one-armed joint on Munda
To the place where Pappy dwells,
To those pre-dawn takeoffs that we loved so well;
Sing the Black Sheep all assembled,
With canteen cups on high,
And the magic of their singing casts a spell.
Yes, the magic of their singing
Of the songs we knew so well:
Mrs. Murphy, One-Ball Reilly, and the rest;
So we'll serenade our Pappy

While life and breath shall last,
Then we'll pass and be forgotten like the rest.
We are poor little lambs who have lost our way,
Baa, Baa, Baa;
Little Black Sheep who have gone astray,
Baa, Baa, Baa.
Gentlemen Black Sheep off on a spree,
Damned from here to Kahili;
God have mercy on such as we;
Baa, Baa, Baa.

The rendition brought at least one grimace to the face of the CBS man in charge of the show.

A couple of weeks later, in Washington to receive his "posthumous" Medal of Honor from President Truman, Boyington was the guest of honor at a company-sponsored reception at the sedate Carlton Hotel. With him as his aide was the Black Sheep intelligence officer, Major Frank E. Walton, a rugged Los Angeles cop whom the squadron had quickly nicknamed "Flat." An Olympic backstroke champion (unfortunately a contemporary of Johnny Weissmuller), Flat Walton had long been a tower of strength and good judgment for Boyington and the Black Sheep.

Boyington and Walton arrived in Stratford, Connecticut, on October 24, 1945, amid a flurry of local publicity. Vought's top officials — Rex Beisel, Bert Taliaferro, and Jack Hospers — guided them through the big plant and served as hosts at lunch in the company dining room. Next came publicity visits to the offices of Stratford Town Manager Harry B. Flood and Bridgeport's popular Socialist Mayor Jasper McLevy. The latter, the soul of thrift, was best known for this midwinter remark on the city's shoddy snow removal. "The snow?" he told a reporter. "It'll go away." (It finally did, in late April.)

Today Pappy Boyington leads a new and purposeful life.

"I'm busier than ever before," he said recently. "I've been traveling the commercial airlines for better than a year, maybe two trips a week, appearing at air shows, opening supermarkets, and all of that. I give talks, selling my book, and of course it all helps the TV show. I've been going day in and day out. I'm way behind in my correspondence."

At first, beatings with rifle butts and baseball bats punctuated his life as a prisoner, but Boyington soon learned it was best to say nothing....

Pappy's varied interests, enthusiasm, and good health show through as he talks. "Even though I'm now a bona fide senior citizen of 65, I feel fine," he says, "much better than I have a right to feel." He'd just as soon discuss his golfing difficulties at the 1978 Crosby Pro-Am Tournament as the rewards and frustrations of the TV show, "Black Sheep Squadron." Although he still holds a commercial license with instrument and multi-engine ratings, and membership in Fresno's Sunnyside Country Club (his home overlooks the 14th fairway), he doesn't get a chance to fly or play golf as much as he'd like. He and his wife Josephine spent a week at the Crosby, which he described as a "welcome break" despite the troublesome links layouts there.

The original Black Sheep TV show, "Baa, Baa Black Sheep," was cancelled in March 1977 at the end of its first season, but was brought back in December of that year under the new title "Black Sheep Squadron." The show's revival was mainly the work of Robert Conrad, the rugged and handsome veteran of five TV series, who plays Boyington. Conrad, as aggressive in show business as Pappy was in the war, simply talked the NBC brass into reversing their earlier cancellation.

Of Conrad, Boyington says, in his candid way, "I don't know of anyone more ideally suited for the role. He's a feisty guy and a good athlete. He doesn't like to come in second, and it shows in the script. Robert is 42 but looks no more than 33. Bodywise he's better than a lot of guys in their early twenties."

In an interview at the time of the show's revival, Conrad noted the similarity between his and Pappy's personalities. "A man can give you the impression of being overbearing or obnoxious," he said, "or extremely aggressive when he has a peculiar talent that is his. Boyington's talent was that he was one of the finest pilots that ever lived."

Boyington says he is "really happy" with the new show, which he feels is "more adult and greatly improved over the earlier episodes, which seemed more directed at the kid audience."

Pappy's participation in the show tapered off once the series got well under way. "I'm technical adviser," he says, "which includes a multitude of duties. But I don't spend as much time on this as in the beginning, which was 100 percent.

Then I went over story lines and scripts and was on hand for all of the shooting, day and night. Once you get your crew broken in, there's not a great deal you can do there. So now I'm free to go peddle my papers, as it were. I can sell books and take fees for making appearances and giving talks."

The technical "experts" who send him letters of criticism both surprise and annoy Boyington. "People expect us to duplicate World War II," he says, "but that's impossible, physically impossible. For example, there were no split-deck

Pappy Boyington at 65, photographed in 1978 at the time of the television series "Black Sheep Squadron."

aircraft carriers in World War II, yet that's the only kind we have today. So what are we to do — build a whole new carrier and spend millions instead of thousands to shoot a scene? Yet people keep writing in their complaints about such technicalities — real nitpickers. In the Admiral Yamamoto episode we used P-51 Mustangs to shoot him down. We know it was a P-38 that did the job, but there are lots of P-51s around today, and no P-38s. So we got letters on that. Another time a camera panned the inside of a Corsair cockpit and sure enough one expert spotted a piece of electronic equipment which did not exist until 10 years ago. And sure enough I got a letter from him!"

Others have spotted an F4U-4 Corsair on the new series. The F4U-4 has a four-

bladed propeller in contrast with the three-bladed props used on all the other Corsairs, which are F4U-1s. "Of course we knew that there were no F4U-4s with us in the South Pacific," Boyington says. "There are only eight F4U-1s in flying condition in the whole world, and we've got all eight under contract. So I wrote those people, asking them to let me know if they found any more three-bladed models we could use."

Others complain that they never see more than five Corsairs in flight at any one time. "We've got the others down for maintenance," Boyington says. "In the war we never had the whole squadron in flight condition at any one time; there were always a few down for repairs. People who write such letters think they're so smart; they don't know anything about making movies."

While fighting for the show's revival in 1977, Conrad monitored its fan mail. "The records showed," he said, "that 'Bionic Woman' got the most mail, 'Six Million Dollar Man' was second, and 'Baa, Baa' was third. But half the letters for 'Bionic Woman' and 'Six Million Dollar Man' were in crayon!" The records also showed that "Baa, Baa" did not do well in New York, but very well elsewhere, especially in the South.

Pappy Boyington, happy traveler and certified extrovert, has come a long way from his days as maverick leader of the Black Sheep and nemesis of the Marine Corps brass. Yet he remains as tough-minded and straight-talking as ever.

"Roosevelt had seen something about me in an Ed Sullivan column," he said recently. "And that's how I got recommended for the Congressional Medal. So the Marine Corps, thinking I was dead, gave me the Navy Cross. They'd never given me anything before, not even a Purple Heart."

In his book Boyington tells of a fellow pilot who, in prewar days, toasted him as "the luckiest unlucky man I know." Maybe that phrase still fits. A more apt evaluation, however, might be that the qualities that served Pappy Boyington so well in combat, chiefly his indomitable spirit, are what have seen him through to his personal triumphs, professional achievements, and ultimate happiness as a civilian.

*The late Lowell Ames Norris wrote many articles for Yankee during the 1960s
(as has his son, Curtis B. Norris, since then). Here, however, is the one readers seem to
remember best. It concerns a Memorial Day meeting of a Massachusetts
Grand Army of the Republic post — conducted by the last
surviving member before empty chairs.*

Last of the G.A.R.

BY LOWELL AMES NORRIS

Memorial Day always brings back many memories to me. I remember the G.A.R. parades when I was a small boy, and bands moving along beneath the elms on Washington Street in our town. White-haired veterans of the Civil War, clad in faded blue uniforms with black slouch hats, decorated the graves of their comrades. Also not to be forgotten was the annual appearance of one or two of these veterans before the grade-school pupils.

By 1927, the years had reduced the Grand Army of the Republic to a mere handful of men scattered across the country. It is of one of them I wish to speak, a man whom I still remember vividly. At the time I was a feature writer on the *Boston Sunday Herald*. Paul Waitt was the Sunday Editor.

In some way he had heard of the doings of A.E. Lincoln, who was Commander of a Grand Army post in Kingston, Massachusetts, a town adjoining Plymouth. Although then the sole survivor, this man had been holding monthly meetings of the post, rallied by the spirits of his comrades who had passed on.

"I want you to get a story from him," he ordered, "and sit in on his annual meeting, which is today. You can take [Alton Hall] Blackington with you for photographs."

So we hurried from the Herald Building, which was situated then on Mason Street off Tremont. It was an exhilarating spring day. The leaves had not fully emerged, and although the sun wasn't very hot, there was already a tinge of summer in the air.

Around Kingston, we learned that at one time the Martha Sever Post, No. 154, had been one of the most flourishing and energetic posts on Boston's South Shore. Organized in 1893 with 25 charter members, it had grown steadily in size and importance. Then time commenced to take its toll of the members. Yet the remaining veterans continued to hold meetings in the old G.A.R. Hall on Summer Street.

Finally only three were left!

The old hall, which had housed them for almost half a century, was dismantled and turned over to the American Legion.

Commander A.E. Lincoln of the Grand Army of the Republic conducted a regular meeting of Post 154 in 1927.

Most of the relics were taken away. There was even some talk of disbanding entirely and surrendering the charter and the post colors. But Commander Lincoln bitterly opposed this suggestion and it was finally dropped.

So it came about that the Martha Sever Post was reestablished at the home of Commander Lincoln on Cross Street in Kingston. We headed for the new quar-

ters. As we drew up before the old-fashioned farmhouse, Commander Lincoln hobbled out to greet us, cane in hand. In his faded blue uniform and corded black slouch hat with the insignia "G.A.R.," he looked every inch a soldier. We introduced ourselves.

"You came just in time for the meeting," he said, leading the way into one of the large rooms on the lower floor, which had been transformed into a typical G.A.R. post.

There was the coveted charter hanging upon the wall and a flag-draped altar had been set up in the center of the room. A little apart and on raised platforms were seats for all presiding officers. Beside the commander's desk were the post colors, worn and torn from 40 years of service. Beyond were row upon row of vacant chairs. Commander Lincoln hobbled a little way ahead and looked around him.

"We used to have mighty cheery times together," he chuckled. "Used to sit close to that old parlor stove during the long winter months, exchanging experiences." He turned to us. "As you can see, the room is small and cozy." He hesitated, and then went on after clearing his throat. "We didn't seem to miss our absent comrades quite so much.

"We held our monthly meetings with a great many good-time jamborees in between. There was three of us who moved from the old hall here: John Thompson, Captain George H. Bonney, and myself." He paused as if in thought. "That was some years back. Time slipped along, and John went. Our little circle was narrowed down to two. A few more months, and Captain Bonney rejoined John. I was alone.

"Folks told me I ought to give up the charter now that I was the only member. I couldn't see myself surrendering our colors while there was a single member of the post left to fight for all the good things the Grand Army stood for. And so I refused.

"Besides, I got into the war during its last years. I was too young to join before and I didn't get much chance for service. Then the war was over, and we came home. Now that they've all gone, I feel it's my turn to give the service I didn't have the chance to give back in those war days. I know as long as I hold monthly meetings and keep my reports, they can't take that charter away from me." He straightened up with an effort. "And now, if you'll excuse me, I'll call the meeting to order."

He motioned us to some seats set apart from the rest. Then he turned to the vacant chairs. "Well, comrades," he said. "What do you say we get down to business?"

We watched as, before a silent assembly of vacant chairs in a room bright with spring sunshine but pregnant with memories, the annual meeting of this post, which once boasted 66 members, began.

His uniform lending reality to the scene, Chaplain Lincoln, Adjutant Lincoln, and Sergeant-at-Arms Lincoln opened the meeting with a prayer, standing beside the flag-draped altar on which rested the open Post Bible guarded by crossed swords.

In a voice that was not always steady, the old soldier sitting in the adjutant's seat called the roll before reading the report of the last meeting. Name after name he called: "Tom, John, Fred, Arthur" — all old friends and neighbors. Down page after page of the age-yellowed roster, he read. Commander Lincoln sat back. He was satisfied. All present and accounted for. Somehow he knew and we felt they were bearing with him in silent sympathy. Every chair seemed occupied by a living and vibrant personality.

Next he read orders from Departmental Headquarters in Boston and put to a vote in a formal parliamentary way invitations for many events. All but one were voted down. Then came the election of officers. Soberly he wrote down his name beside every office on the ballot and presented it to himself as adjutant. It was then voted to have the adjutant cast one ballot. This was done.

The gavel of the commander fell on the marble slab on his desk with a sharp knock. The 43rd annual business meeting of this one-man Grand Army post stood adjourned.

For months Commander Lincoln had held these meetings, transacting the regular business of the post, alone except for

"The last of the rear guard," Commander Lincoln raised the American flag in front of his home in Kingston, Massachusetts.

Soberly he wrote down his name beside every office on the ballot and presented it to himself as adjutant. It was then voted to have the adjutant cast one ballot. This was done.

the memories of those comrades who had passed down the Long Trail ahead of him. Every Memorial Day he visited their graves and saw to it that they were properly decorated. He helped in many other ways to keep alive the splendid spirit of patriotism, and he worked hand-in-hand on programs of the future with American Legion officials.

In the desk of the adjutant were the records of the post, including the old parchment-bound register. The 80-odd year old opened the book. All of the 66 members had their names inscribed. Some of them had interesting sidelights of wounds received at Gettysburg and other famous engagements. One or two were ripped by bowie knives during the sharp encounters in the Blue Ridge Mountains. Over all the names but one a heavy line had been drawn.

"I am the only one left of these brave men and kindly neighbors," he told us as

he rose stiffly from his chair and accompanied us to the door. "I am the last of the rear guard staying behind to complete our duties." His tone was matter-of-fact, and he smiled. "Soon I will rejoin them and we shall all stand reunited in the Camping Ground of the Sky.

"I have seen the Grand Army of the Republic grow from a small group to be one of the most influential organizations in the country," he concluded. "The Grand Army closes its books on a patriotic career which has been successful in bringing about One Country and One Flag. I hope when the last member of the now flourishing American Legion closes its books there will be spread on its records a career which has accomplished the termination of wars and a United States of the World."

Commander Lincoln died in 1931.

– photographs from the Blackington Collection

Most articles on the Shakers cover their history, their theology, something about their craftsmanship, and so on. For the May 1980 issue, Yankee Executive Editor Tim Clark embarked on a more difficult task: to determine the real situation now and, for good or ill, what form Shakerism will take in the future. It remains one of the pieces of which he's most proud. (In our opinion, deservedly.)

Shattering the Shaker Image

BY TIM CLARK

"At the Shakers' house in Harvard, I found a spirit-level on the window-seat, a very good emblem for the Society; but unfortunately neither the table, nor the shelf, nor the window-seat were plumb."
— Ralph Waldo Emerson, 1842

One day last summer I was preparing to visit the Shaker community at Sabbathday Lake, Maine. The temperature was hovering near 100 degrees, and I was debating what to wear. The practical garb — shorts and a T-shirt — was clearly out of the question. After all, I was visiting a religious community, one with more than 200 years of history and tradition, a celibate community, moreover, that rejects any suggestion of carnality.

Shorts, I decided, had a slightly irreverent, even carnal air about them. So I drove up to Sabbathday Lake wearing a short-sleeved shirt and slacks, and put on a tie just before going in. There I was greeted by my Shaker host — who was wearing shorts.

We all come to the Shakers with certain preconceived notions — that their tables will be plumb, that shorts will not be worn. We carry an image around in our heads of an austere, highly disciplined, perhaps fanatical sect, living in nearly bare rooms with pegs on the walls, speaking in stilted Old Testament English, refusing to have any truck with the corrupt and worldly 20th century. Those of us who have done a little research before visiting may have read the Millenial Laws of 1821, which regulated the lives of the brethren and sisters down to the most picayune details — it was "contrary to order" to "have right and left shoes," or "to shake hands with the

'world' [outsiders], unless they first tender their hand," or "to put the left foot on the stairs first when ascending."

But what we discover, when we arrive, are people, not caricatures. They wear shorts when it is hot, and blue jeans when they work in their herb gardens. They have right and left shoes, drive cars, read newspapers, talk on the telephone, and even shake hands with the world. They continue to practice their religion, founded in 1774 by the Englishwoman called Mother Ann Lee, which stresses simplicity, possession of all things in common, and separation from the world. But it is separation from "the sense and feeling of the world," not from the world itself. "We can't separate ourselves from the world," one Shaker told me. "God made the world. The world is a good place." They may still say "Yea" and "Nay" instead of yes and no, but it is a fond tradition, not an affectation. The Shakers of today are proud of their past, but they live in the present.

It is a glorious past, to be sure. The Shakers have the distinction of being the longest-lived religious communal society in American history. Begun in 1774 as an outgrowth of even earlier experiments by French mystics, the Shaker experiment survived the explosion of revivalist thinking in New England known as The Great Awakening, flourished during the millenial fever of the early 1800s, and was a model to secular socialists of the same period. It outlasted such famous communes as Brook Farm and New Harmony. And though the socialists rejected the Shakers' strict celibacy (which they called "absurd" and "disgusting"), they raved about the Society's material success. "They are the only dealers in

Part of the Shaker Village in Canterbury, New Hampshire. At far right is the 1792 Meeting House, first building erected in the formerly 100-building village. Now open to the public, the Canterbury Shaker Village, which is still home to two original Shakers, has undergone extensive restoration since Tim Clark's article was written — and includes a quality gift shop and art gallery.

– Todd Smith

America who have known how to make honesty pay," reported English socialist George Holyoake. "Some say they are the only tradesmen who have attempted it. Utopianism makes money — a thing not believed in England."

Shaker communities were a magnet for political and literary luminaries. "A visit to the Shakers in the 19th century was obligatory," remarks one modern scholar. Lafayette, Tocqueville, Monroe, Hawthorne, Cooper, Emerson, Dickens all paid calls. Tolstoy corresponded with Elder Frederick Evans. Abraham Lincoln summoned a Shaker elder to the White House to investigate the sect's refusal to fight in the Civil War, and after hearing the Society's case, reluctantly freed Shakers from military service. "We need regiments of just such men as you," he sighed.

The list of Shaker inventions is awesome, considering that their numbers never exceeded a few thousand. Shakers built the first circular saw and the first washing machine, improved the water-wheel, and came up with many ingenious laborsaving devices, including the common clothespin. "Feeling that their primary reason for being was a religious one, Shakers were always ready to seek and adopt devices which would save time and energy and allow them to devote themselves more fully to the things of the spirit," writes a Shaker scholar. And another historian says, "If they were around today, they'd be in computers."

But they *are* around today, though occasionally they feel pushed back into the past, made into living artifacts, exhibits in a museum. I went to a two-day seminar on Shakerism in New York City last

fall, where a number of historians and curators made speeches about various aspects of the Shaker experience. The speakers were brilliant, or dull, or irrelevant, but they all seemed curiously unaware of those members of the audience who actually *were* Shakers. They made their assertions, were applauded, and sat down while the Shakers listened politely, and then one of the visitors from Sabbathday Lake got up and said that much of what had been asserted was false. The Shaker past, he said, was not so important as the present and the future, and it made him feel like an anachronism to be constantly discussed in the past tense. "The work goes on," he said, adding, "perhaps the best thing to do with the Shaker image is to shatter it completely."

Whenever Shakers read about themselves in newspapers or magazines, they see the words "heritage" and "legacy" — as if Shakerism were the equivalent of a rich uncle in poor health, whose relatives were already eyeing the silver. There is something a little ghoulish about all the articles predicting the extinction of the sect. Sister Frances Carr, a jolly lady in her middle years, recently put on a slide show depicting daily life at Sabbathday Lake, remarking that, "Every slide show we've ever seen about our community has made a point of showing the cemetery. As a refreshing change, we've decided to leave it out."

* * *

In 1957 Shakerism was reaching the bottom end of a long decline. For eight decades, Shaker communities had, one by one, been dissolved, consolidated, or sold, as the number of Believers steadily dwindled from a mid-19th-century peak of 6000 souls in nearly 20 communities. You can check the history books for the reasons why, but the first one that might occur to you — celibacy — is not one of them. In fact, as any immigration official will tell you, the convert usually brings far more enthusiasm to his adopted nation or creed than the person who is born into it and takes it for granted.

As the number of Shaker communities was reduced, much of their property — cash, real estate, and investments — came under the control of Eldress Frances Hall of Hancock, Massachusetts, who, when she died in 1957, was the titular head of the Society. Leadership then passed on to Eldress Emma King of Canterbury, New Hampshire, along with the Society's assets, which were substantial.

The Eldress in Canterbury was worried about all that wealth, and what to do with it. She consulted professionals outside the Society, among them the distinguished Manchester, New Hampshire, law firm of Sheehan, Phinney, Bass, and Green. Upon their advice the money was placed in what is called the Shaker Central Trust Fund, under the direction of what was initially a six-member board of trustees. Each of the three then-surviving communities was represented by a Shaker and a non-Shaker attorney, who were appointed for lifetime terms. In 1960 the last of the Hancock Shakers died, so the board now consists of two Shakers — Eldresses Gertrude Soule and Bertha Lindsey, representing Sabbathday Lake and Canterbury, respectively — and three attorneys — John Sheehan and Richard Morse of the Manchester law firm, representing Hancock and Canterbury, and Walter Foss of Portland, Maine, representing Sabbathday Lake. According to Morse, the money is managed by a "substantial financial institution," acting on behalf of the trustees.

How much money was there? Newspaper reports pegged the amount at either $2 million or $3 million — a figure that trustee Richard Morse describes as "greatly exaggerated." Nevertheless, it was enough money to worry Eldress Emma King, and in the eyes of some Shakers, it was enough to trigger the serious problems that beset the society today. "I wish they'd never found it," said one Shaker sister.

In the six years following the establishment of the trust fund, the feeling grew in Canterbury that the money was a threat to the purity of the Shaker faith — a threat because it might attract new members more interested in the money than in "bearing the cross," the Shaker term for a life of sacrifice in the Lord's service. In 1965 the eldress at Canterbury, on the advice of her Manchester lawyers, decided to close membership in the Society. The practical effect of that decision, in a celibate order, was to ensure that the living Shaker faith would not survive long, if at all, beyond the end of this century.

Why was this decision, so drastic in its implications, made? Eldress Emma King cannot explain — she died in 1967. The current leaders at Canterbury, Eldress Bertha Lindsey and Eldress Gertrude Soule, who moved to that community from Sabbathday Lake in 1971, may be able to shed some light, but their attorney, Richard Morse, told me they do not wish to discuss it. Morse also refused to answer questions about the Shakers, but agreed to review this article for factual errors.

But in 1973 Eldress Gertrude Soule explained the decision to a reporter from the *Portland* (Maine) *Sunday Telegram.* She tied the move to the death, in 1961, of the last male Shaker, Elder Delmer Wilson of Sabbathday Lake. "His death meant that we could not admit a new male member because we would not have a male counselor to instruct him," she said.

"We ruled against accepting young women as members because young people do not want to accept the discipline, the rules and regulations which govern our way of life," she continued. "Young people are interested in and attracted by the Shaker religion and faith, but the discipline of our living is not acceptable to them. We have had bad experiences in some Shaker communities."

But the decision did not mean a complete end to Shakerism, she added: "Young people are greatly interested in reading and studying it. . . . It is only the Shaker way of life in a Shaker family that will come to an end. I wish it were not so. I wish that every room in every Shaker residence were filled. However, our religion was started by God; God will see it continued in some way. He will take care of it."

Manchester attorney Richard Morse says the decision to close membership was made "after extensive consultation with all the remaining members of the then two societies," and by joint agreement of the eldress at Sabbathday Lake — Gertrude Soule — and the eldresses at Canterbury.

But every Shaker did not agree with the decision. Sister Mildred Barker of Sabbathday Lake flatly opposed it, telling the same Portland reporter in 1973 that, "No one has the right to shut the door of the church on anybody who sincerely seeks to enter." She was not alone. Other sisters at Sabbathday Lake opposed the decision, which they say is contrary to the language of the Covenant of the Society, and to the terms of the agreement setting up the Shaker Central Trust Fund. Their disagreement led to open defiance when, in 1972, they refused orders from Canterbury to eject a man who had been living at Sabbathday Lake for 10 years.

Theodore Johnson is a big bear of a man in his late forties, with silver-gray hair and beard, and a light, high voice in which he speaks softly. But he carries a big intellectual stick. A Colby College

... the making of the Shakers into Americana is a violation of that Shaker virtue we claim to cherish most — simplicity.

For nearly a half century, Shaker meetings were the scene of both ecstatic dancing and the odd jerking and twitching movements that gave the sect its name. But by the time of this photograph, around 1890, such behavior had disappeared.

graduate and Fulbright Scholar, he did postgraduate work at Harvard, and was, for a short time, president of a small college in Lewiston, Maine. Born in Massachusetts, he can recall visits to the Shakers at Canterbury as a child, but it was not until the mid-1950s that his path crossed that of the Believers again.

As Johnson tells it, he was working as a branch librarian in the Boston library system when a high school student came in asking for information on the Shakers. Johnson started finding books and documents for her, and reading them on his own before sending them back to the central library. Within a few months, he estimates he had read 50 books by or about the Believers, and, stimulated by what he had learned, he visited the then-surviving community at Hancock.

That was in 1956. The Hancock community, though still alive, was moribund. But he discovered the thriving community at Sabbathday Lake, where there were still almost a score of Believers, plus a number of children. "My interest and concern continued to grow, and my visits became more frequent," Johnson says, "until I found myself living here. I decided this was where I would be happy."

Johnson says he had considered joining a religious community before he met up with the Shakers at Sabbathday Lake, and might have joined an Anglican com-

munity had he not. But the Anglican community was "still pretty medieval," he recalls. "I found that Shakerism represented all of the good things in religious community, and was lacking many of the bad things — the medievalism, the desire to live in the past. I find Shakerism very modern — able to cope meaningfully with the problems that human beings have at this particular time."

Johnson was not married when he decided to join the Shakers, and he says his mother, who passed away shortly thereafter, approved his decision. "My father, although he has come to accept the life very much more, thought I had given up too much — the opportunity for a natural family, a career, perhaps, of some academic promise. I think he has come to understand that, for me, I have a family, and really a larger one than I would have in the world. . . . I think, too, that he has come to accept my view that academic preferment, money in the bank, a house, a boat, a car, are not important to me, and really would not have been important had I not come here."

Although Johnson had been living at Sabbathday Lake for several years before the Canterbury sisters decided to close membership, he is still not recognized by them as a member of the Society. The Canterbury position, as explained by their lawyer, Richard Morse, is that there are only nine living Shakers, all of them

women — three at Canterbury, and six at Sabbathday Lake.

The Shaker sisters in Maine, however, accept Johnson as a brother in their community. Johnson is reluctant to comment on the controversy, except to say that "the important sanction is that which comes from those with whom one is involved in living." He also points out that conflict is not unprecedented in the Society. "On one issue, for example, in the 1870s, when musical instruments began to be introduced into the communities, and the community at East Canterbury bought an organ, Elder Otis, of this (Maine) family, records in his journal his utter consternation over such a move. He wrote, 'The human voice is still a full and sufficient instrument for the worship of God!'

"To be sure," Johnson added after a moment, "the difference of which you speak may be in some respects more fundamental. But in all truth, it does not really affect our daily lives, because we are doing what we think is right, and we do what God has led us to do."

Ted Johnson is not the only man living among the Shakers at Sabbathday Lake these days, but he remains, for some, the most controversial, perhaps because of the increasingly public role he plays, almost as a spokesman for the Shakers. He established the Institute of Shaker Studies at Sabbathday Lake in 1967, offering annual courses, seminars, and lectures on Shaker history and thought. He edits and publishes *The Shaker Quarterly*, a periodical of wide circulation in academic circles since 1961. He is director of the Shaker Museum at Sabbathday Lake, and speaks on Shaker history, thought, and customs in seminars and colloquia in outside institutions.

To some outsiders with Shaker interests, Ted Johnson is "the resident scholar and sage of Sabbathday Lake." To others, his presence is more disquieting. "He believes, and I think sincerely, that he can save the Shaker religion," says one scholar, "but I don't think he can. I don't think he's the type of person that is capable, or qualified, or just fitting."

Regardless of the personalities involved, the Shakers today are a deeply divided community that, throughout its history, has placed a high value on unity. "For whereas there is among you envying, and strife, and divisions, are ye not carnal and walk as men?" wrote one Shaker in 1818. The problem of the Sabbathday Lake community is compounded by the fact that they feel they lack

The debate is not over a church's policy or procedure, but its very definition: who is a Shaker?

genuine representation on the board of trustees of the Shaker Central Trust Fund. Eldress Gertrude Soule, who is the official Shaker representative of the Maine community, moved to Canterbury in 1971, and still lives there. Attorney Foss, who is supposed to represent Maine interests on the board, was asked to step aside by the Sabbathday Lake community in 1972, but he has not given up his seat on the board.

The conflict may even have resulted in punitive action against the Sabbathday Lake community by the parent ministry at Canterbury. The sisters at Canterbury live off an income from the Shaker Central Trust Fund, as did the community at Sabbathday Lake until 1973. Then the trust fund cut off the $3000 monthly payments it had been making to Sabbathday Lake, while continuing to pay taxes, insurance costs, and a small allowance — less than $10 a week — to each of the sisters recognized by the parent ministry.

Ted Johnson says Sabbathday Lake is financially self-sufficient on the income from its herb industry, its agriculture and timber sales, and the proceeds from the museum and tours. Since 1974 the Maine community has also received help from a group of "interested individuals" around the nation calling themselves Friends of the Shakers, which has

paid for electronic security systems in several buildings, and for repainting and refurbishing them.

The conflict has moved beyond the borders of Maine and New Hampshire as academics and others with interests in the Shakers choose up sides. When the Museum of American Folk Art in New York City announced it would hold a Shaker seminar last fall, featuring Ted Johnson as a speaker, its president, Robert Bishop, received several "threatening" phone calls and letters from Richard Morse — behavior that Bishop called "appalling." And several of the listed participants in the conference heard from Morse, too. The seminar went on, but was boycotted by the Canterbury Shakers, who had been invited to attend.

If the conflict remains unresolved, serious legal questions could arise in the future. The two Canterbury eldresses on the board of directors of the Shaker trust fund are both in their eighties. According to published reports, when the last Shaker dies, the trust fund is to be converted to a charitable trust that would finance scholarships and historical research into Shakerism. But if all three of the Canterbury sisters should pass away before those officially recognized sisters in Maine (as seems likely, in view of the respective ages), would the Maine sisters

be allowed to take part in the management of the trust fund?

And who is to decide the future of the buildings and property at Sabbathday Lake, when the last of the "recognized" Shaker sisters living there is gone? In 1972 the entire village of Canterbury was turned over to a nonprofit corporation run by a large board of directors, whose president is Eldress Bertha Lindsey. When the three elderly sisters living there now are gone, it will become what executive director Jack Auchmoody calls "a living museum," where visitors (there were 15,000 in 1978) can see craftspeople simulating Shaker works in genuine Shaker dwellings.

If any of these questions should ever be brought before a court (and the courts have in the past tried very hard not to get involved in religious matters), legal precedent has generally dictated that decisions made by church leaders are binding on church members, provided that those decisions are made in the religion's customary fashion. But in this case the debate is not over a church's policy or procedure, but its very definition: who is a Shaker?

What it seems to boil down to is a debate over continuity. Those who favor the decision to close membership seem to think it would be better for the living Shakers to disappear rather than risk contamination of Shakerism by the admission of new members. Those who wish the membership rolls to remain open say that change is not something to be feared. Ted Johnson: "I have always liked what Eldress Anna White said to a reporter in the early days of this century. He asked her what she thought was the classic period in Shakerism. She hesitated for a second, and then said, 'I would say that the classic period in Shakerism is that which has begun to evolve at this minute.' "

Gerald Wertkin, a New York attorney who heads Friends of the Shakers, thinks the conflict will be amicably resolved. He points out that individual Shakers continue to communicate with each other, and that the disagreement has not resulted in personal animosity. He has talked with both sides and is confident they will be reconciled. His own position in the dispute is clear — he regards the Covenant of 1830, which states "the

– Todd Smith

Now in her nineties (1985), Eldress Bertha Lindsay has lived at the Canterbury village for over 80 years.

door must be kept open for the admission of new members into the Church" as the equivalent of the U.S. Constitution — a higher authority than the decisions of any particular elders. "Shaker life is not intended to be static," he wrote in a recent article.

But never in the history of the Society have worldly persons had so much influence as the Manchester lawyers, or Jack Auchmoody, or Gerald Wertkin. In addition to Friends of the Shakers, there are other nonprofit groups involved in protecting or preserving Shaker villages and artifacts: The Shakerton Foundation in Massachusetts, The Shaker Historical Society in Ohio, the Shaker Heritage Society in New York, the Friends of Pleasant Hill in Kentucky. All are part of a large and growing complex of academicians, museum curators, history buffs, antique dealers, and, yes, journalists like me, who interpret the Shaker experience to the rest of the world.

But this complex — call it the Shaker Industry — is not the same thing as the Shakers, and even as it strives to uncover the truth about Shakerism, it warps and distorts that truth in its own interest. Academicians need to publish articles and books, give seminars and papers, teach courses. They sell their own perceptions about the nature of Shakerism. Museums want to attract more visitors, so they preserve and play up the most attractive features of Shaker life in their exhibits and restorations. Antique dealers and collectors rely heavily on professors and museums to authenticate their possessions and thus enhance their value on the $6 billion annual antique market in this country. And let's not leave out writers and reporters, who look for new angles to the often-told "Shaker story."

The result is that the picture of the Shakers presented by the Shaker Industry — the Shaker Image — is never quite complete. It is edited, enhanced, packaged. It is made into that curious beast called "Americana," which like all the other "-ana" — railroadiana, baseballiana, Kennedyana — is a vain effort to capture some unpossessable spirit. Americana is to America what nostalgia is to history. And the making of the Shakers into Americana is a violation of that Shaker virtue we claim to cherish most — simplicity.

But somehow I am confident that a faith that survived mob violence in the past ("They Were Made to Suffer Greatly," *Yankee*, August 1974) will survive the corrupting affections of this carnal

Eldress Gertrude Soule, Lead Minister of the United Society of Believers, moved to Canterbury from Sabbathday Lake in 1971. "Young people are interested in and attracted by the Shaker religion," she says, "but the discipline of our living is not acceptable to them."

world. I can say that because I have seen Shaker simplicity triumph even in the midst of one of the most carnal places on earth — New York City.

I saw Sister Mildred's radiant integrity on a rainy night a few blocks from Broadway, when she sang "Simple Gifts" to a crowd of sophisticated New Yorkers, and made their glitter look cheap. She has been a Shaker for most of this century, and a leader of other Shakers, but she is too modest to define her faith. "It took me a long time to find out what Shakerism really meant," she told me. "You don't get it in one reading, in one day's work, in one struggle. You have to go over it and over it again and again. It takes more language than I have to really tell you what it has meant to me."

And I saw it again on a Sunday morning in the soaring neo-Gothic vastness of Manhattan's Trinity Church, where the small party of Shakers and their worldly friends gathered for a service — a Shaker

service — in a setting so riotously unsimple that the enterprise seemed doomed from the start.

But we got up in turn, and spoke, and prayed. We sang together — the cheerful, childlike tunes, calling on Believers to bow and bend like the willow, and shake, shake out of them all that is carnal.

> 'Tis the gift to be simple,
> 'Tis the gift to be free,
> 'Tis the gift to come down
> Where we ought to be.

I watched, and listened, and struggled with my own self-consciousness, which is the great enemy of simplicity. And suddenly my eyes were stinging, and the huge church seemed to shrink to the dimensions of a plain meeting room, and the noise of the city was transformed into the musical silence of Maine, and I felt for a moment that I had come down to where I ought to be.

126

Barney Roberg's Impossible Choice

A True Story
by L. Michael McCartney

Thinking back on it, Barney said, it's a good thing he stopped when he did that morning to repair the part of the old logging road that had been swamped out by the changing October weather. "Otherwise I wouldn't be here to tell you about it today," the former lumberman claims.

Bernard B. "Barney" Roberg, who now lives and works at the John Galanek Lumber Company in Southwick, Massachusetts, was telling a story that hasn't been reported since 1956, but one that made him a folk hero among woodsmen from Bangor to the Canadian border. Ralph "Bud" Leavitt, executive sports editor for the *Bangor Daily News,* calls it "one of the greatest stories I've ever covered" in a career that has spanned more than three decades. Maine sportswriters were so impressed with Barney's courage 23 years ago that they named him corecipient of the "Sportsman of the Year" award along with world champion prizefighter Rocky Marciano. When sportscaster Mel Allen arrived to make the presentations, Leavitt recalls telling him, "You're going to hear a story tonight like you never heard before."

Barney, now approaching age 65, calls himself "the black sheep son" of a Litchfield, Connecticut, educator and judge who wanted his oldest boy to become an engineer. "He sent me to M.I.T. [Massachusetts Institute of Technology]," Barney reports, "but I just couldn't stay

there. I was always a restless sort and I couldn't take all that sitting around in classrooms and libraries. All I ever really wanted was to be out in the woods. So I quit school at the end of my second year and went out and taught myself the lumber business."

In the early autumn of 1956 he was working the woods outside of Portage Lake, Maine. He stayed with other loggers at Dean's Motel in that town, but he generally worked off by himself, wandering alone into the deepest reaches of the forest, searching the edges of woodland frontiers to probe the limits of the New England timber industry.

"This particular morning I left the motel in my four-wheel-drive jeep and headed up this deserted old logging road. Partway in I ran into a quagmire of muck and water and sank down to my axles. I just about got through it. I thought for a minute I was going to have to winch myself out. But when I got clear of it I said to myself, 'Well, Barney, you'd best stop right here and now and fix that little marsh because you sure aren't going to feel like doing it on the way home tonight, after a day's work.' "

So Barney cut some poles and saplings and threw them across the swamped-out portion of road until he'd satisfied himself that he'd have enough traction to drive back through without trouble at day's end. Then he continued on a distance of about five miles until he reached

"Nobody knew exactly where I was, and I knew nobody'd even begin to miss me until nightfall, so it was pretty clear right from the start that I'd bleed to death if I just waited for help."

127

"I just kept telling myself, 'Barney, you can't give up. If you give up you're a dead man, no two ways about it.' I had to stop and think a long time about what to do next."

the end of the trail. He parked his jeep, took his axe and chain saw, and walked about another two miles deeper still.

Barney scanned nature's offerings and decided to fell a pine tree that he guessed was better than two feet in diameter. As it began to topple, Barney realized that it was going to lodge itself in the branches of an equally big tree in the path of its fall. He began to walk around behind the falling timber. Just as he was directly behind it, the tip of the falling tree slammed into the boughs of the other, bending it backward like a huge bowstring. The standing tree recoiled under the weight of the falling pine, but suddenly it thrust itself forward again and shot the trunk of the tree Barney had dropped backward off its stump like a gigantic bow firing a monstrous, blunt arrow.

The huge pine popped off its stump and flew directly backward, seizing Barney's right leg in its flight. The backward thrust smashed the logger's leg up against another pine, crushing skin, muscle, and bone and pinning Barney, trapped and seemingly helpless, against the dark wall of pine.

Barney recalls, "I nearly went into shock. I had to fight, at first, just to stay conscious. The pain was ferocious. It was sweeping over me in waves. I knew I had to stay conscious and I knew I had to get my wits about me. When I'd managed that I took a look at my circumstances, and I can tell you they didn't look promising. I tried to pull myself free, but that tree had me pinned in there so good there was no way I could yank myself out. Nobody knew exactly where I was, and I knew nobody'd even begin to miss me until nightfall, so it was pretty clear right from the start that I'd bleed to death if I just waited for help."

His next thought, when it fought its way through the tides of pain and nausea that engulfed him, was to chop himself free. "I'd dropped my axe right next to me, so I reached down and picked it up and began whacking at the tree trunk. But, you know, when you're in an awful fix like that you've got more strength than you ever knew you had. On the third or fourth swing I busted that axe right off and the head went flying. I said

to myself, 'Well, you've really gone and done it now. You just lost your best friend.' "

Barney rested and tried to develop another plan. The force of the blow from the tree had driven his chain saw right into the ground, partially burying the blade. "I knew if I could get hold of that saw I still had a chance," Barney said, "so I took what was left of the axe handle and, little by little, I dug out the chain saw, and inch by inch I nursed it over to where I could get my hand on it. I knew if I lost touch with that saw I was a goner for sure."

Finally, sure of his grasp, Barney hoisted the saw up, rested it on the trunk of the tree that had made him its prisoner, yanked the cord, and started the engine. The top of the fallen tree was still lodged in the upper branches of the one that had shot it backward into the logger's leg. It arced down at an angle of about 45 degrees from its tip to the butt end that held Barney captive against the other pine.

"Well, sir," Barney remembered, "I thought for a minute that I had it made. I started to cut into the tree, but I'd no more than started when I was disappointed again. The angle of that tree was such that as soon as I started cutting into it my saw started to bind up on me. I knew if I went in any farther the pressure of the wood converging on the blade would bind the saw up so bad that I'd never be able to get it out. I couldn't risk losing the saw. I was in a real pickle and I knew it. I just kept telling myself, 'Barney, you can't give up. If you give up you're a dead man, no two ways about it.' I had to stop and think a long time about what to do next."

Even now, so many years later, Barney still paused before revealing his next move. He was sitting in the Houndshead Pub in Westfield, Massachusetts, sipping one of the two bottles of beer he permits himself after work each day. He was wearing the heavy woolen, red-and-black-checkered shirt common in lumber camps, and the shoulders were covered with sawdust, the epaulets of the lumberman. Pale blue eyes looked out of his brown leathery face with a distant expression.

"I finally decided there was just one thing for me to do," he continued, "and I knew I had to do it. Thinking about it wasn't getting me anywhere, and I was getting weaker all the time. So, I did it. I took the chain saw and cut my own leg off, just below the knee. I won't go into the gory details. I just took the saw and cut off my own leg."

He fell to the ground, removed the rawhide laces from his work boots and tied a tourniquet around the leg to stem the flow of blood. And there he sat. Having amputated his own leg he was still two miles over rugged terrain from his jeep and another five miles from that to the nearest source of help. "At first I thought of trying to make myself a pair of crutches," Barney said, "and I fooled around with that project for a while. But there was no way I could do it. I had to head out of there fast because I was starting to fade in and out of consciousness. I decided I just had to crawl."

The overland journey on his stomach, clawing along the pine needle floor of the forest, was continuously interrupted by horrendous pain and lapses into unconsciousness. "At that point I had only one thought," Barney said. "I figured I was going to die out there, but when they found me I wanted them to know that I'd given it one hell of a fight. Every time I'd come to, I'd keep crawling again until I passed out, just saying to myself, 'Barney, every yard you make it back toward that jeep you'll have proved to them you didn't quit. When they find you they'll know you gave it all you had.' "

It took him, as nearly as he can figure, four hours to cover the two miles, but at some point in the afternoon he made it back to the jeep. He was almost too weak and too awkward on the one remaining leg to drag himself up into the driver's seat. When he finally managed that he faced another problem — he had to teach himself how to drive the jeep with only one leg. After a dozen agonizing attempts to operate accelerator, clutch, and brake with his left leg, he got the jeep turned around and headed back down the old logging road.

Only moments before he hit it, Barney remembered the marsh. "Oh, God!" he

remembers imploring. "After all this don't let me get stuck in that quagmire!"

He floored the accelerator. "The jeep hit the swamp like a tank," he remembers. "It splashed and spun and twisted and it was throwing mud and saplings 30 feet in the air. Then it started to skid and bog down. I'd just about lost it. I figured right then and there I'd driven myself right into my own grave. And then, at the last possible second, the front tires grabbed onto firm ground and I got through. For the first time since I'd cut myself loose from that tree I began to think I was going to make it."

A recent photo of Barney Roberg, who, despite his artificial leg, has returned to his trade of woodsman.

When he arrived back at Dean's Motel he called a woman over to the jeep to ask that she go inside and get him help. When she saw what had happened to his leg she was horrified. "She threw her hands over her face and began to scream," Barney said with an understanding smile. "That was all I needed. I said, 'Lady, whatever you do, please don't do that.'"

John Galanek and his son came out of the motel, along with a doctor who was in the area because of an injury suffered by another logger that day. He told the Galaneks to rush Barney to the hospital in Eagle Lake, but first, he said, he would give him something for the pain. He took a syringe and a vial of clear liquid out of his medical bag.

"Make it a good one, Doc," Barney said to him.

"I'm giving you enough to knock a horse flat," the doctor promised.

"Just before I went under," Barney recalls, "I said to myself, 'It's a good thing you aren't a horse, old boy, or they'd be putting you to sleep for keeps.'"

When he next regained consciousness he was in an Eagle Lake hospital bed, confronted by an elderly physician who told him, "Fella, it ain't too good. I'd sooner trust my money to a Democrat than bet on your chances of making it."

"I made it this far," Barney told him.

"Well," the old doctor said, "the only chance you got, and it's a slim one at that, is if I amputate the rest of this leg off up above the knee. Otherwise, sure's cats have kittens, gangrene's going to set in and that'll be the end of you."

"Listen here, Doc," Barney answered, "I done all the cutting on that leg that's going to be done. I got it trimmed up just the way I want it. You leave it alone."

The old doctor shrugged. "Suit yourself," he said, "but if I was in your place I don't think I'd be so all-fired stubborn."

Barney kept the knee and six weeks later walked out of the Eagle Lake hospital on crutches. The townspeople took a collection and paid off his medical costs. Two weeks later Barney was back at work driving a bulldozer and in a few months he went to Boston and was fitted with an artificial limb.

"Works good, too," Barney said. "Watch this."

He got off his bar stool and punted it 10 feet across the pub with the wooden leg to demonstrate its effectiveness.

Somebody offered to buy him a shot of whiskey. "God, no," Barney protested. "I'm not even supposed to be drinking this beer. Doctor's orders, you know. I'm diabetic. The doctor says beer will kill me." The leathery face crinkled around the smiling blue eyes. "I guess I told him a thing or two about what can and can't kill old Barney Roberg."

☞ Memorable thoughts, quotes, and assorted tidbits from the last 50 May issues. ☜

MEL'S GOOD-BYE

(On June 28, 1983, writer Lynn Franklin was killed while on assignment for Yankee. In the following May issue, Yankee Senior Editor Mel Allen wrote about Lynn and their friendship over many, many years. Here are the last four paragraphs. . . .)

☞ He had not filed a flight plan. Nobody knew where to search any more than if Lynn had been a wild bird that had not returned to the nest. On Saturday a pilot on a sightseeing tour of the mountain spotted the wreckage. Searchers found Lynn, 400 feet below the 3165-foot summit, strapped into the plane that had broken in two and burned. Lynn had died on impact. It was how everyone expected Lynn to go, probably the way he would have chosen. It was just too soon. He was only 46.

Lynn would have enjoyed his funeral. We shared Lynn stories and laughed at his foolishness and his recklessness and his eccentricities, like his penchant for going into Howard Johnson's with a thermos and

Lynn Franklin.

asking people for their leftover coffee. He had been everyone's naughty boy, everyone's Peter Pan. I think it was why we loved him so much. It was a lot more fun growing older with Lynn around to remind us to be young.

I climbed the mountain with Lynn's nephew Ken and his friend Sharon. The plane lay there crumpled among the trees and rocks. We stood quietly on the rocks looking down at the lakes glistening below. At 21 Ken resembled the youthful Lynn. He was

tall and wide-shouldered and already making his way as an adventurer. He was a falconer, a mountain climber, a white-water canoeist, and had decided to be a writer. He looked at the plane and then he laughed and you could hear Lynn in that laugh.

"He'd be so angry with himself," Ken said. "I can just hear him. He'd say, 'Next time, Franklin, next time we fly *over* the mountain!' " (*From "Ode to a Bold Pilot" by Mel Allen.*)

THREE REAL ESTATE ADVERTISEMENTS FROM THE MAY 1939 *YANKEE*

☞ Handsome Home, Equipt Farm — 110 acres, about 55 miles Boston; 190 fruit trees, 50 acres field, on improved road: splendid 2-story 10-room Colonial, electricity, marvelous views; good barn, 4-car garage; catalog price $5000 cut to $4400, part down, including 13 cows, heifers, bull, machinery, 1½-ton truck, milk route, etc. Here is grand val-

ue, pictures page 15. Free 100-page catalog. Strout Realty, 810-AP Old South Bldg., Boston, Mass.

☞ 85 acres. 1000 cords wood. Near large town. Good markets. New house, barn for 18 head, other buildings. Orchard, $2650. Terms. 4 acres. On Lake. Good Buildings. $2250. Easy terms. A.H. Knight, West Warwick, R.I.

☞ Hopkinton, Mass., 26 miles from Boston, bus passes door. Stores, churches, schools close by. 15 rooms, steam heated. Bathrooms, electricity. Owner occupies 9 rooms, balance always rented. Monthly income $47. 5 garages, 7 hen houses, 1 acre. Price $6500. Will exchange for village or country property. Frances Young, Hopkinton, Mass.

Tim Love, Governor of the Penobscot Nation: The Early Years

☞ He and some other kids from the island got together and formed an Indian organization, Nee-Dah-Beh, "the friends." Tim began telling them that there were things they didn't have to take from white kids or teachers or anyone; that girls didn't have to put up with being called "squaw"; that boys should not be pigeonholed in shop courses just because they were Indians.

In homeroom one morning Tim refused to hold his hand over his heart and salute the flag. In the principal's office he was lectured about all those "others" who were paying for the Indians' education. He remembers that it brought to his mind the Passamaquoddies, who were starting to press for the return of their own land. After that, he wouldn't

Governor Tim Love, 1981.

even stand when the other kids were saluting the flag, and the principal threw him out of school. Then Tim Love went out and got himself a lawyer.

The lawyer was Tom Tureen, who still remembers the day he accompanied Tim

to the principal's office. "Even then he was rational about it all. What he did was a matter of principle. He's grown sophisticated, but he hasn't changed."

Tureen got Tim back in school, but in 1971, just four months short of graduation, Tim quit and moved to Springfield, Massachusetts, where he lived in a tiny apartment and drew welfare. "I wanted to go down as a statistic, another Indian dropout," he says. "I wanted to show the failure of the system."

But before he left the island, he crept down to the riverbank one night with his bow and arrows. Across the river were the lights of Old Town, the houses of white men in a white man's town. He had nothing against those particular houses or the people in them; they were just nearest.

He struck a match and held it to the wrapping on his first arrow until it caught. Then he raised the bow and let fly. But the river was wide, and neither the bow nor the archer strong enough. The arrows, one after another, fell with a hiss into the black water. (*From "Now the White Men Call Him 'Sir' " by Willis Johnson.*)

What Do You Do for Fun in Eastport?

☞ "We used to make our own fun when we were kids. There were games we played: ever heard of Heist the Green Sail? No? How about Pippy? It was a game we played with sharpened clothespins. I guess nobody plays Pippy anymore.

"Now my daughter-in-law in New Hampshire pays money and drives her kids to play hockey. It's a different way of life, I guess.

"My father used to have a 'trucking' business. He hauled things from the fish factories in his wagons. He used to tell me to quit playing tennis and get to work. Yep, there used to be a tennis court in Eastport. Isn't anymore, though. No tennis court. No movie. No bowling alley.

"What do people do for fun in Eastport? Nothing. That's what they do: *nothing*." **Harry Turner, postmaster in Eastport, Maine.** (*From "Eastport, Maine: The Same Salty Whiff" by Lois Lowry.*)

On Memorial Day and Always — Remember

☞ Late last summer Michael Daly returned to Germany for the first time since World War II. At 58 he was slender with serious gray eyes. He had been invited by the young commander of Company A, 15th Infantry, 3rd Infantry Division, his old outfit, "to boost morale." They gave him the Audie Murphy Suite, but he woke before daylight, uncertain whether he had slept at all. "Faces came back to me," he said. He dressed quickly and walked across the parade grounds to a small memorial park where plaques were set in boulders. He stood alone, watching the sun streak the sky until he could hear faint stirrings in the distant barracks. He was remembering, fighting against forgetting, fearing that if the memories dimmed he would become a stranger to himself.

He gave a speech at an officers' banquet. He was asked to wear his blue embossed medal and he did. He had always wanted to give a speech

Michael Daly, 1982.

like this, to soldiers; so often the speeches he gave at home seemed not really understood. No speech he had given before, he felt, would mean as much as this one. He spoke about the infantry and the men he had lost, and at times his voice cracked. Towards the end he quoted the Antarctic explorer Captain Scott, who wrote to his son from his deathbed, "Courage is the thing. Everything goes if courage goes." As he finished the men stood and applauded.

"Remember us," he told them, "as long as you can." (*From "Only Afraid to Show Fear" by Mel Allen.*)

– Merle Nacht

"WHAT HAPPENS TO ALL THOSE HOUSES YOU FEATURE IN 'HOUSE FOR SALE'?"

Let's take one example, the town of Kokad-jo, Maine, featured in the May 1981 issue. It was nine acres, a store with apartment, and eight sporting camps, all on Lake Kokad-jo up in Maine's moose country. Several weeks after the May issue came out, the owner gave us a report of the results.

☞ There were 93 inquiries from 26 states, including New England, Maryland, Michigan, Ohio, Florida, Indiana, and Wyoming. Occupations of callers included doctors, attorneys, writers, stockbrokers, schoolteachers, a policeman, a pilot, a machinist, a policewoman, a chemist, a potter, businessmen, and many others.

The first person to call, the very day the May issue was on the newsstands, was obviously inebriated. He said how interested he was and how he loved the place. Then, 10 minutes later, he called back to ask why someone had called him, because he wasn't "at all interested in real estate."

Walter Gibson, author of "The Shadow," called. He was 83, still writing, and looking for a retreat. He'd seen the place in 1912.

A man afflicted with an unfortunate stutter telephoned to make an appointment to see the property. The owner was away, and, since the answering recorder was on for only a half minute for each call, he had to telephone over a dozen times to complete his message and he utilized the entire recording tape.

The seven California callers were all looking to "go East." As the owner remarked to us, "Looks like the gold rush is over."

A Washington, D.C., man and his partner said they wanted to move to Ko-

kad-jo because "we are a couple of burnt-out executives."

And so on.

The man who bought Kokad-jo, George Midla of Cold Springs, New York, had seen it when he bicycled through the area a year before with his son, John. At the time, he'd remarked how wonderful it would be to live there. Then, when he saw the place featured in *Yankee,* he felt fate was working overtime. He called to determine how much down payment was needed and a week later said he had the money and would be at Kokad-jo three days later to wrap it up. The day before traveling to Maine, he walked into the Con Edison plant in which he had worked in public relations for the past 25 years and quit. "George," his boss said, "you don't just sever yourself from a corporation after 25 years like this." George replied, "You don't, huh?"

After signing the papers up at Kokad-jo the next day, George and his son embraced and danced for 10 minutes. He said it was the best he had felt in 48 years:

"Free," he said. "Free at last."

A PIE WITH A POINT

☞ My grandfather was recently in a Maine restaurant where he ordered a piece of blueberry pie (where better to get blueberry pie than Maine?) and a cup of coffee. While he was eating the pie, he came across a bone hairpin. He called the waitress over to complain. She examined the pin, looked my grandfather in the eye, and said, "Baked right in the pie, warn't it?"

Mrs. R.W. Banfield, Sr.
Biddeford, Maine

– Stephen Whitney

G. Earl Taylor, 1969.

IT'S NOT HARD TO RIG AN ELECTION IF...

☞ Taylor City is more a state of mind than a geographical location. According to its lean, laconic "mayor," it runs "down by the brook and over to the other side of the hill." More accurately, it straddles two states. It is composed of Parsonsfield, York County, Maine, and South Effingham, Carroll County, New Hampshire.

About 1950, the history and uniqueness of Taylor City was in danger of being forgotten by the younger generation, so G. Earl Taylor decided to run for "Mayor of Taylor City."

Taylor won the "election" overwhelmingly — after all, the entire population of Taylor City is composed of Taylor's relatives. One exception is the Crabtree family, and they have stopped being "outsiders" since their son married a Taylor.

Summer campers in the area have protested this form of small-town democracy. Every year they advance an opposition candidate of their own — to no avail. For the past eight years the leading opposition candidate has been Mr. Robert Womboldt, a writer for the *Boston Herald.* "They say he's got the entire weight of the paper on his side, but it doesn't do him any good," said G. Earl Taylor. "It's always a dirty election and we rig it from beginning to end." (*From "The Mayor of Taylor City" by Audrey Lynch.*)

YANKEE SNOBBERY DEFINED

☞ I remember asking a member of the Tavern Club, one time, what he did, and he answered, "I carve ducks." This intuitive debasement of personal merit spared him an enumeration of the banks of which he was a director, and the corporations on whose boards he sat, but it also reprimanded me for bringing up a mercenary thought in a social context. An illusion of shyness was part of it, but mainly it served to emphasize his success, good breeding, and modesty, and to reassert that a true gentleman is never proud. Above all, the remark possessed wit, and derived from his firm opinion that whatever he did was all right. Only from a position of security and satisfaction could such a remark come.

I have concluded this to be the warp and the woof of Yankee snobbery. It depends on a pleasant willingness to let everybody else be different, which is not at all like being different yourself, and with an inner approval that permits a gentility of comparison. Yankee snobbery never seems to be harsh, and is often subtle rather than quiet: a Texan may be a braggart, but he can't be a snob. (*From "The Insiders" by John Gould.*)

P.S. Three months after the above appeared, we received the following letter....

Dr. John Gould's scholarly paper on Yankee snobbism in the May 1971 issue of *Yankee* omits the most salient example of this art ever perpetrated anywhere. A good number of years back, when John Gould was just starting to be a household word as an authority in all fields of human endeavor, he was automatically incorporated into *Who's Who in America* along with such other eminent individuals as folks might want the address of to write to. Young John (he is older now than what he was then) saw his chance to get himself once for all onto the highest peak of snobbism, where he would be impregnable to attack thereafter. Accordingly, he got himself identified under the heading of Occupation as "farmer." All you have to do is to take a good squint at any issue of *Who's Who,* and you will see the supreme example of the Yankee art of snobbism preserved for all time right alongside the name of John Gould.

Richard V. Clemence
Wellesley, Massachusetts

THE FASTEST (AND MOST DANGEROUS) PLANE ON EARTH

– courtesy of Sheryl Seyfert

Charles Lindbergh congratulates Bayles, winner of the 1931 Thompson Trophy.

☞ But the big one was still to come. The Thompson Trophy race was set for the next day.

("Granny fretted for fear we'd taken too much out of the Model Z in the smaller races. And we'd been hearing about Jimmy Doolittle and his new Super Solution — we'd heard it had a 20 mph speed edge on the Gee Bee. It was a tense night!")

When morning broke, the planes began lining up for a racehorse start. Bayles in the Model Z lined up beside Doolittle's threatening racer. Spread out beyond were Jim Wedell in a Wedell-Williams Special, Ben O. Howard and his Pete, Dale Jackson in a Laird Solution, Bill Ong at the controls of a Laird Speedwing, Ira Eaker flying a Lockheed Altair, and Bob Hall in Maude Tait's Model Y Gee Bee. Granny knew the Model Y was outclassed, but anything could happen in a race.

The Thompson consisted of a 10-lap, 100-mile course. Engines revved, the racers trembled against nervously held brakes. Sweat poured down Bayles' face while the rest of the Granville crew stood back waiting.

The starter's flag dropped and eight of the fastest planes in the world thundered into the air toward the scattering pylon a mile away.

Jimmy Doolittle was first around the pylon and back onto the course. Bayles was right behind, with the Gee Bee's eight-foot prop gnashing at Jimmy's rudder. Wedell, Jackson, Hall, Eaker, Howard, and Ong trailed in that order.

As Jimmy Doolittle brushed past the pylon, leveling off into the second lap, his Super Solution began trailing black smoke. It was later found that he had broken a piston, but Jimmy paid no attention to it. In the same lap, Dale Jackson struck a tree, but he, too, kept going.

Halfway down the back stretch of the second lap, Bayles pulled ahead of Doolittle. Then, as Jimmy's plane began to lose power, the Gee Bee widened the gap. By now the smoke from Doolittle's engine was obscuring the racecourse, but still he managed to hold second place. In the seventh lap, Doolittle's engine could no longer take the punishment, and Jimmy was forced down.

Bayles was never seriously threatened by the others. The "City of Springfield" took the checkered flag with an average of 236.2 mph. (*From "Wings, Wood and Wire: The Gee Bees" by Sheryl Seyfert.*)

"How much would you expect to pay for Rhode Island and Providence Plantations? Wait, don't answer, because we'll also include this miracle maize processor and three-piece set of deluxe steak knives. NOW how much would you pay?"

133

CHAPTER 6

June

A lthough few readers selected their "all-time favorites" from the "weddings" and "college graduation" editorial categories, those two subjects were always foremost on our minds in the early days of compiling our June issues. Not just any college graduation, however. Until he died in July 1970, Yankee Magazine founder Robb Sagendorph (his portrait is included in the painting on the front cover of this book) made sure it was always something to do with Harvard's graduation. (He was Class of '22.) But even Robb enjoyed tossing the occasional gentle barb at his alma mater, often pointing out three popular misconceptions about Rev. John Harvard. "One is that he founded Harvard College," he'd say. "Another is that he's buried beneath his monument in the Old Phipps Burial Grounds in Charlestown, and the third is that the statue in Harvard Yard is he!"

The "weddings" category was more wide-ranging. We utilized everything from old wedding portraits to wedding-cake recipes to abandoned churches in "House for Sale" (such as "How to Have a Church Wedding in Your Own House" in 1980) to the occasional fiction piece involving wedding ceremonies that, according to a fairly predictable number of angry subscribers, "came too late."

In the following 22 pages, neither of these June categories appears. The top vote-getters involve lobstermen, Staffordshire china, a trip on a barge, and the Massachusetts lady who remembers going down with the Titanic! June weddings and Harvard College just didn't stand a chance!

No heat, electricity, fresh water, sewage system, or safe way to get into this 1984 "house for sale" — Chatham Rock Lighthouse in the middle of Stamford, Connecticut's harbor. A New York banker paid $230,000 for it, saying he'd always wanted a lighthouse.

– photograph by David Witbeck

Marjorie Newell Robb of Westport Point, Massachusetts, holding photographs of her father, who went down with the Titanic, and her mother, who spent the rest of her life in mourning.

*Here's a magazine editor's dream! A living person — right in
Westport Point, Massachusetts, no less — who had actually been aboard the* Titanic!
*Although 92 years old at publication (the June 1981 issue), she remembered
fascinating personal details of the disaster, too.*

I Took a Voyage
on the R.M.S. *Titanic*

BY SCOTT EYMAN

At the age of 56, Mr. Arthur W. Newell of Lexington, Massachusetts, had finally attained that station in life to which he had long aspired. Born in Chelsea to poor parents, he had risen by dint of his unquestioned integrity and single-minded attention to detail to be chairman of the board of the Fourth National Bank of Lexington. A somewhat distant, austere man with a Vandyke beard, a student of the Bible, a mediocre-to-poor keyboard player, he had a tendency to bring the office home with him. When that happened, his wife and three daughters would form a quartet and play some classical music to relax him and bring him out of his shell.

In 1909, Newell had taken his family on a European trip, one of those leisurely three-month junkets that people had time and money for in those days. Late in 1911, he decided to repeat the adventure, but his wife, who had a delicate disposition, and a daughter, who shared her mother's temperament, begged off, having found the arduous embarkings and disembarkings infinitely wearing.

So it was that in February of 1912, Arthur Newell and daughters Madeline and Marjorie set sail for Europe. They traveled to the Pyramids (Marjorie Newell celebrated her 23rd birthday in Cairo), and made exhaustive investigations of the Holy Land: Port Said, Jaffa, Bethlehem, Jericho. After taking a ship to Marseilles and traveling thence up to Paris, the Newells arrived in Cherbourg, where they were to start the voyage home.

There the daughters found one more surprise awaiting them, for A.W. Newell had booked first-class passage for himself and his daughters on the maiden voyage of the world's largest ship. She was 11 stories high, a sixth of a mile long, weighed over 46,000 tons, and had a top speed of 24 to 25 knots. Their trip home would encompass another week or so of sumptuous luxury and a triumphant arrival in New York harbor before the glorious vacation would be over.

The Newell girls would certainly have something to tell their grandchildren: what it was like to sail on the world's greatest ship, to travel in the company of some of the world's richest men, like John Jacob Astor, or Isidor Straus of Macy's Department Store, or Benjamin Guggenheim. In short, Marjorie and Madeline Newell would have had the inestimable pleasure of having sailed on the White Star Line's crowning achievement, one of the jewels of the post-Edwardian age, the R.M.S. *Titanic.*

"It was a most beautiful ship," says Marjorie Newell Robb, today in her low-ceilinged 200-year-old house, originally built for a minister, in Westport Point, Massachusetts.

She is 92 years old now, only slightly hampered by her years, endlessly gallant and feisty about life and frankly hesitant to recall the events that irrevocably altered that life. Even now, almost 70 years later, a feeling of intense melancholy comes over the former Marjorie Newell as she recalls the last days in the short life of the ship they called unsinkable.

"The *Titanic* was a massive affair in every way; four enormous smokestacks, carpets that you could sink in up to your knees, fine furniture that you could barely move, and very fine paneling and carving. Everything on the ship was of the finest quality.

"We were, I think, five days out of Cherbourg; I do know that it was Sunday night. We had finished a lavish dinner in the corner of the magnificent dining room and had gone up to one of the foyers. We just sat there for a while, feeling very refreshed and invigorated after this lovely trip. My father smiled and said, 'Do you think you can last till morning?' You see, we had rather large appetites, and he was kidding us about whether we'd need more food. While we sat there in the foyer, I distinctly remember that John Jacob Astor and his wife walked by, looking very affable and distinguished.

"Well, as the evening wore on, my sister and I decided to retire, so we went to our rooms.

"I don't honestly remember how long we'd been down in our rooms, but we suddenly felt and heard a great vibration; its size was just staggering."

It was 11:40 P.M. on April 14, 1912, latitude 41°46'N, longitude 50°14'W. The grinding, tearing sound that had awakened Marjorie Newell and her sister was made by an iceberg shearing a 300-foot gash in the *Titanic*'s bow, helped along by the ship's rapid 22.5-knot speed and the fact that a half-dozen warnings about drifting ice had been more or less ignored by the captain.

Marjorie Newell sat up in bed, won-

"We suddenly felt and heard a great vibration;
its size was staggering."

> **"Very soon after the noise, there was a knock at the door. It was Father. 'Put on warm clothing and come quickly to the upper deck,' he said. We obeyed. We always obeyed Father."**

dering what had happened. Far below, in the ship's boiler room, what seemed like the entire starboard side of the ship collapsed, the sea flooding in over the watertight bulkheads.

On the upper decks, little seemed to be wrong at first. The *Titanic* lay dead in the water, three of her four funnels blowing out steam with a large, thundering noise. Yet somehow Marjorie Newell's father knew something was terribly wrong.

"Very soon after the noise, there was a knock at the door. It was Father. 'Put on warm clothing and come quickly to the upper deck,' he said. We obeyed. We always obeyed Father."

Several minutes later, the Newell sisters arrived on the top deck. There was no moon that night, but through the thickish fog that surrounded the ship it could be seen that the sky was full of stars, and she remembers that the water was perfectly clear, perfectly smooth.

On the starboard well deck, near the foremast, lay several tons of ice that had been shaved off the iceberg by the recent collision.

"When we arrived on the top, there were really very few passengers about; I believe we were among the first. And it was quiet; everybody was so stunned and frightened that hardly anybody was speaking at all."

Slowly the decks began to fill with people wearing incongruous combinations of clothes: bathrobes, evening clothes, turtleneck sweaters, fur coats.

About 25 minutes after the crash, the ship's crew began preparing the wooden lifeboats, 16 of them, eight to a side, as well as the four collapsible canvas lifeboats. If filled to capacity, the 20 boats would hold 1178 people. But on that cold April night, there were 2207 people on board the *Titanic*.

Distress rockets began to be fired and the ship's "CQD," the forerunner of SOS, was picked up on the Cunard ship *Carpathia* at 12:25. The *Carpathia* was 58 miles away and radioed that she was "coming hard."

By one o'clock in the morning, the bow of the *Titanic* was slowly moving deeper into the water and the ship had developed a nasty list to port. Passengers and crew alike moved over to the star-

board side in an attempt to restore her balance. Slowly the wounded ship regained its equilibrium. Still there was no panic; rather, the busy, scurrying silence had taken on an intense, dreamlike quality. And Marjorie Newell was about to leave the *Titanic* under considerably less glorious circumstances than her father had anticipated.

"I believe we were in the second boat to be lowered. The ship was listing rather badly, and we were at a great height. The boat we were on had only one boatman. There were no supplies and everything was ill prepared. My father said, 'It seems more dangerous for you to get in that boat than to stay here,' but he hustled us into the boat anyway. Father stood there just as stately and calm as if he were in his living room.

"We were lowered. Most of the people in the boat were women and they were very frightened; nobody was saying anything. I thought to myself, 'You have to help where you can,' so I took hold of an

oar and rowed and rowed. I was young then, and strong.

"We got a distance away and we could see the ship was listing badly; people were in the water, gasping and yelling for help; one rocket after another was going up."

At 1:55 A.M., the last distress rocket was fired and all the lifeboats but one had been launched. By this time, the ship was at something approaching a 25-degree angle, with the forecastle head very close to the water, and the remaining passengers and crew moving towards the stern of the ship. In her lifeboat, Marjorie Newell looked on with mingled horror and fascination.

"In a way, it was beautiful; every light on the ship was on, and each porthole was illuminated. And then, across the water, came this enormous, awful roar."

As the bow had plunged deeper, the stern had tilted higher. The sound resembling some monstrous metal beast in battle that came across the water to the waiting lifeboats was nothing less than

– Culver Pictures

Every light was on, each porthole illuminated, as the liner went down.

everything on board the ship breaking loose. As Walter Lord describes it in *A Night to Remember*, "Twenty-nine boilers ... 800 cases of shelled walnuts ... 15,000 bottles of ale and stout ... tumbling trellises ... the fifty-phone switchboard" — everything went tumbling end over end.

Now, finally, the *Titanic* rose up, almost majestically, perpendicular to the water, sending people on board catapulting, skidding, sliding, and screaming into the water. The lights of the ship flickered once, flashed again, and finally went out.

And there, after a minute or two at a 90-degree angle, the ghastly rumbling roar mixing with terrified screams, the hull outlined now only by the red and green running lights and the clean white light of the stars reflecting on the placid water, the *Titanic* began to go down, moving at a slant, picking up speed as she went. When the water closed over the flagstaff on the stern, it was 2:20 A.M.

"I can remember, to this day, the noise the ship made as it went under," says Marjorie Newell Robb, trying hard to maintain her composure. "You could actually feel the noise, the vibrations of the screams of the people, and the sounds of the ship.

"I don't really know what happened on board after we left. People have asked me if the ship's orchestra was playing 'Nearer My God to Thee' as the legend has it, but I don't think so. I know I didn't hear it, but that may be because we were far away by that time, as far away as we could get."

As the morning broke, the *Carpathia* arrived, and the survivors, some 705 rowing, floating, sobbing, shocked men, women, and children, could at last see just where they were.

The lifeboats were scattered over four square miles of water. Surrounding them and separating them were dozens of small icebergs as well as three or four large ones 150 to 200 feet high. Off to the north and west, five miles away, there began a field of ice that stretched on forever. The spot where the *Titanic* had gone down was marked only by flotsam: crates, deck chairs, rugs, a few life belts, and one dead body, all rapidly being dispersed by the gentle waves.

Slowly, the survivors began boarding the *Carpathia*.

"Seeing all the icebergs around shocked us; it proved how dangerous our passage had been, and how irresponsible the *Titanic*'s Captain Smith, who went down with his ship, had been. Anyway, we wanted to get aboard the *Carpathia* as fast as we could, so we could be reunited with our father. It never occurred to us that Father hadn't gotten off; we didn't realize how few had been saved.

"We climbed onto the ship and there was a silence like a funeral. The *Carpathia* by that time was loaded with *Titanic* survivors. People were lying all over the deck, trying to find someplace to rest.

"Father wasn't there. But I was so proud of him, that he'd abided by the rule of the sea: women and children first. Some men didn't. I know I sat beside a man on the *Carpathia* who had shoved aside women and children to save his own life. Why, even John Jacob Astor got his wife on a boat, but never got off the ship himself."

Shortly after nine o'clock the *Carpathia* had picked up everybody left alive and turned towards New York. Arthur Newell, who just 12 hours before had paused to muse on his daughters' healthy appetites, was listed among the missing.

"We reached New York on Thursday and were hurried over to the old Manhattan hotel where my mother and other sister were waiting. My mother had seen lists of those who had been saved, but she was hoping that there had been an oversight. I can see her now in the hotel corridor, her arms outstretched, giving a howl of despair when she saw that only her two daughters had been saved and not her husband.

"Mother turned down an offer of a settlement from the White Star Line. No, she never asked us for details; she didn't want to talk about it, and she forbade us ever to speak of that night. She wore black or white for the rest of her life. When she died, at the age of 103, she was still in mourning."

Two weeks after the *Titanic* disaster, the body of Arthur Newell was washed up on a Newfoundland beach. Identified by some distinctive jewelry and a pocket diary, he was buried in Lexington's Mount Olive cemetery.

Six years later, Marjorie Newell, who had been misidentified as "Alice" on the list of survivors, married and began her own family, her own life. Throughout her married and professional life, raising her children, helping to found the New Jersey Symphony, she respected her mother's wishes and refused any and all inquiries about her experiences on the *Titanic* with a polite but firm, "I don't like to talk about it."

And, in truth, she doesn't. A most definite-minded, jut-jawed, matriarchal woman, whose strength of character is complemented by a distinctly coquettish femininity, Marjorie Newell Robb still grows noticeably upset, almost distraught, when she recalls that endless night of almost 70 years ago.

Still, there are some things that have to be faced, and the daughter was not at all like her brooding, isolated mother.

In 1960, after the deaths of both her mother and her husband, Marjorie Robb took a trip to Europe. The itinerary included a stop in Litchfield, England, the hometown of the *Titanic*'s Captain Edward Smith.

"Of course, as far as I'm concerned, Captain Smith is a very unpopular man. I wanted to see the statue of him they have at Litchfield, but the main reason I was going there was to see the exquisite cathedral they have there, with its gorgeous carving.

"As I went into the cathedral, the organ, a favorite instrument of mine, burst forth into magnificent music, flooding the church.

"I walked down the aisle and stood there, terribly, terribly moved. I didn't even seem to be on earth; I was somewhere else. It was as if I was ascending. I felt that here, at long last, was the end of the *Titanic* story. My father had given his life to save me, and now that I was free of everything else, it was up to me to make the decisions as to what I wanted to do with the rest of my life. But the *Titanic*? For me, it was over with."

So now, Marjorie Newell Robb, like Melville's Ishmael, is left to tell of the mighty ship. Considered unsinkable, it sank on its maiden voyage, taking with it all the interlocking assumptions about modern man and the perfectability of his works, the smug, hubristic self-assurance of the Gilded Age. For along with A.W. Newell and 1502 others, the *Titanic* took with it an entire insulated way of life.

"The irony of it all is so striking," says Arthur Newell's last surviving daughter. "The unsinkable ship, all the money that those men had that was of no use to them at all. And the irony even touched my father. One of the ways we identified his body when it washed up was an onyx ring that he always wore. One of my grandchildren wears it now. And on that ring, you see, is a carving of Neptune, King of the Sea."

Although these observations appeared in Yankee *back in June 1976, nothing has basically changed since then. And everyone has always told us it was the only true (some said "painfully honest") description of the Maine lobsterman they'd ever read.*

Maine's Offshore Renegade

BY LEW DIETZ

Lobstering has been called Maine's largest "little business." Although "business" is hardly the word for this operation, its annual landed catch of around $27.5 million must be accepted as a boon in a state where only the woods can be classified as "big."

Not so easily translated into figures are the spin-off assets this seagoing industry brings to coastal Maine. California offers Disneyland as a prime tourist attraction and New York has its Rockefeller Center. Once in Maine, travelers are likely to head for the first lobsterman. They may not find what they expect, for as one local observer put it recently, only a show-off will say "ayuh" in front of a stranger.

It is reasonably safe to believe anything about this coastal breed since there's a modicum of truth in anything one may hear. The Maine lobsterman is the salt of the earth and the sock in Mrs. Murphy's chowder. He works from dawn to dark for a hard buck and he makes such a good thing from his profession that he knocks off work for three months of the year to avoid a confiscatory tax bracket.

One common misconception should be scotched, however. The myth of taciturn lobstermen you can forget about. Occasionally you may run into some waterfront codger who considers a grunt sufficient response to a question, but, by and large, Maine lobster-catchers are as vocal a breed as you'll find on the face of the earth. Not only will lobstermen talk; they will argue, protest, pronounce, and state their personal views at the drop of a bait bag.

Although the lobsterman is not congenitally a dissembler, he's not above peddling misinformation upon occasion. Phil Haines was overheard telling an innocent visitor that what he used for bait were bricks soaked in kerosene, adding that sometimes in the shedding season lobsters hanker for peanuts.

Voluble though he may be, there is one thing a Maine lobsterman will not discuss. He'll never tell you how well he's doing. He most certainly won't admit he's doing well. If he says he's "catching a few," you may multiply a "few" by any given number and arrive at the approximate truth. He considers his day's catch classified information and will go to elaborate pains to avoid close scrutiny when he dumps it into his lobster car.

Says lobster buyer Herb Elwell, "I'd tear my right arm off before I'd tell what anyone is catching or how many traps

he's fishing. If I couldn't keep a secret I wouldn't be buying lobsters very long."

A Texan may be tempted to exaggerate his affluence: the Maine lobsterman does everything he can to minimize it. It appears to be a tenet of his credo to perpetuate the canard that Maine lobstermen live on a bare subsistence level. They call their traps "poverty boxes" and wear their clothes until even the patches are threadbare. Making good money, certainly anything into four figures, is an embarrassment.

Some years ago I mentioned in a story about a Winter Harbor lobsterman that he owned a Lincoln Continental and a grand piano. I thought the fact was interesting. The subject of the article considered the revelation an invasion of privacy and said so in no uncertain terms.

Unreasonably perhaps, Maine lobstermen accept the Internal Revenue Service's interest in their incomes with little grace. They term an investigation of their books harassment. In the course of a recent investigation, the Maine IRS director stated, "the degree of noncompliance with tax laws we found among lobstermen was most disturbing."

For their part, the lobstermen find such bureaucratic scrutiny not only disturbing but farcical. One lobsterman made the acerbic point that IRS men don't know the first thing about lobstering. "I deducted $1000 for twine I use to make trap heads. This fellow tried to tell me that twine was for tying up packages and that I couldn't have tied up that many packages in a year."

The fact that the Internal Revenue Service finds Maine lobstermen difficult should surprise no one. If a brief may be made presenting Maine as America's last frontier, the Down East lobster-catcher should be Exhibit A. The phrase "rugged individualist" fits him like a glove. He is freewheeling, free-living and freethinking. Like the Old West homesteader, the Maine lobsterman lives by unwritten laws and is not reluctant to enforce them in his own way.

The "wars" that have been going on for decades between the fishermen of Vinalhaven and Matinicus islands over fishing territory prompted one local newsman to remark, "When people get tired of seeing Westerns on TV we can always give them some 'Easterns.'"

According to Maine laws, anyone with a proper license may fish for lobsters in any waters under the state's jurisdiction. The tight fraternity of lobstermen has custom-hallowed laws governing the matter, and anyone wishing to break into the profession had better believe it.

A carpenter may become a carpenter by investing in a set of tools. Lobstermen view any newcomer as an interloper and treat him accordingly. And the fellow who proceeds without thought to the traditional proscriptions is in trouble. If he moves into occupied territory or if he sets his traps too close to those of an established fisherman he may be given the courtesy of a warning — typically, two half-hitches around one of his buoy spindles. If such a broad hint isn't enough, he might find his traps damaged. Repeated transgressions may bring the ultimate reprisal — offending traps may be cut off and rendered irretrievable.

For a number of good reasons, offenders are seldom confronted personally. First of all, trap-cutting is illegal and, even by the lobsterman's private code, reprehensible. In fact, Maine lobstermen are slightly paranoid in the matter of tampering with the traps of another. When his traps aren't producing as he thinks they should, the lobsterman's first thought is that someone is pilfering them. Hoping to confirm his suspicions, he may tie invisible threads on his trap door, or tie a slip knot on his warp. He prefers to take care of the matter in his own way, but he may go so far as to notify a coastal warden.

The concept of territoriality has existed among Maine lobstermen for a hundred years. Extralegal though the system may be, it's difficult to envision how any semblance of order could be maintained without it. All things considered, it's amazing that there's no more trouble than there is. As one lobsterman put it, "How do you think a bunch of farmers would get along if they all planted potatoes in the same field?"

The main service such a system performs is to limit membership in the competitive profession. Even so, the estimated 1.8 million traps being fished today in Maine is more than double what it was 10 years ago. This suggests that there *are* ways for a newcomer to enter the guild despite the obstacles.

The simplest way to break into the lobstering trade is to have a lobsterman father. If you have a grandfather lobsterman as well, all the better. Although there exists no legal footing, fishing territory may be inherited, and so rooted is the custom that no one has even attempted to take issue with it.

Take the case of Sherwood Cook of Martinsville. Both his father and grandfather were lobstermen, and the rights to the fishing ground around Little Green Island accrued with their ownership of that island. Cook, a graduate engineer, was working in New Jersey when his father died. Since lobstering rights have no legal sanction and traditionally cannot be held except by use, Cook had to decide whether to come home or allow his rights to lapse. It didn't take him long to conclude that a productive fishing territory in Maine waters is not something to turn one's back on. He came home and claimed his patrimony.

Although they seldom agree among themselves, lobstermen of each Maine cove tend to band in a loose confederation to maintain surveillance over the precinct. If a youngster in high school wants to put out a few traps his presence is usually suffered so long as he obeys the code. Once out of school, he's not apt to find much resistance if he decides to become a full-timer.

An outsider isn't accorded the same tolerance, and an "outsider" in Maine is anyone living beyond the outskirts of town. Nor is a local adult who goes into

(continued on page 144)

The fact that the Internal Revenue Service finds Maine lobstermen difficult should surprise no one.

– illustrations by Mark Kelley

141

In June 1979, America's most famous lobster cook,
Bertha Nunan, revealed to Yankee Editor Mel Allen . . .

The Secret to Cooking Perfect Lobster

From the weekend before Memorial Day until the last weekend in September, Bertha Nunan, perhaps America's most famous lobster cook, begins her days at dawn in the tiny fishing village of Cape Porpoise, Maine, not with crustacean but with crust.

This is when she begins the first of her 25 daily pies. In the corner of her house she calls "my pie shack," she bakes apple, blueberry, and chocolate cream pies. She has started her summer days like this since 1956. Sometimes she wonders "what all my pies would look like stacked together."

When the pies are removed from the oven and set to cool, she starts work on her brownies. And when the brownies are cool it is time to think of the evening ahead, when the pastries, along with their maker, will go to Nunan's Lobster Hut, a nondescript clapboard building sandwiched between Route 9 and a salt marsh in Cape Porpoise.

The kitchen is small, filled with the sweet fog of lobsters and clams steaming in blue enamel pots. A tank is filled with local lobsters, many caught by Bertha's 19-year-old son, Richard, who begins his days, as his father and his grandfather once did, hauling traps from the icy waters offshore.

From this humble setting emerged one of only three four-star ratings awarded by traveling gourmets Jane and Michael Stern to restaurants in New England. To the regulars who forsake the fancy lobster houses in the Kennebunkport environs for the hard wooden booths of Nunan's, the recognition came as a mixed blessing. It's never been easy to get into Nunan's in summer. With *Newsweek* sending their readers there as well, the possibilities for these lobster lovers seemed disastrous.

In a good year (and the definition of a "good year" in the lobstering industry is revised downward each year) Maine lobstermen will sell some 20 million pounds of lobsters. Only a tiny fraction of those

Bertha Nunan, of Cape Porpoise, Maine.

will be cooked the way lobstering families have cooked lobsters for generations. It is the way Bertha Nunan learned from her father-in-law, Captain George Nunan, the way she cooks lobster today.

"When people ask me the secret," Bertha says, "I tell them. Then they look at me and say, 'But we don't cook them that way.' And I think, 'Well, they will now, I bet.'

"The secret to cooking lobsters is not to murder them. Give them a nice, slow, respectable way out. Don't put them in boiling water, and don't drown them in too much water.

"Boiling them in a lot of water just boils their flavor out and too much water waterlogs them. I put in two inches of water, whether I'm cooking two lobsters or 14. I take a salt container and with the spout open I pour it three times around the pot, then, plop! at the end (about three teaspoons). When the water is boiling, put in the lobsters, put the lid on, and steam them for 20 minutes. Not a

minute less or a minute more. That's how Grandfather (Captain George Nunan) showed me and I've done it his way ever since.

"When they're done," she adds, "draw up your butter and serve the lobster with a dish of vinegar as well. Now the next step is what a lot of people, and practically all restaurants, ignore. It's why people tell me our lobsters taste the best of any they ever had.

"I always wash the pot after cooking each lobster. Lobsters are scavengers and they can get pretty greasy from the bait. Look in the pot the next time you cook them and you'll see a sediment from the shell. So I always put in fresh salted water for every batch of lobsters.

"I'll never stop being surprised at what some people will do to a lobster. Some folks, to save time, precook their lobsters. When people arrive, they throw them in boiling water for a minute. That's the worst thing you can do. The lobster just fills with water. If you're eating lobster in a restaurant and when you crack it open water spurts everywhere, you can bet they just threw a precooked lobster in boiling water.

"When you buy lobsters," she says, "you should know that from winter to summer the lobsters are hard-shelled. They're packed full of meat then, and you need fewer lobsters for a pound of meat if you're making a stew. But I prefer them when they're soft-shelled. They're sweeter then."

Cooked lobsters are placed on trays next to a bag of potato chips and a hard roll and butter. "We're not frilly," says Bertha without apology. There are few frills inside the eating area either. Heat is provided on cool summer evenings with ancient gas space heaters. There are several sinks along the walls with a roll of paper towels for butter-smeared hands. A refrigerator filled with soft drinks and beer sits in the open, and newspaper stuffed into a crack above a window ledge is dated June 13, 1973.

But no matter. The spartan atmosphere inside reinforces the impression, felt immediately upon entering, that dry land has been left behind at the door; inside the Hut you are afloat in the seafaring legacy of generations of Nunans.

The wooden lobster buoys dangling from the ceiling are emblazoned with a slash of crimson against white — the Nunan trademark for three generations of lobstermen. Strong, thick netting from the days when Nunan men gill-netted off the Grand Banks is stapled to a wall, and faded photographs of sturdy men in fishing togs line the walls as though the restaurant has become their public album.

The painting of the *Sadie Nunan* draws the attention of the customers, who, in this informal atmosphere, roam about, bibs beneath their chins, tracing the yellowed history of their hosts. The *Sadie Nunan* was the greatest in a fleet of seven Nunan schooners that Bertha describes proudly as "making Cape Porpoise prosper."

If they look closely at the photos, people will notice the short, sturdily built man standing beneath a stately elm tree. The tree, which was in front of the present restaurant, is gone, and there is no way for the curious to know that their meal and Bertha Nunan's methods of preparation really began under that tree, when Captain George Nunan decided one hot summer's day to sell some lobsters, the way kids sold lemonade, from his front yard.

"Captain George left gill-netting and came home to Cape Porpoise to go lobstering in 1932," relates Bertha. "About 1951 he just set a kettle and cooking stove beneath that elm tree and cooked up a batch of his lobsters the way I do now. People passing by stopped. He'd sell the first one for $1.25, then 80¢ for every one after that.

"People told him they were the best lobsters they'd ever eaten. Pretty soon he had more people stopping by that elm tree than he could handle. In 1953 he converted his garage into a kitchen, where we work today. He built a tiny dining room with benches lined up along the walls.

"I came along," she says, "in 1956 when I married his son Clayton. Clayton had grown up next to where the Hut is now. He was a fine lobsterman; he fished 200 traps and in summer brought all his catch here. I started working at the Hut that summer. I scurried around so much

Grandfather called me 'Hoppy' and the name stuck. Even today when people come in and ask for Bertha, my girls will say, 'There's no Bertha here.' "

Bertha seems as proud that her restaurant is considered a family place where friends come to say hello and then pitch in to help as she is of its reputation. "The girls who work for me are very dear to me," she says. "They call me mom. People ask me if they're my daughters, and I always say yes."

Her son Richard, now finishing his final year of high school, will soon marry his high-school sweetheart, who has worked at the Hut for five years. Richard has the quiet ruggedness of a fisherman. Though the business, with its 10,000 customers a summer, has grown too big for his 75 traps to supply all the lobsters, his contacts with local fishermen assure the Hut of the freshest lobsters around.

Richard got his own lobster license at the age of nine. Fishing with his grandfather and father he learned the seal-dotted waters off Cape Porpoise as well as his backyard. And when it was necessary to fish in earnest, he was ready.

"We lost Captain George in 1972," Bertha says, "and two years later we lost Clayton, too. It was on Father's Day and Richard was 14. He was determined he'd take his father's place. The *Little Roxanne* became his boat then, and he would leave the house at five, fishing for the Hut. My friends told me I had to open up. They said if I didn't open up within a week, that I'd probably never open up. I guess they were right. It's a good thing Captain George taught me everything he knew about cooking and Clayton taught me about the business. He must have known something."

Lobster Stew

¼ pound butter (not margarine)
1 pound freshly picked lobster meat
1½ quarts milk

Melt the butter in a fry pan. Let lobster meat simmer in the butter, cooking slowly. The meat should get very juicy and there should be no butter left in the fry pan. Meanwhile, heat the milk slowly, not letting it boil. When the lobster meat is finished it should be beet red. Add it to the milk. If you make it right you won't need any seasoning, or paprika for color.

This recipe will make four large servings. It will taste even better if put in the refrigerator overnight and then reheated.

"Frozen lobster meat can be used for a stew if necessary," Bertha says, "but I

don't like it for anything else. You can keep it only about a month before it gets rubbery."

Baked Stuffed Lobster

"When I have a crew party late in August this is what I make. I used to be able to eat two, in my young and foolish days. But I would suffer afterwards, because they are so rich. This recipe will serve four."
4 lobsters, 1¼ to 1½ pounds apiece
1 cup tomalley (the liver of the lobster, what people call "the green stuff")
½ pound butter
1 stick margarine
3 stacks saltines (¾ of a 1-pound box)
1 tablespoon Worcestershire sauce
1 tablespoon cooking sherry
1 tablespoon mayonnaise

Cook the lobsters. Split each down the middle. Remove the intestinal tract and the "lady," the small sac near the head. For the filling mix the tomalley (can usually be obtained at a lobster pound, or use the tomalley in the cooked lobsters), melted shortening, and the crackers, well crumbled. Add the Worcestershire sauce, the cooking sherry, and the mayonnaise. Mix well. Put in the split body cavity and pad over the top. Wrap the claws in tinfoil so they won't dry up. Bake at 400° until stuffing is crisp on top.

Corned Hake

"One of my favorite meals."
2½ pounds hake
Table salt
Salt pork
Boiled potatoes
Stewed tomatoes

Put the hake in a flat pan. Salt liberally. Leave overnight in a cool place and rinse off the next day. Taste the fish. If still salty, rinse again. Boil hake 15 minutes. While fish is boiling, fry salt pork slowly. Serve hake with salt pork, boiled potatoes, and stewed tomatoes.

Sautéed Lobster

Cut two or three slices of salt pork into small pieces. Add ½ teaspoon vinegar to cut-up lobster meat. Use all the meat from the lobster; when you sauté just the tail you don't get the nice red color you want. Sauté slowly, letting flavors absorb into the lobster.

"How do you think a bunch of farmers would get along if they all planted potatoes in the same field? . . ."

(continued from page 141)

lobstering as an avocation greeted with enthusiasm. It is the muttered conviction of the lobster establishment that such part-timers are taking unfair advantage by holding down two jobs and taking bread from the mouths of those who depend upon lobstering for a living. Also, there is the abiding suspicion that the fellow who puts out a few traps on the side is often using this as an excuse to be at sea so he can raid the traps of honest fishermen.

Crucial to any understanding of this salty breed is the point that lobstering is not so much a business as a way of life. The profit motive is operative and indeed as healthy a force as you're likely to find in our entrepreneurial economy, but it isn't the money that attracts the Maine man to the profession. The Maine lobsterman likes being a lobsterman. More to the point, few who have tasted the lobsterman's life are capable of adjusting to any other.

As Pete Rogers of Bailey's Island said, "I'm my own man. No one tells me when to go to work or when to quit. And no one can fire me. No amount of money could get me ashore. I'm not fit for it anymore."

Like the farmer, the Maine lobsterman is a prime producer. But unlike the farmer, who must drudge to replenish his soil, the Maine lobsterman demonstrates only passing concern for the future of his industry. He reaps but neither sows nor fertilizes. Only when faced with steadily

decreasing stocks does he consider the very real possibility of a depleted resource. Even then, the typical Maine lobsterman is reluctant to compromise his independence by banding with his fellows in an attempt to do something about it.

There are roughly 10,000 licensed lobstermen in Maine, and of these no more than 2000 are full-time operators. About 30 percent of these hardcore professionals are members of the Maine Lobsterman's Association (MLA) and the Southern Maine Lobsterman's Association, trade groups that were organized to speak for the lobsterman.

Quite clearly, the majority of Maine lobstermen don't care to have anyone speak for them; they prefer to speak for themselves. Nonmembers of the MLA are much in evidence at legislative hearings, but so fragmented is the lobster lobby and so diverse are suggestions and opinions that little comes out of such gatherings. This lack of concord caused one legislator to lament, "If only we knew what the lobstermen want, we might be able to do something for them."

Ed Blackmore, the current head of the MLA, obviously does not speak for the majority of fishermen when he pumps for marketing cooperatives as the answer to the industry's economic woes, since all but a few attempts in this direction have failed abysmally. His organization must always work around the lobsterman's inherent suspicion of rules and

regulations. Just as the lobstermen's lifestyle has given them little more than contempt for landlocked bureaucracies like the IRS, so too has it made many hesitate to join the MLA or a co-op, or to regard with anything but distrust the biologists who for years have tried to set up controls and establish conservation measures with an eye to saving the resource from overexploitation.

Donnie MacVane, a Casco Bay lobsterman, expresses his disapproval of state and federal interference in fundamental terms. "Here we have the state trying to impose trap limits, and then the federal government trying to give us more money to buy traps. I'll tell you, God will take care of trap limits. We don't need the state!"

In all fairness, the Maine lobsterman has some reason to be wary. He takes more than his share of the gamble inherent in this uncertain and speculative industry. The wholesale market traditionally has been dominated by a few dealers who can set prices within the boundaries of supply and demand and with due regard to personal economy. The dealer sees his handsome slice of the profit pie as legitimate since he acts both as wholesaler and speculator. He may be holding $10,000 worth of lobsters in his pound and lose his shirt in a collapsing market.

The Maine lobsterman points out that not only does he take all the personal risks attendant to his profession, but that he can get wiped out in a single storm.

144

– illustration by Mark Kelley

The lobsterman cannot accept as just the wide spread between the price he is paid for lobster and the cost of a lobster dinner at some posh restaurant.

Undeniably, lobstermen are exposed to occupational hazards in the conduct of their profession, but the fishermen themselves tend to minimize the dangers and attribute most of the fishing fatalities to carelessness. Men who work close to nature acquire a respect for her unpredictable crotchets. When seas run high or fogs close down, the prudent leave their boats at their moorings and let their traps "set over."

It's not so much that the lobsterman fears for his life as for the sizable investment he has in his boat. For, by and large, the Maine lobsterman is a fatalist: it's his philosophy that he'll go when his number comes up and not before.

The fact that few of them can swim is surely an expression of that fatalism. Of course there is the very good point that offshore water in Maine is no place to go swimming. In 40-degree water the swimmer and nonswimmer have approximately the same chance of survival.

The Maine lobsterman, for all his passion for independence, does operate on a loose version of the "buddy" system, if only because he's forever mindful of his vulnerability. A few years ago, a Casco Bay lobsterman fishing with his son sighted a boat going wide open with a pair of rubber boots upthrust over the transom. "Son," he said, "that just don't look right to me."

He was quite correct, as he discovered after rushing to the rescue. What had happened was that the confrere had got tangled in his stern lines and while he was reaching for his knife his foot had slipped. He'd gone over the side feet first and there he was, head in the icy water and hanging on for dear life.

Then there was that day when an Owls Head lobsterman failed to return to port. The local lobstermen to a man turned out for the search. When the missing boat was found adrift with no one at the helm and death by drowning was ruled, every boat in the cove remained at its moorings as the town's fishing fraternity attended the funeral.

The structure of the Maine lobster industry is as old-fashioned as the men who conduct it, and it's unlikely that this will change appreciably in the foreseeable future. A few years ago the Dead River Company, Maine's largest industrial conglomerate, went headfirst into the lobster business with the hope that substantial venture capital and sophisticated management techniques would streamline the operation and bring in some profits. When the considerable investment returned nothing but headaches, the corporation sold out and put their capital into less speculative and more manageable enterprises.

It would appear that the Maine lobster industry by its very nature is incapable of adjusting to modern streamlining. Technical advancement has made some changes, of course. Instead of the sweet-lined sloop of his grandfather's day, the typical Maine fisherman now runs a 30- to 40-foot power boat. Hydraulic pot-haulers have taken some of the bone labor from the job, and synthetic rot-resistant nylon serves for potheads and warps. But the oak-lathed trap hasn't changed basically for a hundred years and the lobster-catcher baits his traps and works his strings in much the same way as did his father and grandfather.

The Maine lobsterman may be aware of the uncertainties that lie ahead. He is mindful that 90 percent of the legal inshore lobsters are harvested each year; that the annual Maine lobster production has dwindled from a high of close to 25 million pounds to well under 20 million pounds. Individually, there is little the Maine lobsterman is willing or able to do about it. More efficient fishing methods and more sophisticated marketing techniques would only hasten the decline of the limited lobster resource. He's willing to submit to increased fees and to agree (if grudgingly) on some form of limitation on the number of traps he may fish, but yielding further to state and federal dictates would so compromise his independence as to render his traditional way of life unacceptable.

Those who choose the sea for a life and a livelihood have seldom been accepted as full-fledged members of our earth-bound society. Nor do their basic needs easily accommodate to the demands of the marketplace. The Maine lobsterman battles not only against the sea, but he is at odds as well with an economic system that rewards bigness and conformity and penalizes all forms of singular behavior.

It is inconceivable that the Maine lobsterman will renounce his anarchistic independence and settle for corporate security. More likely, he will continue to speak his mind and struggle along on his old course, guided by his own personal views of the inalienable rights to life, liberty, and the pursuit of happiness.

Antiques to Look For

Old Blue —
the Poor Man's China?

BY JANE GOYER

There was a time, not too long ago, when antique shops almost everywhere in the country would be pretty sure to have on display at least one vivid blue plate, platter, or bowl with a border of shells, flowers, leaves, scrolls, or eagles; on the face would be a view of some historic place. The authentic name of this particular dinnerware is "Historic Blue Staffordshire."

Today, most of this ware is in museums, where it rightly should be. If you should happen to find a piece, you would probably consider the price prohibitive. Pieces that used to sell for nickels, dimes, or quarters are now priced in the hundreds of dollars, and, in a few cases, up to a thousand dollars or more.

What makes this old ware so important? Some of the pieces are beautiful and impressive-looking, but many are not. The first early ware was crudely made, and the indigo blue color was used chiefly to cover the defects. It isn't even china — it is earthenware. It cracks and chips easily, which is why so little of it was preserved, although it was brought here from England in great quantities, especially following the War of 1812.

Staffordshire is a district of England known as "The Potteries." In this district lived the Wedgwoods, Enoch Wood & Son, Whieldon, James and Ralph Clews,

Stevenson, Stubbs, the Ridgways, T. Mayer, W. Adams, and others. These would be the names to look for on the underside of the pottery; Enoch Wood was the most prolific. The names of the towns would also be imprinted in the "biscuit": Burslem, Trent, Longton, Hanley, Tunstall, Stoke-on-Trent.

If your own mother was a china collector, she would probably not have any of this ware around — nor would your grandmother. The china they collected would be lovely Old Bristol, or new Wedgwood, or Haviland from France, or Leeds from England, or Irish Beleek. Or it could be Limoges, or Sevres, or Meissen. But the "old blue" had gone out of fashion and had been discarded. The ware your grandmother's mother had loved was put up in the attic, or brought out to the barn. It was called "the poor man's china," not fit for use.

Why, then, is it so important today? It is important because it is our heritage. On it are portrayed all the humble beginnings of our country as well as the brave and proud accomplishments — the early bridges, the first public buildings, the waterways, the ferries, the parks, the schools, the churches, the happenings, and the important people.

It has been said that if we could get together in one place all these platters

and plates and bowls, we would have the most comprehensive history of our country — a vast panorama revealing, as no textbook ever could, the achievements of our forefathers. There was no photography in those days. If a building was destroyed by fire or other means, it was gone forever. If any records were kept (and often there were none), they too were destroyed. Every once in a while a plate is found with a view of a building of which there is no record.

There are many fine books written about "old blue," so it would be foolish to go into details about borders, manufacturing methods, etc. This is far too lengthy a subject. Each potter used his own individual border, which was sometimes sold to others, or borrowed by others, which can make things pretty confusing if the maker's name is not on the piece. A great deal of study is required to become even a little knowledgeable on the subject. Most people find it more interesting to know how I became interested in the ware, and how I acquired the pieces in my collection.

I think my interest can be traced back to the time I accompanied my parents on a visit to my great-grandparents, who lived in New Bedford, Massachusetts. I was about five years old at the time. They lived in a small house with weath-

"Landing of the Pilgrims," by Enoch Wood, was made in 1820 for a banquet in Plymouth celebrating the 200th anniversary of the Mayflower's arrival. Samoset and Squanto are portrayed on it, and John Alden stands on the rock in the center.

ered shingles and a stone fireplace along one wall. Over the fireplace was a shelf that held five deep blue plates my great-grandpa had brought from over the sea. I fell in love with those plates. Great-grandma promised to leave me one of them when she passed on, but I never saw them again. In later years, I thought of them often, and wondered what had happened to them.

Years later, after I married, my husband and I bought an old house in a New England town. There was an old barn connected to the house, and it was full of odd things — old trunks full of old dishes, one of them a plate, deep blue,

marked "Harvard College, University Hall" by Stevenson and Williams, 1815. I was thrilled; I wanted to learn all I could about this plate. I went to the American Antiquarian Society building in Worcester, Massachusetts, where a very comprehensive collection of "old blue" hung on the walls — easy to study. I went again and again, and I bought books on the subject.

I began haunting antique shops and junk shops. Every vacation jaunt became a hunting expedition for "old blue" china. I warn you — if you once become interested you are hooked.

A memorable occasion was the visit to

a lovely old home in Falmouth on Cape Cod, which had been turned into an antique shop. Seeing nothing I wanted, I asked the proprietor, "Do you have anything in 'old blue'?" "Nothing very nice," she answered, "just a few old dishes I've been feeding the cat out of." "May I see them?" I asked. She went into the kitchen, and came back with two light blue plates, one a soup plate. They were dirty, chipped, and stained. But my heart jumped. I had seen those views somewhere. "How much?" I asked. "Oh! Give me a quarter, not worth much. Glad to get rid of them." I wasn't sure, not positively sure, but I insisted

Pieces that used to sell for nickels . . .
are now priced in the hundreds of dollars. . . .

---

that she take five dollars. She looked at me as though I were a bit of a nut.

I couldn't get back to my room fast enough. I got out my "Larsen," an authority, and flipped the pages. There it was: "Deaf and Dumb Asylum, first in country, Hartford, Connecticut, by Ridgway." Furthermore, the text in the book revealed that the view was rare. I still have that plate. It was my first big find and I'd hate to part with it.

Another pleasant memory is the time when I was on vacation in Maine, as usual indulging in my favorite pastime, searching for "old blue." There was a sign posted on a tree — "For Sale — Old Things and Stuff, at corner house, in garage." There was a table there, piled high with old dishes. Among them was one with a border of shells. That was Enoch Wood's border, and I dug it out. Oh no! It couldn't be! But it was: Castle Garden, Battery, New York, about 1820. It was a beautiful plate, deep blue.

Another plate I was thrilled to find, this time in an antique shop, high up on a shelf where it had rested unnoticed for a long time, was Wood's "Landing of the Pilgrims." This plate in light blue was made by Wood in 1820 for a banquet in

Plymouth to celebrate the 200th anniversary of the landing of the Pilgrims. The table was set with this ware, which pictured Samoset and Squanto, two Indians, and John Alden standing on a rock. The border is not a typical Wood shell border, but one of medallions and ships, with names in the medallions. This plate has been widely reproduced.

It's a funny thing, but you seldom do find one of these plates in the locale where it should be; that is, in the state for which it was made. But I found my "Landing of Lafayette" plate right in the proper spot — New York City. This is a very important plate, made by James Clews, one of the earliest potters in the Staffordshire district. Americans loved Lafayette, and the English trade took advantage of this; a deluge of blue china bearing his likeness was shipped over from England.

This plate of mine is one of a complete set of dinnerware. The scene on each piece depicts Lafayette's landing at Castle Garden in 1824. In the foreground are three sailing vessels and a tugboat. On one side are the Castle Garden (once a fort) with flag waving, and the long, long bridge from the Battery. Underneath all

are the words "Welcome Lafayette, the Nation's Guest, and Our Country's Glory." Also at the bottom is the title, "Landing of Lafayette at Castle Garden, New York, 16th August, 1824." The border is flower clusters.

I never thought I would possess one of these precious plates, and how I came upon one is an interesting story. I was invited to appear on a TV program in New York City. One of the other guests owned an antique shop there. Talking together, we found we shared a love for old china. He had, he told me, a few very old blue plates. Would I like to see them? What a wonderful time we had looking over those plates, one of which was my "Lafayette"; and when he sold it to me at a very reasonable price, I was overjoyed. It is mended, but still valuable; although many of these pieces were made, they are scarce today.

One of the most interesting plates in my collection is one portraying a church in Bradford, Massachusetts. It is one of those mystery pieces, for there is no record of such a church at that time. It is a lovely deep blue, with a Stevenson border. There were itinerant artists from England traveling around drawing scenes and buildings such as this one. William Guy Wall was one such artist; another was William Henry Bartlett. There were others, but there is very little information about them. The name Barber appears on some plates.

The "States" plates and platters were made by Clews. The deep blue border consists of names of the thirteen original states in medallions, separated by stars and loops of ribbon. In the center of each piece is a view of an important building, or a portrait of a hero of the day. Washington is on one and Jefferson is on another. I hunted for one all over the country, and I finally found it in an old barn, under a pile of junk. This one has the usual "States" border, and a picture of University Hall of Harvard College, sheep on the lawn, with a man standing on the left. The owner of the barn was an impoverished old lady who was selling all her possessions. She had thrown all the "undesirable stuff" on the floor in the barn. She was speechless when I offered her five dollars for it, and very grateful, too. "I almost threw it out," she said. And this one is perfect.

The "States Arms" plates and platters are usually confused with the "States" plates. These, too, are by Clews, and very beautiful in deep indigo blue. I have never been able to find one, but I have seen one or two in museums. The engravings

This plate by James Clews features a view of Harvard's University Hall, and the deep blue, star-studded "States" border.

were by Thomas Sully. The "Arms of Pennsylvania" is an exceedingly beautiful platter. The border is leaves, fruit, and flowers. The picture is of two horses rampant, a plow, a sheaf of wheat, scales, and a ship.

There is a story — how true it is I do not know — that molds were made for "Arms" plates and platters for every state that was in the union at the time of manufacture. But the one for the state of New Hampshire has never been found. If anyone could produce one, it would be worth a small fortune. I have searched all over the state but no one there has ever seen one.

Another memorable incident I will never forget happened at an open-house party in Groton, Massachusetts, given for a women's club. It was in a charming old house, with satiny floors and cupboards full of old dishes. Knowing my weakness, the hostess invited me to look around as much as I pleased. There were pieces of Lowestoft with armorial designs, very old cups without handles, lovely lustre pitchers of copper and silver hues, and samples of old willow ware and Canton china.

But what caught my eye and sent a flutter to my stomach was a large blue pitcher on the floor in a dim corner of the porch. It was filled with dusty strawflowers. "Oh, may I see that?" I asked the hostess. She looked at me in surprise. "That's just an old pitcher — it's chipped, and it's been hanging around for ages." I took it up and wiped off the dust and grime. I just couldn't believe it. It was a gorgeous blue, with a border of large flowers and a view of the Boston State House. It had a beautifully designed handle and lip and impressed in the "biscuit" was the name Stubbs.

Even though it had a chip on the rim, it was a wonderful find. I tried to tell my hostess what she had, but she was so skeptical, I think I could have bought it for a few dollars right then and there. I gave her the name of a nearby dealer to bear me out. She called me a few days later and said, "You were right — that dealer offered me $800 for the old thing." I would have given more if I could have afforded it.

There were many plates, platters, and bowls made in the early 1800s to illustrate the stories that were so popular at the time. Many of them were by Clews. The story of "Don Quixote" was transferred to many pieces with many different views. There was the "Wilkie" series too, each piece telling a story of simple everyday life in the early 19th century. There were views of the "Dr. Syntax Adventures," such as "Reading His Books," "Returning From His Tour," "With The Gypsies," and so on. They were made in bowls, cups, and tureens, as well as in plates and platters.

Most of these literary pieces are in museums now, but I acquired one in a most unusual way. I was asked by the editor of our local paper to interview an old man who lived alone in the woods, a hermit really. He was living in a shack, very dirty, and eating mainly out of tin cans. He had kept only a few of his former possessions, a few dishes in an orange crate. There was a vegetable bowl with a beautiful flower border in deepest blue and, on the inside, a view of Dr. Syntax "Home From His Tour." It was cracked and crudely mended, but still lovely. He told me that his mother had loved it, and he could not bear to part with it. Naturally, I did not ask him to. But not too long afterward, he brought it to the newspaper office. He was going into a home, and he wanted "that nice lady to have it." I was so thrilled. And of course I saw to it that he got reimbursed for it. I had it mended by an expert, and it has a place of honor in my daughter's old home. It has no mark on it whatsoever (many pieces didn't) but I have verified its authenticity from pictures in books.

Joseph Stubbs made a specialty of scenic views: New York Bay; Mendenhall Ferry; The Highlands; East River View, New York; Schuylkill River; Nahant Hotel, Boston; Hoboken, New Jersey; and many others. Ridgway, too, made many lovely views, and so did Jackson. Ridgway made the "Beauties of America" series, considered the very finest, artistically, of all the blue china. These were by J. and W. Ridgway, John and William. Borders are medallions of roses and leaves. There are 22 views in the series. I do not have one.

I found Stubbs' six-inch plate "Fairmount Park" in a dusty barn antique shop that had mostly junk. This is a pale blue plate with a border of scrolls and flowers, the view showing "Dam and Waterworks, Fairmount, Philadelphia." It is a charming piece showing a maiden in white seated on a rock, and a man standing nearby.

There was a plate made by J. & J. Jackson, a six-inch plate, "Bunker's Hill Monument." In the foreground is a group of people, and in the center the Quincy granite monument, surrounded by a fence with trees at right and left. The background looks like a row of three-story apartments. This monument was erected on Bunker Hill, Charlestown, Massachusetts, where the battle was said to have taken place. Lafayette laid the cornerstone for the memorial on June 17, 1825, but it was not completed until March 1843. There was a great deal of controversy over it. Many claimed that the battle was never fought there. Nevertheless, wouldn't it be wonderful to find such a plate for your very own, at this time of our 200th anniversary?

1985 Prices for Historic Blue Staffordshire

☞ Prices go up so rapidly that it is difficult to tell what a perfect historic blue piece might bring. The prices below are approximations by experts David and Linda Arman, whose absentee auction brochure is available by writing them at Box 353 A, RR1, Woodstock, Conn. 06281.

Landing of the Pilgrims (Wood Plate)	$100
Castle Garden (Wood cup plate)	195
Deaf and Dumb Asylum (16″ Ridgway platter)	650
Landing of Lafayette (10″ Clews plate)	210
Landing of Lafayette (Clews coffeepot)	1500
City Hall, N.Y. (10″ Ridgway plate)	185
Dr. Syntax (10″ Clews plate)	175
Fairmount Park (6″ Stubbs plate)	185
10″ States Plate (Clews)	275
10″ States Arms Plate (Clews)	550
Arms of Pennsylvania (21″ Clews platter)	7000
Boston State House (Stubbs pitcher)	650

Some fine books on the subject:
American Historical Views: Staffordshire China by Ellouise Baker Larsen
Standard Catalogues by Sam Laidacker
The Blue China Book by Ada Walker Camehl
Staffordshire Pottery by Thomas H. Ormsbee
Something Blue by Catherine Fennelly

Some 40 times a year a tug pushing an oil barge and 600,000 gallons of oil leaves Rensselaer on the Hudson and, 32 hours later, ties up in Burlington, Vermont. During the trip the two crews live in a special world all their own, although, in June 1982, they allowed our writer-photographer team to share it with them.

Bound for Burlington

BY LIONEL ATWILL
photography by Carolyn Bates

On a hot summer night on Lake Champlain when fog clings to the water like cotton candy to a gingham dress, you will hear the sound, feel it, too: DUM-DUM-DUM-DUM-DUM-DUM, a primitive throb coming from the air, the shore, the lake. The pulse is fast, your heart's rhythm on an uphill run. You may think it is Champlain's heart until someone who has seen the source by daylight tells you: barge.

In the morning you may see one in the middle of the lake. The profile is unremarkable — long, bulky, squat to the water. You can tell which way the barge moves not from bow spray or wake but from its changing relationship to the shore; the barge appears to stand still while the background rolls by. Unless you look with binoculars, you may not notice that the barge is nuzzled at her stern by a tugboat. The tug's great diesel engine makes that sound.

People who live along Lake Champlain — New Yorkers and Vermonters — grow accustomed to the barges. They know they carry fuel to Plattsburgh and Burlington — gasoline, kerosene, aviation fuel, and heating oil. They know they run from early spring through late fall. They know little beyond that, for the barges tend to their business with a monotony that stifles curiosity, and they are upstaged at every wave by spinnakered sailboats and flashy cruisers. The barges are simply . . . barges. DUM-DUM-DUM-DUM-DUM-DUM.

On board, however, a world of its own spins round.

August 6, the Pittston Oil Company dock in Rensselaer, New York, on the Hudson River: in the background sprawls the city of Albany; directly across the river a Chiquita banana boat off-loads. The barge *Stony Brook* and her consort, the tug *Laurie Kehoe*, are

Left: *From the pilothouse of a tug, pushing a 243-foot barge through the narrows of Lake Champlain looks difficult, but it is child's play compared to threading the barge through 60 miles of canal and 12 locks.* Above: *The crew calls Burlington a good port — "They don't treat you like an outsider."*

moored to the dock. The barge is discharging ballast — Lake Champlain water she carried when returning empty from Burlington so she would stay low in the water and fit under the bridges spanning the Champlain canal. The Hudson here is tidal, and as the tide comes in and the ballast goes out, the barge rises above the dock, showing her bulk. She is 243 feet long, 43 feet abeam. Loaded, her keel is 10 feet below the surface, her deck only four feet above it. The tug is 87 feet long and two-thirds the width of the barge. Subtract the 20 feet where the tug's bow tucks into the cleft in the barge's stern and the two vessels together are still longer than a football field.

When the 12 holding tanks are empty, dockmaster John Perkins, barge captain Bill Taylor, and Bill's assistant Charlie Cook crank valves and recouple the eight-inch feed line to take aboard No. 2 fuel oil — 113,400 gallons an hour. They monitor the transfer closely. Not a drop of oil spills. Only the heavy, noxious fumes wafting up through the tank vents reveal the cargo.

Five hours and 35 minutes later, the barge has taken on her full load — more than 600,000 gallons. She could hold more, but not without grounding in the canal, which is only half-a-catfish deeper than 10 feet. The pump shuts down. By measuring from the surface of the oil in each tank to the top of the vent, Bill and John compute the volume of fuel aboard. They double-check each other's calculations, factor in the temperature, and come up with an exact figure: 613,496 gallons of No. 2, enough fuel to fill over 980 tractor trailers, enough fuel to heat my house — maybe yours — for 1000 years.

The tug crew is on board now, captain, mate, two engineers, two deckhands, and the cook. They have stowed their bags in small cabins flanking the engine rooms and stored the groceries in the galley, which spans the tug's stern. The engineers coax the throb from their 1200-horsepower diesel; the deckhands scurry about taking up the cables linking barge to tug and stowing deck clutter; the cook fires his galley stove for coffee and caresses the carton of fresh tomatoes he has brought aboard; the mate and captain take to the pilothouse, ready to get underway. With no fanfare, the order comes down: "Shove off." The 86-inch prop churns the water and the tug swings away from the dock, pirouetting the barge around her bow line, then backs into the river until the barge swings through 180 degrees and points up-

stream. At 8 P.M. the trip to Burlington has begun.

Life on board settles in. The barge men, John and Charlie, who have minded the pumps all day, now have some time off to eat and relax in their quarters in the barge's stern. The tug crew, which functions independently of the barge — separate quarters, galley, and jobs — takes up watches: 6 to 12, 12 to 6, a routine broken only by hour-long meals straddling shifts to accommodate the men going on watch and those coming off. This 12-hour-a-day work schedule — work six, off six, work six, off six — will continue for a week; then the crews will rotate off tug and barge for seven days ashore.

In the galley Guido Liberatore, the chef, rustles up a light meal, light because it is now 8:30, three hours off the dinner schedule, and schedules on board are all. Full meals are served only on a change of watch; anything in between is

---

The deckhand's hourly rate adds up to $1172.04 for seven days' work, cabin (next to the engine room) and grub included. . . .

---

considered "light." On a narrow, built-in table extending the breadth of the galley are bowls of rice, potatoes, peas and carrots, sliced tomatoes, bread, and Wiener schnitzel — Guido's personal recipe. The off-watch eats first, then spells the rest of the crew. Meals — even light meals — are important on a tug.

It is dark now, and the lines controlling the spotlights forward on the barge are run up like giant clotheslines (which, in fact, they are) atop the pilothouse, where the captain, Jim Kehoe, stands watch. Jim, the son of Clayton Kehoe, who owns the *Stony Brook* and the *Laurie Kehoe* (named after Jim's younger sister), is not a stereotypical ship's captain. He is 31 years old, stands 5'9", has curly blond hair that fights to escape the grip of a baseball cap, a wispy mustache, and animated blue eyes. In the pilothouse he has the slightly nonchalant, one-hand-on-the-wheel manner of a weekend boater, but anyone on a barge will tell you he is as good a captain as you will find. Jim has spent two-thirds of his life on tugs; he has held a captain's ticket for a dozen of those years.

The first lock, the Troy lock at the entrance to the Champlain canal, confirms Jim's expertise. Maneuvering a football field of oil into a lock only a few feet longer and a foot wider than that football field is like threading a grocery aisle full of fat people with a three-wheeled cart loaded with beer — only harder. The barge responds to wheel and throttle in a laggardly fashion. If you want to turn left *now,* you should have cranked the wheel a minute ago. To complicate matters, as the barge approaches the confines of a lock, its 10-foot draft acts like a piston, piling up the water in front of it, water that fights back by shoving the barge astern or to the sides. Piloting a barge is not a skill to be learned overnight.

Three hundred yards before the lock, Jim slacks off on the throttle and eases the barge toward the left wall with gentle nudges of the wheel and considerable body English. The body English must help, for the barge kisses the wall, then, guided and eased along her course by deckhands wielding huge rope fenders, she slithers into the lock. The gates close. The lock floods. The barge and tug rise 14 feet and continue up the canal.

Before breakfast the next morning, the barge negotiates four more locks, rising a total of 68.3 feet. But then a fog rolls in, a creamy-thick fog that coats the water and shore with amorphous gray. The captain is called to the pilothouse. He takes the wheel from the mate and negotiates the invisible canal like a cat creeping down a dark alley. His whiskers are the radar screen and his knowledge of the water. When the fog lifts, the sixth lock comes into sight. "How did you get in here?" yells the lock tender. "I could hardly see the road *driving* to work this morning." Jim smiles, waves, and sips his coffee. Twenty years on the canal is the answer, but no one says a thing.

After breakfast and the change of watches, the workday begins. On the barge Bill and Charlie break out paint and brushes and set about the never-ending job of keeping things shipshape. On the tug the deckhand on watch, Clayton Kane, falls to the nautical ritual of chipping rust. The engineer coddles his engine, throbbing away at 800 rpm. The cook finishes the breakfast dishes and starts in on lunch, which is dished up as the barge passes through the ninth lock. Lunch is *not* another light meal: creamed corn, potatoes, bread, fish, clams casino, cole slaw, tomatoes, noodles, noodles with clam sauce, strawberry shortcake, and Kool-Aid. Guido is sort of a hero on board. He nurtures his boys with tender loving calories, and they, in turn, sing his praises to the radar mast. "You wouldn't believe some cooks," says David Blair, the mate. "Couldn't boil water. Couldn't *burn* water. But Guido, he's a *chef.*" "Just your basic seven-course meal," says Guido, blushing down to his white shoes.

Later, in the barge galley where Bill and Charlie must sling together their own meals, Bill comments on Guido's talent with a nautical aphorism: "You'll never find footprints on his grub receipts," meaning that unlike some cooks who blow most of their expense money for food on high times ashore and fill the galley with hot dogs and Spam with the leftover change, Guido buys honestly and serves the best. The bellies on all the crew — save those of the engineers who spend their watches in the saunalike engine room, where temperatures may peak at 125 degrees on a summer day — testify to that.

The Champlain canal runs 60 miles, from Troy on the Hudson to Whitehall at the foot of Lake Champlain. It was built in 1823, a 40-foot-wide, four-foot-deep channel. Since then it has been deepened and widened considerably, and its original locks have been replaced with massive concrete structures, wider now than the original canal. But the lock mechanism remains basically the same. When a boat or barge enters the lock from downstream — the low end — the gates close behind it. Valves are opened on the upstream side, allowing water to flood the lock, and the craft floats upward at four feet per minute. When the water in the lock reaches equilibrium, the gates are opened and the craft moves on. Going downstream, the procedure is reversed: the boat enters a flooded lock, the downstream valves are opened, the lock drains until the water level inside drops to the lower level, and the boat moves on.

There are 12 locks along the canal. Sailing, motoring, or steaming from the Hudson to Champlain, a boat is lifted by nine locks a total of 138.8 feet and, once over the height of land, lowered by three more locks a total of 43.5 feet. Thus a football field full of oil can climb from sea level to the 95-foot height of Lake Champlain.

For the rest of the afternoon the *Laurie Kehoe* and the *Stony Brook* move through those locks. Under bridges (the pilothouse lowers hydraulically to pass under the lowest bridge without decapitation) and parallel to roads they chug along at a sedate pace. Only once is there

a break in the routine when the barge hangs up on the canal bottom on the inside of a turn where debris and silt have piled up. She is not there for long; 1200 horsepower sees to that. The prop is reversed, the engine run up. The water foams like a giant chocolate soda, and ever so slowly tug and barge back away.

By supper time the barge has passed through the last lock at Whitehall and into Lake Champlain. The sailing is peaceful here — no locks, good water. Passing through the narrows of the lake where great blue herons peer down from skeletal trees, the off-watch gathers on the stern of the tug for a cup of coffee, a smoke, and talk of the things all seamen discuss: good ports (Burlington: "They don't treat you like an outsider there") and bad ones; pay ($16.32 per hour for a captain to $12.21 for a deckhand with time and a half on weekends) and union rules; amiable shipmates and miserable ones, who can make an 87-foot tug seem

smaller than a rowboat and a week's trip longer than a hitch in the Navy. There are stories of other tugs, other canals, other journeys. There are complaints about life on board, but underneath it all there is an unspoken understanding that no other life will do. Everyone in the crew travels a good ways to work the tug or barge; several come from around New York City, a few from as far away as Pennsylvania and North Carolina. They put up with the travel and the week away from home for the money, certainly — the deckhand's hourly rate adds up to $1172.04 for seven days' work, cabin (next to the engine room) and grub included — but there is more to it than that. There is a romance to boats, as Mark Twain attested. It gets in your blood, and, in fact, most of the men come from boating families or have married into them: Bill Taylor is Jim Kehoe's brother-in-law; Clayton Kane's dad captained a tug for years; David Blair's father cooks on one still.

In the pilothouse Jim Kehoe is at the helm again. He does not have the luxury of sipping coffee on the stern, of watch-

ing the herons fly by, of reminiscing about other tugs and other trips. He has the *Laurie Kehoe* to worry about. "We've had this tug only a few months," he says, throwing some body English to starboard in preparation for a right turn a half mile ahead. "She's mechanically sound, even though she's pushing 34 years old, but there's a lot of cleaning up to do. All that rust on the stern. The paint on the brass portholes. Lots of cosmetics. She sat at the dock for a year, and when you let a boat sit like that — don't keep right at her — she goes fast. But I'll get her cleaned up." He calls down to the deckhand to bring him a cup of coffee, then adds, "Get a rag and some brass polish, too." As the sun drops and the tug threads the buoys of the lower lake, Jim sips his coffee, nudges the wheel, and keeps one eye on the radar screen and the other on the deckhand, polishing brass.

The lake opens now; the difficult part of the trip is over. Unless a heavy fog rolls in or the lake kicks up a storm, the barge should be in Burlington before dawn.

And she is — 32 hours and 30 minutes after pulling away from the Pittston dock, the *Laurie Kehoe* and the *Stony Brook* tie up to the offshore pilings in Burlington harbor. The barge crew is bustling about in the dark. The moment the barge is secure, they couple the eight-inch line and start the barge's pumps. The oil is flowing before the sun cracks the horizon.

It will take eight hours to unload. Some of the crew may take the H.M.S. *Guido*, the rowboat stored on the stern of the tug, and visit the good port of Burlington for a few hours. Jim plans to don scuba gear and check the prop. Once the oil is off, however, the barge will pull out and head right back to Rensselaer. Without those 600,000 gallons of oil to push, they will make the return trip eight hours faster than the voyage up the lake. There they will fill up and make the trip again, repeating the schedule over and over until the storage tanks at Burlington are full or the canal freezes sometime in late fall, some 40 trips in all.

Only then is the routine broken; only then do the *Laurie Kehoe* and the *Stony Brook* head south, down the Hudson River and into the harbor of New York to serve their winter duty shuffling oil about the city.

Only then does the heartbeat of Lake Champlain, the DUM-DUM-DUM-DUM-DUM-DUM of the ever-present barge, fade.

A·JUNE
SAMPLER

WHAT TO DO WHEN YOUR CAR STEERING WHEEL COMES OFF

☞ Perhaps you have seen this situation depicted in old-time "comic" movies. As one who has survived this experience can testify, however, in the brief period between your perception of what has happened and the outcome, happy or tragic, there is little to laugh about. A feeling of surprise is quickly superseded by a feeling of utter helplessness. Endeavor to make this phase as brief as possible, and get on with the question of what to do. Note where the break has occurred, and if a sizable stub of wheel spoke remains attached to the column, you may be able to steer to some extent.

– Tom Payne

Or you may seize the nut that held the steering wheel (no pun intended) with the vise grips you should always keep handy, to improvise a tiller. Before trying these maneuvers, however, look over the road and the traffic situation. Is the car holding a reasonably straight course now that it's free to go whither it listeth, or is it veering to left or right? A reasonably quick thinker can cover these points in seconds.

Here is where most drivers make their mistake. If you have reason to believe you may get away with a fender bender or cut lip, you may spend your time bracing yourself, or trying to remember what your insurance covers. But if things appear hopeless, do not waste time on these trivialities, but proceed immediately to review your past life. Drowning persons have more time for this, and generally do an adequate job of it. If you waste too much time, you may not get beyond the time you flunked algebra, and may have to cut it short in order to allow a second or two to wonder whom your wife will marry, and time for a final curse, or commitment to the Almighty, depending on your religious persuasion. Some drivers do not review their lives, but, adhering to a custom common among American Indians, sing a death song. (*From "The Gentlemen's Manual for the Old and New Touring Cars" by Frank J. Smith.*)

THE BEGINNING OF MAINE'S VERSION OF "THE GRAND OLE OPRY"

☞ Jennie Shontell didn't set out to be a star. It happened quite by accident. Her husband, who had been a cook in Bangor, died in 1962. A few years later, when a small television station in Bangor decided to fill the late-night airwaves with a country amateur hour, Jennie was one of the first to appear.

The song she sang on that first show was "Bouquet of Roses," a standard country ballad. She fit right in with the flavor of the show, which was, in a word, loose. No one ever rehearsed. From a technical standpoint, the show looked as if someone had mistakenly flipped on a TV camera at a jam session when no one was watching. People walked in front of the camera as if it weren't even there. Sometimes it seemed as if the cameraman had fallen asleep when the picture

stayed with the host while someone could be heard singing. And with only a few microphones to go around, it sounded as if the band was playing underwater.

To everyone's surprise, the show caught on. Harry Stockley, another of the Jamboree regulars, says the show is popular because "Everybody doesn't try to be somebody else. We just get up there and play."

Stockley admits that perhaps the troupe would sound better if they occasionally rehearsed. But because most of them have regular day jobs and live in scattered places — Bucksport, Old Town, Cherryfield — rehearsals are difficult to arrange. "The only time we see each other is on Saturday," he explained.

Dick Stacey, a service station owner who took over the show after its first few

Stacey's Country Jamboree, featuring Jennie Shontell.

– Kip Brundage

years, agrees with Stockley. "We don't pretend to be anything we're not. If we're bad, we're bad." (*From "She's Singing Their Song" by Dennis Bailey.*)

THE CRACKERS YOU COULD STRANGLE ON

☞ I grew up in Vermont, not far from Montpelier, and remember the Cross crackers from my childhood in the late twenties and early thirties. You could still buy them in bulk, but I remember that mostly we bought them in large, oblong cardboard boxes that held several dozen crackers. My family always had a supply on hand. Everybody did. If there was ever a universal, multiuse food, the Cross cracker was it.

Those crackers were crumbled into milk as a breakfast cereal, and for lunches, too, crumbled into meat loaf and casserole dishes, split in halves and toasted to be served with melted cheese or creamed codfish, or they were just split and spread with fresh Vermont butter, honey, homemade raspberry jam or strawberry preserves, or a tuna and onion mixture. I sometimes spread a heavy layer of butter on the cracker halves and topped it with peanut butter, having learned from experience that one

The original cracker-barrel cracker.

simply could not eat those crackers spread with peanut butter alone without strangling. (*From "Death of a Cracker" by Lawrence F. Willard.*)

Since this article, excerpted here, was published, Vrest Orton's Vermont Country Store in Rockingham and Weston, Vermont, has purchased the old Cross cracker-making machinery and has these old-fashioned "Vermont Common Crackers" available for purchase.

– Austin Stevens

BOSTON GLOBE — Simmons is introducing the beauty rest adjustable bed. Press a button and it lifts your head to read or snack or watch TV. Other buttons cause vibrations for the massage of tired muscles and the lifting of feet over the head. . . .

NEWS ITEM: R. WILCOX DUBLIN, N. H.

...AND IF YOU CAN'T RAISE ANYBODY IN THEIR BOSTON OFFICE, TRY BEAUTYREST, INC. IN CHICAGO...

GOOD NEWS, BAD NEWS

☞ "At his best, Roosevelt was a political genius. But his very ability enabled him to lead our country into disaster when he was wrong." **William Christian Bullitt, then (1936) ambassador to France.** (*From "Do You Remember the Nation's Most Glamorous Career Girl?" — an article about "Missy" LeHand, F.D.R.'s secretary — by Joyce Palmer Ralph.*)

A · FAVORITE LETTER

THE LANGUAGE OF LOVE

☞ Reading "Hitler's Afrika Korps in New England" in the June issue was an opportunity to learn the facts behind a memory. As a young girl I worked in the Rexall Drug Store in Marsh Hill, Maine. Each morning when the POWs were transported from Houston to the farms to pick potatoes, the truck would stop there for the guards and driver to pick up their *Bangor Daily News* and coffee. I'm afraid they got very little attention from me because of one particularly innovative prisoner. As I looked out the huge storefront window, he would sing beautiful songs with soulful gestures. Though the songs were in German, the language of love is universal. As the days moved further into fall he progressed to dancing for me and holding up paper hearts, etc. His fellow prisoners apparently enjoyed his "windowpane" courtship and would crowd into one end of the truck to provide him with his tiny dance floor and would clap and stamp at appropriate moments.

Perhaps there is a middle-aged man somewhere in Germany who has told his children of the young girl in northern Maine, just as she has told hers.
Rita Stitham Gavin
Hastings-on-Hudson, New York

– Jan Hahn

Miss Alice Charry had her doubts about Captain Slocum's navigation.

So What If He Sailed Around the World?

☞ Some weeks later, as if in oblique apology, Captain Slocum invited the same crowd to sail from Fairhaven to Newport, for the races.

"I should have known better," Miss Charry said, "but the prospect was too exciting to miss."

Again they boarded the *Spray* on a fine summer day. Again Captain Slocum weighed anchor, and they put out in a light southwest wind.

"We sailed and sailed and sailed," Miss Charry sighed. At noon they opened the picnic baskets with which they had prudently provided themselves, and shared the contents with Captain Slocum. At night, to no one's particular surprise, they made port at Marion, 42 miles east of Newport.

"Father put his foot down after that," the Fairhaven woman recalled. "He said he didn't care if Josh Slocum had been commanding vessels for 25 years. I'd taken my last trip aboard the *Spray.*"

Why did a mariner of Captain Slocum's reputation allow this double fiasco to happen?

"I don't suppose he meant to," Miss Charry replied matter-of-factly. "I think he just got lost."

Champions of Slocum, bristling when told this tale, point out that he was seldom in much of a hurry to reach a destination (he dawdled for a month about starting around the world while a keyed-up press fumed and importuned) and that he doubtless went to Marion on purpose, because the *Spray* had a head wind.

"He was more writer and philosopher, sort of a seagoing Thoreau, than a navigator anyway," they add defensively.

To which Miss Charry was wont to counter, with polite but precise finality, "I don't know about *that.* All I know is that I don't understand all this fuss about his being a *sailor.*" (*From "Slocum Was No Sailor" by Genevieve M. Darden.*)

The Man Who Prowls the North Country

☞ It was in Worcester two years earlier where he first got on the trail of Rich Gedman, who in only his second year as a minor league catcher for the Red Sox is already being compared to Carlton Fisk and Jim Rice.

But two years ago he was a high school first baseman and pitcher, an enormous kid who stood 5′11″ and weighed 250 pounds. He had tremendous batting power, and for awhile the scouts hovered thick as flies. Then they left, disenchanted with his physical condition. He was painfully slow, and nobody could figure out where he could play.

Except Bill Enos. In his mind's eye he shifted Gedman to catcher, where his bulk could be useful. Though Gedman had never caught, Enos encouraged him to make the switch in a summer league, and while the scouts were on the scent of other prospects, Enos watched. Week after week young Gedman began shedding the excess weight. He grew another inch, and the huge hands and arms that had impressed Enos from the start now exuded strength, finally freed from fat. Towards the end of the summer Gedman smashed a home run over a basketball game in progress beyond the center-field fence. Once again he was a bona fide prospect and the scouts returned.

Because he had not been chosen in the major league player draft Gedman was free to sign with any team. Enos staked a claim on the Gedman living room. As each phone call came from a rival team, Enos would turn to Gedman's father and say, "Where are they? I don't see anybody else here." And the Red Sox got their man. (*From "A Scout for All Seasons" by Mel Allen.*)

– Carole Allen

Red Sox superscout Bill Enos.

Nightmare Over the Mianus River, Cos Cob, Connecticut

☞ Suddenly there was a blinding flash. The bridge lights went out, and brake lights flashed on the trucks and the little car ahead of Anderson's car. The truck directly in front of Anderson was braking so hard that the cab was veering toward Weldon's Toyota.

"They're going to crash!" Shannon Kelly cried. Anderson slammed on his brakes. Tires were squealing. Sparks spewed from under the Paces' careening truck as its trailer began to lurch over on the right side. Then abruptly the entire truck just dropped out of sight.

Bill Anderson was standing on his brakes with all his strength. His tires shrieked as they burned along the pavement, but the car held the road and he skidded to a halt only six to eight feet from a black abyss.

Below on the boat in the Harbor Marina, Dale Shelton's reverie had been shattered by "an incredible explosion" followed by a blinding flash of light and a mushrooming cloud of orange dust.

At first Shelton thought that a truck must have struck a guardrail, but as he stared incredulously, he saw a large section of the bridge starting to fall. First the left side broke away. Then the right side followed. With a rumble that built to a reverberating roar, a 300-ton slab of the bridge, 35 feet by 100 feet, three lanes wide, dropped 75 feet into the river. With it fell a huge trailer truck, headlights blazing. In another moment, a second truck came "nosediving" down into the water. (*From "The Night the Bridge Went Down" by Evan McLeod Wylie.*)

– Ron Cioffi

Scene of the grisly 1983 Mianus Bridge disaster, in which three died.

A·FAVORITE LETTER

OK, This Is How "OK" Began

☞ The earliest known written use of OK to indicate approval was by General Andrew Jackson in the War of 1812 for endorsing documents. It was a shortened version of the often-used expression "I don't care" which indicated a form of approval.

After Jackson had served two terms as president of the United States he was succeeded by his vice-president, Martin Van Buren. Van Buren was born in Kinderhook, New York, and was affectionately known among his friends as "Old Kinderhook." This became a slogan in his campaign for reelection in 1840. Old Kinderhook was shortened to OK, and the cry was "Van Buren is OK!" OK Clubs were organized throughout the country and use of "OK" became common.

A casual study of etymology shows how words can grow. "Hocus-pocus" is said to have originated when untrained priests tried to say *"Hoc est Corpus"* (Latin for "This is the Body") in serving the bread at Holy Communion. *Martin Chambers, Winston-Salem, North Carolina*

"I'm Not Alone"

☞ We were quiet for a moment, then I asked her if she could foresee going back to her medical practice.

"Yes. When we've got rid of the bombs."

"But even if there is no war, that might take longer than you live to accomplish," I observed.

"Then I've lost my life," she said. "I've lost my vocation. I feel very resentful toward the bomb makers who have done this to me. And I'm not alone." Her eyes were very direct and, for once, the smile was gone. **Tim Clark interviewing Dr. Helen Caldicott of Newton, Massachusetts.** (*From "The Doctor Who Scares People."*)

– Don Bousquet

"Remind me to fine-tune the tension adjustment on Uncle Roy's up-an'-at-'em rocker. . . . "

CHAPTER 7

July

*J*uly has usually been like a firecracker explosion, with bits and pieces flying everywhere. It was, for instance, the month an arrogant college professor challenged New England's dowsers to prove they could find water. They couldn't. But the photo of the professor laughing so hard that tears came to his eyes raised everyone's hackles, including ours (July 1964).

It was the month we tried to solve the controversy as to the location of the birthplace of the American Navy (July 1972). Was it Marblehead, Beverly, or any one of five other places? It was the month we reported on New England's only albino chickadee (July 1970), thus precipitating an onslaught of additional sightings; explained who put the "Macaroni" in "Yankee Doodle" (July 1967); sold off Lizzie Borden's house for $79,000 (July 1978); offered a rock in Assonet as Massachusetts' answer to "The Old Man of the Mountain" (July 1967); and published works written especially for us by Erle Stanley Gardner (July 1960) and Pearl Buck (July 1971).

If all that didn't generate enough fireworks, July was also the month of two horrendous errors. The first was publishing a photograph of "Charmaine, taking all sorts of daring liberties," to accompany an article about Boston's famed "Old Howard" theater (July 1960). The second one was saying that Calvin Coolidge was "the only U.S. President to be born in Vermont" (July 1972).

July's "favorites," however, begin with perhaps the saddest and most horrible of all stories we've published in any month. . . .

The Inn Street Mall, Newburyport, Massachusetts.

– photograph by Bohdan Hrynewych

The Fight to Save Kevin Wessell

BY MEL ALLEN

Shortly after 9 A.M. on Wednesday, January 5, 1983, a pale young man, accompanied by his father, stepped rapidly into the emergency room of Waltham Hospital, 10 miles west of Boston, and with a wild, anxious look in his eyes said that his chest and back hurt, that he could not catch his breath, and that at least once every minute, for reasons he could not explain, he was overtaken by an urge to gasp, as if frightened — a gasp so powerful it made him tremble. He could not swallow without gagging — "I feel like I'm choking," he said — and he added he had been unable to sleep.

His name was Kevin Wessell. His parents lived just down the street from the hospital in the maroon, wood-framed house where he had grown up. He was 30 years old and handsome, remarkably so, dark-haired and mustachioed. His 5'10" frame was lean and hard from grueling eight-mile runs in the Nigerian bush, where for nearly four years he had helped manage a rock quarry for a Waltham architectural company for whom he had worked since high school. He told the nurse that two days earlier he had received booster shots for cholera, typhus, and typhoid — he was due to fly to Africa that night. He reasoned he might be having a reaction to the shots. Privately he thought that what he called his "Nigeria Blues" had gotten the best of him.

He had come to dread the awful heat, the insects, the snakes, and the isolation of the quarry deep in the bush. He was engaged to Mercedes B., the beautiful daughter of a prominent Boston physician; he called her "Mercy." She had come to Africa that spring, settling down to life in the porter camp. A friend gave them a puppy, a Doberman they named Pepper. Kevin and Mercedes returned to Massachusetts in July for his sister's wedding, and when he went back to Africa, Mercedes stayed behind. In October Pepper died, leaving Kevin even lonelier than before.

"Twice a year, summer and Christmas, he came home," his mother Dorothea says. "The week before he'd leave to go back was always the worst. So much anxiety. He'd be gagging. I'd say, 'Kevin, what are you doing it for?' and he'd say, 'Ma, I told them I'd do it, so I'll do it.'"

Besides, he had planned his life with an architect's precision — the payoff for his loneliness was the money he was saving. In 10 weeks, on March 14, he would be leaving Africa for good, coming home to work for the company. This Christmas had been a breathless round of future plan-making. His wedding was set for June 4; reservations were made at the Copley Plaza for the reception. He'd bought land, two acres about 40 miles north in New Hampshire; he and Mercedes had shopped for furniture, and he'd filled a notebook with designs for the house to be built in the summer after the honeymoon.

"It was the beginning of great times for all of us," his mother says. And though she thought he seemed a little jumpy, his eyes a little too big ("kind of bulgy"), she kept it to herself. Then, just before New Year's, Kevin seemed to come down with a cold.

"He complained of being tired," his mother says, "of wanting to lie down, which wasn't like Kevin. He started sweating. His nose ran. He said he must have a bug." He went to Boston New Year's Eve, to the Marriott Hotel, and the next day complained to his mother of a tingling in his arm.

"Which arm?" she asked sharply. He held up the right. "Don't worry," she said, "not your heart arm." The next day he received his shots, and the day after, Tuesday, he awoke with chills. "Must be the shots," his mother said. That night, trying to drink a cup of hot cocoa Mercedes had made him, he brought it to his lips and could not drink. He jerked back as if slapped, holding his throat, which was in spasms, as if a hand had closed around it and was squeezing it tight. He was awake all night. By morning his heart was racing and he was gasping for breath. Alarmed, his father drove him to the hospital.

In the emergency room, the nurse saw he was breathing too rapidly, hyperventilating — a classic symptom of an anxiety attack. She gave him a paper bag, made him sit down, and told him to breathe deeply, nice and slow, into the bag. Then she summoned the doctor on call.

Dr. Douglas Butman was making his morning rounds when he answered his page. The son of a Waltham druggist, he

---

That night trying to drink a cup of hot cocoa, he brought it to his lips and could not drink. He jerked back as if slapped. . . .

was, at age 68, one of the hospital's senior physicians. "Just an old-fashioned GP" he likes to say, "who still makes house calls." In four decades there was little he had not seen in medicine, but he was stunned when he saw Kevin Wessell in the emergency room.

"I'd given him his shots on Monday," Dr. Butman recalls, "and except for the jitters he always felt before going back to Africa, he said he was fine. Now here he was, obviously in great distress — and he had a plane to catch in a few hours! Kevin asked if it might be a reaction to the shots. I doubted it. Then he wondered if his not drinking milk for several years might be the problem. I said I didn't think that too likely either.

" 'Then it must be my Nigeria Blues,' Kevin said. And I thought of a syndrome discovered in World War I, Neurocirculatory Asthenia. Doctors called it 'soldier's heart,' or sometimes, 'nervous heart.' It was caused by emotional stress and gave soldiers all the symptoms of heart patients — shortness of breath, palpitations, chest pain, feeling of faintness. It reminded me of Kevin. So I gave him an injection of Valium. But to be safe I ordered an electrocardiogram. I found aberrations in the electrocardiogram that were just unreal. Nothing diagnostic, but dead wrong for a boy in his physical condition. I couldn't let him get on a plane that night. I said, 'Kevin, I've got to put you in the hospital. I don't know what's wrong — yet.' " At about noon Kevin was wheeled into room 412 on the Nichols medical-surgical ward.

At dinnertime Dr. David Duhme, covering for Dr. Butman, received a call from a nurse that tranquilizers were not helping Kevin Wessell. He seemed extremely anxious. He was spitting copious saliva into a basin and kept saying he was choking. He refused to eat or drink.

"I saw him about 7 P.M.," Dr. Duhme recalls. "These were strange symptoms. He described it as trouble breathing — but it was not what anyone else meant by trouble breathing. He said it was a sudden urge to take a gasping breath, and that certain things stimulated it. Water for example.

"He said the sight of water made him have trouble breathing. So I brought a glass of water and his whole body recoiled in spasms, with sheer terror on his face. The same thing happened when I took out my throat stick. It certainly seemed like a severe anxiety reaction. He was so tense, so fearful. I had the feeling he was ready to go off in any direction.

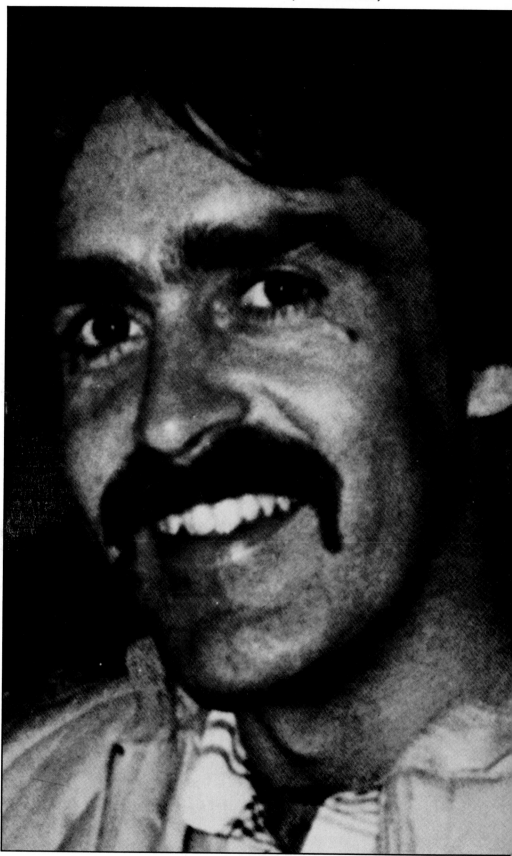

Only a few days after this photograph was taken, Kevin Wessell was in the local hospital complaining of symptoms that baffled doctors at first.

161

But something didn't figure, because while we talked he remained calm and reasonable. You don't see that in many patients who have to be hospitalized for anxiety.

"He admitted he got nervous before going away, but this didn't feel like that, he said. So we just sat there talking, and I was asking him about his life in Africa, frankly stumped, when out of the blue, and very calmly, he told me about his dog Pepper."

One day in October something curious had happened. Pepper, standing by the edge of the camp, ignored Kevin's breakfast calls, then loped away and did not return. Searching for two days, Kevin found his dog caught in a steel leg-hold trap set by native tribesmen. Though bleeding and weak, Pepper wagged his tail and whimpered a greeting. Kevin released him then and knelt to check the leg. Without warning and before running off, Pepper attacked. "His teeth went through my arm like butter," he wrote Mercedes.

Bleeding badly, Kevin drove an hour to the nearest medical help, a German clinic, figuring the pain of the leg wound had driven Pepper mad. He had vaccinated the dog for rabies, so he was not worried about that; nevertheless, the doctor gave him two shots. One, Kevin

"I was asking him about his life in Africa, frankly stumped, when out of the blue and very calmly he told me about Pepper."

figured, for tetanus, the other for rabies, with boosters a week later.

Dr. Duhme asked Kevin's family, who were in the room, to find his vaccination certificate. He examined Kevin's right wrist. Only thin, white lines, barely discernible, remained from the perfectly healed wound. "And Pepper?" he asked.

"I found him lying in the grass, dead," Kevin said. "I buried him." Quietly Dr. Duhme scanned the vaccination chart. He expected to find a notation for rabies serum; he found instead, on October 8, the words "tetanus" and "tetanus immune globulin," both vaccines repeated a week later.

"I had this sudden sinking feeling," Dr. Duhme says today. "The old image of rabies — hydrophobia — struck me. Here I'd been trying to evaluate his fear of drink!" He told Kevin he wanted some other doctors to look in on him. Then quickly he stole away to the medical library.

David Duhme was 37; his specialty was internal medicine. He was recruited by the hospital in 1979 from a Boston neighborhood health center and asked to join Dr. Butman (who hinted at retirement) in his practice. Hurrying down the hall he was excited, fascinated, though fearful. "Sometimes I'd wondered what it would be like to treat rabies," he says. In the United States it ranks as one of the rarest (averaging one to five cases a year) and most hopeless of human infections. Its symptoms are, perhaps, the most frightening and bizarre in medicine. The madness, the frothing, the violent reactions to water, end inevitably in death. (Only three survivors worldwide have been recorded.) If Kevin Wessell had rabies, David Duhme wanted to whip the curtain off the ancient scourge and see its face. This morbid curiosity, he figured, had been kindled at age three. In St. Louis, a city then rife with rabies, he had been bitten by a cat and had undergone the traumatic series of 21 shots — three rows of seven beneath the skin in the abdomen — which left him swollen and badly bruised.

Duhme was unsure that Kevin's problem was rabies. In fact, he was inclined to believe it was not. The word comes from the Latin, 'to rage', and Kevin did not seem sick enough. "My image of a rabid person is someone who would need restraints," he says, "and we had just had a perfectly cogent conversation." There were other possibilities. Diptheria was remote, but had to be considered, as did a host of tropical infections. Once he had had a patient who had swallowed a test-tube cap, causing spasms in the throat. Something lodged in Kevin's esophagus could perhaps explain his inability to swallow. There might be pathology in the neck, or it might be a thyroid problem.

Probability too weighed against rabies. A human is naturally resistant to rabies virus — a person bitten by a rabid dog and left untreated still has only a 15 percent chance of being infected. Simple washing of the wound with soap and water reduces that risk to only one percent. It had been 50 years since the last case of human rabies in Massachusetts; it seemed unlikely that it had turned up here in Waltham. Yet, as he perused the literature, he felt he was reading symptoms right from Kevin's chart.

". . . the intervals between the bite and the appearance of symptoms range from nine days to over a year, but in 90 percent of cases it lasts between two weeks and three months, tending to be longer after

Kevin sent this snapshot of the dead Pepper to his fiancée, and told her not to worry, that both Pepper and he had received proper shots.

bites on the limbs than after those on the face. . . .

"The first sign is often a vague feverish illness resembling influenza, a common cold, or a sore throat. A feeling of tension, inability to sleep, have all been described. None of these features is particularly suggestive of rabies. . . .

"The majority of patients develop a symptom which is, however, highly suggestive of impending rabies. They feel an abnormal sensation radiating from the site of the bite wound, which by now will have healed. A tingling . . . lasting for a few hours to a few days."

To Dr. Duhme it was all there on Kevin's chart, like a light trying to penetrate the fog. He called Dr. Donald Thompson, a neurologist (rabies attacks the nerve endings in the brain), and Dr. Susan Aoki, infectious disease specialist, and asked them to see Kevin.

"The neurologist said that Kevin had been able to spell 'world' backwards," recalls Dr. Duhme. "And a person with dementia could not do that." Dr. Aoki noted that Kevin, when he relaxed, seemed to be swallowing normally. An Iraqi doctor who knew rabies also came in. "He said emphatically that this was not rabies," Dr. Duhme says. "He was too well."

Nevertheless, late that night, Dr. Aoki phoned the Center for Disease Control in Atlanta, the nation's clearinghouse for disease information, and asked for advice. "Close observation" was the reply. As a precaution, nurses were told that there might be a problem; Kevin's secretions were to be double-bagged and incinerated. Still, when the Wessells asked what was wrong with Kevin, Dr. Duhme admitted that, while rabies had to be considered, he just did not know.

At 6:30 Thursday morning Dr. Duhme found Kevin smiling, calmly sipping water, wondering if he could jog in the hallway to stay in shape. Dr. Duhme's internal debate continued. Rabies ravages the nervous system so severely that the average patient, without heroic lifesaving procedures, is dead within a week. So Kevin should be getting steadily worse, but, if anything, he was improving.

Only a few hours later, when Dr. Duhme was off, a lab technician asked Kevin to swallow barium for a throat X ray. Kevin flung it away, shouting, "You're trying to kill me," and this time there was no calming him down. He began crying out continually, "I don't want to go back," and "Mercy, Mercy." A doc-

tor changed his sedatives, thinking perhaps they had backfired and excited Kevin instead. He sat shaking on the side of the bed, now up, now down, unable to rest. His thrashing pulled out his intravenous needle, but he was too agitated to have it reinserted. His mother watched his wide, staring eyes and thought they reflected not just fear, but fury and shame, as the saliva he could not swallow frothed down his chin. The room had become a nightmare, and his roommate was removed.

Mrs. Wessell was confused and angry with the doctors, who still seemed to think that this was a nervous reaction. She knew her son was no psycho. But she knew something inexplicably horrible was happening to him. "That's not my son," she told a nurse.

"He was delirious," she recalls. "I said he had to have a nurse stay with him all night. They said it wasn't possible, it had to be arranged ahead of time. I said, 'Okay, but no way am I going to leave my son until I know what's wrong.' He was burning up. I wet a cloth and put it on his face, when all of a sudden he stands right up on the bed. Now I'm screaming for a nurse because I can't hold him. The nurses come in, and Dr. Butman and everybody's trying to calm him down, to get him to lie down, but I know my kid is in another world. The next thing I see he's not breathing, his eyes are back. I hear 'Dr. Blue, Dr. Blue' [code for respiratory arrest]. Then everyone came running into the room."

It was at 10 P.M. and about a week after Kevin had first complained of "catching cold" that the doctors' debate ceased. No longer was there any question of this being a case of anxiety. Kevin had just suffered a grand mal seizure.

"I'm afraid," Dr. Butman told a distraught Mrs. Wessell, "that what we fear may be true."

By midnight a web of tubes and catheters probed his body; Kevin lay in isolation in the intensive care ward, semiconscious, with ice packs beneath his arms. His temperature read 106 degrees. A call was made to Atlanta's Center for Disease Control.

"The CDC said to take a tissue sample from the base of the neck. That's where the virus would be, exploding outward from the brain," Dr. Butman says. "No one wanted to do the biopsy. People were afraid. There was no surgeon around, but being an old GP I'd done an awful lot of surgery myself. And, anyway, I'm an old crock, so it made no difference to me. I said, 'Oh, hell, give me the knife.'

"Dr. Aoki and I drove the sample packed in dry ice to the airport. It was 4 A.M., like when I delivered babies. What flabbergasted me was how quiet Logan was, just some cleaning men getting ready for morning. And I had this eerie thought — if something happened to the plane and an animal got into the box, we could start a rabies epidemic right here. I felt that I was sending a time bomb."

Waiting in Atlanta for the lab reports was a soft-spoken, 35-year-old physician named Ken Bernard. An authority on diseases transmitted directly from animals to man — Q fever, typhus, rabies — he was the CDC's medical epidemiologist, Division of Viral Diseases, charged with overseeing the care of rabies patients anywhere in the country. At 4 P.M. Friday word came: Kevin Wessell had rabies. Immediately, Bernard phoned Waltham Hospital — extreme caution must be taken because Kevin's saliva was potentially lethal. (Within hours, Mercedes and a doctor who had been splashed in the eye with saliva began immunization with a new $500 vaccine flown in from Florida, so potent it required only five injections in the arm. In addition, the hospital identified 132 people who had had contact with Kevin. Though no doctor or nurse had ever contracted rabies from a patient, 30 asked for immunization — "mostly to still their fears.") Then Bernard booked a flight to Boston and went home to pack.

Ken Bernard knew nearly everything about preventing rabies. The science was little changed since July 6, 1885, when Louis Pasteur saved the life of a child, mauled by a rabid dog, with his untested vaccine. But he did not know how to cure it. In that, he was heir to a fragmented history. For centuries, doctors all but drowned their patients, thinking that if a patient could but endure four minutes underwater, his hydrophobia could be cured. One doctor, hoping to extract "the poison," put gunpowder on the bites, then lit it. Bezoars sold for great sums; found in the stomachs of sheep, goats, and deer, they were said to have great powers on the bites of mad dogs and thus were called madstones. But the most common treatment was euthanasia, "to stifle the poor wretch between feather beds."

In 1970 in Ohio, on the night of October 10, a six-year-old farm boy woke up screaming, a rabid bat clinging to his thumb. Two weeks after completing rabies shots, he lay comatose in a hospital. Rabies experts at the CDC theorized that if intensive care could keep a patient alive long enough, perhaps the body itself could provide the cure. Until then rabies victims died within a week; the immune system needed more time to fight back. Skunks and raccoons and foxes sometimes survived rabies, so it was possible. Young Matthew Winkler was given anticonvulsants, fluid was extracted from his brain to relieve pressure, a respirator helped him breathe. After a week he began to emerge from the coma; weeks later he was discharged, hailed as the first human rabies survivor. But hope for intensive care as an answer proved premature. There have been only two more recorded survivors since. Each year 20,000 people, nearly all in poor, developing countries, die of rabies.

The last time Ken Bernard had treated rabies was in August 1981. An American living in Mexico had been bitten by his dog. Several weeks later he was seized with terror at the sight of water, "so that I wanted to drown the fear out of me," and came to a hospital in Tucson, Arizona. Soon afterwards the CDC diagnosed his condition as rabies.

Bernard put his hopes on interferon. Extracted at great cost from human white blood cells, interferon seemed to fight any viral infection, much as some antibiotics kill any bacteria. At the time it was being hailed as the wonder drug of the eighties, possibly even a cure for cancer. After 10 days of interferon, the man had died.

Saturday morning Dr. Bernard stood by Kevin's side, a soda straw hidden in his hand. Some Waltham doctors, having seen Kevin grow alert enough to write notes to his family, remained unconvinced of rabies. Dr. Bernard trusted lab tests, but he trusted his own test more. Lifting the straw to his mouth, he blew a gentle stream of air onto Kevin's face. The reaction was spontaneous and violent, as though Kevin's whole body were a raw, inflamed nerve.

Bernard said to the surprised doctors watching, "Aerophobia. More diagnostic than hydrophobia." He knew Kevin's was an advanced case of rabies. The only hope he could offer was another go at interferon, already on its way from California. He sensed the family and the hospital had great hopes for the drug, but he harbored no illusions; he felt nearly as helpless to save Kevin as if all he carried was a handful of madstones.

That afternoon a hole was drilled into Kevin's skull, and a tube passed into the brain which would drip every evening five million units of interferon (twice that would be injected into his arm). Ke-

Drs. David Duhme (left) and Douglas Butman called Kevin's case the most extraordinary they had seen in their careers.

vin could neither swallow nor cough; every few minutes a nurse would suction his foam. A few feet outside his door, at the nurses' desk, the rhythm of his heart beeped across a screen. A respirator sighed beside his bed. IVs dripped like rain. There were no windows, only a glass door curtained against the curious. Lights were dimmed to perpetual dusk. There were drugs for blood pressure and fever, convulsions and sleep, and fear. There was a specialist on call to monitor every organ. Kevin's family wore gloves to hold his hands, looked at him through goggles, spoke to him through masks. Late at night a nurse asked if he was afraid. He nodded yes. She asked if he wanted not to be left alone. He nodded again. She sat down, took his hands, and held them for an hour, two hours. Before leaving she made certain someone would be there when he awoke.

The next morning Dr. Duhme exulted, "He looks remarkably well; he's making use of sign language." Nearly everybody, including Kevin, seemed buoyed by the change.

Kevin's family and friends stayed by his side. They murmured to him, "You've got things to do, you've got things to do" — as though incantation could throw into retreat the virus that hour by hour was canceling all plans. By Tuesday Kevin's kidneys showed signs of complications. An infection began in his eyes. The eye drops terrified him. "It's as if he can't help resisting," a nurse wrote. "He appears to be trying very hard to cooperate."

The days passed, as if by metronome, filled with the routine of critical care.

Kevin, hallucinating, would smile or wave, shake a fist at the ceiling, bang on his chest with both hands, grimace at eye drops, snatch at lights constantly shined in his face to monitor the eye infection. He would clamp down hard on the suctioning tube, teeth clenched in a tug-of-war with nurses trying to relax his grip, until, reluctantly, Dr. Duhme ordered a powerful paralytic, rendering him helpless, unable even to blink. A week after beginning interferon, Kevin needed his first blood transfusion. Every day, like gradually encroaching winter, Kevin lay quieter, slept longer, until on Sunday, January 16, he was caught in the long, solid grip of coma.

Kevin's story had become terrible but irresistible news to reporters throughout New England. They were drawn by the contrast, the modern wonder drug versus a disease that seemed, as Dr. Duhme said, "out of the Dark Ages of medicine." He told reporters, "We have to be optimistic. The few who have survived went into coma, too. All his organs are functioning well. Improvement with interferon should come within two weeks. January 24 is the critical date."

The eye worsened, the infection perforating the cornea. "The worst I'd ever seen," says Dr. Duhme. "He was going blind." Despite Kevin's coma, failing kidneys, and beginning pneumonia, on January 21 he received a cornea transplant. "If you're going full blast to save a life, you must do everything," explains Duhme. "We couldn't have him survive rabies and say, 'Sorry, you're blind because we lost hope.'" Wherever the doctors looked they saw crises; no sooner would one be quelled than another broke out; treating one problem often worsened another. His white-blood-cell and platelet counts were becoming dangerously low, possibly a side effect of interferon. It was unclear to Drs. Bernard and Duhme whether Kevin was being helped or harmed by interferon.

"We debated," recalls Duhme. "One theory was that the immunological response to rabies is just as lethal, maybe more so, than the virus. The antibodies attack the disease in every cell of the body, in every brain cell, until the body dies. Some autopsies find no rabies virus at all. And the hypothesis was that interferon helped temper the antibody response. So that could be good. On the other hand, Kevin had the dubious honor of being the first person to culture rabies virus from his cerebrospinal fluid. It seemed the virus was going wild without antibodies to kill it."

Shortly after midnight on Thursday, January 27, an exhausted Dorothea Wessell left Kevin's room. He was bleeding from his nose, mouth, and breathing tube; she kept cleaning his face. His hands lay on pillows, his heels, turning blue, lay elevated on water balloons. At 1:10 A.M. the heart monitor at the nurses'

station sounded an alarm. As if in response to his cries for "Mercy" of three weeks earlier, this time there were no attempts at resuscitation. The autopsy found virus everywhere. A hospital spokesman said it had been decided not to go into detail. The report stated only that Kevin Wessell had died of rabies on January 28, 1983.

A week later, in Michigan, a five-year-old girl said her right arm hurt. Diagnosis was a sprain. She grew irritable, stopped eating, and the arm grew weak. By February 17 she was comatose, and her parents remembered that late one August night she had screamed that a bat was biting her. "Only a nightmare," they had reassured her. Her death of rabies came March 9, the first human rabies case in Michigan since 1948.

In the summer Ken Bernard flew to Kenya, where a 23-year-old Peace Corps volunteer was dying. She had been bitten by her puppy in May. "He's been acting strange," she wrote in her diary. "I hope he doesn't have rabies." In neither case did consulting physician Bernard choose to recommend interferon.

David Duhme thinks back to one missed signal — when Kevin asked if he could jog. "I took it as a healthy sign," he

says. "It was only later that I realized he was about to go mad. You don't jog in a hospital."

One of Kevin's critical care nurses needed time off after his death. "You see a lot of people die," she says, "and you're not supposed to get involved — but he wanted so much to live." When she returned she found she was more sensitive and kinder to her patients. She still walks in the cemetery behind the hospital, following the path along the river to where the new graves are, and places a fresh flower by Kevin's stone.

Dorothea Wessell works for a florist down the street from her house, making arrangements for weddings and funerals. "I don't make plans anymore," she says. Though it is extremely painful for her to speak of Kevin's death, she feels she must. She tells of an epidemic of raccoon rabies 500 miles to the south that experts predict one day will reach New England. She hears of people who live nearby with unvaccinated dogs and cats; her face tightens and very quietly she says, "People don't understand what happens. I thought it was only a dog bite. But it changed everything."

RABIES: SOME OF THE FACTS

☞ Rabies has been cloaked in mystery and superstition for so long that man's ignorance of the disease is one of its greatest dangers.

With few exceptions, rabies in man is caused by the bite of an animal with virus-laden saliva. Unbroken skin protects against the virus; however, cuts, open wounds, and mucous membranes allow the virus to penetrate. Once embedded, the virus travels along peripheral nerves, reaching the spinal cord within 24 hours. At the rate of three millimeters per hour, it moves toward the brain. It is the destruction of brain tissue that leads to the bizarre symptoms of madness.

One myth is that rabid animals are always frothing, snapping dervishes. In fact, the "furious" stage of the illness often lasts just a few hours. Often an animal grows lethargic, stops eating, and retreats to a dark, secluded place. It is when people bend over to inspect the "injured" animal that they are bitten. Another myth is that if a sick pet drinks water, it cannot

have rabies. Only man suffers from hydrophobia — and even then, some human victims of rabid bats die of paralytic rabies, free from throat spasms and manic behavior.

Because human rabies is so rare in this country, it is easy to be lulled into complacency about a disease that among wildlife is actually exploding. One government physician termed the outbreak of raccoon rabies in the Washington, D.C., area "the greatest rabies threat in 20 years."

The virus has endured for centuries because it has the unique ability to infect any warm-blooded animal. Its spread can thus be rapid and nearly unstoppable. In 1919, for instance, a dog incubating rabies was smuggled into Scotland past quarantine officials. Soon an epidemic swept Scotland, spreading to southern England. Not until thousands of animals were shot and poisoned was Britain again free of rabies — three years later.

After 8000 dogs became rabid in the U.S. in 1946, health officials

cracked down, and nearly all states enforced vaccination regulations. Now the domestic dog is all but eliminated as a rabies threat (125 cases a year). But no such regulations apply to cats, and in the past few years cat rabies has doubled. "The cat is now a much greater rabies threat to man than the dog," says Gus W. Thornton, DVM, director of Boston's famed Angell Memorial Clinic.

The last serious outbreak of animal rabies in New England was in 1971, when rabid foxes ran rampant in Maine. Though the epidemic abated, pockets of rabid foxes still linger. Insectivorous bats are found in all New England states. Testing shows about five percent carry rabies.

Dr. Thornton cautions that there is no barrier to the chance of rabid raccoons sweeping northward. "New England is sitting on a powder keg," he warns. "We are surrounded by wildlife. It's just a matter of time."

Summer Nights, When the Band Plays

BY INGEBORG LAUTERSTEIN

All the summer nights when the band plays seem like one great celebration: a merry-go-round of children and dogs tumbling, dancing, running around and around the circle of light and music, around the cluster of instruments and musicians surrounding the dark grasshopper back of the conductor.

There is always a march and a parade of little ones — thin ones, fat ones — heads bobbing, arms waving, feet stepping it out; dogs march along, tails high as flags. And older sisters, little mothers, baby-sitters run behind toddlers that have just learned to walk. Little Jane carries a bottle, another small girl in grass-stained white pajamas turns somersaults; a sprite in a grayish, very long nightgown drifts as though puffed about by the trumpet.

Yes, everyone who has an instrument can join the band — "Concert Under the Stars" — anyone who wants can come, find a chair, bring one, spread a blanket, prop up against a car. Or stroll about to officiate, or say a few words to this one, avoid another one. Perhaps to say, "How are you? Band's better than ever this year. More instruments."

In town for the summer, a day, an hour, a life, it seems easy to forget to be a stranger while the music plays. Did the moon always rise to three-quarter time, or really just once? Just once the two ladies, their hair the color of the moon, take each other by the hand. They turn slowly, earnestly, remembering, as they dance. Faces unfamiliar and familiar swirl past. The blankets with families are little islands on the grass. The music is the waltz, their waltz. They hold each other gently and dance around a purple beach towel where a young mother discreetly nurses her newborn. When he grows up there might be dancing for everyone again, a waltz, the turning together: holding one another with reverence without getting giddy — or dizzy — a long-forgotten art.

When the waltz ends, the clapping hands, honking car horns, barking dogs voice approval. The white-haired dancers seek the dark side behind the chairs to say: "Well, I don't know what they'll think, but wasn't that fun!" There is the smell of popcorn, exhaust, whiff of low tide, a shawl perfumed with lavender. The conductor introduces the next piece — an original flute solo.

The music starts again. The first sound of the flute brings a husky up the steps to the stand. He raises his head with those pale eyes and the strange mask, howls three times, then slinks off towards the dark corner where his young master is engaged in playful warfare among the young knights of the town.

The girl flutist sways up there among gleaming instruments as little revelers begin to rub their eyes and seek mother's lap. Last piece before the anthem. Women look at each other over heads of sleeping children and their smiles are bouquets given and received. This night, all other nights, festive as long as there is a band, as long as another summer will come for us. ⁊

Band Concert, Rutland, Vermont *by Cecil C. Bell, courtesy of the Cecil C. Bell Estate.*

*Here is a revealing reminiscence by Henry Villard,
later to attend Harvard (Class of '21), become a career diplomat,
and author many successful books, who was hospitalized in the bed next to
Ernest Hemingway in the summer of 1918. Published in Yankee on the 50th
anniversary of A Farewell to Arms, it shed considerable light on exactly how autobiographical
the plot of that novel really was. (Another immediate result, perhaps not
even worth noting, was that the photograph, shown herewith,
from our July 1979 issue, appeared that summer tacked up on the office walls
of no less than five of our younger editors and designers!)*

A Prize Specimen of
Wounded Hero

BY HENRY S. VILLARD

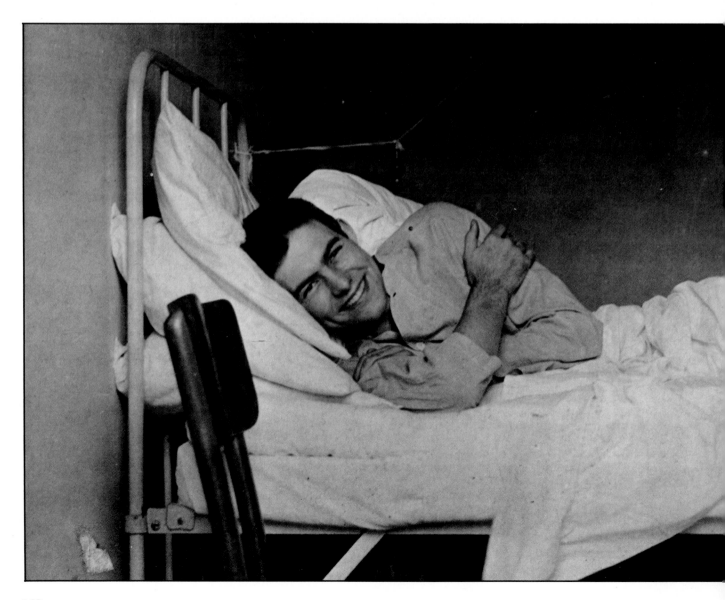

It was late at night when I reached the hospital in Milan, sick and tired and dirty, after a day-long journey from my base at Bassano, 45 miles northwest of Venice at the foot of the towering Dolomite Alps. I had been driving an ambulance for the American Red Cross that sultry summer of 1918, attached to the Italian army with the assimilated rank of second lieutenant, and I had just congratulated myself on having come through the recent heavy fighting unscathed, when I was stricken with a high fever accompanied by a queasy feeling in the pit of my stomach.

American Red Cross headquarters at 10 Via Alessandro Manzoni, where I had been instructed to report, were closed when I got there, and the hospital section, a short distance away at 3 Via Borchetto, did not look in the least like what it purported to be. A moderate-size stone-and-stucco structure with big rectangular windows, it had formerly been used as a *pensione;* except for the familiar emblem over the doorway, the old-fashioned mansion had nothing to indicate that it housed the first medical and surgical institution ever to be opened by Americans on Italian soil.

"Why, hello there! I guess we've been expecting you." The fetching night nurse who answered my ring at the landing smiled cheerfully. "Do come right in. We have a room all ready for you."

I didn't have to be asked twice. It was the first feminine voice with an American accent I had heard since leaving the States and it belonged to a tall, slender, chestnut-haired girl with friendly blue-gray eyes, who seemed to combine brisk competence with exceptional charm. Ill as I was I couldn't help responding to her encouraging welcome. What luck, I thought, to encounter such an attractive person instead of some grim, sour-faced matron! Her loose-fitting, ankle-length uniform, open at the neck, with belt and Red Cross arm band, was crisp and white; a starched white cap perched like a butterfly on the back of her head.

We tiptoed down a corridor enclosed by glass doors and windows, something like a sun parlor, till we came to a pleasant, airy room, whitewashed in a soft tint, with a single bed and a French window opening on a small balcony. Curtains of bright cretonne, an armoire of oak, a wash basin with hot and cold running water, a night table, and two chairs completed a picture of calm and privacy.

I caught sight of myself in the narrow, full-length mirror on one half of the armoire and was startled at what I saw: the fever danced in my eyes and the color of my face was a ghastly yellow-green. Suddenly, I realized how exhausted I was.

"All the rooms connect with one another. You can walk right through, like in a ward. And still, you can be all by yourself if you want. Get undressed, please, and I'll draw you a hot bath. You can have an eggnog if you're hungry." Then, to my surprise, she added, "What kind of a cocktail would you like?" She gave me an impish glance and stuck a thermometer in my mouth.

I wasn't sure whether I had heard right, but on the chance she meant it I ran over in my mind the agreeable possibilities, the drinks I had begun to experiment with at college: An orange blossom, a Bronx, an Alexander, a stinger — finally settling for a very dry martini. And that was what my attentive night nurse brought me — none of your insipid European vermouths with a whisper of gin, but a clear, cold, American-style cocktail. Only there was a joker: at the bottom of the glass, instead of an olive, lurked a fat glob of castor oil. I managed to smile wryly and downed it at a gulp.

Just before she switched off the light, I asked the name of the angelic creature who had admitted me into this little spot of heaven.

"Agnes von Kurowsky," she said, "from Washington, D.C."

As I drifted off, I kept thinking how sympathetic and lovely she was — dou-

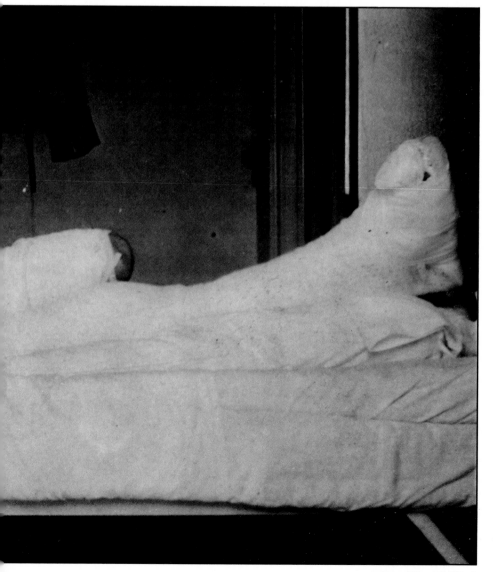

– courtesy of Henry S. Villard

"Hemingway was a good-looking son-of-a-gun, I thought, lying there fresh-faced and clean-shaven on the white-painted iron bedstead . . . . He had a strong jaw and a wide, boyish grin that revealed an even row of dazzling white teeth, and his jet black hair and dark eyes contrasted starkly with the snowy pillows that propped his broad shoulders."

bly attractive so far from home. All right, she was a few years older than I, but then older girls are quite likely to appeal to young men who have lately turned 18.

When I awoke next morning, I found that another nurse had taken over where the lissome Agnes had left off. Elsie Macdonald was not so beautiful, not so young as Agnes, nor was her figure so tall and slim, but her kindliness and good humor were unmistakable. "You can call me Mac," she said in a motherly tone, fussing with my pillow. "There'll be a glass of milk for breakfast, and that's all until the doctor sees you." I felt at ease with her at once.

Dr. Sabatini, attached to Milan's *Ospedale Maggiore* with the rank of *capitano,* was a short, red-faced man, happy to be consulted by an establishment whose regular physician was off caring for refugees in the north. He had no need of the inevitable black satchel to diagnose my case as jaundice. "Maybe touch of malaria, too," cocking his head judiciously. "That no dangerous. But for yellow disease — must rest, obey rules, take medicine. If not" — his stern expression was belied by the twinkle in his dark-lashed eyes — "I WASH my hands from you." As he spoke he suited his gesture to the words.

I felt dizzy and weak after the doctor left, but Mac thought I might as well become acquainted with the patient who was my next-door neighbor — I would be seeing a lot of him, she said — Second Lieutenant Hemingway. An ambulance driver, too. From Section Four. He had been the first patient to be admitted after the hospital was opened and he was badly wounded, as I would see for myself. She knocked, and without waiting for a reply opened the door to a room in every respect like mine, except that it was larger. "Ernie," she said, familiarly, "I'd like you to meet a new arrival: Lieutenant Villard from Section One."

Hemingway was a good-looking son-of-a-gun, I thought, lying there fresh faced and clean shaven on the white-painted iron bedstead, and good natured too, considering that he appeared totally disabled. He had a strong jaw and a wide, boyish grin that revealed an even row of dazzling white teeth, and his jet black hair and dark eyes contrasted starkly with the snowy pillows that propped up his broad shoulders as he reclined at full length, one leg in a plaster cast, the other swathed in bandages. I judged him to be about my age or a little older. Whatever the extent of his injuries, there was no question about his magnetism or his mental alertness. "You'll like it here," he said warmly, taking my hand in a vigorous clasp. "They treat you royally."

"They" had counted 227 shrapnel wounds in his legs, explained Mac, hovering around like a wet hen. "But he's doing fine. He's the first of our boys to be wounded in Italy — and we're very proud of him." This was no ordinary patient, I surmised. Judging by the worshipful look on Mac's face, she, and, I assumed, the other nurses, regarded him as their special pet, a prize specimen of wounded hero.

"Sure thing," I responded. "Great place, this hospital." And I meant it — it had far exceeded my expectations. "How long since you've been laid up?"

"Since July the eighth. That's when I was wounded. Arrived here the 17th. Where's your home?"

"New York," I told him. "The big city. Where's yours?"

"Oak Park, Illinois — place you never heard of." He laughed a boy's laugh. "That's near Chicago. Out where the West begins. Maybe I should say Kansas City — I was working on a newspaper there." He had sailed on a ship named, by coincidence, the *Chicago.* "When did you come over?"

"Middle of May," I said. "Had a week or so in Paris. Got to Bassano on the 30th — Memorial Day. In time for all the excitement on June 15th."

"Me, too. Got to Schio with a few days to spare — the 'Schio Country Club.' " I could see he was sizing me up with those lively, penetrating black eyes, glad of a chance to talk shop with a fellow driver. "Left New York May 11th but didn't make Section Four till the 10th of June. Paris and red tape, temporary duty here in Milano. Some show put on by the Austrians. But you guys at Grappa saw lots more action than we did around Pasubio. That's why I had to get down to the Piave, to see what was happening — and that's where I got mine," glancing at his legs.

I didn't try to prolong that first encounter; my head was swimming.

"Come back when you feel like it, Villard. You don't have far to go." Hemingway's voice was strong and resonant, his grin cordial and infectious. I had the impression he was eager to receive visitors and would always be ready for a chat.

For the first few days I was too sick to do anything except doze or play an occasional game of solitaire on the bedspread with cards that Agnes brought me. To my regret, I didn't see as much of Agnes as I would have liked, for she didn't mind the night duty that the others were inclined to shun and was seldom around in the daytime; but the plump, warm-natured Elsie Macdonald — as Scottish as her name implied — looked in frequently to see how I was getting on. When Agnes did appear, the entire place seemed brighter because of her presence.

Every day through the half-open door I could see Hemingway holding court with her and whomever else happened to drop in, guffawing and joking about the multiple wounds that had incapacitated him. "Look — are they going to amputate just one leg, or two?"

Agnes or Mac would be laughing and kidding back. "Two, of course. What good's one leg?"

"All right, make it two. When do we start?"

"Maybe today, maybe tomorrow. Maybe next week. When the sawbones are good and ready."

"Christ, I'm ready now."

I knew it was banter because I felt sure he would never let them cut off his limbs, no matter how long it might take to extract, piece by piece, that awesome collection of metal fragments from his flesh. From Agnes in one of her spare moments I learned the details of how he had been hit by the explosion of a trench mortar lobbed over from the Austrian lines — what the soldiers called an "ash can" — that burst on contact and scattered pieces of junk steel in every direction; in addition, he had been wounded in the right knee by machine-gun fire. The Red Cross had officially labeled all except 10 of his injuries as "superficial," but that didn't prevent me from admiring his intestinal fortitude in enduring pain, not to speak of the excruciating tedium of lying immobilized for weeks on end. And in spite of his own strong-willed attitude, the possibility of amputation seemed to be always present if things should take a turn for the worse.

As soon as my temperature dropped

and the dreadful yellow color began to fade under a milk-and-egg diet, I was allowed to take the few steps through the connecting door and sit at Hemingway's bedside in my dressing gown. I looked forward to this ritual as much for the companionship as for taking a turn, like everyone else, in helping the wounded warrior — so much worse off than I — to while away the hours and forget his plight. He was generous with his time — he had plenty to spare — and he was insatiable in his desire to hear what was going on at the front. Nothing escaped his interest — names, places, dates; his own memory for detail seemed remarkable. It was almost as if I were being quizzed by a lawyer for the prosecution; years later it would occur to me that this probing was the instinct of the born storyteller.

We were quickly on a first-name basis; it wasn't hard to strike up a friendship with Ernie. That was what most of us called him, though I preferred the more masculine-sounding Hem. I liked this big bear of a fellow from the start and I think he liked me. He had celebrated — if that's the word — his 19th birthday, confined to bed, on July 21; which made me the youngest inmate of the hospital by a good eight months. Actually, we had a lot in common. For one thing, we were both volunteers in the ambulance service, both hospitalized in a strange land far from home, neither of us old enough to have been in a hospital before — a bond unconsciously felt but not openly talked about. We shared also the unique experience of being attached to a foreign army with the honorary rank of *sotto tenente* while scrupulously preserving our allegiance to the American flag — for we looked at the war through American eyes and knew that nothing could lessen our attachment to and pride in our own country. America, only America, could show the world what had to be done to rout the Teutonic hordes and bring the Kaiser to bay, and we shook our heads, groaning in unison, when we spoke of the spirit of defeat that pervaded Italy's army after Caporetto the previous year.

We were American to the core, too, in our preoccupation with the great game of baseball, quickly slipping into the idiom of the sport like the most avid fans. Hem was a stalwart supporter of the Chicago White Sox, who were destined to win the National League pennant that season; I of John J. McGraw's New York Giants. Baseball scores from the U.S. were hard to come by, and we devoured what scraps of information came our

way about the rival teams' standings or about the performance of Babe Ruth, Sultan of Swat, who was making history by hitting a record number of home runs. One of us — I forget which — came up with some doggerel that provided us with no end of amusement:

Here lies the body of Mary Jones
For her life held no terrors;
She lived a maid and died a maid
No hits, no runs, no errors.

The last line we adopted as a form of riposte to any inquiries as to how we were faring in the hospital, where one hot, uneventful day was very much like another — "No hits, no runs, no errors. Thanks very much." And in amateur strategy sessions or arguments about the war, we kept track of reports from the front in terms of box scores or innings, as if we were loyal rooters for the home team against visitors from out of town.

I was struck particularly by what Ernie had to say about journalism, for I had ambitions in that field myself. His brief career as a cub reporter on the *Star* in Kansas City, the job wangled for him by an uncle, impressed me enormously: six months of covering the police blotter, the morgue, the city hall, and the railway station spelled volumes of experience to me, and I looked up to him as an authority on what I thought might one day be my own profession. Next to watching a war, he would say, newspaper work was the best way to learn to think for yourself, and the best way to learn to write was to write about what you yourself actually *saw* and *felt*. When I remarked that one of *my* uncles was editor and publisher of the liberal *New York Evening Post,* he promptly accepted me as a literary aspirant: "Christ, Harry, we talk the same language!" Maybe he would have been intrigued to learn, a year later, that he had not encouraged me in vain and that I had in fact become a reporter and an editor of my college daily, *The Harvard Crimson.*

I took it for granted that Ernie would continue writing after the war — *dopo la guerra* — though he was never specific on the form his writing would take. A college-type education didn't seem to interest him; firsthand experience in a sphere like journalism was schooling enough. He had contributed a number of pieces to his high-school newspaper and magazine — that too commanded my respect — and he hinted at the satisfaction of seeing his stories in print, but he never mentioned a novel as one of his goals. There was no hint that he might

use the war or the hospital as background for a book someday, or that he intended to go in for fiction in preference to anything else. He was basically a reporter, and that was that.

Hem didn't hesitate to point with pride at what he liked to call his army of "dead men" — empty bottles of brandy, vermouth, Cointreau, or plain "red ink" — stashed away in the big oak armoire against an opportunity to have them smuggled out by the porter, who had brought them in for a small bribe in the first place. If the nurses didn't exactly countenance his tippling, as visiting friends did, they tolerated the habit as long as he kept it under control and didn't exhibit signs of intoxication. Not so, however, with Miss Katherine C. de Long, the establishment's dignified, able supervisor, with whom Ernie had more than one run-in on the subject of alcoholic beverages. He had an unlimited capacity to swallow a bottle's contents without betraying the fact that he had been drinking — but he couldn't disguise his breath, and Miss de Long was adept at detecting this telltale sign.

Under the stimulus of one of those periodic libations, Hem would embark on a long-winded discourse — about the conduct of the war, the sporting life, or the ineptitude of Italy's soldiers — which would be interrupted only by an addition to his audience or the appearance of a nurse on some hospital chore. At such times, as likely as not, he would break out with a "Christ Almighty! What is it now?" or a "Come in, goddamit, and listen to this." Despite his usual ebullient good humor, despite the disarming smile that won him so many friends, male and female, Hem could be imperious if not downright irascible. He was in fact far from being an easy patient to handle. One of the nurses, Mrs. Charlotte M. Heilman, would observe years later in a letter to Red Cross headquarters that he was "impulsive, very rude, 'smarty,' and uncooperative," that he gave the impression of being badly spoiled, and that he "always seemed to have plenty of money, which he spent freely for Italian wine and tips to the porter who brought it."

If Hemingway was the invalid luminary, then Agnes scintillated among the nurses. She had a sparkle the others didn't possess: fresh and pert and lovely in her long-skirted white uniform, moving lithely as she went about her tasks, wasting no time yet never seeming to hurry, she radiated zest and energy. Obviously her work took precedence over everything else, and just as obviously she liked her work. I came close to having a real crush on Aggie — or Ag, as she was called by those who grew to know her best — but then, all the boys fell for Aggie in some degree. Little wonder; in the close quarters of our top-floor ward we couldn't help being conscious of her comely presence. It was evident, however, that Ernie had been smitten to a far greater extent than the rest of us, and I knew that he had the inside track to her affections when I caught him holding her hand one afternoon in a manner that did not suggest she was taking his pulse.

"Catherine Barkley was greatly liked by the nurses because she would do night duty indefinitely," says Lieutenant Henry, the hero of A Farewell to Arms. *"She had quite a little work with the malaria people, the boy who had unscrewed the nose-cap was a friend of ours and never rang at night unless it was necessary, but between the times of working we were together. I loved her very much and she loved me. I slept in the daytime and we wrote notes when we were awake and sent them by Ferguson. Ferguson was a fine girl. I never learned anything about her except that she had a brother in the Fifty-Second Division and a brother in Mesopotamia and she was very good to Catherine Barkley."*

Often taken wrongly to be the exact counterpart of Catherine Barkley in *Farewell*, Agnes Hannah von Kurowsky was born in Philadelphia in 1892 and moved to Washington with her family at the age of 13. There in due course she found employment in the catalogue department of the public library. "But that was too slow and uneventful," she told me. "My taste ran to something more exciting. So I went into training as a nurse at Bellevue in New York, and asked for an assignment abroad as soon as possible." Ferguson, or "Fergy," the "fine girl" in the novel, was most likely inspired by Agnes's sidekick, the Scottish Elsie Macdonald, former head of the Nurses' Infirmary at Bellevue, and fondly referred to as "the Spanish Mackerel" or "Spanish Mac" by Hem, whom she in turn would call her "Ernesto."

Life was especially bearable for the convalescents when one or more of the girls, off duty or pausing in their rounds, would join the group lounging on the terrace "to chew the fat" — as Ernie would loudly proclaim — over a glass of milk or orange juice (both rarities at the front), to crack a few jokes, to pose for an amateur snapshot, or to listen to a favorite record or two. Somebody had introduced a parody of "Smiles," that immensely popular song hit of the war years 1917 and 1918; it was called "Styles," and the words were considered delightfully risqué for mixed company; we hummed them with a glint in the eye when the nurses were present:

> There are styles — that show the an-kle,
> There are styles — that show the knee,
> There are styles — that show the vaccination,
> There are styles — that hadn't ought to be.
> There are styles — that have a certain mean-ing,
> Which the eyes — of love alone may see.
> But the styles — that Eve wore in the garden
> Are the styles that appeal to me.

As I gained strength with the addition of oatmeal and boiled chicken to my diet, I began to think seriously of the day when I could aspire to asking Aggie out to dinner. The prospect of a tête-à-tête meal with her was a standing incentive to the guys to get well quickly, and the vision of a splendid restaurant where I could have her all to myself for an evening was enough to set my spine tingling. Here, I thought smugly, I had the advantage over poor handicapped Ernie, for it would be many more weeks before he could expect to get out of bed and hobble around on crutches.

A milestone was reached in my recovery on August 10, when I was allowed to step into the street and take a short walk in the teeming city. On the same day I made note in my diary that "Hemingway was operated on early in the morning." The air was tense in the hospital; a lot depended on this, the second operation for its Very Important Patient: would he be able to walk again, and if so, how soon? Everyone was concerned about the outcome; but much to everyone's relief, Hem came through with flying colors, and the *Red Cross Bulletin*

reported that he was "progressing toward complete recovery." Captain Sammarelli, the attending surgeon, deftly removed the machine-gun slugs from his knee and foot and presented them to him as a souvenir; they went into a basin at the side of his bed which contained an impressive assortment of shrapnel he had picked out of his legs with a penknife during his long convalescence and had saved for the edification of visitors.

When at last I found the courage to ask Aggie for a date, I was not aware that, in conformity with Italian custom, the Red Cross frowned on unchaperoned social contact between the sexes.

We had agreed to meet in the Galleria on the afternoon of her day off for a carriage drive around the *Giardini Publici* before dinner. I could hardly wait for the red-letter day. I had my uniform pressed, cocked my overseas cap at a rakish angle, and took a last critical look at what I hoped would pass for a mustache in the mirror. But the wind suddenly went out of my sails when Agnes approached, for to my consternation she had Elsie Macdonald in tow. "We have to travel in pairs, you know," she said disingenuously. Not that I didn't enjoy Mac's company, but, well, three *is* a crowd.

Agnes herself was impartial in the way she encouraged her patients, making them feel individually that she really cared about their welfare. But one couldn't help noticing that Ernie received an extra share of her attention, partly because of the special fondness that was developing between them, partly because Ernie had a compelling — not to say a demanding — way about him that required her attendance on every conceivable occasion. Agnes would be the first to agree that he was not an easy patient to handle, that he could assert himself with no little authority if matters weren't exactly right or if he found the unrelenting discipline of Miss de Long too irksome. At times, it would take all the sympathy and tact that Agnes possessed to calm him down and keep him from scolding. Yet, as Bill Horne was to observe in later years, "her romance with Hem was a beautiful thing to watch," even if, as proved to be the case, the love light was burning a lot more brightly in his eyes than in hers.

Hemingway was to make excellent use of that hospital setting when he came to write *Farewell* 10 years after the war. Quite obviously, the author identified himself with the protagonist, Lieutenant Henry; but equally clearly, the nurse Catherine Barkley does not rightly reflect the flesh-and-blood Agnes. The dif-

---

I knew that he had the inside track to her affections when I caught him holding her hand one afternoon in a manner that did not suggest she was taking his pulse.

ference between fact and fiction is most strikingly apparent in the chapters describing the progress of the liaison between the two lovers.

She looked toward the door, saw there was no one, then she sat on the side of the bed and leaned over and kissed me. I pulled her down and kissed her and felt her heart beating.

* * *

You mustn't, she said, you're not well enough.
Yes, I am. Come on.
No. You're not strong enough.
Yes, I am. Yes. Please.
You do love me?
I really love you. I'm crazy about you. Come on, please.

* * *

All right, but only for a minute.

Night after night, while everyone else is asleep, the affair flourishes, notwithstanding the physical handicap of Henry and the presence of other patients next door. *That was madness,* says Catherine — in what must surely be the understatement of the war — after their first amorous encounter, which sets the tone for their subsequent meetings.

It would indeed be farfetched to assume that the romantic attachment between Ernie and Agnes ever approached such lengths; at most, their regard for one another was expressed in notes and letters, in words rather than deeds, perhaps in more visits to Ernie's room by Agnes than were strictly necessary, perhaps in a harmless, occasional kiss. Aside from that, the fictional lovemaking occurs under conditions that, to say the very least, would require the partners *to be awfully careful,* as Catherine puts it. It would be hard to imagine circumstances less propitious for the clandestine carryings-on that reached their climax in Catherine's pregnancy; no more awkward or improbable environment could have been devised for illicit dalliance than the vigilantly supervised, sanitized quarters such as Ernie and I occupied at the American hospital in wartime Milano. One can draw only one conclusion: the torrid scenes of the novel, whether laid in the patient's room or later in some hotel, all chronicled in terms that were scandalously explicit for the day, were the product of some particularly ardent and wishful retrospective thinking on the author's part.

Late in August, I was granted a short convalescent leave and spent it at the picture postcard resort of Rapallo, on the coast south of Genoa — an ideal change

Henry Villard, the author of this article, and Agnes von Kurowsky on the occasion of their famous afternoon on the town, spoiled somewhat by the addition of Elsie Macdonald, who acted as chaperone for the couple.

– courtesy of Henry S. Villard

of venue. From the terrace of the Kursaal Hotel there was nothing to remind one of war except a squadron of noisy flying boats that patrolled the adjacent waters. There was swimming off the rocks; there were English *permissionaires* to talk with; an English-speaking *contessa* to dance with, to an unreal background of music, moonlight, and roses; the ancient harbor; the sea; and the mountains veiled in a midnight mist.

I stopped in Genoa on the way back to inspect an assembly plant for U.S. Army ambulances, a portent of what was to come, which made me wonder how much longer our Red Cross units would be needed. In my absence, the hospital on the Via Borchetto had become engaged in the "vigorous activity" for which it had been intended with the advent of American troops; there wasn't a spare bed, and I found I would have to sleep under the stars on a mattress laid out on the terrace.

The first thing I did was to pay my respects to Ernie. He seemed to be in the same general state of incapacity as when I had left, but the broad grin and cheerful frame of mind were there as usual. It wouldn't be long before they would measure him for crutches. What was Rapallo like? What about it as a place to recuperate? Had I met any snappy-looking dames? Was there any interest in the war down there? I told him about the seaplane base, the ambulance camp near Genoa, the sociable evening on the Kursaal ter-

race. "Maybe I should go there when I get out of here, Harry." I had the impression he was more enamored of Aggie than ever, but I couldn't tell how she felt; with the influx of new arrivals there was not time for her to talk with me.

On the morning of the second day Dr. Sabatini pronounced me cured and fit to resume my duties at the front. I went into Ernie's room again to say good-bye. It would be almost exactly a month later that I was to hear he had chosen for *his* convalescent leave not Rapallo but Stresa on Lake Maggiore, where the luxurious Grand Hotel would one day supply part of the background for the second half of *Farewell.* We exchanged a few jokes; our laughter was a bit forced, as it is with newfound friends uncertain whether fate will ever bring them together again. It was time to start back for Bassano and Section One. We toasted each other with that vulgar Italian ode to man's basic pleasures in life, the words redolent of army slang:

Aqua pura, vino fresco
Bella fica, cazzo duro.

Then we shook hands and wished each other luck, hoping we would meet *dopo la guerra.* That, however, was not in the cards. It was the last time I was to see Ernest Hemingway.

Portions of this article appeared in the August 1978 issue of Horizon.

In awarding "Eliza's Punishment" the 1981 Yankee Fiction First Prize, poet and novelist Rosellen Brown wrote us that it has in it "not only the magic of live language but some of the complexity and pain that we find in real family struggles." She went on to say, "I like the sense of the end, too, that the mystery of personality endures, even overwhelms, duty, jealousy, vengefulness. . . . Good and bad are not easy to isolate in Wilson's story, and that's the way I like my morality. Nobody ever said life was simple."

Eliza's Punishment

FICTION BY SYLVIA ENGEN WILSON

Lorenzo went first. What a child he was! Our only boy — handsome, strong. He would hold onto my fingers and I would raise him straight up out of his cradle, and him laughing all the time. My man, William, was proud of his little Lor. What a back that baby had, strong legs and hands that gripped hard. The girls, all but Phoebe, loved the baby. Them as are next a young one often get a cankering. So it was with Phoebe, but I knew time would get her over it. When Lor died of lung fever, my heart was skinned naked as a shore rock.

You can't blame a little girl. Phoebe wasn't much over five, but still she should have had better sense. She let Lor crawl into a tide pool, out in the cold wind and wet to the skin. Eliza, my oldest, was 13 at the time. She had a sharp tongue and a quick hand for slapping. I was at Sally Randall's to help her with a birthing. I didn't hear about it till later when I got home.

"Phoebe was mooning along with a fistful of purple thistles. She wasn't paying any attention to Lor. He was cold as a fish, and chewing on a crab leg. I was so mad I gave her a crack across the face. I told her it was like to be the death of the baby, wet and in a cold wind like that."

Eliza spoke true. It was the baby's death. It hit Phoebe hard. She was never the same child again. A wrenching thing it was, Lor burning with the fever and Phoebe whimpering in the corners. When the baby died, Phoebe tried to climb into her father's lap, but he pushed her from him. Not a mean man, it was his grief made him do it. For all he tried, William never could undo that doing. Phoebe lived inside herself from that time on. So quiet she was, you'd never guess she was around.

Wind and sun don't bother with their feelings. They keep on with their work and I kept on with mine. I had thought I was done with bearing, then I got heavy with Judson. I prayed for a boy, and a boy I got. William was pleased, and the girls, Eliza, Jane, and Mary were happy. About Phoebe, I couldn't tell.

A cliff falls into the sea, tearing rock from rock. So it was when I lost my man, so much was he a part of me. William died and Phoebe disappeared. Nowhere could she be found. Eliza said, "It would be like her to throw herself into the sea. She's that kind." Eliza had a bad feeling for Phoebe since Lor's death. So Phoebe wasn't at the burying — a sore thing. Worry for her kept me from my grief, and it still sours in the bottom of my soul. It never did get out of me. Two days later, Eliza found Phoebe under a bed. She was trembling when Eliza pulled her out, but not a word did she say.

"Shows how much you loved your father!" Oh, that Eliza could be hard.

"She loved him most of all," I said. Something was showing on Phoebe's face that made me think she might come back. But she went inside herself and nothing ever happened on her face again, not as I know of.

Extra good often comes with the extra bad. The Lord had given me Judson. What a man he was, though he had only 12 years on him. Such kindness, such strength. We all depended on him. God had given him special powers. With Judson Phoebe would talk. Not in the house, but I would see them out on the rocks.

"Why has she stopped talking to us?" I would ask him. They were close, the two of them, and I thought he might know. He didn't. "What do you talk about?" It was not that I wanted to pry. I longed to help Phoebe out of her prison.

"We talk about gulls and clouds and barnacles. She says she's becoming a gull. Some day she'll be going back to the sky, she says."

A few years after my man died, Judson got the sickness in the lungs and he died, too. The Caswells were not made to be shoalers. Their chests couldn't take the wetness and the cold winds. Since Judson died, life's been a slow going downhill for me. Only Phoebe's still here.

Eliza married a Portsmouth man. They have one little girl and a fine big house. Summers she comes visiting us. Jane and Mary are still on the island with their families. At times I take care of their young ones. I wish they wouldn't say, "Don't leave the baby alone with Phoebe." Back of that still face she wears, I know she is alive and paining.

Phoebe

Lor was an ugly baby, slobbering on himself and peeing in his pants. Eleven

Is it true that if one wishes for something hard enough it will come true? Even if it's a horrible wish?

174

– illustration by Gordon Morrison

175

– illustration by Gordon Morrison

months old and he couldn't even talk. A crybaby, too. But no one ever scolded him for it. Not even Eliza. She was mean enough to scold an angel. If an angel were to fly down from heaven and come into the house Eliza would say, "What you doing here? Don't track in the dirt. We got enough work to do around here."

Where was Lor? Take your eyes off him a minute and he was gone. There he was. In a tide pool getting himself all wet. She was the one who'd be blamed for it.

"Don't you know better than that?" She tried to sound like Eliza, but that Lor was a dumbhead. He didn't even know he was being scolded. He held up his arms when she pulled him out of the water and hugged her around the neck. In some ways he was a sweet baby.

"We ought to go back to the house, now, but if we do, Eliza will slap us. Shall we wait till Mam gets home?" Lor made noises. She might have known she wouldn't get a sensible answer from him. He seemed to be happy. Phoebe put him down. He crawled right back to the tide pool. The water was warm to her hands. "I'll let you play in the water today, but don't do it when you got dry duds on, understand?" He was slapping at the water with his hands.

Now to get back to the thistles. Like little purple brushes they were, not as nice smelling as roses, but a lot prettier.

Prickles make them hard to pick, even hard to hold. She would get a big bunch for the Randalls' new baby. They had had one that died. Reverend Tucke had said in a deep voice, "May the Lord have mercy on his soul." It had a grand sound. Phoebe tried it on a gull. It flew away to tell another gull.

Oh, oh. There was Eliza coming on the run, making straight for Lor.

"What's the matter with you, letting the baby play in the water? It could be the death of him, wet and in the cold wind." Eliza slapped her across the face so hard it made Phoebe cry. "When Mam gets home she'll hear about this. Stop your sniveling." Lor had begun to cry. It was Eliza's angry voice scared him, Phoebe knew. It scared her, too.

Mam didn't scold when she got home, but Phoebe could tell something was in Mam like scolding held back. "He's beginning to burn," Mam said. She had Lor in her arms.

Pap didn't kiss Phoebe good-night, didn't tell her she was his sugarplum. He always did that, but not that night. That night his eyes were angry with her.

"Lor is going to die and it's all your fault." That's what Eliza said to her. And Lor died. He stopped pulling at the covers, stopped the hoarse whimpering. Eliza, Mary, Jane, Pap, and Mam began to cry. Would Pap forgive her? She put

her hands on his knees. He did not look down. She began to climb into his lap. He pushed her away. How can you live when you have done something so bad your own Mam and Pap hate you?

Gulls live in a good world. They glide across the sky, be it blue or gray, through wind and quiet air. They utter cries she learned to understand. Not right away, but over the years it came to her gradually, "Phoebe is a gull, one of us. Soon she will be gliding through the skies, blue or gray, through wind and quiet air." They loved her. She loved them.

Judson was a gull. She knew it and the gulls knew it. He died. When a gull dies, it is sad, so sad you can hardly bear to go on living.

Eliza

"Go out and see what Phoebe's up to," Eliza ordered Mary.

"Don't be so bossy. Lor's all right with her."

"For a five year old, that Phoebe doesn't know beans," Eliza answered. She should have gone out herself, gone right away. Something told her to do it.

But rendering fat is messy, and what with one thing and another, time went by. The first thing she noticed when she did go out was how cold the wind had become, blowing across the rough water. Was that a tide pool Lor was playing in? Fear

Gulls, their droppings, their squawkings, the high and mighty way they sailed through the air as though they owned both sea and land — how Eliza hated them.

clutched at her. She began to run. The baby was soaking wet.

"What's the matter with you?" She slapped Phoebe across the mouth. Eliza had not meant to hit so hard. Her hand left a red mark. "It's like to be the death of him, wet and out in the cold wind. Mam will hear about this when she gets home." She scooped Lor into her arms, wrapping her shawl around him and running for the cottage.

"Mary! Mary!" she called. Mary must have gone over to the Randalls' to get Janie and find out about the birthing.

Quickly Eliza peeled off the baby's wet garments. His body was cold. She laid an ear to his chest like Mam did. Was a croupy sound beginning? She could not tell. That Phoebe, a big girl of five! She should get a whipping. Pap was always too easy on her, and so was Mam. If ever there was a spoiled child, Phoebe was the one. Where was she now?

"Phoebe! Phoebe!" There was no answer. Something was under the table. Phoebe had worked her way along the wall and was hiding underneath. "What are you doing down there?" The look of fright on Phoebe's face stopped Eliza. She gentled her voice. "I'm not mad at you. Come on out." But Phoebe stayed under the table until Mam came in with Jane and Mary.

"It's another girl," Jane called out. Always she had to be first with the news.

Mam came over to the table. "Why are you dressing Lor?"

"That Phoebe!" Eliza's anger returned. "She was supposed to be taking care of him. I went out and found Lor paddling in a tide pool, wet to the skin and Phoebe mooning along the rocks picking thistles, paying no heed to him at all. Don't be creeping out grabbing Mam's skirts. You ought to get a whipping. I'll save you the trouble of tattling on me. I gave her a good one across the face, Mam, but she had it coming."

Mam was laying an ear on Lor's chest. "He's working hard at his breathing. How long was he out in the cold?"

Her fault pressed heavy on Eliza. She should have checked on Lor long before she had. "I was busy with the fat, Mam. I told Mary to go, but she's always such a lazybones. You can never get her to do anything."

"Don't be so busy with your blaming, Liza. How long was he out in the wind?" Phoebe pulled her face out of Mam's skirts. "Long enough for a gull chick to pip through his shell."

"Long enough for Lor to catch his death, that's how long it was." Eliza spoke savagely. Her hand itched to slap Phoebe again.

Gulls, their droppings, their squawkings, the high and mighty way they sailed through the air as though they owned both sea and land, how Eliza hated them. If ever a bird was of the devil, it was the gull. Phoebe, of course, loved them. They let her walk among them without scattering, even let her pet their chicks. It was the gull in Phoebe that Eliza hated.

Mam was pulling a wool nightshirt on Lor. "He's beginning to shiver. A fever is starting up."

"Can I hold him?" Phoebe whispered.

"You've done enough harm already. He's like to have caught his death. It's all your fault."

Eliza's tongue was a scourge and she was whipping Phoebe with it, a whipping that was long in the coming, for neither Mam nor Pap would ever give it to her. They had not been so tender with her when she was a young one.

"Have done!" Mam said sharply. She sat down in the rocking chair, cradling Lor in her arms. Phoebe was pressing against her. "Don't bear so close, Phoebe. Lor's getting the croup. It's hard enough for him to be pulling in the air."

Mam's voice had an edge to it. She was anxious. The trace of sharpness cut right into Phoebe. Eliza was watching her face. Phoebe's face was like a shallow tide pool that catches every cloud on a bright day, and the living creatures in their water worlds are naked for all to see. It isn't decent to have such a face. To show all the things that come and go inside. Hurting Phoebe. The thought of doing it filled Eliza with a pleasurable excitement. Why should hurting Phoebe give such delight? Eliza's thoughts bolted in another direction. Pa called Phoebe his sugarplum. He kissed her every night. Never had he done that to his firstborn, never in her whole life. Once Eliza had asked Mam about it. "Pap has never kissed me, never once held me on his lap."

Mam said, "You just don't remember."

Eliza remembered all right. Pap did not like her. He said, "You've a sharp tongue like your granny. You even look like her." He meant her Granny Newcomb. "If that witch is in my house, I'll spend the night in my boat with the fish." That's what he said about Granny Newcomb. And Eliza was a Newcomb. Phoebe was a Caswell. Phoebe was a sugarplum, snugged up to every night. How would Pap like it when Phoebe's doing cost Lor's life? It would be worth a peck to see how he took it.

Lor was a strong baby yet he went in one night. Mam would say he must have had the makings of the lung fever in him before he went out that day. But Eliza knew why he went so fast. God read her mind. He sent death to Lor because that's what Eliza was praying for. His death would square off Phoebe.

"I don't want Lor to die. I love Lor," she explained carefully to God, but God knew her thinking and the thinking was in her. Why does God always answer bad prayers?

"You hate Phoebe more than you love Lor. You want him to die. I give you what you want." She could almost hear God saying it.

The rasping of Lor's breath stopped when the cock crowed outside. Eliza thought of Christ on the cross. "If I am to blame for your sending death to Lor, forgive me for Thy Son's sake. But it isn't fair to give me all the blame. Phoebe has a lot to answer for, too."

Forgiveness never came. She could never forgive herself. Her hatred for Phoebe grew with her growing. Eliza could hardly abide being in the same house. She was glad to marry a Portsmouth man.

There are dyings and birthings, and she lives through all of them. She sees Mam and Jane and Mary on summer visits to the shoals. Phoebe is always out on the rocks with the gulls so she is spared the sight of her. Life is good, or it looks that way from the outside. God never gives up His punishing. Only one child has she been able to get, a little girl who is the spit of Phoebe, acts like her, talks like her, thinks like her. Sometimes Eliza forgets and calls her Phoebe. Anastasia says, "I like it when you call me Phoebe. I love Aunt Phoebe more than anyone in all the world."

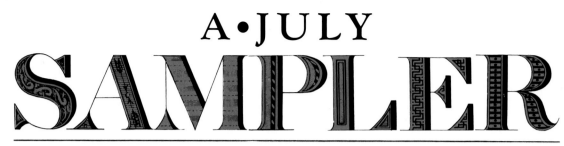

A•JULY
SAMPLER

☞ Memorable thoughts, quotes, and assorted tidbits from the last 50 July issues. ☜

STORY BY A STORYTELLER

☞ "My wife died five o'clock this morning," the man said in a flat, expressionless Down East drone. He had thick, dark hair and a lean, lined, anguished face.

"Spent the rest of the morning making her a coffin," he continued in the same unemotional tone. "Ran out of nails, twice."

The audience giggled.

"Split three covers before I got the fourth one nailed down tight. Bruised my thumb with the hammer. Pulled my back lifting the coffin into the wagon. Broke the halter as the horse pulled the wagon out of the barn, so we had to go into town pulling crooked." Another ripple of laughter.

"Got out of control going down

The late Marshall Dodge.

— Charles W. Collier

---

that last hill, and my wife just shot right off the back of the wagon. (Louder laughter.) Crashed through the post office window. (A roar.)

"I jumped off, run inside to make sure no one was injured. There was Tut Tuttle, the postman, staring at me through the stamp window. Said 'Lucky I had the grating down.' (Volley of guffaws.)

" 'Sure was,' I replied.

" 'Did you pass the preacher and the undertaker heading out your place this morning?' he asked.

"I said, 'Tut, I come into town to see if I couldn't find them.'

"He said, 'I guess you missed them.'

"I said, 'I guess I did.'

"I said, 'Tut, you know — my day's been one . . . long . . . fizzle from beginning to end.' " (Helpless hysteria and applause.) **The late Marshall Dodge, at a gathering of Maine storytellers at the 1978 Maine Festival in Brunswick.** (*From "Funny as an Elm Tree" by Tim Clark.*)

A•FAVORITE

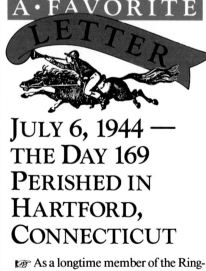

JULY 6, 1944 — THE DAY 169 PERISHED IN HARTFORD, CONNECTICUT

☞ As a longtime member of the Ringling Bros., Barnum & Bailey Circus, I was interested to read the account of the Hartford fire (at which I also was present) in the July *Yankee*. Many have been praised for their coura-

geous action during the fire, but to me the real heroes were a Catholic priest and Merle Evans' circus band.

Right after the famous Wallenda Troupe of high-wire artists had finished their act on that particular day of tragedy, Merle Evans, a veteran of over 25 years with the Big Top, could see that something was wrong on the other end of the tent, and he started the band playing. The thought came that it could be the seats had collapsed or an animal had run amok, but the picture was so confusing he could not be sure. Glancing up at the speck of light, he saw that it was growing larger and larger, working its way along the canvas. When he realized that the Big Top was ablaze, he kept the band playing. Merle picked up his trumpet and gave out with several bars of his famous triple tongue technique, keeping one eye on the flame eating its way through the top, as it seemed to devour everything in its

path. The air was filled with the pitiful screams of the children and the crash of the poles dropping to the ground as the ropes dissolved in the heat, but the band went on playing!

Circus workers ran in to guide the crowds through the haze of smoke. Clowns Emmett Kelley and Felix Adler, followed by Saluto, the midget clown, came out leading a group of children as the smoke got thicker and the light grew dim.

It was almost impossible to breathe without choking, when out of the darkness came a priest and two nuns with seven crying children. Leaving the children safely outside with the nuns, the priest rushed back into the flaming top. A moment later he came out carrying a crippled child with another youngster clinging to his coat-tails. Faces blackened, eyes red from the blinding smoke, they struggled to catch their breath as the priest stumbled into the fresh air.

THE SPEECH NO ONE REMEMBERS

☞ But suddenly the interest of the weary delegates quickened — Alexander Hamilton, the young delegate from New York, whose spectacular career was known to most of them, had the floor. Hamilton began by stating he feared they would not approve his plan, that it was based on the English form of government, which he considered the finest in the world. Showing great promise at the beginning, Hamilton's plan provided for a bicameral legislature in which the assembly was to be elected by popular vote for a term of three years. Though he did not mention the word "king," the chief executive was to be chosen for life and to have the power of absolute veto over all laws passed by the state and national legislatures. The senators must all be men owning large, landed estates and were to be elected for life — not directly by the people. Only those of means were to be permitted to vote for a group of "first electors." As the plan unfolded, it was apparent that the people were to be permitted little participation in the government, as they were "not competent to govern themselves."

For five hours Hamilton talked, quietly and without oratory. The convention sat as if stunned, the only sounds in the hall being Hamilton's voice and the rustling of his papers. When he sat down, there was a deathly silence — no one moved — no one spoke. Finally, as if released from a trance, one of the delegates made a comment upon an entirely different matter — and the convention came back to life. It was as if Hamilton had never spoken. Only Madison came to him later to ask for a copy of the speech for his notes.

However, later that day, outside the hall, a goodly number of the more conservative delegates congratulated the daring young man, which prompted Johnson of Connecticut to remark: "The gentleman from New York is praised by every gentleman but supported by no gentleman." (*From "The Great Compromise" by Emily Ross.*)

The scene described here took place during the convention in Philadelphia in the summer of 1787, at which the United States Constitution, after months of work, disagreements, and compromise, was finally adopted.

Mrs. Lincoln Clark of Chelmsford, Massachusetts, and Mrs. Margaret Mills of Belfast, Maine, observe the reenactment of the Battle of Penobscot Bay in July, 1979.

THE WOMAN'S ROLE IN REVOLUTIONARY WAR BATTLE REENACTMENTS

☞ "Always bring your sewing," one veteran camp follower was admonishing a less experienced neighbor. A baby began to cry, and a number of faces wore the familiar look of women putting up with inexplicable male behavior. "This is getting to be a tedious battle," huffed a mobcapped matron, who got up and shuffled back toward the fort.

Although a number of women get dressed up as men and take part in the hostilities — just as some did during the actual Revolution — for the most part, women are relegated to secondary roles in reenactments. One lady present at Penobscot — "I'm a wench," she explained — said she enjoyed the encampments more than the actual battles. She was looking forward to returning to Fort George for the second phase of the battle, where she would be "cooking, polishing gaiters, getting attacked, and what-not." (*From "When the Paraders Meet the Button-Counters at Penobscot Bay" by Tim Clark.*)

"Here, Father, take my hand!" I shouted. But he braced himself momentarily and pulling out his rosary beads, held in blistered hands, he walked deliberately into the fiery Big Top. As he did so, the tent was crumbling, the fire now 10 feet from the bandstand, and I could see the priest make the sign of the cross and give the last rites.

Now the musicians were standing to play those last few notes as Merle shouted "Coda!" — a musical term meaning "cut, the end" — and waved for them to jump. The musicians jumped and raced for the outside, some leaving their instruments — the bass drum, the tuba, along with Merle's priceless collection of circus music, all of which were burned to a crisp in a few seconds.

It had taken only 10 minutes, but it seemed like eternity. That was the last time I saw the Catholic priest, and I've never learned his name. But his

Photo taken seconds before the entire top of the tent erupted in flames.

contribution, like that of Merle Evans and his band, was truly heroic.

Albert Tucker
Sarasota, Florida

There was no doubt in the minds of any of those present as to who had committed these crimes. In fact, the murderer stood gleefully surveying the results of her handiwork.

She was Captain Frances G. Lee, a woman in her eighties who delights in perpetrating crimes that baffle the shrewdest brains in investigative work today.

None of the bodies was more than six inches in height, and the environment of the crime was spectacularly true to life. They were all housed in glass boxes. The stories told by the witnesses had been neatly typed. Where a miniature State Trooper stood holding a notebook, spectators could be assured that, despite the fact this notebook had been fashioned at the scale of an inch to the foot, the miniature pencil which the State Trooper held in his hand actually had a microscopic lead and that notations which had been written in the notebook had actually been made with this pencil.

Where the crime was committed in the garage in the dead of winter, the snow melting on the roof on the south side of the garage had resulted in more icicles and less snow than on the north side of the garage.

For many years now, select groups of state and foreign police — some from the famed Scotland Yard, some from as far away as India — have gathered to match wits with Captain Frances G. Lee and to try and solve her miniature crimes.

So far, no one has ever been able to detect any error.

Captain Lee is a perfectionist. (*From "The Perennial Crimes of Captain Lee" by Erle Stanley Gardner.*)

These are the opening few paragraphs of Erle Stanley Gardner's July 1960 Yankee article about Captain Frances G. Lee of New Hampshire. When we asked Mr. Gardner if he would accept our $87.50 article fee, standard for us in those days (and calculated to appear as if we had meticulously "figured out" the amount), he replied, "No, you can pay me either $1000 or nothing." We opted for the latter, and Mr. Gardner happily conceded that to be the only "true Yankee" choice.

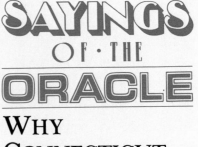

– Anthony Anable

Captain Frances G. Lee as she appeared in Erle Stanley Gardner's 1960 article.

THE MURDERER STOOD AMONG THEM

☞ A group of highly trained police officers stood looking at the scene of the murder.

These men represented the cream of the crop. They came from half a dozen states and had been selected on the basis of merit by the highest state and police officials. But now, as they stood looking at the corpse in the garage, they were plainly puzzled.

The physical evidence on the ground simply didn't check with the story that had been told by the witnesses. Moreover, a late fall of snow had covered the ground with a telltale blanket, which had made it impossible for anyone to have entered or left the garage without leaving tracks. Yet the tracks that were present couldn't be explained by any rational theory that coincided with the stories given by the witnesses.

A short distance away another corpse dangling at the end of a rope was puzzling a similar group of picked officers of the State Police. Here was a man who had apparently climbed up on a fruit box, adjusted a rope around his neck and then crashed through the box into the oblivion of death when the slender slats had given way.

SAYINGS OF · THE ORACLE

WHY CONNECTICUT IS CALLED "THE NUTMEG STATE"

☞ *Dear Oracle:* Could you, by chance, publish anything that might help to dispel the stigma suffered by the state of Connecticut regarding the libelous tale of the wooden nutmegs? Of course you know that there is no basis of fact for it. CONNIE.

Answer: Now, now, Connie! We have been assured by the best authorities in Connecticut that it is a cussed lie, but there is a basis of fact; oh yes there is!

Back in the early 1800s, in the town of Waterford, the minister, Rev. Jacob B. Spofford, was invited to tea by Mrs. Elishib Peterson. The Reverend was very fond of boiled rice sprinkled with sugar and nutmeg, and Mrs. Peterson had prepared that dish for him, or so she thought. But just before teatime, her servant, Amanda, came and whispered that there was no nutmeg in the house.

"Run over to Mrs. Hammersley's and borrow one!" directed the distracted hostess, and the servant disappeared. Tea was served, the rice with it, plenteously sprinkled with what looked like nutmeg, and the Reverend consumed it with apparent relish.

A day or so later, having purchased some nutmegs, Mrs. Peterson told Amanda to return the one she had borrowed. "Why M'is Peterson," exclaimed Amanda, "I didn't borrow any. Mrs. Hammersley didn't have any, either."

"But what did you use, then?" demanded the lady.

"Why," explained the servant. "I knew that your party would be ruined without it, and so I just grated on the handle of a buttonhook!"

So you see, Connie! **Joseph Chase Allen, who answered reader questions in Yankee for over 35 years in a column entitled "Sayings of the Oracle."**

BOSTON GLOBE — Dr. Harrison T. Rogers and his sexmobile rolled up to the Prudential yesterday to attempt to eradicate "one hundred years of prudery." The Bureau of Sexological Investigation has four such sexmobiles that tour the East and carry the message that sex is "normal and fun. . . . "

NEWS ITEM: NANCY MILLER·
BOSTON, MASS.

A · FAVORITE LETTER

STATUS IN A BASKET

☞ Not to upstage Damon Ripley, your roving reporter, whose article on Nantucket basket-makers caught my eye in the May issue — but the first Nantucket baskets were made, topless, by the Wampanoag Indians on the island. They taught the new white settlers. The lightship crews took up the art from the islanders. The refinement of the decorative tops was perfected by José Formoso Reyes, now the dean of basket-makers.

During the summer months, when the island population swells from 5000 to almost 25,000, cocktail-party talk invariably brings the question: Is your basket a Reyes, a Roop, a Macy, an Elder, a Sevrens, a Sayle, a Chase, a Whitten, a Brown, or a Kane? There is a pecking order of basket-makers maintained by every owner of one of these authentic gems. Naturally the owner's personal artisan is number one in the order! Owners of an original can spot a Hong Kong import on Main Street from two blocks away. And the snobbery of silence in passing can sometimes be devastating to the interloper with the imitation — Nantucketers have their own status symbol. Above all, for neophytes, never refer to it as a pocketbook or a handbag. A Brahmin nose would not be long enough to look down at you for your indelicacy.

John L. Grey
Boston, Massachusetts

THE MAINE WAY TO MAKE BEAN-HOLE BEANS

☞ "This recipe of mine should feed eight people but probably won't if they are really hungry. You need two pounds of beans — make sure they're last year's crop, or they might be too tough. Wash the beans. Mix ⅓ cup of good molasses, one tablespoon of salt, one tablespoon of dry mustard, and one tablespoon of white pepper — black pepper looks dirty in beans. Add to the beans and fill the kettle with water. Parboil until tender, about half an hour with a rolling boil, if you've got good beans. Then add a good slab of salt pork, washing off all of the salt first. Put this on top of the beans to brown as they bake. Of course you will have had your fire going in the pit overnight until the firebricks or rocks are red-hot. The beans should be in the ground for at least 10 hours, well covered with sand. It's hard to overcook them. If you fill the kettle with water just before covering, it will never boil dry. Try it and you'll see why the Maine lumberjacks always sent the cook on 24 hours ahead into a work area. They wanted hot bean-hole beans waiting for them when they got there. There's nothing

Charles "Doc" Hall.

– Lawrence F. Willard

that better represents the state of Maine." **Charles "Doc" Hall of South Paris, Maine — for years the bean-hole baked bean chef supreme at the Oxford Hills Bean-Hole Bean Festival attended by thousands of bean lovers each July.** (*From "If You're Planning Baked Beans for 1000 or More" by Ezra Huckleby.*)

– Margo Letourneau

CHAPTER 8

August

A *ugust issues should be read in a hammock. Even in the shade of the two trees or porch to which it's slung, the temperature is too wonderfully warm to do much beyond gently swinging there — and reading about nature, about life, about memories of long ago, and perhaps about ships that can take you to faraway places in your dreams. Accordingly, August issues have seldom generated controversy of any kind, unless one counts the August 1977 cover painting of a teenage lass walking along the seashore with a man's shirt covering her bathing suit or, as some complained, covering nothing at all.*

As Yankee's *circulation grew, however, we noticed that some August features did more harm than good. We wanted to bring to our readers some of the comparatively unknown, unpublicized, quiet local happenings of August — town picnics, band concerts, blueberry-pie bakes, clambakes — but found we ruined them! As a result of the publicity we generated, too many people would descend upon the affair and, though certainly well-mannered (as are all* Yankee *readers), wreck it through sheer numbers. So, for instance, we refrained, year after year, from featuring the lighting of more than 300 antique Japanese lanterns out on the famous old campgrounds at Oak Bluffs on Martha's Vineyard, an annual August event known locally as "Illumination Night." Then, in 1983, we found a way. We shared "Illumination Night" with our 3½ million readers that year through photography — but stated clearly that the date would not be divulged by anyone until two nights before. Some of the best solutions to problems are the simplest!*

Little Compton, Rhode Island, as seen from Sakonnet Point.

– photograph by Paul A. Darling

183

Dr. Bennett is a diver, a scientist, and a writer, the ideal combination for revealing, as here, in August 1975, the complicated inner workings of a lake.

What's a "Two-Story" Lake?

BY DR. SHAUN BENNETT

Slowly, slowly I rise to the surface, keeping pace with the expanding bubbles that surround me. I've been exhaling for almost 45 seconds and it feels strange — all my normal reflexes are telling me to take a breath — but as I rise the pressure decreases and the air already in my lungs is expanding; I know that I must let it out or risk bursting my lungs. At about 20 feet from the surface it is so much warmer than the zone I've just left that the water feels like a warm bath to me.

There's a fisherman up there. I can hear his motor and I look up as I rise so that I don't bang my head on his boat or mine. He shouldn't be so close to a diver, but he doesn't mean any harm — he's just curious. John will warn him off if he gets too close.

Finally my head, encased in a black neoprene wet suit and masked behind an oval plate of glass, breaks the surface. The fisherman spots me immediately. He's been watching my bubbles roil the surface. He asks the inevitable question.

"See any fish down there?"

I don't know why fishermen aren't more imaginative, but this question never varies so much as a word. Concentrating on their sport, I guess.

"Naught ah whun," I gurgle back through the mouthpiece of my regulator, shaking my head.

A bass will come right up and stare you in the eye, but these are trout waters, and the shy trout is usually gone before I spot him.

"How deep is it?" comes back the invariable question number two.

"Hitty heet," I gurgle.

"Fifty feet," translates John, who is not gagged with a mouthpiece. He has learned my strange language over the months we have worked together. Question three is phrased more as a statement, but it's always the same, and the fisherman always wants me to confirm or refute it.

"I heard there's a hole in this lake so deep there's no bottom to it."

This idea creates in my mind the image of a long tunnel in the lake's bottom, the other end of which opens in the bottom of a similar lake somewhere in China. It's the only way I can conceptualize a bottomless hole. I spit out the mouthpiece for this one.

"Is that so? Well, I haven't run across it yet. I'd say it was 50 feet at the deepest."

If we weren't busy collecting data, I'd probably take a few minutes to explain to him that all the lakes I've ever seen have had very gentle, regular bottom to-

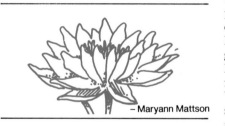

– Maryann Mattson

pography with nothing resembling a hole except near an occasional rock outcropping, which can create something like a cliff. It's also a bit difficult to say precisely how deep the lake is until you define exactly what you mean by the bottom. Many lakes, like this one, have bottoms covered by a soft, gelatinous ooze that has developed over the centuries. A continual "rain" of the bodies of microscopic creatures from the surface waters, as well as dust and pollen that fall into the water, forms layers that may be many feet thick. If you measure the depth by sounding with a weighted line, your weight, depending on its size and shape, may sink some considerable distance into this ooze before it finally stops.

The bottomless hole concept is a scary one. Once I even thought I had fallen into the bottomless hole. I had just started diving, and I was working on a biological project in which I made observations at the lake's bottom. It was my custom to "spread-eagle" horizontally in the water and to sink slowly to the bottom with plenty of time to think about what I was doing. At 30 or 40 feet a lake is very dark, and it may take a minute or two for a diver's eyes to adjust so that he can see at all. Well, I sank into the darkness for what seemed an interminable period and still I did not strike bottom. Finally, I could take it no longer; I wasn't going any farther down. It was already so completely dark that I knew I'd have difficulty just determining which direction to take back to the surface. As I began to swim for my life, I was surprised to find that my limbs moved as though through pudding, and then suddenly there was a dim light. It was then that I realized what had happened. I had floated down so gently in my temporary blindness that I had landed on the soft bottom and had not felt it through the thick wet suit. With my mask buried in the muck, I had simply lain there, experiencing terror after terror as I calculated that I was sinking untold fathoms into an abyss.

Diving like this teaches one to see all types of water bodies as complex, functioning, ecological entities rather than as so many categories in a dull, though not dry, system of classification. Most water bodies can be distinguished on the basis of how they work, the way they function physically and biologically, as well as by the way they look. A pond, for instance, is merely a small lake in which the littoral zone, a shallow region where plants can root in the bottom while also extending to the surface, where they stand (like rushes) or float (like lilies), occupies a relatively large proportion of the total area. The law, on the other hand, recognizes no such biological distinction and it classifies any body of standing water that is greater than five or 10 acres (depending on the state) as a Great Pond, and hence public property.

One of the most graphic lessons for a diver in New England lakes is his first

184

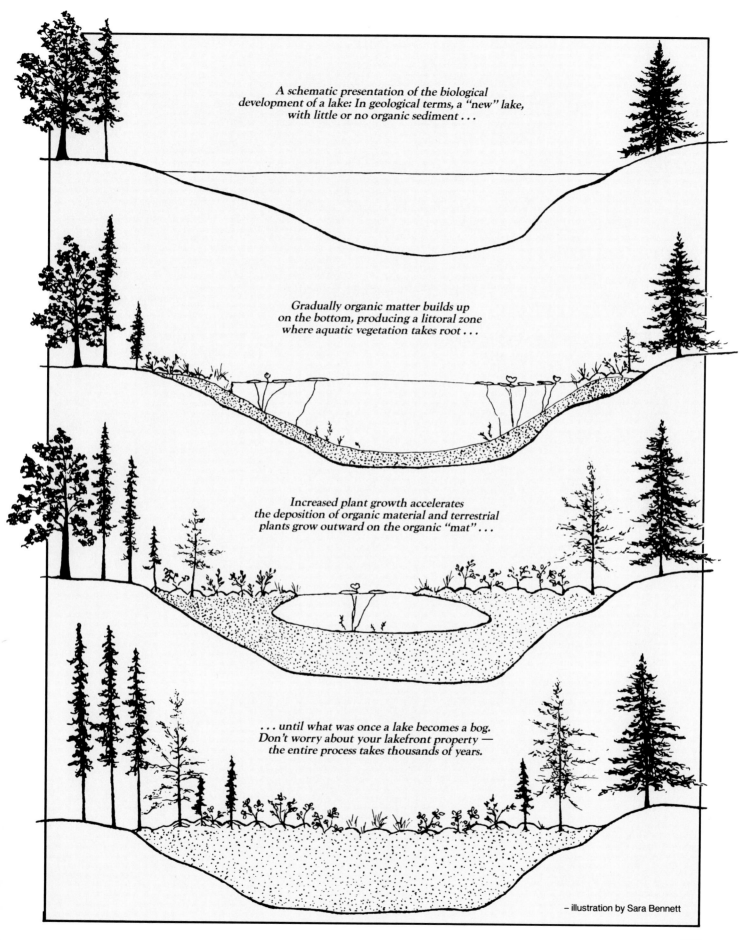

A schematic presentation of the biological development of a lake: In geological terms, a "new" lake, with little or no organic sediment . . .

Gradually organic matter builds up on the bottom, producing a littoral zone where aquatic vegetation takes root . . .

Increased plant growth accelerates the deposition of organic material and terrestrial plants grow outward on the organic "mat" . . .

. . . until what was once a lake becomes a bog. Don't worry about your lakefront property — the entire process takes thousands of years.

– illustration by Sara Bennett

185

Over the centuries such a lake tends to fill itself in and become shallower....

encounter with the "thermocline," a layer of water in which the temperature drops very rapidly as one goes deeper. Beneath the thermocline is another layer which limnologists call the "hypolimnion," a five-dollar way of saying bottom layer. The hypolimnion is uniformly cold, around 40 degrees Fahrenheit. A diver encountering the thermocline and hypolimnion unawares is in for a real shock. He cannot spend much time in these waters without a good wet suit to protect him from the cold.

The upper waters of a lake are known as the "epilimnion," which means surface layer. The epilimnion and thermocline form in the spring and develop ver-

tically throughout the summer, because the sun and wind warm the cold water at the lake's surface. The warmed water expands slightly, and thus becomes lighter and tends to "float" on the denser, colder waters beneath. The result is a stable situation with light, warm water (the epilimnion) floating above heavy, cold water (the hypolimnion), with a zone of sharp temperature change (the thermocline) in between. Imagine one of those inflatable children's toys that has a weight in the bottom, so that no matter which way it is punched or tossed, it always turns upright. This is analogous to the stability of a thermally stratified lake.

The stability of a stratified lake, or its

resistance to mixing, forms a barrier between the upper and lower layers and produces what Fish and Game people call a "two-story" lake. Since the layers cannot mix, the supplies of certain substances critical for living organisms cannot be renewed. Oxygen, for instance, cannot reach the bottom layer from the atmosphere because of the intervening barrier of epilimnion and thermocline. Thus, the oxygen in the hypolimnion at the time of stratification is an entire summer's supply. Similarly, nutrient materials are concentrated in the sediments and deep waters of the lake and are prevented from moving into the surface water. Microscopic algae living near the surface,

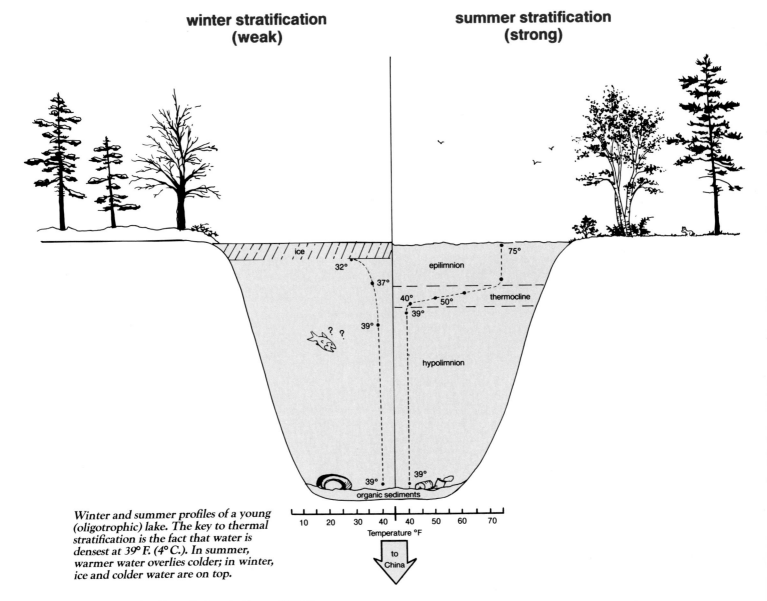

winter stratification (weak)

summer stratification (strong)

Winter and summer profiles of a young (oligotrophic) lake. The key to thermal stratification is the fact that water is densest at 39° F. (4° C.). In summer, warmer water overlies colder; in winter, ice and colder water are on top.

– illustration by Sara Bennett/redrawn by Maryann Mattson

186

where there is abundant sunlight for them to use in photosynthesis, eventually exhaust the supplies of nutrients there. The result is a sort of "brake" on the organisms in the epilimnion; their processes of growth and reproduction slow as their nutrient supplies are depleted.

The density difference between the warm- and cold-water layers may also create a barrier of another sort. Some objects, microscopic algae for instance, may become dense enough to sink through the epilimnion. However, unless they are also heavy enough to sink through the thermocline, they may become trapped there. I have seen literally billions of such algae in a blanket, a few inches thick and many acres in area, "floating" eerily on the thermocline 15 or 20 feet below the surface.

When a lake begins to cool in the fall, the water in the epilimnion contracts slightly, gradually becoming heavier. If water behaved like most substances, one would expect the denser water to sink to the bottom and to cool until it eventually became ice. But water is a curious substance, because after cooling to a certain point, four degrees centigrade or 39.1 degrees Fahrenheit, it no longer contracts on further cooling but, instead, expands slightly, becoming *lighter*. Thus, the densest water in a lake is that closest to 39.1 degrees Fahrenheit. As the epilimnion cools and contracts, it eventually reaches the same density as the hypolimnion, or even becomes slightly heavier. When this happens the lake is no longer stable in its stratification. Then a late October or November wind circulates the water and mixes it from top to bottom in a phenomenon known as "overturn." Sometimes the upper waters become significantly heavier than the lower ones before mixing and they sink with enough force to stir up the bottom sediments and produce turbid water, where only the day before the water was relatively clear.

Later on, in December usually, ice begins to cover the lake. Ice can be thought of as a lid on a lake, a barrier that holds back oxygen and, if the lake is snow-covered, blocks out light. It is under such circumstances, when no oxygen can reach the water and no light reaches the algae, which might otherwise replenish the oxygen supply through photosynthesis, that fish may suffocate — the so-called winterkill. Nevertheless, it is fortunate that ice does form at the surface rather than sinking to the bottom, where it might never melt. It is the expansion of ice to a volume about 10 percent greater

than that of an equal weight of water that accounts for ice's ability to float. Next time you walk across a frozen lake, consider that you are actually supported by a floating raft rather than by a rigid bridge.

Just below the ice the water is 32 degrees Fahrenheit, and from there toward the bottom it warms and becomes denser, reaching a uniform temperature in the vicinity of 39.1 degrees Fahrenheit. The lake is again stratified, but this time colder and lighter water is floating on denser, warmer water. There is no thermocline in winter, and the stratification is relatively weak because of the small temperature differences (about seven degrees) compared to those of summer (as much as 40 degrees). However, the lid of ice prevents anything from disturbing the stratification, which persists until ice-out in the spring, when the

– Maryann Mattson

surface waters warm again to the temperature of maximum density and stratification again breaks down. Then winds circulate the water a second time, replenishing nutrient supplies and oxygenating it. Thus, New England lakes mix twice each year, once in the spring and again in the fall, a pattern limnologists refer to as "dimictic."

Over the centuries such a lake tends to fill itself in and to become shallower. Some of the sediments will be carried in by streams from the surrounding area, but, more importantly, the remains of many of the creatures that live in the lake will create organic sediments.

There are also various contributions of human origin to the sediments. In certain lakes where trolling or other relatively sedentary forms of boating are common (as opposed to canoeing or sailing, which take a lot of work), the lake bottom is likely to have a remarkably dense population of beer and soda containers. Of more interest on the bottoms of New England lakes are numbers of sawlogs all cut and limbed. After the 1938 hurricane, it was simply not possi-

ble to saw all the downed timber before it rotted, so many lakes were filled with logs to preserve them until they could be made into lumber. Many of these sank first, and they were lost until recently, when at least one New England diver started making a nice living by raising them and selling them.

Eventually a lake may fill with sediments to the point that the hypolimnion disappears; that is, the water becomes so shallow that it can be warmed all the way to the bottom in summer. When this "aging" occurs, the body of water becomes a "one-story" lake, and nutrient materials can be regenerated from the sediments all summer long to replace those utilized by plants and algae. Now the brake on living things is removed and growth escalates rapidly, as does the creation of materials to form more organic sediments. It will be a relatively short time, as these things go, before the lake becomes completely filled in and resembles the terrestrial habitats around it.

This biological development of a lake, which scientists insist on obscuring with the title "eutrophication," used to take thousands of years. But in recent times man has greatly accelerated the process by supplying huge amounts of nutrients to lakes, both intentionally in the form of municipal and industrial wastewater, and unintentionally in the form of runoff from fertilized agricultural lands. These huge amounts of nutrients are effective aquatic fertilizers and they encourage tremendous growth of algae and other plants. Occasionally these accumulations of algae die, and their decay depletes the water's oxygen to the point that fish also die of suffocation. It should be remembered, however, that it is precisely this overactivity of living organisms that depletes the oxygen. When the oxygen is completely gone, other living organisms that do not require it take over the decay process.

John and I have finished for the day and we are at the landing, laboriously carrying equipment from the boat to the trunk. We are tired. A fisherman with a small boat on a trailer drives up. He's going to take advantage of the long summer twilight for a few hours of fishing. John struggles to stow my last scuba tank before the fisherman spots it, but it's too late; he's seen it. He swoops like a hawk.

"See any fish down there?"

"Nope. But there's a hole out there you wouldn't believe. Must go clear to China."

⟨⟩

Our August 1983 issue with this article came out the week Scott Nearing, coauthor of Living the Good Life, *finally passed away at age 100. It was widely quoted in the subsequent obituaries in newspapers across the country.*

Leaving the Good Life

BY MEL ALLEN

Helen and Scott Nearing, whose book, *Living the Good Life,* is the bible of the back-to-the-land movement, live on a windswept spit of land on Penobscot Bay in Hancock County, Maine, 20 miles from the nearest stores and banks, in Blue Hill. She is 79; he will be 100 on August 6 (he was born the same year as Franz Kafka), and for 50 years they have had little use for towns or stores or banks.

They began homesteading in 1932 on a run-down, 65-acre Vermont farm at the foot of Stratton Mountain, which they bought for $300 down and an $800 mortgage. Scott Nearing was nearly 50 and broke, living in New York City with Helen Knothe, a beautiful young violinist who later became his wife. In the stove in their East Side apartment they burned copies of his pamphlet, "The ABC's of Communism," for warmth. A leading Socialist, he had run for Congress and had sold out lecture halls debating Clarence Darrow. A professor of economics and sociology, he had been fired from three universities for taking stands against child labor and for his pacifism during World War I. His textbooks had been withdrawn and publishers refused his new work. The move to the country was for survival.

They had no electricity and, except for a battered pickup truck, no machinery. They fortified the soil with compost, heated with wood, and built a house of stone. They kept no farm animals and had no children. They ate only the vegetables they raised and the grains and fruits they bartered for. From their sugar bush, they boiled maple syrup for cash. But in 1952, feeling crowded out by

---

A few weeks before his 100th birthday, Scott Nearing gave a talk to friends and relatives visiting Forest Farm. "He was his old self," said his wife Helen.

Stratton Mountain ski developers, they moved to Maine, to another run-down farm on 140 acres of isolation. He was 70, she 49. They were starting over again.

One cold misty morning late last May, I visited "Forest Farm," now a garden spot that attracts several thousand people a year. Whenever I feel age descending and hopes receding, I think of Scott Nearing and I am cheered. I had seen him twice, in person, giving talks on gardening and the coming collapse of capitalism. His deeply tanned, wrinkled face atop a straight, sturdy body made me think, somehow, that he would scythe his meadow, chop his wood, and plant his garden forever. I did not have to buy his theories on socialism to feel that he was a heroic man. But this was a melancholy drive down the Maine coast, for I had just received a letter from Helen Nearing that said that Scott was dying. "He's in no pain," she had written, "just getting ready to leave a worn-out body."

There is a sign nailed to a pine tree at the end of the gravel driveway: "Visitors 3–5. Please help us to lead the good life." They are famous for their stone buildings, all done by hand with stones they have gathered obsessively on walks through the fields, in the woods, or along the shore. When I park I see a garage, a storage shed, an outhouse, the beautiful balconied house completed when Scott was 95, and a five-foot-tall wall surrounding the garden, all of stone, giving me the impression that I have dropped in at the estate of an English lord.

Instead it is Helen Nearing, with her white blouse torn at the shoulder, a faded red sweater, and blue corduroys, who greets me. Scott, her barber of 50 years, has not been able to cut her hair; a few strands stick out from her forehead like quills. She is weary, her face drawn, and when she sits down at the long wooden table in the kitchen to talk, her attention wanders, her ears cocked to the living

room, where Scott is sleeping. A fire burns in the cookstove. Herbs and onions hang from an oak beam and a breeze rustles chimes.

"I've never known him a day sick in bed," she says. "Never, never. We've never had a doctor. He was still working outside half a year ago. But one morning he just took to his bed and started to sleep. I think it was November; like he was hibernating. He was restless for a time, shouting out suddenly at night. Now he's contented. He doesn't complain. But sometimes he'll look at me and say, 'I wish I could carry the wood in for you.'"

She walks into the living room. The floor is stone, the walls paneled, and a massive wooden table sits before the picture window that looks out upon their cove. There is a woodstove in a corner, and on the other side of the room where bookshelves span the walls, Scott Nearing lies in a hospital bed with the sides up, like a crib, and beside the bed is a cot where Helen has slept the past several months. "This is my job now," she says quietly. "This is it."

He stirs at her approach. "What do you want, dear?" he says. His face is softer than I remembered, still tanned and weatherbeaten but as peaceful as a baby's, and above his lip is a thin white mustache.

"Someone's come to see you," she says to him.

Blinking, he focuses on me. "Well, good," he says. "Good."

I tell him I have found a whole batch of his early books and pamphlets in a secondhand bookstore.

"Thrown away?" he asks.

"No," Helen says. "They've gone to a good person who will keep them."

"I'm going to have them reprinted," he says. He takes a deep breath and coughs. "Sure, sure," Helen says, comforting, and pulls a second blanket over him. He looks out the window to the calm, gray sea. In a moment he is asleep.

189

"That we ate no meat was in itself strange, but during our 20 years in Vermont we never baked a pie."

They met when Helen was 24. She was independent and beautiful, a student of Eastern mysticism who had recently returned to the family home in Ridgeway, New Jersey, after studying violin abroad. At her father's request she invited Scott Nearing, then separated from his wife and living in Ridgeway, to speak at the Unitarian Church. Nearing liked her and took her for a drive. Like Helen, Scott had been born to a wealthy family. Raised in the coal-mining town of Morris Run, Pennsylvania, he was the grandson of Winfield Scott Nearing, the despotic ruler of the company town. Young Scott sided with the working class. He had a horror of riches and fancy living. When his first wife decorated their home with lace doilies and cut glass, he bought himself a wooden bowl and spoon and refused to eat from anything else.

"That first night he said, 'Do you believe in fairies?'" Helen tells me. "I thought, what kind of guy is this? Of course I believe in fairies, and I told him so and he was very interested. I was going with four or five fellows at the time, but I

was taken with his integrity, his purpose in life. Even those who disagreed with him responded to his warmth. And he was a vegetarian, as I was. I still tease him that if he hadn't been a vegetarian we wouldn't have hooked up."

We are in the kitchen and she laughs. "Can you imagine my parents? A Communist, a married man, and a man 21 years older. It turned their hair white!"

He told her to live poor for a while before she came with him, so she moved to a slum and found work in a Brooklyn candy factory. He told her to return to the glitter of Europe, to be sure she wanted his life. She did. When he asked her to return to the cold-water flat in New York City and help him research a book on war, she cut her long, dark hair and took a boat home.

Soon she was a subsistence farmer in Vermont, where they evolved a system that would continue the rest of their lives. They worked four hours every day producing their food and shelter, four hours at their professions — his writing on social issues, her music — and spent

four hours socializing. The latter was a little tricky in the hill towns of Vermont.

"Our ways amused the neighbors, baffled them, or annoyed them," Helen has written. "That we ate no meat was in itself strange, but during our 20 years in Vermont we never baked a pie."

There was little time for what Scott considered idle amusements. Once when an acquaintance invited him to play miniature golf, he replied, "When I lose my physical capacities, I will take up golf. When I lose my mental faculties, I will play *miniature* golf."

In 1946 Scott's wife died. "I told him 'I want your name,'" Helen says. "It's a bad name and I want it." In 1947 Scott and Helen were married. "And we've endured, haven't we?" she says. "And we're so different. His thinking is so pedantic, like he's always at a blackboard: 1,2, 3,4,A,B,C,D. And he gets hooked up with me, who sings, plays the fiddle and the organ, and yodels. And he doesn't even like music." She sighs and stands up. "Let's see if he's awake," she says.

"Scotto, open your mouth," she says,

Left: *Helen knits with Scott nearby.* Right: *The young couple visited Russia in 1931. They wed 16 years later, after Scott's estranged wife died.*

– courtesy of Helen Nearing

Lunch outside the Maine farmhouse included "nothing that walks or wiggles."

propping up a pillow. "I'm giving you some rose hip juice."

"That's nice of you."

"Rose hip juice you made yourself. Picked them and pressed them."

He takes a sip. Then another.

"Would you like some more?"

"Is it handy?" he asks.

"Yup. Right here."

Helen wipes his mouth and smooths his mustache. "He has a mustache now only because I'm too lazy to get in under his nose and shave it. He hates affectation. He heard William Jennings Bryan speak once, and he thought he was such an affected ass that he came home, shaved off his mustache, and gave away his dress suit. And he hasn't had either one since then."

We are speaking in the kitchen about families and the personal price one pays to be Scott Nearing. "People write to Scott," Helen says, "telling him he is a great man, an inspiration. But he had three sisters and two younger brothers who were ashamed of him. They thought he was a failure. We'd send them his books, and they'd come back unopened. He had two children. His son Bob is still friendly, but Scott severed relations with John in the sixties. He worked for Radio Free Europe, broadcasting propaganda to Europe. Scott said, 'You're working against the things I'm working for.' That was it. His son was John Scott Nearing, but then he dropped the Nearing.

"I asked Scott once if he would have lived his life differently. He said not in the big decisions, but in his personal relations. I think he meant he wishes he could have gotten along better with his son. But John died, so there's nothing to be done."

Past Scott's bed a door opens into a small, narrow room furnished with a desk, a typewriter, a bookcase. On the wall is a painting of Scott from a photograph by Lotte Jacobi. This room is the Social Science Institute, the publisher of many of Scott's 50 social science books. Though *Living the Good Life* was a success, Helen and Scott never touched the royalties for living expenses. All the money went here, to the Institute, to finance the research and publication of *Civilization and Beyond; USA Today; The Conscience of a Radical; Freedom, Promise and Menace.*

"I'd like someone to do a book of the early writings of Scott Nearing," Helen says. "Not just excerpts, but great chunks of writing. There are things in there, *important* things that will never be read by anyone."

We step back into the living room. Scott is sleeping. His right hand rests on his forehead, as though he is deep in thought. She says softly, "I wonder where the real Scott Nearing is now."

We are eating lunch in the living room, sitting before the picture window on a bench made from a slab of driftwood dragged up from the cove. There is eggplant soup, an enormous ceramic bowl of popcorn, a bowl of steamed millet, peanuts, peanut butter, honey, apples, and bananas. Helen Nearing's motto of cooking is: "The most nourishment for the least effort."

"Scotto, we have soup and popcorn," she calls. She sits for a moment to crack some peanuts, then leaps to her feet to feed him handfuls of popcorn, returns to the table for more peanuts, then leaps up again to give him soup. I think of a mother bird feeding her nestlings, all that flying off and returning.

"Finish your soup," she tells me. "I'll give you Scott's Emulsion." Into my bowl she drops a couple of spoonfuls of peanut butter and a thick dropper of honey. "Work that down like cement," she says. She adds a scoop of the millet and some apple slices. "We eat this every day." She laughs remembering a letter from a man who, after reading *Living the Good Life*, insisted on eating from a single bowl. "His wife divorced him. She said she wasn't going to eat like a dog."

A car drives up. It is a nurse to give Scott a bath.

"We were in the hospital for 12 days," Helen says. "I stayed with him in the room. When we got home, I thought I could take care of him, but I fell with him once. When I realized I couldn't, I just bawled because I thought I had to put Scott Nearing in a home. We went to a home for a while. I stayed with him, and they were very nice to us. But this is where he belongs."

Since girlhood Helen had collected stones with bands of black or white around them. She called them "wishing

"We never talked about Scott going first. He was so vital, so strong. We were equals."

Asked what they did for fun, the Nearings replied, "Give us a good-size job of building with stone and concrete."

– courtesy of Helen Nearing

stones" and felt that with them she had powers of divination. One day, knowing they must leave Vermont, she tied a wishing stone to a string, dangled it over a map of Maine, and closed her eyes. She imagined a saltwater farm, isolated enough so Scott could write in peace, run down enough to be cheap. Over Penobscot Bay the stone circled in an ever-tighter arc. That is where they found their present Forest Farm. And it was then that Pearl Buck, who had wanted to buy their Vermont farm, suggested that they write a book about their home-steading adventure.

"It had never occurred to us," says He-len. "It was just how we lived." They coauthored *Living the Good Life.* It sold 3000 copies in 1954, then went out of print. In 1970 Schocken Books reissued

it to a new generation. It was compared to *Walden,* sold 170,000 copies, and made the Nearings celebrities as Scott approached 90. When the energy crisis hit in 1973, TV networks sent nattily dressed reporters to the farm. Scott would take them to his woodpile, hand them a saw, and put them to work. He'd smile into the camera. "No crisis here," he'd say.

We are upstairs on the balcony outside Scott and Helen's bedroom, so close to the sea you seem to touch it. "I sit up here," she says, "and wonder where I'll go when Scott goes. I think of Switzer-land or Holland, where my mother is from. But then I ask myself, what could I get anywhere that I don't have here?

"I've remade my will so that the house will not go into the real estate market. I

want it to be a homestead educational center. People could come and see where Scott Nearing lived."

"Not where Helen Nearing lived, too?" I ask.

She laughs. "I'm just 'Helen and,' " she says. "When we sign books he signs his name and hands them to me and I write 'Helen and.' If I write my autobiography that will be the title, 'Helen and.' "

We walk into the guest room overlook-ing the garden. It is used by Nancy Rich-ardson, a 32-year-old Pittsburgh woman who made a pilgrimage to the farm seven years ago, remained in the area, and now helps Helen care for the garden and for Scott. Like others in the house, the room is sparsely furnished. The walls are deco-rated with Japanese prints, a photograph of Helen's cat Pusso (killed by a fisher in

October, and for which Helen mourns so much she cannot bear to look at it), and a painting of the stone house in Vermont on which this one is modeled.

"I learned detachment when we left Vermont," Helen says. "I thought if I ever have to leave anywhere again it won't be as hard as this. And when I went back a few years ago and saw that our house had become a ski chalet, well, I said, it's time to build its sister."

Bookshelves fill two walls of the room. "We've never had radio or television," she says. "I'd knit and he'd read to me or he'd shell beans and I'd read to him. If he tried one of his economics books I fell asleep. He liked Robert Louis Stevenson and anything by Tolstoy. I'd slip a science fiction in sometimes. Or stories about animals. Anything about animals."

She leans down and plucks a book from the bottom shelf. It's a biography, *Scott Nearing: Apostle of American Radicalism,* by Stephen J. Whitfield. She grimaces. "I don't like this at all," she says. She opens it. She has crossed out paragraphs with a marking pen. She reads the words under her lines:

"This is not an intellectual portrait of Scott Nearing. I expect that his thought cannot bear the weight of intensive scrutiny." She shuts the book loudly. "I wouldn't let Scott read it. I said, 'Don't bother yourself with it.' "

In the corner of the room are two boxes stuffed with photographs, letters, notes. She says with satisfaction, "It's all here, a treasure trove. Someday I'll give them to a sympathetic biographer."

Stacked on a shelf are metal card files crammed with 5 x 7 index cards, their headings ranging from "The Future of Civilization" to "Composting." "He took notes on everything," she says. "He taught me his system. 'Don't put information in books,' he would say, 'where you can't get at it.' So I take notes, writing down pithy quotations."

Among her quotations is this one: "No meal is as good as when you have your feet under your own table." Beside that she has written, "Scott Nearing, an opinion, 1970."

We start downstairs. I see four words burned into a plank nailed to the wall: "Sunshine — birdsong — snowfall — trees." She looks in on Scott.

"Your eyelashes are growing into your eyes," she says. "Here, close your eyes." She snips quickly.

"Thank you very much," he says.

We go through a door into the woodshed. It can hold eight cords. A cord or so is left from the past winter. "He cut and stacked all that last year," she says. "Incredible, isn't it?"

A 50-foot-long stone storage shed stands beside the house. Inside, cardboard cartons filled with books are stacked four feet high. "Thoreau had a library of 600 *Walden*s. We have 6000 Nearings." In a corner are boxes filled with letters from hopeful homesteaders. "The cruel thing was that more than anything he wanted to teach one class with the same students and watch them grow," she says. "And that was denied him. But he had more influence than if he had been a college president, don't you think?"

In the next room are the tools that Scott loves — his axes, including a double-bitted axe he has had since 1900, bow saws, teeth sharp as razors, and wheelbarrows, as clean as if they were in a museum. "Scott has a favorite wheelbarrow," Helen says. "Whenever we were building with stone, that was the one he used to mix the cement." He never left a tool in a field. Even if he were only pausing for lunch, he'd wipe it clean with burlap sacking that hung from a peg in the toolshed. He once wrote, "Order in the woodshed, the woodlot, toolshed, yard, and home are essential . . . . Care and artistry are worth the trouble."

We walk to the nearby farm where Helen and Scott lived for over 25 years before building their new stone house. A few years ago they sold it to Stan Joseph, after already selling many acres to other homesteaders. "We have only four acres left," Helen says, puffing slightly from the climb past boulders. "I wanted Scott to be relieved of the burden of cutting the grass and trimming the trees and weeding the garden." She looks at me. "But I never expected that none of the people who bought our land would stay our friends. We never see them. We were too organized, too methodical for them."

Soon the farm comes into view. A stone wall that took Helen and Scott 14 years to build surrounds the garden. Helen yodels, approaching the house, and we are welcomed inside by Stan Joseph's girlfriend. Helen has come to look at photos of Scott. There is one she would like copied. The two of them are walking down the road holding hands.

Stan Joseph comes in from the garden. He is a large man with a beard, a large hole in his checked, flannel shirt. There is an exchange of greetings. He points out a checkerboard hanging on the wall. "Look at that," he says. "I paid only a dollar for it at the flea market. I bet I can get $30 for it in the city."

"You know what you might like to give me is some mint," Helen ventures. "We have lost ours. I kept giving it away and now we have none left."

"Sure, Helen. We could work something out. What have you got to swop?"

We walk back to the house, and at 1:30 the mailman comes. He has a package of blankets sent by a Hollywood producer who is interested in making a movie based on their lives. She scoffs: "Can you imagine?" But she is excited, walking into the house. "Our mailman has read some of Scott's books," she says. "He says he wants more. He wants a list so he can check off the ones he wants."

It is time to leave, and I go to Scott Nearing to say good-bye. I have a friend whose courage to build her own house came after reading *Living the Good Life,* and she asked me to be certain I thanked him for her. So I did.

"You're welcome, I'm sure," he says. "I hope it turns out all right."

We shake hands. His grip is still firm.

"Will I see you again?" he asks.

I say I hope so. I say I would like to.

At the kitchen door Helen presses a dozen book lists in my hand. "Take them to bookstores. Tell them for God's sake to stock this man." She hands me a pamphlet of six pages with "SCOTT NEARING" at the top in bold letters. Beside it in smaller type, "August 6, 1883–" with space for one last date and this brief statement:

Scott lived a long and purposeful life. He was dedicated to research and to serving. He searched for knowledge and the truth, while he dedicated himself to serve his fellows. From the ideas on death that appealed to him I have selected some which show the direction of his thought. He undoubtedly goes on researching and learning, and knows more now. This much, at least, we can share of his thoughts.

There would be no ceremony. His body would be cremated and the ashes spread on the garden.

"We planned everything," she says, "but I stupidly didn't expect it. We never talked about Scott going first. He was so vital, so strong. We were equals."

She stands on a knoll while I drive away. In other times she bade farewell to visitors with a ringing yodel, but as I look back she waves good-bye in silence before she turns back to the house. Later it struck me that Scott Nearing was giving Helen his final act of kindness, leaving the good life as he had lived it, slowly, patiently, one step at a time.

FOUR FAVORITE ESSAYS

A Shadow on the Moon

What better vantage point for watching a lunar eclipse than to be in a boat
in the middle of Lake Winnipesaukee?

BY JOANNE CAPEN HAMLIN

It was after midnight when my husband George and I, armed with down quilts and binoculars, left our dock on Little Bear Island in Lake Winnipesaukee. We stopped the boat about midway between Little Bear and Whortleberry directly across from us. With the motor off, the silence was broken only by the lap of the water against the hull and the occasional cry of the loons from their sanctuary on Hurricane Island.

It was a cloudless summer night: the full moon dimmed the stars and cast a coppery reflection on the lake. The trees on Little Bear were etched against the deep blue of the sky. I leaned back in the boat and looked up, feeling something akin to vertigo, as though I were falling up into space. We wrapped the quilts around us and waited.

We could hear laughter, voices, and music from the mainland, though it was at least a mile away. George and I muttered about that, but as the minutes passed, the voices and music ceased, and we welcomed the feeling of being utterly alone. We pulled our arms out of the cocoon of quilts to pass the binoculars back and forth, looking for a change in the bright circle above us.

It was perhaps half an hour before we noticed it. Almost imperceptibly a faint darkness appeared to flatten one edge of the moon. I blinked, looked away, and saw dancing orbs before my eyes. When I looked back, I saw a definite shadow.

"Look," I whispered to George.

"Yes," he whispered back, and I felt a surge of excitement as I realized that the earth we rode on was throwing that shadow on the moon. Suddenly, a loon's call pierced the night, and from across the water another answered urgently.

For the next hour we watched as the faint shadow moved inexorably, taking a larger and larger bite out of the shining

disk. As the light faded, more loons flung their laments across the lake, and answering calls ricocheted back. Gradually the copper splash on the water dimmed, and the sharp stars brightened. The moon's color deepened from white-gold to apricot.

In the final minutes, as the eclipse reached totality, the keening of the loons rose to a crescendo. Their cries echoed across the lake, engulfing us in sound as thick as the surrounding darkness. Only the stars and the feeble aurora outlining the tarnished coin of the moon gave any light. Sudden tears stung my eyes.

We waited until a glow brightened the end of the moon as the earth moved on, carrying its shadow into space. George started the motor, barely engaging the throttle, loath to intrude a mechanical sound, and the boat slipped slowly back to our dock. We gathered up the quilts, surprised to find that they and every surface of the boat were now wet with dew. I hugged the damp quilts while George tied up the boat; then we walked silently up to the house. The night was already brightening, and the panic of the loons had passed.

How to Take a Swamp Bath

The ancient cartographer's warning "beware ye olde quagmire"
holds no threat for this author.

BY JONATHAN VON RANSON

For my cabin site I picked a spot near a swamp. I know swamps breed mosquitoes. Their poor behavior goes further: into spirochetes, reptiles, and decay. But something inside me reacted to the richness of the geography:

a mountainside swamp in a cozy vale, room-size boulders, a southern exposure, and rising ground with fair drainage — though perhaps a bit bony. I figured I could live with the decay.

I pitched my tent on leaves near a cliff.

All summer I labored, logging in the woods and building a stone cabin. Almost every day I broke off work in the afternoon for a swamp bath.

The swamp and I developed our relationship out of curiosity. I loved the fea-

– illustrations by Christopher Tremblay

tures of the rough land and felt the urge to become intimate with all of them: cave, oak and pine stand, blueberry patch, old cellar hole, swamp, and all. The more I confronted and tamed my uneasiness, the more inviting the swamp began to look. In my isolation, it became like an exotic stranger at a party: her presence was felt even when you were dancing with someone else.

One day late in the spring I interrupted my cabin-building and walked out to investigate what lay beneath the surface of the swamp. Soon I was digging in circles, sucking oversize core samples out of the opaque water with my long-handled shovel. Slithering parasites were no doubt in there; they were just cleverly avoiding my gaze.

After several feet of muck and slimy sticks I found a layer of gray sand. It was resting on a ledge three feet below the surface. I felt as if I had found the 10,000-year-old calling card of a friend, the same practical, artistic one who had arranged the boulders around my cabin. "Glacial sand," I said knowledgeably.

Over the next few weeks of spring I contemplated the gray sand. It changed my impression of the swamp. Underneath the muck, flecked with bright red spores, under the sticks, leaves, and branches held in suspension to rot anaerobically, lay a footing of sterile gray sand. Almost like beach sand.

By early June I decided the time had come to create a hole big enough to bathe in. Wearing sneakers and shorts, I kept ahead of chilblains by excitement and fast work. I created a large bathtub or tiny pond, as you will, and having done so, waited impatiently over the next week as the silt settled.

Out of my first bath in my new facility developed a summertime ritual.

I begin by peeling off my soiled work-clothes. I grab a bar of Ivory soap, a washcloth, and a towel. The towel I snap around my body to dislodge mosquitoes, beside themselves at the opportunities suddenly presented. The towel's vortex feels cool and sensuous. I'm like the suburban homeowner stepping out of the cabana at midnight for a skinny-dip in his pool.

On a good day the mosquitoes let me concentrate on the bath. On a buggy day I go through with it — but just for spite.

Suddenly lighter, freed of my sweaty clothes, I float over the path, long leaps alternating with bursts of fast footwork around the sharpest stones.

The ground becomes flat. It's spongy underfoot. From digging — both in-ground and in-library — I can say with fair certainty that my swamp was once a pond, from the glacier's withdrawal 10,000 years ago practically until the present. It was fed by surface runoff and seepage along the ledge that forms this geologic cup. Gradually the pond edges crept inward and the floor upward, building year by year on silt and the carcasses of last year's vegetation. The construction work met in the middle, where with glacial speed an earnest would-be geologist again displaced it.

Hanging my towel and glasses on a hemlock branch, I mentally rehearse the next steps. I advise every swamp bather to do this. In my swamp, there's a pain threshold that must be surmounted. In contact with the ledge that holds up my mountain and shaded by tall hemlocks, the water retains numbing coldness until late July.

One also has to keep the silt in mind. Only the right moves will permit the swamp bather to step down a slippery, decaying hummock into the water without stirring up silt.

Usually the left foot gets elected to go first into the thick, tannic water. I've found it doesn't send forth as rich a pain signal as the right. I save my best foot to put forward for the climb back out.

Swamp water (here I'm shooting from the left hip) isn't volatile like ordinary water. It's more akin to mercury or liquid nitrogen; it leans toward the solid. That makes it feel colder.

Deliberately, the right leg is raised, brought forward, and lowered vertically into the water like a heron's. I'm standing in swamp water crotch-deep, and I could do a report for the Army Corps of Engineers on minute changes in the level from the last bath. At this point you have to remind yourself of the sensuousness of swamp bathing.

The washcloth is saturated, applied against the bar of Ivory, and used to persuade dried sweat from forehead, cheeks, neck, and chin. Rinsing, eyes closed, I momentarily lose my balance. A step to adjust reminds me that my legs are losing feeling. Tempo picks up: washcloth again soaped up and applied over the entire body. Not acceptable to omit the armpits.

I rinse with the same frigid washcloth, then, as an authentic swamp bather, prepare for the plunge.

You could probably take a swamp bath without the plunge. But in the plunge one confronts the very essence of swamp bathing, the symbolic return to the primeval ooze.

For the plunge, I put my hands on the rim and lower myself in, breathing heavily to fuel my bodily furnace, which I mentally stoke.

Of course I'm out by now — I exited while the reader was on that business about the bodily furnace — and I'm toweling myself off. The air caresses me erotically, the birds applaud, the body feels clean and the spirit rejuvenated.

A sense of well-being suffuses the swamp bather. No reason to analyze any further why; there are 24 comfortable hours until he has to think about another swamp bath. ॐ

(continued)

The Tramp and the Titanic

Give a child a new point of reference and he'll remember it the rest of his life. For instance. . . .

BY LEVERETT CARTER

People often tell me of early childhood experiences that they are able to recount in great detail. Evidently I was somewhat retarded, because I can recall only a few events and these were at the advanced age of six or seven.

We lived in a small house whose granite front step was directly adjacent to the footpath that bordered the Boston Post Road. Behind the barn, the end of our hayloft was quite close to the New York, New Haven and Hartford Railroad tracks. On occasion I would go down to wave at the freight engineers or beg partially burned flares and unexploded rail torpedoes from the section hands. Usually I played about the front of the house and I recall with some discomfort an incident that involved my use of a Guilford Fair souvenir buggy whip on a passing cyclist. Also I have some memory of waving a Yale banner from the stone wall at the caravans of Locomobiles and Stanleys en route to the Yale-Harvard boat races. I had saved a few gunpowder caps and torpedoes from the Fourth and would cause one to explode behind the wall, whereupon the nearest vehicle would come to a stop and the duster-clad occupants dismount to inspect the tires. This afforded me much delight as I had a typical Yankee fondness for anything with wheels, engine, or sails. All in all, without ever having been told, I gather that I was a charming, wide-eyed child.

Because of our location on the direct route between New Haven and New London and because Mother said we had a mark on our house, tramps frequently knocked at our back door for a handout. I searched carefully for the tramp mark but never found it, not even when I asked one of the travelers where it was. Mother always obliged them with a mug of coffee or root beer and a hunk of cold roast between diagonal slices of homemade bread. (She was left-handed and sliced everything at a decided angle.) Mother insisted that the tramps sit on the back steps to eat and objected vigorously whenever one seemed inclined to pocket the sandwich. I generally sat there too, with a similar edition of the lunch.

Just before noon one day in May (I know it was May because I had had a birthday cake a few days before), a sturdy man, older than my father, came to the door. He had a sea bag over his shoulder and asked if he could have a drink at the well and maybe a "biscuit to soak it up." Mother was wringing the wash on the rear porch but, because of the modest request and her sympathy for seamen, she dried her hands and fixed the man the usual generous lunch plus a fat molasses cookie with a wedge of store cheese. I was wearing my treasured and somewhat battered sailor hat with *Maine* on the headband and "Manila Bay" on the ribbons. My Bridgeport aunt, an admirer and political supporter of the admiral, had found it somewhere among mementos and had felt it a suitable incentive for a boy of my talents. I took my cookie and sat down on the steps not far from our caller.

"You be a bit of a ship's boy, I see," said the man.

I nodded and then asked shyly if he had a ship.

"Ay, once."

Instinctively I withheld more questions until he had finished his bread and meat and picked up the cookie.

"Were you a captain?"

"Dynamite gunner on the *Vesuvius* out of Philadelphia," he replied and finished off his coffee.

I had held some hope that he was a whale catcher like the one in the picture that went with "W" in my alphabet book. However, I did have a fair notion of dynamite from my familiarity with the "Katzenjammer Kids," so a dynamite gunner seemed quite acceptable. As the now-established sailor rose to his feet and headed for the well with his mug, I tried once more.

"Are you going to your boat now?"

"Bound for the Groton shipyards," he answered and returned to the steps with the rinsed-out cup.

The man picked up his sea bag, thanked Mother again, and started for the sidewalk with me at his side. I was reluctant to part with such a romantic figure, so I asked him the only question I knew that related to current affairs.

"Do you know about the *Titanic?*"

The gunner stopped then and looked down on me with what I interpreted as grown-up respect.

"Ay, a sad maiden voyage for a monstrous ship near three times the length of your *Maine.*"

"How big is that?"

"Can you count, boy?"

I was quick to reply that I could count all the way to one hundred and could read all the alphabet words in my picture book. My new friend paused and seemed to be thinking or reckoning in his mind.

"I'll step off the *Titanic,*" he said. "You stand fast where I am now and as I shove off down the towpath I'll count one hundred just short of three times. When I swing around and give you a hail, there lies the *Titanic.*"

He left with a grand stride and I tried to count the steps, but after the first hundred I could not keep up. Near the road where the railroad underpass started, my sailor turned, swept his free arm over his head as a signal, and left me the huge ship as he continued his course to the east.

Since that time I have been subjected to many kinds of visual education and several varieties of measurement comparisons, but this so-called tramp gave me my first memorable lesson. Probably that is why it is my dearest recollection from childhood.

Of Fire Hazard and Piranhas

A brief study in the infinite complexities of decision-making. . . .

BY ARTURO VIVANTE

They were driving along a lonely country road in Vermont, he, his wife, and younger daughter, back from a visit to the elder one at her school, when he threw the lighted stub of a cigarette out the window.

"You should use the ashtray," his wife said. "The woods are dry."

He took in what she said but didn't answer. Should he stop and turn back and look for the cigarette and stamp it out, he wondered? Perhaps he should. Yet he kept driving.

"You just aren't very public spirited, are you?" she said.

That wasn't quite true, he thought, and saw himself walking down Via Cavour, in Rome, the year before, by a pet shop with big picture windows, stopping, and looking at some fish inside a large glass tank. "Piranhas," a label said, and he stared at them in fascination. They were larger than he had imagined, about a foot long, and they had strong, scoop-like lower jaws. He had imagined them minuscule, no larger than a small insect and as fearless, and able to eat you up just because there were so many of them. A million tiny jaws at work, each about the size of the tooth of a hacksaw, shredding you up. Instead they were good-size. He had heard about their voracity, of how schools of them made some South American rivers almost impassable and devoured any animal that tried to wade across, and that the water quivered, rippled, seemed to boil, go mad, as they bit into their prey, no matter how large, till the animal — cow, squirrel, or man — would drop as bones down to the bottom and the rest quite disappear, become piranhas; and that to cross the riv-

ers the natives sometimes would throw an animal in, then follow a moment after in the hope that in that time the fish would be too busy with their prey to attack them; and of how women, washing clothes by the riverbank, often had their feet and ankles bitten by piranhas and bore bad scars. Now he looked at the infamous creatures in their tank. They seemed perfectly harmless there. Tigers in a cage. Assassins in a cell. Pitiful. Pathetic. Sad. Bleary-eyed. The might of their jaws useless. And indeed he read later that they never bit you as pets inside their tanks, not even if you put in your hand and held it there.

Well, he had wondered about them long after walking down that street. What if the eggs of the fish flowed into a river? In Italian rivers they wouldn't hatch and thrive; the water was too cold in winter. But in Africa? There might well be pet shops, like the one he had seen, in their cities, in some African cities perhaps, in Africa that was free of the scourge of the piranhas. And what if some eggs accidentally went down the drain and into a river like the Congo and reproduced there? An accident of that sort might change the whole fauna of the continent, there where they had no natural enemies. The giraffe, the hippopotamus, the elephant, the zebra — already so scarce — might become extinct, and countless animals die, be horribly slaughtered, disappear in the roiled waters. The bloodshed, in his mind, was fearful. Oh, he must do something about it, write a letter. And he *had* written a letter, expressing his apprehension and urging they do something to forbid the export of piranhas, to F.A.O. — the U.N.

Food and Agriculture Organization in Rome, where he knew there was a large fisheries department, and after a long time — several months — he had got a letter back thanking him for his interest and informing him that any action of the sort he had described was not in their power to enforce, that they couldn't interfere in the internal affairs of any country, and that they could only make recommendations. Would they? They didn't say, and he had gone on worrying about piranhas.

I did write that, he thought, defending himself in his own mind from accusations of irresponsibility. But why wasn't he consistent? God, the whole forest might go up in flames; the smoke rise so you could see it for miles; the birds, the deer all flee, or try to. And he wouldn't even know about it, unless he sent for a local paper or phoned, and what good would that do? He remembered a charred park he had seen near Plymouth, the black stumps, hill after hill.

He had gone at least two miles since dropping the lighted stub, and every moment made his stopping and turning back more difficult. He slowed down a little as if to give himself time and make a decision easier. Surely it was a bit excessive to turn back. The cigarette was probably on the asphalt, probably burnt out. Probably? Could he take a chance? Oh dear, this was ruining his journey.

"Why are you going so slowly, Daddy?" his daughter said.

"I think I must turn back," he said.

"Why?" his wife said.

"That cigarette."

"You'll never find it."

"I remember the spot."

"It will be out."

"That's what I hope."

So he stopped and turned back and retraced the miles to the place where he thought he had thrown the stub, and there he got out of the car and looked around. He couldn't find it. He waited a while and looked for smoke. He saw no smoke. He saw the trees with their fresh, green leaves; once in a while a bird darting from a branch — and hippos wallowing in the Congo.

– illustration by Christopher Tremblay

To do this story, Mel and Carole spent over a week with an elite group of men at the Bath (Maine) Iron Works. They discovered that their specific work was mostly done at night, that it was the hardest, meanest, coldest, and certainly most hazardous work in the entire shipyard, and that few of the men involved would ever want to do anything else.

The Men Who Launch Ships

BY MEL ALLEN
photography by Carole Allen

The most uncertain, stressful journey a big ship will ever make is the first sprint down the ways when it is launched. The stress is shared by the workers in a shipyard, for whom months of work could be squandered if the launching proves a disaster. Once in a great while a ship will capsize when launched. Sometimes, too, the greased ways will catch on fire from the friction, the flames leaping at the ship. In Japan some years ago a big tanker upon its launching plunged across the channel and did not stop until it had plowed into an opposing shipyard, stern high off the ground, bow thrusting through the trees.

Twelve years ago in Ontario a 9300-ton cargo ship lurched free from its stays on the bank of the Georgian Bay, 15 minutes before the scheduled launching, while 125 men still worked beneath. Two died; 40 others were seriously injured.

I learned these things, eventually, because I happened by chance upon a ship launching last December at the Bath Iron Works (BIW) in Bath, Maine.

It had been a bitter morning, and I sat among the other spectators shivering through the speeches by admirals, politicians, and BIW officials. When the champagne burst upon the bow, however, the ship's descent was so sudden, the space left so vast, it was as though a mountain had vanished. The band played "Anchors Aweigh," and to my surprise I was stirred.

I walked to the edge of the platform and looked down. Where the ship had been there remained only concrete and slabs of grease as thick as my arm. A knot of men wearing hard hats stood by the water's edge watching the tugs bring the ship around. Others leaned low from a small boat, grappling with the cradle that had ferried the ship down and now floated in the river, timbers askew.

I had not known there had been anyone down below, by the ship. It was as though I had overturned a big rock and stolen a glimpse at the teeming world beneath. I learned they were BIW's launch crew, 15 men who worked for the boss of the carpentry shop, who by tradition is the launch master.

Their work, I was told, was done almost always at night, and was the hardest, meanest, probably the most dangerous in the yard; but it was also the work most steeped in tradition and history. There were some on the launch crew who had done nothing else for years but launch ships, and they had refused to work elsewhere in the shipyard.

I was intrigued. So I came to Bath the first week in April to learn more about the little-known world of a launch crew. On Saturday, April 4, at high slack tide, 12:22 P.M., a Navy guided-missile frigate, *Stephen W. Groves*, would be launched into a stretch of the Kennebec River called Long Reach, where, it is said, more ships have been launched than anywhere else in the country.

On the afternoon before the launch I visited an old launch master named George Costain. He was nearly 80 and before he retired as launch master at BIW he had launched 177 ships, more than anybody before him. "You don't forget some launchings," he said. He lingered over the names of the ships, and the dates they were launched and what they looked like and what they weighed, as though they were old sweethearts.

He told me of his early days, when the launch crew were nearly all old men. They would knock the timber triggers loose beneath the ships and have only a moment to dive into a hole before the ships came thundering down, only a few feet above. He told of the terrible creaking the ships used to make when they would be tied to the land by cables. "It was like it was full of ghosts," he said. And he told about "the awful stillness" just before he let the ships loose, when, if anything went wrong, he would be powerless to correct it. "I'd be so nervous, I couldn't eat," he said. "It's the only job I know where if you make a mistake there are no second chances. There was always the fear, 'Did I forget something?' "

"I'd always warn the children," said his wife. " 'Now your father has a launching this week, so be quiet.' "

He said he would wait by his window on Saturday listening for the whistles in the yard to blow, the signal for a successful launch.

"Until then, I never knew. People don't understand. It's not *natural* to move something so big."

Rain was moving in and the night had no stars. The gray, sleek hull of the frigate rose from its blocks at the river's edge, dwarfing the men who from time to time gazed upward as though contemplating an immense sculpture. The ship was 445 feet long, 3700 tons, with a draft of 24½ feet. At $200 million, it was the Navy's top-of-the-line destroyer-size ship.

The ship had been built on a declivity of 13 degrees, a precisely engineered angle. The launch crew knew how fast the ship *should* slide, how deep the stern *should* go when it hit water, how much pressure *should* bear on the bow when the stern first lifted in the water, the most

About 200 workers from all over the Bath Iron Works shipyard reported at 6 A.M. to pound the wedges that lifted the Stephen W. Groves off its cribwork and into its cradle, ready to launch.

The river was 40 degrees, matching the air. "Cold?" Albert Doughty said. "It's 60 degrees warmer than our last launch."

critical moment in a launching. What they didn't know gave every launching its drama — the weather, the current, the absoluteness of the calculations.

The river was 40 degrees, matching the air, and the wind sucked the cold off the river. I said I was cold. "Cold?" Albert Doughty said, wool vest snug across his chest, wool hat tucked beneath his hard hat. "It's 60 degrees warmer than our last launch."

Doughty was the assistant foreman of the carpentry shop on second shift. Until Ed 'Sonny' Murphy, the launch master, arrived in a few hours, he was in charge. In 29 years Doughty has never seen a launching ceremony. He's always been under the ship waiting by the trigger.

We walked beneath the ship, heading aft towards the propeller. The men crawled like spiders among the timbers, hauling chain saws, cant dogs, wrenches, and sledges before them. A rat poked out from under the timbers, nosing its way upwards from the rising tide. A line of light bulbs had been strung on the ground the length of the ship's belly; their glare reflected harshly off the hard hats of the men, and off the rat's fur, still dripping from the river. There was no sky, no perspective, just a tangled forest of shadows. It was a world, I felt, in which perhaps only coal miners would also feel at home.

"We'll get half a dozen rats in here sometimes," Doughty said, "and skunks. Plenty of raccoons, too. Don't know what you'll find sometimes."

Beside us a man leaned his weight on a long-handled lug-all wrench, another held it in place, another yanked free a three-foot-long, half-inch-thick iron bar, covered with grease. For weeks the bars had kept the weight of the timbers from squashing out the grease. They had to pull 72 such grease irons. It was hard work, because the pressure had locked the irons fast and the space was cramped. They worked deliberately, with the steady movements of men accustomed to overtime. They grunted and when they bumped into a girder they cursed. As soon as an iron was pulled the grease rolled out, dark on top, light yellow on its side, looking like an exotic custard.

"Once you've pulled the grease irons," said Doughty, "you've had it. No matter

what the weather's like, we've got to go ahead with the launch."

Someone knocked a shoring timber loose on the side of the ship. Bursts of light flared across the ship, then darkened as the bracket that held the timber was ground off, the *thud, thud, thud* of the tool against the hull ripping the air.

We stepped from under the ship near the water's edge. BIW's 400-foot crane loomed over us like a giant mantis. The headlights of cars crossing the Carlton Bridge twinkled in the distance. From behind the timbers, I could hear the coughing and the hoarse laughter of unseen men.

I remarked to Doughty how immense the ship was, seen so close. I found that Doughty, a taciturn, strongly built man who has launched 19,000-ton ships, possessed a sense of proportion that perhaps is unique to those who launch ships.

"This ship's just a *baby*," he said.

It takes 7000 man-hours to launch a guided-missile frigate. The cradle was built like an elaborate club sandwich, layer upon layer, using enough timber to build about 40 medium-size ranch houses.

Twelve hundred pounds of boiling wax were first poured down the concrete ways. On top of the wax the men spread two tons of special launching grease mixed with fish oil to keep it from freezing. Grease irons were then put down. Now the timbers that would actually slide the ship down could be laid.

Twelve slides were bolted together along each side of the ship. They were in sections 30 feet long and two feet wide, dimensions that were carefully figured so that only 2000 pounds per square foot would rest on the grease before launching. On top of the bottom slides they placed hundreds of wedges.

A top layer of timbers was placed on top of the wedges, bolted to the bottom and connected to the slides on the opposite side of the ship by long steel rods.

A huge "shock absorber" was built under the bow and extended to the midsection of the ship. When the ship was launched, and the stern first rose in the water, the weight on the rest of the ship would suddenly increase to over 10 tons per square foot. If it were not for the

"shock absorber" the ship could break its back. Thick steel bands girdled the ship, and blocks of wood were fitted both to the hull and to the sliding timbers. By late March the work was done, and the *Stephen W. Groves* was packed as carefully as a 3700-ton piece of china.

The cradle would serve as ferry, sled, carriage. It might seem that, once having completed the cradle, the work would be finished, the uncertainties accounted for. Nothing, however, could be further from the truth.

By 4 A.M. the first glimmer of color, pale purple, appeared over the spruce trees on the Woolwich shore. Gulls wheeled low over the long, flat buildings in the shipyard, caught the breeze and flew above the ship, out into the river where six destroyers were docked, distinguishable one from another only by the numbers painted on their hulls.

The grease irons had been pulled and the slides tightened. Some wedges by the stern had been pounded up, taking pressure off the keel blocks that had supported the ship since September. Using their sledges the men knocked the blocks free, passing them out hand to hand as they balanced on grease-soaked supports.

"The cranes can't help you once you're under the boat," Doughty said. "It's a $200 million ship but it takes brute strength to free it." He called a break, and the men drifted into the carpentry shop for coffee. They sat on the edge of tables, taking the long, slow inhalations on their cigarettes that night workers substitute for sleep.

We talked about all the things that could go wrong. A big cargo ship was launched here a few years ago and its cradle splintered and got skewered in the river. As the men fought the river to break it apart one man jammed a spike through his hand, another sliced the tips off his fingers, and a third broke his neck when hit by a falling block, and has been disabled ever since. "It's tough work," Doughty said.

Doughty sipped his coffee. "We launched the *Arizona* a few years ago (a 19,000-ton cargo ship) and the wind came up all of a sudden, tremendous gusts, just before launching," he said. "No way we should have launched, but the ship was squashing all the grease out. We had to.

"We'd put great steel 'barn doors' on the stern to slow it up. When it hit, the wake was so much it broke the lines of the *Maine* (another cargo ship) docked nearby. The electrical lines broke and the sparks set the circuit box on fire. The gas lines had broken too. If it wasn't for Tommy York, who jumped down and turned off the gas, we might have had some serious problems."

"Could've lost the whole yard," someone said.

"That wasn't the end of it," Doughty said. "The wind pushed the *Arizona* to the bridge. Nine tugs straining with all their power couldn't hold it. People were running from the bridge seeing that big ship heading right for them. When the tugs brought her around, there couldn't have been more than 50 feet left."

Someone mentioned the *Maui*, a 720-foot container ship, the largest ever built at BIW, launched during a snowstorm in 1977. "Now that ship was just too heavy for what we'd put under it. When the

stern pivoted in the water, the saddle (steel bands around the ship's belly) gave way. The bow actually bounced. It scraped the cement, sparks shooting up. Sometimes when that happens a ship just stops."

The *Maui* made its way down the ways safely, but I wondered what they would have done if it had just stopped, its stern waterborne, its bow landlocked. "We probably would have had to burn its bow off," Doughty said.

At 6 A.M. the workers gathered, 200 strong, assembled from all departments in the shipyard. It was time for the ritual called "rallying," when the wedges would be driven, prying the ship off its building blocks and settling it securely into its cradle. Driving rams had been placed the length of the ship in front of the wedges.

One strapping man tugged on his hip boots. "I always draw the mud," he grimaced, referring to his position by the water. "How was the mud starboard?" someone asked. "Soft," came the reply. "Foot and a half of it. You'll be down on your hands and knees."

At one time or another nearly everyone works the rallies. At a shipyard where the ships are assembled piece by piece like puzzles, it is the only time that they can truly feel they are working on a *ship*. The men (and some women) worked in threes, for the rams that drove the wedges weighed 150 pounds apiece. Each team was responsible for one of the 34 wedging stations along each side of the ship.

Sonny Murphy, the launch master, had arrived an hour before, and at 6:12 he gave the signal to a woman sitting on a stool, clutching a stopwatch. A buzzer rang the length of the ship. For three minutes the air swirled with the concussions of the ship being driven a few inches upward, the noise held in by the steel hull. Seven-minute break. The buzzer rang again.

"We have to slow them down," Murphy said. "The old-timers know to let the rams do the work for them. And you can't lose your concentration." He told about one young man who lost his for an instant and then caught his hand between the wedges and the ram.

The buzzer rang. Three minutes of

Right: *A detail of a fore poppet. When the stern first pivots in the water the weight on the bow is tremendous. Multilayers of soft wood packing and steel saddle bands absorb the pressure. The concrete cap is used for ships that are larger than guided-missile frigates.*

Below: *The profile of a ship resting in its cradle, ready for launching. Grease is smeared between the ground ways and the sliding ways. The trigger, just aft of midships, holds the ship secure in its final hours before the launch.*

STEEL BRACKETS
CONCRETE CAP
SOFT WOOD PACKING
STEEL SADDLE STRAP
TIE ROD
SPREADER
CROSS BRACES
CRUSHING STRIPS
TIE BOLT
WEDGE
RAM

– illustrations by Ray Maher

FORE POPPET
GROUND OR STANDING WAYS
TRIGGER
SLIDING WAYS

> ## "Once you've pulled the grease irons," said Doughty, "you've had it. No matter what the weather's like, we've got to launch."

Rallying is hard work. The rams weigh 150 pounds each and need three people to supply power. They pound in the wedges for three minutes without stopping, then rest for seven. After several rallies, the ship lifts slightly and the building blocks are removed.

pounding. Rang again. Break. "It's the hardest work I've ever done," said one young man.

Murphy circled the ship, peering at the cradle, his ears alert. "If we've done it right," he said, "she'll lay in the cradle as quiet as can be. But if not she'll start to sag. It'll tell you what it's doing by the noise it's making. When those timbers start to expand and you hear the creaking you get a very funny feeling. Because if it ever comes out of the cradle, you know not where it's going."

Rally three. Rally four. The strain began to lift from the building blocks, and began to show in the faces of the workers. The blocks were heavy and were passed from deep inside the cribwork to the daylight world outside.

Murphy surveyed the scene with his predecessor, John Shaugnessey, now assistant to a vice-president at BIW. "A piece of cake," Shaugnessey enthused. "She'll go easy." Murphy glanced at the

bunting being draped over the platform.
"She better," he said.

Sonny Murphy had been at BIW 30 years — like many others he had followed his father into the yard. He was known for his temper, his strength, his stamina, and, most important for a launch master, his coolness under pressure. He was a no-nonsense, hard-nosed boss, a wide-shouldered, square-jawed six-footer, intimidating to some, with the deeply lined face of an outdoorsman.

He stood by the trigger lever 20 minutes before launch. It was noon, but in this world it was forever twilight. There have been other launchings when every minute was squeezed dry, racing the tide, to get everything free. This one, so far, had been almost too smooth for comfort.

"The morning goes so slow once you've driven up," he said. "You need

the time, but once you're done you're just watching the tide rise."

Shaugnessey stood back a few feet, talking on a walkie-talkie to BIW's captain on the bridge of the ship. Five tugboats waited 200 feet out in the river, hovering like anxious parents on the end of a sliding board. "Sonny knows he's got a winner," Shaugnessey said. "He knows he's done everything right. But he doesn't know the unexpected. And that's the game he gets paid to play. You watch him when that ship is in the water, and it's upright and the cradle is free. He'll be a different man."

Sonny Murphy checked a gauge that showed if the ship had moved since the blocks were removed. It had — a quarter of an inch.

"Good," Murphy said. "She's lively and compressing a little aft. We know it's not stuck down. Sometimes we get too much movement. A few years ago a tanker was creaking real bad. Shaugnessey called the platform and told them they had 60 seconds to get through with the speeches and cracking the bottle. He was sending the ship. Even if they had to talk into a big hole, he needed the safety of the ship."

Albert Doughty stood by the trigger with Murphy. They didn't talk, but watched the men they had sent to remove the trigger safety pins. Once the trigger pins were removed, the ship could be launched by holding down the trigger lever, which released the cam-shaped brakes.

"All that's holding the ship now," Doughty said, "is one piece of steel."

All we could hear was the drone of words we could not make out coming from the loudspeakers at the platform. I asked if the speeches were on time.

"Don't know. Don't care," Doughty said, his face lined with fatigue. "That's fanfare over there."

Over the walkie-talkie crackled the message: "Invocation starting." I stepped back away from the trigger. The sky was gray. To my right the crowd peered intently at the 88-year-old minister, a former neighbor of Stephen Groves, who was offering a prayer for the ship. The launch crew waited impassively to my left. The river brought the day's flotsam splashing lightly against the propeller. Everyone seemed frozen, waiting.

It was not entirely devoid of ceremony by the trigger. A trim, attractive woman, the wife of a BIW vice-president, took her place alongside Murphy to share the honor of setting the ship free. She wore a white coat and white gloves, and she clasped her hands below Murphy's dirt-caked grip. He set his feet. He waited.

Mariam Groves, the niece of the ship's namesake, strode to the ship's bow. She gripped the ribboned bottle as tightly as Murphy, 300 feet away, gripped the trigger. "In the name of the United States Navy I christen thee *Stephen W. Groves*," she shouted. The bottle cracked, spraying champagne over the bow. A button was pushed on the platform. A bell rang at the trigger.

"Here we go," shouted Murphy. He pushed the lever down 90 degrees, nearly lifting the white-coated woman off her feet. We could hear "click, clack, click," the sound of the cams releasing, like trains running over a track. The ship began its slide.

The sky opened behind us. Faster and faster the ship pulled away, and a rush of wind, which had been held back for months, blew over everyone.

The preparations for launching took months, but the Stephen W. Groves *was in the water 31 seconds after the champagne bottle cracked across the bow.*

The stern hit the water, pivoted upwards. Murphy stared as the bow rode down without a ripple of trouble, and in 31 seconds the ship was in the water, the tugs circling her. The snagging cables jerked the cradle free. Whistles blew throughout the yard. I thought of the old launch master, George Costain, waiting by his window, smiling.

Murphy and Doughty walked to the river. Murphy would be around until 9 P.M. The *Stephen W. Groves* would be

berthed and parts of the cradle would be hoisted free. Murphy was already thinking ahead. In a shipyard, once the shouting and the cheers have died out, a launching, after all, means another ship can begin on the ways.

"Now that sugar barge," he said, referring to a 14,000-ton ship to be launched in February, "we've never done one of those. That will be *challenging*."

AN·AUGUST
SAMPLER

☞ Memorable thoughts, quo... b... e last 50 August issues. ☜

STUCK IN THE PORCH

– Mark Kelley

☞ One spring a chauffeur-driven limousine pulled up at the farm, and an enormously stout and stately dowager emerged. She was looking for a possible lodging for some friends she was expecting later, and Ma told her to go ahead and look around as much as she liked.

The poor woman happened to step on a rotten board in a neglected section of the porch. One leg went straight down, just about to the hip, while the other slid forward. She was cast as solidly as our old mare the time her hind leg went down through the stable trapdoor. The chauffeur couldn't budge her, and there was nobody else around the house. Ma finally found Al, a painfully shy farm boy of 18 who was working nearby.

"Come quick, Al," Ma yelled at the top of her voice. "There's a fat woman stuck in the porch — get a saw!"

When Al appeared with the saw and beheld the awful prospect of the task he was to perform, he nearly defected, but Ma spoke firmly. "Just saw around her leg, Al," she commanded, "And get her out of there!"

So Al started sawing, and when the woman was freed, he, the chauffeur, and Ma heaved her up on her feet.

"It only scratched her leg a little," Ma said afterward. "I told her she should thank her lucky stars she hadn't been really hurt, but she went off in a huff. Good riddance." Then she added, "But oh, my goodness, she did look *so funny,* with that big flowered hat, sitting down on the floor — I had to keep telling poor Al to open his eyes, so he wouldn't saw right into her leg. . . ." *(From "How Not to Run an Inn" by Newton F. Tolman.)*

ESPECIALLY THE MALE SEX

☞ "I do think that the human race has an enormous amount of inbred, or inborn bellicosity. Especially the male sex. From what I can tell, fighting has been a more frequent activity than anything except agriculture in the history of man. People are always fighting somewhere. I think it has to do with identity. You don't feel like a group unless you have an enemy. That makes you feel like 'us', and they are 'them.' People fight to give themselves a tribal identity." *(From "Barbara Tuchman [quoted here], In Search of Mankind's Better Moments" by Tim Clark.)*

HOUSE WITH THE BEST OF ALL VIEWS

☞ *On 50 acres in Garfield, Vermont, this new (in August 1981) sun-heated house faced southwest to Camel's Hump and a myriad of other mountains. It and another smaller house on the property went together for $250,000.* – photo by Patricia Whitcomb

204

A STERN LESSON FOR A DEAR OLD SOUL

☞ Mrs. Smith was famous as a long-winded talker. She was a dear old soul, living out the sunset years with her son's family. When Mrs. Smith got on the line with a phone pal, she was good for half an hour or more. We all liked Grammie Smith, but we all complained of her telephone calls.

I was home from college and feeling my oats. "I'll fix her," I said confidently to Mother. "You don't have to take this sort of treatment."

"No, don't trouble her," Mother answered. "The poor soul needs the telephone. Still, I wish she would hang up."

"I'll fix her," I repeated. I remember Father, resting on the kitchen sofa, opened an eye and smiled. Sister Edith said, "Go ahead. She needs a lesson."

I walked over to the phone, took off the receiver, and jammed the hook down with my shoulder so I couldn't be heard.

Then I made a speech. "Mrs Smith," I said, "This is Haydn Pearson, the minister's son, and I am speaking for my mother and the whole town. You are mo-nopolizing the telephone. You are inconveniencing all the subscribers on this line. In plain English, you are being extremely selfish."

I thought Mother would faint until Edith walked over and whispered in her ear. I went on for a few minutes and then hung up. "There," I said. "That should fix her. You won't have any trouble from now on."

It is about 40 years since that afternoon. And I still wonder. I would swear I had pressed the hook down. But the fact stands. After that day, Mrs. Smith rarely talked over 10 minutes. (*From "That You Mabel?" by Haydn S. Pearson.*)

EVEN EXPERTS MAKE MISTAKES

– Bill Wagner/"The Daily Astorian"

Tim Black (stern) and Peter Macridis (bow) at the start of their voyage.

☞ The canoe was found the next morning at 8:00, washed ashore upside down. Members of both families arrived, still hopeful, because an elite rescue team failed to turn up any traces of Tim and Peter, believing, as Doug Williams said, "They were incapable of flipping and drowning in a river. It was impossible." They thought perhaps they'd gone exploring deep in the woods, not aware their canoe was gone; perhaps they had hitched a ride on a tugboat and the canoe was being towed when it came loose. More ominous were reports of bitterness between the Indian fishermen and the white authorities over fishing rights — had the boys unknowingly stumbled into conflict?

It was an agonizing time for the families. Weeks passed and all they knew was that Peter and Tim were "presumed drowned." On April 11 shortly before 4 P.M. Tim's body washed ashore at the mouth of Wind River. On May 6 Peter's was found nearby. There were no signs of foul play. All that remained was Michael Black's haunting questions: "Why didn't they wear life vests? Why heavy boots? Why didn't they tie down their equipment to prevent shifting and loss of balance? Why did they break all the rules they had themselves taught so well to others?"

There are no sure replies, of course, but perhaps it is enough to say that they planned for everything but their own cockiness — without others to watch over they let their guard down, assured of their skills to watch over themselves, as though their youth and their dreams afforded their own protection from harm. There were, in short, no plans for death. (*From "They Planned for Almost Everything" by Mel Allen.*)

A · FAVORITE LETTER

YANKEE SENTIMENTALITY

☞ The August 1973 issue of *Yankee* Magazine contains a letter re the supposed dearth of sentiment in Maine men. Apparently, this applies to all New Englanders.

My New Englander is of doubtfuller-than-Maine origin, being's he's from Massachusetts, and *he* nearly choked on the marriage vows that he recited, being's they contained the word "love." "You look all right," is the highest compliment I ever get, and once when I bawled (all right, so I was younger then) and said he never said he loved me, he muttered darkly, "I show it in other ways," and went back to whittling on his woodcarving.

There is some evidence that he may be mellowing, however. One night last winter he got out of bed to go to the bathroom, and I think he must have thought I was asleep, which I almost was, being barely aware he was up, because when he came back to bed he said out loud, "I love you!" It startled me awake so's I got up and wrote down the date and time (1:10 A.M.), but I'd appreciate if you'd omit to print my name and address if you print this letter, as I'd hate for his relatives back in Massachusetts to get the idea he's become maudlin.

CHAPTER 9

September

Labor Day. Back to school and college, summer's gone in an instant, memories of a hurricane (no anniversary of the one in '38 has ever passed us by), time to pick potatoes up in Aroostook County, Maine, close the summer camp, stack the wood, haul out the boat, reorient living rhythms back indoors to fireplaces once again — that's been our general mood when compiling September issues. Of course the last great surge of tourists begins late in the month, so these issues have continued to feature travel-oriented material as well. For instance, 1972's September issue described a beautiful route for "leaf spotters," the famous Mohawk Trail that winds around from Greenfield over to North Adams, Massachusetts. We called the article "Drums Along the Mohawk," and went on to say that most of the souvenirs — meaning the various Indian tom-toms and facsimile tomahawks found in the little tourist traps along the route — are made in Taiwan. A week after publication we received a collect call from Chief Eagle Fire in Cherokee, North Carolina. We accepted the call. The next few minutes were spent agreeing as often as possible to the deepest and fiercest of angry voices, which informed us of the error of our ways. Most Mohawk Trail tom-toms, we have since been quick to say at most any opportunity (like this one), are made in Cherokee, North Carolina.

The 220-acre Modern Dairy Farm, a Williamstown, Massachusetts, landmark.

– photograph by Carole Allen

*In a small graveyard on Mt. Desert Island, Maine, is a granite marker that reads,
"Ronald E. Alley, 1922-1978." What it does not say, of course, is that Ronald E. Alley
was the only officer in this century to be imprisoned by the U.S. Army
for collaborating with the enemy. When we published the following article in
September 1980, we said it was "a story with an ending perhaps still to come."
It came in July two years later — see "The Aftermath," page 212.*

A Soldier's Disgrace

BY DON J. SNYDER

Long after they had met and fallen in love and raised a family I came to know Erna and Ronald Alley — long after their best years were done. It was the beginning of 1978 and I was editor of the newspaper in Bar Harbor, Maine, where they had lived for 23 years. A small, self-contained town on an island off the coast, Bar Harbor bends over backwards for summer people from June till September, selling a lot of film and lobsters. In this community people still call the evening meal "supper," and a stranger when he meets you might rummage through his wallet to show you his American Legion card just because it matters that much to him.

Erna and Ronald Alley came to see me that winter of 1978 because they had a story to tell and I was, it seemed, always looking for stories then. What they told me and what I learned about them will not let me be. And looking back I believe they came to me because it was late and they knew they were running out of time.

Ronald Alley had grown up in Bar Harbor in an old clapboard house where there were too many children and not enough food. Eager to leave home and to make something of himself, he joined the Army just as soon as he could. He fought in Germany during World War II. A big, strapping young man with sandy brown hair, he was a captain by 1946, assigned to the military government in occupied Germany. He came to that place with many thousands of other Yanks like him. They had done the right thing for the right reason; there was dignity among soldiers then, and Ronald expected his career in the Army to be bright and honorable.

That spring Ronald met Erna Laulies, a beautiful German girl with crystal blue eyes. They fell in love and when the Army gave them permission to marry they did so right away. Then they sailed to America on an Army transport and rode the train to Schenectady, New York, where Ronald was assigned to a reserve unit as an instructor. They bought a stove and an old Ford. Erna gave birth to a daughter and then a son. They had their best years there.

The best years did not last long. In July 1950 Ronald received orders for a transfer to Korea. On August 2 Erna drove him to the airport, where he held her and said good-bye to the children, then boarded a plane.

At first the fighting went well in Korea and in his early letters home Ronald wrote casually, asking Erna to renew the car registration, reminding her to balance the tires. But in late November the Chinese entered the war, and American forces pushing northward were caught off guard. For days, in brutal fifty below zero weather, American troops fighting near Chosin Reservoir in North Korea struggled to hold out. They were surrounded, caught in a death trap where many American soldiers died. In a desperate attempt to retreat many more were taken prisoner. Late in the afternoon of December 1, as he held a wounded South Korean soldier in his arms, Captain Alley was captured by four Chinese who ordered him to march, and promptly shot two bullets into the head of his helpless comrade.

For 33 months he was a prisoner of the Chinese, who moved him from one camp to another throughout Korea. He suffered dysentery for months at a time; he coughed up blood and lost 40 pounds. And in the long days without occupation and the nights of fear and horrible abuse he watched many of his comrades die before finally the war was finished and he was returned to American hands. Unlike the other POWs, who boarded Army transports for the trip home, Ronald was flown immediately to Tokyo for medical treatment. From there he went to St. Albans Naval Hospital, where, lying on his back, his gaunt face covered with a sterile mask, he saw his wife and kissed her for the first time in three years. He had been promoted to the rank of major, and there was much to be grateful for.

It took two years of hospitalization and repeated surgery before Ronald was well enough to be released. During the time of his convalescence he twice refused a full medical discharge from the service, telling attending physicians that he had 30 good years left in him to give to the Army.

In January 1955 Ronald wrote Erna from the Valley Forge Military Hospital telling her he would soon be released and would be coming home to Maine for an extended leave. By this time Erna had moved to Bar Harbor and she made excited preparations for his homecoming.

Discharged from the hospital, Ronald traveled first to Washington, D.C., to pick up his orders for a new assignment. But there was no new assignment. Instead he was ordered to attention, read a list of formal charges filed against him by the Army, and placed under house arrest.

He was charged with collaborating with the enemy while a prisoner at Camp Five in North Korea. The prosecution claimed it would prove Major Alley had given the enemy military information, led Communist-sponsored propaganda discussion groups, and participated in activities to foster "Red propaganda" and portray the United States as an illegal aggressor in Korea.

November 3, 1955 — escorted by a military policeman, Major Ronald Alley emerges from the courtroom, having just been sentenced to 10 years at hard labor.

Two men were there on their knees —
"No pulse! I get no pulse!" one of them was saying.
Then she saw the soles of Ronald's shoes. . . .

After 33 months in a North Korean prison, Alley had lost 40 pounds.

Ronald said the charges were preposterous. When his defense counsel, Lt. Col. William T. Logan, advised him to secure civilian attorneys, Ronald refused. Logan then confided to Erna that the atmosphere was unfavorable and that the deck might be stacked against her husband. He urged her to talk to him, make him change his mind. But Ronald was adamant. He said he had done nothing wrong. He said the Army would know that.

On August 22, 1955, the general court-martial of Ronald Alley convened at Fort Meade in Maryland. For two and a half months the prosecution, presenting more than 50 witnesses, argued that Ronald had behaved dishonorably as a prisoner of war.

Defense witnesses took the stand to contradict these accusations. They stated that Ronald had been a loyal officer, that he had done what was necessary to support his men in the difficult conditions. They explained that all prisoners had been forced to participate in activities that created the illusion of cooperation. In interviews with the press, several defense witnesses accused prosecution witnesses of lying on the stand in order to protect their own careers.

Throughout the interminable proceedings, Army prosecutor Major Joseph M. Kelly questioned witnesses about Ronald's political inclinations. Two prosecution witnesses stationed with Ronald prior to his Korean assignment testified that they had heard him speak of the advantages of socialism. These oblique references were used to characterize Ronald as a man with Communist sympathies; they established a motive for his alleged misconduct. In the prosecutor's final remarks he demanded that a maximum sentence of life imprisonment be imposed.

On November 1, 1955, a court-martial of 10 officers, all but one above the rank of major, none having ever been a prisoner of war, deliberated for four hours before finding Ronald guilty of four counts of collaborating with the enemy. Ronald sat motionless in the courtroom as the verdict was read.

Two days later the court-martial sentenced him to 10 years at hard labor and dismissed him dishonorably from the Army. Erna sobbed as he was led from the courtroom to the stockade at Fort Meade. From there he was transported to the Leavenworth Military Prison in Kansas, where he became the only officer in this century to be imprisoned by the Army on collaboration charges.

At Leavenworth he was stripped of his major's uniform. He was soon informed that his defense counsel had been tranferred and would not be able to prosecute his appeal. The counsel assigned to him appealed only one minor technicality, and the conviction was upheld by the Military Court of Appeals.

Ronald was released from Leavenworth after serving three years and seven months of his sentence. On June 13, 1959, nine years after he had left his family at the airport outside Schenectady, Ronald came home to them in Bar Harbor. In the newspapers he had been called a "turncoat" and a "Red friend." A defeated man, he faced months of confusion and lassitude at home before he finally bought a suit of clothes and found work selling Fuller Brushes door to door.

In the years that followed Erna and Ronald raised their family and struggled to reorder their life together. They continued to seek help to overturn Ronald's conviction. Dozens of politicians expressed interest in the case, but were disinclined to pursue it. At the Harvard Law School, the Committee on Military Justice, a nonprofit private organization that offers legal aid to veterans, took on Ronald's case, but eventually ceased their efforts when they were unsuccessful in securing from the Army information vital to his defense. Maine's young congressman, William S. Cohen, offered to seek a presidential pardon from Richard Nixon, but Ronald turned down the offer, saying a pardon would imply guilt and he was not guilty.

Twice Ronald ran and was defeated for a seat on the Bar Harbor Town Council. During one of his campaigns someone fired a shotgun at the Alleys' car while it was parked in the driveway of their home. Local authorities never produced any suspects.

During the final days of the Ford administration, the Bar Harbor Vice-Commander of the Legion wrote an appeal for help saying, "We all felt they just picked out one guy. He was just looking out for his own men. If you know Ronny long enough, you know. If a guy is square here, he had to be square down there [Korea]. A leopard can't change spots that easily."

Three times Ronald requested that the Army Board for the Correction of Military Records (based in the Pentagon) review his case. Three times his request was denied.

Vowing they would never give up, Erna and Ronald tried to interest publishers in writing a book. They consented to newspaper interviews and met with journalists whenever they would listen. Again and again they told their story, but nothing happened.

On Thursday, January 19, 1978, three weeks after I took the job as editor of the *Bar Harbor Times,* I received a call from Ronald Alley, whose name I had never before heard. He explained that he was a candidate for Congress, running as an Independent. I told Ronald I would be glad to interview him on Friday and we set an appointment at one o'clock. By the time I left the office Thursday afternoon it had begun snowing and the wind was slanting sharply through town.

It was still snowing the next morning. I

walked to work and was making myself a cup of coffee in the back room when one of the boys from the print shop approached me from his press. "Seeing Alley today?" he asked laconically, as he wiped ink from his hands with a badly soiled rag. I told him I was.

"You know the Major?" he asked, with the unmistakable look of triumph an island native gets when he's about to tell you something you'd already know if you were an island native.

"No. We've never met," I said, waiting for him to continue.

"He's done some time. Know that?"

"Time?"

"He was a turncoat in Korea. Spent some time in the slammer for helping the enemy," he said flatly, stuffing the rag back into his pocket. "You might want to ask him about that."

Alley made his way to my office, walking the length of Cottage Street. He was a big man, taking big strides and wearing no hat. Inside the front door of the newspaper he stomped the snow from his boots and we shook hands.

"Looks as if it could snow forever," he said in a clipped-off baritone. He wore tan khakis top and bottom and the shine on his boots had been worked at. We spoke very briefly about his campaign and once, by accident I believe, I called him Major.

"You know about my trouble with the Army?" he asked quietly, and his eyes darkened.

I said I did not, but when he began to recount his story, the telephone on my desk rang with a call from a fisherman who was standing at the dock watching the swollen ice rip one of the summer restaurants from its cedar posts — "If I was you, boy, I'd get down here with that camera of yours and get one great picture," he said.

I explained to Ronald and he agreed to return to the office Monday morning. We shook hands, and when he had gone I hurried down the street to the dock.

The routine of Ronald Alley's mornings seldom varied. That Monday morning he patted Erna's back as he left the bed. She heard him running the shower. She listened for the teakettle then drifted back to sleep until she heard him open and close the kitchen door. He would be going outdoors to walk and she could close her eyes and lie still a while longer before breakfast. There was no light in the bedroom and she let herself sink back into sleep.

When she awoke it was after seven o'clock. But why hadn't she heard Ronald come back inside? She held herself very still and listened for him. She pulled on a bathrobe and went downstairs. Opening the back door she spotted the morning paper folded in half on the steps. Two men were there on their knees. "No pulse! I get no pulse!" one of them was saying. Then she saw the soles of Ronald's shoes, and then all of him lying face down in the snow.

Living out his greatest fear, Ronald Alley died that day, January 23, still known as a collaborator with the enemy. He had not had time to clear his name.

Eager to write my first novel, I resigned my position at the *Bar Harbor Times* and left the island in September. Twice I had attempted to begin a book on Ronald, abandoning the idea when the story seemed to me too big and intractable. Then late in 1978 Erna sent me the names of two officers who had served in Korea with Ronald who wanted to help clear his name. Both assured me he had been a competent and loyal officer who often jeopardized his own safety in order to protect his men. One of the officers, Captain Frederick Smith, insisted that the most serious charge against Ronald had been false. The Army had claimed that Ronald had given the Chinese information about artillery manuals. But Captain Smith, who told me he had been in the hut with Ronald during the Chinese interrogations, swore they had both tried to present phony information only to have the Chinese produce a stack of artillery manuals dating from World War II, when China was an ally of the United States.

A year later I secured portions of an FBI file kept on Ronald. The file revealed that J. Edgar Hoover had been personally involved in monitoring Ronald's life from the time he returned from Korea until 1970. Memos from FBI field workers frankly referred to Ronald as a Communist. Then, when I arranged to review taped recordings of interviews conducted with Ronald by CBS and NBC news in Boston and New York City, I discovered the tapes had been inexplicably erased.

I wrote another novel in 1979, but the Alley story was under my skin and I continued to devote time to it. I was convinced that we had gone to war in Korea with only a vague understanding of what was at stake there. Without a clear definition of which American interests they were fighting to protect and without a firm consensus at home that these interests were worth fighting for, American

– UPI

Erna Alley outside the courtroom where her husband was sentenced. She told the court, in a tearful appeal, that she could not support her two children if her husband went to prison.

As he held a wounded South Korean soldier in his arms, Captain Alley was captured by four Chinese who ordered him to march, and promptly shot two bullets into the head of his helpless comrade.

---

soldiers had been confused by the war and by the absence of solidarity that had bolstered soldiers in other wars. They had tried to fight an enemy they could barely identify under political constraints they could not begin to understand. As a result, the war had not been won. It may be said that it had been lost. The Army was under pressure to explain why things had gone so poorly.

This military establishment, still staggering from the heat of Senator McCarthy's rhetoric, was anxious to improve its image. Somewhere it was decided that the POWs and their misconduct in Communist captivity provided the best evidence of what had gone wrong. They were soft, the Army said. Softness lost the war; softness was punishable.

The Air Force, Navy, and Marines refused to prosecute their own men. The Army eventually excused all but 14 of the 3493 troops held by the enemy. Of these 14 men, eight enlisted men and three officers were court-martialed, convicted, and sentenced. During Major Alley's trial President Eisenhower endorsed the

Army's actions, saying, "American fighting men must toughen up."

All of this I learned, and late in 1979 I returned to Mount Desert Island and went to Ronald's grave. In a cemetery resting on the side of a shabby brown hill not far from an abandoned pile of railroad ties, granite slabs, and discarded automobile parts they buried Ronald Alley. This is not where Erna would have buried him, but it was the family's wish and she consented.

It was a raw, gray day. Someone from the Legion post had marked the veterans' graves with small plastic American flags. Ronald's was torn, and the wind had shaken a corner of it loose from its wooden stake. At the head of the grave a granite stone read: Ronald E. Alley, 1922–1978. An American flag and the Shrine emblem were engraved below his name. Alongside him were the graves of his father, Howard O. Alley 1896–1979, and mother, Thelma P. Alley 1901–1978. A lot of death crowded into a few years. A lot of family crowded into a few square yards of earth.

I had dinner with Erna that evening and she read me a letter from a former sergeant in the Army, Clyde Wilson, Jr., living in Kentucky. Wilson was writing to say he had just learned of Ronald's death, and he was deeply saddened. He wrote of how he, too, had been captured near Chosin Reservoir in December 1950. He said Captain Alley had been the officer most responsible for keeping them alive that first horrible winter. In the last paragraph he wrote: "I will help in any way to clear the record of one who suffered along with us in Korea and then had to suffer all over again after his return to the States."

Before I left Bar Harbor I promised Erna that I would find out why Ronald had gone to prison and that I would write the book she had spoken so often of writing. I told her we would not stop until we were sure of the truth. And for several hours we spoke of this word "truth," certain that it existed, certain that it could be found and that I would find it.

§∾

The Aftermath . . .

From the November 1980 issue . . .

IN DEFENSE OF RONALD ALLEY

☞ I read with interest "A Soldier's Disgrace" in your September issue.

I knew Ronald Alley. Shortly after I was captured I was put into a group of 13 officers that included Ronald Alley, and we were together until our release in 1953.

Prior to the "Peace Talks" that began in the summer of 1951, life was very hard. The Chinese Communists and North Koreans were making no effort to keep us alive and healthy; prisoners had the highest death rate per capita in the history of the United States, including the Civil War. When I was captured, I weighed about 175 pounds, and in three months I weighed 70 pounds. I had beriberi, jaundice,

dysentery, night blindness, and pneumonia. This was very common, not the exception.

When things were the most difficult, Ronald Alley and another officer were taken out for interrogation and kept in a Korean house just outside of our compound. We could observe them daily and could see them drinking tea and eating — what they were eating we could not know or see. Many prisoners were willing to believe that the two men were collaborating with the Chinese, but we had no way of knowing this. Those of us who knew Ronald could not believe that he would do anything that would help the Chinese, while those who did not like him were willing to believe otherwise. Ronald was quite ill at this time, but he always did his share of duties and never complained.

When men are cooped up under very poor conditions, it is easy to hate and to like. Ronald had an odd personality, and those who did not

know him felt he "knew it all," but this was not true. He was an excellent officer and very proud of his military service.

At the time of our release, Senator Joseph McCarthy had everyone running scared, including Hollywood and the United States Army. Every returning POW was suspected of collaboration, and we had no security clearance, could not attend school, be promoted, etc., until we were cleared.

At the time Ronald was being court-martialed, I was not well, but did attend the proceedings. Those of us who were to appear as witnesses for the defense were quartered in an old enlisted barracks, the porch of which was rotting away. We had no heat nor hot water and no way to safeguard our personal possessions. The witnesses for the prosecution were quartered in a hotel in Washington and were having one big party.

I could see that Ronald Alley did not have a chance; it had been determined before the trial that he was to be found guilty. He did not receive a fair trial — there was no way he could have under the circumstances. There is no evidence to show that the court ever considered the physical condition of Ronald Alley, or duress; and they did accept hearsay evidence. They did not give adequate recognition to those who testified in his behalf; they wanted to find him guilty.

I really feel like crying when I think of the ordeal that Ronald Alley and his family faced, not because he was a traitor or guilty of misconduct, but because the court wanted to show Washington and Senator McCarthy that they had taken action to rid the Army of Communists.

In the 33 months that I spent as a POW, I never saw or heard anything that would make me feel or believe that any POW was a traitor. I did see what I thought was poor judgment, but who can judge men who are in ill health, being starved and mistreated? The conduct of the POWs in North Korea was such that all services may be proud of them.

I pray daily that someone who has the authority will set the record straight and remove this terrible stain on the Alley family; they do not deserve it. Ronald Alley was a good American, an excellent soldier, and did much more for his country than most of us.

Charles L. Peckham
Lt. Col. (Ret.)
King City, California

From the December 1981 issue . . .

A NEW HEARING

☞ After twice denying his requests while he was alive, the Pentagon's Army Board for the Correction of Military Records announced on September 25, 1981, that it would grant a formal hearing on the case of Major Ronald E. Alley, whose story first received widespread publication in the September 1980 issue of *Yankee*. Don Snyder, author of that article, has now written a book, and the results of his research for the book (funded by the Washington-based Fund for Investigative Journalism) helped persuade the Army Board to review

the case. The author; the major's widow, Erna Alley; and her attorney, Gerald Williamson of Brockton, Massachusetts; are seeking an honorable discharge for the deceased Major Alley. The formal hearing will be held at the Pentagon during the first week of January 1982, approximately 27 years after Major Alley was court-martialed and sent to prison. Maine Congressman David Emery and Senator William S. Cohen have joined in the appeal for Major Alley's honorable discharge.

From the October 1982 issue . . .

THE FINAL ENDING

☞ Just after nine o'clock on the morning of July 13, a telephone call finally came from Congressman David Emery's office in Augusta, Maine. "I'm afraid I have bad news for you," were Mike Danforth's first words.

I listened as he read the Army's official statement to me. By a vote of three to two the Army Board for the Correction of Military Records had denied the honorable discharge for Major Ronald Alley. After more than five months of deliberations the Army ruled that the 1955 court-martial of Major Alley had been "manifestly correct."

I asked Congressman Emery to request the Pentagon not to release any

press statements until I was in Bar Harbor with Mrs. Alley. Then I telephoned Erna's son Gary. He said he would meet me in Bar Harbor, but not until late in the day; he wanted me to get there first. "If it's all right," he said apologetically, "would you be the one to tell Ma?"

Erna was out on the front porch of her home in Salisbury Cove, and as I walked toward her I glanced at the sign that said "No Vacancy" at Erna's German Motel. "I knew you'd be coming today," she said solemnly. "I kept one room for you, Don." She knew why I was standing there in front of her.

When Gary arrived we went along to Major Alley's grave. The grass in the cemetery had just been cut, and the men from the Legion Hall had remembered to put a small flag on the grave. I stood off to the side and watched as Gary pulled away the blades of grass that grew close to the granite headstone. "He'd have been some proud standing there in the Pentagon. That's what I keep thinking. Why didn't the Army give him the hearing while he was alive? Now that he's dead why do they want to hurt us anymore? The man's dead," he said.

Erna busied herself picking the red geraniums that had died in their pot. Finally she folded her hands and drew in a deep breath. "I did the best I could," she whispered. "You'll have to understand, honey."

And that was all.

Courtesy of Don Snyder

Still bitter after 30 years, Erna Alley calls her husband's trial "a circus, a farce" and blames the Army for his death.

The First Frost
"...was it just the moonlight playing tricks?"

A friend of mine used to tell how his father, a third-generation Vermont farmer, would wait for the trefoil, his one cash crop, to ripen: he would sit in a straightback chair next to a window that faced the field dotted with bright pink clover blossoms, elbows on his knees, fingertips tapping time, eyes roaming the wide field, waiting for that moment — he couldn't say what it was but he knew it when he saw it — when the blossoms had opened just so, and were ready to be harvested. I think I've felt that tension, mostly when the temperature drops into the thirties at night and the shortened days have a hard time knowing whether they belong to summer or winter. Without a garden I marked the passage of the seasons on paper: calendars or dates at the tops of letters. But with a garden, dates go back to being numbers and the drama of waiting for the first frost becomes a game that seems to change its rules and timing every year.

I'm a long way from having the kind of knowledge, the intuition, that my friend's father had, so I have to rely on every other resource I can, including weather reports, my record of the dates of the first frosts of the past several years, and the advice of my neighbors who've been at it a lot longer than I.

Some people say the arrival of the first frost has to do with the position of the moon, that a full moon often brings it on; some say that it's a combination of the moisture in the air and the temperature. I've also been told that the valleys get frosted first — the hilltops get it last. But then I hear that it happens the other way around. I have no guesses. Living on the side of a slope that descends into the Connecticut River valley, I've seen the depth of the valley frosted first and the hilltops next — all the while leaving my tomatoes to ripen. I've also seen it happen the other way around. And I've seen the frost come within a few feet of my garden, which lies in the protective southern shadow of my house, the crystal whiteness stopping as if in respect to some invisible boundary line. On a few mornings, I've found the thermometer to be below freezing, but still no frost. I have no guesses.

Our weather report comes from a radio station in Hartford, more than a hundred miles to the south, close enough to put me on guard when they predict frost, but far enough away so that I know I'll have to take my own gambles. Last year, I wrote in my garden journal: "The radio warned 'frost in the low-lying valleys' for tonight so, after I got home from work, I went out to the garden with the flashlight and the wheelbarrow, filling it to the brim with tomatoes in all stages of ripeness, eggplants whose pale purple was just shy of the rich black I was waiting for, butternut squash still striped at the neck, peppers I'd passed over before because they were too small. I gathered the zinnias and marigolds in huge bundles and later put them in jars around the house. I left the broccoli, with several good heads starting to form, parsnips and carrots which the frost won't bother, and some buttercrunch which it might take with it."

Frost never came that night. In fact, it didn't come for another two weeks. My plants were left to thrive, fruitless, in the warmth of an unexpected Indian summer. And the vegetables I'd taken in ripened in the wheelbarrow on the porch.

This year, time got away from me. The fall came warm and indulgent. It was October before I knew it, yet still no frost. I should have been ready. This morning, I woke up early. In the distance I could hear the Amtrak Montrealer — which passes through the valley around 4:30 A.M. — whistling its way north and I could see its headlight pan up from the valley across the bedroom ceiling. As the trumpet of the train passed, it grew completely still outside, the moonlight so sharp it seemed that all the tomatoes I'd left unpicked could ripen in its light. I got up and looked out the window: in the bright of the setting moon I thought I could see the earth turned white, or was it just the moonlight playing tricks? I went out to the garden, the frost alive under my feet. Tomato and squash vines lay brown and slumped, the squash leaves dangling from the stalks like black tissue. But the zinnias, the eggplants, the ferns around the garden — all had kept their colors, there in the first light of the morning, crystallized in frost, not yet taken by the inevitable rising sun.

– Edie Clark

*As the first woman in the nation to become a licensed pilot
and the first to fly the English Channel, beautiful Harriet Quimby deserved her title,
"Queen of the Air." But she didn't deserve the horrible fate that met
her at Harvard Field in Squantum, Massachusetts. (A fate, as
it turned out after publication, witnessed by a Yankee subscriber — see letter, page 221.)*

What Killed Harriet Quimby?

BY FRANK J. DELEAR

N o one remembers Harriet Quimby. It's as though she never existed."

So wrote syndicated columnist Michael Kilian of Chicago in March 1977. His column, a poignantly touching tribute to Harriet Quimby, may have stirred a few vague memories here and there.

Yet its brevity left many unanswered questions as well as the nagging thought that Miss Quimby merits more than a fleeting nod of remembrance. So, this is to report that Harriet Quimby *is* remembered and has not been, as the columnist feared, "thrown out with the old newspaper clips." She lives, first, in the pages of

a dozen or more encyclopedias and aeronautical histories as a talented writer and drama critic (of *Leslie's Weekly,* in New York); as the first licensed woman aviator in the United States (1911); as the first woman to fly an airplane across the English Channel (1912); and as a fearless young woman who happened to have more than her share of intelligence, ambition, personality, and beauty. Still, the references to her tragic finale — the horrifying accident in the summer of 1912 — seem surprisingly sketchy and inconclusive.

Harriet began writing in 1902 for the *Dramatic Review* in San Francisco, but she also wrote for *Leslie's* and in 1906 moved to New York as that magazine's drama critic. Her interest in aviation began with her attendance at the Los Angeles International Aviation Meet in January 1910, the first air meet in the United States. It soared to enthusiasm in October that year when she attended the big international air meet at Belmont Park, New York, the nation's third such meet (after the Harvard-Boston meet of a month earlier). She cheered with the rest as John B. Moisant upheld the honor of the United States by flying his Bleriot to the Statue of Liberty and back (36 miles in 34 minutes) to defeat the best that Europe could offer. Harriet Quimby decided to learn to fly.

She enrolled in the Moisant Aviation School at Garden City, New York, in the summer of 1911, competing with Moisant's sister, Mathilde, to become the nation's first licensed woman pilot. Both flew Moisant monoplanes, copies of the famous Bleriot design.

Would her bosses at *Leslie's* frown on their drama critic's unwomanly activities? Harriet dodged the question by taking her flight lessons at dawn and concealing her femininity in a flying suit and face-shielding hood. The secret was short-lived. After 33 lessons, involving only four and a half hours in the air, instructor André Houpert soloed his mysterious student, and on August 1, 1911, Harriet received Aero Club of America license number 37 (beating Mathilde by two weeks).

Two days later Harriet won headlines by making a moonlight flight over Staten Island, New York, to the amazement of a crowd of 20,000, a feat for which she received $1500.

In the spring of 1912 another "first" tempted her — a flight across the English Channel. Since Louis Bleriot had first flown it on July 25, 1909, other famous male fliers had followed. But no woman (there were several European female fliers at the time) had dared to challenge the channel.

In New York, Harriet agreed with *Leslie's* request for exclusive American rights to a first-person account of the proposed flight, obtained a letter of introduction to Louis Bleriot, and, in March 1912, sailed for England. In London she concluded an agreement with the *Mirror* to finance her flight, at "a handsome inducement," as she later described it. Meeting Bleriot in Paris, she made another wily move, ordering a new 70-hp plane and at the same time arranging to borrow a new 50-hp Bleriot for her

Early in the morning of April 16, 1912, spectators hold Harriet Quimby's Bleriot monoplane in check as she enters the cockpit to attempt a crossing of the English Channel, the first woman to do so.

– Smithsonian Institution

Then the horrifying and unbelievable occurred. Willard was seen to hurtle clear over the nose of the plane, followed a second or two later by Miss Quimby.

flight. Both were two-seaters, and the borrowed craft was the same general type she had flown in America.

It may be difficult today to see why the 22-mile channel hop could be hazardous. Yet it was, and several fliers had already been lost in the attempt. For Harriet, this was her first flight in a Bleriot, first with a compass, and first across water. Add to that a flimsy plane that warped its wings to turn, an engine that needed prayer as well as fuel, and fog that hid the water for most of the flight.

A worried group of friends saw Harriet off early on the morning of Tuesday, April 16. Heavily clad against a chill, damp day, she wore under her satin flying suit (as she later wrote), "two pairs of silk combinations, over it a long woolen coat, over this an American raincoat, and around and across my shoulders a long wide stole of sealskin."

Airborne at 5:38 A.M., Harriet climbed in a wide circle over land, reaching 2000 feet before heading out over the channel. She caught a brief glimpse of the *Mirror*'s tugboat jammed with reporters and photographers before running into a fog bank. She climbed through the mists to 6000 feet, seeking

---

Left: Miss Quimby poses a few minutes before boarding her plane for the channel flight.

---

clear sky, but found only more mists and a "bone-chilling cold."

The little monoplane was flying at 200 feet when it broke into the clear. Harriet sighted a deserted stretch of beach dead ahead and soon passed over the Cape Grisnez Lighthouse. She flew briefly toward Boulogne, then spiraled down to a landing near the Bleriot hangar at Hardelot, some 25 miles south of her intended destination, Calais. Despite the Bleriot's cruise speed of almost 60 miles an hour, the flight had taken nearly an hour because of the climbing and landing spirals and the long slow ascent to 6000 feet, as well as the course variation.

Harriet, now "Queen of the Air," returned to the United States as a celebrity on two continents. In demand at air meets throughout the country, she entered the 1912 Boston meet held at Harvard Field in Squantum on the shores of Dorchester Bay. It was a troubled affair from the start, with the management, a group of local promoters, squabbling with the Aero Club of America, the rules-maker for such competitive meets. The meet eventually ended $25,000 in debt and with the licenses of seven aviators suspended for the rest of the year. Worse, it ended in tragedy.

Monday, July 1, the second flying day of the meet, went quite well, with, said the news accounts, "some good flying

during the day." Just before 6 P.M., with the competitive events concluded, Harriet took off with a passenger, William A.P. Willard, the meet manager, for a flight to Boston Light, about eight miles out in the island-dotted harbor.

Taking off, Harriet and Willard circled the field and headed east toward the Light, climbing to a height of 5000 feet. Harriet sat forward in the new 70-hp Bleriot (the ship she had ordered in Paris), the plane's white wings extending just below and to either side of her. Willard rode in the rear cockpit about three feet back of the pilot. The plane's center of gravity was forward at the wings so Willard's weight kept the fuselage level, replacing sandbags carried to prevent the tail from rising too high when Harriet was flying alone.

Returning from the Light some 20 minutes later, the Bleriot descended in a wide circle and, headed east, reached a point near the mouth of the Neponset River, midway between the Squantum and Dorchester shores. The plane, already in a steep glide, suddenly slanted even more steeply down and started a turn to the left, presumably to make its final approach to the field. Then the horrifying and unbelievable occurred. Willard was seen to hurtle clear over the nose of the plane, followed a second or two later by Miss Quimby. Both plunged into

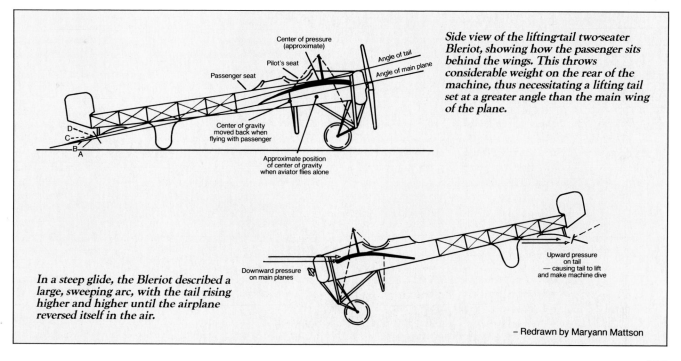

In a steep glide, the Bleriot described a large, sweeping arc, with the tail rising higher and higher until the airplane reversed itself in the air.

Side view of the lifting-tail two-seater Bleriot, showing how the passenger sits behind the wings. This throws considerable weight on the rear of the machine, thus necessitating a lifting tail set at a greater angle than the main wing of the plane.

- Redrawn by Maryann Mattson

Willard, enthusiastic over Miss Quimby's splendid performance, for a moment forgot the danger of moving. . . .

Mathilde Moisant (left) and Harriet Quimby were friendly rivals and fellow students at the Moisant Aviation School in Garden City, New York, in 1911.

the muddy river 1000 feet below, which, with the tide out, was barely three or four feet deep. Death was instantaneous. The plane dove into the river 100 feet away and flipped upside down. Though badly smashed it was intact enough for a later inspection of its controls.

Harriet's flying career spanned a scant 11 months and she was 28 when she died.

What caused the tragedy? Hardy, Miss Quimby's French mechanic, was one of several to advance his theory: "Too steep

a glide. The machine lost its balance." He voiced strong doubt that there had been any mechanical failure. "I personally tested every screw, bolt, and wire before we pushed the machine from the hangar," he said. "I always did that, for I would never allow Miss Quimby to get into the seat, much less allow her to carry a passenger, unless I was satisfied that every part of the machine was perfect. But what could have happened? I can only say: what has always happened to

Bleriot monoplanes. . . .Most of the accidents to Bleriot types have happened almost exactly alike. They all have lost their balance."

A reference in the *Globe* of July 3 added support to Hardy's words. "It appears," said the item, "that an accident similar to this one has occurred many times in France — always with fatal results and nearly always in the Bleriot monoplane. The French government is at present engaged in an investigation of this kind of accident with the Bleriot. It is supposed to be due to the curve at the entrant edge of the plane."

In its August 1912 issue the magazine *Aircraft,* a leader in its field, devoted almost four pages to the accident. Included were articles by Walter H. Phipps on the Bleriot's dangerous instability, and by Denys P. Myers, who conceded the instability, but agreed with Earl Ovington, a leading flier of the day and one of the first to inspect the wrecked plane, that the main cause was jammed controls. Included also were reports from four key eyewitnesses — two favoring instability as the cause, a third (Ovington) who clung to his jammed-control theory, and a fourth who suspected a broken "forward truss wire" under the wing, but offered virtually no proof.

Phipps' article, "The Danger of the Lifting Tail and Its Probable Bearing on the Death of Miss Quimby," has a convincing ring of fact. Phipps pointed out that the fixed horizontal tail surface of the two-seat Bleriot was actually a small cambered wing, similar aerodynamically to the craft's main lifting wing. Further, he explained, the tail surface was set at a higher lifting angle than the main wing to help carry the weight of a passenger who sat well back of the plane's center of gravity. His article, complete with photographs and drawings, showed how the combination of a lifting tail and difference in angle created a situation of great potential danger.

A. Leo Stevens, Miss Quimby's manager, wrote that he believed the accident was caused by "Willard suddenly straining forward to speak to Miss Quimby." Stevens, a friend of the Wright brothers and a famous balloon pilot, said he had twice warned Willard before the flight not to leave his seat under any circumstances. "This warning I was very particular to give," he wrote, "because I knew him to be a man of sudden impulses. Many a time while talking with him I have known him to suddenly leap from or lean forward in his chair to com-

Smiling confidently, Harriet Quimby receives last-minute advice before her channel flight.

municate an idea that had flashed into his mind. . . .I believe that as the flight drew to its conclusion, Willard, enthusiastic over Miss Quimby's splendid performance, for a moment forgot the danger of moving and suddenly stretched

forward to shout a word of congratulation to her."

Harriet Quimby was a victim of aviation's age of innocence. Surely the cards were stacked against her that sad summer day. Whatever the triggering cause

— too steep a glide, sudden shifting of the passenger's weight, even a fouled rudder wire — no doubt can remain that the Bleriot was a terribly unforgiving aircraft, even for pilots of far more experience than Harriet Quimby.   ᔓᕽ

Two months after the above was published in September 1979, we received the following letter from a subscriber.

Investigators examine the wreckage of her Bleriot monoplane in an attempt to determine the cause of her fatal plunge into Dorchester Bay on July 1, 1912.

☞ I read with great interest the article in the September issue on Harriet Quimby and her accident. As a boy of 16 I was a witness to that tragedy. Another boy and I had borrowed my father's rowboat and had gone down to watch the planes at the Squantum air meet.

Miss Quimby's plane was almost overhead when we saw her passenger and Miss Quimby both fall out. She hit the water not more than a hundred feet from us. Several men waded out from the shore and I rowed over close to where she fell and they placed her body in my boat. I rowed over to a nearby wharf where the men took her body ashore.

Needless to say it was a dreadful experience for me, and in all the years since I have never forgotten it.

G. Myron Savage
West Wareham, Massachusetts

221

We'd always heard that what the Ganges is to the devout Hindus, the Nile to archeologists, and the Mississippi to Mark Twain, so the Batten Kill in Vermont is to certain fly fishermen. It was lucky for us that writer Geoffrey Norman just happened to be one of those — or at least he developed into one. Or did he? Anyway, to all our fisherman readers this seems to be the all-time favorite.

Mystery of the Batten Kill

BY GEOFFREY NORMAN

The river seeps out of two thick alder bogs, one to the east of my house and the other a little north and west. The two branches run roughly parallel for perhaps seven miles, sparkling little streams that pass through beaver country and gravel pits without losing their character; then join up in Manchester to become the main branch of a river large enough for the name. Then it is on downstream, mile after gentle mile, through cow pastures and stands of shrubby second-growth timber, before crossing the state line and emptying, finally, into a worthy river, the Hudson. This is the Batten Kill.

I heard about the river long before I moved to its suburbs. In New York, where I worked and suffered, other frustrated fly fishermen remembered weekends on the "Kill" and told me their stories. Several of us would gather from time to time to eat lunch and commiserate, and I would hear descriptions of big native fish almost too wise to be taken, vast hatches of mayflies, solitary pools and rising fish. It sounded like paradise.

Better, certainly, than the Catskill streams I was driving to almost every weekend. Those streams were heavily stocked and heavily fished — largely by other men who made their livings in Manhattan and who had the manners to prove it.

But the Batten Kill was five hours away and you didn't drive up there for a weekend of fishing. In their stories, the men I ate lunch with never mentioned crowding or fishing pressure. So I assumed that it didn't exist. That raised the unseen river still further in my esteem. In fact, it counted for almost as much as the big native brown trout.

Perhaps the single most alluring datum about the river was the "Hendrickson rate." I came on this at one of my lunches, amid all the talk of rods and fly patterns, leader tapers and faraway rivers. Individual streams are as beguiling to the devoted fly fisherman as European cities are to the serious traveler. A fisherman can rhapsodize for an hour about the friendly gravel bottom of his favorite Michigan stream or the fecund weed beds of a gentle spring creek.

The "Hendrickson rate" came up when the Batten Kill was under discussion. It seemed that cabins along the river that normally rented for $50 a week could not be had for less than $500 during the early part of May when the little brown mayflies called ephemera — or more commonly, Hendricksons — were hatching. The river was that good. And, the man telling me this added, "you just can't get one of those cabins unless you make your arrangements a year in advance. Otherwise, your best hope is to do a favor for somebody who already has a place reserved and hope that he'll invite

Fishing at Sunset by Richard Earl Thompson, courtesy of the Richard Thompson Gallery in San Francisco.

... the Batten Kill was, and is, a fine bamboo piece. I own one and I love it so much that I have made special provisions for it in my will. No bass bugger or bait fisherman will ever own that rod.

you along to share expenses — and the hatch — with him."

When my wife told me that she was pregnant and *Fly Fisherman* announced that it was looking for an experienced editor, I made my first trip to the Batten Kill — for a job interview.

But the part I felt most keenly was the prospect of actually seeing the Batten Kill, and perhaps even *fishing* it, though it was late summer and there was no reason to expect the fishing to be very good. It seems foolish now: to want so much in a river. There was so much more at stake. But that is the nature of passions: they overwhelm more fundamental, rational concerns. That is why they so often lead to disaster. I loved fly fishing in those days and almost never got to do any. Frustration only excited my passion, which is one of life's great dangers. And . . . I had heard so much about that river.

My first look was, of course, disappointing. Once I reached its banks, the Batten Kill looked very much like any other shallow, rocky Eastern stream. In fact, it seemed a little sluggish and dark, with some of the vulgar virtues of a bass river. There were a lot of logs that had fallen into the river and some very deep, almost still water. The Catskill streams were easily more beautiful, I thought. But then, a common exterior could conceal lovely, exotic secrets. So I rigged my fly rod and got into my waders.

I had an hour to fish before I was to meet my wife and a real estate agent to look at some houses. The afternoon was reserved for my job interview. It was a most frustrating hour. The stream was deep in many places and could not be waded. But there was no good bank to fish from. I would need a canoe, I decided, when I moved to Vermont.

When I found a stretch of water that could be waded, I watched and, glory of glories, in a few minutes I saw the unmistakable ripples and splashes made by fish feeding on surface insects. *Rising fish.*

What they were feeding on, however, was the microscopic mayfly that hatches in the early mornings of late summer. It is so small that the entire insect, head, body, and wings, could fit inside the circumference of a dime. I tied on an imitation and worked a few fish, but the combinations were just too dainty for me.

The leader was delicate as silk sewing thread; the fly was too small to see; the fish were wary and suspicious. One or two rose to my fly but detected the artifice and did not strike. I could feel the hook bite when I finally got one small fish to strike, but I was too forceful and broke the leader. But there would be time, I thought like Prufrock, when I moved to Vermont. Then, I could learn the intricacies of small flies and fine leaders on the legendary Batten Kill.

Although I never did go to work for *Fly Fisherman* magazine, my wife and I moved to Vermont in the late fall. I saw and studied the river as I ran the errands that included taking my wife to the hospital and bringing her home with a baby girl. Even through all of that, the river was always in my mind, just beneath the conscious surface. I could not wait for spring to come.

It came, and with it came the famous Hendrickson hatch. Early May, I'd been told — that was the time to look for it. Make sure you were ready. Have your tackle cleaned and rigged, waders patched, fly box full. I did all of that in April, and bought a license. I was ready.

Fishermen came up from Boston and New York for the hatch, but none of them paid a special rate. I found that out from a real estate friend who laughed when I asked her about it. And it was a good thing, too, since there were more fishermen than mayflies on the river. "Shortest Hendrickson hatch on record," one Batten Kill regular I know said. "Must have gone on for 10 minutes on a Thursday."

I never saw a Hendrickson fly, much less a pool full of trout feeding with abandon on the hatching insects. Nor did I talk to anyone who had done either of those things. I told a friend that if the fall came and the leaves did not change color, I was going back to New York.

Well, even rivers have slumps (though you don't expect them on legendary rivers) and you can come up with all sorts of theories to explain them. There were dozens traded around to account for the nonappearance of the Hendricksons. Too much snow. Too little snow. Early runoff. Late freeze. Pollution. Beaver dams. Radiation. Meanwhile, spring wore on and then it was summer and the trout season was still open. The river was still there and I kept fishing in spite of the

failure of the Hendricksons, which was beginning to take on the dire aspect you would expect if the swallows failed to show up at Capistrano.

I'm no great fisherman but I knew that trout would go on eating, Hendricksons or not. . . . It is that or die, and nothing in nature commits suicide or goes on hunger strikes. So I tried all of the tactics on the Batten Kill that I had learned in Michigan, Colorado, and the Catskills. I went fishing early and late in the day. I fished with dry flies, wet flies, streamers, and nymphs. I was tempted to try live bait but resisted. I was not *that* bad at fishing and I would not let the river humiliate me. I fished on, sticking with artificials. I worked deep pools and shallow riffles, cut banks and sweepers. I tried exotic little flies that imitated flying ants and beetles. I tried grasshoppers and crickets. I talked to other fishermen and read books and followed all advice. It was August before I caught a respectable fish. Then I went to Africa on a job and, before I returned to Vermont, trout season was over.

I did not think much about the river that winter. It had beaten me and I was sore about it. I sulked. It was childish, but just the same I felt cheated.

Then I made a short trip to New York and met up with some of my old lunch friends. They asked about the Batten Kill right away. Their voices were full of a kind of nonmalicious envy. They looked at me the way a group of former Little Leaguers might look at an old teammate who had made it all the way to the "bigs" and is starting for the Orioles. I hated to disappoint them.

"Well," I said, "I had a tough season."

"Sure, sure," one of them said. "The good rivers are always tough; not like these stocked canals we're used to. Nothing but native fish in the Batten Kill. You've got to work for them, am I right?"

"Hard to argue with that," I said.

"But that's what makes it great. You catch one of those beauties and you've done something."

"Absolutely."

"I can't tell you," one man said solemnly, "how much I would like to have the chance to fish a really first-rate river regularly. You know, if you just go up for a weekend now and then, you never get a chance to really study the stream and get to know it. You look at the surface of that river and it is just like looking at a mirror. All you see is reflection and glare. But if you fish that stream day in and day out, when you look at it what you see is clear glass, like a windowpane. You can see everything going on down there under the surface. *That's* the way to fish."

"For sure," I agreed quietly. I went back to Vermont and the Batten Kill chastened. Perhaps it was my fault. I had expected too much, provided too little. This season I would try harder. I would go to the river with a little humility.

I was mercifully out of the state for opening day and the Hendrickson hatch. A friend sent me a telegram:

HENDRICKSONS HATCHED TO-DAY STOP ONE CAME TO TRAGIC END ON WINDSHIELD OF A DODGE STOP THE OTHER IS STILL AT LARGE STOP WANT TO BUY A COUPLE OF SLIGHTLY USED FLY RODS STOP

I pressed on in spite of this discouraging news, and the equally disturbing news that Lee Wulff, one of the foremost fishing writers and experts in the country, no longer fished the Batten Kill. He enjoyed catching fish too much. And his reputation depended on it.

I was shut out the first few times I went out on the river and I couldn't honestly say that I had learned anything for my time and frustration. I dreamed of other rivers that I had fished, especially some mild Michigan streams full of native fish, to be sure, but sweetened also by enough hatchery trout to make sure the fishermen had a chance. I also thought about moving to Montana.

It was in the midst of a spell of brooding that I came on a clue to what I was beginning to think of as "the mystery of the Batten Kill." That river was getting to me. It was like going to Disneyland and watching the kids have a rotten time. Something was out of joint.

But then a new tackle shop opened in Manchester. It was called the Bamboo Rod and it franchised Leonard fly rods, generally considered the finest you can buy today, certainly the most expensive. You should have $500 to spend before you start shopping for a Leonard. For reference, you can buy a fine glass rod for less than $100. You can get an adequate bamboo rod for $200 or so. The fish do not know the difference.

Before the Bamboo Rod opened its doors, Manchester was already the site of what is perhaps the world's most famous tackle store since the passing of Abercrombie and Fitch — Orvis. It is almost a generic term in fishing circles. Anything you need in the way of fishing tackle, you can find at Orvis. It will be good quality — the finest — and expensive.

One of the best fly rods you can buy at Orvis — a beautiful bamboo piece — is called the "Batten Kill." It was once the top of the line from Orvis. It has been eased out of that spot by graphite rods, the latest technological wonder. But the Batten Kill was, and is, a fine bamboo piece. I own one and I love it so much that I have made special provisions for it in my will. No bass bugger or bait fisherman will ever own that rod.

Think of hundreds of thousands of adolescents around the country sitting in small suburban rooms dreaming of Broadway. They are not conjuring images of Orange Julius stands, live sex shows, trashy novelty shops, and prostitutes too young to get a driver's license. Their vision is of perfectly ordered lights, row after row of them. Muted limousines. Elegant women and correct gentlemen. The theater — the life. One of those dreamers makes it now and then, and once he has been through the ritual of disillusion — seen the filth and borne up under the indignation — he learns to love Broadway once again. It is never the same, of course. It is once-burned, eyes-open love.

And so I stopped looking for the Batten Kill of my dreams, a river that existed, if ever, sometime before I was born, when fly fishing was something that only a few men did and all of them wrote books about. Nothing is as good as it once was. There are too many fishermen, not enough fish, too many people in canoes, not enough Hendricksons. The only thing that gets better is the fishing tackle.

So the Batten Kill became another river. I learned to fish it when I felt like killing a couple of hours. Big fish lived there. Bait fishermen caught them all the time. Maybe I would get lucky one day. Maybe not. But at least I was fishing and not talking about it.

One evening I slipped into the river near dusk. I was dressed in a work shirt and patched-up waders. I had fallen that far from the ideal. I was going fishing. It was cool, as it almost always is in the evenings in the Green Mountains. The water was clear and a little low — it had been a dry spring. I took a spot in a long flat section of the river and began casting. I was using a fly that is called a Henryville. It is made of some brown hackle and green feathers, tied up to look sort of like a lot of things but nothing in particular. I was careful about my leader, using 14 or 15 feet tied down to a 6X, which is about as fine as you can get and still be practical about the thing.

I shivered when I first got into the stream, then warmed as I began casting. Nothing much happened for the first 15 minutes. I watched a mink prowl the banks. That was diverting. As my attention wandered, my casts got flabby and I tangled my leader. It took a couple of minutes to work the knots out. Just at sunset, some insect activity began — slowly at first, then a little more rapidly. Something was hatching on the surface here and there, tiny insects that dried their wings, then popped free of the water's film and flew up into the corridor of light above the river and disappeared in the gray gloom. Some trout began feeding on the insects. I made a cast to the nearest fish and caught him — a small brook trout. I threw him back and cast to another. I caught him, too. Before the light died completely I caught half a dozen brook trout and one fair brown. I took the last two fish home to my wife, who made a late supper of them.

I fished the Batten Kill on a few other occasions that summer. As I fished I developed a new and more refined feeling for the river, the kind of affection I suppose a farmer must feel for marginal land that produces, but only after long hours of arduous cultivation. I know a few dozen places to fish now. They are not especially popular, so I can be by myself even during the fabled Hendrickson hatch. One pool where I go has a fish that must weigh seven or eight pounds. I've seen him and I hope some day to hook him.

I catch a few fish. During the late season I can catch small brook trout almost to order for my wife. The scenery is especially lovely then, with the leaves changing and matching the spawning colors of the little brookies. I even know of a couple of places where I can fish from the bank and where my wife and I can picnic and play with our daughter while we watch the moody water and wait for a sign of something worth casting to.

Now and then I'll be visited by an old friend from the city who inevitably asks about the river. If he persists, I'll give him directions and loan him what tackle he needs. These friends always go off to the river with the eager look of a kid going on his first overnight hike. I stay behind and caution, "It's not all it's cracked up to be." Then to myself I say, "And thank God for that."

A·SEPTEMBER SAMPLER

☞ Memorable thoughts, quotes, and assorted tidbits from the last 50 September issues. ☜

THE STORY THAT HURTS TO READ

☞ On Monday, returning wearily from the woods at dusk, Ron tripped and fell heavily in a deep gully. His ankle turned bright purple and swelled to twice its size. Though ordered off his feet by a doctor, he continued to end a day's woods search at his familiar post in front of the loudspeaker calling his son's name into the forest. In desperation, friends laced his coffee with tranquilizers. Wednesday night, his fourth night without sleep, the drugs finally took effect. His speech slowed, and he sat gripping the loudspeaker close to his mouth, unable to speak, until finally his head dropped as he gave in to his shattering fatigue. "He was the toughest man I've ever seen," said Duane Lewis. "Just unbelievable stamina."

The C-130H gunship flew a three-hour mission Tuesday morning, failing to detect a trace of Kurt. The plane was hampered by the low-hanging clouds and heavy rains that grew so bad searchers could not see their way in the woods and had to be pulled out. Hovering over the search area in the helicopter, Jill would call, "This is Momma. I want you to go to where you can see the sky. Come and wave to Momma." As the rain and fog continued into the fourth day, hopes dimmed that Kurt could be found alive, and the strain on Jill was growing almost unbearable.

"If someone had asked me beforehand how I would have acted," she would say later, "I would have said I'd go to pieces. But something happens to keep you going. You find reserves you didn't know you had. I kept telling myself it wasn't going to do Kurt any good if I wasn't able to function. It seemed that every time I turned around the wardens were pulling Ron out of the woods because I was upset. Finally I said, 'Look, I'll tell you if I

Jill and Ron Newton, 1981.

need him. But I'm going to cry. There's no way I'm not.' "

She preferred to search on her own with a few friends, "going on gut instincts. I kept thinking I'd find him whimpering behind the next tree." One day she found some holes by the horse hovel that bothered her, one in particular large enough for a child to have crawled through and way down under. Lacking a flashlight, she began clawing at the ground, desperately trying to see in. Looking up she saw a group of National Guardsmen recently activated to search. " 'I've got to have help,' I said, and three or four of them started digging. I was panicky by then, saying, 'Oh please God, he's got to be in there.' And I looked down and this guy crawls out from the hole and he says, 'There's nothing there,' and I said, 'He's got to be,' and he said no and tears rolled down his face." (*From "The Day Kurt Newton Disappeared" by Mel Allen.*)

On Labor Day weekend, 1975, Kurt Newton, aged four, vanished from his parents', Ron and Jill Newton's, campground at Coburn Cove, Maine, resulting in the most extensive woods search in the history of Maine before or since. The article excerpted here was published four years later and resulted in an avalanche of mail, including a half dozen sincere readers who wrote to say they'd recently "seen Kurt." Each of these leads was meticulously followed up by the Newtons — to no avail.

"Think you k'n handle this one, Earl? . . . I just don't feel up t' bein' a crusty old New England character so early in the mornin'. . . ."

226

Linnea Calder in 1982.

ONE WAY NOT TO HAVE TO TAKE A BATH

☞ There was no end to chores in this crowded house, where most of the time the 18 bedrooms were full — many of them occupied by the Roosevelt children and their friends. FDR referred to his sons Elliott, John, James, and Franklin Jr. as "a bunch of wild Indians," a description Linnea seconds. "They were always up to something," she recalls. Noting a wood chest in the back hall, she chuckles, "I remember a game of hide-and-seek when one of the boys hid in there, with a stick holding the lid barely open for air. One of his brothers spotted the stick, removed it, and sat on the lid." She opens the door to a dumbwaiter. "And once when somebody hid in the dumbwaiter, one of the boys ran upstairs and dumped a glass of ice water down the shaft!" She shakes her head, grinning. "One of their favorite tricks was to get guests to use all the hot water — so there wouldn't be enough left for the boys to take their own baths." (*From "The Last Campobello Survivor" by Bill Hennefrund.*)

This was an article about Linnea Calder, historian of the Roosevelt home on Campobello Island. For nearly 60 years she had been part of the summer help there.

THE DISCOVERY OF A MAINE FOLK SONG

☞ I can report that, along with the respect it has always commanded in New England, Harvard has also instilled a healthy irreverence in New England folk. My valued friend Samuel Eliot Morison was in Maine and heard someone singing in a field. Deciding it must be a Maine folk song, he went to some trouble to memorize it. He later sang it to a friend who told him, "Why, Sam, somebody's pulling your leg. That's nothing but 'Home on the Range.'"

Sam told him where he'd heard it, and the friend, who knew the farmer in question, went around and asked him why he did that. The farmer said, "He's a professor down at Harvard. I wanted to see how much he'd take." **Walter Muir Whitehill, former Director and Librarian of the Boston Athenaeum.** (*From "The Irascible Iconoclast" by Richard Meryman.*)

WHO'LL PAY THE PRICE?

☞ "Very few people are willing to pay the cost of their real life, to say 'this is what I have to do to become myself,' and act upon it, whatever the consequences." **Poet May Sarton**. (*From "In Love With Solitude" by Deborah Stone.*)

THE MOST POPULAR OF ALL SEPTEMBER "HOUSES FOR SALE"

☞ If you'd like a house on an island in Maine and your taste runs to simple, century-old houses, country life, and equipment such as a never-failing well, a kitchen pump, and kerosene lamps — read on. The name of the island is Matinicus, on which is situated the Red House, owned by Miss Doris P. Merrill of Blue Hill, Maine. The setting is eight acres of spruce, lilac bushes, and an aged apple orchard — plus sand beaches and the whole Atlantic Ocean. The red clapboard house boasts a 25-foot kitchen with windows on three sides, a living room with open Franklin stove, a study, and four bedrooms. There is an oil unit for extra heat if needed and a gas range for cooking. What more do you want? A workshop? The weather-shingled barn included on the property takes care of that. The price covering this entire offer is about what you would pay for a new car these days — $3500. Write Miss Merrill for further information.

Miss Merrill received hundreds of replies to the above (from the September 1959 issue) and finally sold to the sender of the earliest postmark on one of over a dozen letters containing the full asking price, sent sight unseen.

"Captain, if you mean it when you say you have not yet begun to fight, I sure as hell could use a little help here!"

C.H. ("Clif") Peasley of Hillsboro, New Hampshire, has dealt with draft horses all his life. For our September 1974 issue, Richard M. Bacon interviewed him for the "Forgotten Arts" series. Here we excerpt some of what Clif said. . . .

Working with a Draft Horse

I f you can locate one, it will sell for from $200 to $1000. But you won't get much of a horse for $200 today. But compared to tractor prices, the horse looks pretty darn good."

* * *

"About eight to 12 years is a good starting point. After you get experience, you can go for something younger and spunkier. Start with a proven workhorse. There is enough to learn about handling a horse without having to break all of its bad habits."

* * *

"Go for a grade that can do a little of everything and not too much of anything. It doesn't have to be a swaybacked plug. But avoid any horse that has been trained for pulling contests. It'll take off with any equipment you hitch it to."

* * *

"More important than either cost, age, or breed is the horse's disposition. Unless you want a horse only to impress your neighbors, you're better off, if you're a beginner, finding a good-natured horse, especially if you have any children around."

* * *

"Working with a horse is a cooperative business. Your habits and hers will both take some getting used to. If you work her a little every day and let her see what you can do, as well as discover what the horse can do, you'll learn before you know it.

"Finding a bred mare holds a further advantage, but even her ability to foal (in about 11 months) should not outweigh the horse's nature."

* * *

"For the home-production farm, there is very little a single, medium-size workhorse can't do. It's better to hire the heaviest work done than to try to find enough for a team to do yourself. Pro-

The above photograph and the one at right were taken by Stephen Whitney at Draft Horse Field Day in Cornish, New Hampshire, held each year in conjunction with the Draft Horse Institute at Indian Summer Farm in Cabot, Vermont. (Several readers have said the photo at right is their "all-time favorite Yankee photo"!)

vided you're not in a hurry, a single horse can do practically any job you set her to, including ploughing up sod land. You know, you can cover a lot of ground in a wagon. The same with a mowing machine. But you'll have to learn that you'll both need to rest."

* * *

"It's possible to work a horse too hard. A sweat is as good for a horse as it is for you. The only thing you don't want to do is work her to a lather. It's something you'll be able to judge when you get to know the horse."

* * *

"Horses have to be well fed to get the best from them, just like everything else. A medium-size workhorse will take about one-quarter bale of hay morning and night and two to three pounds of grain while she's working. Some feed their horses at noon, too. Horse feed is pretty high now — same as everything

else — but if you keep a cow, a horse will eat cow feed just as well.

"It's also a good idea to supplement her diet with daily vitamins and have plenty of salt and water available."

* * *

"You want to get a good, sound horse to begin with. She'll have to be wormed twice a year, and have the vet inoculate her for encephalitis, a disease humans can get. Unless she goes onto the pavement, there's no reason for shoeing her. Of course, some horses go through shoes quicker than children. It all depends on the horse."

* * *

"Every horse is different, just like every man and woman is different. With enough experience, both the horse and the man will learn to anticipate what the other needs."

"CVEEYANSTON"??

– Bruce Hammond

RULES FAW PRONOUNCING RHODISLAN

☞ To pronounce *r* aw not to pronounce ah, these ah the rules:

Rule 1: *r* is neva pronounced before a consonant. For instance, say "four o'clock," but "faw boys" and "fawth of July." It's "the fahmer in the dell," but "fahma Jones."

The glaring exception to this occurs when Rule 3 applies. If a plural ending must be used, but the *r* glide would apply if the word were being said in the singular, then it is stuck before the plural, as in "His idears ah good," or "Those umbrellers ah handy." This does not happen with words that are spelled with *r* as theah final sound. No true RhoDislan speaka would eva say "fahmers," for instance, only "fahmas."

Rule 2: (a) If a word ends in *r*, do not pronounce it if the word is said alone or in lists, or if it comes at the end of an utterance. For instance, "What a great dance flaw," or, counting, "one, two, three, faw, five. . . ."

(b) Even if the next word does staht with a vowel, an *r* at the end of a word might not be pronounced **if** the word is being emphasized, as in "Come heah, Annie!" **or** if there is a long pause befaw the next word.

Rule 3: If a word ends in the sounds "a," "uh," or "aw," and the next word stahts with a vowel, put in an *r* even if it isn't spelled that way, as in "Ma-r-ate," "umbrella-r-is," "thaw-r-it out." *(From "How to Speak and Understand RhoDislan English" by Elaine Chaika.)*

"HELLO, SUCKER!"

☞ As a Pulitzer Prize winner, T. W.'s evenings in London were filled with engagements with writers, publishers, and old friends. His phone rang constantly. "Let my epitaph read," he said, "here lies a man who never refused an invitation." But we could never persuade T. W. to join us at a nightclub, although he did not disapprove. A few years later, when he was teaching at the University of Chicago, he became an irregular customer at Texas Guinan's famous speakeasy. "Hello, sucker!" was her loud, raucous greeting to everyone who came in, but Texas had a soft spot in her heart for T. W. One night, so Thornton told me years later, she was entertaining three members of the Capone gang. They were dressed to kill: $200 suits, diamonds and sapphires on their fingers, immense gold cuff links, pearl stickpins, and, in their pockets,

pearl-handled guns. Texas introduced Wilder as the famous author he was. "Have any of you mugs read *The Bridge of San Luis Rey*? And don't any of you lie and say yes, because I know you haven't. The only things you guys read are the Most Wanted notices. But things are going to be different. You gotta bring some tone to my joint." She whispered an order to a waiter. He soon returned with three copies of *The Bridge of San Luis Rey*. "Thornton," she said, "autograph these books for these gorillas." And he did. They looked at Wilder and one, speaking for all, said, "This is real good. Real nice of you. Anything we can ever do for you. . . ." "Anybody you want rubbed out?" Texas whispered to Thornton. "They might start with Jed Harris," he replied with a Cheshire-Cat smile, referring to the director of his play, *Our Town*. *(From "To Us He Was Always 'T.W.' " by Clark Andrews.)*

WANTED: A NICE FAT FASTBALL

☞ It was after my sophomore year at Boston College when three of us boys on the football team went down to Ohio to play an exhibition game against the legendary Jim Thorpe and his Canton Bull Dogs. Before the game Thorpe and I put on a kicking contest, and that was a real thrill for me — particularly in retrospect. I could kick really well in those days, but Thorpe beat me. I never saw anyone anywhere, before or since, who could kick a ball so far.

Babe Ruth was a powerful man, too, but I had a little better luck against him. Old Magnet Haley, a promoter from Portland, Maine, with a mouth a mile long, got Babe Ruth's traveling exhibition baseball team to come to Portland for a game. Magnet had heard of my pitching at Boston College and he got me to come up to Bayside Park to pitch against the Babe and his team. It was a Saturday afternoon, and Bayside was a great park for baseball. I was pretty nervous about the whole idea, but I did all right. I pitched and we beat Babe's team. And in the four times I faced Babe he didn't get a hit. He popped up twice to right field. One of them was a mile high, the highest fly ball I ever saw. The other two times, believe it or not, I struck him out. He was up there swinging with that great big swing of his, and I was giving him all curve balls. I changed the speed on them, but they dropped *two feet*, and he couldn't touch them. He was in Portland that day to show how he could hit the ball a mile, so he was waiting for a nice fat fastball — and I just wasn't going to give it to him, that's all. When the game was over I went on over to shake hands, but he wouldn't turn around. In fact, he wouldn't even speak to me. What he didn't know was that I would have been just as thrilled if he'd hit a home run! In fact, many times in the years since then, I've sorta wished I'd served him up a fastball.

James Fitzpatrick,
as told to Don J. Snyder

THE LAST ANYONE EVER SAW OF THEM

☞ One thing is certain. After three years of planning, numerous delays, canceled departures, and the expenditure of $100,000, *The Free Life* rose grandly from its mooring that Sunday in September from George Miller's meadow, fronting on Accabonac Creek and Gardiner's Bay, after a series of staccato ballast drops. It taxied a few hundred yards in this manner, then Malcolm Brighton gave the command "lift off," and crew members on the ground let the craft slip from their clutching fingers. It flew upwards majestically, seemed momentarily to sink dangerously behind a row of scrub pines, and then quickly became a tiny dot in the sky to the northeast, the desired direction.

The last anyone saw of them, Malcolm had leaped up on the rim of the gondola and was waving to the crowd, looking like Burt Lancaster about to do the triple from the high swings in that circus flick. Pam had turned the tables on the photographers and was filming the crowd for a movie the trio hoped to make about the flight. Rod, Tiparillo in his teeth, was smiling that happy birthday smile and flapping both arms like a stoned seagull.

High-pitched emotions emanated from their many friends in the crowd. Cries of "We love you, Malcolm,

Rod, Pam" were lofted on the light breeze that caused the Union Jack and Old Glory to flutter from the straps that stretched from the gondola to the nylon outer balloon. And then, while everyone was still shouting, and the crew on the ground had their arms about one another, the aeronauts vanished into the heavens. (*From "The Tragic Last Voyage of The Free Life" by Alan D. Haas.*)

—I REMEMBER—

THE REUNION

☞ A while ago a neighbor of mine met a trenchmate of his on a visit to Boston. The two fellows, who were in World War I together, hadn't seen each other for years. So they went into a bar to have a few drops and catch up on the years that had passed. After nursing their drinks for quite some time, one of them, rather glassy-eyed by then, looked into space and said, "It's not clear to me whether it was you or your brother who was killed in the War — which one of you was it?"

Lee Winslow Court

AND NOW, FOR EVERYONE WHO BELIEVES THE JAPANESE HAVE NOTHING TO OFFER FOLKS FROM MAINE!

SOLID STATE COMBINATION CALCULATOR, QUARTZ CLOCK, AM-FM STEREO, TWO INCH COLOR TV, SWISS ARMY KNIFE AND CHAIN SAW

– Don Bousquet

BLACKLISTED CHEESES

☞ Our Daily Bread, like 90 other western Massachusetts co-ops, buys cheese and grain from Western Massachusetts Cooperatives, a federation, or "co-op's co-op" headquartered in a warehouse in Easthampton. WMC is big enough to own its own refrigerated delivery truck and to offer short-term credit to its members, along with 395 different items ranging from Sylvania light bulbs to Jarlsberg cheese — a product that used to be on many co-ops' blacklists because of its connections with Nestle, the giant Swiss corporation that has been criticized for selling infant formula to many Third World nations.

I was surprised to see the Jarlsberg at the WMC warehouse, and mentioned it to my guide, Alan Surprenant, a tall, slender, soft-spoken member of the collective that operates the warehouse. He explained that the boycott of Jarlsberg cheese was no longer operative for complicated reasons, adding, "It's hard to find a good Swiss cheese that's politically acceptable." (*From "Land of Dissenters and Dreamers" by Tim Clark.*)

EXACTLY WHY THE LEAVES TURN

☞ During the summer, leaves are busy manufacturing food. This food — starches, sugars, and proteins — is distributed by chlorophyll, the green coloring matter in leaves. When the chlorophyll captures the rays of the sun, it transforms the carbon dioxide in the air and the water in the soil into food. This, then, is distributed throughout the plant.

In the autumn, as a result of cooler weather and shorter days, the food manufacturing process is slowed down. This results in a chemical breakdown of the chlorophyll, so that the starches and other foods go into the branches, limbs, and trunks of the trees to be stored for spring use. When the green chlorophyll breaks down in the process, it becomes colorless, thus permitting the colors already present in the leaves to reveal themselves. (*From "This Miracle of Fall Color" by George Taloumis.*)

CHAPTER 10

October

No other month in New England is quite like October, for it is summer going out with all banners flying, a triumphal passing. The slow fire spreads from the blazing maples to the gold of the birches on our high slopes. The threat of winter is not yet upon the land, but rather a sense of awakening from the sultry bondage of summer, — and the Red Gods call. The smell of burning leaves in the still dusk, the bells of night-wandering cattle, brittle limbs on enormous moons, mists aglow in the valleys — these and a hundred such will always be New England October. And to them even the dullest heart must make some answer. But the heart answers, too, to something deeper than these.

Somehow at this season it is easier for us to shed intolerance, to put aside our feuds and walk in spirit with all fellow men. For we, too, are part of the infinite wisdom that patterns the seasons — winter and spring, the discordant summer, the temperate fall. This fall, hope for peace in a better world seems, at last, to have some meaning and certainty. Its symbol and promise is on all our land.

The above was written by Benjamin M. Rice, an associate of Yankee founder Robb Sagendorph from the very beginning, for the October issue in 1945. In our opinion, it has lost nothing in the passage of 40 years. Such is the enduring nature of October — and of ourselves.

Ben went on to be associated with Yankee as an editor, writer, and consultant for the rest of his life, which ended peacefully in 1978 on his beautiful 140-year-old ancestral farm (featured in the December 1983 issue) out on Windy Row in Peterborough, New Hampshire.

An October morning, Danville, Vermont.

– photograph by Richard Brown

233

The Angel Shooter

BY TIM CLARK

Like another American legend, this story begins with a cherry tree. Unlike the moral fantasy of George Washington and his hatchet, however, this story is true, and it is not about honesty, but faith.

On October 19, 1899, on a farm outside Worcester, Massachusetts, a young man named Robert Hutchings Goddard climbed a cherry tree to do some pruning for his grandmother, who owned the farm. Pruning may have been only an excuse; the young man's diary, which he started keeping the year before and would keep religiously until his death, is full of references to climbing and sitting in trees. It is a pleasant thing to sit in a tree and dream.

He had turned 17 two weeks before — a quiet, serious boy, interested in science, who read his father's *Scientific American* as well as the *Youth's Companion,* who built a "chemical labritory" and blew it up trying to make artificial diamonds. He was an avid reader of science fiction: Jules Verne, H.G. Wells, and a book by Garrett Serviss called *Edison's Conquest of Mars.*

In his leafy reverie Goddard was suddenly struck by "how wonderful it would be to make some device which had even the possibility of ascending to Mars, and how it would look on a small scale if sent up from the meadow at my feet." He imagined a sort of whirligig propelled by centrifugal force — an idea his cousin, who went to Harvard, later told him would never work — but he could almost see it in the hazy splendor of that autumn afternoon. "I was a different boy when I descended the tree," he wrote years later. "Existence at last seemed very purposive."

Such flashes of childhood revelation are a literary convention of sorts, common to biographies and autobiographies, and usually self-glorifying myths. In fact, Goddard's diary for October 19, 1899, reads: "Trimmed large cherry tree in afternoon." But in his diary for that date in 1900 is "Climbed cherry tree," and the words "Anniversary Day." He would write "Anniversary Day" under October 19 in his diary for the rest of his life, and whenever possible he would go back to climb the tree or just touch it on that day. He was in New Mexico when the great New England hurricane of 1938 finally toppled the tree. On the day that news arrived he wrote: "Cherry tree down. Have to carry on alone."

Goddard never lost faith in the vision he had seen from the cherry tree, the vision of a machine that could fly to Mars and beyond. The boy whose father called him "the angel shooter" was obsessed

---

"I never heard but two rockets take off in my whole life," he said finally. "But they were the *first* two."

---

with the idea of interplanetary flight or, as he more modestly and cautiously put it before the public, "a method of reaching extreme altitudes." Curious about many things, he would in time conceive of advances in radio and solar power which, had he pursued them with the zeal he put into his rocket experiments, might have made him a rich man. But he never took his eyes off the sky. "The years forever fashion new dreams when old ones go," he copied out in his diary one day after being jilted by a sweetheart. "God pity a one-dream man!"

But what a dream! Goddard was not the first to imagine flights to the moon, but he wrote out the formulae for the amount of energy needed to do it, and by 1909, when he was 27, he had outlined half a dozen different methods of space propulsion, all of them wildly imaginative in his day, all of them either in use or under consideration in ours. He considered atomic power for space flight 10 years before atomic disintegration was experimentally proven. His notions of spacecraft driven by light-catching solar sails and ion-stream engines are studied seriously today as methods of cheap transportation between planets. A vehicle literally blown upwards by exploding bombs was anticipated by Goddard.

Best of all, in his private notebooks you can find detailed description of a winged "car" driven by "explosive jets of liquid hydrogen and liquid oxygen," steered by "side-jets," which could circle the earth doing experiments in astronomy and meteorology and return safely by means of "tangential re-entry" into the atmosphere, protected from the heat of friction by "layers of a very infusible hard substance with layers of a poor heat conductor between" — in other words, a space shuttle.

My first impression of *Columbia,* seen close up, was that the world's first reusable spacecraft is beginning to *look* used. The white paint job is getting dingy. The main external fuel tank, atop which the orbiter perches like a bird on a rhino's back, is no longer painted at all, but is left the reddish brown color of the spray-on foam insulation covering it to save money and weight. From a distance it looks as if *Columbia* is fastened to a king-size rusty muffler pipe.

The dowdy look is heightened by the tower next to the spacecraft and its boosters, a 350-foot jumble of walkways, stanchions, railings, elevators, and cranes, some covered loosely by flapping canvas and plastic awnings.

"Is that thing still called the gantry?" I asked our NASA press guide.

"No, it is actually two separate structures," she replied crisply, "the Rotating Service Structure, or RSS, and the Fixed Service Structure, or FSS."

"If NASA couldn't use acronyms, they'd be speechless," another reporter grunted.

I pondered that as we got back on our

bus and drove around Launch Complex 39 for another look. Desiccated technological jargon is an old story, but here in NASA-land it can be overwhelming. Even reporters bandy phrases like "longitudinal dynamic oscillations," so that at press conferences the questions are sometimes as hard to understand as the answers. One interesting side effect is that the occasional lapse into English — for example, the ditch that bisects the launch pad in order to deflect exhaust gases away during lift-off is simply called "the flame trench" — begins to sound like poetry.

We passed clusters of remote cameras staring up at the pad like the Artoo-Detoo Fan Club, and two enormous spherical fuel storage tanks for the superchilled liquid oxygen and liquid hydrogen that power the shuttle's main engines. They are really just giant Dewars, or vacuum bottles, identical in principle if not in size to the ones Goddard used to carry his precious LOX, a then-rare substance produced as a by-product of the manufacture of welding gas. Goddard used two liters of LOX for his first liquid-fueled launch in 1926. *Columbia*'s main engines burn half a million liters in less than nine minutes during the lift-off.

Fuel economy is not a major concern at NASA. We passed one of the two crawler-transporters, six-million-pound hot plates on gargantuan tractor treads, that carry moon rockets and space shut-

tles from the Vehicle Assembly Building (VAB) to the launchpad. Top speed with such a load is one mile per hour, and fuel consumption is measured in gallons per mile (*hundreds* of gallons per mile!), not the other way around. The VAB, when it was built, was the largest building in the world, and still holds the record for the largest doors ever constructed — the United Nations building would fit through them comfortably.

Even such mammoth structures remain vulnerable to bad weather, however, and the space center is located within the second-most lightning-prone area in the country (only Tampa Bay, across the peninsula, is hit more often). As we drove away from the pad, loudspeakers were blaring an "adverse weather advisory," warning workers to take cover. The western half of the sky was the color of a bruise, and when the storm struck, blotting out our vision of the launchpad, the rain made the metal dome of the press center ring like an alarm bell. It was a genuine emergency: hail was falling on the launchpad, scoring *Columbia*'s fragile heat-resistant tiles and threatening to

---

Goddard's faith in rockets was tested by many apparent misfires, including this 1929 attempt, which discouraged his staff (including the young Percy Roope, at right), but not Robert Goddard (second from left), who could learn as much from failure as from success.

halt the countdown. For all its might, the shuttle is still not an all-weather vehicle.

A flash rainstorm had ruined an important demonstration of one of Goddard's rockets, sending distinguished visitors home from New Mexico disappointed. A cold snap caused ice to crystallize in the fuel lines, causing another shot to fizzle, and the 1938 twister smashed both rocket and launching tower without warning. Everyone but Goddard was in despair afterwards, but his wife Esther recorded that "as he came in last night, almost staggering, the undefeatable was still in his eyes, and made me ashamed."

The hailstorm did not stop the countdown. During an eight-hour built-in hold overnight, workers frantically checked each of the 27,000 tiles for damage, repairing more than 200 dents and chips with a special slurry. The countdown resumed the next morning on schedule, and as I sat in the press grandstand in the stifling heat, reporters and guests cheered the passage of each crucial point in the checklist. Everything was proceeding smoothly, which added an element of wonder to the suspense. The biggest roar came at T minus 28 seconds, when the four primary computers on board *Columbia* took over control of the launch sequence without a hitch — an earlier countdown was halted at just this penultimate moment, causing screams of frustration — and all present

Robert Goddard took the concept of rockets from a gravity-bound state to a vision of a machine that could fly to Mars and beyond.

– illustration by John Kilroy

realized with glee that STS-4 would be the first launch in the history of the manned space program to go off exactly on time.

At T minus 7 seconds, the shuttle's main engines fired, their bright red flames barely visible in the steel thicket of service structures obscuring our vision. Then, as the clock displayed all zeroes, the two solid-fuel boosters lit off, drenching the pad in white gold as clouds of pale smoke billowed winglike on either side of the flame trench. The rusty pipe slipped smoothly out of the thicket before the first sound reached us, three and a half miles distant — only a murmur at first, hardly heard above the shouting, then a crescendo that shook the grandstand under our feet. The sound was more impressive than the sight. The air vibrated in distinct waves — blap blap Blap BLap BLAp BLAP BLAP — as the rocket rushed into a low cloud. The vibrations slowly diminished and once again the cheering was audible, the cheering of a million people who had come to Cape Canaveral for the show.

Within seconds the rocket was only a glowing dot on the distant tip of a writhing tentacle of vapor. In less than a minute it was more than five miles high, and two minutes after lift-off, when those of us with binoculars barely observed the puff of the solid-fuel boosters being blasted away, spent, *Columbia* was 30 miles above the earth. In all his life Robert Goddard never fired a rocket that exceeded an altitude of 9,000 feet.

Launch Complex 39 looked like Dresden in World War II, covered with black smoke and flickering with internal fires. But the photographers were still looking upward, the deadline reporters had stampeded to their phones, and the show was over. It was time for me to go see Percy Roope.

The old man listened with intense interest to my description of the noise of the lift-off. "I never heard but two rockets take off in my whole life," he said finally. "But they were the *first* two."

Dr. Percy Roope retired to a pleasant home in Cambria, California, just a Frisbee-toss from the Pacific, 20 years ago, but before that he was a professor of physics at Clark University in Worcester.

It was there, as a freshman in 1916, that he met Robert Goddard, whom he would eventually succeed as chairman of the physics department.

Roope had intended to major in chemistry, but from the first day in Goddard's physics class he was hooked. "Goddard was the greatest teacher that I have ever known," he says firmly.

Roope went on to become Goddard's assistant, and on March 16, 1926, he was present in Auburn, Massachusetts, when the world's first liquid-fueled rocket was launched. Goddard was there, of course; the farm on which the experiment took place belonged to his Aunt Effie. Esther, his young wife, came along to film the test with her French movie camera, which could record only seven seconds of action without rewinding. The fourth witness was Henry Sachs, mechanic and metalworker who, along with Goddard, an accomplished welder and glassblower in his own right, actually built the rocket.

It was an ungainly contraption, with the engine stuck up on top of the fuel tanks in what appears now to be a backward configuration. Goddard thought it would be more stable that way, with the engine pulling the weight rather than pushing it aloft. The engine had been tested while clamped down at the lab, but no one was sure it would actually lift the unlovely beast into the air.

Sachs ignited the engine by means of an ordinary blowtorch on the end of a long rod, and Esther started her camera — prematurely, as it turned out, for the film ran out before the rocket actually lifted clear of its metal framework. There wasn't much of a roar, and Goddard was surprised by the absence of smoke and by how small the flame looked. But it rose 41 feet before turning its nose downward and crashing into Aunt Effie's cabbage patch, 184 feet away. The whole flight lasted two and a half seconds.

Esther thought it looked "like a fairy or esthetic dancer." To Roope, "it sort of wobbled up and then plopped into the ground." Dour Henry Sachs observed that he could throw a baseball a lot farther. Goddard beamed. He may have been the only one there who realized the implications of what had happened on Pakachoag Hill — an Indian name meaning "a turning point."

"I certainly didn't have any idea what the future would bring," Roope told me in Cambria the day before *Columbia* was to land a couple of hundred miles east of us. "I knew the rocket would go up eventually. We were just happy it worked."

It was more than three years before the second Goddard rocket worked, and that one attracted more attention than its inventor desired. In July of 1929 the new rocket went a little higher — about 90 feet — then blew itself up after hitting the ground about 60 yards away. As usual, Goddard was ebullient. In a photograph taken by his wife, Goddard and his four assistants, including Roope, are standing over the twisted wreckage. Everyone looks glum except for Goddard, who is smiling broadly.

The smile disappeared when a cloud of dust appeared over the hill and a dozen cars came roaring up with two ambulances in the lead. Aunt Effie's neighbors, hearing the explosion, thought a plane must have crashed and called the police. Goddard explained the situation and said it was a routine experiment. Could the whole matter be kept quiet? In answer, the policeman pointed to two men hurrying toward them and said, "They're reporters."

Goddard had already had some runins with the press, notably in 1919, when he tried to stop publication of a *Worcester Gazette* story claiming that the local professor had perfected a rocket capable of destroying military targets 200 miles away — "a terrible engine of war." The publicity-shy Smithsonian Institution, which was bankrolling Goddard's experiments at that time, was not amused. The Smithsonian attempted to deflate the excitement over the story by publishing a release describing Goddard's research as meteorological in nature, but reporters picked out a portion of the announcement stating that Goddard hoped to land a rocket on the moon and set off a powder charge visible from earth. He was instantly dubbed "The Moon Man" — a nickname he hated, especially because he was more interested in going to Mars.

After the 1929 furor the headline in the *Boston Globe* read: MOON ROCK-

---

He was instantly dubbed "The Moon Man" — a nickname he hated, especially because he was more interested in going to Mars.

ET MAN'S TEST ALARMS WHOLE COUNTRYSIDE. Goddard and his team were disgusted. "They ain't done right by our Nell," said one of the mechanics, referring to a popular melodrama, and from then on, all of Goddard's rockets were fondly known as "Nell."

The Massachusetts fire marshal ordered Goddard to cease testing his infernal machines in the commonwealth. The scientist got permission to go on with his work on federal property at Fort Devens, but it was 25 miles away over rough roads, and the jolting damaged the delicate rockets.

The bad publicity had a silver lining, however. In November of 1929, Goddard got a phone call from Charles Lindbergh, still the toast of the nation two years after his solo flight to Paris. Lindbergh was interested in rockets, had seen the news accounts of Goddard's tests, and wanted to know more. Could he pay a visit?

"Esther, I had an interesting call today from Charles Lindbergh," Goddard said over dinner.

"Of course, Bob," she replied. "And I had tea with the Queen of Rumania."

Lindbergh and Goddard got along well, and the flier eventually persuaded financier and aviation enthusiast Daniel Guggenheim to grant Goddard $100,000 for four years of rocket research. The Carnegie Institution also kicked in $5,000, and Goddard was at last able to leave his teaching duties and devote full time to rockets. He moved to Roswell, New Mexico, in 1930, where the weather was usually fine and there were few nosy neighbors.

Over the next nine years Goddard refined his inventions, making them bigger and more powerful, adding gyroscopic stabilizers to keep the rockets flying vertically. He conducted over 100 static tests and almost 50 flight tests. Still, progress was slow, largely due to his refusal to work with other scientists, even when his financial backers criticized his "lone wolf" attitude. While Goddard tinkered with new nozzles and high-speed pumps, well-financed teams of German scientists with the full backing of their government were catching up and eventually moving ahead of him. In 1923, when the German theorist Oberth had published a paper on rocketry closely paralleling Goddard's earlier work, Goddard had predicted that rocket research would become a race between the nations. Now the combination of official skepticism (Goddard tried to interest the War De-

partment in a bazookalike antitank rocket in 1918 without success) and his own stubborn individualism had put the Germans into the lead.

"Goddard was always ahead of everybody else, and he wanted to stay ahead of them," said Percy Roope. "He wanted to do it himself."

Roope is in his eighties now, and since the death of Esther Goddard last summer he is the last witness to the first rocket tests. "And I won't be here much longer," he said cheerfully. He stood up slowly — a small, bent man with the same mobile, humorous face of the young man in knickers in the old photos. "You can hear me creak. A friend bought me a cane," he added, gesturing across the room, "but I haven't had occasion to use it." And he laughed.

Captured German rocket scientists, impatient with the ignorance of their American interrogators, asked, "Why don't you ask your own Dr. Goddard?"

"I never saw Goddard discouraged," he went on, sitting again. "We would go out on a trial and the rocket would explode. We'd all say, 'Gee, this is terrible,' but Goddard would say, 'No, we learned something today. We've made real progress.' Goddard had faith in himself and in the rockets; he had that faith until the end of his days.

"It's like my hollyhocks," he said. "When I came out here from Massachusetts, I couldn't grow them. I kept trying, though, and now look." He led me out into his backyard and pointed proudly at a hollyhock 10 feet tall.

That evening I drove from the coast to the high desert of Mojave, where the space shuttle would land the next morning. A crowd of half a million was expected to join President and Mrs. Reagan in welcoming the astronauts back; every hotel and motel for miles around was full. It must have been a similar scene in Worcester in 1911 when the first airplane ever seen there landed at the fairgrounds. "Every hill in or near Worcester was swarming with humanity eager for their first glimpse of a real airship in flight," said the *Worcester Gazette.* Goddard, laconic as ever, wrote "Quite a sight" in his diary.

I slept in my car under the weird blue-white lights of Edwards Air Force Base, and awoke to the glory of a desert dawn — great batts of pink-orange clouds lined up in the eastern sky as if somebody were trying to insulate the heavens. There was something refreshing about this spot in contrast with Cape Canaveral. Maybe it was the cool dry desert air instead of subtropical humidity, or the raffish informality of the old test-pilot base as opposed to the white-shirt-and-tie corporate atmosphere at Kennedy. Maybe it was just the wild beauty of the land itself, the dry lake beds ringed with mountains shimmering in the mounting heat. A portion of the Kennedy Space Center is given over to a wildlife refuge where I saw egrets and alligators, but still there is a manicured, Disney World feeling to it. The idea of a wildlife refuge at Edwards is laughable — the air base is a people refuge in the middle of an indomitable wilderness.

The future of the space shuttle is at Kennedy, though. Soon *Columbia* and her sister ships *Challenger, Discovery,* and *Atlantis* will land as well as take off there. These desert landings are the last hurrah for Edwards, where rocket-powered aircraft were first tested and the phrase "the right stuff" was coined. It will be sad when it's over.

Columbia fired her main engines — the "de-orbit burn" in space pidgin — over the west coast of Australia and did a half gainer into the atmosphere. Actually it was more of a belly flop, putting her heat-resistant underside forward to absorb the 3000-degree-Fahrenheit fury of reentry. "An advantage of this method," Goddard scribbled in his notebook in 1909, "is that no energy would be necessary to land. The car could circle the planet . . . and after the velocity has been cut down sufficiently, the planes (wings) could be made to slow it down in the upper atmosphere, and thereafter the car could be guided where desired."

Part of the charm of *Columbia*'s reappearance in the skies over California was its unexpected, almost magical quality. The launch, though exciting, went rigidly according to schedule and was drained of surprise. It seemed inevitable and therefore anticlimactic.

At Edwards we were all raking the western horizon with our binoculars, looking for the first trace of the returning spacecraft ("Watch for the contrails of the chase planes," one veteran advised me), when suddenly BAM BAM came two sonic booms, and somebody from behind us shouted, "They're over *there!*" We all spun around and looked up to the east. There they were: two glittering dots of the chase planes etching the blue sky with contrails and ahead of them the bulkier white dot of *Columbia* without a contrail (no engine), already skidding into a 180-degree turn for landing. A cheer went up and *Columbia* seemed to return the salute by venting some sort of vapor trail — a giant exclamation point.

Our mistake had been that we expected *Columbia* to fly towards us like an airliner on an approach. *Columbia* flies like a brick. It was only in the last few frightening moments of her steep and speedy approach that she turned up her blunt nose and became a light and airy creature, skimming a few feet above the runway as if reluctant to touch down. Then her wheels scratched the desert, and *Columbia* whizzed past us, less than a mile away, as a long line of camera shutters popped like a volley of champagne corks.

That moment of grace was illusory and brief. Once she had rolled to a halt, resting on her spindly landing gear, nose down and tail up, *Columbia* looked like a moving van that had sprouted wings. And when you stop to think about it, that's exactly how the space shuttle should look.

Afterwards, President Reagan told a merry audience of contractors and their families, most dressed in red, white, and blue and waving flags, that the landing was like the driving of the golden spike that connected the East and the West by railroad. Mattingly and Hartsfield appeared and spoke in astronaut dialect ("The vehicle performed well . . . it's a super vehicle . . ."); the new orbiter *Challenger* swooped past on the back of the 747 that would take it to Kennedy for the next launch; and the President sent everyone home laughing by saying that the experience "sure beat firecrackers!" It was a very satisfactory Fourth of July celebration, except for the massive traffic jam that occurred when everyone tried to pilot their RVs back to Los Angeles at once.

It was a less rousing Independence Day 40 years earlier, when Goddard finally left New Mexico and his high-altitude research for good. The war was going badly, and Goddard had volunteered his services in whatever way Washington felt would be most useful. The world's leading authority on rockets was assigned to a naval base in Annapolis, Maryland, where he would try without much success to develop a rocket-assisted takeoff system for seaplanes. The wet air of the Chesapeake Bay made his tuberculosis worse. By 1944 he could barely speak, and had to tap out instructions to his shop hands in Morse code with a pencil stub. One night lightning struck the cottage next door, setting the empty house ablaze, and though Goddard called the telephone operator for assistance, she couldn't understand a word of his anguished whisper.

Perhaps it didn't matter — the world wasn't listening to the Moon Man anymore, even though captured German

Esther and Robert Goddard relaxed in the New Mexico sun at their ranch home, about 1937.

rocket scientists, impatient with the ignorance of their American interrogators, asked, "Why don't you ask your own Dr. Goddard?" The German V-2 turned out not to be the Ultimate Weapon after all. That belonged to the U.S., and it was exploded for the first time in the New Mexico desert not far from the spot where Nell and all her sisters had flown, or fizzled, or just sat.

Goddard returned to Worcester for the last time in May of 1945 to accept an honorary degree from Clark University — the only college that so honored him. In June throat cancer (which had also killed his father) was diagnosed, and on August 10, four days after Hiroshima, he died in Baltimore. "Darling Bob slipped away," Esther wrote in his diary, the last entry. "The end of a love story."

The rocket story was not over, though. Russians and Americans put their captured Germans to work, and soon a new space race was under way. As the importance of Goddard's research became clearer, the honors he never won in his lifetime began piling up. In 1951 NASA paid Esther Goddard and the Guggenheim Foundation $1 million for the use of 200 Goddard patents dealing with rockets and space flight. The American Rocket Society put up a monument on the golf course where Aunt Effie's farm used to be, and NASA named its main tracking station in Maryland the Goddard Space Flight Center. In 1969, the day after Apollo 11 left earth orbit for the moon, the *New York Times* ran an editorial recalling that 49 years earlier the paper had sneered at Goddard's contention that rockets could operate in the vacuum of space. "The *Times* regrets the error."

In 1978 astronomer Carl Sagan came to Clark University, where the Robert Hutchings Goddard Library now stands, and told the graduating class that Robert Goddard had "irreversibly changed the world." He reminded them of the cherry tree story, and pointed out that although "Goddard never lived to see the beginnings of rocket astronomy or high-altitude meteorology, much less flights to the moon or planets . . . all of the essential engineering, in a practical sense, goes back to Goddard."

The dictionary says that to witness is "to see or know by personal presence." Goddard could not witness a flight of a space shuttle as I did, nor even as Percy Roope witnessed those first feeble tests in Massachusetts. But there is another sense of the word, used in a religious context, in which to witness means to testify to the truth revealed by faith. In that sense Robert Goddard, angel shooter, lone wolf, one-dream man, was a witness. He operated all his life on a mixture of facts and faith, as volatile as liquid hydrogen and liquid oxygen; it fueled the engine of his will.

At a low point in 1932, when the Depression had choked off his Guggenheim funds and he had to return for a while to Clark and his teaching, Goddard wrote to H.G. Wells, whose visions of space travel had ignited Goddard's own imagination. "How many more years I shall be able to work on the problem, I do not know," he wrote. "I hope, as long as I live. There can be no thought of finishing, for 'aiming at the stars,' both literally and figuratively, is a problem to occupy generations, so that no matter how much progress one makes, there is always the thrill of just beginning."

239

*We held our breath after our October 1977 issue came out.
It seemed certain to us we'd be deluged with subscription cancellations
because of "The Bracelet." We'd already decided, after considerable soul-searching, the story was
special enough to warrant the storm it would cause, but the surprise was on us.
While, yes, there were a few complaints, there was no "storm." To this day
we're not sure whether or not that was due to reader sophistication — or because
few people read it carefully all the way through to the end!*

The Bracelet

FICTION BY PETER MEINKE

At first she had felt like a white fleck of foam in a black sea. She would bob along the crowded streets of the old cloth market in Ibadan, looking at the bolts of bright fabrics piled higher than her head in front of the open shops lining the narrow dirt thoroughfares. She had been afraid to buy any of the beautiful material with the mysterious names — *adire, adinkra, kente, kyemfre* — because she didn't know how to haggle over prices and didn't want to pay too much. So she would just flow along with the crowd, small and wide eyed, the lanes sometimes so jammed and narrow that her feet would be lifted from the ground and she'd be carried like a piece of driftwood with the tide.

But that was 10 years ago. She had come to Nigeria as an archeologist, working on her Ph.D. from Harvard. She had done some reading on the Old Kingdoms of the Yoruba and wanted to study them firsthand, particularly the Kingdom of Oyo, one of the traditional centers of Nigerian culture. So Ibadan had seemed the natural place to go to, an important city with a new university; and it was less than 20 miles from Oyo, where slaves and eunuchs were still reputed to guard the Oba's palace.

When she arrived, Sally Warren was 26 years old. She was very shy and quiet; at the same time, nothing much frightened her. She had clear brown eyes in a no-nonsense face that she didn't waste time gazing at.

Her plan had been to spend one year researching the Kingdom of Oyo and then return to Cambridge and write her thesis. And then she supposed she'd get married. Her fiancé Jim was opposed to the trip entirely; he had wanted to get married right away. There was nothing wrong with Jim: he was fine, he was ambitious, he played a decent game of tennis. He was the type of young faculty member who was sure to advance, get tenure, and become chairman of his department. He had it all planned. Eventually they would have two baby archeologists, a boy and a girl.

Sally was a reflective woman, but not a complaining one, even to herself, so the first time she realized that Jim bored her was when she was flying to Africa. They were flying over the vast expanse of the Sahara Desert; for an hour she looked at the unchanging, almost colorless sand. *Why, that's just like Jim,* she thought, and crossed him off.

Perhaps that was why Africa had given her such an enormous sense of freedom. She had no sooner taken a room at the university when her past years washed away like so many ridges of sand at high tide. Her room, on the second floor of the dormitory, was tiny: a bed, a desk, a wardrobe. An open passageway ran in front of it; she could bring a chair out there and look into the white flowers of a large frangipani tree growing in the courtyard next to the building. In the evening its jasmine-like fragrance flooded her room and seemed to insist that she think of nothing but the fragrance itself. That was what Africa was like to her: it demanded attention to the texture of her life.

For a while she pursued her studies at the university, with occasional field trips to Oyo, always made with great difficulty because of the irregularity of the bus system. To stay overnight in one of the cheap hotels was uncomfortable; she would be the only woman there, a white woman walking through a maze of small rooms where men sat silently drinking palm wine or chewing on kola nuts. At least they were always silent as she walked by, and even when she lay alone in her bed she seemed to feel them staring at her, their gazes a positive weight on her skin.

So her studies became diffused. As she got to know people at the university, some of whom had cars, she began visiting whatever places they were driving to. If they were going to Oyo, good; if they were going somewhere else, like Abeokuta or Oshogbo, that was good too: off she went. She was learning a great deal about the Yoruba in general but not making much progress on the research for her thesis.

She made one marvelous find, by accident. She had been taken by one of the professors in the Institute of African Studies to visit an old shrine for Shango, the God of Thunder, which had been destroyed in a war but was still regarded as a holy place. It was outside of Meko and the jungle had almost reclaimed it. On the way back from the shrine she had gone off the overgrown trail to look at a small crimson flower she saw glowing in the shadows. As she knelt down by the flower her eye was caught by what seemed to be a tin can buried in the ground. When she pulled it up and brushed off the dirt and leaf-mold, she found it was a brass bracelet about six inches high, with intricately wrought figures and a series of small bells attached to either end.

Her companion was greatly excited. At first he thought it was ancient, but as they cleaned it he decided the bracelet must be between 50 and 75 years old, one of the ornate decorations worn by the priestesses of Shango or some related deity. He wanted Sally to bring it to the institute for appraisal.

But when she took it back to her room, and worked on it for several hours, using a bottle cleaner, brass polish, and finally her toothbrush, she found she didn't want to give it up, or even let it out of her hands. The bracelet was a perfect fit, feeling heavy and snug on her sturdy arm. There was a long mirror on the inside of her wardrobe door; she stood in front of it with the bracelet on, and then slowly took off her clothes and looked at herself for a long time. *Maybe I'm going off my rocker,* she thought, and smiled. But she began doing this every night, sleeping naked under the mosquito netting, wearing only the bracelet.

The months were sliding by. She made two good friends, both of them dancers, with whom she would take her meals in the university dining hall. Andrew Cage was a 30-year-old Englishman who had studied medicine at Oxford and switched to dance late in his student career. He had danced with several of the major companies in England and America, and had come to Ibadan two years ago to study African dance. Like Sally, he found much that fascinated him, but his specific studies went slowly. Unlike Sally, however, whose money was running out, Andrew seemed to have a decent independent income, and indeed he often paid for all three of them when they went out together.

The other dancer was Manu Uchendu. Manu was the son of a chief of one of the larger villages in northern Nigeria. Despite his small stature, he was a commanding presence: slow and oracular in talk, dignified and erect in carriage, he looked the part of a chief. His eyes were deep set and yet prominent, almost pop-eyed. *High blood pressure,* said Andrew. But he inspired confidence; when Manu spoke in his measured, musical tones, people leaned forward to listen.

When Andrew spoke, people tended to laugh. He was cynical and worldly, and often drunk. Sally thought he might be homosexual. Once she asked him why he had never married.

"It's the old story," he told Sally, "I loved her. She loved her." And that was all she could get out of him on the subject. But he was careful not to be alone with her at night. Once Sally brought him to her room to see the bracelet; he was edgy and uncomfortable.

"Yes," he said, when she put it on. "You're a natural priestess. I wish you'd put a curse on old Millers." Millers was the rather stuffy director of Andrew's dance project. "May his tongue swell and his genitals wither." But he wouldn't sit down in those close quarters. He went out on the passageway and stared at the frangipani tree that stood trembling in the moonlight.

One Sunday Manu told them that the fetish priest of a small village near Oshogbo was going to perform, that this was "the real thing" and they should try to see it. "We'll have to bring him some sort of gift, like a bottle of schnapps, that's customary."

"I've got a bottle of Gilbey's gin," said Andrew. "I can teach him how to make a martini."

"Gin will be all right; just let me handle it."

They drove in Andrew's car. The village consisted of several clusters of mudbrick huts with rusted corrugated tin roofs sprawled around an open market. One cluster enclosed a small courtyard where a crowd of villagers, mostly women, were already assembled. Manu spoke to one of the elders, who placed the gin by a large hand-carved chair with wooden snakes forming the legs and arms. The three visitors sat down at the edge of the circle of people.

Four drummers had been playing softly in the background; now their beat became faster and more insistent. The crowd stirred as the priest entered the compound. He was a little old man completely covered with a gray claylike substance, snakes wrapped around his neck, wrists, ankles. There was something wrong with his face: eyes and mouth twitching, limbs trembling like an advanced case of Parkinson's disease. He sat in the chair, one gray leg still shaking violently, and received gifts from the village women: yams, cloth, pineapples, a large white chicken. He brandished a pair of brushes, made of cowtails; beside him a young man held a basin of white powder. As each woman presented her gift, she would touch the ground in front of the priest, and he would chant to her, dipping the cowtails in the powder and brushing her shoulders.

"He is curing sickness," Manu whispered. "And barrenness, and bad luck. He can do it only when he's possessed."

"I don't feel well," said Andrew. "I could use some of that gin."

Sally was spellbound. She was trying to commit every detail to memory. She wondered if she would be frightened if this were at night.

The drums became more and more excited. Suddenly the priest stood up and began to dance, stamping and shuffling in a circular motion. He took a banana

– illustration by Rich Ferraro

241

and rubbed it over his face and body, then did the same thing with several eggs. Now his young helper handed him the fluttering chicken. The drummers leaped up and began playing in a frenzy; the priest whirled around, swinging the chicken over his head. He stretched the chicken to its full length, and sank his teeth into its neck, tearing at it until he put the chicken's head into his mouth and bit it off. Blood streamed down his neck and torso. Still dancing wildly he again swung the chicken around, ripping off its wings and legs, blood spattering the spectators.

As the tempo of the drummers slowed, he turned and stopped in front of Sally. Without hesitation she stood up, then touched the ground with both hands as she had seen the women do. He brushed her shoulders with the white powder, chanted for a minute, and it was over.

Back in the car, they were silent for a long time. After a while Sally asked, "What did he say to me?"

"He wished you good health and asked the gods to watch over you here in Nigeria," said Manu.

"It turned my stomach," said Andrew. "I've read about geeks in American carnivals, old winos who bite the heads off chickens for a few drinks. I don't know how you managed to stand up when he came to you."

But Sally was elated. She felt that she had done the right thing, that something significant had happened.

Not long after, Manu became Sally's lover. He seemed to expect it, he didn't press her. They were in her room, talking about her plans, about the experience with the fetish priest; she was wearing the bracelet. When he held out his hands, she went to him, her body pushing at him of its own volition while her mind thought *Why not?*

It didn't seem to make any difference in her life. They were careful; she wasn't swept away by passion. Sally had learned long ago to dismiss all generalizations: they were fine, you needed them to hold a decent conversation, but they never applied to a particular case, to her case (even this generalization, she realized, was suspect: perhaps some did apply to her case). Jim had been a great generalizer; he had theories about everything. But she had never understood theories. As soon as she uttered or wrote one, the exceptions would start to crowd into her mind like a mob of unruly children clamoring for attention.

So one day at a time the year disappeared. Harvard renewed her scholar-

The monkeys had moved back in to the third floor and were her pets. At night they would look out the windows when the young men stood before the house, silent in the moonlight.

ship for a year, but even so she was hard pressed for money. Jim's letters, frequent at first, had slowed down to a trickle, though he threatened to fly to Ibadan to find out what was wrong with her. But Sally was sure he would never do such an extravagant thing, even for love.

After about a year and a half at the university she began looking for a job. She worked for a while as a cataloguer in the university museum: this wasn't bad work, but consumed a lot of time. Work on her thesis had virtually stopped.

Then one afternoon Andrew came in with a great announcement. He had discovered a large abandoned house outside of Oshogbo, near the Oshun River. Years ago many people in the house had died of the plague, and the natives believed it to be inhabited by evil spirits. But the chief of that district paid a man and his wife to guard the house, and they lived in a little hut on the same property. Andrew was sure that if Manu would speak to the chief, Sally could live in the house for nothing, and they could fix it up for her. It was the perfect place for an archeologist as there were many shrines, both active and abandoned, in the area around the river.

Gradually, it was all arranged. Near the end of the second year of her stay, Sally moved into the Oshogbo house. It was a three-story affair, with an ornately carved roof, and a porch on the second

floor as well as the first. A dirt road around three miles long joined it to the main highway leading into Oshogbo and it was less than an hour's drive from Ibadan and Oyo. The three friends painted it and fixed the windows, and chased away the family of monkeys living on the third floor. They stocked it with food from the university commissary; Andrew brought over what looked like a five-year supply of bandages and other medical provisions, and a 10-year supply of candles.

For a short while Andrew and Manu stayed with Sally, Andrew sleeping in a room on the first floor, and Manu and Sally sharing the master bedroom on the second. They swam (and washed) in the slow-flowing river, explored the territory and the neighboring shrines, and in the evening danced by candlelight in the large and empty main room on the ground floor.

It was a good time, but when the men left to return to their studies, Sally looked around at her house and felt strangely exultant. She thought that she always knew that people were essentially alone, and she liked it that way. She remembered being puzzled by movies and books in which men were punished by being placed in solitary confinement. She didn't think that would bother her at all; she would prefer it. And she would raise her arms and whirl around the room, the bracelet picking up the candlelight and reflecting it on the ceiling and walls as she danced.

A few days after Manu and Andrew left, Sally heard activity in the courtyard. A man and woman were erecting a series of bamboo poles near the native hut. These must be the caretakers who were not in evidence when she moved in; Sally hurried down to greet them. The woman turned slowly around and bowed her head. She was a large woman, a head taller than Sally, and her hands and feet were stained a dark blue. Her name was Vida; she and her husband Ayi had gone into Oshogbo when Andrew's car appeared and had just today decided it was safe to return.

By now Sally could speak some Yoruba, and Vida knew a little English from three years in a government school, so they were able to communicate without difficulty. Ayi was a farmer who worked a small plot of land about two miles from the house. He planted mostly yams, but also grew corn and beans and sometimes melons. Ayi even owned several kola trees and sold the kola nuts as his main cash crop.

Vida brought in some money by mak-

– illustration by Rich Ferraro

242

ing the traditional Yoruba cloth called *adire,* which accounted for her blue hands and feet. One reason she and Ayi stayed on a place thought by most to be haunted was the great profusion of the *elu* plant on the property. Vida would take the fresh green leaves of the plant and pound them into a blackish pulp, making a high pile of dye balls about the size of tennis balls. Sally was fascinated by the whole process of dyeing and soon was regularly helping Vida with her work. Andrew or Manu would arrive for a visit and find her tying or folding the lengths of white cotton that Vida would then dip in the large dye pots half buried in the ground. Around the courtyard lengths of the beautiful indigo blue fabric with their intricate designs were drying on the bamboo poles.

"I love doing this," she told Andrew. "I could do this forever. I can already tie the Osubamba design." She pointed to some drying panels with large white circles surrounded by many small ones. "Big moons and little moons."

"That's all very well," said Andrew, "but I'm not sure how I'll like you with blue hands and feet." The *adire* dye was very hard to get off; the ground by Vida's hut was stained a permanent blue.

Sally tried to get Ayi and Vida to move into the house with her, but they would have none of it. They thought Sally especially blessed by the gods to be able to live in the house unscathed. In fact, it was clear they saw their roles as handservants to her: Ayi brought her food from the farm, Vida cooked it; once every four days they would clean the first floor of the house for her, though it scarcely needed it. They wouldn't go upstairs, and they wouldn't enter the house if Sally weren't in it. They had very set ideas as to what kind of work was appropriate for her. It was fine for Sally to work very hard tying and folding the *adire* designs, and helping with the dyeing process in general, but they didn't like her to carry things, to cook, to sweep, to pound the yams and cassava for the *foofoo* that was their staple meal. In a very short time the three of them established a peaceable and efficient routine.

Sally liked walking to the cloth market outside of Oshogbo, where Vida would sell their work and buy the raffia string and the white cotton they used. One afternoon on the way back from the market, she met a woman with a sick child. The little girl was burning up with fever. Sally brought them home with her and treated the child as best she could, giving clear directions to the mother for contin-

ued treatment. A few weeks later the woman returned and left two large water pots on the porch. As the year progressed there were more of these incidents; sometimes women from the small neighboring village would bring their children to the house. They were afraid of the large hospital in Oshogbo, though they would go there if Sally told them to; and they would never stay in her house.

"They think you're a priestess of Oshun," Manu told her, looking at the pots, carvings, little brass figures, and river-worn stones that were collecting on her porch. Oshun is the Venus of Yoruba, light skinned and beautiful; if she felt like it she could cause or cure dysentery, stomachache, and other minor disorders. "She was a wife of Shango and is famous for her lovemaking."

Manu had studied the art of divination and he taught the rudiments of it to Sally, using 16 kola nuts, which could be thrown or arranged in any number of combinations. In college, Sally had learned to do the *I Ching,* and this was similar; she memorized the verses and chants for the different combinations with great ease. "You're a born diviner, a *babalawo,*" he told her. "It's in your bones."

Sally believed in it, in her own way. She thought it as good a way of regulating one's life as any other. She remembered reading about one of those English archeologists with the hyphenated names like Pritchard-Evans or Evans-Pritchard, who lived with a tribe somewhere that made its decisions by poisoning chickens with a poison called *benje,* and then deciphering the circular patterns in which the chickens ran as they died. The Englishman had lived this way himself for a year and claimed it was as efficient as trying to reason things out (Shall I go to market today? Shall I plant my vegetables? Should I marry Alice when I return?).

In this way, time had gone placidly by, like the Oshun River flowing by her house. Tonight, holding Jim's letter in her hand and looking back on her 10 years in Africa, Sally had difficulty remembering what had happened when. Andrew was dead, she knew that; he had gone back to England and then died. And she hadn't seen Manu for a long time: he had returned to his village in the North to become its chief. He told Sally that she could be one of his wives, any time she wanted. She thanked him and thought she'd rather not.

"You could be one of my husbands, though."

"Yes, I'd like that." But it had been several years since she had a visit from

Manu. Now her house was truly like a shrine, surrounded on all sides with the artifacts of Yoruba life and religion. The monkeys had moved back in to the third floor and were her pets. At night they would look out the windows when the young men stood before the house, silent in the moonlight; occasionally, the door would open and one would enter.

The university had long since severed its connection with Sally, so she had been totally surprised a month ago when its mail truck came bouncing down the road with a thick letter from Jim, and one from her father. Sally's mother had died, they wanted Sally to come home; her mother had left her $10,000. It seemed strange to her that she had parents; they had never captured her imagination, either positively or negatively. Jim had apparently never married; he had been engaged (engaged? Sally could barely understand the word) several times but it had never worked out. He was a disappointed man. He wanted to see Sally again. When she opened the mail her hand trembled; she didn't know how she felt. After reading the letters she took out her sixteen cowry shells and began to arrange them, searching for an attitude. She loved the small, brightly colored shells that someone had left for her to do her divinations with. She would hold them in her hands for hours, their smooth, highly polished surfaces somehow comforting her, joining her with the ageless rhythms of the sea. But the shells had said nothing but "Wait," and so she hadn't answered the letters.

And now Jim's second letter had arrived today. He and her father were at the university and would be coming to get her tomorrow. They were terribly worried, they had heard awful stories, they feared for her very life. Sally smiled as she read this.

The moon was caught in the branches of the God-tree, the three-forked tree leaning over the river, which flowed silently and irresistibly toward the great ocean. She walked upstairs to her room, and stood for some time looking at her face in the mirror. She piled her long hair on top of her head. She was wearing one of her *osubamba* cloths around her waist; multicolored beads which the women had left for her hung between her naked breasts, and the bracelet felt cool and solid on her arm. Then she took out the narrow file she had borrowed from Vida, and began filing her front teeth into the traditional M-shaped gap of Yoruba women.

This is the introduction to a book by Elizabeth Coatsworth entitled Personal Geography, *published in October 1976 by The Stephen Greene Press. We published it, with permission, the same month, and readers still speak of it to this day. . . .*

I Am an Old Woman Now. . . .

BY ELIZABETH COATSWORTH

I have always loved journeys long or short, but this journey on which I shall some day embark — is it long or short? No one seems to be able to tell me.

The bristlecone pine is supposed to be the oldest tree in the world, older even than the sequoia. One measures the age of a tree on a cross-section whose rings show the amount of growth the tree enjoyed each year. There is a wide circle for good years, and a very narrow one, sometimes almost none at all, marks the years of drought. I know that we show no such physical proofs of our experience, but I think our lives are not unlike those of the trees. Some years are good years, and we expand in them; some years are bad ones, and the most we can do is to hold our own. But good or bad, like the trees we are still ourselves, growing out from the heartwood of our youth, which I believe is a combination of our inheritance and our upbringing. Like the trees, we may be able to correct a bend or knothole which shows in youth; we may cover over the scar of an injury which, however, will always be there, though it may be hidden from sight.

I like this sense that all my life and experience is contained in me. I am a five-year-old child in Egypt; I am a schoolgirl in a very strict private school on Park Street in Buffalo; I roam the beaches of Lake Erie, barefoot all summer; I explore the winter countryside around Vassar more thoroughly than I do its curriculum; I go to the theatre and art shows in New York and climb California mountains; later I travel in the Far East and around the Mediterranean with a piercing pleasure (and as always the more uncomfortable trips, the more dangerous moments, are the most clearly remembered).

I settle with my mother in an 18th-century house in Hingham overlooking Boston Harbor (how I love that house!). By this time travel has jarred me into writing, and writing has become almost as much a part of me as eating or sleeping. Then in my mid-thirties I marry a man both handsome and perceptive, and we have two little girls and buy a Maine farm overlooking hayfields and a lake. Life never stops. The daughters grow up and marry, each has four children. My husband, who is five years older than I, begins the long struggle with old age, and for years I fight that inevitably losing battle with him. He dies, and for eight years I have lived the diminished life of a widow, with one daughter living in Alaska and the other in California, but one or both visiting me each summer.

I am an old woman now, fighting my own losing battle with age, but with time to enjoy life along the way, as Henry always did. Naturally I think of death. I don't want to die, because even in this narrower radius there are so many people and things still to enjoy. I do not fear death itself, I think, but I often do not like its approaches. Only the other day I first formulated for myself the truism: "You cannot conquer death, but perhaps you can conquer the fear of it."

All these things and a thousand more are embodied in me, the good years and the bad, the wide rings of growth and the narrow. Our past is not something we leave behind, but something we incorporate. When I write a story for children I am a child, with perhaps a grown-up person's powers of criticism (as least so I hope). When I lunch with a group of young middle-aged people, I feel no difference between us; when I walk in to my neighbor's, watching every step for fear I may trip on something (my sense of balance is irretrievably lost!), I greet her as an equal as she sits in a big chair tatting, with her walker in front of her. Outwardly I am 83 years old, but inwardly I am every age, with the emotions and experience of each period. The important thing is that at each age I am myself, just as you are yourself. During much of my life I was anxious to be what someone else wanted me to be. Now I have given up that struggle. I am what I am.

To leave your boat in New England waters for
October sailing is to press your luck. . . .

"She's Loose! She's Goin' on the Rocks!"

A Personal Experience
by Joseph E. Garland

It was seven Sunday morning, October 26, 1980, too late in the season to keep a cruising sailboat on a mooring out in front of our house on Eastern Point. But I'd been pushing my luck for years for the chance Indian summer spins out there on the dazzling blue of Gloucester Harbor.

The wind had mounted from the south during the night, then veered to sou'west in gusts shooting the needle on the gauge up to 53. Four- to five-foot waves rushing and roaring in by the end of the breakwater bore right down on her, the only boat left out.

Bow and bowsprit were jumping up and down on that mooring line like a guy sawing firewood. I'd kept a nervous watch out the window and had fidgeted all night, but there was no way I could launch the dinghy in those seas, let alone row out to her. I knew the mooring, an old steam engine bed, would hold, and the day before I'd double-checked the chafing gear where the heavy line passed through the bow chock.

I was on the phone in the kitchen when Charlie Lowe, an old friend and the ace photographer for the Gloucester *Daily Times,* beat on the back door. His clothes were flapping in the wind, and he was waving his arms and panting, "She's loose! She's goin' on the rocks!"

I dashed to a window. The cove was a fury of whitecaps. Downwind, in line with the wild raspberry patch and still

coming, I saw old *Cruising Club*'s mast swaying as if signaling me that she was still afloat. I covered the hundred yards to the beach in three leaps.

She had grounded, all six tons of her, a few feet outside of a massive rock. She was still intact in four feet of heaving water, but the tide was coming, and every wave lifted her a few inches closer to what the pit of my stomach told me was her destiny.

I raced back to the house and phoned the Coast Guard without the least shred of hope. "Sorry. We can't go out unless someone's aboard, in danger. Regulations." Which I knew. Called the police, heart pounding. Ditto. Called Larry Dahlmer, the young East Gloucester boatwright who had done so much loving work on her, all 51 years of her. He hung up and jumped into his car.

I got into my sea boots and slicker. Larry screeched up and we ran for the beach. She was just outside that rock now, but still upright, her decks and cockpit swept by the surf. Charlie was there with his beat-up Nikon, up to his knees in the water.

Larry waded out, pulled himself aboard, and broke out the anchor. Our one foolish chance was to carry that hook and all the chain I could drag parallel to the shore and pray for the superhuman strength to kedge her off, to pull her by her own anchor away from the rock to where she'd be carried in free by the tide

---

The author (foreground) and boatwright Larry Dahlmer struggle against wind and rising tide to keep Cruising Club *from being crushed against the rocks.*

– photograph courtesy of Joseph E. Garland

247

The battle sadly lost, the two men resignedly pack up their gear and let nature have its way with the battered remains of Cruising Club.

The author hurries to salvage the portholes before scavengers can pick the wreck clean.

and left high and dry on the shore without too much damage.

Into the surf I plunged, damn near to my chest, and Larry handed me the anchor from the bow. The next wave almost knocked me off my feet. With Larry feeding out the chain, I lurched off through the white water up to my hips, hauling chain like Marley's ghost gone berserk. I kept losing my footing as I stumblebummed along. The lengthening chain grew heavier and heavier, snagging on unseen small rocks, me yanking it, shouting out imprecations to the gale, springing it free with the anchor and stumbling on. Out of breath, out of strength, I felt my heart sledgehammering inside me, arms pulling off at the shoulders, legs turning to rubber.

One more stagger and I'd have dropped. I let go the anchor in the surf and, God help me, ran in my boots, full of water, back up to the house. I broke out a block and tackle and ran back down. We slacked off the blocks and hooked them onto the chain a couple of fathoms apart, and then we hove and hove and hove on the rope, slipping and sliding in the surge of the seas, trying in ludicrous despair to drag six tons of dying boat through solid sand.

– photographs courtesy of Joseph E. Garland

She was nudging now against that rock, helped along by each wave. Whoosh — GRUMP. Whoosh — GRUMP. We straightened up and looked at each other. I unhitched the tackle and Larry grabbed the anchor, and we packed it up. The tide and the wind and the waves, fulfilling their nature, just kept acoming.

Another few minutes and she lay over to port, way over, like some dying creature, crashing between rock and sea. As the tide rose, she capsized, her spars in the raging water, and her sails and a tangle of lines like the black carcass of a beached whale.

Then she just came apart and spilled out her guts. The wind and the waves bore them ashore, hatches, dishrags, wooden spoons, life jackets, stove kindling, socks, coffee cans, sleeping bag, spare pants, paint cans, charts, a book or two, union jack, and there at my feet half a bottle of rum, courtesy of the recently deceased for the benefit of the wake. So we toasted the old girl, boots awash, right then and there.

The word had gone out over the police radio, I guess, and the road above the beach was crowding with cars. She was a pretty famous boat, and the last of her nine owners had written a book called *Lone Voyager* about her first owner, a man named Howard Blackburn, dead 50 years, some say the greatest Gloucester fisherman who ever lived. Ah, it was Blackburn who froze his fingers rowing a dory with the frozen body of his dorymate 65 miles into the coast of Newfoundland in the winter of 1883, five days without food or water, who sailed alone across the Atlantic twice, who built this sloop of 32 feet in 1929 in honor of being made an honorary member of the Cruising Club of America. Blackburn, The Fingerless Navigator.

Charles Freyer, master mariner, had sailed *Cruising Club* single-handed to England and back, through the Canal to San Francisco and back, down to Brazil and back, and home at last to Gloucester where he sold her to me, the guy who wrote the book, in 1976. No, she never let us down, any of us, and here she was, a hundred yards from her mooring, from the safety of her bed. . . .

Lord, how many thousands, tens of thousands of miles under that old keel? Reribbed, refastened, repaired, recaulked, rerigged, repainted, resuited with sails, hundreds of voyages, generations of owners, 51 years of it. Two days before, we'd gone for a little sail, our last as it turned out. A sweet October after-

noon, hardly a breath of wind. We got no more than a quarter of a mile from the mooring when the wind gave out altogether. Do you think I could coax her home? Not on your life. Had to start up the engine. She knew.

Yes, there was quite a crowd. Some came to wonder, some to stare, some to catch the irony of the scene on film, some to weep, some to help, and some to help themselves, say, to one whole side of the cabin trunk when it came floating in and nobody was looking, and to what else I will never know.

When the tide ebbed and left the fractured frame, there was I with my axe, crazy mad, chopping out the portholes from what was left of the cabin before the vultures got them. All kinds of friends pitched in, working into the dark

at low tide. We dissected out the engine and slung it under the busted boom like a trussed boar, carrying it in flashlit safari up the beach.

Ah, those precious summers sailing the coast of Maine. Sultry southeaster, smoky sou'wester, shiver of sail, creak of gaff, rush of hull, clang of bell, thick of fog, splash of anchor, cry of gull, scent of pine, whiff of stovesmoke, lap of wavelet, lying in the bunk, moonbeam shifting, slanting through the skylight.

Two years went by. We recovered the mast and restepped it as a Blackburn memorial flagpole at the edge of the porch, to raise the stars and stripes where every passing craft can see whence the wind blows — and how hard.

Cruising Club's first owner, Howard Blackburn. In 1883 he rowed his dory 65 miles to the coast of Newfoundland, molding his frozen fingers around the oars.

The author and final owner at Cruising Club's helm near the entrance to Gloucester Harbor. In 1976 he wrote a book about Howard Blackburn's exploits.

Last Day at Fenway Park

BY JOHN HELYAR

"It was the frozen twilight moment as Yaz walked to the plate . . ."

I have this thing about Red Sox closing days.

I go to them — nine out of 10 of them since 1969. Mostly I go alone. I have friends who are good baseball fans, but even they do not readily understand this exercise, this mixture of reflection, celebration, mourning, and beer. But then they do not stubbornly cling to a baseball autographed by Dick Radatz in 1964 either.

Many more people, of course, pride themselves on getting to every opening day, at the other end of the long season. Politicians go for exposure, businessmen for status, schoolboys for glee. But opening day is not so much a ball game as a ritual of renewal. As with most rituals, the anticipation almost always exceeds the actual event.

On closing day the game itself is the thing, for nearly always there is surely nothing else. The crucial series have come and gone, been won or lost; the batting averages are all but frozen, the standings are settled; and a just-for-the-fun-of-it feeling prevails.

Closing day is for opening up the senses an extra notch, being, for a change, superalert for all the sights and sounds of the day. In the sultry afternoons and soft evenings of summer it is easy to stop looking for the little things that make baseball the best game. Familiarity breeds laziness, and a July game unmarked by special heroics can be a mild disappointment.

But not on closing day, when the billboard on Brookline Avenue shows no coming attractions, and the only thing left is Now. The urgency is not to win, but to crystallize and catalogue it all, ensuring that something has been tucked away that can be brought out for inspection on barren, bitter cold winter nights. It is the last chance for memories.

But the events of one year ago, October 2, 1978, belong in a compartment all their own. It was the least typical of closing days in one respect, for up until the final swing of the bat it was not clear it *was* to be closing day. Yet it brought forth the essence of the season being ended — only so much more vividly and wrench-

ingly, its like will almost surely never again be seen.

To appreciate the pattern of the game it is important to know the pattern of the season. The Red Sox jumped out ahead — way ahead — of the Yankees and the rest of the division. But the advantage began to dissipate in late July and then was abruptly wiped out altogether, almost violently, in mid-September when New York invaded Boston for a four-game, no-contest sweep, seemingly leaving no survivors.

Somehow the Sox regrouped and revived, winning their last eight straight to pull even on Sunday, the final regular game of the season. I came away from the box office afterwards with precious tickets to the play-off Monday.

One of the tickets was for my friend Bill, who had not given a second thought to winging in from upstate New York for one afternoon of baseball. I met him in the early afternoon in a crowded Kenmore Square, where the Indian-summer air was electric with excitement, people surging toward Fenway, straining for their first look at which way the center-field flag was blowing; scalpers testing the marketplace and the ticketless appealing for handouts; radios blaring the pregame show from stands where vendors were shouting 10 times a minute, "Hey, SOUVENIUHS"; people chattering speculation on what amazing events might unfold on this gleeful reprieve of a

day when the passions and wills of decades of bitter rivalry would meet head-on. ("Tell you what Zimmer oughta do," Clif Keane was saying. "He oughta have somebody warming up as soon as Torrez throws his first pitch.")

Our seats were in the right-field stands near the foul pole. We watched the green-trimmed, low-slung country grandstand slowly fill, the players go through their perfunctory warm-ups, and a few puffs of white clouds go scudding across the perfect blue sky.

The game finally began, one of quiet tension interspersed with bursts of drama. The first came in the second inning when Yastrzemski caught a Ron Guidry fastball flush, stroking it in a long line drive out our way, just fair around the foul pole for a home run.

I abandoned the careful nursing of a searing sore throat and was screaming, "YAZ, YAZ," and less intelligible things while repeatedly jumping up and down for joy for the first time since I couldn't remember when.

Then came the slow accumulation of innings: Bill and I exchanging sporadic, shorthand appraisals; Mike Torrez, after all his stretch drive disappointments, mowing down the hated Gothams; another Boston run in the sixth.

The grandstand and light-tower shadows were beginning to cut deeply into the field, the sun lowering to the blinding treachery level for right fielders, when in the seventh New York for the first time put together two straight hits.

That brought up the less-than-fearsome Bucky Dent, who looked even less fearsome sitting on the ground for several minutes after fouling a pitch off his shin. We were speculating on who would pinch-hit when he finally hobbled back to the plate.

Torrez came into the stretch, looked back at Chambliss on second base and over his shoulder at White on first, then pitched.

Dent swung and lofted a fly ball toward left. The grandstand overhang blocked its flight from view, and I watched Yastrzemski looking up, looking up, as though setting for the catch.

Then he turned around, still looking up, and staggered.

The ball did not come down. The worst had happened. Fenway Park was silent except for the pockets of Yankee fans emerging from their closets, on their feet shouting with glee.

The score mounted to 5–2 with a Reggie Jackson eighth-inning homer, and now I was not so much tired as empty.

"It's gone," I said, watching Jackson's well-practiced October Cadillac trot.

"I don't know," Bill said bravely. "I think we're going to see a real garrison finish. It's the pattern of every classic game — go ahead, fall behind, come storming back."

I held my skeptical tongue and watched him proven correct. The game, the season, had one more twist.

The league's best reliever, Rich Gossage, had been overpowering on entering the game in the seventh, but Boston was rocking him with singles in the eighth while the revitalized Fenway Faithful rocked in approval: Yaz driving in another run, Fisk fighting off fastball after fastball before singling to keep the rally alive, before, finally, George Scott fanned to strand two runners.

Still, we were down only 5–4 now, and the top of the ninth was only an occasion for recharging voices. I looked at my scorecard. One batter, just one batter on, and Rice would have another shot.

With one out in the last of the ninth Gossage obligingly walked Rick Burleson. Jerry Remy followed with a line drive to right and my eyes quickly riveted on Lou Piniella, 150 feet away squinting into the sun, standing frozen.

"He's lost it," I shrieked, a piece of intelligence unfortunately lost on Burleson, who was rooted between first and second. The ball hopped directly to Piniella, and he threw toward third. Burleson rounded second, then came skidding to a halt and retreated.

Now the wildest fantasy I could have spun way back in March, when I was listening to the first exhibition game on the car radio, the snow stacked high on either side of Route 2, was unfolding — the whole season coming down to Rice and Yastrzemski coming to bat with the tying and winning runs aboard.

"Swing at the first one and I'll personally strangle you," I hissed as Rice stepped in, for fearsome hitter as he is, he often does not wait for the optimal pitch. He watched the first pitch go by, but the best he could then do was fly deep to right and move Burleson to third.

And then there was one. The roar rolled down from the stands and tumbled over the field as Yastrzemski came out of the on-deck circle, the noise swelling to a near-insupportable din as he approached the plate.

Yaz. Thirty-nine years old. A rookie when I saw my first game, the one link to all that history since.

Tom Yawkey was dead, Tony Conigliaro was off somewhere being a TV sports announcer, Rico Petrocelli was on call-in radio, Orlando Cepeda was in jail — and Yaz was peering out at Gossage, his bat cocked.

Everyone in the park was standing, now, for this final exquisite agony, our best against theirs, another season of giddy highs and abysmal lows, all hanging in the balance in the Back Bay gloaming.

Gossage was ready. The first pitch rode in; 32,925 people winced. Ball one.

The crowd roared anew, and a thought sprang loose in my mind — my God, this could happen. I was suddenly assaulted with mixed feelings. Could I handle winning? Had I become so adept at rationalizing close-but-no-cigar, so comfortable with second-guessing and speculating, that I didn't in my heart of hearts want anything else? Did I want it to end cleanly and honorably right now so that I would not have to face the pressures of a stake in the Series? I was, after all, the one who missed Fisk's legendary foul-pole home run in 1975 because I had gone to bed early, unable to endure the tension.

On the mound, Gossage was looking for his sign.

And then another random thought: "Bobby Thomson." He of the 1951 playoff-winning homer for the New York Giants. I had always envied Giants fans the eternal ecstasy of that moment, had run through many a daydream of something like it in Fenway one day. Now the day was here and I was thinking, "No, thanks"?

I looked out at Paul Blair in center, waiting, and pictured Yaz ramming one over his outstretched glove. Remy would be flying around the bases for the winning run, I would be pounding on Bill, he would be pounding on me, and the general eruption would make the '67 homer seem like afternoon tea at the Copley.

I decided, with an exhaled heave of breath, that I could take a stab at living with victory.

Gossage set and fired again. Yastrzemski uncoiled a full swing, and I could not see where the ball had gone. Then I saw Gossage jumping up and down on the mound and beyond him third baseman Nettles backpedaling.

"I was thinking," Bill said in a darkened Brattleboro, Vermont, bar months later, "I was thinking I saw Brooks Robinson drop one just like that in 1970."

But Nettles did not, and within seconds the tableau between batter and pitcher had dissolved into a swarm of joyful Yankees near third base, the cheers of Yankee fans echoing thinly around the park, while the rest of us were abruptly gagged.

John Kiley started playing the organ, and with that cue the park emptied quickly. It was as though you had pulled the plug on something. Bill and I stayed put, staring at the people bunched up in the aisles and past them at the line of ushers and cops around the perimeter of the field, unaccountably guarding against an invasion of jubilant fans.

I started filling out my scorecard box score methodically, deliberately totaling the at bats, runs, hits, and RBIs, trying to make the statistics a cushion against everything else.

The score came out the same every way I added it.

Finally the ushers started moving in on the stragglers, and Bill and I got up slowly and headed for the exit. I went down the ramp and away from the 1978 season without the usual last, lingering look. I knew I already had the vision that would stay with me.

It was the frozen twilight moment as Yaz walked to the plate through the gathering din, the sudden collision of all memory and hope, the confrontation cementing the game's place as a classic, the setting from which I would spin my dreams of different endings.

Outside Fenway the day had lost most of its sparkle. Commuter and ball-game traffic had met and snarled. The smell of exhaust and the blasts of horns were rising to meet the first leaves falling from the trees along Park Drive.

Bill finally spoke.

"It was the best game I ever saw," he said.

"The best," I said.

There was nothing else to add, and we walked along in silence.

I was wondering why Remy's hit had to bounce to the blinded Piniella, neat as you please. I was wondering why storybook endings hardly ever happen outside storybooks.

I was wondering, just like every other year, why winter had to come so soon.

New England is home to an extraordinary number of superb craftspeople, many of whom we've featured in our monthly "Small Business & Crafts" column, edited by "Damon Ripley," a name created by Yankee founder Robb Sagendorph and used by a total of nine editors at different periods over the past 50 years. The text and photography here, however, were provided by Lionel A. Atwill (and that's his real name!).

Porter and Mary Brown Carve Birds

Porter and Mary Brown are raising the indigenous American art of bird carving to a new plane: beyond workmanship, above refined skill, to fine art. Within a span of nearly six years, the Browns have progressed from an early, somewhat awkward effort at a stiff-legged sandpiper to regal ospreys in flight, wild turkeys exploding from cornfields, hawks and owls and grouse so perfect in detail, so precise in conformation and coloration that collectors will gratefully pay $10,000 and more — much more — for one of their works.

It isn't the money that inspires the Browns. "People are always asking me what one of our birds costs," says Porter, a former NASA engineer who retired to Pawlet, Vermont, in the early seventies, "and when I tell them that an osprey goes for ten grand, then they want to know how long it took us to do that bird. You can just see the wheels turning. They're trying to figure out what we make per hour at this. It's not much."

Porter maintains that it takes him three days to carve a single feather in a wild turkey, a bird that has 70 primary feathers. That's 210 days of carving feathers alone, just part of the bird.

They work on each project jointly, Porter doing the meticulous carving and Mary, who studied painting at Parson's School of Design, painting the sculptures to capture the delicate play of light on the feathers and the subtle blending of hues from beak to feet. As a team, they say they work together with an almost uninterrupted harmony that began after their retirement, when Mary gave Porter a set of carving knives with the suggestion that he try whittling something. He whittled a sandpiper that he later assessed as "just a *hunk* of a bird. But then Mary took it and painted it, gave it feathers and texture. She gave it life!"

That was the start, at which point Porter admits he didn't know basswood from cactus, ordering expensive little blocks of basswood, a smooth, tight-grained wood that Porter prefers, from a wood-carver's supply house. By chance, he found out from the state bee inspector that his house was surrounded by basswood trees. "We were sitting in the kitchen and he told me the biggest tree in sight was a *basswood.* Then I knew we were doing the right thing."

The Browns' work has skyrocketed from those early experiences to shows at galleries in Vermont and Florida, as well as commissioned work, including a wild turkey they're now working on for the company that makes the bourbon of the same name. With characteristic honesty, Mary worries that she won't capture the colors the way they should be. "You know turkeys look just brown from a distance, but when you get up close to them, you see that their feathers shimmer, changing colors from bronze to gold to green, depending on how you look at them. I've been so scared I couldn't do that, but now I think I've come up with a way to capture that effect, so when you look at our turkey, he'll turn colors, too." She pauses, then adds, "But I'm not going to tell how."

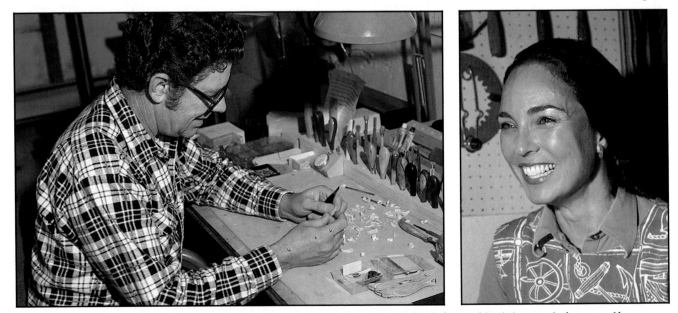

Porter and Mary Brown, shown above in their studio, observe and photograph birds from a blind they made from a golf cart. Mary does the detail work and painting on each feather Porter carves. Porter even designs and makes his own knives to execute with meticulous realism birds like the owl (reaching for the tail of a mouse) on the opposite page.

– photographs by Lionel Atwill

AN·OCTOBER
SAMPLER

☞Memorable thoughts, quotes, and assorted tidbits from the last 50 October issues.☜

CHAPPAQUIDDICK WASN'T MUCH OF A STORY

☞ Somebody said to me, "I suppose the Chappaquiddick affair was the biggest story the *Gazette* would ever have." I said no, it wasn't a particularly big story for us. Our main interest was in how the mainland papers and radio and TV stations covered it, because that was really an invasion, with the big television vans and the vestry of the Methodist church filled with telephones — there must have been 150 telephones installed in there. The church is right across from the courthouse, and they rented space to the newspapers for phones. It was very profitable for the church. It was quite a sight.

For us, the 1938 hurricane was a much bigger story, something that affected us directly with great damage from the tidal wave. In 1944, too, there was a lot of damage and we lost our power for a couple of weeks. The *Gazette* came out, only a little late. We set the type in New Bedford and ran the paper on the presses at Plymouth. Those things which make a difference in the life of the Vineyard are important stories. **Henry Beetle Hough, Editor of the *Vineyard Gazette*.** (*From "Island Man" by Lawrence F. Willard.*)

Norman Simpson, author and inn observer.

— Elizabeth Einstein

ADVICE TO THOSE YEARNING TO RUN A NEW ENGLAND INN

☞ "If your marriage is shaky, forget it. You'll run into lots of problems that may destroy your marriage as well as your business. Even if your marriage is solid, you're going to discover some cracks you didn't suspect were there. And if you have an alcohol problem, the problem will increase. Your lounge will make a baroque variety of liquor available to you, and somehow you'll think you're not even paying for it. Moreover, you'll find lots of reasons for drinking — the strain, and stuff like, 'I have to entertain the guests. . . .' "

* * *

"The two most questionable reasons I hear from people who want to start an inn are these — I love people and my wife is a good cook. Now, nobody knows whether they like people until they find themselves in a position of having to serve them day and night. And as for thinking your wife is a good cook . . . well, doesn't everybody? Even if she really is above average, cooking for a family and cooking for 70 people are two entirely different things."

* * *

"People expand, usually in their third year of ownership. We call that the 'dangerous year.' They think they've made it, so they expand quickly and their added expenses and mortgage make the whole thing top-heavy and then they go down the tube." **Norman Simpson, author of *Country Inns and Back Roads*.** (*From "So You Want to Be a New England Innkeeper" by Austin Stevens.*)

— Lawrence F. Willard

The late Henry Beetle Hough, Editor, Vineyard Gazette, *Martha's Vineyard, Massachusetts (1972).*

SOMEHOW, NOT THE SAME IN BOSTON

☞ . . .but there was, I found, a reason for her bitterness towards garden showings. Years before, at a time when things were far more decorous than they are today, she had unwittingly caused a considerable scandal in Garden Club circles. Captivated by the gay informality of the little vine-covered gardens of Italy, she decided to reproduce in her Beacon Hill garden some of this wayward European charm. She therefore caused long clotheslines to be strung out over her garden and, just before the Annual Tour of garden-lovers arrived, she ordered hung up on the lines a casual array of her own immaculately laundered undergarments.

It was meant to be a reproduction of a gay, informal Neapolitan scene; but somehow, in Boston, the effect was not quite the same. Moving about under a flapping cloud of Mrs. C.'s skivvies, Beacon Hill visitors felt distinctly ill at ease. Were you supposed to look? And how could you *not* look?

It made history. (*From "Beacon Hill: The Hub of the Universe" by Frances Minturn Howard.*)

23 SPECIAL WORDS FOR THE FIRST COLUMBUS DAY

☞ One hot August evening back in 1892, a young editor by the name of Francis M. Bellamy, a former minister from Rome, New York, sat down in his Boston office of *The Youth's Companion* and proceeded to write "The Pledge of Allegiance." He did it at the request of the *Companion*'s editor, James Bailey Upham, who, several months before, had gone to Washington, D.C., for an appointment with the president of the United States, then Benjamin Harrison. Accompanied by Henry Cabot Lodge, Upham had persuaded the president to ask Congress to declare Columbus Day, October 12th, a national holiday in honor of "the discovery of America" exactly 400 years before. On June 20 the resolution passed.

But Upham wanted to do more. "The flame of patriotism is dying out in this country," he told Bellamy on his return to Boston, "and I believe the place to revive that intense spirit is among America's schoolchildren."

So, through the pages of the *Companion,* Upham and Bellamy initiated a national program to have an American flag flying over every schoolhouse in the country in time for the first Columbus Day celebration in October. Then one evening in August, as the two editors were having supper at the Thorndyke Hotel in Boston, they began to discuss the idea of printing in the *Companion* some sort of patriotic loyalty vow for schoolchildren across America to recite as they raised their new flags.

"I can't seem to come up with the right flavor," Upham told Bellamy and suggested that Bellamy return to the *Companion* office that evening and try his hand at it. Bellamy agreed, and a few hours later had the following 23 words on paper: "I pledge allegiance to my flag and to the Republic for which it stands, one nation indivisible with liberty and justice for all." And those are the exact 23 words, unsigned by Bellamy, that appeared in the September 8, 1892, edition of *The Youth's Companion.* A month later, on October 12th, those are the words that were roared by over 12 million schoolchildren across the land.

Later, the wording was revised to read "the flag of the United States of America," and in 1954 the words "under God" were added between "nation" and "indivisible."

A rather remarkable postscript to the story is that for a number of years it was generally thought that the author of the Pledge of Allegiance was a man in Cherryvale, Kansas, who in 1896 lifted the Pledge from the old 1892 *Youth's Companion* and entered it as his own work in a school essay contest. This bit of chicanery not only won him the school prize for the best essay, but it also established him as the author of the Pledge of Allegiance. And here's the *really* remarkable part. The Cherryvale, Kansas, man's name was none other than Frank Bellamy!

It was only through years of research in the 1930s by one Margarette S. Miller of Portsmouth, Virginia, that enough evidence was gathered to persuade The United States Flag Association to conduct a formal investigation of the confusing facts. Their final report, rendered by three outstanding historians of the day, was completed in 1939, and it conclusively established the Frank Bellamy of Rome, New York, and *The Youth's Companion* as the true author of the Pledge of Allegiance.

J.D.H.

A·FAVORITE LETTER

MARDON ME, PADAM!

☞ Read the short piece about spoonerisms in the 1978 *Old Farmer's Almanac* and I wanted to chide you for overlooking the "Nervous Usher at the Church Wedding." "Mardon, me, padam! Are you a friend of the gride or the broom? May I sew you to a sheet or would you rather take a chew in the back of the perch?"

Ian M. MacDonald
Leominster, Massachusetts

– Austin Stevens

HURRICANE ISLAND, MAINE (UPI) — For about $550, a tired business executive can be dropped on a deserted island without food. This vacation is sponsored by Outward Bound and offers an opportunity to regain self-confidence. . . .

LIKE HARD INNER TUBES

☞ "They never touch. I've been rocked by the cavitation from their great flukes but never touched. The flukes lift up and over you. If you reach out to touch them, they pull the pectoral fin in, just the way they avoid you with the flukes. Not quickly, but slowly. They're not frightened, but they don't want you touching them. The eye follows you. You can't read the mood. They're not expressive eyes. You can see only one at a time, for one thing. They look right through you. That one eye. That grapefruit eye.

"You feel a shock wave when a whale passes by. If you are close, say six feet, there is a gentle rocking if you are in the path of the down circle of its fluke. When I touch them — which I very seldom try to do — they feel like hard inner tubes. But one move toward most whales and they turn and are gone. You can't imagine that an animal of that size can turn in such tight circles or maneuver so delicately, but whales do. Fin whales, for example, are incredibly elusive. You see a brief flurry of motion, and that's all. I've

Bill Curtsinger readying his cameras on a dock overlooking Biddeford Pool, near his home in Maine.

— Stephen O. Muskie

never really gotten a good photograph of one. Right whales, however, are curious. They will come over to you. You can swim toward them.

"You can hear the right whales, but not like you hear the humpbacks. You hear the right whales just once in a while — theirs is a guttural sound, rare and private. But the humpbacks! At the right time of the year you can hear a humpback in Hawaii when you are miles and miles away from the whale that is singing the song. If you are close enough to a singing whale, you can feel the vibrations in the water." **Bill Curtsinger**. (*From "He Swims with Whales" by Lynn Franklin.*)

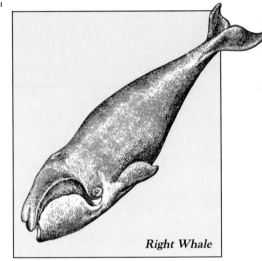

Right Whale

ALL IN THE LIFE OF A TROMBONIST

☞ I remember a rehearsal of the BSO under Serge Koussevitzky when our second trombonist was almost destroyed. We were rehearsing the Russian Easter Overture of Rimsky-Korsakov, which has a declamatory passage for the second trombone. As soon as he had finished it Koussey stopped the orchestra and expressed his approval:

"I have conducted this piece many times, and never have I heard it played better. Bravo!"

All of us then dutifully applauded our colleague.

"Let us do it again," Koussey said, and the inquisition began.

"No! It is too fast! Please again. No! The second note is too fast! No! The phrasing is wrong. And now it is out of tune!"

Each time our colleague would start again, and each time he would get nowhere. Finally, when he had been completely broken down, Koussevitzky announced, "It is the most baddest I have ever heard!" and left the stage. The rehearsal was finished for the day and so was our second trombonist. (*From "I Know You're in the Boston Symphony Orchestra But What Do You Do for a Living?" by Harry Ellis Dickson.*)

— Austin Stevens

GETTING THE MESSAGE

☞ The wrestlers teamed off and went through several standard maneuvers — scissor kicks, head holds, leg drops. The whole time Walter moved counterclockwise around the action, mumbling encouragement or barking, "No, no, nooooo." Once he stopped the proceedings between Chris and Burt. Chris was trying to learn a maneuver where he ducked under his opponent's advancing arm, reversed his direction with a balletic spin, and took his opponent's legs out from under him. Kowalski walked through the move three times in a row, pausing with each strategic grip. "You *see?* This, *see?*" He repeated. "Not *there.* Not down there. That's *sloppy....*" Each time Chris tried, he got it wrong. So Walter had Richard perform the move on him. The result: The Killer went slamming to the mat, sending powerful reverberations through the entire stage floor. For several seconds the Killer lay prone, motionless. Then he lifted his head, scowling in pain.

"I think you pinched a nerve," he growled. The students exchanged anxious glances. Richard offered the teacher a helping hand. The Killer seized the hand and flipped Richard over violently onto his back. Kowalski popped to his feet and grinned. The students looked stunned.

"Always expect the unexpected in life," Walter shouted. Then he relented, smiling. "That's the message." (*From "The Killer Retired" by James Dodson.*)

THE LIBERATED TOWN

☞ Weston is proud of its Village Green and its fame is far and wide. Some years ago, I wrote a short account of how this Green was maintained by nine women, which appeared in the journal of the Boston Women's City Club. A few weeks later, a tourist came into our Vermont Country Store and said to one of our women clerks, whose husband was, at the time, one of the three town selectmen, "I have come a long way to see the Town of Weston, owned and maintained by nine old ladies!" (*From "Green is for Weston" by Vrest Orton.*)

A MOMENT OF BIRTH

☞ From about 6:30 on, Gigi was in hard labor, the muscles in her abdomen visibly contracting, the great bulge of her belly moving downward. Much of the time she sat up in the climbing bars, holding on with hands and feet clenching on the bars as the contractions intensified. She frequently held her head with both hands, as if it were also hurting. The labor had by now lasted much longer than expected, and the observers were becoming concerned.

The moment of birth, at 10:43 P.M., caught everyone by surprise. They had been expecting the slow progress of a human infant's appearance — first the head, then a shoulder, and so forth. But Gigi's baby popped out of her all at once, while she was in a standing position. As the humans all sucked in their breaths, Gigi made a grab for the infant as it fell, but missed, catching the umbilical cord instead. She looked surprised. Then she dropped the baby onto the concrete floor, still attached to its mother by the cord.

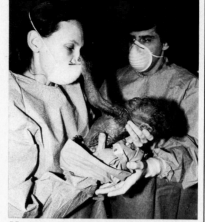

Veterinarians examine the gorilla Gigi's baby at the Stoneham, Massachusetts, zoo in 1981.

The infant, a male who later weighed in at six and three-quarter pounds, unusually large for a gorilla baby, opened his eyes within a few seconds of birth, and began to cry. It was not a tentative sound, but a wail of such volume that the human observers at first were confused as to the source of the sound, looking around to see if someone had brought in a human infant. (*From "Born in Captivity" by Tim Clark.*)

THE BEST APPLE PIE RECIPE

As judged by Barbara Radcliffe Rogers in October 1978 (and eight of her New Hampshire friends who were not allowed to vote for their own pies).

The crust:
    2 cups pastry flour
    ¾ teaspoon salt
    ⅓ cup chilled lard
    ⅓ cup chilled butter
    ⅓ cup ice water

Sift flour with salt. Cut in lard and butter very quickly until it is in little pieces. Sprinkle water over, 2 tablespoons at a time, stirring gently until pastry can be gathered into a ball. Wrap and chill 1 hour before using. Experienced cooks can tell when the amount of shortening is right for the flour, and do not have to measure the water, but until one learns to recognize the right feel of the pastry, measuring is a help.

The filling:
    2 pounds of apples, peeled, cored, and sliced evenly
    ¾ cup sugar
    1 tablespoon flour
    ½ teaspoon cinnamon
    ½ teaspoon fresh ground nutmeg
    ¼ teaspoon salt
    Dash of cloves
    3 tablespoons butter

Arrange the apples in the bottom crust, on which you have sprinkled 2 tablespoons sugar. Sift flour and seasonings with remaining sugar and sprinkle over the apples. Cut butter into small pieces and dot the top. Cover with remaining crust, seal edges well, and cut steam vents.

Bake at 450° for 15 minutes. Reduce heat to 350° and bake 30 to 45 minutes more, or until crust is nicely browned.

"JUST PICKIN'"

☞ When the sun rose at quarter of six on October 7, 1931, Donald Parker started out his day bending over the hills and plucking spuds from the sandy loam of the Reed Brothers Farm in Fort Fairfield, Maine, scuttling them into barrels and hefting the barrels into wagons. Eleven hours later, as the sun sank and Donald stood and stretched and dusted his hands off, he'd drawn 38,016 pounds of potatoes from the thin Maine soil. That's about 17 tons, several tons more than he picked most days. Paid by the barrel, Donald collected his $7.56 and headed home for supper, pleased that he'd brought in a bit more than usual but not knowing that his day's take of 216 barrels had set the world record for potato picking, a record that's not since been broken and that Donald, now 80 [in October 1980], doesn't think is likely to be challenged, ever again.

Was he hustling to break a record on that cool October day back in 1931? "Nope. I was just picking."

CHAPTER 11

November

*A*lthough Halloween comes a week or so after our November issue is published, that's still October's fare. November's principal focus is Thanksgiving and, in its behalf, we've had everything from Bill Conklin's exploding turkey to turkey hunts to a Bath, Maine, lady who could bone an entire raw turkey in eight minutes flat; we've also run enough cranberry, turkey stuffing, and pumpkin pie recipes over 50 years to last every subscriber for a lifetime of solid Thanksgivings! Other typical November themes: the World War I Armistice, now observed as Veterans Day; Indian Summer (it can only occur sometime between the 11th and the 21st); trees and home heating; politics and elections; the Harvard-Yale game, known simply as The Game; and ghost towns. Yes, ghost towns — or often ghost farms. November has always somehow seemed to be the appropriate time to include descriptions of meanderings back into the now-bare forests in search of old cellar holes, stone walls, barn foundations, isolated gravestones, and lone apple trees among thick stands of birch, oak, and poplar. In our November 1972 issue, for instance, Kenneth Andler wrote how stone walls found deep in the forest "speak out to anyone who half listens to the toil that went into them, rod by sweaty rod, the sort of manual labor almost impossible to comprehend today." And yet, he observed, "there is no stillness to compare with the quiet where people have once lived and live no more."

Moosehead Lake, Maine.

– photograph by Carole Allen

When this story came to Yankee we were all so surprised by it that we wrote the author asking him if it was true. He answered saying: "As to its verity, I can only attest that it was recounted to me some years ago as being completely true by a woman whose honesty could not be doubted. This wonderful person, Mrs. Nesta Weir, was one of the foremost real estate agents in Easton, Maryland, and was well known throughout that entire area for her integrity, warmth, and general astuteness. By no means was she a 'Teller of Tall Tales.' Mrs. Weir told me that she and her daughter-in-law actually witnessed the event in the story, which I have tried to preserve because I felt compelled to do so."

The Swan of Ice

BY HOWARD D. WOLFE

It was bitter cold. The night before an unexpected northeast gale had left a skim of ruffled ice on the bays and backwaters, which were now blinking and shimmering in the morning sun. A paralyzing blast from the arctic had swept through the region, immobilizing everything in its path and leaving in its wake a stillness that was broken only by the faint creaking of the ice crust on the water as it resisted the currents below.

About a hundred yards out in the bay, in the lee of a marshy point of land, there was a tousled blob of white that obvious-ly did not belong there. It looked like a man's dress shirt tossed away and left to stiffen in the frozen water.

At first it made no movement at all, but then a faint twisting motion could be discerned. A head with a coal-black bill rose feebly from a pile of snow-white feathers and then fell back exhausted. It was a whistling swan, trapped as it slept, unaware of the impending danger and the quick, relentless crystallizing of the brackish water into ice.

An anguished sound, almost a repeated moan, was heard as the swan struggled to be free from its icy bondage. Its triple-noted whoop, normally so confident and strident in the winter air, was now muffled and pitifully weak. Yet it was audible as the swan rotated her head to scan the sky, pleading for some sort of recognition.

Suddenly this plaintive calling increased in tempo and in volume. The head stiffened, gazing far up into the steel-blue sky, which revealed nothing to the human eye.

A little later a wavering "V" of small, dark specks appeared very high over the western horizon. Almost simultaneously a raucous clamoring rang out to signal the presence of a flock of Canada geese, honking their celebration of conquest over the storm just passed.

This feathered arrow sped unswerving through the frigid air, becoming larger and yet larger as it neared the point. Soon each goose was clearly defined against the sky and each powerful wingbeat could be counted. There were nearly 30 geese in the flock, each calling to one another and responding to their leader with harsh yelps of allegiance.

As they raced across the sky, the lead goose, almost without warning, dropped and wheeled sharply, while his followers hesitated briefly above him, slowing their wing beats, waiting to discover what their altered destination would be.

The leader banked slowly, losing altitude gradually, and the flock still faltered above him. Abruptly the gabbling of the flock ceased, and a few deep, resounding honks from the old gander directed their sharp and rapid descent to the mute white figure fast in the ice below them. One by one they plummeted down.

Tumbling from the air with wings full-set and backing, the leader first, and then the rest behind him, they hit the ice with poised grace, expecting welcoming water to ease a normal landing.

Astonished squawks rent the air as the surprised geese skidded and slipped over the ice in a flopping mass of badly ruffled feathers that twisted to a writhing, struggling stop far past the calling swan.

Spread out in scattered bunches, the geese, one by one, slowly stood up on the unfriendly, frozen surface, smoothing their disarranged feathers and shaking away the embarrassing indignity of their ludicrous landing. For a moment they remained standing quietly, blinking at the feeble sunlight, as if questioning the wisdom of tarrying at all. They were all silent until composure returned and the leader, with short, low barks, indicated his will and intention.

Without hesitation they formed a straggling line that made its way across the treacherous ice, back to the pinioned swan. Carefully they formed a tight, compact circle around the white bird.

The swan croaked guttural recognition. Her raised head swung slowly from

---

As they raced across the sky, the lead goose, almost without warning, dropped and wheeled sharply, while his followers hesitated briefly above him. . . .

---

side to side, expressing both wonderment and apprehension.

Swans and geese are not friends. Neither are they enemies. They tolerate each other, sometimes somewhat grudgingly, and seldom rest within hundreds of yards of each other. They prefer to feed by themselves and do not seek out each other's company. The swan's nervous clucking reflected the uniqueness of such close proximity.

The lead goose growled a few low orders and bent to the ice, his powerful bill hammering at it with steady blows that chipped away small pieces and formed an ever-widening circle of cleared water in front of him. The other geese, after watching him for only a few seconds, crouched to a similar task. The air was filled with the rapping of their relentless mandibles slashing at the frozen crust. Bit by bit the ice gave way.

The tiring job continued as the geese proceeded, closer and closer to the swan, pecking fiercely and with enormous force, until the bulky body, so much larger than theirs, was floating free.

The swan now paddled timorously with great labor and struggled to raise her vast wings, which were still frozen to her flanks and sides and covered with a firm film of ice. She was unable to fly, and her desperate yawps gave voice to her wild distress.

The geese chuckled soft reassurance.

They swam slowly forward to her until their bills were touching her neck and back. Slowly and steadily they began to run their bills down the length of each glistening feather, freeing them one by one from their icy covering.

At times many of the geese were engaged in this delicate, time-consuming procedure. Sometimes they worked singly or in pairs, their blue-gray bills sliding gently and continuously across the long primaries, then to the secondary, smaller feathers, and finally to her tail. The swan did not move.

After endless minutes of this meticulous and painstaking preening the geese finally drifted back away from the swan, leaving her alone in her bright circle of shimmering water. No sound could be heard at all.

First one great pinion of the swan raised, then the other. The broad, heavily tendoned wings strained and then extended to their entire length, stretched and trembling in the fresh new wind. A few very slow but powerful, whooshing wing beats moved the swan ahead. Then a few more, almost imperceptibly faster and much stronger.

The heavy white body raised in the water and slid over the ice. The crazily dangling legs clacked clumsily over the frozen surface, rising inch by inch above it until, after nearly 20 yards, they retracted, and the full seven feet of churning wingspan lifted the freed swan up into the clean, cold wind.

Steadily she rose, higher and higher, and then she banked in a slow circle over the geese. As she wheeled, the sun shone through the enormous breadth of her wings, revealing each newly released feather, glowing almost transparently against the brightness of the day. A double whoop, grateful, and clear and strong now, drifted down the wind to the bunched geese watching intently from the water below.

As the swan continued to circle in an ever-increasing orbit, a busy babble of honking, brisk and purposeful, indicated the time for departure. The geese lifted, jumping off the water as a flock, faltered briefly, then climbed rapidly, forming a flying wedge that propelled itself swiftly towards the horizon.

Very soon the wedge was only a small, dark spot in the sky, moving directly towards its original destination. A wild chorus of joyous honks floated softly through the winter sky behind it.

Described by best-selling author Stephen King as "one of my personal favorites," this story begins slowly, ends like an onrushing tidal wave, and, according to so many who wrote us after reading it in our November 1981 issue, it "stays with you forever."

Do the Dead Sing?

FICTION BY STEPHEN KING

"The Reach was wider in those days," Stella Flanders told her great-grandchildren in the last summer of her life, the summer before she began to see ghosts. The children looked at her with wide, silent eyes, and her son Alden turned from his seat on the porch where he was whittling. It was Sunday, and Alden wouldn't take his boat out on Sundays no matter how high the price of lobster was.

"What do you mean, Gram?" Tommy asked, but the old woman did not answer. She only sat in her rocker by the cold stove, her slippers bumping placidly on the floor.

Tommy asked his mother: "What does she mean?"

Lois only shook her head, smiled, and sent them out with pots to pick berries.

Stella thought: *She's forgot. Or did she ever know?*

The Reach had been wider in those days. If anyone knew it was so, that person was Stella Flanders. She had been born in 1884, she was the oldest resident of Goat Island, and she had never once in her life been to the mainland.

Fall set in, a cold fall without the necessary rain to bring a really fine color to the trees, either on Goat or on Raccoon Head across the Reach. The wind blew long, cold notes, and Stella felt each note resonate in her heart.

On November 19, when the first flurries came swirling down out of a sky the color of white chrome, Stella celebrated her birthday. Most of the village turned out. Hattie Stoddard came, whose mother had died of the pleurisy in 1954 and whose father had been lost with the *Dancer* in 1941. Richard and Mary Dodge came, Richard moving slowly up the path on his cane, his arthritis riding him like an invisible passenger. Sarah Havelock came, of course; Sarah's mother Annabelle had been Stella's best friend. They had gone to the island

school together, grades one to eight, and Annabelle had married Tommy Frane, who had pulled her hair in the fifth grade and made her cry, just as Stella had married Bill Flanders, who had once knocked all of her schoolbooks out of her arms and into the mud (but she had managed not to cry). Now both Annabelle and Tommy were gone and Sarah was the only one of their seven children still on the island. *Her* husband, George Havelock, who had been known to everyone as Big George, had died a nasty death over on the mainland in 1967, the year there was no fishing. An axe had slipped in Big George's hand, there had been blood — too much of it! — and an island funeral three days later. And when Sarah came in to Stella's party and cried, "Happy birthday, Gram!" Stella hugged her tight and felt love swell her heart . . . but she did not cry.

There was a tremendous birthday cake. Hattie had made it with *her* best friend, Vera Spruce. The assembled company bellowed out "Happy Birthday to You" in a combined voice that was loud enough to drown out the wind . . . for a little while, anyway. Even Alden sang, who in the normal course of events would sing only "Onward Christian Soldiers" and the doxology in church and would mouth the words to all the rest with his head hunched and his big old jug ears just as red as tomatoes. There were 95 candles on Stella's cake, and even over the singing she heard the wind, although her hearing was not what it once had been.

She thought that the wind was calling her name.

"I was not the only one," she would have told Lois's children if she could. "In my day there were many that lived and died on the island. There was no mail boat in those days; Bull Symes used to bring the mail when there was mail. There was no ferry, either. If you

had business on the Head, your man took you in the lobster boat. So far as I know, there wasn't a flushing toilet on the island until 1946. 'Twas Bull's boy Harold that put in the first one the year after the heart attack carried Bull off while he was out dragging traps. I remember seeing them bring Bull home. They brought him up wrapped in a tarpaulin, and one of his green boots poked out. I remember. . . ."

And they would say: "What, Gram? What do you remember?"

How would she answer them? Was there more? Did it mean something?

On the first day of winter that year, a month or so after the birthday party, Stella opened the back door to get stove wood and discovered a dead sparrow on the back stoop. She bent down carefully, picked it up by one foot, and looked at it.

"Frozen," she announced, and something inside her spoke another word. It had been 40 years since she had seen a frozen bird — 1938. The year the Reach had frozen.

Shuddering, pulling her coat closer, she threw the dead sparrow in the old rusty incinerator as she went by it. The day was cold. The sky was a clear, deep blue. On the night of her birthday four inches of snow had fallen, had melted, and no more had come since then. "Got to come soon," Larry McKeen down at the Goat Island Store said sagely, as if daring winter to stay away.

Stella got to the woodpile, picked herself an armload, and carried it back to the house. Her shadow, crisp and clean, followed her.

As she reached the back door, where the sparrow had fallen, Bill spoke to her — but the cancer had taken Bill 12 years before. "Stella," Bill said, and she saw his shadow fall beside hers, longer but just as clear-cut, the shadow-bill of his shadow-cap twisted off jauntily to one side just as he had always worn it. Stella

felt a scream lodged in her throat. It was too large to touch her lips.

"Stella," he said again, "when you comin' across to the mainland? We'll get Norm Jolley's old Ford and go down to Bean's in Freeport just for a lark. What do you say?"

She wheeled, almost dropping her wood, and there was no one there. Just the dooryard sloping down to the hill, then the wild white grass, and beyond all, at the edge of everything, clear-cut and somehow magnified, the Reach . . . and the mainland beyond it.

Gram, what's the Reach?" Lona might have asked . . . although she never had. And she would *have given them the answer any fisherman knew by rote: a Reach is a body of water between two bodies of land, a body of water which is open at either end. The old lobsterman's joke went like this: know how to read y'compass when the fog comes, boys; between Jonesport and London there's a mighty long Reach.*

"Reach is the water between the island and the mainland," she might have amplified, giving them molasses cookies and hot tea laced with sugar. "I know that much. I know it as well as my husband's name, and how he used to wear his hat."

"Gram?" Lona would say. "How come you never been across the Reach?"

"Honey," she would say, "I never saw any reason to go."

In January, two months after the birthday party, the Reach froze for the first time since 1938. The radio warned islanders and mainlanders alike not to trust the ice, but Stewie McClelland and Russell Bowie took Stewie's Bombardier Skidoo out anyway after a long afternoon's conversation with Brother Jim Beam, and sure enough, the Skidoo went into the Reach. Stewie managed to crawl out (although he lost one foot to frostbite) but the Reach took Russell Bowie and carried him away.

That January 25 there was a memorial service on the island. Stella went on her son Alden's arm, and he mouthed the words to the hymns and boomed out the doxology in his great tuneless voice be-

"No, I've never felt I needed to leave the island. My life was here. The Reach was wider in those days."

fore the benediction. Stella sat afterward with Sarah Havelock and Hattie Stoddard and Vera Spruce in the glow of the wood fire in the town hall basement. A going-away party for Russell was being held, complete with Za-Rex punch and nice little cream-cheese sandwiches cut into triangles. The men, of course, kept wandering out back for a nip of something a bit stronger than Za-Rex. Russell Bowie's new widow sat red-eyed and stunned beside Ewell McCracken, the minister. She was seven months big with child — it would be her fifth — and Stella, half-dozing in the heat of the woodstove, thought: *She'll be crossing the Reach soon enough, I guess. She'll move to Freeport or Lewiston and go for a waitress, I guess.*

She looked around at Vera and Hattie, to see what the discussion was.

"No, I didn't hear," Hattie said. "What *did* Freddy say?"

They were talking about Freddy Dinsmore, the oldest man on the island (two years younger'n me, though, Stella thought with some satisfaction), who had sold out his store to Larry McKeen in 1960 and now lived on his retirement.

"Said he'd never seen such a winter," Vera said, taking out her knitting. "He says it's going to make people sick."

Sarah Havelock looked at Stella and asked if Stella had ever seen such a winter. There had still been no snow; the ground lay crisp and bare and brown. The day before, Stella had walked 30 paces into the back field, holding her right hand level at the height of her thigh, and the grass there had snapped in a neat row with a sound like breaking glass.

"No," Stella said. "The Reach froze in '38, but there was snow that year. Do you remember Bull Symes, Hattie?"

Hattie laughed. "I think I still have the black and blue he give me on my sit-upon at the New Year's party in '53. He pinched me *that* hard. What about him, anyway?"

"Bull and my own man walked across to the mainland that year," Stella said. "That February of 1938. Strapped on snowshoes, walked across to Dorrit's Tavern on the Head, had them each a shot of whiskey, and walked back. They asked me to come along. They were like two little boys off to the sliding with a toboggan between them."

They were looking at her, touched by the wonder of it. Even Vera was looking at her wide eyed, and Vera had surely heard the tale before. If you believed the stories, Bull and Vera had once played some house together, although it was hard, looking at Vera now, to believe she had ever been so young.

"And you didn't *go?*" Sarah asked, perhaps seeing the reach of the Reach in her mind's eye, so white it was almost blue in the heatless winter sunshine, the sparkle of the snow crystals, the mainland drawing closer, walking across, yes, walking across the *ocean* just like Jesus-out-of-the-boat, leaving the island for the one and only time in your life *on foot* —

"No," Stella said. Suddenly she wished she had brought her own knitting. "I didn't go with them."

"Why *not?*" Hattie asked her, almost indignantly.

"It was washday," Stella almost snapped, and then Missy Bowie, Russell's widow, broke into loud, braying sobs. Stella looked over and there sat Bill Flanders in his red-and-black-checked jacket, hat cocked to one side, smoking a Herbert Tareyton with another tucked behind his ear for later. She felt her heart leap into her chest and choke between beats.

She made a noise, but just then a knot popped like a rifle shot in the stove, and neither of the other ladies heard.

"Poor *thing,*" Sarah nearly cooed.

"Well shut of that good-for-nothing," Hattie grunted. She searched for the grim depth of the truth concerning the departed Russell Bowie and found it: "Little more than a tramp for pay, that man. She's well out of it."

But Stella barely heard these things. There sat Bill, close enough to the Reverend McCracken to have tweaked his nose if he so had a mind; he looked no more than 40, his eyes barely marked by the crow's feet that had later sunk so deep, wearing his flannel pants and his gum-rubber boots with the gray wool socks folded neatly down over the tops.

"We're waitin' on you, Stel," he said. "You come on across the Reach and see the mainland. You won't need no snowshoes this year."

There he sat in the town hall basement, big as Billy-be-damned, and then another knot exploded in the stove and

he was gone. And the Reverend McCracken went on comforting Missy Bowie as if nothing had happened.

That night Vera called up Annie Phillips on the phone, and in the course of the conversation mentioned to Annie that Stella Flanders didn't look well, not at all well.

"Alden would have a scratch of a job getting her off-island if she took sick," Annie said. Annie liked Alden because her own son Toby had told her Alden would take nothing stronger than beer. Annie was strictly temperance, herself.

"Wouldn't get her off 'tall unless she was in a coma," Vera said, pronouncing the word in the downeast fashion: *comer.* "When Stella says 'Frog,' Alden jumps. Alden ain't but half-bright, you know. Stella pretty much runs him."

"Oh, ayuh?" Annie said.

Just then there was a metallic crackling sound on the line. Vera could hear Annie Phillips for a moment longer — not the words, just the sound of her voice going on behind the crackling — and then there was nothing. The wind had gusted up high and the phone lines had gone down, maybe into Godlin's Pond or maybe down by Borrow's Cove, where they went into the Reach sheathed in rubber. It was possible that they had gone down on the other side, on the Head . . . and some might even have said (only half in fun) that Russell Bowie had reached up a cold hand to snap the cable, just for fun.

Not 700 feet away Stella Flanders lay under her puzzle quilt and listened to the dubious music of Alden's snores in the other room. She listened to Alden so she wouldn't have to listen to the wind . . . but she heard the wind anyway, oh yes, coming across the frozen expanse of the Reach, a mile and a half of water that was now overplated with ice, ice with lobsters down below, and groupers, and perhaps the twisting, dancing body of Russell Bowie, who used to come each April with his old Rogers rototiller and turn her garden.

Who'll turn the earth this April? she wondered as she lay cold and curled under her puzzle quilt. The wind gusted, rattling the storm window. It seemed that the storm window was talking to her, but she turned her face away from its words. And did not cry.

"But, Gram," Lona would press (she never gave up, not that one, she was like her mom, and her grandmother before her), "you still haven't told why you never went across."

"Why child, I have always had everything I wanted right here on Goat."

"But it's so small. We live in Portland. There's busses, Gram!"

"I see enough of what goes on in cities on the TV. I guess I'll stay where I am."

Hal was younger, but somehow more intuitive; he would not press her as his sister might, but his question would go closer to the heart of things. "You never wanted to go across, Gram? Never?"

And she would lean toward him, and take his small hands, and tell him how her mother and father had come to the island shortly after they were married, and how Bull Symes' grandfather had taken Stella's father as a 'prentice on his boat. She would tell him how her mother had conceived four times but had only carried one child to term: her, Stella Godlin. How she had grown up, gone to the island school through the eighth grade, and how she had decided on Bill Flanders instead of high school. She would tell the children these things, but perhaps it would really be Lois she was talking to. She would tell them that she herself had conceived four times, but one of her babies had miscarried and another had died a week after birth — she would have left the island if they could have saved it at the mainland hospital, but of course it was over before that was even thought of.

She would tell them that Bill had delivered Jane, their grandmother, but not that when it was over he had gone into the bathroom and first puked and then wept like a hysterical woman who had her monthlies p'ticularly bad. Jane, of course, had left the island at 14 to go to high school; girls didn't get married at 14 anymore, and when Stella saw her go off in the boat with Bradley Maxwell, whose job it had been to ferry the kids back and forth that month, she knew in her heart that Jane was gone for good, although she would come back for a while. She would tell them that Alden had come along 10 years later, after they had given up, and as if to make up for his tardiness, here was Alden still, a lifelong bachelor, and in some ways Stella was grateful for that because Alden was not terribly bright and there are plenty of women willing to take advantage of a man with a slow brain and a good heart (although she would not tell them that last, either).

She would say: "Louis and Margaret Godlin begat Stella Godlin, who became Stella Flanders; Bill and Stella Flanders begat Jane and Alden Flanders and Jane Flanders became Jane Wakefield; Richard and Jane Wakefield begat Lois Wakefield, who became Lois Perrault; David and Lois Perrault begat Lona and Hal. Those are your names, children: you are Godlin-Flanders-Wakefield-Perraults. Your blood is in the stones of this island, and I stay here because the mainland is just too far to reach. Memory is so wide and so deep, and I cannot cross. Godlin-Flanders-Wakefield-Perrault."

That was the coldest February since the National Weather Service began keeping records, and by the middle of the month the ice covering the Reach was safe. Snowmobiles buzzed and whined and sometimes turned over when they climbed the ice-heaves wrong. Children tried to skate, found the ice too bumpy to be any fun, and went back to Godlin Pond on the far side of the hill, but not before little Justin McCracken, the minister's son, caught his skate in a fissure and broke his ankle. They took him over to the hospital on the mainland where a doctor who owned a Corvette told him, "Son, it's going to be as good as new."

Freddy Dinsmore died very suddenly just three days after Justin McCracken broke his ankle. He caught the flu late in January, would not have the doctor, told everyone it was "just a cold from goin' out to get the mail without m'scarf," took to his bed, and died before anyone could take him across to the mainland and hook him up to all those machines they have waiting for guys like Freddy. His son George, a tosspot of the first water even at the advanced age (for tosspots, anyway) of 68, found Freddy with a copy of the *Bangor Daily News* in one hand and his Remington, unloaded, near at hand. Apparently he had been thinking of cleaning it just before he died. George Dinsmore went on a three-week toot, said toot financed by someone who knew that George would have his old dad's insurance money coming. Hattie Stoddard went around telling anyone who would listen that old George Dinsmore was a sin and a disgrace, no better than a tramp for pay.

There was a lot of flu around. The school closed for two weeks that February instead of the usual one because so many pupils were out sick. "No snow breeds germs," Sarah Havelock said.

Near the end of the month, just as people were beginning to look forward to the false comfort of March, Alden Flanders caught the flu himself. He walked around with it for nearly a week and then took to his bed with a fever of 101. Like Freddy, he refused to have the doctor, and Stella stewed and fretted and worried. Alden was not as old as Freddy, but that May he would turn 60.

The snow came at last. Six inches on Valentine's Day, another six on the 20th, and a foot in a good old norther on the leap, February 29. The snow lay white and strange between the cove and the mainland, like a sheep's meadow where there had been only gray and surging water at this time of year since time out of mind. Several people walked across to the mainland and back. No snowshoes were necessary this year because the snow had frozen to a firm, glittery crust. They might take a knock of whiskey, too, Stella thought, but they would not take it at Dorrit's. Dorrit's had burned down back in 1958.

And she saw Bill four times. Once he told her: "Y'ought to come soon, Stella. We'll go steppin'. What do you say?"

She could say nothing. Her fist was crammed deep into her mouth.

"Everything I ever wanted or needed was here," she would tell them. "We had the radio and now we have the television, and that's all I want of the world beyond the Reach. I had my garden year in and year out. And lobster? Why, we always used to have a pot of lobster stew on the back of the stove and we used to take it off and put it behind the door in the pantry when the minister came calling so he wouldn't see we were eating 'poor man's soup.'

"I have seen good weather and bad, and if there were times when I wondered what it might be like to actually be in the Sears store instead of ordering from the catalogue, or to go into one of those Shaw's markets I see on TV instead of buying at the store here or sending Alden across for something special like a Christmas capon or an Easter ham . . . or if I ever wanted, just once, to stand on Congress Street in Portland and watch all the people in their cars and on the sidewalks, more people in a single look than there are on the whole island these days . . . if I ever wanted those things, then I wanted this more. I am not strange. I am not peculiar, or even very eccentric for a woman of my years. My mother sometimes used to say, 'All the difference is between work and want,'

and I believe that to my very soul. I believe it is better to plow deep than wide.
"This is my place."

One day in middle March, with the sky as white and lowering as a loss of memory, Stella Flanders sat in her kitchen for the last time, laced up her boots over her skinny calves for the last time, and wrapped her bright red woolen scarf (a Christmas present from Hattie three Christmases past) around her neck for the last time. She wore a suit of Alden's long underwear under her dress. The waist of the drawers came up to just below the limp vestiges of her breasts, the shirt almost down to her knees.

Outside, the wind was picking up again, and the radio said there would be snow by afternoon. She put on her coat and her gloves. After a moment of debate, she put a pair of Alden's gloves on over her own. Alden had recovered from the flu, and this morning he and Harley Blood were over rehanging a storm door for Missy Bowie, who had had a girl. Stella had seen it, and the unfortunate little mite looked just like her father.

— illustration by Bob Giuliani

She stood at the window for a moment, looking out at the Reach, and Bill was there as she had suspected he might be, standing about halfway between the island and the Head, standing on the Reach just like Jesus-out-of-the-boat, beckoning to her, seeming to tell her by gesture that the time was late if she ever intended to step a foot on the mainland in this life.

"If it's what you want, Bill," she fretted in the silence. "God knows I don't."

But the wind spoke other words. She did want to. She wanted to have this adventure. It had been a painful winter for her — the arthritis which came and went irregularly was back with a vengeance, flaring the joints of her fingers and knees with red fire and blue ice. One of her eyes had gotten dim and blurry (and just the other day Sarah had mentioned — with some unease — that the firespot that had been there since Stella was 60 or so now seemed to be growing by leaps and bounds). Worst of all, the deep, gripping pain in her stomach had returned, and two mornings before she had gotten up at five o'clock, worked her way along the exquisitely cold floor into the bathroom, and had spat a great wad of bright red blood into the toilet bowl. This morning there had been some more of it, foul-tasting stuff, coppery and shuddersome.

The stomach pain had come and gone over the last five years, sometimes better, sometimes worse, and she had known almost from the beginning that it must be cancer. It had taken her mother and father and her mother's father as well. None of them had lived past 70 and so she supposed she had beat the tables those insurance fellows kept by a carpenter's yard.

"You eat like a horse," Alden told her, grinning, not long after the pains had begun and she had first observed the blood in her morning stool. "Don't you know that old fogies like you are supposed to be peckish?"

"Get on or I'll swat ye!" Stella had answered, raising a hand to her gray-haired son, who ducked, mock-cringed, and cried: "Don't Ma! I take it back!"

Yes, she had eaten hearty, not because she wanted to, but because she believed (as many of her generation did), that if you fed the cancer it would leave you alone. And perhaps it worked, at least for

a while; the blood in her stools came and went, and there were long periods when it wasn't there at all. Alden got used to her taking second helpings (and thirds, when the pain was particularly bad), but she never gained a pound.

Now it seemed the cancer had finally gotten around to what the froggies called the pièce de résistance.

She started out the door and saw Alden's hat, the one with the fur-lined ear flaps, hanging on one of the pegs in the entry. She put it on — the bill came all the way down to her shaggy salt-and-pepper eyebrows — and then looked around one last time to see if she had forgotten anything. The stove was low, and Alden had left the draw open too much again — she told him and told him, but that was one thing he was just never going to get straight.

"Alden, you'll burn an extra quarter-cord a winter when I'm gone," she muttered, and opened the stove. She looked in and a tight, dismayed gasp escaped her. She slammed the door shut and adjusted the draw with trembling fingers. For a moment — just a moment — she had seen her old friend Annabelle Frane in the coals. It was her face to the life, even down to the mole on her cheek.

And had Annabelle winked at her?

She thought of leaving Alden a note to explain where she had gone, but she thought perhaps Alden would understand, in his own slow way.

Still writing notes in her head — *Since the first day of winter I have been seeing your father and he says dying isn't so bad; at least I think that's it* — Stella stepped out into the white day.

The wind shook her, and she had to reset Alden's cap on her head before the wind could steal it for a joke and cartwheel it away. The cold seemed to find every chink in her clothing and twist into her; damp March cold with wet snow on its mind.

She set off down the hill toward the cove, being careful to walk on the cinders and clinkers that George Dinsmore had spread. Once George had gotten a job driving plow for the town of Raccoon Head, but during the big blow of '77 he had gotten smashed on Thunderbird and had driven the plow smack through not one, not two, but three power poles. There had been no lights over on the

Head for five days. Stella remembered now how strange it had been, looking across the Reach and seeing only blackness. A body got used to seeing that brave little nestle of lights. Now George worked on the island, and since there was no plow, he didn't get into much hurt.

As she passed Russell Bowie's house, she saw Missy, pale as milk, looking out at her. Stella waved. Missy waved back.

She would tell them this: "On the island we always watched out for our own. When Gerd Henreid broke the blood vessel in his chest that time, we had covered-dish suppers one whole summer to pay for his operation in Boston — and Gerd came back alive, thank God. When George Dinsmore ran down those power poles and the Hydro slapped a lien on him, it was seen to that the Hydro had their money and George had enough of a job to keep him in cigarettes and wine ... his father kept him fed, at least. Now Missy Bowie's alone with another baby. Maybe she'll stay here and take her welfare and ADC money here, and most likely it won't be enough, but she'll get the help she needs. Probably she'll go, but if she stays she'll not starve ... and listen, Lona and Hal, if she stays, she may be able to keep something of this small world with the small Reach on one side and the big Reach on the other, something it would be too easy to lose hustling hash in Lewiston or donuts in Portland or drinks at the Nashville North in Bangor. And I am old enough not to beat around the bush about what that something might be: a way of being and a way of living; a feeling."

They had watched out for their own in other ways as well, but she would not tell them that. The children would not understand, nor would Lois and David, although Jane had known the truth. There was Norman and Ettie Wilson's baby that was born a mongoloid, its poor dear little feet turned in, its bald skull lumpy and cratered, its fingers webbed together as if it had dreamed too long and too deep while swimming that interior Reach; Reverend McCracken had come and baptized the baby, and a day later Mary Dodge came, who even at that time had midwived over a hundred babies, and Norman took Ettie down the hill to see Frank Childs' new boat and although she could barely walk, Ettie went with him, although she had stopped in the door to look back at Mary Dodge, who was sitting calmly by the idiot baby's crib and

knitting. Mary had looked up at her and when their eyes met, Ettie burst into tears. "Come on," Norman had said, upset. "Come on, Ettie, come on." And when they came back an hour later the baby was dead, one of those crib-deaths, wasn't it merciful he didn't suffer. And many years before that, before the war, during the Depression, three little girls had been molested coming home from school, not badly molested, at least not where you could see the scar of the hurt, and they all told about a man who offered to show them a deck of cards he had with a different kind of dog on each one of the 52. He would show them this wonderful deck of cards, the man said, if the little girls would come into the bushes with him, and once in the bushes this man said, "but you have to touch this first." One of the little girls was Gert Symes, who would go on to be voted Maine's Teacher of the Year in 1978, for her work at Brunswick High. And Gert, then only five years old, told her father that the man had some fingers gone on one hand. One of the other little girls agreed that this was so. The third remembered nothing. Stella remembered Alden going out one thundery day that summer without telling her where he was going, although she asked. Watching from the window, she had seen Alden meet Bull Symes at the bottom of the path, and then Freddy Dinsmore had joined them and down at the cove she saw her own husband, whom she had sent out that morning just as usual, with his dinner pail under his arm. More men joined them, and when they finally moved off she counted just one under a dozen. The Reverend McCracken's predecessor had been among them. And that evening a fellow named Daniels was found at the foot of Slyder's Point, where the rocks poke out of the surf like the fangs of a dragon that drowned with its mouth open. This Daniels was a fellow that Big George Havelock had hired to help him put new sills under his house and a new engine in his Model A truck. From New Hampshire he was, and he was a sweet talker who had found other odd jobs to do when the work at the Havelocks' was done ... and in church, he could carry a tune! Apparently, they said, Daniels had been walking up on top of Slyder's Point and had slipped, tumbling all the way to the bottom. His neck was broken and his head was bashed in. As he had no people that anyone knew of, he was buried on the island, and the Reverend McCracken's predecessor gave the graveyard eulogy, saying as how this

Daniels had been a hard worker and a good help even though he was two fingers shy on his right hand. Then he read the benediction and the graveside group had gone back to the town hall basement where they drank Za-Rex punch and ate cream-cheese sandwiches, and Stella never asked her men where they had gone on the day Daniels fell from the top of Slyder's Point.

"Children," she would tell them, "we always watched out for our own. We had to, for the Reach was wider in those days and when the wind roared and the surf pounded and the dark came early, why, we felt very small, only dust motes in the mind of God. So it was natural for us to join hands, one with the other.

"We joined hands, children, and if there were times when we looked too long at the summer's flowers, it was only because we had heard the wind and the waters on long winter nights, and we were afraid.

"No, I've never felt I needed to leave the island. My life was here. The Reach was wider in those days."

Stella reached the cove. She looked right and left, the wind blowing her dress out behind her like a flag. If anyone had been there she would have walked farther down and taken her chance on the tumbled rocks, although they were glazed with ice. But no one was there and she walked out along the pier, past the old Symes boathouse. She reached the end and stood there for a moment, head held up, the wind blowing past the padded flaps of Alden's hat in a muffled flood.

Bill was out there, beckoning. Beyond him, beyond the Reach, she could see the Congo Church over there on the Head, its spire almost invisible against the white sky.

Grunting, she sat down on the end of the pier and then stepped onto the snow crust below. Her boots sank a little; not much. She set Alden's cap again — how the wind wanted to tear it off! — and began to walk toward Bill. She thought once that she would look back, but she did not. She didn't believe her heart could stand that.

She walked, her boots crunching into the crust, and listened to the faint thud and give of the ice. There was Bill, farther back now but still beckoning. She coughed, spat blood onto the white snow that covered the ice. Now the Reach spread wide on either side and she could, for the first time in her life, read the

**There was Bill, farther back but still beckoning. She coughed,
spat blood onto the white snow that covered the ice . . .**

"Stanton's Bait and Boat" sign over there without Alden's binoculars. She could see cars passing to and fro on the Head's main street and thought with real wonder: *They can go as far as they want . . . Portland . . . Boston . . . New York City. Imagine!* And she could almost do it, could almost imagine a road that simply rolled on and on, the boundaries of the world knocked wide.

A snowflake skirled past her eyes. Another. A third. Soon it was snowing lightly and she walked through a pleasant world of shifting bright white; she saw Raccoon Head through a gauzy curtain that sometimes almost cleared. She reached up to set Alden's cap again and snow puffed off the bill into her eyes. The wind twisted fresh snow up in dancing, filmy shapes, and in one of them she saw Carl Abersham, who had gone down with Hattie Stoddard's father on the *Dancer* in 1941.

Soon, however, the brightness began to dull as the snow came harder. The Head's main street dimmed, dimmed, and at last was gone. For a time longer she could make out the cross atop the church, and then that faded out too, like a false dream. Last to go was that bright yellow and black sign reading "Stanton's Bait and Boat," where you could also get engine oil, flypaper, Italian sandwiches, and Budweiser to go.

Then Stella walked in a world that was totally without color, a gray-white dream of snow. *Just like Jesus-out-of-the-boat,* she thought, and at last she looked back but now Goat was gone, too. She could see her tracks going back, losing definition until only the faint half-circles of her heels could be seen . . . and then nothing. Nothing at all.

She thought: *It's a white-out. You got to be careful, Stella, or you'll never get to the mainland. You'll just walk around in a big circle until you're worn out and then you'll freeze to death out here.*

She remembered Bill telling her once that when you were lost in the woods, you had to pretend that the leg which was on the same side of your body as your smart hand was lame. Otherwise that smart leg would begin to lead you and you'd walk in a great big circle and not even realize it until you came around to your backtrail again. Stella didn't be-

lieve she could afford to have that happen to her. Snow today, tonight, and tomorrow, the radio had said, and in a white-out such as this, she would not even know if she came around to her backtrail, for the wind and the fresh snow would have erased her tracks.

Her hands were leaving her in spite of the two pairs of gloves she wore, and her feet had been gone for some time. In a way, this was almost a relief. The numbness at least shut the mouth of her clamoring arthritis.

Stella began to limp now, making her left leg work harder. The arthritis in her knees had not gone to sleep, and soon they were screaming at her. Her white hair flew out behind her. Her lips had drawn back from her teeth (she still had her own, all save four) and she looked straight ahead, waiting for that yellow and black sign to materialize out of the flying whiteness.

It did not happen.

Some time later, she noticed that the day's bright whiteness had begun to dull to a more uniform gray. The snow fell heavier and thicker than ever. Her feet were still planted on the crust, but now she was walking through five inches of fresh snow. She looked at her watch, but it had stopped. Stella realized she must have forgotten to wind it that morning for the first time in 20 or 30 years. Or had it just stopped for good? It had been her mother's, and she had sent it with Alden twice to the Head, where Mr. Dostie had first marveled over it, and then cleaned it. Her watch, at least, had been over to the mainland.

She fell down for the first time some 15 minutes after she began to notice the day's growing grayness. For a moment she remained on her hands and knees, thinking it would be so easy just to stay here, to curl up and listen to the wind, and then the determination that had brought her through so much reasserted itself and she got up, grimacing. She stood in the snow, looking straight ahead, willing her eyes to see . . . but they saw nothing.

Be dark soon.

Well, she had gone wrong. She had slipped off to one side or the other. Otherwise she would have reached the mainland by now. Yet she didn't believe she

had gone so far wrong that she was walking parallel to the mainland or even back in the direction of Goat. An interior navigator in her head whispered that she had overcompensated and slipped off to the left. She believed she was still approaching the mainland but was now on a costly diagonal.

That navigator wanted her to turn right, but she would not do that. Instead, she moved straight on again, but stopped the artificial limp. A spasm of coughing shook her, and she spat bright red onto the snow.

Ten minutes later (the gray was now deep indeed, and she found herself in the weird twilight of a heavy snowstorm) she fell again, tried to get up, failed, tried again, failed, and finally managed to gain her feet. She stood swaying in the snow, barely able to remain upright in the wind, waves of faintness rushing through her head, making her feel alternately heavy and light.

Perhaps not all the roaring she heard in her ears was the wind, but it surely was the wind that finally succeeded in prying Alden's hat from her head. She made a grab for it, but the wind danced it easily out of her reach and she saw it only for a moment, flipping gaily over and over into the darkening gray, a bright spot of orange. It struck the snow, rolled, rose again, was gone. Now her hair flew around her head freely.

"It's all right, Stella," Bill said. "You can wear mine."

She gasped and looked around in the white. Her gloved hands had gone instinctively to her bosom, and she felt nails of fear scratch her heart.

She saw nothing but shifting membranes of snow — and then, moving out of that evening's gray throat, the wind screaming through it like the voice of a devil in a snowy tunnel, came her husband. He was at first only moving colors in the snow: red, black, dark green, lighter green; then these colors resolved themselves into a flannel jacket with a flapping collar, flannel pants, and green boots. He was holding his hat out to her in a gesture that appeared almost absurdly courtly, and his face was Bill's face, unmarked by the cancer that had taken him (had that been all she was afraid of? that a wasted shadow of her

268

husband would come to her, a scrawny concentration-camp figure with skin pulled taut and shiny over the cheekbones and eyes sunk deep into the sockets?), and she felt a surge of relief and love.

"Bill? Is that you?"

"Course."

"Bill," she said again, and took a glad step toward him. Her legs betrayed her and she thought she would fall, fall right through him — he was, after all, a ghost — but he caught her in arms as strong and as competent as those that had carried her over the threshold of the house that she had shared only with Alden in these latter years. He supported her, and a moment later she felt the cap pulled firmly onto her head.

"Is it you?" she asked again, looking up into his face, at the crow's feet around his eyes which hadn't sunk deep yet, at the spill of snow on the shoulders of his checked hunting jacket, at his lively brown hair.

"It's me," he said. "It's all of us."

He half-turned with her and she saw the others coming out of the snow that the wind drove across the Reach in the gathering darkness. A cry, half joy, half fear, came from her mouth as she saw Madeline Stoddard, Hattie's mother, in a blue dress that swung in the wind like a bell, and holding her hand was Hattie's dad, not a mouldering skeleton somewhere on the bottom with the *Dancer*, but whole and young. And there, behind those two —

"Annabelle!" she cried. "Annabelle Frane, is it you?"

It *was* Annabelle; even in this snowy gloom Stella recognized the yellow dress Annabelle had worn to Stella's own wedding, and as she struggled toward her dead friend, holding Bill's arm, she thought that she could smell roses.

"Annabelle!"

"We're almost there now, dear," Annabelle said, taking her other arm. The yellow dress, which had been considered Daring in its day (but, to Annabelle's credit and to everyone else's relief, not quite a Scandal), left her shoulders bare, but Annabelle did not seem to feel the cold. Her hair, a soft, dark auburn, blew long in the wind. "Only a little further."

She took Stella's other arm and they moved forward again. Other figures came out of the snowy night (for it was night now). Stella recognized many of them, but not all. Tommy Frane had joined Annabelle; Big George Havelock, who had died a dog's death in the woods,

walked behind Bill; there was the fellow who had kept the lighthouse on the Head for most of 20 years and who used to come over to the island during the cribbage tournament Freddy Dinsmore held every February — Stella could almost but not quite remember his name. And there was Freddy himself! Walking off to one side of Freddy, by himself and looking bewildered, was Russell Bowie.

"Look, Stella," Bill said, and she saw black rising out of the gloom like the splintered prows of many ships. It was not ships; it was split and fissured rock. They had reached the Head. They had crossed the Reach.

She heard voices, but was not sure they actually spoke:

Take my hand, Stella —
*Take my hand, Bill —
Annabelle . . . Freddy . . . Russell
. . . John . . . Ettie . . . Frank . . . take my
hand, take my hand . . . my hand. . . .*

Will you take my hand, Stella?" a new voice asked her.
She looked around and there was Bull Symes. He was smiling kindly at her, and yet she felt a kind of terror rise in her at what was in his eyes and for a moment she drew away, clutching Bill's hand on her other side all the tighter.

"Is it — "

"Time?" Bull asked. "Oh, ayuh, Stella, I guess so. But it don't hurt. At least, I never heard so. All that's before."

She burst into tears suddenly — all the tears she had never wept — and put her hand in Bull's hand.

They stood in a circle in the storm, the dead of Goat Island, and the wind screamed around them, driving its packet of snow, and some kind of song burst from her. It went up into the wind and the wind carried it away. They all sang then, as children will sing in their high, sweet voices as a summer evening draws down to summer night. They sang, and Stella herself going to them and with them, finally across the Reach. There was a bit of pain, but not much; losing her maidenhead had been worse. They stood in a circle in the night. The snow blew around them and they sang. They sang, and —

— and Alden could not tell David and Lois, but in the summer after Stella died, when the children came out for their annual two weeks, he told Lona and Hal. He told them that during the great storms of winter the wind seemed to sing with

almost human voices, and that sometimes it seemed to him he could almost make out the words: "Praise God from whom all blessings flow/Praise him, ye creatures here below. . . ."

But he did not tell them (imagine slow, unimaginative Alden Flanders saying such things aloud, even to the children!) that sometimes he would hear that sound and feel cold even by the stove; that he would put his whittling aside, or the trap he had meant to mend, thinking that the wind sang in all the voices of those who were dead and gone . . . that they stood somewhere out on the Reach and sang as children do. He seemed to hear their voices and on these nights he sometimes slept and dreamed that he was singing the doxology, unseen and unheard, at his own funeral.

There are things that can never be told, and there are things, not exactly secret, that are not discussed. They had found Stella frozen to death on the mainland a day after the storm had blown itself out. She was sitting on a natural chair of rock about a hundred yards south of the Raccoon Head town limits, frozen just as neat as you please. The doctor who owned the Corvette said that he was frankly amazed. It would have been a walk of over four miles, and the autopsy required by law in the case of an unattended, unusual death had shown an advanced cancerous condition — in truth, the old woman had been riddled with it.

Was he to tell David and Lois that the cap on her head had not been his? Larry McKeen had recognized that cap. So had John Bensohn. He had seen it in their eyes, and he supposed they had seen it in his. He had not lived long enough to forget his dead father's cap, or the look of its bill, or the places where the visor had been broken.

"These are things made for thinking on slowly," he would have told the children if he had known how. "Things to be thought on at length, while the hands do their work and the coffee sits in a solid china mug nearby. They are questions of Reach, maybe: do the dead sing?"

On the nights after Lona and Hal had gone back with their parents to the mainland in Al Curry's boat, the children standing astern and waving good-bye, Alden considered that question, and others, and the matter of his father's cap.

Do the dead sing?

On those long nights alone, with his mother Stella Flanders at long last in her grave, it seemed to Alden that they did.

The Man Who'd Sooner Lamps

BY EDIE CLARK
photography by Ozzie Sweet

Forty-six years ago, at the age of 16, Herb Young bought a night lamp for a quarter and, without knowing it, started his collection of oil lamps that today numbers 377 — possibly the largest, most complete collection on the East Coast.

A stocky, gravelly voiced Yankee, Herb Young lives at the edge of one of New Hampshire's clear, cold lakes in a house that he built as a summer camp when he came home from World War II. As years went by, he added to it, insulated and tightened it up, and he now lives there year-round. It is just the right size for him and his collection, which includes angle lamps and double angle lamps; skating lanterns; float lamps; a lamp with a cast-iron font; lamps with carved, tin-lined wooden fonts; night lamps and miniature lamps; hanging lamps and station lanterns; a lamp with a chimney designed to heat hair curlers; a lamp that can be used as a vaporizer; peg lamps; camphine lamps; a piano lamp signed by Handel; a "Gone with the Wind" lamp that was a wedding present to his grandparents; lamps with fonts made of carnival glass and of Sandwich glass; lamps with glass fonts blown into patterns of beads and fans and flutes and tweeds; maps in patterns known as eyewinker, icicle, fishscale, eyebrow, and feather duster.

All these plus many, many more are displayed on the walls of the bedrooms, the living room, and the porch; on tables; on shelves in the kitchen; in a cabinet in the bathroom; even on the slate path to the driveway. All of them are complete and clean and in the evening some are lit. "If I can't display them and enjoy them, there's no use in having them," Herb says. The drawers in the bureaus are filled with miscellaneous burners, extra wicks, and varieties of chimneys in every size. "I'd been collecting all those years, kind of on the side. But when my wife died seven years ago, my interest really picked up. It gave me something to do. Right now, if I had a wife, I wouldn't have space for my lamps."

Herb has been an electrician all his working life and he has changed over many of the homes in his area from kerosene to electricity. In his work he is often in the cellars and attics of homeowners and has sometimes bargained for a lamp that caught his eye through the dust and cobwebs.

Although much older, this wedding gift to Herb's parents is often called a "Gone with the Wind" lamp, because it resembles props used in the movie.

Oil lamps were all there were when he was growing up in Wilton, Maine, back when kerosene was 9¢ a gallon. When he bought that first night lamp, a brass wall-mounted "glow" lamp that burns a wick no bigger than a shoestring and today hangs by itself on the wall of his bedroom, he says he bought it because he liked it. Even today, that personal appeal is the criterion he uses more than any other for buying a lamp to add to his collection. It is the reason why he does not collect the primitive and compara-

tively drab-looking rush lamps and Betty lamps, nor the popular Aladdins.

What sets Herb Young off from other collectors is that he is not a man of means. He does not peruse the catalogs of Sotheby Park Bernet and he has never bought out anyone else's collection, a common way for a collector to increase his inventory. And, in a field where the price of a single rare lamp can reach as high as $1000, possibly more, the most he has ever paid for a lamp is $275. Many of his lamps are worth multiples of that. His collection is a result of knowing what to look for, persistence, a lot of time spent scouting, and hours spent at auctions where only one or two lamps might be put up for bid.

Herb used to have the field pretty much to himself. Though a huge percentage of the world's population still lives by kerosene lamplight, the kerosene era in the United States spanned only about 60 years (depending on the area of the country), from 1860 to 1920, with new designs falling off sharply after 1900. Most people, when they converted their homes to electricity, either stuck the lamps in the basement or attic, where they often were broken, or else threw them out altogether. This is why, in so many cases, matching bases and shades are hard to find, and why there is a scarcity of old chimneys, which can be distinguished from new ones by their thickness and the smoothness of the rims. Some say that if it weren't for the occasional fallibility of electricity, there wouldn't be any lamps left at all.

Popular interest in collecting lamps has come up only recently, along with the energy crisis in the early 1970s. Novice collectors discovered an enormous variety in lamps, both in style and in function. Artistically, glassblowers had competed for unusual designs, of which there are thousands. Functionally, tinkerers had come up with a seemingly endless variety of burners, all designed to create

Lamp collectors refer to these as "three-paneled two-panel lamps." They were made in the late 19th century in colors to match glassware goblets in table settings.

"I'm more interested in the history of the lamps than I am in their value. At night I don't watch TV. I read up on lamps."

a brighter flame through different draft assemblies. At the turn of the century, the search for a brighter flame could only be compared with our current compulsion to increase miles per gallon. Burners seemed to come in every imaginable design, and there were so many patents pending at that time that it must have seemed that there was a man with an idea for a better burner in every village. Some burners had many perforations around the base, some had only a measured few; some had unusual thumbscrews or different ways to make the wick go up and down; some had two wicks or a wick that went in a circle or a wick that was round like a rope; some opened out like a jaw so the wick could be trimmed without removing the chimney. Nearly all had a variation on the prongs that hold the chimney. There was also wide variation in chimneys, all produced in efforts to create a better draft and achieve a brighter, smokeless flame. Some were thin and tapered like wine bottles, others were squat and bulbous. Many were made with fancy inscriptions, ornate designs, and beaded tops. If old burners are hard to find, those old chimneys are next to impossible. There are several antiques dealers around New England who specialize in antique oil lamps, but most of them emphasize that lamp parts aren't something worth parting with: a burner that could bring them only $5 might be the missing link to complete a lamp worth $100. They advise the collector to look at flea markets, shows, and especially in shops that *do not* specialize in oil lamps, where chances are better for finding parts.

That's what Herb Young does. Weekends and days when business is slow, Herb visits flea markets, antiques shops and shows, yard sales, and auctions. In the summer he packs his Model A (which is his service truck: he has put 23,000 miles on it over the past two years) and takes off for two or three days, traveling in a roundabout way up to Bangor, Maine, looking for lamps, lamp parts, and lamp literature. He takes this trip three or four times in a summer and considers it his vacation.

Though his collection was recently assessed by an antiques expert as being extraordinary because it has examples of so many different types of lamps, Herb's

selection is personal and principled. He is something of a purist in that he will not electrify a lamp if he thinks it will ruin it; he does not like to see brass polished to a bright gold or wooden fonts refinished. And "make-do" lamps, which have been reassembled incorrectly, Herb regards as an insult.

Herb knows almost instinctively when a lamp base and the font are mismatched or when the shade is off-color, partly because he grew up around lamps. But he also has a collection of catalogues and advertising brochures that tell him, through pictures and text, exactly what part goes with what lamp. These are as valuable to him as his lamps, and he's always on the lookout for others. "I'm more interested in the history of the lamps than I am in their value. At night I don't watch TV. I read up on lamps."

A typical lamp consists of seven different parts: base, stem, font, collar, burner, wick, and chimney. It can sometimes take several years to find all the right parts to a single lamp — and some of that time is spent just finding out what those parts are. Over the years Herb has stored up a large assortment of old parts essential to his collection and increasingly hard to find. "If you could go out the first day and find everything new," he points out, "there wouldn't be any fun to it. You've got to have a goal." Herb has a lamp base of patterned glass that's missing a shade. "I've had this base for several years and I know the shade I need to match it. I haven't found it yet." Another item he puts on his shopping list is a match holder made of milk glass, an accessory to the lamp that hangs over his dining-room table. He's been looking for that for 10 years.

One Sunday last winter I went along with Herb to an antiques show in Concord, New Hampshire. He had heard that a certain lamp would be there, one that he wanted in his collection. "It's got a special kind of draft setup, with holes in the stem and a kind of funnel that goes up through and feeds directly into the burner. Supposed to make a brighter flame," he told me on the way. I asked him if he'd pay any price for it and he said, no, he never will. "I believe that in time, whatever lamp it is, I'll have it at the right price. If I don't, I wasn't supposed to have it. Besides, I've got the

Yankee in me: I'm quite apt to dicker."

In fact, Herb always dickers. Often his friend, Stanley Bennett, goes with him to the shows and they operate as a team, fanning out as soon as they get there, making a quick assessment of which lamps, if any, might interest Herb, and which ones are worth bargaining for. Stanley is not a collector but, from being

Herb Young adjusts the flame on one of his 377 oil lamps on display throughout his house. He polishes and lights one or two of them every evening.

with Herb, he knows how to spot something that Herb might like.

Herb's source has told him that the lamp will be on a table up near the stage,

CONNECTICUT'S KEROSENE LAMP MUSEUM

☞ Overlooking the "green" in Winchester Center, a small village in northwestern Connecticut, is the Winchester Center Kerosene Lamp Museum, which opened in the fall of 1981. The museum has 500 kerosene lamps dating from 1856, when kerosene first came into use in this country, until 1880. The brainchild of George Sherwood, a retired aeronautical engineer, the museum has its collection displayed on the first floor of a former country store. Hundreds of lamps and lamp parts hang from the ceiling and walls, while other items are shown on tables and in glass display cases. Mr. Sherwood hopes eventually to restore the entire building to recreate a home of the late 1800s, complete with period furniture and kerosene lamps.

The lamps in the museum's collection have been acquired by Mr. Sherwood over the past 25 years at tag sales and auctions around the country. Many are from Connecticut, which at one time had a flourishing kerosene lamp industry with companies in Thomaston, Bridgeport, Meriden, and Waterbury. The Winchester Center Kerosene Lamp Museum is situated on the Old Waterbury Turnpike (Route 263), only four miles from Winsted, and is open daily. There is no admission charge, and George Sherwood will prove a most amiable guide as he demonstrates the beautiful lamps in his collection.

Leonard A. Schonberg

and that's where he heads as soon as we arrive at eight o'clock sharp. At the table, from a relatively large assortment of hand lamps and pedestal lamps, Herb delicately picks up the lamp with the unusual draft assembly. It is marked $90 and looks to be in excellent condition. Holding the chimney in place, he upturns it and inspects the bottom. Perfora-

tions in the stem reveal a bit of tampering: one of the holes has been enlarged ever so slightly, just enough for an electric cord to run through. Though disappointed, Herb still walks away from the table and says to me in a conspiratorial tone, "I like it. I'm going to own that lamp." He first sends Stanley in to offer the dealer $70, but she shakes her head

One of the signs he looks for . . . is wear marks on the bottom.

disinterestedly. It is still very early in the show. Shortly Herb returns, offering the woman, who appears to know who he is, $80. She accepts and puts the lamp aside for him until he's done with his picking.

Among the displays of quilts, early American toys, glassware, and tinware, there is a good selection of lamps for Herb to inspect. He stops at a table spread with early glassware and picks up the font to a hand lamp that looks convincingly old to me. He turns it over and mutters "reproduction," puts it down, and moves along. One of the signs he looks for, especially in a hand lamp, is wear marks on the bottom, the kind of wear common on old milk bottles and returnable Coke bottles. Herb remarks that some dealers, eager to hike up the price of a repro, will sometimes rub the base with sand. "But it never looks the same — it just comes out looking like a lot of scratches."

By 10:15 he's scoured the four huge rooms of the show, the tables of some 230 dealers, and stopped to chat with some who apparently know him and his collection. By noon he's back home, finding a spot on the crowded shelves for the newcomer.

Herb Young is a modest man. If asked about his collection, he might say, "I don't claim to have a very good collection, but, well, I've got a couple." If pushed, though, he'll confess that lamps are his obsession. "I don't drink. I don't smoke. I don't really have much to spend my money on," Herb says in defense of his habit. "Right now, I am in need of a new hearing aid. But I'd much rather have a new lamp."

Catherine M.V. Thuro is considered the authority on oil lamps. Her book, Oil Lamps: The Kerosene Era in North America, *is available from Wallace-Homestead Book Company, 1912 Grand, Des Moines, IA 50305. Few collectors, including Herb Young, would go picking without it: it includes a periodically updated price guide.*

Above: *All of these lamps once burned camphine (a mixture of turpentine and alcohol) except the lamp second from left, a peg lamp that burned whale oil and nested in a candleholder.*

Left: *Two miniature lamps adorn a bureau. The one on the left is known as a Nellie Bly. The lamp on the right has a diamond puffed pattern.*

*Over the years, we've learned one ought to be a bit more
cautious about accepting too quickly articles submitted for November publication.
For some reason — maybe because it's sandwiched between Halloween
and the often-dreaded "holiday season" — it seems to be a time for spooks, and spoofs.
Here are two of the latter, remembered by many, that got by us.*

A Useful
Home Guide to Firewood

BY FRANK HEATH

We'll skip the comparisons of a gallon of oil vs. a scuttle of coal vs. three bulbs of electricity vs. seven days of July sunshine. Those puzzles can only be solved by 11-year-old mathematics whizzes or 45-year-old engineers who have homes with electric heat. If you bought a woodstove because it seemed like a good idea, then you're ready to think wood.

A BTU, by the way, is something the British invented, and they are not known for being warm and cozy. If they were concerned about heat, they'd have moved to Bermuda while they had the chance. One reason the British drink so much tea is to keep their hands warm. Fortunately, that practice works well in this country, too.

A BTUH, should you fall across one before you realize what you're reading, is just the sound an old-timer makes when he spits tobacco juice at the potbelly stove. A BTUH can't be British because they didn't have potbelly stoves. They didn't even have Franklin stoves until after Ben Franklin invented them.

But about that wood: over the past couple of years there have been more articles and guides and pamphlets and leaflets and books listing the advantages and drawbacks of each kind of firewood than there are leaves on a hop hornbeam. Or hackmatack, for that matter.

But not one of these helpful aids means a thing if you can't tell maple from birch from ash from a hole in the ground. And many people can't. For lots of people, there are grass, bushes, and trees. Grass is short, bushes are middle size, and trees are big.

One solution is to take a forestry course. You'd learn the significance of a running cord vs. a rick cord vs. a face cord vs. a dump-truck load vs. a pickup full vs. all you can pack in your trunk vs.

– illustration by Tom Payne

a tied-up bundle of pine stick kindling from North Carolina. You'd learn that in the forestry course — not here.

Another solution involves gathering all the articles, guides, pamphlets, leaflets, and books and burning them; BTU-wise, you'd do all right, and help with the litter problem, too.

All the wood heat literature emphasizes that dry wood burns better than wet wood. It's the sort of thing you might have thought of yourself. Firewood wants to be dry on the inside as well as the outside. If it's still wet inside — green — you'll have to boil it before you can burn it. Boiling or steaming wood isn't what you're after. You won't get enough of those BTUs and it makes the stove hiss, which a stove shouldn't do. Who wants to sit around of a winter evening and listen to the stove hiss? Disheartening, somehow.

So that leaves you with two choices: either (1) get some green wood — the

hard kind — and put it under cover where it can dry out for a year or so — your garage is nice if you don't mind leaving your car out; or (2) burn wood that is already good and dry, wood that you already have, wood that you can identify without special training.

For instance, rocking chairs. Any rocking chair that creaks is prime firewood. That creak means dry. It also means it will probably fall apart anyway, so you might as well get it first. And here's a bonus, a chance to practice some one-upmanship. Any fool knows the difference between a Boston rocker, a carved oak rocker, and a cane bottom rocker. So when the boys at the general store get to talking about oak vs. maple vs. hickory, you can chime in that you burn only rockers. And if you mention that last year you went through two rick of rockers, that should slow them down considerably.

So here's the first truly useful guide to

276

firewood ever published. There's something here for everyone. You need only look around you.

Louis Quatorze furniture — wonderful stuff for the stove. Old enough to be very dry, big, heavy, with good burning woods. Sometimes pieces of marble will be left over. Heat them up and take them to bed with you. Waste not, want not (B. Franklin).

Louis Quinze — still good and dry, but not quite as much wood, and you'll have pieces of metal and porcelain to get rid of. (See above.) Still, if you've got it, you can burn it. Not the upholstered parts, though. Probably smell bad, and shredded it makes good garden mulch.

Louis Seize — light and maneuverable — the sort of thing your wife can use if you're still down at the general store.

Queen Anne — very high rating. About the only remaining dependable source of good walnut firewood.

Chippendale — relatively easy to come by and good stovewood, though it stands to reason a highboy is preferable to the chairs. Still, if it's a long winter, you'll get it all. A couple of Chippendale chairs have been known to warm a cool April evening in satisfactory fashion.

Hepplewhite — not recommended. You'll find yourself running to the stove all night. Hepplewhite chairs look all right, but there just isn't that much wood in them. You'll go through a set of six before midnight. Again, a chest will last a little longer.

Sheraton — doesn't seem too good for potbellies, but works admirably in the box stoves.

Golden Oak — very popular right now, and as good a source of heat as you'll find.

Bentwood — remember that someone else already boiled this stuff to bend it. For you, it'll burn.

TV and stereo consoles — with rare exception this is fake wood. Still there's enjoyment in watching anything connected with TV go up in flames, so throw it in. Take the tubes and metal out first. They have no pH value later when you throw the ashes on the garden.

Card tables — not a good deal. Card tables are usually cardboard. Strictly penny ante stuff that can euchre you out of a bundle of BTUs.

Toothpicks — be real careful here. Though they are handy, a lot are made from white birch. (They take the bark off so you can't tell.) White birch gives little heat, and at 19¢ a box, it could ruin you. Still, they burn readily and are pre-cut.

Matches — another special case. Matches share many of the attributes of toothpicks, but the EPA might object to all that sulfur in the air. Also, a friend in New York reports he wore out the right pant leg of both his new and old suits striking the matches as he threw them in the fire. It's something to think about.

Shutters — depends whether it's a shutter that shuts. If it shuts, it could help you keep what heat you get. If it bangs, burn it.

Love seats — quite a debate here whether a love seat produces more heat in the stove or in the parlor. Don't confuse the love seat with the back seat. The back seat produces more heat, hands down. If necessary.

Lincoln Logs and Tinkertoys — real fine stovewood, easy to handle, nearly everyone has some. Experience shows, though, they burn best late at night after the kids' bedtime.

Clothes poles — probably maple and obviously dry. Go ahead.

Bamboo porch and window shades — real fine. Nothing more suitable — you'll need the shades only in the summer, and you use the stove only in the winter. A hand-in-glove arrangement.

Pianos — still another special case. Pianos contain a great deal of champion firewood. Many people will hesitate, but if you can't find middle C and haven't had it tuned for more than five years, well . . . that iron harp in there makes a wonderful doorstop, and the piano wire is great for making hard-boiled egg slicers, or for building a suspension bridge to the outhouse.

Banisters and spindles — they burn well, but do it only as a last step.

Following this guide by itself should get you to spring. Add to it yourself and you're good for a couple of years.

Another advantage is that this method frees you of axes and old saws. But one old saw still applies: Firewood warms a person twice — once when you carry it in from the living room, or bedroom, or parlor, and again when you burn it.

A Test to Determine
Your Dog's Personality

BY JAMES T. PENDERGRAST

At one time or another every dog does something that makes you wonder just what goes on in his or her canine brain. Not an easy question. The following quiz may help you begin to understand your pet better.

THE TEST
(*To be completed by your dog within a 24-hour time limit.*)

1. You have been inside all day. You have done everything you could possibly do, twice, taken a ridiculous number of naps, chewed everything you can chew without endangering your position as man's best friend, and you "had to go" two hours ago. Your master finally comes home, gets out the leash and takes you, bladder bursting, out for a walk. You would (lick, scratch, or otherwise mark just one):

☐ A) Throw caution, and possible outdoor playtime, to the winds and relieve yourself at the first opportunity.

☐ B) Do some minor exploring, until you can tell from your master's voice that he's becoming impatient.

☐ C) Go for the record, see how long you can hold out, and how much more territory you can cover, aiming for a quarter block farther each day.

2. Your master has some people over for a visit, and you want to do the most perfectly natural thing, which is to smell their crotches. How do you proceed?

(continued)

277

– illustration by Tom Payne

5. You have never had sex in your life, and the way things are going, it doesn't look too likely that you ever will (being a pet is sort of like being a monk). Your master has taken you to the park and removed your leash, and you have wandered behind a little group of bushes, where all of a sudden you see the most gorgeous creature you have ever laid eyes on. All of the proper overtures have been made and you are ready for your own *Summer of '42,* when you hear your master calling you.

☐ A) Trusting that your master knows best, you drop the idea and go around the bushes, wagging your tail, thankful for three squares a day and your Snoopy water dish.

☐ B) Figuring this may be your only chance, you go ahead with the plan, hoping not to be discovered until it is too late, and also hoping your partner is not a "moaner."

☐ C) This is the last straw. You decide to run away from home, encouraged by the other dog (who will always run with you until *its* master calls). The two of you take off, ready for a life on the road, leaving your master standing there, hollering the silly name he gave you and waving your leash.

☐ A) Wait a while, act cool, as if smelling their crotches was the last thing on your mind, and hope to ingratiate yourself to the point that you will later have lots of leisurely sniffing time.

☐ B) Bounce around the room when they come in, feigning excitement, and take quick little whiffs as you "accidentally" get near the desired area.

☐ C) Go right for the crotch the minute they walk in the room and risk getting yelled at.

3. You have invited a few friends over to play and one of them has an "accident." What do you do?

☐ A) Knowing you're going to have to take the rap anyway, you wait patiently for your master's return and the inevitable whacking you will receive with that stupid newspaper. You look appropriately sorry, even though you know that "since you've already relieved yourself," you won't get to go out for a few hours.

☐ B) You know what's coming, but you hope beyond hope that you will be able to convince your master that you are not at fault, and try to figure out the best combination of tail wags, body shakes, and whining that will prove your point.

☐ C) Anyone would know, even a *cat,*

that it isn't your mess, but you're sure that, in spite of the obviousness of the point, your master will miss it, and you will be punished. You lie down in your favorite spot and try to think of the best object you can chew up in order to even the score.

4. Your master is eating a steak. Suddenly the doorbell rings and your master gets up to answer it, leaving the tender, juicy steak unprotected on the table. You would:

☐ A) Not even think about the steak, and follow your master to the door to see just who could be calling at this hour.

☐ B) Think about the steak a lot, and even get up on your hind legs to be able to see it better. Before you make up your mind, you hear your master approaching and hurriedly go back to all fours. You have to go over and take a few bites of your stale, dry dog food in order to absorb some of the excess saliva that's collected in your mouth.

☐ C) Wait until your master has disappeared, jump up, grab the steak, and down it. Delicious. Then you jump back in your favorite chair and pretend to be asleep. You don't have the slightest idea what happened.

SCORING

Give your pet one point for each A, two for each B, and three for each C. Now total the score, and check below for results.

5 or less: Your pet is a perfect example of *Canis familiaris,* with the emphasis on the latter. If it is a small dog, it probably barks almost all the time; if a large dog, there is likely to be a place set for it at the table. It is completely domesticated and probably owns a sweater.

6–10: It tries to tread the thin line between its natural instincts and the desires and requirements of you as its master. This never works, of course, and it ends up being frustrated almost all the time.

11–15: Your pet is completely aware of the fact that it is a dog, and that's just the way it likes it. It is determined to get its doggy way. For example, if it is thrown off the bed a thousand times, it will sneak back on it a thousand and one times.

A Word of Warning for Pets Scoring in the 11–15 Category: If you aren't careful, you could wind up on the street eating stale Big Macs from the garbage can and avoiding the dogcatcher.

Writer Lynn Franklin was killed (see "A May Sampler," page 130) while on assignment for Yankee a year and a half after he wrote this article about "living legend" Lester E. Blodgett, Jr., for us. It's the perfect Lynn Franklin article — up in the country he loved and about the sort of remarkable individual he, along with everyone else, truly admired.

The Finest Woodsman of Them All

BY LYNN FRANKLIN

Foremen for the international paper companies, such as Great Northern Nekoosa and Scott and Boise-Cascade and International Paper, say that Lester E. Blodgett, Jr., is the finest woodsman in Maine and in all of New England. There may be challengers to his title, but none so far has earned it, and it's not likely anyone will — not on Lester's terms, anyway, which are those of a purist and a traditionalist in a tough trade fast going mechanical.

For one thing, Lester likes to work alone. Foremen, unless they know as much or more about the woods than Lester knows, tend to rile him. They tend to be company men on salary, earning about half of what Lester earns (about $25,000 a year) on piecework, strictly according to the wood he cuts.

Lester has put out 90 cords of wood in a five-day week. He has put out 92 cords in 40 hours, tree length, and there are many weeks on record in which Lester has produced 40 to 50 cords of four-foot pulp to the stump plus his logs. That's working alone. He is in the woods before 6 A.M., rain or shine, working a 10-hour day in what seems to be effortless slow motion, making every move count.

Lester lives north of Bingham, Maine, at Moscow near Austin Stream where it flows into the Kennebec River. He lives in a newly painted, immaculate five-room house alongside Highway 201, with his wife, Glenda, and their 13-year-old son, Lester III. There are twin red 1000cc Harley-Davidson motorcycles in the garage beside twin, coal-black, gleaming four-wheel-drive pickups, also brand-new. Polished and greased, under cover, are twin snowmobiles waiting for winter to arrive.

His blue eyes express, as do his face and movements, great independence and directness of purpose. He chews winter-green-flavored Beechnut tobacco and he wears black, silicon-tanned lineman's boots and farmer's coveralls over a T-shirt in the summer and a wool shirt in the winter. The veins in his arms stand out, pressed against his skin by hard muscles that flicker up and down his arms as he works. He is deep voiced and when he speaks it is with urgent sincerity, pausing to emphasize the reality of his recollections.

It seemed to me that the logging, dangerous and endless, must have given Lester a kind of strength that something that has come easily does not give. I was to learn that Lester is larger than life, a living legend. And why he could say, "I don't think there's a man living that likes to cut wood as much as I do."

My father was a woodsman," Lester said. "He took me into the woods with a hatchet when I was five. When I got big enough to handle a bucksaw and a horse he separated me from him. We'd go in with a pair of horses and each take one. Father expected me to put out the same amount of wood as he did. And I could. When I was 14 I could match any man in any camp with a bucksaw, and I still can.

"My old man figured 50 cords to a horse a week — every week. Raining? Wear a suit. Deep snow? Dig and throw the wood on a slug. Work at night? We put a lantern on the hames and slung the grain on the other side. We always grained good, and the horses had it easier than we did. We had two teams so they didn't have to work but every other day.

"We had a small farm and raised everything. We milked 10 or 12 cows. We'd get the chores done at night and come in for dinner. Then my father would light the lanterns and we'd go back down in the yard and saw with a bucksaw until 11 o'clock. Once I got distemper and went in behind the stove to lie down. Dad got me up. Sick or not, he said, we work just the same. Dad was a harsh man. That's why, when I got to be 14, I just left. I didn't send a postcard or a letter and I've never been back.

"I had a bucksaw and an axe and what clothes were on my back. I went from farm to farm cutting wood. When it came fall and cold weather I went to an old fellow's in Hinckley, Maine, on the Kennebec. His name was Jim Green. I'd work at the sawmill if we had custom sawing and in the woods jobbing if we didn't. I stayed three years. Then I struck out for the woods camps. I was on my own again.

"I went into camp for a small jobber. It was winter and an awfully cold night. He moved me into camp and went off and left me. Water had come down the stovepipe and the stove was right full of ice. Everything was frozen. The brook was frozen two feet and I had to chop to get a drink of water. I couldn't get the stove going right. I was just a kid. I got pneumonia and I hiked out and got back to Jim Green's and stayed until I got well again. I don't remember what camp I went into after that, but I went from one job to the next and I worked all around the country.

"If there were Canadians in camp, they'd steal my stockings. We'd sleep in shacks and the snow would blow in all over your blankets.

"Finally I got sick of working with Frenchmen because none of them would speak English, so I started working by myself. All by myself, all day. I always work by myself now.

"If I can find a real good man, OK. But good men are hard to find. Also, working alone, whatever you get is yours and you can work the hours you want. I can walk into any lumber camp and pick out the good men from the poor ones without even talking to them. I can tell just by the way they dress and the way they handle themselves. There are some things you can't tell a man. It's got to be in you so you know it. I can pick it out when I see it. I'll try to tell a man how to do right in the woods. But if he's doing things wrong and making moves against us, I just can't put up with it.

"I'd rather have a good twitch horse to work with in the woods than a lot of these men I've worked with. If you get a good horse you can hook him up with a load, send him into the yard, and the man in the yard will send him back. A good twitch horse, well experienced, can back up and set over by himself if he gets hung up.

"One time I had a man working for me in the woods. We had a John Deere crawler, one of the first they came out with. It was in '52 and we were cutting logs up toward Johnson Mountain. I sent this fellow out with a twitch behind the tractor and I could hear the tractor thrashing. I said, that's funny. That road is swamped good. That man ought to be able to get out there and back without thrashing the tractor like that. I walked out a ways and I saw what was going on. He was right to the end of the cable, about 75 feet. He was down behind a two-foot drop and the logs were behind him lodged against a big rock. He was coming onto that tractor just as hard as he could. I told the man, I guess you've had it. You might as well go home. I've got horses that know more than that. This is why I work alone.

"There is a courtesy in the woods among good men. But it isn't like it used to be, nowhere near. Good men take pride in themselves. For one thing, you never touched a man's tools in the woods, and I don't like to have a man take mine. I've got my tools filed to suit me and when I pick them up I know what I'm doing with them. You've got to have sharp tools. You've got to file a chain saw just the same way you file a bucksaw. And filing is something you can't tell a man. You can watch an expert file and you won't be able to do it. If you haven't filed right you are pushing hard and wearing out your saw, the bar, and the chain and the motor. I say filing is the main thing in cutting wood. A lot of fellows go through one saw after another, but a good man gets more out of his saw. Not only that, but he's making his money a lot easier.

"I learned to file a bucksaw on Satur-day nights when I was a kid. That was the only night the old man left us alone. We'd listen to the radio. It was WQXR, Wheeling, West Virginia. And while I listened I'd get my bucksaw and file bucksaw blades. When I was working for Jim Green there was a Frenchman named Rene LeBree who could file so fast I thought I'd never file that well. One time I took my bucksaw to his shed and hung up my saw and I took his. I knew he'd be mad at me, but I knew also he wouldn't do anything to me. When I came back, he let me know about it.

"The worst accident I ever had in the woods was with another man's axe when I was a kid. We had logged a big white birch. I didn't want to bother to get my axe when his was right handy. So I picked it up and made a swipe with it. Now every axe is hung different, and I wasn't used to this one. The blade struck the side of the tree and glanced off and spun around and cut me right below the knee and laid this whole leg open.

"We were staying in a camp, this fellow and I. He was a big, rugged character, a single fellow, and I figured I was just as tough as he was. I never had that cut sewed up and I worked every day, and it kept tearing open. It got kind of smelly in camp because that wound wouldn't heal. I had no antiseptic, no doctor, no nothing. But I was young and I'd got to prove I was as tough and rugged as the other fellow. It was a good part of the winter before that leg healed.

"Another time I was cutting over in Starks. It was back in '65. I was in the swamp and it was quite a long yard. I'd cut a big rock maple, an old growth, and it had three or four crotched limbs on it. I had an old 10-20 Homelite chain saw that had an accelerator pump on the side of the carburetor and it would idle no matter if you flipped it upside down. As I was cutting the last limb off I had my leg in between. She flipped quick and come over it and pinned me. I couldn't get up. My leg was twisted so bad I thought it was broken. The only thing that kept that tree from killing me was a little white maple about four inches through that it struck against.

"I could just reach my saw with the tips of my fingers. It was still running and I got it over my leg. Now that limb had my other arm pinned, too, so I had just one arm. I got the saw on the limb and bore down on the back of it and I sawed the limb off. And I got out. I was lucky. It was pretty near a year before I would walk good, but I never missed a day in the woods and I never went to a doctor with it. I was no hand for a doctor, never.

"Another time I broke off the end of my top rib. It swelled right up. It was in the wintertime, and every time I pulled on that twitching cable, it felt like that rib was coming clear through in front. But I worked, I never lost a day with it.

"Now, wherever you will find real good men, they won't hang on to the job too long before something will happen and they will have to get out. Jobbers don't want good men. If a man puts out a lot of wood and he's right there steady and he makes a lot of money, he's not apt to be there too long. He'll have to move. The reason, I would say, is jealousy. It's an awful thing to say, but any good man will tell you it is true. What they'll do if they see you can produce a lot of wood and do it easy, is put you in a hard place where they know the other fellows can't make a living. And they will do this all the time you work there. They will never change where they put you.

"And there are other reasons for making it hard on a woodsman. When I worked for Scott Paper I always carried my Maine Woodsman's Association decal on the side of my pickup for all to see. It didn't bother me a mite, no more than any good man is bothered to speak right out for his interests. Now the Scott foreman was a salary man and I was a pieceworker. When you get that combination it causes friction, because a good man is making more than the foreman. And if the foreman is inexperienced, that makes it even worse.

"Now we were bringing out our wood the way he told us to. That was to push it up over the stumps and break it up so that when the crane came it would be all crossed and a third of it would be left lying there. Well, I suggested we put it lengthways at the side of the road. There was plenty of room. It would be a lot easier on the equipment, wouldn't break up our wood so much, and there wouldn't be so many busted chokers and blown-out tires, stuff like this. Added to that I saw the foreman was cheating on our scales about 10 cords a day and giving it to the other men. We were watching the crew right beside us and we knew how many chokers they had and how many twitches. We knew where that wood was going because we'd just loaded the board.

"And then he crossed me for coming in early to work on Friday morning, which is half a day in the woods. I like to get in early on Friday to get a good half a day. The boss came in and gave the other fellow I was working with a hard time

– Lynn Franklin

Hard-working, highly experienced, independent woodsmen like Lester Blodgett, above, are paid according to the wood they cut, twitch, and pile. Although such woodsmen traditionally know — perhaps precisely to the quarter-cord — how much wood they have piled, their wood is officially scaled when a truck hauls it to the mill where it is weighed. Scott Paper Company in the Jackman area of central Maine, for example, reckons a cord at 4480 pounds. That scale is recorded on a slip numbered according to the jobber or contractor for whom Lester works. The jobber paid Lester about $10 a cord in 1981. If Lester used his own skidder ($40,000 to $60,000 at 1981 prices) instead of the boss's, he would have been paid about $18.75 a four-foot cord.

and then he came and tapped me on the shoulder. I'd taken all I could from him, and I just dropped him right there. He asked for it and he needed it and he had it coming to him. Years ago you didn't push good men. You came and talked to them and you asked them if they were doing something wrong. Years ago, the bosses wore the same clothes as you did. You knew that you were dealing with a man who knew as much about the woods as you did or more or he wouldn't have that job. Today when you walk into a woods camp and the boss comes up to you, look and see what he's wearing. He won't be dressed like you are. He won't look like a working man. There's nothing about him that is a working man. I'm not saying all of them. There are still some good woodsmen and good jobbers, but not so many as there used to be.

"An American woodsman can't get into a lumber camp where it's all Canadians and Canadian bosses, because the American will not get a fair shake. I have been in a good part of the lumber camps around this country and I've never seen it fail. You can be the best woodsman you are able to be and they will test you out for a week or two and then you are going to get it. The Canadian boss is going to favor the Canadian and an American boss is going to be scared of his job and he's going to favor the Canadians, too. I'd like to see some of these foremen make a living in some of the holes they put us in. But they'd never take a challenge like that.

"The Canadians keep the price of wood down. The companies don't admit it, but everybody knows it. I'm not saying the Canadians are not good men — they are. We've got American woodsmen just as good, only the Canadians can work cheaper. They have more benefits than we do and they get extra on the exchange in Canada of the American dollar they get for pay. The authorities are not upholding the law that says Canadians can't be hired in these woods if there are American woodsmen unemployed. The authorities have no intention of enforcing the law. The paper companies are powerful and the politicians are afraid of them. There is a lot of our money going into Canada.

"I'd like to see the American woodsmen stick together. If you've knocked around the woods as long as I have and taken the beatings in the woods that I've taken, it doesn't bother you a mite to say something to a man and stand up for what's right."

281

*We've probably read this more than a dozen times. But never without
a lump in our throat at the end. In fact, even thinking about it has the same result.
Maybe because we have long-ago memories that are so very similar. . . .*

At the End of the Lane

BY AMES POIRIER

When I was born in Peth Village, Vermont, on a cold February morning, Fido was then one year old. And when a few years later I moved up on the mountain to live with my grandparents on the farm, I met Fido there, and we grew up together.

It was just a hill farm and as such did not make Grandfather wealthy, but, oh, what a place for a boy and a dog!

Bear Hill Road, running north and south, divided the farm. On the east side of the road was the Night Pasture with its swamp and the beginnings of Bear Hill Brook, which ran down the hillside past the Big Field on the way to Ayer's Brook and White River.

The Big Field was one of Gramp's prized possessions. After first being shown the Morgan horses, all visitors then had to take a tour of this field. It was very large and surprisingly flat for being at such a high elevation. (Standing in the middle of the freshly mown field, I used to raise my arms to the sky and thrill to the freedom of this great open space.)

To the west of the road were the farm buildings: the old farmhouse, the cow and horse barns, and several outbuildings. Beyond these was a patchwork of small fields that hugged the slope up to the woods.

The cow lane started at what we called the "Flat" behind the cow barn. From there cowpaths meandered to the north fenceline, then turned west and climbed steeply to a knoll at the height of the lane. At this point all the paths converged into one, which entered the woods leading to the Big Pasture.

Of all the places on the farm, the Big Pasture brought me the greatest pleasure, for it was there that Fido and I had our own little adventures.

It is difficult to describe Fido after all these years. He was part collie, part shepherd, and part something else. Of medium size, he was nevertheless powerfully built, with a broad chest and strong legs. He was reddish brown in color except for his white chest and underside. Although he was short haired, his neck and chest fur was long, and I loved to bury my face in its soft, silky thickness.

I often spoke of Fido as being "my dog," but of course he wasn't. He was Gramp's cow dog and all-around hunter. In a way, though, he belonged to everyone on the farm, and we all loved him.

He was a proud dog, with a dignity that I respected. He was affectionate and liked to be petted — but only to a point. Then he would shift his weight restlessly from one front paw to the other; I would notice this and say, "All right, Fido, you can go." Then off he would trot to one of his favorite haunts.

Fido was a wonderful companion but also a good workdog. He was one of those exceptional cow dogs who could search out the cows even when they were out of sight of the barns. I always enjoyed watching him do this.

Gramp would take Fido to the flat behind the cow barn; there Gramp would listen for the sound of the cowbell and then, pointing, would say, "Fido, get the cows." Fido would run up the lane, and we'd see him enter the pasture woods. Shortly thereafter we would hear his bark, and the cows would begin emerging from the woods in single file. Fido would appear and sit on the knoll while Gramp counted the cows. If there were some missing, Gramp would wave his arm back toward the pasture and shout, "Go back!" Fido would then return to the woods.

(Quite often some of these pesky critters could sense the approach of milking time and would hide in a spruce thicket. I called them "Hiders.")

This time there would be a frenzied barking when Fido found the missing cows, and they would come out of the woods pretty fast because Fido didn't like "Hiders."

As I grew older, more and more I began to accompany Fido in search of the cows, and finally it became a customary thing — something we both looked forward to at the end of day.

Well in advance of milking time, I would get my trusty slingshot and a pocketful of pebbles from the roadway. Fido, watching these preparations, would get all excited and jump around and bark loudly. Then we would start our stroll up the cow lane.

This was the most beautiful time of the day — the afternoon breezes dying and the sun's rays lengthening across the valley. The meadowlarks, vesper sparrows, and other songbirds sang clearly in the stillness of the evening.

We had a steep climb and went slowly, always stopping at the height of the lane to sit on the knoll, our "resting place."

From here, when the sky was clear, we could see far, far away — across Randolph Valley, south to Mt. Ascutney, west to Killington and Pico, and on and on for miles and miles.

After awhile, rested, Fido and I would enter the pasture woods. If the cows were nearby, we would send them down the lane quickly and return to go looking for game. If they were at the far end of the pasture, we would tarry along the way to do our hunting.

We had to venture forward very cautiously — there was so much game we could surprise. In the beech or butternut groves, there were those cussed squirrels always giving away our presence with their darned chatter. I would sling a pebble after one, rarely hitting it but coming very close! And scaring that squirrel half to death, it seemed.

Approaching each clearing we had to be especially careful. For here were the woodchucks, and the trick was to catch one far from its hole.

We never did catch Old Hoary, though — he was too clever for us. This big, gray chuck had a hole on high ground at the base of a large elm tree and, because of this, I guess he could see us coming from a long way off. Only once did we surprise him when he had strayed too far. It was a

282

close race between Fido and him for the hole, but in the end Old Hoary won out.

Along with hunting there were dark caves and mysterious glades to explore, small brooks to wade in, and springs to drink from. I had glass jars on wooden stakes at each spring, but in the end preferred to get down on my hands and knees to drink from the pool alongside Fido, who lapped up the water noisily.

Entering the head of our little valley, a trough between two ridges, we were sometimes lucky to see deer feeding at the far end. Fido, at my side, would look up at me inquiringly, and I would say quietly, "No, Fido," for we taught him not to chase deer.

To the far west of the pasture was the Northfield Gulf. The slopes were thick with spruce, and in this heavy cover the big snowshoe rabbits gave Fido a merry chase. Once in a while he would bring one around in front of me, and I would zing a pebble after that darned rabbit, missing him by only a hair.

At last, unable to delay any longer, we would find the cows and herd them back to the barn.

All the seasons in Vermont were delightful — even the long, long winters, so dreaded by some.

In the spring, the main activity was maple sugaring. My chore was to gather the sap buckets and bring them to the gathering tank being hauled by our Morgans, Ned and Babe. Fido would bound along in the deep snow opening up paths for me.

In the summer came haying time. In those days it was extra hard work cutting, raking, and bunching hay, loading it on the hay wagons and unloading it by hand — not too pleasant for a boy who kept thinking of better things to do, such as fishing or swimming. But when the haying season was over, the fields neatly cut and the barns full, there was a sense of accomplishment, and there was the reward of a short rest before the harvest.

Bear Hill School (with about 10 pupils) was a mile walk up the road. When school opened early in September, it took me away from Fido most of the day, but returning over the crest of the hill in late afternoon, I'd see him seated in the middle of the road by the farmhouse waiting for me. I'd call to him and he'd run to meet me. Then we'd leave the road to wander about the swamp, hunting for turtles and frogs.

The old farm was a wonderful place to visit in those days, especially in the fall

– illustration by Austin Stevens

Of all the places on the farm, the Big Pasture brought me the greatest pleasure. . . .
. . . Wonderful springs, summers, and autumns have come to the mountain
and many snows have drifted deep in the dooryard —
and now I, too, am old. . . .

---

after the harvest. The men, relaxed after a hard summer's work, would sit in the evening on the front porch, where they could enjoy the view of the valley while they smoked their pipes.

On one of these evenings, Gramp noticed me seated by Fido, an arm around him, talking to him and stroking his soft fur. Gramp said to the other men, "Look at those two. Did you ever see such a close pair? Let me tell you of the time Fido saved the boy." I pretended to be embarrassed, but secretly I was pleased to hear the story retold, for it made me feel closer to Fido.

It happened on a bright, wintry morning. The night before a blizzard had struck the mountain, and high winds had howled through the bare maples and under the eaves of the farmhouse. On rising, we children had all rushed to the window and shouted happily at what we saw. The road and dooryard were completely blocked with high drifts of snow. This meant no school!

We hurried through one of Gram's good breakfasts, then, warmly bundled up, ran outdoors to enjoy the new snow. It was too dry for making snowballs, but we darted around, shoving and pushing each other into snowdrifts. All the while, Fido, in our midst, leaped and barked for the sheer joy of it all.

In the end, tiring of this, we decided on making an igloo and chose the larger of the drifts for the start. While I tunneled into the snow with a small scoop, the others with snow shovels heaped more snow on top of the huge drift. Just as I reached the center of our igloo, the whole mass of snow collapsed on me. The children, too young to know what to do, simply jumped up and down screaming for help. Gramp at last came running from the barn to my aid. But by this time Fido, digging furiously, had found me, and now, with his powerful jaws clamped on the seat of my britches, was tugging and pulling with all his might. Gramp reached down, grabbed me by my boots, and completed the rescue.

I like to think, though, now that I look back on it, that Fido could have done it all by himself.

The seasons came and went — the years rolled on so happily that I have only the fondest memories of them. Maybe Gramp and Gram had their problems and worries, but for a small country boy this little world on top of the mountain was all I ever wanted.

Then the autumn morning and the moment I had long dreaded was at hand. A car awaited me in the dooryard to take me down country, where I would live in a big city. I bid good-bye to Gramp and Gram and the others. Then, fighting back the tears, I took Fido aside on the lawn and knelt beside him.

"Fido," I said, "I'm going far away and won't be back for a long, long time. Be a good dog, now, and go get the cows alone." I added the last part because lately I had noticed he was hesitant about getting the cows without me.

As our car went down the hill, I turned for one last look at the farm. Fido was still seated on the lawn where I had left him, his eyes following the car on the road. The morning sun, shining through the maples, brilliantly lit his beautiful reddish brown fur against the green of the lawn.

I said to myself, "He doesn't understand, of course. He probably thinks I'm only going down to the village and will return in a short time. But no, I won't be back soon, and tonight Fido will be getting the cows alone." At last the flood of tears came, and Fido and the farm were blurred from sight.

It was a long, difficult winter, made bearable only by the many letters that came from the farm telling me of the doings there — and of Fido.

But spring finally arrived, then the last day of school, and I was on the train on my way north to Vermont. Gramp met me with his Model T Ford at the Randolph Depot and, on the way back to the

farm, brought me up to date on the happenings there. And when we drove into the dooryard, what a great reunion with Fido! As I stepped from the car, he recognized me immediately and came bounding into my arms. We rolled over and over on the lawn. I was so happy that I laughed and cried at the same time.

Gramp freed me from chores for the rest of the day so Fido and I could get reacquainted. The first thing I did was dig a can of worms from behind the barns; then I got my fishing pole and headed for the brook.

Now, wherever I went on the farm, I wanted Fido with me. However, there were times when he didn't make a good fishing companion. The reason: Fido liked water too much.

I would approach my favorite pool very cautiously and then, keeping as hidden as possible, would carefully lower the baited hook into the foam by the waterfall, hoping some brook or rainbow trout was lurking there. Then, splash! There would be Fido — right in the middle of the pool! I would say, "Now, Fido, look at what you've done!" And Fido, shoulder-deep in water, would hang his head and try to look properly guilty.

Another summer passed, and then another. I missed Fido very much the other times of the year when I was away, but we made up for it in the summer — that was our best season for fun, anyway.

All those years Fido was such a good companion, so loyal, so faithful — and so obedient until that day in September.

Haying was done, the barns were full, and the lull before the fall harvest had again arrived. That day had been spent on the woodpile, sawing the wood into stove lengths. My share of the work was to stack the chunks in the woodshed, and, as I had not yet finished by milking time, Gramp decided to send Fido after the cows alone. He led him out to the flat behind the cow barn. I stepped outside the woodshed to watch.

Gramp listened for the sound of the cowbell, pointed, and said, "Fido, go and get the cows."

Fido walked slowly up the lane a ways, then turned and sat down.

Again Gramp said, and this time loudly, "Fido, go get the cows!" And again Fido walked up the lane a short distance, turned, and sat down.

Now Gramp picked up a stick and, with his arm raised high, advanced threateningly on Fido.

I was frightened. I had never before seen Gramp beat Fido — maybe he was only threatening now, but then, I couldn't be sure. . . .

I rushed forward, crying out as I ran, "Gramp! Please, Gramp, don't! Don't hit Fido! Look at him — he's too old to get the cows anymore!"

Gramp stopped short, lowered his arm, and the stick slipped from his fingers to the ground. Then he knelt by Fido and stroked his head for some time. When he finally rose, his face was very sad, and, without saying a word, he walked back to the house.

I guess Gramp realized, just as I had at that moment, that Fido's cow-getting days were over.

I went after the cows alone that day.

From then on Fido went into retirement. He had always been given the best of care, but now he was treated royally. "Fed right from the table, like the rest of us," as Gram would say.

Fido still joined in the farm's activities, but he remained close to the buildings, and more and more took siestas in the warm sun on the front porch.

Once, seated on the porch with Gramp, I noticed Fido's legs were moving in his sleep. "Look, Gramp," I said, "Fido's running in his dream!"

And Gramp, taking his pipe from his mouth, nodded sadly, "Yup, still hunting, I guess. Maybe chasing a fox."

One evening as I walked slowly up the lane on the way for the cows, I sensed something behind me and turned to see Fido on the cowpath trying so hard to keep up with me. While I waited patiently for him, I thought, "Oh, Fido, how awful to see you this way! From now on, I must put you in the house before I go for the cows."

When he reached my side, we walked together the rest of the way to the height of the lane, where we sat down on the grassy knoll.

The view of the valley was so beautiful — it should have put me in a peaceful mood, but something was troubling me, something that had been on my mind for a long time and now needed to be spoken. I leaned aside, put my arm around Fido, and whispered in his ear, "Fido,

you're my dog. All the others — they love you — but not as much as I do."

Fido, embarrassed at this extra attention, stirred uneasily, then raised his head and licked my face.

High in the sky, crows were battling a hawk. I turned to see if Fido was watching this. But no, he was looking down at the woods by the little pond. Did dogs have memories, I wondered? For there, many years ago, Fido had treed a bobcat. We had been awakened that night by Fido's barking. Gramp had said, "Fido's got something up a tree and it's not a coon." And off we had gone into the dark night with our lanterns.

Down at Bear Hill Brook Fido and I had often bathed together in the cool pools on hot summer days, and under the birches bordering the Big Field we had sat many times in the shade waiting for the next hay wagon to load.

And over there — suddenly I was overwhelmed with sadness and buried my face in the soft fur of Fido's neck crying, "Oh, Fido, when you go, I'll miss you so!"

After awhile, I dried my tears, rose, and said, "Stay, Fido, stay," and went into the woods to bring back the cows.

In the spring of '31, the sad news came from the farm.

Fido had been failing in health all that winter. Gramp and Gram could no longer bear to see him suffer, so they called Kurt, the farmer from over the hill, to come and take him away. Some years later Kurt told me what happened that day.

When he walked into the dooryard, Gramp and Gram had just given Fido his last meal and were saying good-bye to him. Kurt led Fido away on a rope, and Gramp and Gram, both in tears, went into the house.

It was strange that Kurt chose the cow lane for Fido's last walk. Kurt had intended bringing Fido into the pasture woods, but on reaching the knoll at the top of the lane, for some reason unknown to Kurt, Fido sat down and refused to be led any farther.

So, while Fido sat there looking over the valley, Kurt dropped the rope and stepped back. The rifle shot echoed and reechoed along the mountain ridges.

Fido was buried where he fell, on the knoll, our "resting place."

Oh Fido, since you have gone, wonderful springs, summers, and autumns have come to the mountain, and many snows have drifted

The author in March 1923. "Fido would open paths for me in the deep snow."

deep in the dooryard. The years have gone by all too quickly and now I, too, am old.

In the spring of each year I return to the mountain to wander about the old farm, now long deserted. Bear Hill Brook still runs down the hillside, pool to sparkling pool; but the meadows, unmown, are not the same, and our beautiful pastures have gone back to forest.

In all these years I have searched and searched but have not been able to find a dog quite like you.

And now, when I go slowly up the lane, following the faint traces of a cowpath, I go alone.

But as my steps take me higher and higher, memories of our days keep coming back to me clearly — so clearly that I imagine you are once again by my side. The cows are just ahead — in the stillness of the evening we can hear the tinkling of a cowbell in the pasture woods.

Now, we reach the height of the lane, and turn to rest on the knoll.

From here, when the sky is clear, we can see far away — across Randolph Valley, south to Ascutney, west to Killington and Pico, and on and on for miles and miles of lovely green mountains.

A·NOVEMBER SAMPLER

☞ Memorable thoughts, quotes, and assorted tidbits from the last 50 November issues. ☜

A TRUE STORY TO THINK ABOUT
(or, perhaps better, to not think about!)

☞ Flames will not destroy it — or so it is believed. The two-story white stucco house on Roxbury Street in Keene, New Hampshire, is fireproof from top to bottom. It has steel girders, plaster walls and ceilings, floors of a heavy tile immune to fire, and thick iron doors in every room.

Fred Sharby, the owner of a chain of motion picture theaters in western Massachusetts, New Hampshire, and Vermont, designed the house, and decided what materials should be used in its construction.

"My father had a fear of fires," recalls Pauline Sharby Bulman, Fred Sharby's daughter, now living in Greenfield, Massachusetts. "Two of the theaters he owned — one in Brattleboro, Vermont, and the other in upstate New Hampshire — had burned to the ground. He had the entire place rebuilt according to his specifications. Steel girders were put up, and they were covered with stucco on the outside. The walls were plastered, and he tested several types of floor tile before he finally selected one he was convinced was fireproof. The furnace had thick cement walls around it, and all the doors were solid iron."

Sharby, his wife, and Pauline, who was in her teens at the time, and three other children moved into the plush fireproof house in 1939. Their son, Fred, was an exceptional athlete, and three years later he was the star of the Keene High School football team. He is still remembered at the school today. Every year, the team presents the Fred Sharby Trophy to the top football player.

The elder Sharby was naturally quite proud of his son's gridiron accomplishment. "I'm taking you to Boston," he told him, "to see the best college football team in the country."

Thus it was that Sharby, his wife, and young Fred went to Boston one Saturday in late November to see Boston College, the top-rated football team in the nation

Fred Sharby, whose dread of fire impelled him to tear down his Keene, New Hampshire, home and completely rebuild it with fireproof materials.

at the time, play Holy Cross. But Holy Cross trounced B.C. that day in what was then called the football upset of the century.

The Sharbys went to the big game with Clyde and Mabel Clark of Keene, and their daughter, Ann Marie, now Mrs. Joseph Gallagher, who still resides in the city. Ann Marie, known to her friends as Minnie, was young Sharby's girl friend.

"After the game, we had reservations

"The house which flames cannot destroy" on Roxbury Street in Keene, New Hampshire.

– Charles W. Fluhr

for dinner at a big city nightclub," recalled Mrs. Gallagher. "I remember we had a delicious meal. Then I remember going out onto the dance floor with young Fred. I remember we were dancing, and how happy I felt.

"That was the last thing I remember about that night. The next thing I knew I was in a hospital. I was in that hospital for a month before they allowed me to go home.

"A fire broke out that night — November 28, 1942 — and hundreds died in that nightclub. Somehow, young Fred got me out of there, but he was one of those who died. My parents died too."

Hortense Sharby survived the blaze. Her husband did not. Fred Sharby, the man who built a home flames could not destroy, perished in the tragic Cocoanut Grove fire.

by Frederick John

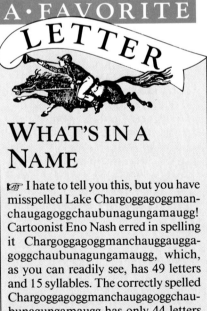

A·FAVORITE LETTER

WHAT'S IN A NAME

☞ I hate to tell you this, but you have misspelled Lake Chargoggagoggman-chaugagoggchaubunagungamaugg! Cartoonist Eno Nash erred in spelling it Chargoggagoggmanchauggaugga-goggchaubunagungamaugg, which, as you can readily see, has 49 letters and 15 syllables. The correctly spelled Chargoggagoggmanchaugagoggchau-bunagungamaugg has only 44 letters and 14 syllables! Incidentally, the accent is on the 12th syllable, for those who like to read aloud.

William D. Feeny
Madison, Wisconsin

IMAGE VS. REALITY

☞ "What's that fella's name?" he asked. "Marshall Dodge? He wanted to film a Maine guide camp the way it would have looked 50 years ago, so he came to Chesuncook, got me to dig out my equipment, and we hauled it over to Cunningham Brook. I had it just right, hot little fire, tight tarps, taut tents. I sat down pleased with myself. Then I looked up. That damned critter was loosening the tarps, pulling out stakes so the tents sagged. He threw green wood on the fire. Said he wanted smoke. He didn't believe the old guides would have had it so neat. Then he wanted me to flip flapjacks!" **Mick Fahey, an old Maine guide.** (*From "Once More Down the River" by Mel Allen.*)

The Third Moose, *an original watercolor by Bill Commerford.*

THE RIGHT MAN

☞ Even more serious was a clash that erupted between Virginia riflemen and Col. John Glover's Marblehead Regiment later in the fall. From an exchange of snowballs this became a riot. When Washington heard the news, he instantly mounted his horse and galloped to the pasture where the troops were battling.

One of his black servants, Pompey, had been ordered ahead to take down the pasture bars, but Washington was on top of them before he could do the job. Without so much as a pause, Washington sent his horse soaring over Pompey and the bars into the midst of the rioters. Leaping from the saddle, he grabbed two brawny soldiers by their throats and lifted them off the ground, one in each hand, shaking them like children while he roared commands to the rest — which instantly extinguished the fight.

John Sullivan, who witnessed this scene, later said: "From the moment I saw Washington leap the bars at Cambridge and realized his personal ascendancy over the turbulent tempers of his men in their moments of wildest excitement, I never faltered in the faith that we had the right man to lead the cause of American liberty." (*From "Washington Takes Command" by Thomas Fleming.*)

⚘ I REMEMBER ⚘

NO ONE EVER GOT THE BEST OF NANA

☞ Anyone else would have hesitated before turning across two lanes of high-speed, oncoming traffic, or at least would have used a directional signal. Not Nana. Only her love of auto jaunts was as legendary in our family as her reputation as a driver.

The car traveling the inside lane managed to squeeze by just ahead of her as she turned into the drive-in eatery. Sitting in the front passenger seat, I have never been so terrified as I was watching the delivery truck in the outside lane ride up on smoking front tires, then skid sideways around the rear of our car, barely missing cars coming behind us. The driver's face, as he slid by, is forever with me. A study in absolute fury.

We motored sedately in to the entrance to the drive-in parking lot as the truck driver roared into the exit, parked his truck with engine still running, its load a jumble, and stamped toward us. Nana honked for the car hop as she adjusted her hair in the rearview mirror. My brother and I slid down in our seats, hoping like chameleons to take on the color and weave of the upholstery. The driver banged on the window, then on the roof of the car. As Nana rolled down the window, all I could hear was, "Lady . . . lady . . . what . . . wha . . . "

"Here to take our order already — you're fast! I'll have a cheeseburger, root beer float . . . and how are your french fries? My grandchildren here will have . . ."

His shoulders dropped abruptly, his face went completely blank, and he turned back towards his truck.

"What a rude waiter," said Nana, watching his retreat. "He's in such a hurry that he didn't even wait for me to finish! . . . "

Robin Leslie

"This month's 'House for Sale' is a converted bowling alley in Orono."

– Bruce Hammond

THE ULTIMATE EXPERIENCE

☞ Then he said we were nearing the jump zone. Those few words were perhaps the biggest obstacle of the day to overcome. That's when the countdown really begins; not when your alarm clock went off that morning; not when you paid your $115; not even when the parachute was cinched tight. But now — you're a step away from dropping your quarter in the jukebox. The selection still must be made. At that moment you become a cautious, conscious, rational human being. You wrestle with the logic of your being up there. Once the door opens, you begin a programmed procedure that you have rehearsed until pure boredom. Self, it is sufficient to say at that moment, just give me another 30 seconds of composure. Placing your feet into the 80-mph wind is instinctive. Getting your body

outside when you hear the standby command is to go beyond the point of no return. The engine power is chopped, and you hear the word: GO.

What I remember is a fuzzy view of the plane above. I forgot to count, though my arch was perfect, and I felt in control. Then came that sweet tug of the chute opening, like swinging on a rainbow. Looking up, I saw everything was all right — no holes, no twisted lines. I grabbed the two toggles. The voice over the radio offered congratulations, then instructed me to take a few practice turns, which was like tacking a sailboat back and forth through the sky. Then silence, and for the first time the events of the last five hours came into perspective. Nearly all of the work was done. The emotional preparation had been successful. The only thing left to do was enjoy the euphoric, sinking journey. Alarm clocks, job, phone bills, taxes — you're above them all. They'll have to wait, because right now you're untouchable, immersed in a powerful stillness. The sense of being alone is unearthly. You can see the mountains of Vermont and the Quabbin Reservoir, and the big sandy landing bowl seems impossible to miss. To make a jump in the autumn, free-falling into the eye of a maple-leaf dream, must be the ultimate experience. (*From "The Day Big Don and I Jumped Out of an Airplane" by Scott Cramer.*)

cated new supplies. Dowsing was part of the style, a style Thomas Jefferson applauded when he declared that cultivators of the land were "the most valuable citizens, the most vigorous, the most independent, the most virtuous, and they are tied to their country and wedded to its liberty and interests by the most lasting bonds."

A real farmer, of course, would never stoop to articulating all this. (*From "Vermont Farms Aren't What You See on Postcards" by Jay Stevens.*)

– Jeff Jacobson

Saving a cow from a breech birth.

I REMEMBER
THE SAFEST PLACE

☞ Usually I don't buy lemonade from children, however appealing, because I'm not exactly sure what I'll be drinking. But it's hard to go by their sidewalk stands, with the carefully hand-lettered signs, and turn a deaf ear to their pleading voices. So I was glad when I came on this especially clean young entrepreneur. I noticed his hands were as clean as his bright and shining face. I thought that was a good omen, and I bought and drank a glass of his lemonade.

Naturally, I asked how business was, and he said it was booming. "Took in a lot of money this afternoon," he said. I cautioned him, but he said his receipts were perfectly safe. "Nobody'd guess where I keep it," he said of his money. I couldn't guess, either. There wasn't any sign of a cash box. It wasn't until I paid him with a quarter that I knew the secret of his safety. He plunged his arm into the big lemonade jug up to the elbow and handed me my change, a bright shiny dime and five dripping pennies.

Ned Comstock

A REAL FARMER

☞ He slapped a haunch to get the last cow moving. He poked her in the tender pink part of the solar plexus, and she ambled off. "You know," he mused, "they say that 50 cows is the best number, because that way a farmer has a chance to know each cow, to understand their problems." He mounted the stairs at the end of the trench and turned out the lights. "Of course, no one can make a living off 50 cows anymore. No real farmer, that is."

I followed him out into the early morning. *No real farmer.* I grew up in the shadow of that adjective. A real farmer rises at daybreak and is in bed an hour or

two after dusk. A real farmer lives close to the natural cycles, and tomorrow's weather is far more important than today's news. A real farmer's praise, when it is paid out, enriches eccentrics like Eddie Morsett, a man who lives near the crest of Bowen Hill and who once kept the Central Vermont engineers at bay with his .30-.30 Winchester until they detoured the power line around his property. Real farmers relish anecdotes of self-reliance — like the time Interstate 91 was blasted into the shale and mica schist of Skitchewaug Ridge, and the dynamite altered the underground water table and dried up the wells. The farmers cut forked apple branches, or, depending on the persuasion, forked willow, and lo-

A HUGE, DARK FORM

☞ "On Friday evening at 6 P.M. in the year of 1947, I was fishing off the northern tip of North Hero Island with two companions. The bass were biting really well and we were about to hoist anchor, having just boated our legal limit. The lake was calm, undisturbed by the slightest ripple, and the air was so clear that Mount Mansfield, Jay Peak, and all other landmarks were outlined against the cloudless sky.

"Suddenly, and without warning, a tremendous splash was heard in the water north of us, instantly diverting our attention in that direction. There was nothing to see at first, save a group of large ripples diverging in concentric circles from a point about 300 yards from our craft. No other boats were in sight at the moment. Then, out of the depths, reared a huge dark form which moved swiftly in a northwesterly direction. Three segments appeared, clearly discernible above the water's surface, separated one from the other by about five feet of water, the overall length of the creature being about 25 feet.

"The segments alternately appeared and disappeared from view, the coordination of movement leading us all to believe that it must be one single inhabitant. It moved with incredible swiftness — about 15 miles per hour — and disappeared altogether in about two minutes. Presently it emerged once more at a more distant point, about a quarter mile from the area where it was originally noted, only to plunge out of sight again, this time for good." **L.R. Jones of Swanton, Vermont.** (*From "In Search of the Champlain Monster" by Brian Vachon.*)

– Alan Ferguson

"*Well, I dunno, Waldo — I don't b'lieve I'd go s'fah as tuh say we gut 'im.*"

BOSTON HERALD AMERICAN — NEWS ITEM: A whistling swan has 25,216 feathers, a Plymouth Rock chicken has 8325 feathers, while a ruby-throated hummingbird has only 940, according to an actual count. . . .

THE SILENCE HEARD 'ROUND THE WORLD

☞ In the November 1964 issue of *Yankee* the article "The Silence Heard 'Round the World" was of particular interest to me. I was a member of the 26th Division from its inception to its mustering out in 1919, Battery B, of the 103rd Field Artillery.

The last day of the war is still vivid in my memory; I was a corporal at the time and was acting chief of the 4th section. We were called into action shortly after morning mess.

We had been in action about an hour when I noticed two men standing on the road about 50 yards from our position, and apparently very much interested in our feeding the gun. My curiosity was aroused, and I beckoned them to come on over. They practically tumbled down the embankment and came to our emplacement. Upon inquiring as to who they were, they introduced themselves as war correspondents. They were from the *Chicago Tribune* and, if I remember correctly, one was Mr. Bert Ford.

For the fun of it, I asked Mr. Ford if he would care to fire the piece. He was more than willing to do so. We instructed him on how to pull and where to stand. With a "whoop and a holler" and a warning to Kaiser Bill, he fired the gun. This was too much for his companion. He asked if he also might fire the piece. We told them they could fire as many rounds as they wished, up to the final shot at eleven o'clock. From that time on our gunner had very little to do. They took turns firing, and each shot was dedicated to a wife, mother, father, sister, and even grandparents, etc.

As the hour of eleven approached, Mr. Ford asked who was to fire the final round. Someone mentioned tying a rope to the lanyard so all could be in on it. With the lanyard lengthened and two minutes to go, all took their places. In their eagerness they leaned against the lanyard too much and, with only five or six seconds to go, the rope broke. In the process of tying the rope back on, eleven o'clock struck and the other three guns of our battery fired. We were then ready and, about three seconds after eleven, our gun spoke — perhaps *the* last shot of the war.

From then on there was no sound of firing from any direction. It certainly was "The Silence Heard 'Round the World." It was an eerie feeling.

L.B.S., Massachusetts

CHAPTER 12

December

*O*ne of the editorial dangers of the Christmas issue is that it becomes just plain TOO Christmas-y. A generous portion of Christmas trees, angels, Santa Clauses, ornaments, lights, and old-fashioned toys is lovely and essential, of course. The trick is not to become so sweet as to be sickening. To provide a little balance, we've always included something like, as in 1984, a first-person account of the Battle of Leyte Gulf, which understandably prompted some readers to ask, "What's that story got to do with Christmas?" The answer was, of course, "nothing," which is the point.

An equally effective (and sometimes better) method of achieving some sense of balance is to gently poke a little fun at some of our Christmas clichés. In 1981, for instance, sleigh riding, so nostalgic a memory for those of us over 50, was rather brutally "exposed." "I have never known what a live buffalo smells like," wrote author Philbrook Paine, his tongue only partially in cheek, "but I can remember precisely the aroma that exuded from a pelt after it had been detached from its owner and made into a robe for sleigh riders. It had vigor and strength and pungency. Once it had become wet — say from falling snow — a sleigher was hard put to decide whether to die of the cold or suffocation. In its damp state, a buffalo robe had all the sweetness and charm of a skunk hit by an automobile."

And yet, no matter what we included for "balance," it seems our December issues, looking back on them, were always overflowing with the spirit of the most beautiful holiday of the year. Perhaps that's simply been something out of our conscious control. . . .

Christmas Eve, 1976 — looking across Boston Common to the John Hancock Building and, farther away, the Prudential tower.

- photograph by S.R. Gilcreast, Jr.   **291**

At the time we published the following (in December 1975), The Society for the Preservation of New England Antiquities in Boston (which is celebrating its 75th anniversary as this book is being published) owned over 60 properties. Morgan W. Phillips was (and still is) a full-time consultant on the historic restoration of many of these as part of the Society's Consulting Services Group, and so it was hard to imagine a better authority on the subject at hand! Readers must have agreed, because the requests for reprints following publication continued for several years.

The 8 Most Common Mistakes in Restoring Historic Houses

(...and How to Avoid Them)

BY MORGAN W. PHILLIPS

1   Don't Destroy the Evidence: Make Tracks.

Old buildings almost invariably consist of material from a number of periods. When a decision is made to remove some recent material and reproduce what had existed at some earlier time, the problem arises of how to find out exactly what the earlier material looked like. Very often a detailed answer can be found in evidence actually on the site. Telltale fragments of missing woodwork may have been reused as a part of later woodwork, or may have fallen into some crevice during the remodeling. A ridge in the paint layers, when illuminated with a light held at an angle, may give the profile of a key piece of woodwork that has been removed.

A common mistake is to proceed with restoration work before gathering all such evidence. The evidence is then lost — removed by carpenters, obliterated by sanding, or thrown away during the overambitious cleanup.

For the same reason that architectural evidence is valuable to us, we should leave a record of our work for the future. New wood should be marked, and a thorough record kept, with text, photos, and drawings or sketches. Measured drawings of the building are the ideal place on which to note all the evidence that has been discovered.

2   Don't Overrestore.

Overrestoration usually takes two forms. First, there is the replacement of old material just because it shows the signs of age and thus looks a little too rough to suit the tastes of a perfectionist.

— illustration by Tom Payne

Old bumpy plaster is replaced with a perfect new job; old fireplace bricks showing some minor heat damage are replaced. A building thus restored loses the patina of age that made it appealing in the first place, and loses the actual materials that make it genuinely old.

A second form of overrestoration is to return the building to its original appearance by stripping away later additions of historical or architectural value. Virtually every old building is a collection of materials from different dates. This is true not only of American houses, but also of the famous ancient buildings of Europe and elsewhere. Sometimes the additions are of more interest than the original parts. A typical example of a valuable later addition is a fine Federal-period mantel built in front of an earlier, larger fireplace. All too often such fine

work is destroyed to expose what remains of the original fireplace.

There is usually a lot of material of no value that can be removed. But the decision about what goes and what stays should be made very carefully, on the basis of a study of the building, and after consultation with others who are familiar with American architectural history.

In general, the best policy is to retain later material: as a real part of the building's past, it has more value than "fake" material put in now. If you don't have time to carry out a study of the building, then the safest policy is certainly to keep later features in place.

3   Don't Make a Building That Never Was.

This is a very common mistake, and a subtle one. It most often happens in one of two ways.

First, it is quite common to see one part of a building restored to one date and another part to another date. As an example, suppose a house of 1810 was heavily remodeled in 1860 — roof raised, new front doorway, new window sash. If today we tear out the 1860 sash and put in 1810-type sash, while retaining the other 1860 features, we have created an appearance that the building never had at any time. Usually this mistake occurs through lack of study of the building, or through the owner's dislike for some part of the later remodeling.

A second example of restoring to a condition that never existed is to restore a building to an appearance that is earlier in character than the building itself — and more primitive. Many old buildings were better finished than we realize. For example, the best 18th-century floorboards were not 18 inches wide and knotty, but six to 10 inches wide, free of knots, and cut across the growth rings so as not to splinter or warp. The use of typically wide, poor-quality attic floorboards in the restoration of formal rooms is a classic mistake.

Probably the most common example of "earlying it up" is the removal of plaster from ceilings so as to expose bare beams, when these beams were never meant to be exposed. Only the earliest or most primitive houses had exposed beams: in most areas from the early 18th century onwards plaster, paneling, and moldings — not beams — were considered beautiful.

In order to avoid making a building look earlier than it ever possibly could have been, it is important to have in mind the actual date of the building. Quite often one sees a fine formal house of, say, the Greek Revival period (circa 1825–1860) marked with a date of perhaps 1750, and sometimes "restored" accordingly. This is apt to happen when the owner has searched the deeds and discovered that a house was built on the site in 1750, but has failed to consider what might have happened to that house. Did it burn in 1790? Was it taken down or moved across the street? Or was the land divided in 1839, so that the 1750 house is really the one next door? The construction of the present house may not be recorded in any documents.

The importance of researching and analyzing a building as a guide for restoration and repair cannot be overemphasized. Documents and the building itself must be studied together. If one trusts only the documents, one can make the kind of mistake just described. If one examines only the building, much information contained in deeds, wills, inventories, old maps, old drawings, and many other sources will never be found. Such information is invaluable in piecing together the whole story of the building and in making the decisions required during the restoration process.

4   Don't Scrape.

The most common procedure in reproducing old paint colors is to scrape clean a sample of the old paint and then match its color with new paint. In many cases the color thus achieved is incorrect, since the old sample has discolored with time. Many unstable pigments were used in early paints, which may have faded over time. The oil in many old paints has

yellowed, often after the paint was covered by later layers, since oil yellows faster in the dark. Thus, many old colors were brighter than we realize.

The analysis of old paints to determine their original colors is very difficult. Short of hiring a professional, the best that a homeowner can do is just to avoid unnecessary stripping of old paint, since this destroys the old samples and means that the research can never be done. And it's not good enough to strip a whole room and leave just one area as a sample: a future researcher will want to look all around the room with a microscope to find one or two well-preserved samples. These are very apt to be little thick lumps of paint near hardware or in crevices, and there may be only a few good ones in a whole room.

Thus, paint-stripping should be undertaken only when absolutely necessary, and as much of the old paint left on as possible. Since most old woodwork was painted from the start, the bare knotty-pine look is apt to be incorrect, anyway. An exception is some types of Victorian houses, where interior woodwork was varnished.

Old wallpapers should be preserved when possible for the same reasons as old paints: they are evidence of changing taste in the building through the years. Many old papers date back as far as the late 18th century and have real value. If a paper has to be removed, you should keep samples large enough to show a full repeat of the pattern. Some wallpapers are important enough to deserve being kept intact on the wall at all costs.

5   Don't Sandblast; Avoid Destructive Repointing.

The cleaning and repointing of old brickwork is seldom done properly.

Old brickwork is often sandblasted to remove paint. Unfortunately, in most cases this also removes the hard skin of the bricks, exposing the much more porous and weaker interior, which often cannot stand up to the weather. Since the skin was formed in the brick kiln, it can never be reformed once it is removed. And after being sandblasted, old bricks absorb much more rainwater and, with freezing temperatures, often start to spall and crumble in a few years or even a few months.

Having removed the bricks' natural barrier to excessive water penetration, building owners are apt to buy a silicone treatment to help keep water out. This treatment can trap in water that has got-

ten into the bricks in any of a variety of ways: through small cracks in mortar joints, from normal interior humidity, or by rising through capillary action from damp soil beneath the building. If this should occur, such trapped water can cause doubly accelerated decay of old brickwork. Silicones are no substitute for the bricks' own skin.

Where old paint is to be removed, one question to ask is whether the paint should be removed at all. Many early brick buildings were originally painted, and the record of the original color is the old paint itself. Once this is removed, the story is lost.

If it is decided to remove the paint, a variety of chemical removers are available. If the right remover is chosen to suit the individual building, this method, although slow, is usually the least damaging to the bricks.

Repointing with Portland cement mortar is perhaps the most common and most damaging error in masonry restoration. Portland cement mortars are made with Portland cement, some lime, and with sand as a filler. If the proportion of cement to lime is high, the mortar is extremely strong, thus being well suited to the best modern bricks, which are also very strong. Together they produce the high-strength masonry needed for modern construction. But old bricks (and many kinds of stone) are much weaker and can be damaged by the very strong, hard mortar used in repointing. A basic principle is that mortar should always be weaker than the bricks or stones that are imbedded in it: thus the old lime mortars — made with only lime and sand — work well with soft bricks and stones. A soft mortar can cushion various movements that occur in masonry: thermal expansion and contraction, expansion and contraction caused by humidity changes, foundation settlements, and so on. Small cracks of no importance may form in the mortar. But when the mortar is stronger than the bricks or stones, the latter give way before the mortar, through serious cracking or spalling.

The formulation of mortar for old buildings requires experience and judgment. Many old limes contained certain impurities that actually made them stronger than today's pure lime. When using modern lime, a relatively small amount of Portland cement is often needed to provide the same durability and strength that the old mortar had. The proportion of cement should be chosen on the basis of the strength of the

The Henry Wadsworth Longfellow house in Cambridge, Massachusetts, built in 1759. The porches on both ends were added 30 years later and are an important addition. They should not be removed, according to restoration experts, simply because they were not part of the original structure. "Virtually every old building," says the author, "is a collection of materials from different dates."

bricks or stones, the severity of weathering actions, and other factors.

New mortar should be color-matched to the old. This requires sand of the right color, and usually some masonry pigments. A great many buildings have been defaced by dark gray Portland cement mortar, when originally the mortar joints were the light warm white of lime. Some manufacturers offer a perfectly white Portland cement, which is extremely useful in mixing new mortar to match the color of lime.

Perhaps the worst aspect of Portland cement mortar in old masonry is that its strength makes it almost impossible to remove without damaging soft bricks or stones. As for removing old mortar prior to repointing, few people realize the damage usually done even in removing a soft, deteriorated lime mortar. Electric-powered cutting wheels are often used, which almost always damage the corners of fine, closely laid old bricks, thus some-

**What do you do when the "experts" disagree? Take enough
time to sort out people who are more expert from people who are less so.**

times noticeably enlarging narrow mortar joints. Only hand tools should be used for removing old mortar, unless in a particular situation a contractor can show that some type of power tool is not damaging in any way.

Old mortar in good condition should not be disturbed. It is normal for old mortar to be weathered back a short way from the face of the bricks; this does not mean that repointing is needed, since having eroded back a little the old mortar may be sheltered by the bricks and may not erode any further.

6 Don't Assume It Can't be Fixed.

With the advent of all kinds of modern products it has become possible to recondition partially deteriorated woodwork, plasterwork, and other architectural material that, 20 years ago, would have had to have been replaced. Thus, an old building can retain more of its authentic material, and more of its value. Often one sees old features that could be saved being carted off to the dump.

This suggestion that modern products are useful in restoration should not be seen as a contradiction of the preceding part of this article, where we pointed out that lime mortar (a traditional material) is generally better than Portland cement mortar (a more modern material) for repointing soft brickwork and stonework. Portland cement *is* extremely useful in restoration — for foundation work, for strengthening lime mortars moderately, and for many other purposes. The point is that both modern and traditional materials are useful, and that any material can be used incorrectly.

Some of the most remarkable progress in the conservation of old buildings is being made in the area of wood preservation by means of epoxies, polyesters, and other synthetic resins. Such resins are the basis of modern waterproof glues, and of many products sold in marine hardware stores for impregnating partially rotted wood or filling holes in it.

The things that can be done with waterproof glue would have amazed an old-timer accustomed to animal glue, which is water-soluble. For example, a roof balustrade of 1806 can have new wood fitted into each baluster wherever the wood is rotted away — and there need be no fear of the patches coming loose because of rain or dampness. Such a balustrade would have had to have been replaced completely prior to the introduction of waterproof glue. Waterproof glue opens the door for the extensive repair of damaged woodwork by skillful piecing-in of new wood.

In the same way, modern resins allow the renovator to restore permanent strength to old, partly rotted wood. In some methods, holes are drilled into the wood to expose the end grain, and the resin soaks into the wood through the holes, then hardens. Not only are such wood-consolidating methods popular in marine reconstruction, but similar methods are also used in the conservation of antique wooden art objects. Resin impregnation is sometimes the only way to conserve a valuable piece of woodwork in an old house: the capital of a column, the bottom of an original door.

Other modern materials can be used for consolidating weakened plaster, readhering peeling paint in wall painting, and many other purposes. Steel is a modern architectural material that, because of its great strength, can be used to permit an old beam to be reinforced, rather than having to be replaced. Very small amounts of steel can form the backbone of an inconspicuous repair that must support a heavy load.

7 Get the Design Right.

Sometimes there is no alternative but to replace something — or a portion of something — that is missing or decayed beyond repair. A basic objective in such work should be to avoid making the new piece a poor parody of the original. Much restoration work stands out like a sore thumb.

The elements of old buildings usually exhibit very specific design characteristics. Although the designs are usually similar to those of other buildings of the same date, there are important regional and individual differences that should be respected.

Old moldings — which include large items such as cornices — were usually designed according to a geometric system, which varied from one period to the next, according to whether the designers of the period were looking toward Greece or Rome or the Gothic era for their architectural details. When an old molding must be reproduced, the paint should be removed from a well-preserved section of the old piece, and the design observed and comprehended. Then, if the work of reproduction is given to a shop or mill, very specific instructions (a precise drawing, model, template, etc.) must be provided.

8 Get Help: Don't Barge Ahead.

How many times have we seen an owner, eager to "restore" a newly acquired house, rush in and tear out large portions of the interior and exterior surfaces, only to discover that the original finishes are long gone and cannot be accurately reconstructed? A professional is then brought in to make sense of a confused jumble of architectural remnants, and the owner sadly discovers, too late, that he has stripped and thrown away valuable portions of his house — the perfectly sensible and aesthetically pleasing Federal remodeling, for example.

All the points we have discussed should make it clear that a restoration or a repair going much beyond ordinary maintenance involves many technical and historical questions. Although elaborate research cannot be done on every old building, old buildings of any quality deserve the best study and care that their owners can give them. In the long run it pays off.

Two simple rules can be followed to improve the quality of repair work at little or no cost. The first is to seek professional advice. At the most basic level this means a visit by someone professionally qualified in the field, and it may save a lot of money from being spent on something that will be damaging or destructive. Even professional people in architectural history and restoration have to consult with each other constantly, according to the specialties that each person has, and there is certainly no way to get the proper information just by reading the books or articles that are available. A tremendous amount of study and experience goes into the training of professional people in the field.

A second basic rule is to take the maximum time possible to make decisions. Getting the technical or architectural history information needed is always a slow process. More disconcerting is the fact that different people supposedly qualified in the field will give different opinions and answers. What do you do when the "experts" disagree? To begin with, by taking enough time to talk to different people, you can slowly sort out people who are more expert from people who are less so.

Even then, knowledgeable people may disagree about difficult problems. But usually, if you take enough time to gather information and opinions, you can learn enough about a problem to determine the best course of action. 〆

– illustration by Mark Kelley

There's always the "last Christmas Junior will believe in Santa Claus," but few parents ever do anything about it. These parents did, and, although we published their account 13 December issues ago, there are still a few longtime subscribers who say it was Yankee's best true "Santa Claus story" ever!

"Whoa, Snitzen!"

BY STEPHEN H. BAMBERGER

Up until my wife's brainstorm of last year, Christmas, to me, was the most cherished of all the holidays.

Easter is lovely, and so is Thanksgiving, but somehow Christmas, with tiny hands reaching for tiny toys and high-pitched voices raised in song, was my favorite. It was, that is, until last year.

It all started out innocently enough with a chance remark by my wife.

"This will be the last Christmas Junior will believe in Santa Claus," was what she said, and while she was only echoing the words of parents throughout the ages, it remained for us, I believe, to be the first parents ever to *do* something about it. Our "plan," if you can call it that, was for me to dress up as Santa Claus and climb up to my son's window on Christmas Eve. Exactly what I was supposed to do when I got up there was never discussed, and to this day I still can't imagine how I ever fell for the idea in the first place.

My son's bedroom, incidentally, opens onto the first staircase landing, which makes it not as high as some low-hanging clouds but high enough for me to have to borrow my neighbor's extension ladder. Also, there is a natural tendency for a house to grow taller at night — but I can't prove this.

Christmas Eve last year, if you recall, was a clear, crisp, moonlit night. We had trimmed the tree in the afternoon and, since we always exchange gifts the following morning rather than at midnight, Junior had little to look forward to after supper, to his knowledge at any rate, other than to hang up his stocking and go to bed and dream.

To save time, I set up the ladder while he was in his bath so that all we had to do after tucking him in and listening to his prayers was to race downstairs to the basement and dress me up.

The costume my wife had purchased was extra large and consisted mostly of pillows, sewn in to prevent slippage.

There was one huge pillow in front and another huge pillow in back, and it was all I could do to buckle my patent-leather belt into the first notch. The mask and peaked hat were conventional, as was the enormous toy sack, also stuffed with pillows, that I was just about able to sling over my shoulder.

A touch of brilliance, though, was the two strings of sleigh bells that my wife, convulsed now and no longer able to talk, thrust into my free hand at the last moment. In other words, I was to be the sleigh as well as Santa. Undaunted, and giddy myself with the spirit of the occasion, I bounded up the cellar steps, shattering the stillness of the Holy Night with what seemed to be a million tinkling sleigh bells.

Bringing my knees up smartly (I blush to think of it now), as I imagined a reindeer might do at the gallop, I bobbed along the length of the house, taking short, mincing steps around the corner, then bobbed some more until I finally came to a halt beneath my son's window.

"Whoa, Prancer!" I roared, still jingling my sleigh bells frenziedly. "Whoa, Dancer! Whoa, Blitzen! Whoa, Snitzen!" and then, letting the bells slip to the ground, I approached the ladder with a hearty, "Ho! Ho! Ho!"

I had originally planned to laugh my way up the ladder, but it immediately became apparent that there was nothing particularly funny about climbing a ladder, accoutered as I was, by the light of the moon. It looked as though I wasn't going to get up there at all until I discovered that my front pillow had wedged itself securely against the rung immediately ahead of it.

Dislodging it with a muffled curse, quickly followed by a "Ho! Ho! Ho!" I took my first step upwards only to have to go through the same procedure with the same pillow all over again, so that to Junior, in his room, I must have sounded like *two* people coming up the ladder, one swearing like a trooper, the other

laughing like a maniac. I wasn't concerned about how I sounded, though. My only thought was to reach his window, before sunup, if possible, and the minute I did I made a wild grab for the sill, inadvertently disturbing the pull on his shade — which shot up out of sight with the crack of an M-1 rifle, scaring me half to death.

It must have scared him too, because the first thing I noticed as my head hove into view was that he was no longer tucked under the covers as we had left him a few minutes before. Rather, he was sitting bolt upright in a rectangle of moonlight and, if you have ever heard the phrase, "eyes wide as saucers," that's exactly the way his eyes appeared at that particular moment. Even his mouth was wide open in an expression that I mistook for one of sheer joy at seeing Jolly Saint Nick practically at the foot of his bed. "Ho! Ho! Ho!" I heard myself saying again.

What happened next, while it may take a little longer in the telling, actually transpired in less than a few seconds. Evidently the last "Ho! Ho! Ho!" did the trick, because the echo of it was still rolling down the valley when there came out of my little boy's throat a shriek so penetrating and so fearsome that I hope I never hear the likes of it again. There was stark terror in that shriek, and panic, and it was delivered with such wild abandon that I momentarily forgot where I was.

Sensing only that flesh of my flesh and blood of my blood was warning his Daddy of impending disaster, I pivoted around to fend off whatever ghastly thing might be headed my way and toppled headlong onto the holly tree below.

That's about all there is to tell about last Christmas Eve at our house. I have no idea what my wife has in mind now that another Season is upon us but, frankly, if it were up to me, I wouldn't even bother putting up a tree this year.

There is a holiday tradition in Wellesley, Massachusetts, in which over 40 women meet on a certain evening and pass around their trays of favorite Christmas cookies. When we published this article about that as part of our "Great New England Cooks" series in December 1982, we made a rather serious mistake. We offered to mail, to anyone who sent a stamped, self-addressed envelope, a printed sheet containing two dozen of the finest of those cookie recipes. In preparation, we printed up 100 sheets. Then someone said maybe that wouldn't be enough, so we went ahead and printed 200. In the three weeks following publication we received just under 18,000 requests for cookie recipes! Publisher Rob Trowbridge, knowing we were going to have to hire extra outside help, asked how much we charged each person for sending the recipes — "50¢ each or a dollar or what?" It wasn't easy to say the offer was free. But we made good on them all (while learning our little lesson).

The Great Wellesley, Massachusetts, Christmas Cookie Exchange

BY SUSAN MAHNKE

It would be like having the cookie jar of your dreams. Every time you'd reach in, you would come up with a different kind of homemade Christmas cookie: frosted sugar plums, rich tea cookies, walnut diamonds, *Zimtsterne* (cinnamon stars); cookies whose recipes immigrated across the Atlantic generations ago from Italy, Germany, France, Poland, Norway; cookies rich with sweet butter and with frosting as lavish as velvet and old lace.

Well, dreams really do come true, at least for the friends, neighbors, and relatives of Mary Bevilacqua and Laurel Gabel who come each year to the annual Christmas Cookie Exchange at Mary's home on Wall Street in Wellesley. This December, for the 11th year in a row, as many as 40 women carrying silver trays of fancy cookies (plus Tupperware boxes for carrying home their booty) will start gathering after supper one snowy evening. They'll greet Mary and Laurel, drift into Mary's candlelit dining room for punch and a choice of luscious desserts Mary and Laurel have made, and then crowd into the living room for the serious business at hand — an exchange of news, Christmas cheer, and, most of all, cookies. Each woman in turn will pass around her tray of cookies (each person makes about three dozen of one kind, from toffee squares and Sacher torte cookies to gingerbread boys, snowflake tarts, and Kifli, with rarely any duplication) while she recites the recipe and explains any idiosyncrasies of the cookie, until all 40 trays have made the

rounds and each cookie exchanger has assembled her own cookie jar of assorted holiday favorites.

"Some people search all year for a new cookie recipe to bring to the exchange," Mary said, "but even people who aren't dedicated cookie makers love to come. Laurel and I always bake an extra batch of cookies in case someone runs out of time to bake but still wants to come. One year we invited three German women who were visiting in Wellesley — they spoke no English, just beamed at us and said '*Danke*.'"

"You can tell the real hard-core cookie exchangers," Laurel added, "by the way they use baggies to separate various cookies so the flavors don't mingle too much. We try to have the party about two weeks before Christmas, so everyone will have cookies on hand for entertaining. Most cookies freeze well and thaw quickly, so lots of us just freeze platefuls of them and bring them out when company walks in the door!"

One of the keys to putting on a cookie exchange seems to be providing enough fancy desserts beforehand so that no one will be tempted to eat the cookies before taking them home. Mary and Laurel,

working together the day before, prepare something for every taste: rich, fruity Clayton carrot cake, light and citrus-y lemon-orange angel dessert, moist chocolate-frosted Yule log, featherweight Pizzelle, and the traditional flamed plum pudding. After some serious sampling, hot cider wassail punch in demitasse cups, cool Christmas punch, spiced tea, and coffee are carried into the living room, and the cookie swopping begins in earnest.

As the dozens of Christmas confections make the rounds and disappear into personal cookie collections, cookie-baking advice flies fast and furious. Here are some of the best tips from seasoned cookie bakers:

• "I always use unsalted butter — it gives cookies a lighter texture."

• "After cutting or shaping cookies, put them on cookie sheets and slip them into the freezer for a few minutes to help them hold their shape when they are baked. This also seems to make cookies a lot flakier."

• "If cookie dough is too sticky, chill it rather than add more flour. Too much flour makes cookies dry."

• "Always use a pastry cloth when rolling out gingerbread boys and other cutout

Hostesses Mary Bevilacqua and Laurel Gabel (foreground, left and right, respectively) and friends encircle a cookie-laden table in Mary's living room at their annual Christmas cookie exchange in Wellesley, Massachusetts.

– illustration by Maryann Mattson

cookies. It reduces problems with handling the sticky dough."

• "Be sure your cookie tins are flat, not warped, so that cookies will bake uniformly. Turn the tins at least once during baking time."

• "Use a flour sifter to dust confectioners' sugar onto cookies."

• "Let cookie sheets cool off between batches — a hot cookie sheet will make dough start to melt."

• "When freezing cookies, place waxed paper between layers, and use good airtight containers — you can reuse the waxed paper and containers every year."

• "Buy expensive ingredients like walnuts and coconut when they are on sale and store them in the freezer."

It was late in the evening at the recent cookie swop when final good-byes were said and everyone headed for home. I walked across the street with Eleanor Homeyer, Mary's neighbor, who has been coming to the cookie exchange since the first year. "I've always made gingerbread boys," she said, "except for one year when I thought I'd try something different. But you should have seen how everyone's face fell when I didn't bring the gingerbread boys! So I'm back to making them again. I've used the same recipe since the 1920s, when I made them with my own mother, always on the first day of Christmas vacation. The dough has to be well chilled, and there are other little tricks you learn over the years. But I think the most important thing is to have little children around to help you put on the eyes, mouth, and buttons — that's what makes it seem like Christmas."

The recipes that follow include some of Mary and Laurel's favorite suggestions for holiday refreshments, including a sampling of the wonderful cookies created each Christmas season in their neighborhood in Wellesley.

Cider Wassail
- 4 cups good fresh cider
- ¼ to ⅓ cup dark brown sugar
- ½ cup dark rum
- 2 tablespoons brandy
- 2 tablespoons apple brandy
- 1 tablespoon orange liqueur
- ¼ teaspoon cinnamon
- ¼ teaspoon ground cloves
- ⅛ teaspoon ground allspice
  Pinch salt
- 1 rounded teaspoon orange juice concentrate
  Whipped cream

Bring cider to boil. Add sugar and stir until dissolved. Remove from heat. Stir in rum, brandy, apple brandy, orange liqueur, spices, and salt. Stir in orange juice concentrate. Heat over moderate heat, stirring, for two minutes. Pour into demitasse cups or wine glasses and top with a generous amount of slightly sweetened whipped cream. (The whipped cream makes a *big* difference in the finished taste of the drink — don't omit.) Garnish with fresh nutmeg if desired. Serves 10 to 15.

Christmas Punch
- 1 quart cranberry juice
- 1 cup sugar
- 2 cups orange juice
- 1 cup pineapple juice
- ¾ cup fresh or frozen lemon juice
- ½ teaspoon almond extract
- 2 cups chilled ginger ale
- 1 pint pineapple sherbet

Blend cranberry juice, sugar, fruit juices, and almond extract. Refrigerate, covered, until serving time. Just before serving, stir in ginger ale and sherbet. Serves 10 to 12.

Lemon-Orange Angel Dessert
- 1 tablespoon unflavored gelatin
- 4 tablespoons cold water
- 1 cup boiling water
- ¾ cup sugar
  Dash of salt
- 1 cup orange juice
- ½ cup lemon juice
  grated rind of one lemon
- 1 angel cake
- 2 cups medium cream, divided
  Nuts
  Shredded coconut

Soften gelatin in cold water. Add boiling water, sugar, and salt; stir. Add juices and rind and stir again. Refrigerate 2 to 3 hours or until slightly jelled and the consistency of unbeaten egg whites. Line a 2-quart bowl with waxed paper. Break cake into small pieces and set aside.

Whip one cup of cream and fold into gelatin mixture. In lined bowl put layer of cream mixture and layer of cake cubes. Repeat, ending with cream mixture. Refrigerate 8 hours or overnight. Invert onto cake plate, peel off paper, and frost with remaining whipped cream. Sprinkle with nuts and coconut if desired. Serves 8.

Christmas Plum Pudding
- ½ cup sifted flour
- ½ teaspoon baking soda
- 1 teaspoon cinnamon
- ½ teaspoon ground cloves
- ¼ teaspoon salt
- ¾ cup fine dry bread crumbs
- ½ cup butter
- ¾ cup packed light brown sugar
- 3 eggs
  One 30-ounce can purple plums, drained and chopped
- 1 tablespoon freshly grated orange rind
- 8 ounces pitted dates, cut up
- 1 cup seedless raisins
- 8 ounces mixed candied fruits, chopped
- 1 cup chopped pecans
- ½ cup currants

Grease an 8-cup pudding mold and dust evenly with granulated sugar. Sift flour, soda, cinnamon, cloves, and salt into small bowl. Stir in bread crumbs. Cream butter and sugar, and beat in eggs, one at a time. Stir in plums and orange rind. Gently blend in the flour mixture, then fold in dates, raisins, candied fruit, pecans, and currants. Spoon into prepared mold. Lock lid in place or cover with foil and tie tightly with string. Place on a rack in a kettle that has a tight-fitting lid. Pour in boiling water to about one-half the depth of the mold. Cover tightly and steam for about 4½ hours or until pudding is firm. Cool pudding in mold for 5 minutes. Loosen around edge with knife. Invert onto serving plate. Allow to stand at least 15 minutes to cool. Garnish with rum sauce. Serve warm.

– illustrations by Maryann Mattson

May be made ahead and frozen. Reheat, defrosted, wrapped in foil, in 400° oven for 30 minutes. Yield: 16 to 20 small servings.

Plum Pudding Sauce

 3 ounces cream cheese
 1 egg
 1 cup confectioners' sugar
 2 tablespoons butter
 1 teaspoon lemon juice
   Pinch salt
 1 cup heavy cream, whipped
   About 2 tablespoons golden rum

Beat cheese until light. Add egg, sugar, butter, lemon juice, and salt. Beat well. Fold in whipped cream and rum just until combined. Store, covered, in refrigerator until serving time.

Best Cheesecake

Crust:
 1½ cups graham cracker crumbs
 3 tablespoons sugar
 ½ teaspoon cinnamon
 ¼ cup sweet butter, melted

Filling:
 3 8-ounce packages cream cheese at room temperature
 1¼ cups sugar
 6 eggs, separated
 2 cups sour cream
 ⅓ cup flour
 2 teaspoons vanilla
   Grated rind of 1 lemon
   Juice of ½ lemon

Crust: Generously grease a 9-inch springform pan with butter. Place pan in center of a 12-inch square of aluminum foil and press foil up around side of pan. Combine graham cracker crumbs, sugar, cinnamon, and melted butter in a small bowl until well blended. Press ¾ cup of crumb mixture onto bottom and sides of pan. Chill prepared pan while making filling. (Reserve remaining crumb mixture for topping.)
Filling: Using an electric mixer at low speed, beat cream cheese until soft.

Gradually beat in sugar until light and fluffy. Beat in egg yolks, one at a time, until well blended. Stir in sour cream, flour, vanilla, lemon rind, and juice until smooth. Beat egg whites until they hold stiff peaks. Gently fold whites into cheese mixture until well blended. Pour into prepared pan. Bake at 350° for 75 minutes. Turn the oven off and allow cake to cool in the closed oven for 1 hour. Remove to wire rack and cool to room temperature. Chill overnight before serving. Serves 10 to 12.

Chocolate Mint Sticks

 2 beaten eggs
 ½ cup melted margarine
 2 squares unsweetened chocolate, melted
 1 cup sugar
 ½ teaspoon vanilla
 ½ cup flour

Frosting:
 2 tablespoons butter
 1 cup sifted confectioners' sugar
 1 tablespoon cream
 ½ teaspoon peppermint flavoring or 1 to 2 tablespoons creme de menthe
 ½ square unsweetened chocolate, melted
 1½ tablespoons melted butter

For cookies: Combine all ingredients except flour and beat well. Blend in flour. Pour into a greased and floured 9-inch square pan. Bake at 350° for 25 minutes. Let sit to cool before frosting.

For frosting: Mix butter, sugar, cream, and peppermint flavoring. Spread over cooled baked layer. When frosting is firm, mix melted chocolate and butter and drizzle over all. Place in refrigerator until firm. Cut into small sticks or squares and put in small cupcake papers. Makes about 4½ dozen.

Mary's Lemon Nutmeg Meltaways

 1 cup sifted cake flour
 ½ cup cornstarch

 ¼ teaspoon salt
 ½ teaspoon nutmeg
 10 tablespoons unsalted butter, softened
 ½ cup confectioners' sugar
 2 teaspoons grated lemon rind

Sift dry ingredients onto waxed paper. Beat butter, sugar, and lemon rind in mixer until light and fluffy. Add dry ingredients. Beat on low speed until mixture is smooth. Shape teaspoonfuls of dough into balls and place on an ungreased baking sheet. Flatten slightly to 1¼-inch circles with the bottom of a glass dipped in confectioners' sugar. Bake at 325° for 15 minutes or until golden brown around the edges. Cool for 2 minutes on cookie sheet and then transfer to a wire rack to finish cooling.

Laurel's Kifli

Dough:
 2 cups flour
 1 cup butter
 2 egg yolks, slightly beaten
 ½ cup sour cream

Filling:
 10 ounces walnuts, ground (about 2 cups)
 ½ cup granulated sugar
 ¼ cup light cream or milk
 1½ teaspoons almond extract
 1 egg, beaten with a little water

To make dough:

Cut butter into flour with pastry blender until mixture resembles coarse crumbs. Add egg yolks and sour cream; stir until just combined. Knead briefly on a lightly floured surface until dough is smooth. Shape into a flat round, wrap in plastic wrap and refrigerate.

To make filling:

Combine nuts, sugar, milk, and extract. Blend well.

Preheat oven to 400°. Grease cookie sheets. On a lightly floured surface, roll out half of dough until it is about ⅛-inch thick, roughly 12 x 16 inches. Cut into 2-inch squares. Use a soft paintbrush to paint the top of each square lightly with egg and water mixture. Spread a rounded half teaspoonful of filling diagonally down center of square. Overlap two opposite corners over filling; pinch to seal. Repeat with other half of dough. Brush tops with egg-water mixture and sprinkle lightly with sugar. Place about 2 inches apart on cookie sheets. Bake until nicely browned, about 15 minutes. Cool on rack. Dust with confectioners' sugar. Makes about 40 cookies.

While "Whoa, Snitzen" (page 296) is considered by many to be Yankee's best true "Santa Claus story," here is fiction's candidate. And yet we've always had the haunting suspicion this might be true as well!

It's Ridiculous to Say He Lives at the North Pole

FICTION BY KATHLEEN LEVERICH

It is not true that he always wears a red suit and drives a team of reindeer. And it is ridiculous to say that he lives at the North Pole. He must be like the wind, like the grass on the ground; he must be everywhere and everywhere be inconspicuous, unremarked. The job requires him to keep a close eye on each one of us, but secretly, so that we don't suspect. He must contribute that sense of security to a place, so that we all relax and are ourselves in his presence, but ineffably, so that no one guesses *why* we can relax: his presence.

Never believe that he enters your life by way of grubby chimneys and cold hearths. That you need do nothing but refrain from lighting a cozy fire, and he will come. That leaving a few stale graham crackers and milk, or even a shot of whiskey and chopped carrot sticks for the reindeer will be enough to attract him. There is more involved to it than that.

He hates snacks and never drinks alone. He invariably eats large meals of local fare in whatever little village or urban neighborhood he finds himself close to or hankering for as mealtime approaches. You will always find him at the table with the crowd that is laughing and intimate, but not self-consciously so. He drinks house wines, beer, and sometimes aquavit — but this is only when it has just finished snowing and the sky is crystal clear. He drinks aquavit, then he goes skating on the river that extends forever.

You can watch him growing smaller and smaller, moving toward the horizon. You wonder, will he ever come back? You grow doubtful, then lonely, then very, very frightened.

Night falls and there is still no sign of him. Probably he has found a more beautiful, a more interesting town, far down the river.

A voice begins to whisper of the dark.

Just then, the door opens. It is he.

This is one time when the overdone remarks about his red cheeks and nose are true. And his laugh. His laugh. You hear it and you forget your doubts and loneliness; you remember your fright. You run to him and bury your head in his chest. He hugs you. He hugs you.

Later when he smokes his pipe — yes, that part is true, too. When he smokes his pipe and you all gather around his knees like cats and dogs, he will pet you to calm your fears. You will be devoted to him.

This is how it is when you know him, when he reveals himself and you recognize him. That used to happen often, but have you noticed? Such times have grown rarer as you've grown older.

Maybe it's a game, you think, and he is making it harder each year. Perhaps he is simply growing old and tired. Or maybe he isn't as

– illustration by P. Henderson Lincoln

The following three days and nights were the worst I'd ever spent. I was afraid all the time. Afraid to be alone ... I kept hearing the voice on the phone ...

amusing and powerful as you thought when you were younger. Children are easily impressed, after all.

Have you noticed that the presents under the tree are not wonderful anymore? You know what they are before you unwrap them; you can tell by the shapes, because you get only things you've asked for. Nothing else.

Where's his imagination, that used to stun with the fulfillment of unutterable yearnings? A phial of water from the spring at Delphi. An incantation against demonic possession from Swabian gypsies. A Sherpa child's doll that moves in its mind in the Himalayas. You get nothing, these days, but what you've asked for. And what wonders can *you* conceive of, these days?

Telephoto lenses and magazine subscriptions. I closed my eyes as I answered my own question, one snowless mid-December evening. Just then my wife came in, noticeably breathless.

"Write down," she said, "what you'd like for Christmas if you could have *things not of this world.* Make a list, and I will, too," she said. There was a glow in her cheeks, and she was half whispering. She might have been suggesting some daring thing we should do before our parents came home.

Telephoto lenses and magazine subscriptions. Not even new magazines; she'd just renewed last year's.

"What's the point of that?" I said. Her excitement made me angry.

She looked frightened and went away to baste the roast. I sat at my desk and looked at the empty hearth. I fiddled with a pencil, and doodling, wrote, "What I want for Christmas" on the top of a fresh sheet of notepaper.

Things not of this world. . . .

"A real Santa Claus," I wrote.

"The Collinses have invited us for drinks tomorrow at six." My wife was carrying holly and the crèche figures over to the coffee table. I crumpled the paper and threw it into the wastebasket.

"Fine," I said.

It never snows anymore.

I went to bed that night feeling hollow. Maybe that's just what he wanted. Maybe it's a game, and he empties us out to fill us up. I lay awake that night and watched the moon rise over the dead lawn. I thought about Christmases when I was a child. I thought of my mother saying to me, "Don't peek in the closet." I had been good; I hadn't peeked inside the boxes, only gazed for long, stolen

– illustration by P. Henderson Lincoln

moments at the presents, stacked on the shelves. Now, as I closed my eyes, I saw my mother. She was as old as she'd been when she died, and she spoke in that short complaining voice, "Where was my closet? Where were my surprises? Did you ever think that I might have inexpressible yearnings, too?"

The next day passed as a dream. I couldn't get my mother's words out of my head. I found myself pacing my office — a thing I never do. My secretary eyed me strangely. Finally lunchtime came. I ducked the crowd from the legal department and went out alone. I had no idea where I was going.

I walked away from the part of town I know. The blocks grew darker and emptier. The wind blew litter along the gutter. It was three days before Christmas, and the sky was threatening rain. It was 45 degrees. Rain.

I passed a door with a cat's-paw decal on the door. A shoemaker. I passed a grocery with stacks of canned garbanzo beans in the window. I passed a door with red curtains covering the top half and a poster paint picture opaquing the bottom. It was a picture of Santa Claus in a sleigh, driving a team of reindeer.

I walked carefully to the end of the block. I argued with myself on the corner for a few moments, then went back.

No one answered when I knocked. I tried the door. It opened. I looked around for someone to accuse me, for someone to stop me. The block was empty, except for people crossing the avenues at either end. I pushed the door farther open and went in.

There was a counter with two dilapidated desks behind it. One had a phone, a blotter, and a pencil holder on it. The other had a typewriter. A bulletin board was tacked all over with what looked like order forms and bills of lading. There were "In/Out" boxes on the counter; both were full, but the "In" box was overflowing.

No one was there. I called out, "Hello," and "Excuse me," and "Can anybody help me?" but no one answered.

The telephone rang and nobody came. I stood waiting. The phone kept ringing. Finally I let out a "Damn it," and went over to answer it myself.

"Walter?" the voice said.

"Who is this?" I asked. My palms were sweating.

"This is Santa Claus, Walter."

Somebody had come into the back room and was shaking bells. There was

music, too. I could hear it beginning very faintly at first, but getting louder.

Those clowns from the office —

"You came here strictly on your own, Walter. Remember?"

The voice was familiar. A smell like a bakery or a kitchen at Christmas hit me, and I thought I was going to pass out.

"I've come to town, Walter. I'm very close to you, so you'd better watch out."

I ran out of the little office without putting the phone back on the hook.

The following three days and nights were the worst I'd ever spent. I was afraid all the time. Afraid to be alone, but distracted in company and afraid people might see that I was distracted, frightened — and frightening. I kept hearing in my mind the voice on the phone in that little office.

On Christmas Eve while my wife was trimming the tree, I put on my coat and walked out. She called down the hall after me, first angry, then crying. I didn't even look back.

I took a taxi downtown, but had it drop me two blocks from the spot, in front of a bar. I thought of going in for a drink, but just looking through the window, through the spray-on snow and tinsel, just seeing the dark figures huddled around the bar in the dim light from the overhead television, stopped me.

I walked down the block. It was windy and, again, felt like rain. It could have been an April evening, except for the occasional holly wreath and burst of canned caroling.

There was a muffled light behind the door. It made the red curtain and the painted Santa Claus glow faintly.

I hesitated with my hand on the latch.

I thought of Nat King Cole on the stereo and a fire burning on the hearth. I thought about mixing one big drink and then calling the neighbors in for another. I thought about dimming all the lights, except the ones on the tree, about putting my arms around my wife's neck and pulling her to me. About making love, slightly drunk, and falling into a dreamless, satisfied sleep. In the morning everything would be all right; the worst would be over. Christmas would be almost over; only the predictable presents to unwrap.

My hand tightened on the latch. I pressed it and pushed in.

There was a suit, boots, a hat, and a pipe lying neatly on the swivel chair behind the desk with the typewriter on it.

On top of the typewriter was an envelope addressed to me, "Walter."

I put on the suit. It felt extremely comfortable, which surprised me, since I have never felt comfortable in red. My wife bought me a red sport coat one Christmas, and it's still hanging in the closet with the tags on it.

The boots were a perfect fit and didn't cramp my feet or make them hot, as I'd expected they would.

Could I get away with a pipe? I'd always avoided pipes on the theory that I'd look affected smoking one. I put this funny old meerschaum in my mouth and looked around for a mirror. There was one over the water cooler. No hint of affectation at all; it looked like part of my face. But the mass of white hair and the beard were partly responsible. I couldn't have gotten away with it before, but now that I had them . . . all perfectly in character.

Somewhere a church clock chimed.

Eight o'clock. I didn't have all night, I reminded myself. I went back to the desk with the typewriter and picked up the envelope. I heard bells, again in the back room, singing and, this time, tapping, like hooves. They sounded restless.

I pulled my spectacles from my pocket, settled them on my nose, and tore open the envelope.

A million letters tumbled out.

"Dear Santa," written in crayon.

"Dear Santa," in pencil.

It is not true that he always wears a red suit and drives a team of reindeer.

"Dear Santa, Are you coming to my house?"

Little girl, I am your house.

And it is ridiculous to say that he lives at the North Pole.

"Dear Santa, What is your real name?"

My real name is Santa, little boy, but people call me Walter and Ann and William and Irene. . . .

The job requires him to keep a close eye on each one of us, but secretly, so that we don't suspect.

"Dear Santa, Can you see me? Can you see me when the lights are out and I'm lying alone in the dark?"

You are never alone in the dark.

I am like the wind, little girl. I am like the grass on the ground, little boy. I am in the next room, always. I am at the window, always.

Listen. I am very close.

We asked Jeanne Rollins of Monhegan Island, Maine, a sternwoman on a lobster boat,
to describe for us one of her typical winter days beginning before sunrise.
Here is her reply, word for word. . . .

All Winter in the Stern of a Lobster Boat

BY JEANNE ROLLINS
photography by Carole Allen

My stride is too short and the gloves are too big. My hands and feet get cold very quickly and I need a four-inch wooden block to help me see out the windshield. If you saw me walking down the road, just barely able to see out of my oilclothes, you would not identify me as a big, hardy Maine lobsterman. Rather, you'd probably pass me off as a back-to-nature city slicker overdressed for the weather. Despite my inappropriate physical appearance, I spend my winters as sternwoman on a lobster boat.

My day starts about an hour and a half before the sun comes up. As Steve rolls over to get another half hour of sleep, I crawl out of the warm blankets and miserably accept the fact that I have to wake up. Probably what I need at this time of the day is a cup of hot coffee. However, fearing the call of nature on the icy sea with its limited facilities, I take my misery in utter loneliness. It takes a conscious effort for me to put the morning eggs on the table instead of in the lunch bag with the sandwiches. Nevertheless, when all is squared away, I can awaken Steve for breakfast. Now when Steve wakes up, he's as wide awake and obnoxious as a playful kitten. It is fortunate that when I bite my lip to protect myself, Steve interprets it as a smile. Breakfast is inhaled while I'm still pouring his coffee, which he drinks as he pulls on his boots. His accelerated pace helps me to forget the biting cold that awaits me outside the door. I finish putting on my six or seven layers of clothes and then stiffly follow Steve. The cold always hits me with an unanticipated shock. When there is a fresh snowfall on the ground I follow Steve's path to conserve my own energy.

Down at the beach there are usually others getting ready to go out. It is still dark, but the sun will provide some light and an effort at some heat before long. If there is a surf at the beach I watch the different styles of launching the skiffs. It usually takes careful timing, a push followed by a quick leap and a scrambling

---

Early morning lobstering duties for Jeanne Rollins include pulling traps, removing lobsters, rebaiting, and washing down the deck.

307

At this point I'm glad that we lobster in the winter: it saves us the odor of hot bait.

When the air is so much colder than the water, the lobsters have to be put into the tank quickly to protect them from freezing.

for the oars. Steve rows while I try to sit as still as possible among the tubs of bait. I shiver as I watch our boat, *My Three Sons,* bobbing heavily on the mooring, weighed down by the ice and snow accumulated overnight.

Preparing to go out is just a matter of setting up the bait tray while Steve checks the engine for any remote sign of weakness that could lead to engine failure. I blow my nose, fork the bait into the tray, and then blow my nose again. At this point I'm glad that we lobster in the winter: it saves us the odor of hot bait. Cold, salted bait causes no trouble as long as the bait was fresh when it was

salted. With the lobster tank full of water, the plugs in the cull box, and the irons baited, I usually get a chance to blow my nose again before we head out.

I watch with terror as Steve grabs at the safety line on his way to the bow to drop the mooring. The deck is often very icy and treacherous. I've worried many times about how I, weighing less than half of what Steve weighs, could ever pull his eighth of a ton (dry weight) from the water and into the boat if he fell in.

Hauling the traps is a matter of teamwork. Steve gaffs the buoy and puts it through the hauler while I pull the warp to the stern of the boat. The warp is a

well-known danger on any lobster boat and must be kept well out of the way to prevent anyone's getting a foot caught in it when the trap is reset. As the trap comes aboard I open it, discard the old bait, rebait it with a fresh bait bag, and plug the lobsters that Steve has measured and put into the cull box. In the winter, lobsters have to be plugged very quickly and carefully to protect them from freezing or shedding a claw. The air is much colder than the water, so we have to put the lobsters into the tank just as quickly as possible.

Plugging a lobster requires a lot of respect for the animal. You have to be firm and let him know who's boss. It may sound from this description that I have no trouble plugging lobsters. In reality, I do. First of all, my outstretched hand measures seven inches from thumb to little finger, compared to nine inches for Steve. I cannot physically hold both lobster claws in one hand. For this reason, I have had to design my own style of plugging. After much trial and error, I have come up with a fast but awkward method. As I grab the big claw with my left hand, I use the back of my right hand to quickly pin the other claw against the corner of the cull box. With the lobster plug already in my right hand, I pull the big claw over close enough so that I can plug it. If the plug breaks I mutter a few unusual words, let the lobster go, and start all over again. With the big claw taken care of, there is no problem in plugging the smaller one. Meanwhile I have to keep my eye on the other unplugged lobsters in the box; they want to bite me just as badly as the one I'm working on does. Frequently I'll be concentrating so hard that I won't notice Steve

Steve Rollins and the author at the end of a lobstering day.

I smile, knowing full well that Steve is going to help finish off a six-pack or have a touch of rum and that supper will sit in the oven . . . It doesn't bother me.

Seals lounge on Eastern Duck Rock on Monhegan enjoying the last rays of sunlight.

sneaking up from behind to grab me. This sends a chill right up my spine, as I imagine that a lobster has taken hold from an unprotected direction. Steve must get great satisfaction from hearing my screams of terror when he does this, for each time he surprises me just as much as the first time he ever did it.

The difficulty of finding warm, waterproof gloves makes plugging lobsters even harder. Winter gloves that are made for lobstering are sold in only one size, men's extra large. That leaves an extra two inches of hard glove that won't allow me to pick up a lobster plug. I must experiment with different combinations of gloves. I still haven't come up with a completely satisfactory arrangement, although I can get by.

We go through the day in this same way, hauling as many strings of traps as we can in the daylight hours. Darkness sets in very early in the winter, so most of

the fishermen try to make the best of the daylight by staying out right up until the sun sets. What a beautiful feeling it is to come around Green Point, the northern end of Monhegan Island, and see the sun setting low in the western sky. In the pink light of dusk, other fishing boats are also finishing up the day's work and heading for the harbor. There are always some seals near Eastern Duck Rock, either peering out of the surf or propped up against a rock, taking in the last rays of sunlight. The half-forgotten chill of the morning wind returns as I busily wash down the deck and bait tray. Coming around the wharf and into the harbor, lights can be seen all around where many of the 14 fishing boats are storing their catches. Steve and I tie up at the mooring and count our lobsters as we transfer them gently into the car. My thoughts drift from the sea to the kitchen; I begin to list the chores that need tending to.

Back on the mooring, I closely watch Steve pulling the mooring chain over the bow. It is just as easy for him to fall overboard in the evening as it is in the morning. With the boat secured for the night, we row ashore with that funny style of rowing that only fishermen use, stern first. Others are also at the beach, where everyone lends a hand at pulling the skiffs up to the fishhouses. Steve takes a big stretch and says, "Well, dear, I think I'll stop in at the fishhouse for a few minutes." I smile, knowing full well that Steve is going to help finish off a six-pack or have a touch of rum, and that supper will sit in the oven until he gets home. It doesn't bother me. After I get my chores done I've got plenty of good books to read and a lot of work left on my needlepoint. Besides, it feels "some good" to be going home.

Right: My Three Sons *heads back to harbor at sunset. "What a beautiful feeling it is to come around Green Point, the northern end of Monhegan Island, and see the sun setting low in the western sky."*

A•DECEMBER SAMPLER

☞ Memorable thoughts, quotes, and assorted tidbits from the last 50 December issues. ☜

WINTER DIVERSIONS ARE FEW

☞ Weather is the talk of the idle and the dull everywhere, but here on Nantucket weather gets more than normal attention. In winter we are especially sensitive to the fact of our separation from the mainland. Although some of us never leave the island short of personal tragedy or serious business to be done over there, we still notice the coming and going of the ferryboats. When a boat is cancelled by high winds or when the harbor freezes and won't let the boat in, that is the talk of the town. Although small planes now carry more winter passengers across Nantucket Sound to Hyannis than "the boat" does, the ferry remains the stronger symbolic link to the mainland.

In winter diversions are few — a common complaint among the year-round residents. Although the island attracts recluses and though people generally stay close to home when it blows, everyone seems to take comfort in the thought that there is something to do just in case they might like to. There is a local dramatic group and occasional visits by performers of music or dance. The high school students put on a thing or two, and there is some limited public recreation for the active of body. But at bottom, Nantucket passes the winter watching television, commenting on the weather, and going downtown for the newspaper and mail. We are most blessed by the cable, which brings not only Boston and Providence channels, but a number of pay-TV channels. And Nantucketers drink, all seasons. Alcohol is very popular here, our 6000 winter residents sustaining four full-time package stores and that many bars. Every small town has its public town drunk; we have at least half a dozen. The exact number depends on whom you ask to recite the census. (*From "Wintering on Nantucket" by Robert Kaldenbach.*)

We must acknowledge that quite a few readers objected strenuously to the article from which the above is excerpted and perhaps this passage caused the bulk of the criticism. So we don't include the excerpt here in defiance of those feelings — but rather simply for those of our readers who say it is one of their all-time Yankee favorites.

John Kenneth Galbraith.

THANKS FOR THE COMPLIMENT, MR. GALBRAITH

☞ "I suppose there is a sort of cultural and political identity to New England. But New England regionalism is kept alive by journalists and magazines like *Yankee* because it is a good story." (*From "John Kenneth Galbraith on New England" by Frederick John Pratson.*)

A•FAVORITE LETTER

THE GREAT PLATE DEBATE

☞ One can hardly fault General John Stark, the hero of the Revolutionary War Battle of Bennington, for the polite letter he wrote in 1809. That year the 81-year-old, New Hampshire-born general advised a group he would be unable to attend a celebration of the American victory at Bennington. In closing, General Stark suggested a toast: "Live free or die; death is not the worst of evils."

Some 170 years later, however, that toast has become the center of another battle, setting at odds two camps in New Hampshire — those who feel the phrase "Live Free or Die" should remain on the state's license plates, and those who think it should not. The slogan, prominently embossed on plates since 1970, was the focus of the recent Task Force on Tourism, which recommended it be dropped. They suggested that the word "scenic" be included in any new plate motto.

Since the task force report, the great plate debate has swelled to include a number of politicians as well as two major New Hampshire newspapers, one of which, the *Concord Monitor*, made several suggestions, including "Eat Your Squash," "Buy Booze," and "Bring Money." Leigh Bosse, one of eight Republicans who sought the gubernatorial nomination, proposed a compromise: "Live Free or Die in Scenic New Hampshire."

Ken Hayward

THE LESSON

☞ That's how it was each Christmas Eve — until the one I remember best. Yes, it was my father up there on the roof each year, crashing about with a broom handle for "hoof clomping," a large string of sleigh bells that he barely wiggled or thrashed about violently to give the various illusions of distance, and wearing heavy, leather-soled riding boots. On this particular best-remembered year, he was also wearing a pair of brand-new riding breeches he had received as a Christmas Eve present from my mother an hour or so earlier.

"Ho! Ho! Ho!" he roared as usual. We were in that phase of the ritual. From the bottom of our beds we heard his heavy footsteps overhead move toward the chimney. "Whoa there!" he shouted as hooves clomped loudly. It seemed he was about to launch into a fresh string of ho ho's

when there was a heavy thump that literally shook the house. This was followed by a loud string of the most wicked curse words you can ever imagine hearing — in a voice both my sister and I instantly recognized.

"That's Dad!" we both shouted, practically in unison, as we emerged from under those many layers of blankets and sprang to the window. Sure enough, there under the bright star-studded winter sky up on our roof was Dad. He'd just risen from the slippery place where he'd fallen and was examining a long tear in the rear of his new riding breeches.

"Dad!" we yelled again. He looked over at us framed in the partially open window. "Hey, kids," he said with a sort of foolish grin, "you're supposed to be in bed."

It was all over. We knew everything there was to know. (*From "The Christmas I Learned Everything" by J.D.H.*)

A PUBLIC RELATIONS NIGHTMARE FOR *YANKEE*

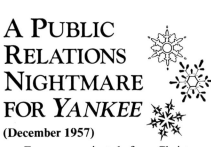

(December 1957)

☞ Every year, just before Christmas, Mr. Edward Rowe Snow packs his plane with Christmas remembrances for his lighthouse-keeper friends all along the New England coast. These he drops into welcoming arms from Maine to Florida.

Last year, as an old friend of this publication, he asked if he could make a similar airdrop over Dublin, where *Yankee* is published. Frantically, a few days before "airdrop" date, he phoned to ask for the name of some local organization that would most appreciate the thrill of these gifts from the sky.

Dublin has a women's club, Grange, Fire Department, and public school, but we felt the most appreciative audience would be our little "Brownies."

These are tots too young for Boy or Girl Scout activities. So we told Mr. Snow our "Brownies" would be just the group — and we told the latter to assemble on the Town Oval on the big day for the event.

Dramatic and pleasurable do not adequately describe the event. The roar of

the propellers, the low-flying red plane, Santa Claus waving in his red and white suit, then the bundles being dropped — all made for a thrill Dublin will not soon forget.

The bundles were immediately retrieved and taken in a truck to the school to await a "grand opening." The *Yankee* staff returned to work, smug and confident in the good deed they had helped to bring about.

But an ominous silence became apparent. No mention of the incident was made. The local minister gave *Yankee*'s publisher only cold stares — the high school principal cut him dead. There were mysterious rumors flying around about "investigations" and that "some local business should be run out of town." Finally, the school janitor told *Yankee*'s publisher what even his best friends had not dared to do — namely, that these bundles had contained razor blades, cigars, cigarettes, dirty magazines, and salacious paperback novels.

It was at that point that Publisher Robb Sagendorph, a Bostonian, too, suddenly remembered that of course the word "Brownies" to most Bostonians means a group of thick-skinned, toughened athletes who make a practice of swimming, come midwinter, in such places as Boston Harbor. Naturally, Mr. Snow had assumed that Dublin had such a group and had made the presents up accordingly. (*From "What Is a Brownie?" by Anthony Anable, then one of* Yankee*'s editors.*)

Edward Rowe Snow, as Santa, circling Dublin, New Hampshire, after dropping presents to the wrong "Brownies."

– Don Bousquet

"When you get to my chimney, you're going to be confronted by an airtight fireplace insert with a three-stage blower manifold and a catalytic combustor. . . . I'll leave the back door ajar."

OUR FAVORITE "HOUSE FOR SALE"

– Stephen Whitney

☞ Many people have asked us during the past 50 years what was the most popular "House for Sale" we've ever featured. There have been so many that we'll simply avoid the issue by saying that our "favorite" was the Garland Mill, the last of New Hampshire's water-powered sawmills operated for profit, which we featured in the December 1973 issue. On Gar-

land Brook in Lancaster, New Hampshire, the property included an 1856 mill in great working order; a nice five-bedroom house; seven acres with the brook, millpond, and wonderful views of Mt. Cabot and the Pilot Range; and innumerable outbuildings, including an old blacksmith shop and two garages. Owner Harold Alden was pretty reluctant to sell this place — he'd lived on it and from it for more than 70 years — but then nobody is particularly happy about some of the decisions that are dictated by advancing years. He was, as we recall, even reluctant to talk price, but eventually allowed as how the whole thing "should fetch nearly $50,000."

The next time we heard anything about it was four years later. A young couple from Philadelphia, Tom and Nancy Southworth, had bought it and were clearing about $7000 a year from it. Not a lot of money — but we envied them.

GOING DOWN WITH THE ONLY SEVEN-MASTER

☞ Old Hoodoo was still with us. We never did pick up Scilly Light, but, by navigation and record of courses sailed, we knew we were somewhere in the vicinity of the Scilly Islands, some 35 miles off the coast of Cornwall, England. It was about the 16th day out, Friday, December 13 (1907), about 5:30 P.M. Others of the crew and myself were forward on the forecastle head straining our eyes and ears for a sight or sound. Suddenly there was the roar of breakers ahead. Breakers it was! Our ears caught sound of it for position, to look, the eye getting a short, hurried view through what was left of the evening dusk at what turned out to be Hell Weather Reef.

With Hell Weather Reef under the bow, off St. Agnes, Annett Island, with no orders given I let go the anchor on my own.

No skipper could face a more trying, difficult nautical situation to pull out of, with the largest steel schooner

in the world under his feet, with seven great towering masts at the mercy of the elements, with little or no sail power to negotiate with in such a tight spot. Inevitably, our bare jury rig was about as useful as the cook's dish towels. Our heavy suit of sail power had blown away.

Chain ran out, anchors hit bottom. We ran plenty more chain through the hawsepipes to check her. The strain soon began to be felt, holding enough to swing her head around, clearing the reef. She swung clear round off Annett Head, but she kept dragging; the anchors wouldn't hold enough to spot her. The big hooks were bumping over rocky bottom.

She continued to drag, steadily contiguous to Annett Island, uninterrupted by good holding bottom. From the time we anchored at sunset the *Lawson* never stopped dragging to loo'ard; the anchors couldn't get a good grip to spot her. It was 11 P.M. the same night when she touched bottom, hard, with a falling tide. It was no sandbank we hit, but a solid, rugged reef. She grounded well aft. All hands were on deck.

Minutes after stranding on the reef,

The Thomas W. Lawson

– The Blackington Collection

all seven masts went by the board. The starboard rigging let go. A heavy sea smacked the ship, and she swung her head round with it, heading straight for and up a cliff. With the masts gone, the big sticks toppling to port carrying the men with them, all was over now, including the hopes of the men borne to a watery grave with the steel sticks of the *Thomas W. Lawson*. It was every man for himself. **Edward L. Rowe of Annisquam, Massachusetts, one of the two survivors of the *Lawson*'s last voyage.** (*From "The Last Voyage of the Thomas W. Lawson" by Captain William P. Coughlin.*)

How I Became Engaged to Cornelia Gould

☞ "Hello," I said.

"Hello, this is Evelyn Austin." My heart sank. It was my mother — the patron saint of interruption, the queen of chaos.

I disguised my voice. "Evelyn who?"

"Stephen, don't be rude — it is your mother."

It developed there was no escape. She would be in Boston within two hours, driving, as I knew she would, in second gear the entire way from Walpole, New Hampshire — first over the old Keene road, bouncing and banging along in her '47 Chevy, nose down, tail up. Her mechanic, having finally solved her constant need for shocks, ended the matter one day in a moment of pique by installing two new ones in the rear of her vehicle that must have been meant for a 2½-ton army truck.

Through Keene she would come, her pace slackened only slightly, a token gesture to its pedestrians. "Have you ever noticed that all the people you see in Keene have a funny frightened look?" she once asked my father.

She would take 119 to Route 2. The police couldn't possibly catch her on such a winding road. She would make good time because she would cut every corner and jump every amber light.

Her plan was full of detail inextricably cross-hatched with my own near future. I was the center of her focus these days, ever since the announcement of my engagement to Cornelia Gould.

I can't exactly name the person who made that announcement. Indeed, I don't even remember proposing. There *was* one evening when the very wealthy Mr. and Mrs. Gould came to dinner. ("They are the Pittsburgh Goulds," Mother had confided to me once when I was six years old. "A fine family. . . .") As usual, they brought their daughter Cornelia with them. I had had perhaps more than my share of the wine when the subject of marriage came up on the level of "wouldn't it be jolly if Stephen and Cornelia one day decided to marry."

I assumed it was all fairly theoretical

– Austin Stevens

— choosing to ignore "Corny's" alternate blushes and giggles, as well as most of the conversation. So when the end of the meal came and mother turned to me and asked, ". . . the week of the seventh or the week of the twenty-first?" I naturally assumed she was talking about a dinner party.

"Why not the seventh?" I said, sweeping the air with my wine glass. That's when they all cheered except old Corny, whose eyes grew large and soft and . . . fixed on me.

Mother's plans for the later afternoon included a trip to Paine's Furniture. I was to meet her there promptly at five to five. One of her wedding presents would be a bed or beds, and there was a problem even in this.

"Well, I don't see why you insist on a double bed, Stephen," she had said less than a week ago. "You'll be much more comfortable in twin beds."

"Double beds are for roommates," I said, "and I'm told that Corny and I are to be married."

Grave then, she looked me in the eye and asked, "You're not marrying Cornelia for sex, are you, Stephen?"

That was the kind of question parents asked offspring in those days. And the whole trouble with answering it was that I wasn't sure exactly what other good reason I might substitute for the one Mother found so abhorrent. *(From "Dinner at the Ritz" by Stephen Austin, a subtle pen name often used by Austin Stevens, then — December 1976 — Yankee's Managing Editor.)*

I Remember

"It Puffed Like Tophet"

☞ Every man over the age of 40 must be able to recall the Christmas he finally got his Weeden engine — the best-known and best-loved old-time toy of them all. In order to have one, you had to sell a certain number of subscriptions to the *Youth's Companion,* a Boston story magazine which arrived every Thursday and was idolized by thousands of boys and girls — and their parents — from 1827 to 1929. The little power plant was devised in 1881 by William H. Weeden of New Bedford, Massachusetts. Its use as a subscription gimmick by the *Companion* began in 1883. Similar engines were made before and have been made since, but the Weeden engine is the one most of us had. Mr. Weeden designed 45 models. An upright, the "Big Giant," was the most popular. It stood on a sturdy metal base. Its shining boiler was filled through the stack, which enclosed a safety valve. An alcohol lamp made the steam. It "puffed like Tophet" as the flywheel spun a grooved pulley, with string for a belt, to run a little grindstone, a tiny lathe, a water pump that splashed happily, a tinker-toy, or a wee music box. Remember?

Courtesy of Frank W. Lovering

WHEN THE OLD RHYMES JUST WON'T DO

Yankee editor Larry Willard hit a responsive nerve in readers who were grandparents with this true anecdote.

☞ Like most grandfathers, I spend more time with my grandchildren than I did with my own kids. They are brother and sister, Tiana and Jason, the girl in nursery school and the boy in first grade. Tiana isn't much for dolls, but occasionally carries one around by the hair. Jason takes things apart (you can never put them together again) and has graduated from toy cars and trucks to rocket ships. They both draw pictures, watch television when we let them, and enjoy being read to. They have not, however, developed much appreciation for the nursery rhymes of my own childhood, such as I recall them, and I will admit that I might be a little bit off here and there. Still, there seems to be a generation gap of awesome magnitude here in this one area. Or maybe kids weren't so critical back then?

The trouble started with the first one I tried to recite.

"Little Miss Muffet
Sat on a tuffet — "

"What's a tuffet?" asked Jason.

"Well, I don't really know. Probably some sort of a hassock."

"What's a hassock?"

"I guess it's sort of a low stool."

"Like my TV stool?"

"Yes, like your TV stool. Anyway — "

"That's a dumb name," said Tiana. "I never heard of anybody with a dumb name like that."

"It's probably a made-up name, to rhyme with tuffet; poets do things like that all the time."

"Why?"

"Look, do you want to hear the rest of it or not?"

"OK."

"Little Miss Muffet sat on a tuffet/ Eating her curds and whey — "

"What's curds and whey?"

"Stuff you get when you make cheese — the curds float around in the whey."

"Sounds yucky," said Jason.

"Yuck," agreed Tiana.

I was beginning to realize that these kids were pretty sharp. How come I

didn't ask these questions when I was their age and somebody read this stuff to me? I even memorized it — more or less. I was beginning to think that it wasn't so much a generation gap as a breakdown in human communication. But I was determined to forge ahead nonetheless.

"OK, so you wouldn't eat it. Miss Muffet *loved* it. Let's go on. I think the rest of the rhyme goes something like this: A great big spider sat down beside her/And frightened Miss Muffet away."

"Not me," said Tiana. "I'm not scared of spiders."

"Boys aren't scared of spiders," said Jason.

"Look," I said. "You kids have started me thinking, I don't think that *is* a very good nursery rhyme. Not for today's kids anyway. How about if I revise it, bring it up to date. Would you like that?"

They said they would, and I let them go for a few minutes, cooked up a new version, and called them back.

"How about this: Little Miss Rosy O'Toole/ Sat on her TV stool/Packing her dinner away/When a great big spider/Sat down beside her/She bashed out its brains with a tray."

"I like that," said Tiana.

"That's pretty good," said Jason. "Do you know any more?"

-- Ted Eastwood

Lawrence F. Willard with his two grandchildren, Jason and Tiana.

-- Carole Allen

Ron Libby calling a square dance in West Falmouth, Maine.

WHAT MAINE'S BEST SQUARE DANCE CALLER DOES IN THE MIDDLE OF THE NIGHT

☞ Sometimes in the middle of the night in West Falmouth, Maine, professional square dance caller Ron Libby awakens and gropes by the bed for a 10-inch-square magnetic board that, he says, "never leaves my side." On the board are eight figures representing the eight square dancers in a "square" or "set" at a square dance. They are two inches tall and stand in pairs of red, green, black, and yellow.

A notebook and pen are next to the board. In the next few minutes after waking, Libby will move the figures across the board in a simulation of the dance he has been dreaming about. In the notebook he writes the impromptu choreography with words that form a code all their own to 6 million square dancers in the United States and 30 foreign countries. "Heads square thru 4 hands . . . Curlique . . . Scootback . . . Follow your neighbor and spread . . . Boys trade, boys run . . . Wheel and deal . . . Allemande left." Having done that, Ron Libby "do-si-dos" back to sleep. (*From "Obsessed with Square Dancing" by Mel Allen.*)

"YOU BLEW IT, BUDDY"

☞ When a person dies there are many things that can be said, and there is at least one thing that should never be said. The night after Alex died I was sitting in the living room of my sister's house outside of Boston, when the front door opened and in came a nice-looking middle-aged woman, carrying about 18 quiches. When she saw me she shook her head, then headed for the kitchen, saying sadly over her shoulder, "I just don't understand the will of God." Instantly I was up and in hot pursuit, swarming all over her. "I'll say you don't, lady!" I said. (I knew the anger would do me good, and the instruction to her was long overdue.) I continued, "Do you think it was the will of God that Alex never fixed that lousy windshield wiper of his, that he was probably driving too fast in such a storm, that he probably had had a couple of 'frosties' too many? Do you think it is God's will that there are no streetlights along that particular stretch of road, and no guardrail that separates the road from Boston Harbor?"

For some reason, nothing so infuriates me as the incapacity of seemingly intelligent people to get it through their heads that God doesn't go around this world with his finger on triggers, his fist around knives, his hands on steering wheels. God is dead set against all unnatural death. And Christ spent an inordinate amount of time delivering people from paralysis, insanity, leprosy, and muteness. Which is not to say that there are no nature-caused deaths, deaths that are untimely, slow, and pain-ridden. But to understand violent deaths, such as the one Alex died, is a piece of cake. As his younger brother put it simply, standing at the head of the casket at the Boston funeral, "You blew it, buddy. You blew it." (*From "My Son Beat Me to the Grave," by William Sloane Coffin, Jr.*)

SIGN OF SUCCESS

☞ "When we had our golden wedding anniversary two bank presidents came by, and they weren't even here to collect money." **Theron Harvey, a farmer in Rochester, Vermont.** (*From "What a Way to Run a Family!" by Fraser Noble.*)

WHO'D WANT TO REMEMBER?

FREEZING IN THE LORD'S HOUSE

☞ Much has been made of New England congregations shivering in the arctic cold of their meetinghouses in bitter winter weather. But the Puritan was happy in proportion to the number of things he could do without, and for over a century he looked upon a stove in the Lord's house as one of these sybaritic items.

Sometimes fur bags made of coarse skins, such as wolf, were nailed or tied to the edges of the meetinghouse benches. Into these bags the worshipers thrust their freezing feet while the hourglass ran out, and was turned over as often as four times during a tedious sermon.

Another expedient on cold Sundays was for each family to bring its "dogg" to meeting, and by laying on his master's feet he warmed at least one member of the household. However, these animal stoves turned out to be a great nuisance. There were so many fights during the services, a dogbeater had to be regularly employed. Finally, any Puritan bringing a dog into the meetinghouse was fined sixpence. If he failed to pay the fine, he lost the dog.

A certain amount of heat was reflected from the pulpit itself, where the emphasis was likely to be on eternal burnings. Some variation of Samuel Moody's description of how it would feel "to lie frying in the hottest fire, world without end" recurred Sabbath after Sabbath. But when fierce wintry blasts rattled the windows and shook the turret, the inmates of the sheep-pen pews may have listened somewhat wistfully to these verbal cracklings of hellfire.

The New England Puritan was nothing if not self-disciplined. Winters he prayed stoically in cold and darkness, and summers he worshiped in a "seething, glaring, pine-smelling hothouse" without curtains or window blinds.

Angela Stuart

– Austin Stevens

WORCESTER (MASS.) SUNDAY TELEGRAM (AP) — Chicago: A proposal that people hold hands in a human chain stretching across the country next July Fourth is making progress, organizers say. The project would link four million people in a 3000-mile human chain. . . .

NEWS ITEM: DEBBIE McCOMB PETERBORO, N.H.

". . . NO, ONLY HENDERSENS WITH AN "E" ARE SUPPOSED TO LINK UP IN VERMONT — YOU'RE A HENDERSON WITH AN "O" – LET'S SEE, I THINK THAT'S NORTH DAKOTA . . ."

The People Who Have Made
Yankee Magazine

Yankee Employees: September 1935 through September 1985

"Thanks for the memories"

Robb Sagendorph
Beatrix Thorne Sagendorph
Gerome Brush
Oliver Jenkins
Beth Tolman Barrell
Fran Tolman
Laurie Hillyer
Phyllis Worcester
Horace Gilbert
Alice Lightenen
Fred Gilbert
Dobbs Putnam
Hugh Hescock
Carolyn Harmon
Benjamin M. Rice
Bernard Thayer
Robert Foote
J. Almus Russell
Robert P. Tristram Coffin
Sidney Paine
Imogene Wolcott
Frederika James
Vera Victoreau
Clifford Scofield
Jacob Bates Abbott
Charles Holbrook
Robert Whittier
Marjorie Mills
John R. Taylor
Horace Wadsworth
Ruth Miller
Irene Neal Railsback
Joseph C. Allen
Ruth Baker
Nancy Dixon
Timothy Fuller
William Clark
Mildred S. Powell
Marjorie Hall
Eileen MacVeagh
Lorna Trowbridge
Edward Van Zile
Carey Walbridge
Richard Merrifield
Mandie M. Martin
Annabelle Dupree
Esther Plimpton
Elaine Pellerin
Alene Rajaniemi
Marilyn Fiske
Marian Leonard

Hallie Burnett
Fran Blake
Jeremy Paulus
Everett Thiele
Alice Herbert
Martha Dakin
Donald Cuddihee
Richard Scribner
Elinor Sherman
C. Robertson Trowbridge
Marjorie Croumie
Marguerite Fournier
Helen Shedd
Maureen Hayes
Janet White
Dennis Dunning
Leona Murphy
Laura Webber
Gloria Blair
Raymond Benoit
Roger Tyler
Ken Fredericks
Jeanette Kear
Mary Sheehan
Juliet Cuddihee
Glenna Eaves
Marie Rajaniemi
Helen Doscher
Alice McKenna
Barbara Strelec
Amy Whitney
Marianne Carney
Al Chamberlain
Harvey Chandler
Gerald Christian
Jacqueline Bower
Jeannelle Moore
Carol Camden
Richard Wasowicz
Faye Carey
Rose Thibault
Priscilla Parker
Judith Baird
Richard Doody
Pamela Holbrook
Linda MacDonald
Cynthia Arnold
Gloria Lucas
Sharon Blanchette
Nancy Rousseau
Nellie Crossley

Jacqueline Pelissier
Carl Kirkpatrick
Richard Heckman
Lauren Libow
John D. Goode
Austin Stevens
Anne Thompson
Stephen Avery
Barbara Horton
Sarah Burbank
Kristen Gould
Linda Greenwood
Ann Grow
Dawn Bochicchio
Marcia Seymour
Margo Letourneau
Darlene Thurston Anable
Mike Anderson
Lilja Keinanen
Norma Pilli
Stephania Ancewicz
Ruthanne Bailey
Joanne Langille
Nancy Brooks
Nancy Gangloff
Patricia Cleary
Vera Elder
Blanche McFarland
Lois Evans
Ruth Johnson
Pauline Gaudreau
Theresa Ducharme
Linda Blanchette
Gail Bradford
Lawrence Spiegel
Susan Walsh
Leslie Luoma
Patricia Poland
Elsa Cuddihee
Ethyl Wenblad
Doris Hill
Mary Butler
Judith Reisert
Anna Manning
Rebecca Sundstrom
Marie Manning
Barbara Howard
Doris Porter
Carolee Barrett
Ronda Knowlton
Edwin Nausbaum

Virginia Perry
Margaret Hutchinson
Ann Raphael
Rita Swanson
Charlotte Telland
Hart Crandall III
Nancy Tripp
Joan Hurst
Katharyn Wakefield
Charlene Lincer
Joanne Blecher
Nancy Aiken
Ingred Nijborg
Ruth Massie
Theresa Welch
Dorothy Fifield
Patricia Caberly
Sandra LaClair
Sandra James
Naomi Somero
Susan Dusinberre
Joyce Farman
Walter Richardson
Janet Sawyer
Clarissa Silitch
Alec Grenda
Ed Phippard
Robert Pettegrew
Bayard Sawyer
Barbara Pond
Jerry Hickey
Janet Blanchette
Helen Sillampa
Joyce Swanson
Fannie Silk
Sandra Prettyman
Karen Tolman
Lynn Spano
Louise Aiken
Donna Thurston
Sarah Thurston
Marie Nason
Donna Basha
Francine Campbell
Marc Hess
Robert Johnson
Gabrielle Salter
Sharon Miner
Florence Perkins
Joyce Miller
Alice Palmer

Caroline Pettegrew
Elizabeth Grant
Dorothy Abare
Betty Creteur
Heidi Swanson
Lisa Blanchette
Jeanette Bortwell
Darlene Bortwell
Janet Kenney
Eileen Magoore
Lois Harper
Karen Hendrickson
Patrice Loves
Marianne Johnson
Grace Mulhall
Lucille Rines
Melissa Stephenson
Mary Ann Sullivan
Sally Ann Lilly
Linda Dunham
Jan Taborelli
Nancy Kemp
David Blanchette
Arthur Wright
Donna Colgan
Mary Smith
Sandy Taylor
Diane Howe
Earl Proulx
Alexandra Schmidt
Susan Clarke
Joseph Palmer
Marshall Pask
John Pierce
Sean Withrow
Anna Larson
Bradford W. Ketchum, Jr.
Richard Livingstone
Bruce Macauley
Judy Fletcher
Lillian Foster
Georgia Orcutt
Jacqueline Jordan
Karen Jones
Ellen Keir
Clifford Blanchard
Harold Shook
Sherry Wilson
Dorothy Cape
Margaret Holden
Irene Blinn

Pamela Campbell
Carol Mellor
Theodore Taft
Roxanne Knowlton
Valerie Dill
Sheila LeGrenade
Karen Longever
Sandra Flagg
Marina Kontos
Kathleen French
Susan Rinta
Marie Faucher
Toni Paoletti
Henrietta Waite
Joseph Cheney
Robert Frazier
Heather Engvall
Lynn Sullivan-Walsh
Sheila Bamford
Janet Groeper
Marion Raynor
Linda Altemose
Dorothy Simard
Georgie Thomas
Irene Harper
Babette Sheehan
Frederick Dexter
Susan Keller
Patricia Evans
Methoda Uzel
Elnora Scribner
Sonja Ducharme
Joan Pedersen
John Kyte
Rita Merrifield
Judith Frazier
Judith Brill
Martha Spencer
Kendra Aldrich
Marie Ward
Aleta Jenks
Freida Day
Janet Weir
Brenda Parker
Dana Hull
Janet Subka
L.M. Deschenes
Erica Boisvert
Eller Egger
Cheryl Cahill
Debra Wright
Lilly Curry
Bruce Hammond
Michele Artese
Marlene Niemela
Diana Carr
Betty Rogers
Sharon Rossi
Susan Shorrock
Mary Reed
Aldene Fredenburg
Lisa Arnold
Wesley Loker
Gaie Hampson
Stephen Smith
Cherry Pyron
Lawrence Pollard
John Fensterwald
Donna Lleger
Taylor Morris

Elliot Allison
Kay Allison
Lendall Fiske
Bill Pierce
Lawrence F. Willard
Annis Lee Tunis
Natalie Morrison
Richard D. Estes
Anthony Anable, Jr.
Blanche Burnett
Priscilla Ayers
Elizabeth Raulett
Judith Jones
Jean Burden
Donald Purcell
Duncan McDonald
Esther Fitts
Richard Latti
Judson D. Hale, Sr.
Judith Stockwell
Beverly McDonald
Joyce Tarr
June Rajaniemi
Christie Smith
Peter Kukish
John Wight
Barry Elder
Linda Rogers
Janice Goodwin
Christine Shook
Mary Doyle
Linda Clukay
Cherilyn Addy
Elaine Fiske
Lorraine Caswell
Jaymia Ryll
Carole Cuddihee
Susan Desrosiers
Peter Sykas
Marie Knowlton
Gloria Nugent
Lida Stinchfield
Nancy Guild
Molly McDonald
Florence Conner
Vivian Ilomaki
Carol Jeffery
Sandra Wojchick
Christine Pratt
Deborah Fossum
Linda Wheeler
Marian Ducharme
Louise Forcier
Sandra Jones
Judith Morrison
Marie Oliver Applin
Joanne Saville
Susan Elliot
Sharon Foley
Phyllis Colburn
Lendra Locke
Madeline Lambert
Jennie Main
Nancy Warren
Patricia Turner
Angelo Sodano
Dianne Johnson
Kathryn Kwicker
Rose Marie Holden
Cynthia Cole

Margo Granfors
Susan Fraser
Theresa Gedenberg
Jean Volte
Denise Blanchard
Dianne Tarr
Nancy Connolly
Carrie Romaine
Candace Lovins
Barbara Richardson
Donna Blanchard
Gayle Steed
Mary Johnson
Jessica Vanni
Jane Black
Heather Ingvall
Lynda Bryer
Marlene Helstein
Sara Stone
Stephanie Leonard
Jane Emory
Karen Grabowski
Pirkko Keinanen
April Stein
Karen Tarr
James Beach
Rose Smith
Carol Merrifield
Lucia Turgeon
Faye Bradeen
P.A. Griffin
Susan Kennedy
Suzanne Korpi
Shirley Lary
Mary Chambers
Valerie Horn
Linda Withee
Sharon Van Valkenburg
Donna Harris
Barbara Davis
Jeanne Shattuck
Janet Mason
Mary Digiacomo
Joanne Crockett
Annette Vincent
Susan Bond
Virginia Blanchette
Kenneth Maxfield
Christine Nerlinger
Lori Miller
William Harris
Susan Shepherd
Ferdie Blackburn
Jennifer Prigge
Ellen Kempner
Janet Auchincloss
Kathleen Stith
Marie Walz
Ann Marie Korpi
Denzel Dyer
Jill Shaffer
Michelle Leblanc
Gary Marco
Ina Urso
Florence Duguid
Marian Pickering
James Lamothe
David Levan
Mary Cornog
C. Edward Buffington

Mary Madden
Raymond Maher
Margo Keating
Christine Aubert
Ruth Lambert
Laurie Stuart
Deborah Balducci
June Ludlum
Pamela Cassidy
Victoria Nevins
Valerie Gill
Frank Wilton
Elizabeth Benes
Madeleine Cleaves
Barbara Hinton
Catherine Whittle
Charles Watson
Linda Keenan
Georgia Gilluley
Guenter Viktor
Robbie Parsons
Kathleen Lombardi
Reynold Weiss
Betty Tewell
Ellen Wright
Brenda McLaughlin
Martha Laflame
Maureen O'Connor
Donna Nason
Harry Peirce
Janet Jespersen
Marion Brumaghim
Carol Caisse
Debbie Blanchette
Margaret Liszka
Priscilla Churchill
Nancy Norton
Muriel Asselin
Mary McDonough
Norma Brouillet
Nora Creech
Helen Lee
Doris Walsh
Cathy Nordberg
Vicky Allen
Susan Galbraith
Kimberly Ann Kolb
Albert Rajaniemi
Ellen Dunbar
Patricia McCarrier
Joan Hanchett
Theresa Mannix
Darlene Josephson
Prugh Roeser
Deborah Leach
Theresa Engstrom
Mary Steiner
Philip Petron
Lewis Fifield
Eve Anderson
Lynn Derr
Susann Rogers
Carol Chamberlain
Katherine Fogg
Blythe Coleman
Meredith Donatello
Judith Kaarto
Barbara Kear
Sheila Heywood
Deborah Hanson

Helen Kemp
Dolores Webb
Jane Patnode
Susan Witt
Barbara Harris
Janet Barter
Nancy Barry
Carol Getty
Chris Tremblay
Leonard Tilton
Cathy Falwell
Tim Clark
Susan Mahnke
Mary Sheldon
Pauline Halvonik
Maureen McHugh
Mike Kukulka
Earl Potter
Carrie Sheehan
Tom Mills
Nancy Hawkins
Isabelle Taft
Hope Davis
Linda Lantry
Brenda Pelkey
Barbara Whitney
Martha Blanchette
Mary Nutting
Jacqueline Irish
Elinor Allen
David Smith
Ann Marie Aldrich
Penny Nichols
Deborah Despres
Douglas Johnson
Brenda Ellis
Susan Tonseth
Stephen Klett
Ruth Wright
Al Lapinsky
Mary Walker
Ronald Burroughs
Robert Nielsen
Roy Pask
Brian Thurston
John Scott
Patricia Pask
Jamien Jacobs
Cynthia Marshall
Susan Medeiros
Brian Barden
Mary Lewis
Jeni Lewis
June Horning
Edythe Clark
Marshall Taylor
Douglas Christensen
J Porter
Dorothea Guy
Donna Jordan
Charlie Jordan
Mel Allen
Carrie Anderson
Betty Doyle
Yolanda Jarvis
Mark Bastian
Stephen O. Muskie
Jean DeLongchamp
Polly Bannister
Maryann Mattson

(continued on next page) **319**

Georgie Jurva
Francine Ojala
Diann Parzini
Penny Patch
Allison Perron
Katherine Wilcott
Jean Tetreault
Lynn Lagasse
Mariann Moery
Joan Smyth
Gerald Christian
John Pawlick
Joseph Hayes
Jeri Kane
Donna Hartwell
Dawn Woodbury
Bonnie MacKeil
Thomas Vannah
Katherine Johnson
Edwin Niskanen
Kathleen McKee
Delores Harris
Jacqueline Christiano
Mark Lancey
Meredith Whitcomb
Sandra Gallagher
Gail Hamblet
Nancy Wienholt
Richard Etling
Joseph Meagher
Beth Tilton
Dolores Worcester
Nena Groskind
David Gumpert
Dr. James Howell
Joi Taylor
Dianne Theall
Jerry Thompson
Jules Thompson
Susan Valaitis
Alice Weir
Margaret Speranza
Denise Goodman
Bill Good
Robert Emmett Ginna, Jr.
Dick Friz
Janet Friedman
Debra Fernald
Len Edgerly
Gordon Early
Laura Dumitras
Paul DeLong
Bob Deming
Debra Stevens
Robert Stickler
John Talbott
Allan Smith
Katherine Snow
Keith Rajaniemi
Kent Sanger
Elizabeth Sanger
Laurie Shulz
Susan Dickson
Wendy Dillon
George Kendall
Richard Head
J. Lang Davison
Maria Churchill
Serena Bliss
Dane Hahn

Theodore Renauld
Ada Parker
Andrew Fox
Ralph Stephens
Jane Young
Suzanne Huberlie
Mary Root
Patricia Gill
Doreen Danhof
Kellee Evans
Bonnie Parker
Martha Henault
Anthony Caron
Joan Nowak
Cynthia Odell
Cheryl Nunemaker
Margaret Trombley
Lois Fredenburgh
Adele Mogavero
Victoria Bartlett
Deborah Davidson
Mary Jane Howell
Alice Pirovanei
Nancy Landry
Mary Norton
Nancy Giacalone
Barbara Garnett
Margaret Shortlidge
Susan Green
Mary Rich
Laura Norton
Judith Pedersen
Katina Trendell
Myrna Fritz
Aaron Webber
Sarah Meath
Christy Menard
Theodore Davies
Deborah Knight
Karen Albrecht
Betsy Hudson
Julianne Luopa
Molly Malloy
Betty Royce
Louise Lawrence
Gary Huber
Gerard Ryan
Barbara Recchie
Robert Tyson
Keith LaPointe
Kerry Alvarez
Martha Chartland
Alta Cheney
Patricia Dodge
Nancy Gorman
Henry James
Maryellen Kelly
Judith Keurulainen
Barbara Murray
Judson D. Hale, Jr.
Clinton Sperry
Ellen Sperry
Wynn Scott
Kristen Smith
Dougald MacDonald
James Trowbridge
John White
Dan Hale
Marilyn White
Paula Noonan

Michael Caron
Amy Chisholm
William Heydolph
Timothy Lewis
Herman Maynard
Anita Mulcahy
Theodora Price
Cynthia Speros
Suzanne Anderson
Andrea Norman Meagher
John Hassan
Stephen Fuller
Janet Benoit
Beth Bishop
Barbara Block
Laura Brown
Richard Bucher
James Dodson
Pamela Burroughs
Mary Cass
Cora Cody
Luellen Cody
Sabra Crownse
Ruth Easton
Heidi Emond
Michele Hobson
Dewey Hutchins
Peter Langley
James Martin
Jean Martin
Karen Poznar
Amy Raymond
Edith Skinner
Susann Tapper
Ray Self
King Herbert
Christine O'Hearn
Kenneth Rowe
Patricia Berlo
Colin Davidson
Henry Drury
Marlene Gagnon
Kendell Kardt
Kenneth Hooker
Eugene Ehlert
Lewis Dabney
Jeanne Nolin
Edwin Morgan
Julianne Perron
Barbara Weil
Douglas Bailey
Jon Bell
Carleen Borges
Claudia Christie
Julie Corvo
Jeffrey Currier
Laura Diamond
Judith Dombrowski
William Donovan
Deborah Flachs
Wendy Morse
Sally Jacobs
Yunghi Kim
Lesley Lloyd
Arthur MacDonnell
Lisa McGurrin
Marianne McLoughlin
Cynthia Newell
Mary O'Friel
Robert Orlando

Jane Simon
Diane Saunders
Marirosa Torres
Kathleen Duffy
Barbara Baxter
Michael Benjamin
Andrea Bergeron
Robert Bliss
Ernestine Phipps
Dennis Christensen
Jane Breschard
Kathleen Comiskey
Charlotte Ehrler
Sharon Hyman
Brian Mahoney
Kathryn Meagher
Kim Nilsen
Christa Price
Sharon Smith
Tim Pritchard
Thomas Nusbaun
Sara Ann Parker
Roger Scott
Diana Micciche
Lauren Sirois
Susan Smith
Deborah Somero
Alice Tarquino
Robert Robinson
Phyllis Ryder
Beatrix Trowbridge
Cornelia Trowbridge
Laurie Walsh
Susan Weller
Priscilla Whitehouse
Jo Ann Sprague
Dana Springfield
Angele Summers
Ann Toussaint
Carolyn Williams
Susan Wood
Benjamin Watson
Joe Timko
Dana Whittle
Laura van Dam
Theresa Verville
Soso Whaley
Mary Ellen Berlo
Virginia Blanchette
Tracy Allen
Paul Belliveau
Neil Cohen
Catherine Cuddihee
Caroline Grady
Samantha Horning
Paul Schlieben
Frances-Anne Frasca
Lorelei Germond
Eleanor King
Jane Koistinen
John Kraichnan
Shiela Kulgren
Ardys Kozbial
Karen Dionne
Alison Bennie
Ann Card
Page Chrystie
Martha Rice
Jane Hoover
Julia Gilbert

Paul Quinn
Lynn Hewitt
John Mitchell
Ellen Brutsch
Kelcy Brooks
Joanna Miller
Michael Schuman
Lila Walz
Anne Hayden
Christine Paananen
Deborah Carrion
Lindsay Churchill
Duyen Williams
Donna Summers
Lynne Rumba
Fran LaFave
Anne Gallop
Laurel Rogers
Patricia Robida
Elizabeth Dadamo
Debra Fish
Florence Pickering
Loris Keating
Cynthia Schlosser
Marie Belanger
Beverly Chamberlain
Kim LaPointe
Jane Adams
Kip Altman
Barbara Green
Ben Barnhart
Anthony Baldo
Mark Browning
Howard Caldwell
Arthur Carveth
Peter Cawley
Bert Charlton
Doran Howitt
Ellen Fitzpatrick
Caitlin Doyle
Veronica Marinaro
Trudy Liek
Eileen McKenna
Cynthia Shaw
Steve Morgan
Bonnie Crytzer
Martha Thomas
Laura Conklin
Charlene Beaulieu
Emily Beauregard
Larry Benson
Paul Biklen
Faye Binder
Linda Bliss
Lora Boyd
Bill Coffee
Nancy Coleman
William Lattanzi
Pat Niska
Bill O'Brion
Patti O'Hare
Sarah Oot
Anita Patten
Richard Poirier
Denise Lobb
Dan Hall
Betty Hull
Elizabeth Sherwin